Ordnance Survey

GW00635212

STREET A
East Kent

Contents

III Key to map symbols

IV-V Key to map pages

VI Administrative and post code boundaries

1 Street maps

206 Town plans of Bromley and Dartford

207 Town plans of Gravesend and Royal Tunbridge Wells

208 Town plans of Sevenoaks and Tonbridge

209 Index of hospitals, railway stations, schools, shopping centres, street names and universities

PHILIP'S

First edition published 1989
Fourth edition published 1994
First colour edition published 1997
Reprinted in 1998 by

Ordnance Survey® and George Philip Ltd., a division of
Romsey Road   Octopus Publishing Group Ltd
Maybush   Michelin House
Southampton   81 Fulham Road
SO16 4GU   London SW3 6RB

ISBN 0-540-07483-7 (hardback)
ISBN 0-540-07276-1 (wire-o)

To the best of the Publishers' knowledge, the information in this atlas
was correct at the time of going to press. No responsibility can be
accepted for any errors or their consequences.

The representation in this atlas of a road, track or path is no evidence
of the existence of a right of way.

**The mapping between pages 1 and 208 (inclusive) in this atlas is
derived from Ordnance Survey® OSCAR® and Land-Line® data,
and Landranger® mapping.**

Ordnance Survey, OSCAR, Land-Line and Landranger are registered
trade marks of Ordnance Survey, the national mapping agency of
Great Britain.

Printed and bound in Spain by Cayfosa

Key to map symbols

Motorway (with junction number)

Primary routes (dual carriageway and single)

A roads (dual carriageway and single)

B roads (dual carriageway and single)

Minor through road (dual carriageway and single)

Minor roads

Roads under construction

Railways

Tramway, miniature railway

Rural track, private road or narrow road in urban area

Gate or obstruction to traffic (restrictions may not apply at all times or to all vehicles)

All paths, bridleways, byway open to all traffic, road used as a public path

The representation in this atlas of a road, track or path is no evidence of the existence of a right of way

45
140
Adjoining page indicators

Dover Castle   **Non-Roman antiquity**

ROMAN FORT   **Roman antiquity**

Acad	**Academy**	Mon	**Monument**
Cemy	**Cemetery**	Mus	**Museum**
C Ctr	**Civic Centre**	Obsy	**Observatory**
CH	**Club House**	Pal	**Royal Palace**
Coll	**College**	PH	**Public House**
Ex H	**Exhibition Hall**	Resr	**Reservoir**
Ind Est	**Industrial Estate**	Ret Pk	**Retail Park**
Inst	**Institute**	Sch	**School**
Ct	**Law Court**	Sh Ctr	**Shopping Centre**
L Ctr	**Leisure Centre**	Sta	**Station**
LC	**Level Crossing**	TH	**Town Hall/House**
Liby	**Library**	Trad Est	**Trading Estate**
Mkt	**Market**	Univ	**University**
Meml	**Memorial**	YH	**Youth Hostel**

British Rail station

Private railway station

Bus, coach station

Ambulance station

Coastguard station

Fire station

Police station

Casualty entrance to hospital

Church, place of worship

Hospital

Information centre

Parking

Post Office

The Canterbury High School   **Important buildings, schools, colleges, universities and hospitals**

County boundaries

Great Stour   **Water name**

Stream

River or canal (minor and major)

Water

Tidal water

Woods

Houses

■ The dark grey border on the inside edge of some pages indicates that the mapping does not continue onto the adjacent page

■ The small numbers around the edges of the maps identify the 1 kilometre National Grid lines

The scale of the maps is 5.52 cm to 1 km (3½ inches to 1 mile)

0		¼		½		¾		1 mile
0	250m	500m	750m	1 Kilometre				

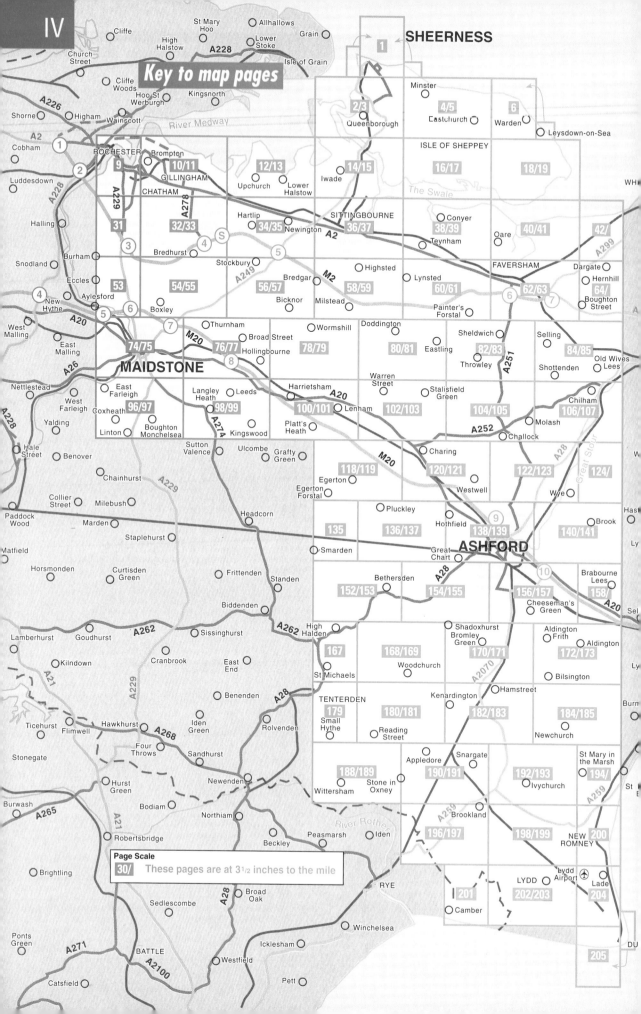

Key to map pages

SHEERNESS

ISLE OF SHEPPEY

MAIDSTONE

ASHFORD

TENTERDEN

BATTLE

NEW ROMNEY

FAVERSHAM

SITTINGBOURNE

ROCHESTER

GILLINGHAM

CHATHAM

Page Scale

30/ These pages are at 3½ inches to the mile

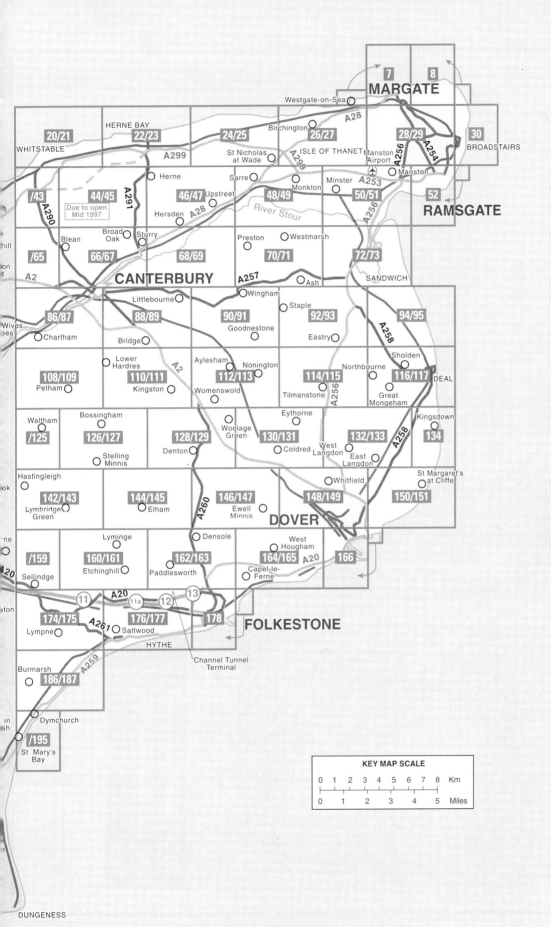

KEY MAP SCALE

| 0 | 1 | 2 | 3 | 4 | 5 | 6 | 7 | 8 | Km |

| 0 | 1 | 2 | 3 | 4 | 5 | Miles |

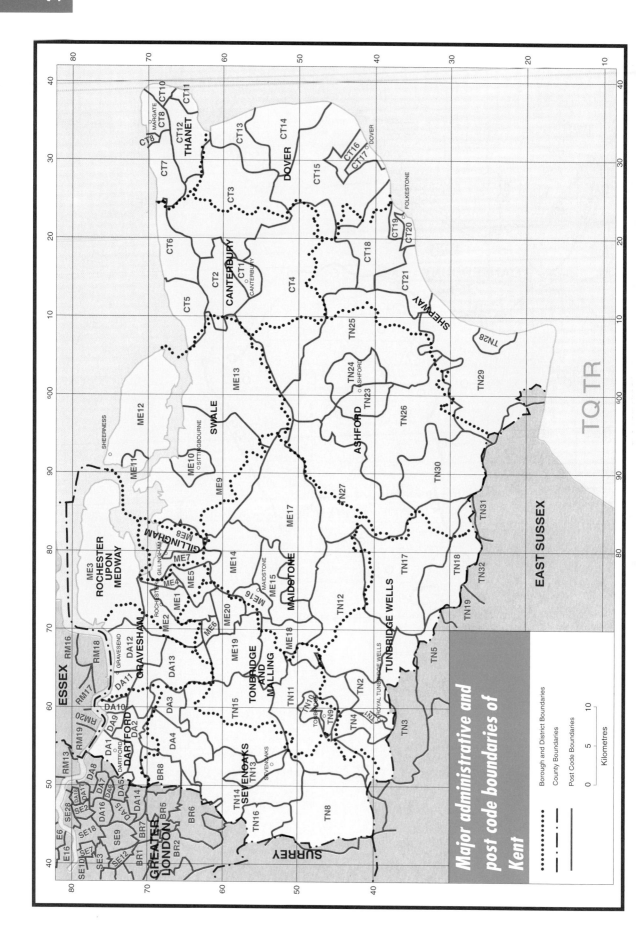

Major administrative and post code boundaries of Kent

Borough and District Boundaries
County Boundaries
Post Code Boundaries

Kilometres
0 5 10

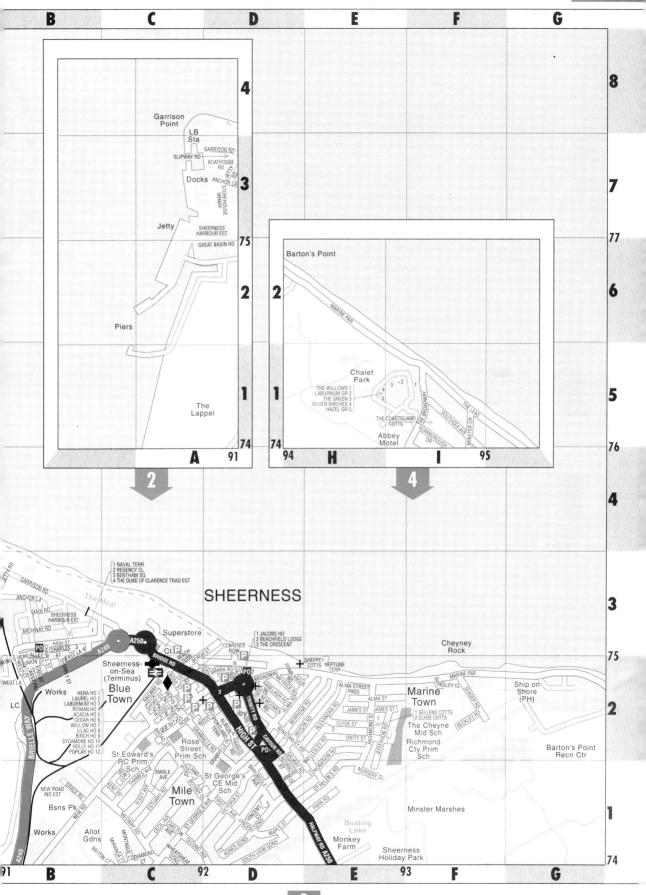

B C D E F G

8

Garrison Point

LB Sta
GARRISON RD
SLIPWAY RD
BOATHOUSE RD

4

7

Docks
ANCHOR LA
STOREHOUSE WHARF

3

Jetty
SHEERNESS HARBOUR EST

GREAT BASIN RD

75

77

Barton's Point

MARINE PAR

2

2

6

Piers

Chalet Park

THE WILLOWS 1
LABURNUM GR 2
THE GREEN 3
SILVER BIRCHES 4
HAZEL GR 5

1

1

5

The Lappel

THE COASTGUARD COTTS

THE BROADWAY
SCARBOROUGH DR
SOUTHSEA AV
MINSTER DR
THE LEAS

Abbey Motel

74

74

76

A 91

94 **H** **I** 95

2

4

4

1 NAVAL TERR
2 REGENCY CL
3 BENTHAM SQ
4 THE DUKE OF CLARENCE TRAD EST

SHEERNESS

3

JETTY RD
GARRISON RD
ANCHOR LA
MAIN RD
The Moat
SHEERNESS HARBOUR EST
ARCHWAY RD

Superstore

Cheyney Rock

75

1 JACOBS HO
2 BEACHFIELD LODGE
3 THE CRESCENT

CLARENCE ROW

SHEPPEY COTTS
NEPTUNE TERR

MARINE PAR

Ship on Shore (PH)

PO
CHARLES ST
A249
A250
BRIDGE RD
BEACH ST
ADELAIDE RD
PARK RD
BROADWAY
POMWELL RD
ALMA STREET PASS

Marine Town

2

KING ST
UNION ST
SHEPPEY RD
Sheerness-on-Sea (Terminus)
Blue Town
RAILWAY RD
Ct
TRINITY RD
Lby
HIGH ST
RANELAGH RD
MEYRICK RD
BERRIDGE RD
JAMES ST
CLYDE ST
RICHMOND ST
ALMA ST

1 SELLENS COTTS
2 CLYDE COTTS

The Cheyne Mid Sch

Richmond Cty Prim Sch

Barton's Point Recn Ctr

2

Works
HERA HO 1
LAUREL HO 2
LABURNUM HO 3
ROWAN HO 4
ACACIA HO 5
CEDAR HO 6
WILLOW HO 7
LILAC HO 8
BIRCH HO 9
SYCAMORE HO 10
HOLLY HO 11
POPLAR HO 12

WOOD ST
ALBION RD
HOPE ST
ROSE ST
GRANVILLE RD
GRANVILLE AVE
WALLESLEY RD
ALEXANDRA RD
INVICTA RD
WINSTANLEY RD
UNITY ST
CONNAUGHT RD
CORONATION RD
ST HELEN'S RD
JEFFERSON RD
NURSERY CL

Rose Street Prim Sch

CAVOUR RD
PO

LC

St Edward's RC Prim Sch

Minster Marshes

BRIELLE WAY

NEW ROAD IND EST

Bsns Pk

Mile Town

St George's CE Mid Sch

THAMES AVE
SWALE AVE
KENT RD
FLEET AV
ESTUARY RD
HOLLAND RD
ST GEORGE'S AVE
SHERIDAN AVE
VICTORIA ST
VINCENT RD
MAPLE ST
PARK RD

Boating Lake

A249
A250

1

Works

Allot Gdns

MEDWAY RD
MONTAGUE RD
CECIL AVE
CARLTON AVE
SECOND AVE
MIRANDA CT
DIAMOND CT
BRITON CT
WHEATSHEAF GDNS
AGNES GDNS
SOUTH VIEW GDNS
HALFWAY RD

Monkey Farm

Sheerness Holiday Park

74

91 **B** **C** 92 **D** **E** 93 **F** **G**

3

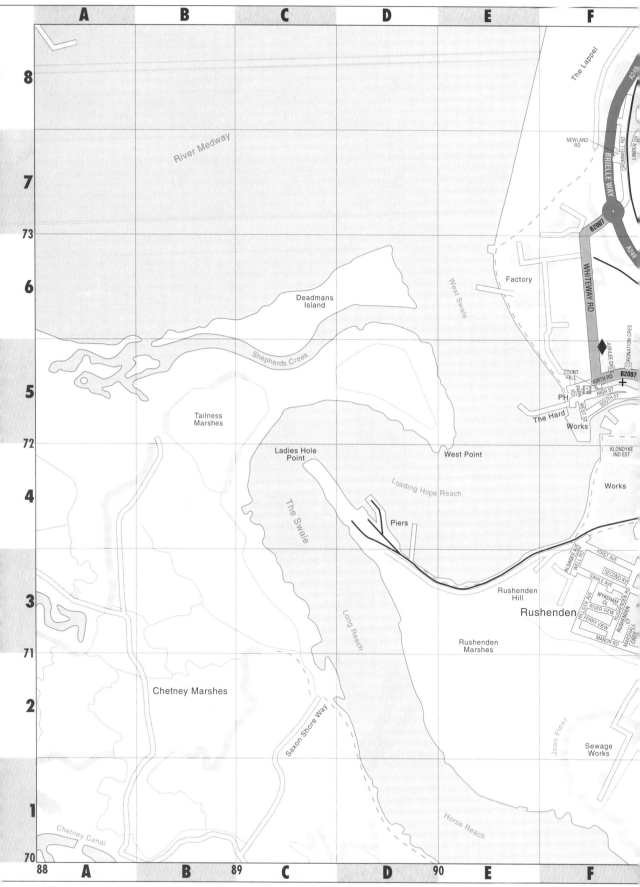

| | A | B | C | D | E | F |

The Lappel

River Medway

NEWLAND RD

CROMWELL RD

LINDEN DR

A249

BRIELLE WAY

B2007

A249

West Swale

Factory

WHITEWAY RD

Deadmans Island

CORONATION CRES

Shepherds Creek

JUBILEE CRES

COURT HALL

NORTH RD

B2007

PARK RD

PH

HIGH ST

WEST ST

The Hard

SOUTH ST

Works

KLONDYKE IND EST

Tailness Marshes

Ladies Hole Point

West Point

Works

Loading Hope Reach

The Swale

Piers

ALSAGER AVE

WELL RD

FIRST AVE

SECOND AVE

SWALE AVE

WYKEHAM CL

HILLSIDE AVE

RIVER VIEW

RUSHENDEN RD

Rushenden Hill

Long Reach

Rushenden

FERRY VIEW

MARSHALL CT

MANOR RD

MARSHALL CRES

Rushenden Marshes

Chetney Marshes

Saxon Shore Way

Joan Fleet

Sewage Works

Chetney Canal

Horse Reach

| 88 | A | B | 89 | C | D | 90 | E | F |

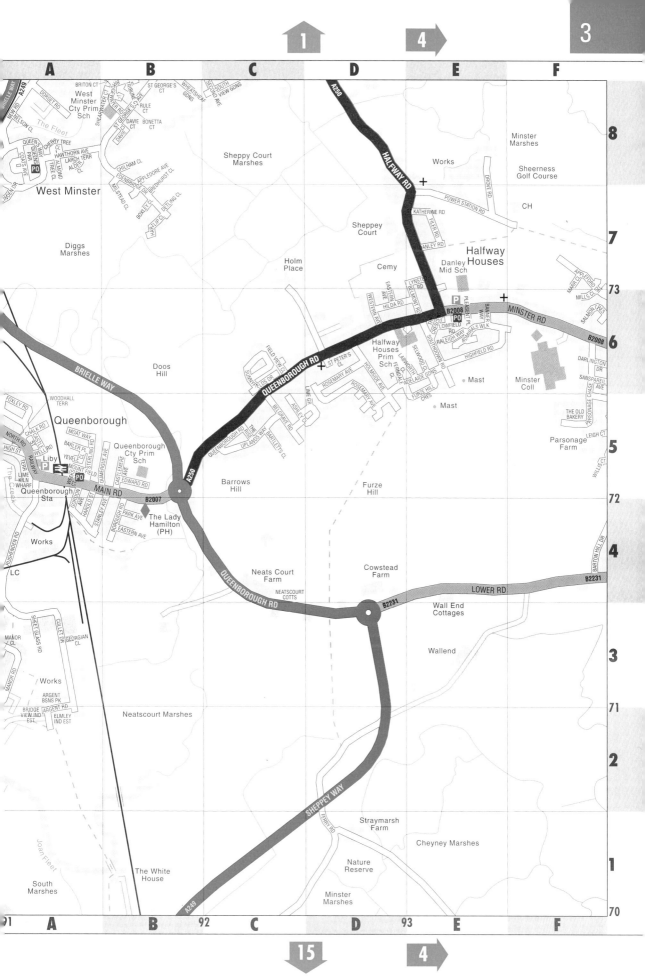

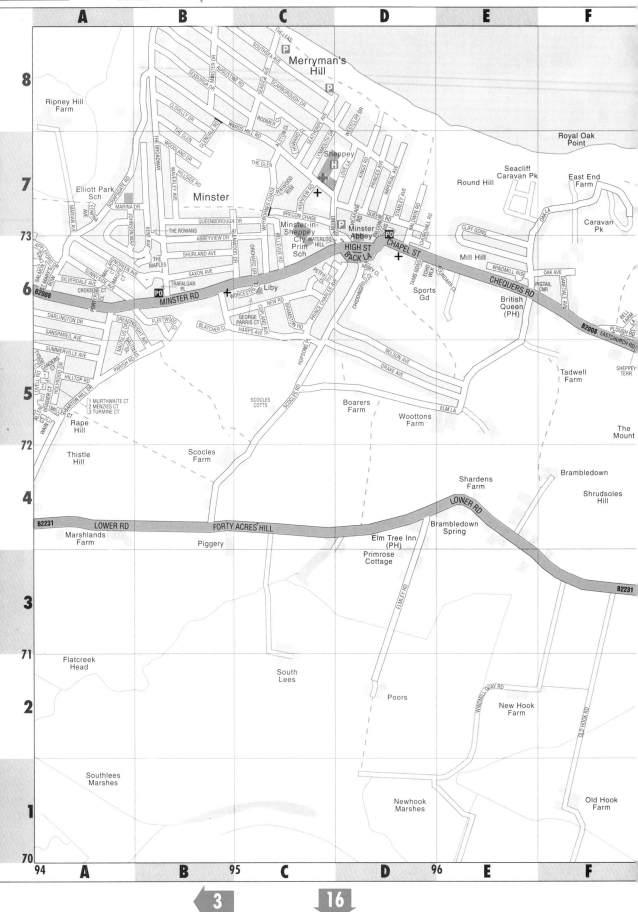

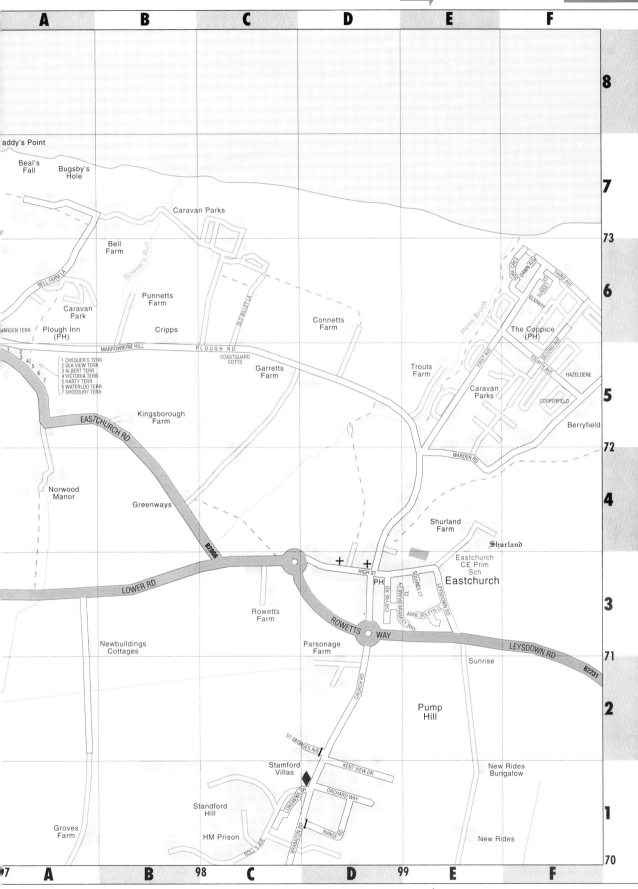

A   B   C   D   E   F

8

71
Leysdown-on-Sea

2
GROVE AVE
P
EASTERN RD
SAND CT
P0
THE PROMENADE
B2231 LEYSDOWN RD
MANOR WAY
THAMES CT
NUTTS AVE
PH   B2231
PRIORY CT
PARK AVE
WING RD

1
Holiday Villages
WING RD
WING RD
SHELLNESS RD

70
SHURLAND AVE
SEAVIEW AVE
WING RD

03   G   H   04

19 ↓

7

73
Fletcher Battery Camp Site
Swanley Farm
Barrows Brook
THIRD AVE
NORMAN RD
SIXTH AVE

6

Warden Point

Cartts Farm
COASTGUARD HOS
MANOR WAY

5
Wheatsheaf Inn (PH)
WARDEN RD
WARDEN WAY
Warden Spring Caravan Pk

72

Barnland
Thorn Hill

4
Warden
THORN HILL RD
CLIFF DR
PRESTON HALL GDNS
SEA APP
ST JAMES CL
IMPERIAL DR
KNOLL WAY
BUCKLERS CL
WATERSIDE
SEASAL CL
EMPRESS GDNS
MELODY
WINDSOR GDNS
EMERALD VIEW
CLIFF VIEW GDNS
JETTY RD
CLARENCE GDNS
ST CLEMENTS
BEACH APP
LEICESTER GDNS
SEA VIEW GDNS
SEA VIEW GDNS

3
Rayham
Mustards
Warden Bay Hotel (PH)
WARDEN BAY RD

71
Holiday Villages
GROVE WAY

2
B2231
MUSTARDS RD
CORONATION DR
ST CLEMENTS CL
B2231
VINCITY RD
Bay View
DANES DR
BAY VIEW GDNS
CLIFF VIEW GDNS
WARDEN VIEW GDNS
LEYSDOWN RD
Cemy

1
Old Rides Farm
HARTY FERRY RD
Rides Farm
Bay View (PH)
Paradise Farm

70

00   A   B   01   C   D   02   E   F

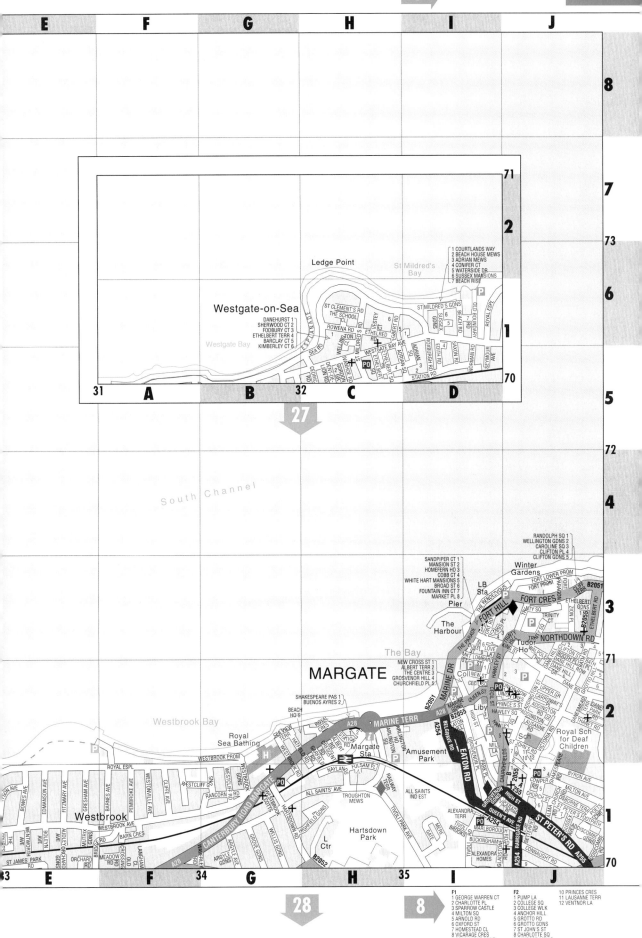

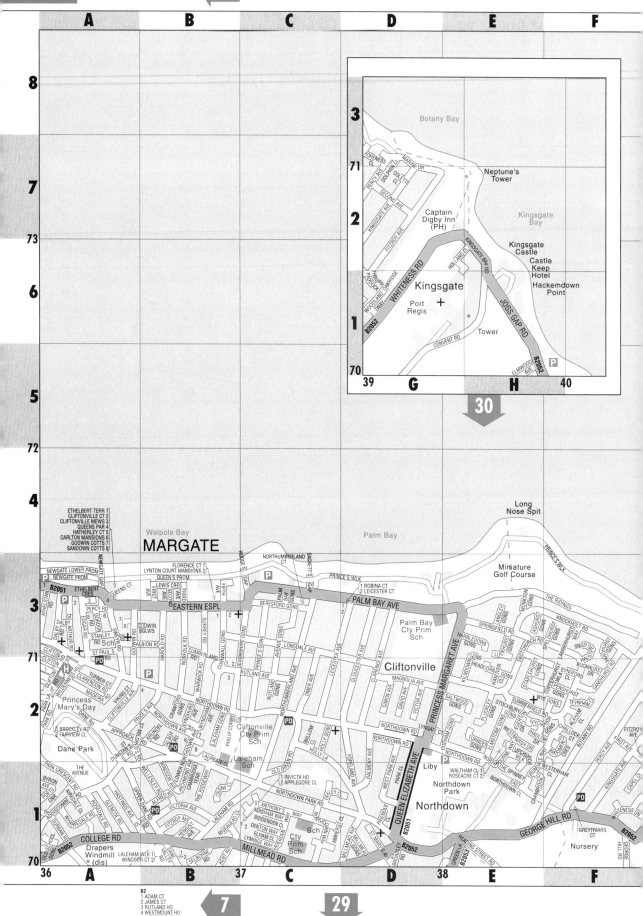

A B C D E F

8

3

71

2

1

70

Botany Bay

Neptune's Tower

Kingsgate Bay

Captain Digby Inn (PH)

Kingsgate Castle
Castle Keep Hotel
Hackemdown Point

Kingsgate

Port Regis

Tower

FORENESS CL
PERCY AVE
MARINE DR
DOLPHIN CL
COLETTE CL
KINGSGATE AVE
SECOND AVE
FITZROY AVE
WHITENESS RD
HOLLAND CL
KINGSGATE BAY RD
JOSS GAP RD
THRUPP AVE
PADDOCK CL
WOODLAND WAY
CAMBRIDGE
CONVENT RD
B2052
ELMWOOD AVE
B2052

39 G H 40

30

73

7

6

5

72

4

3

71

2

1

70

ETHELBERT TERR 1
CLIFTONVILLE CT 2
CLIFTONVILLE MEWS 3
QUEENS PAR 4
HATHERLEY CT 5
CARLTON MANSIONS 6
GODWIN COTTS 7
SANDOWN COTTS 8

Walpole Bay

MARGATE

Palm Bay

Long Nose Spit

Miniature Golf Course

NEWGATE LOWER PROM
Newgate Prom
B2051
Ethelbert Cres
ATHELSTAN RD
DALBY
ARTHUR RD
DALBY SQ
EDGAR RD
STANLEY RD
ST PAUL'S
GORDON
PERCY RD
FIRST AVE
SECOND AVE
THIRD AVE
QUEENS CT
SWEYN RD
ALBION RD
HAROLD RD
NORFOLK RD
SURREY RD
CORNWALL GDNS
DEVONSHIRE GDNS
PRINCE'S GDNS
FLORENCE CT 1
LYNTON COURT MANSIONS 2
Queen's Prom
LEWIS CRES
GODWIN BGLWS
CUMBERLAND RD
WARWICK RD
Northumberland CT
FIFTH
FOURTH
KINGS RD
GAP
SACKETTS GAP
AVENUE GDNS
LONSDALE AVE
BERESFORD GDNS
PRINCE'S WLK
EASTERN ESPL
PALM BAY AVE
1 ROBINA CT
2 LEICESTER CT
LEICESTER AVE
GLOUCESTER AVE
CLARENCE AVE
Palm Bay Cty Prim Sch
HARBLEDOWN GDNS
LANGLEY GDNS
SPRINGFIELD RD
MONKTON GDNS
KNOCKHOLT RD
THE RIDINGS
Cliftonville
CLIFTON GDNS
CLIFTON RD
WILDERNESS HILL
TURNER CT
CLARENDON RD
MADEIRA RD
VIKING CT
CLIFTONVILLE AVE
PRICE'S AVE
CRAWFORD GDNS
NORTHDOWN RD
LYNHURST AVE
WYNDHAM AVE
RUTLAND AVE
NORTHUMBERLAND AVE
OMER AVE
SIMON AVE
DAVID AVE
VICTOR AVE
MAGNOLIA AVE
SALTWOOD GDNS
STOCKBURY GDNS
PLUCKLEY GDNS
SUMMERFIELD RD
ELMSTONE GDNS
WESTMARSH DR
HADLOW DR
IVYCHURCH
READCORN GDNS
HARVEY GDNS
COPPERHURST GDNS
STAPLEHURST GDNS
WYE GDNS
EGERTON DR
TURDEN GDNS
LUCKHURST
NORTH FORELAND AVE
LIPCHURCH
UPCHURCH WLK
PRINCESS MARGARET AVE
HALSTEAD GDNS
LAMBERHURST WAY
SPELDHURST GDNS
ASHURST GDNS
EASTCHURCH RD
HALL ST
BUCKHURST DR
EYNSFORD CL
SANDHURST RD
TEYNHAM CL
CHALLOCK CT
FITZROY
Princess Mary's Day
PARK LA
BROCKLEY RD
FAIRVIEW CL
DANE RD
ST DUNSTAN'S RD
ARUNDEL RD
LAUREATE AVE
Cliftonville Cty Prim Sch
Laleham Sch
Dane Park
THE AVENUE
BYRON AVE
PORTS CRES
ADDISCOMBE RD
AIRDALE CT
WHITEFIELD RD
DURBAN RD
ROSEDALE RD
GLENCOE RD
PARK CRESCENT RD
HASTINGS AVE
UPPER DANE RD
WINDSOR AVE
WILDERNESS HILL
ALFRED RD
LOWER NORTHDOWN AVE
CAMBRIDGE
THE RIDGEWAY
LEGGE LA
Philip Corby
WILLOW
OLD GREEN RD
HOLLY LA
DALMENY AVE
FORELAND AVE
WEST PARK AVE
PARK CL
FRIEND CL
Queen Elizabeth Ave
Liby
Northdown Park
WALTHAM CL 1
ROSEACRE CT 2
Northdown
CRABTREE CT
CRUNDALE WAY
NORTHDOWN CL
CRABBROOK CL
THE SPINNEY
WESTERHAM
PERCY RD
FIRST AVE
COPEL CL
GREYFRIARS CT
Nursery
WHITENESS GN
GEORGE GN
GEORGE HILL RD
B2053
1 ADAM CT
2 JAMES CT
3 RUTLAND HO
4 WESTMOUNT HO
5 HIGHFIELD CT
6 REBECCA CT
7 RICHARD CT
8 LEONA CT
B2
PARK 4
1 BROCKLEY RD
VICTORIA AVE
JUBILEE
FITZROY AVE
HENGIST AVE
LALEHAM RD
RITERSDALE
SELBORNE RD
ST ANTHONY'S WAY
ADISHAM WAY
DENTON WAY
ELHAM CL
LYMINGE WAY
BIDDENDEN CL
KINGSLEY CL
ST MARY'S
AMHERST CL
MILLMEAD AVE
WELLMEAD
BRADLEY RD
B2051
Cty Prim Sch
B2052
READING STREET RD
GREEN LA
COLLEGE RD
B2052
Drapers Windmill (dis)
OLD SCHOOL
LALEHAM WLK 1
WINDSOR CT 2
DANE
MILLMEAD RD
GEORGE HILL RD
HIGH ST
BROCK
1 INVICTA HO
2 APPLEDORE CL
Northdown Park Rd
NORTHDOWN RD

36 A 37 B C 38 D E 39 F

7 29

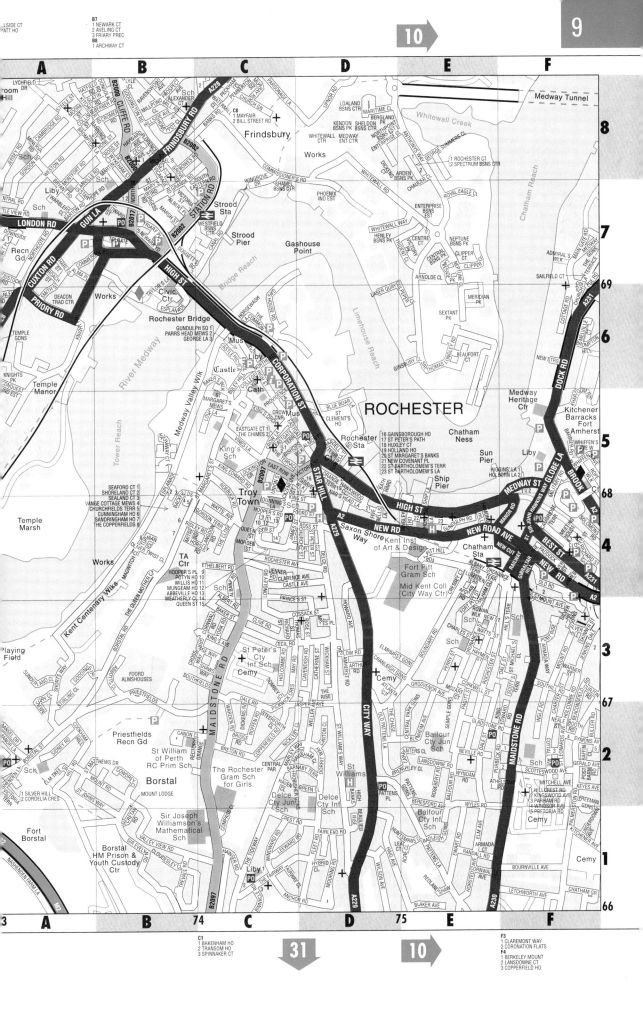

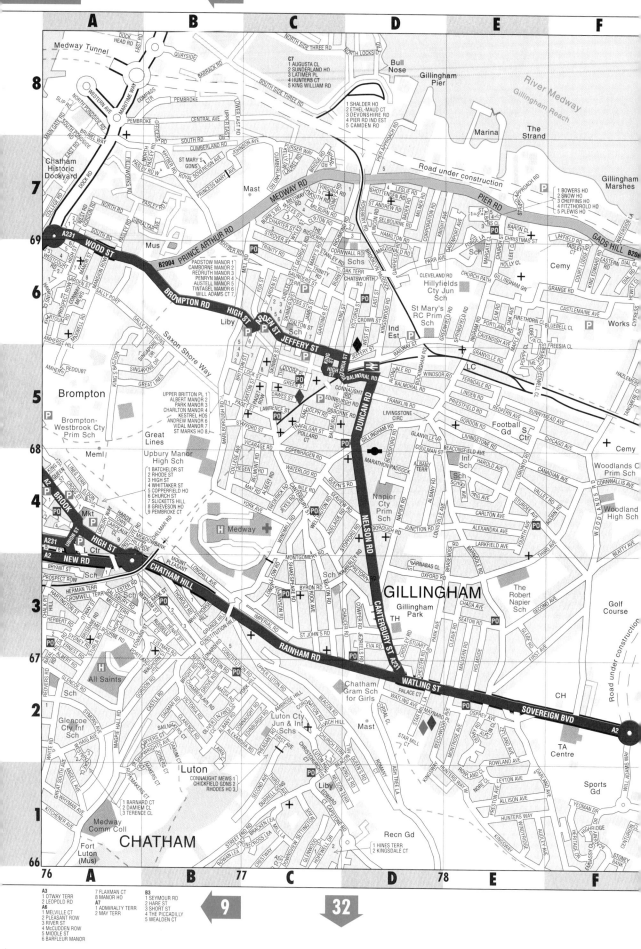

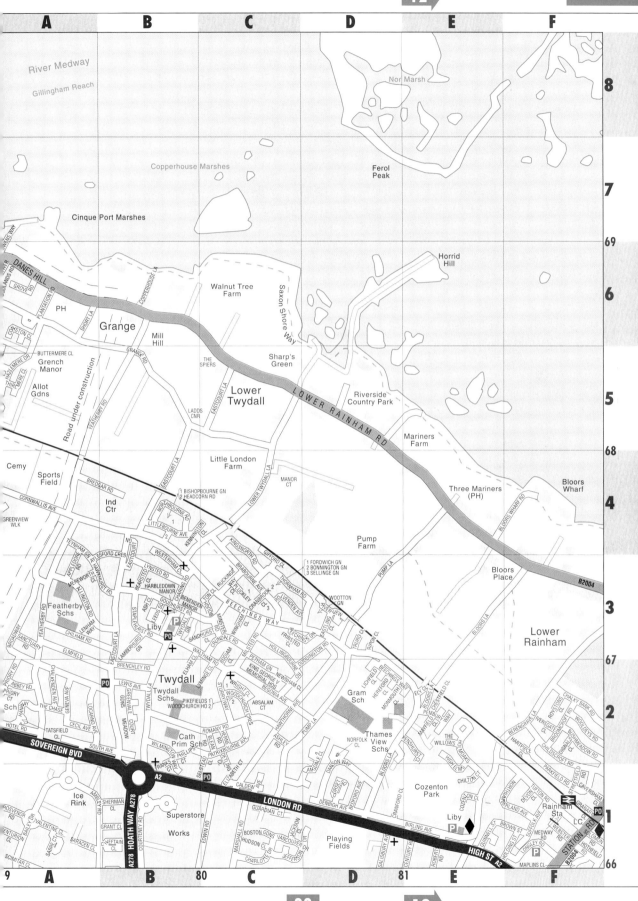

Stray
Marshes

Old Counter Wall

Elmley Island

Windmill Creek

Elmley Fleet

Nature
Reserve

Elmley
Marshes

Sharfleet
Creek

Cockleshell
Creek

Wellmarsh
Creek

The Swale

Main Channel

Peg Fleet

Fowley Channel

Saxon Shore Way

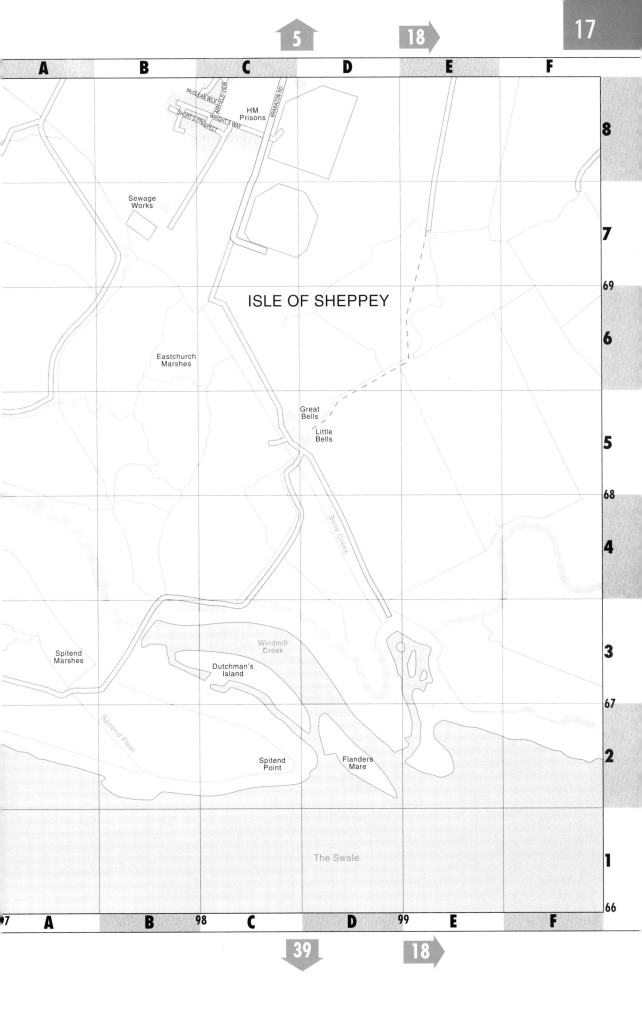

ISLE OF SHEPPEY

Sewage
Works

HM
Prisons

McCLEAN WLK
AIRFIELD VIEW
WRIGHT'S WAY
SHORT'S PROSPECT
BRABAZON RD

Eastchurch
Marshes

Great
Bells

Little
Bells

Bells Creek

Windmill
Creek

Spitend
Marshes

Dutchman's
Island

Spitend Fleet

Spitend
Point

Flanders
Mare

The Swale

A　　B　　C　　D　　E　　F

8

Capel Hill
Farm

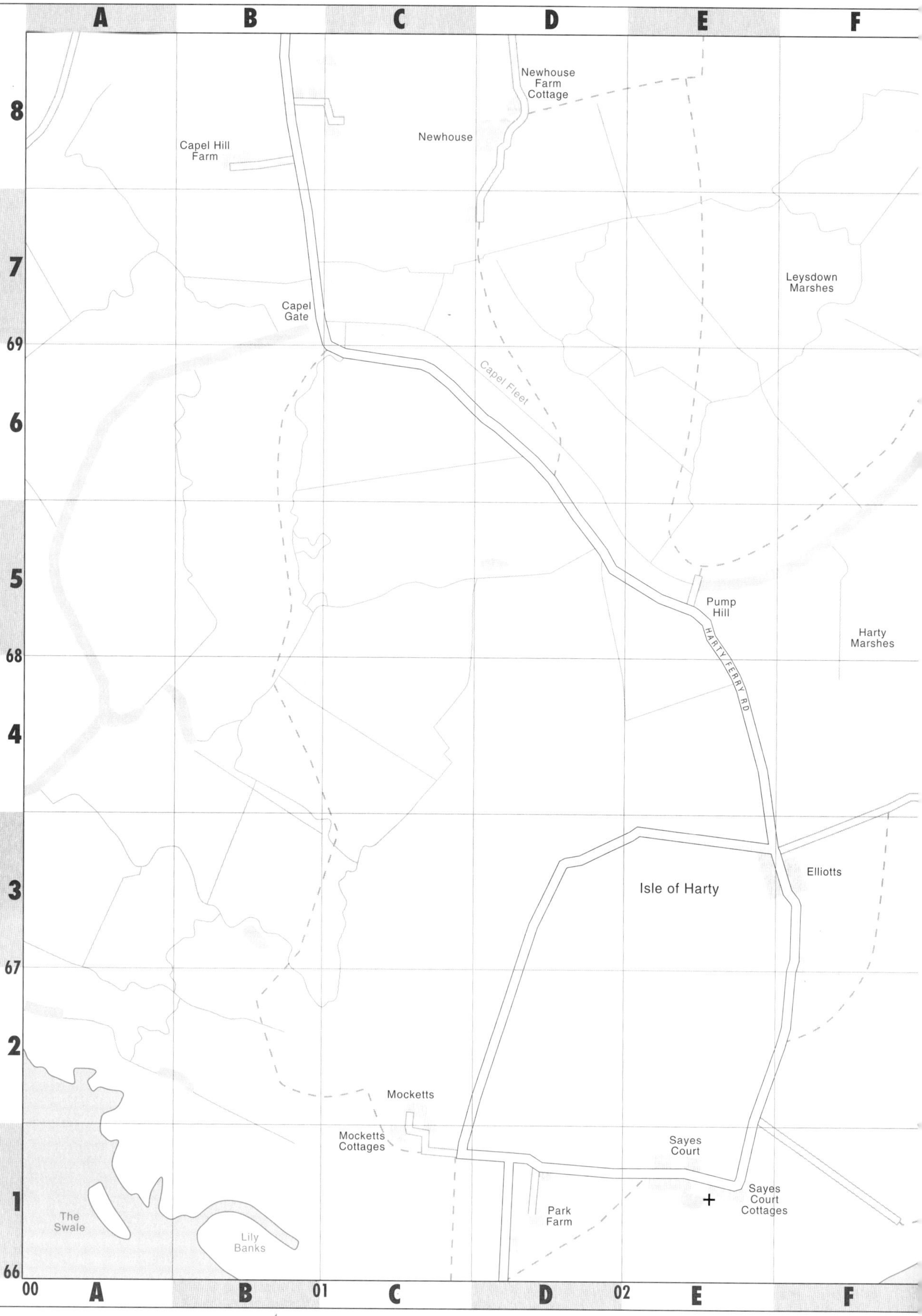

Newhouse
Farm
Cottage

Newhouse

7

Leysdown
Marshes

Capel
Gate

69

Capel Fleet

6

5

Pump
Hill

Harty
Marshes

68

HARTY FERRY RD

4

3

Isle of Harty

Elliotts

67

2

Mocketts

Mocketts
Cottages

Sayes
Court

1

The
Swale

Lily
Banks

Park
Farm

+

Sayes
Court
Cottages

66

A B C D E F

8

Priory
Hill

Coastal
Park

SEAVIEW AVE

WING RD

North
Sea

Leysdown
Marshes

SHELLNESS RD

Muswell Manor
Country Club

7

Capel Fleet

69

6

SHELLBEACH

Harty
Marshes

5

TAMARISK
YELLOW
SANDS

Hamlet of Shellness

68

COASTGUARD
COTTS

Nature
Reserve

4

Brewers
Hill

Shell
Ness

3

67

2

The Swale

1

66

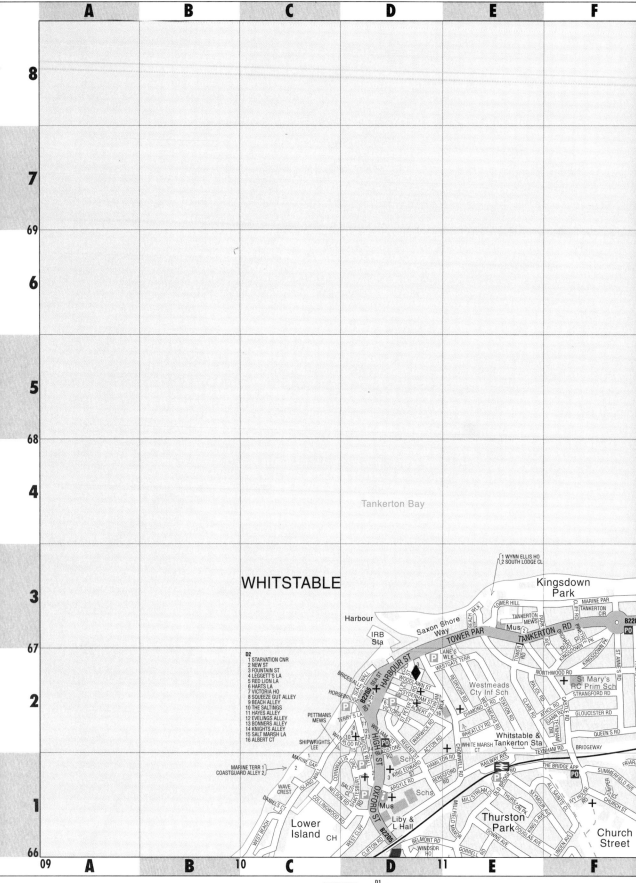

A B C D E F

8
7
69
6
5
68
4
Tankerton Bay

3 WHITSTABLE

Kingsdown
Park

1 WYNN ELLIS HO
2 SOUTH LODGE CL

Harbour

Saxon Shore Way

TOWER PAR

TANKERTON RD

B220

67

D2
1 STARVATION CNR
2 NEW ST
3 FOUNTAIN ST
4 LEGGETT'S LA
5 RED LION LA
6 HARTS LA
7 VICTORIA HO
8 SQUEEZE GUT ALLEY
9 BEACH ALLEY
10 THE SALTINGS
11 HAYES ALLEY
12 EVELINGS ALLEY
13 BONNERS ALLEY
14 KNIGHTS ALLEY
15 SALT MARSH LA
16 ALBERT CT

IRB
Sta

Westmeads
Cty Inf Sch

St Mary's
RC Prim Sch

STRANGFORD RD

GLOUCESTER RD

QUEEN'S RD

2

Whitstable &
Tankerton Sta

BRIDGEWAY

PETTMANS
MEWS

MARINE TERR 1
COASTGUARD ALLEY 2

King Edward

Schs

Whitstable &
Tankerton Sta

THE BRIDGE APP

1

WAVE
CREST

Mus

Liby &
L Hall

Thurston
Park

Church
Street

Lower
Island

66

09 A B 10 C D 11 E F

D1
1 REEVES ALLEY
2 KEMP ALLEY
3 SKINNER'S ALLEY

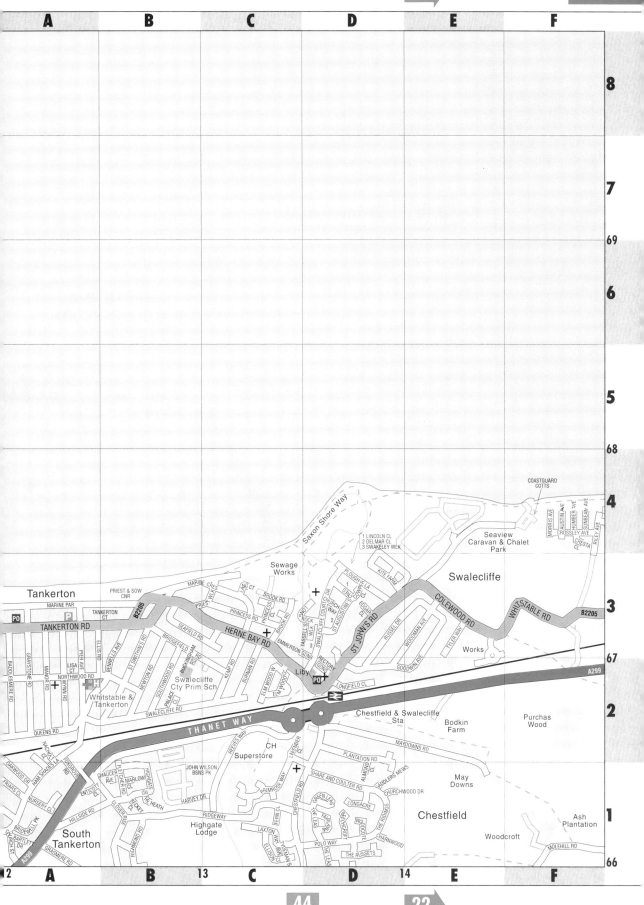

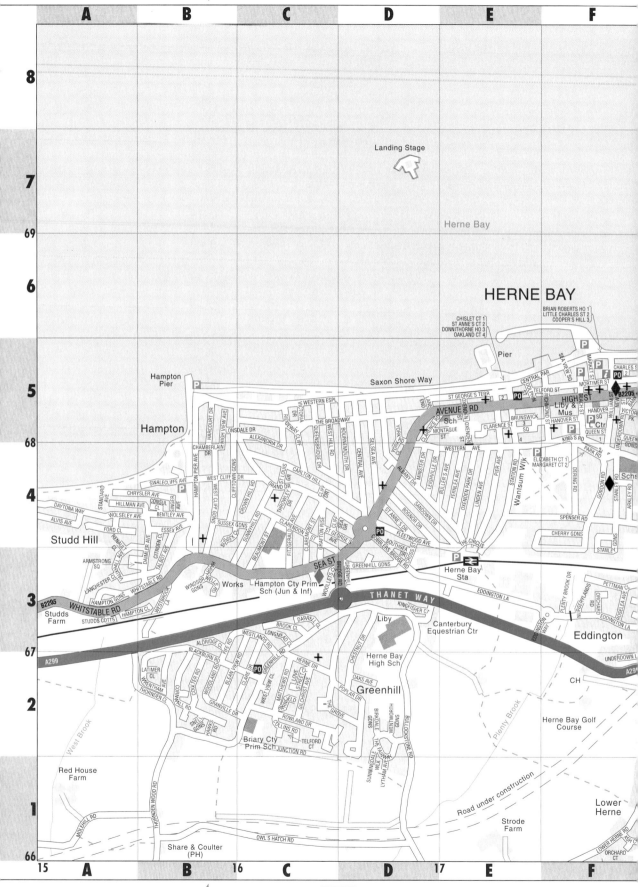

Landing Stage

Herne Bay

HERNE BAY

CHISLET CT 1
ST ANNE'S CT 2
DONNITHORNE HO 3
OAKLAND CT 4

BRIAN ROBERTS HO 1
LITTLE CHARLES ST 2
COOPER'S HILL 3

Pier

Hampton
Pier

Saxon Shore Way

CENTRAL PAR

AVENUE RD

HIGH ST

Liby &
Mus

L Ctr

Hampton

Western Espl

St George's Terr

Telford St

Mortimer St

Hanover St
Brunswick Clarence St SQ Hanover St
Montague
Western Ave
King's Rd
Queen St

The Broadway

Elizabeth Ct 1
Margaret Ct 2

Schs

Studd Hill

West Cliff Dr

Sandown Dr

Wantsum Wijk

Dering Rd

Spenser Rd

Cherry Gdns

Stanley

THE CIRCUS

Herne Bay
Sta

B2205
Studds
Farm

WHITSTABLE RD

Studds Cotts

Works

Hampton Cty Prim
Sch (Jun & Inf)

SEA ST

BRIDGE RD

Greenhill Gdns

THANET WAY

Kingfisher Ct

Eddington

EDDINGTON LA

A299

Liby

Canterbury
Equestrian Ctr

UNDERDOWN L

A29

Latimer
Cl
Wrentham

Herne Bay
High Sch

CH

Herne Bay Golf
Course

Briary Cty
Prim Sch

Greenhill

Plenty Brook

West Brook

Red House
Farm

Road under construction

Lower
Herne

Strode
Farm

MOLEHILL RD

OWL'S HATCH RD

Share & Coulter
(PH)

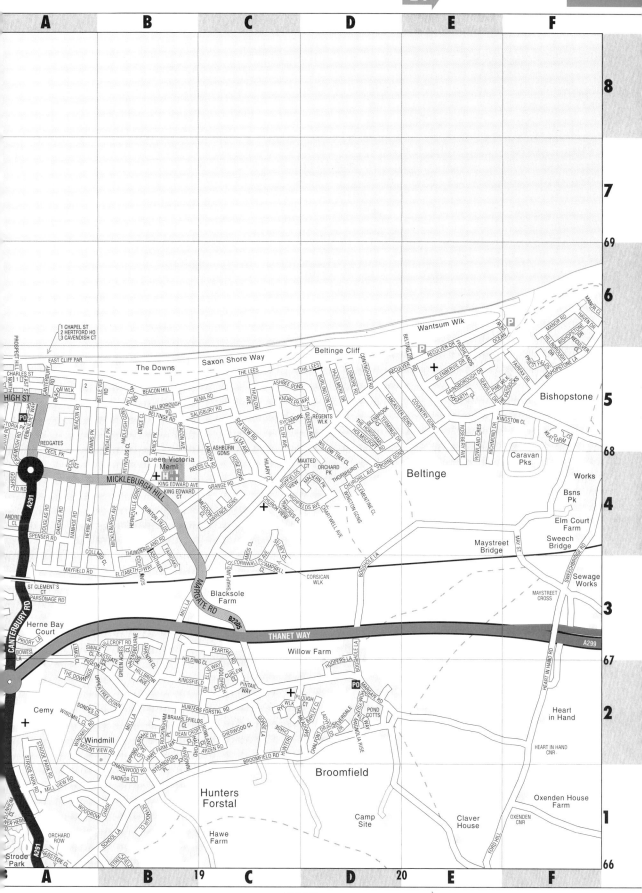

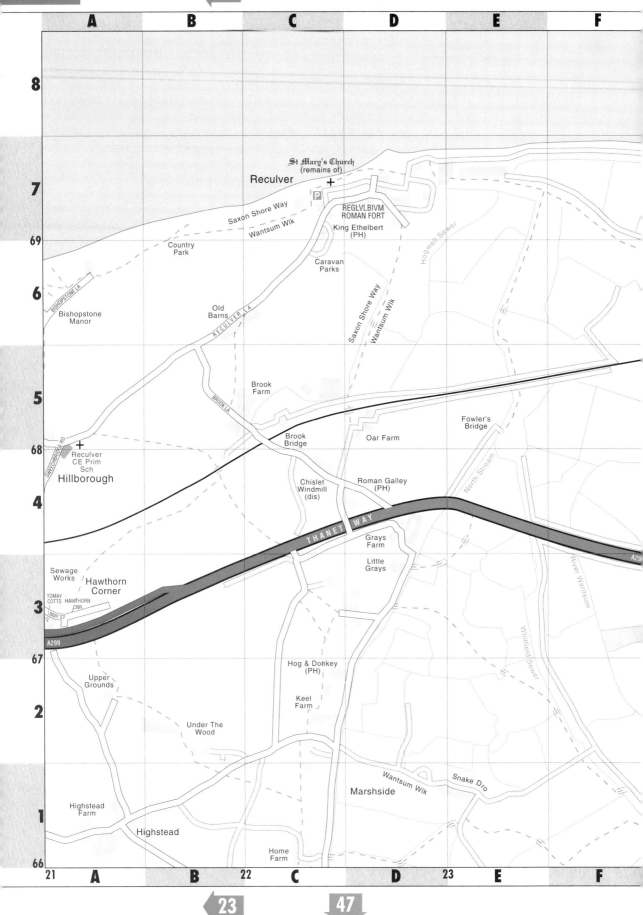

A B C D E F

8

St Mary's Church
(remains of)
Reculver

7
P
REGLVLBIVM
ROMAN FORT
King Ethelbert
(PH)

69
Saxon Shore Way
Wantsum Wlk
Country
Park
Caravan
Parks

Hogwell Sewer

6
BISHOPSTONE LA
Bishopstone
Manor
Old
Barns
RECULVER LA
Saxon Shore Way
Wantsum Wlk

5
BROOK LA
Brook
Farm

Fowler's
Bridge

Brook
Bridge
Oar Farm

North Stream

68
SPEEDBRIDGE RD
Reculver
CE Prim
Sch
Hillborough

Chislet
Windmill
(dis)
Roman Galley
(PH)

4
THANET WAY
Grays
Farm

A29

Sewage
Works
Hawthorn
Corner
Little
Grays

River Wantsum

3
TOMAY
COTTS HAWTHORN
CNR
MAY ST

Whitfield Sewer

67
A299
Hog & Donkey
(PH)

Upper
Grounds
Keel
Farm

2
Under The
Wood

Wantsum Wlk
Snake Dro

1
Highstead
Farm
Marshside

Highstead

66
Home
Farm

21 A B 22 C D 23 E F

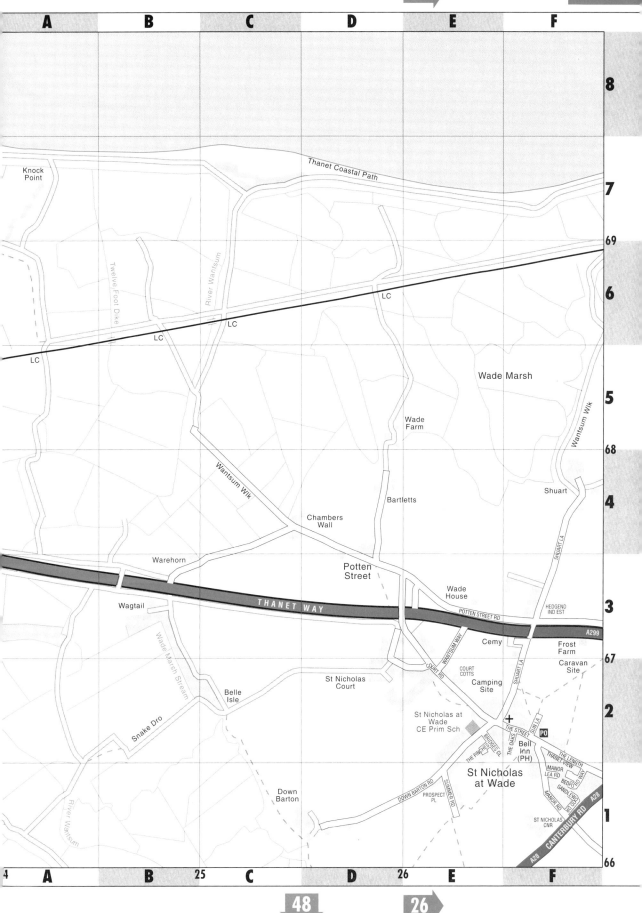

A B C D E F

8
7
69
6

Knock
Point

Thanet Coastal Path

River Wantsum

Twelve Foot Dike

LC
LC
LC
LC

Wade Marsh

Wantsum Wlk

5
68
4

Wade
Farm

Wantsum Wlk

Bartletts

Shuart

Chambers
Wall

Potten
Street

SHUART LA

Warehorn

Wade
House

THANET WAY

Potten Street Rd

HEDGEND
IND EST

3
67
2

Wagtail

A299

Cemy

Frost
Farm

Caravan
Site

Wade Marsh Stream

WANTSUM WAY

COURT
COTTS

Camping
Site

SHUART LA

SHUART RD

St Nicholas
Court

Belle
Isle

SURT RD

Snake Dro

St Nicholas at
Wade
CE Prim Sch

SUN LA

THE STREET

PO

Bell
Inn
(PH)

THE OAKS

THE LENGTH

TRANET VIEW

BRIDGES CL

THE FINCHES CL

MANOR
LEA RD

BEDFO

SANDLEWS

St Nicholas
at Wade

DOWN BARTON RD

PROSPECT
PL

SUMMER RD

MANOR RD

BEDFORD WAY

CANTERBURY RD   A28

A28

ST NICHOLAS
CNR

River Wantsum

Down
Barton

1
66

F8
1 DALLINGER RD
2 CARMEL CT
3 SANDPIPER CT
4 GAINSBORO RD
5 LYELL CT
6 HOMEBIRCH HO

A B C D E F

8

SEA VIEW HTS 1
APRIL RISE 2
BAY VIEW HTS 3
McKINLAY CT 4
RINGSLOE CT 5
FERNDOWN 6

Minnis
Bay

Groynes

Wantsum Wlk
Thanet Coastal Path

7

Darygnton Ave

Dane Rd

Horsa Rd

Ingoldsby Rd

Gore End

Gore End
Farm

Birchington-On-Sea Sta

Birchington

BIERCE CT 1
SANDLE'S RD 2

69

Plumpudding
Island

LC

LC

LC

LC

6

Brooksend Stream

Wade
Marsh

Great
Brooksend
Farm

MILL LA

MILL ROW

5

Upper
Hale
Court

68

Brooks
End

College
Farm

Canterbury Road Birchington

King Edward Rd

4

Hale

Nether
Hale
Farm

Coney
Close

Crispe Rd

3

Monkton Road
Farm

A299

Potten Street Rd

THANET WAY

Canterbury Rd

67

St Nicholas
Rdbt

Seamark Rd

2

A28

Plumstone Rd

1

Manor
Rd

66

A299

27 A B 28 C D 29 E F

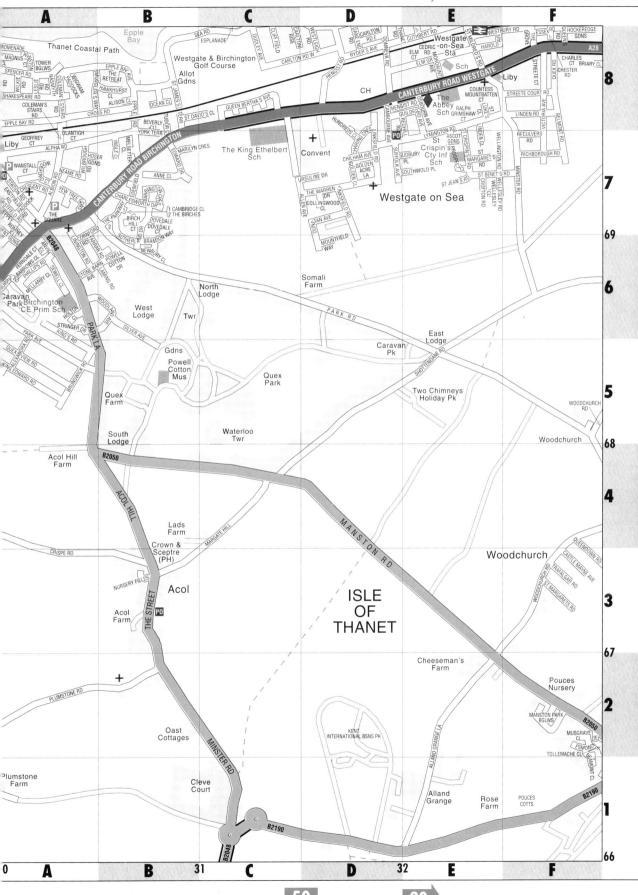

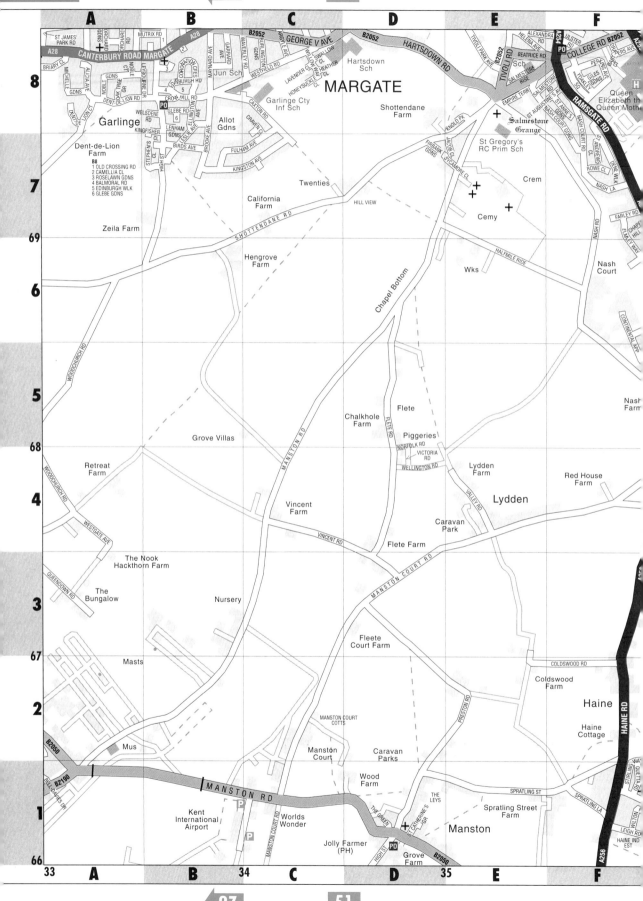

MARGATE

Garlinge

Dent-de-Lion Farm

B8
1 OLD CROSSING RD
2 CAMELLIA CL
3 ROSELAWN GDNS
4 BALMORAL RD
5 EDINBURGH WLK
6 GLEBE GDNS

Zeila Farm

California Farm

Twenties

HILL VIEW

Hengrove Farm

Chapel Bottom

Grove Villas

Retreat Farm

Vincent Farm

The Nook
Hackthorn Farm

The Bungalow

Nursery

Masts

Mus

Chalkhole Farm

Flete

Piggeries

VICTORIA RD

Lydden Farm

Lydden

Caravan Park

Flete Farm

Fleete Court Farm

Red House Farm

Coldswood Farm

Haine

Haine Cottage

Manston Court Cotts

Manston Court

Caravan Parks

Wood Farm

THE LEYS

Spratling Street Farm

Manston

Kent International Airport

Worlds Wonder

Jolly Farmer (PH)

Grove Farm

Salmestone Grange

St Gregory's RC Prim Sch

Crem

Cemy

Wks

Nash Court

Nash Farm

Hartsdown Sch

Shottendane Farm

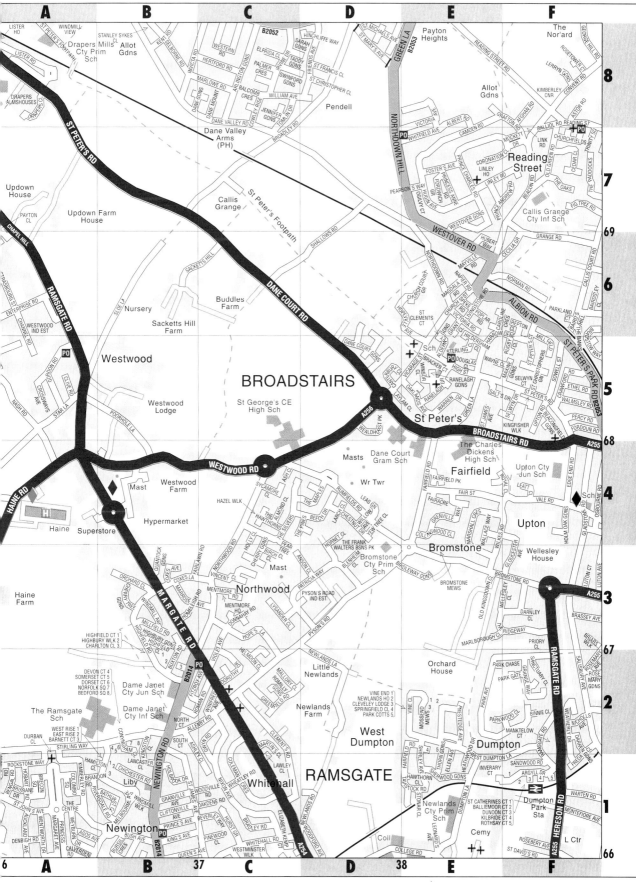

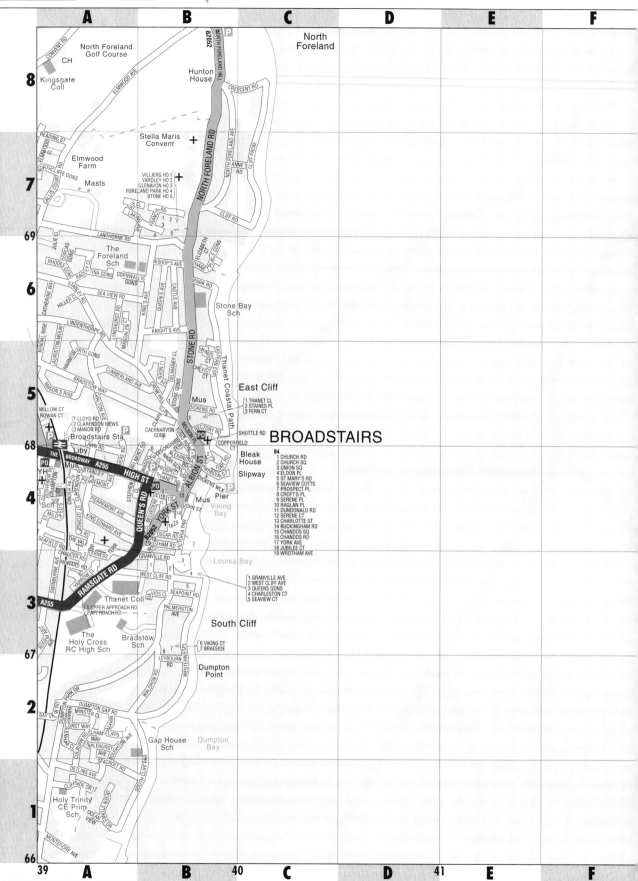

BROADSTAIRS

North Foreland Golf Course

CH
Kingsgate Coll

North Foreland

Hunton House

North Foreland

CONVENT RD
ELMWOOD AVE
B2052
NORTH FORELAND WAY
CRESCENT RD

Stella Maris Convent

Elmwood Farm

Masts

READING ST
ELMWOOD RD
NORTHCLIFFE GDNS
CALLIS COURT RD

VILLIERS HO 1
YARDLEY HO 2
GLENAVON HO 3
FORELAND PARK HO 4
STONE HO 5

NORTH FORELAND RD
NORTH FORELAND AVE
NORTH ANNE'S RD
CLIFF PROM
CLIFF RD

J CL
J GL
FRANCIS ST
LAKING AVE

LANTHORNE RD

The Foreland Sch

ELIZABETH CT
THANE PLACE GDNS
BISHOP'S AVE
PARK RD
CASTLE AVE

JULIE
DORCAS GDNS
DOUGLAS GDNS
RHODES GDNS
TINA GDNS
RADLEY
STANLEY RD
CORNWALLIS GDNS

Stone Bay Sch

CATHERINE WAY
HILLER CL
SEA VIEW RD
KING'S AVE
QUEEN'S AVE
KING'S AVE

KENDAL RISE
LAURISTON MOUNT
HARMEN RD
ORTH GDNS
LINDENTHORPE RD
LYNDHURST RD
MAGDALEN CT
KNIGHT'S AVE

STONE RD
WINGS CT
EASTERN ESP
CHEVIOT CT

MASON'S RISE
BRADSTOW WAY
CARLTON AVE
CUMBERLAND AVE
CLARE RD
CLARENDON GDNS

East Cliff

Thanet Coastal Path

1 THANET CL
2 STAINES PL
3 FERN CT

WILLOW CT
ROWAN CT
1 LLOYD RD
2 CLARENDON MEWS
3 MANOR RD

Mus
DICKENS RD

RECTORY RD
SHUTTLE RD
COPPERFIELD CT

Broadstairs Sta
Liby
Mus
THE BROADWAY
A255 HIGH ST

CAERNARVON GDNS

Bleak House

Slipway

B4
1 CHURCH RD
2 CHURCH SQ
3 UNION SQ
4 ELDON PL
5 ST MARY'S RD
6 SEAVIEW COTTS
7 PROSPECT PL
8 CROFT'S PL
9 SERENE PL
10 RAGLAN PL
11 DUNDONALD RD
12 SERENE CT
13 CHARLOTTE ST
14 BUCKINGHAM RD
15 CHANDOS SQ
16 CHANDOS RD
17 YORK AVE
18 JUBILEE CT
19 WROTHAM AVE

PO
YH
Sch
STANLEY
PIERREMONT
PIERREMONT AVE
KING EDWARD AVE
QUEEN'S RD
YORK ST
ALBION ST
NELSON'S PL

Pier
Viking Bay

MILDREDS
ST GEORGE'S RD
THE VALE
BELVEDERE RD
OSCAR RD
WROTHAM RD
VICTORIA PAR

SEAFIELD RD
CHAUCER RD
HOWARD RD
GRANVILLE RD
WEST CLIFF RD

Louisa Bay

1 GRANVILLE AVE
2 WEST CLIFF AVE
3 QUEENS GDNS
4 CHARLESTON CT
5 SEAVIEW CT

RAMSGATE RD
SWINBURNE AVE
VIDS CL
SEAPOINT RD

Thanet Coll
A255
1 UPPER APPROACH RD
2 APPROACH RD

PALMERSTON AVE

South Cliff

ROSE AVE
The Holy Cross RC High Sch
Bradstow Sch

LEYBOURN RD
WESTERN ESPL

6 VIKING CT
7 BRAESIDE

Dumpton Point

DUMPTON PARK DR
DUMPTON GAP RD
MINSTER CL
WALDRON RD

BAY VW
W RD
HURST WAY
ELHAM WAY
TAPLEHURST
CLIFTON AVE
CLIFFS
STATION AVE

Gap House Sch

Dumpton Bay

DETLING AVE
SEACROFT RD
SOUTH CLIFF PAR

Holy Trinity CE Prim Sch

CLIFFSIDE DR
OCEAN'S DR
OCEAN VIEW

MONTEFIORE AVE

39
40
41

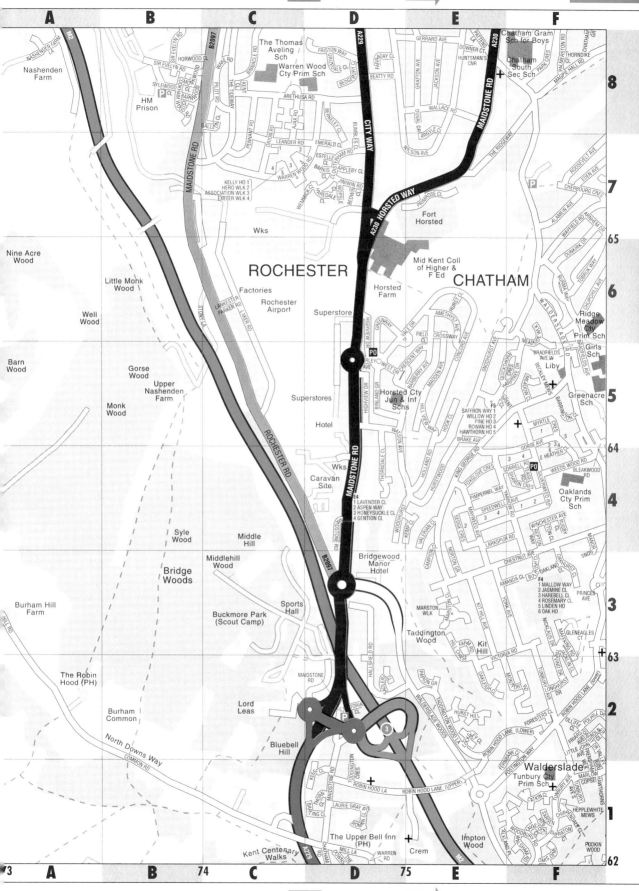

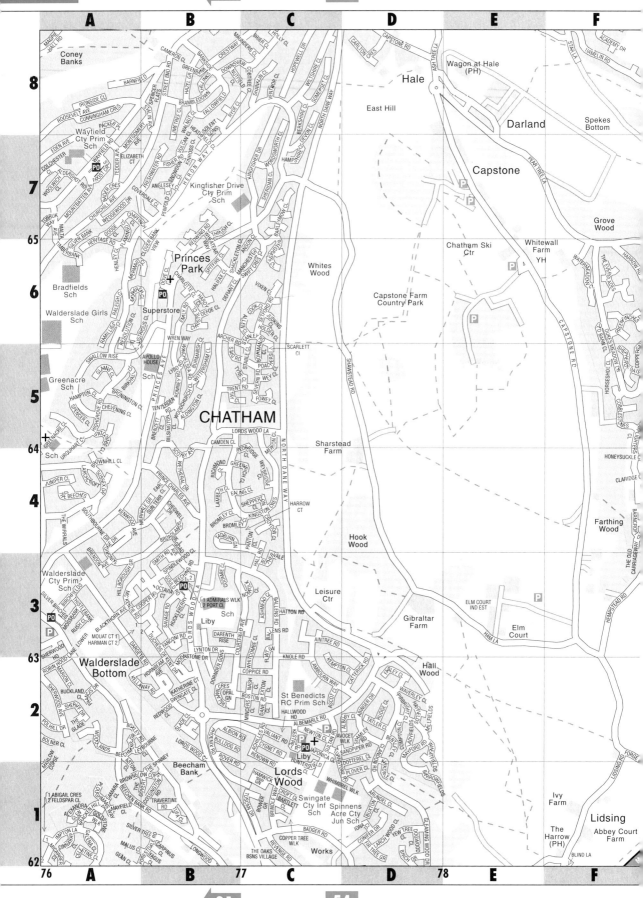

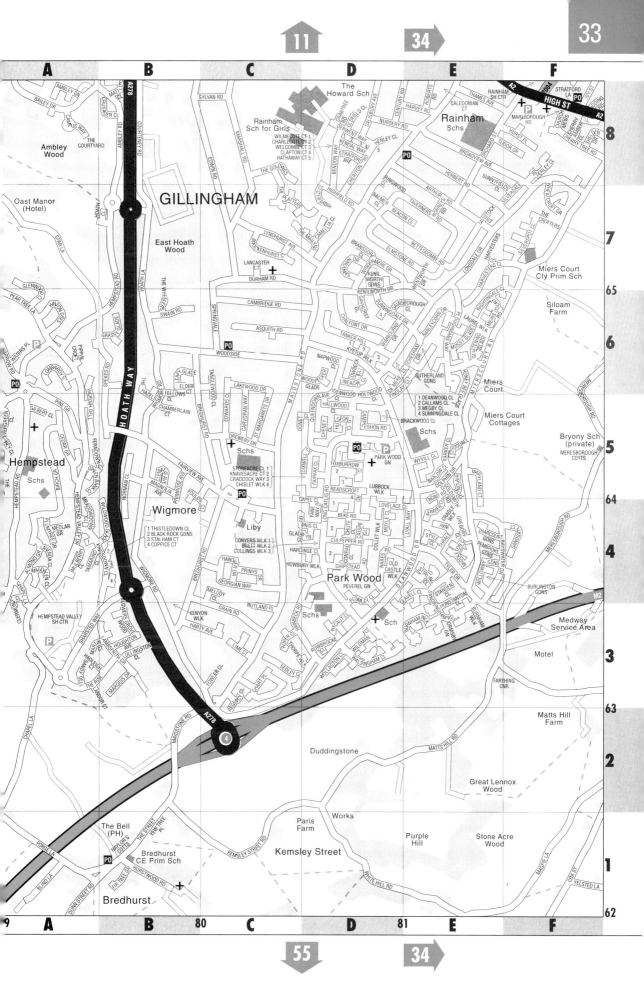

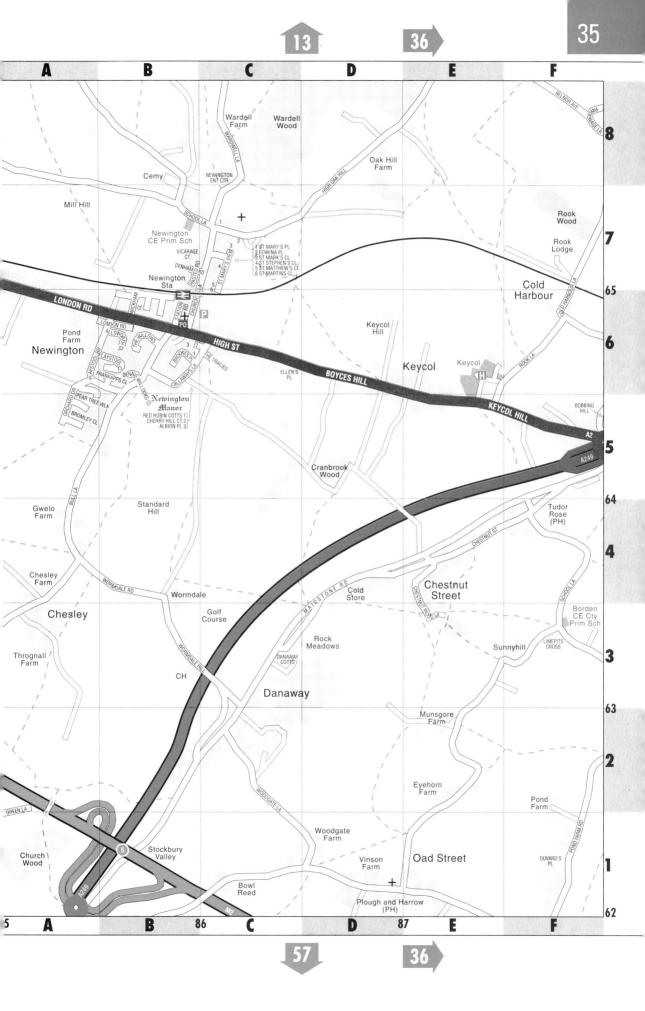

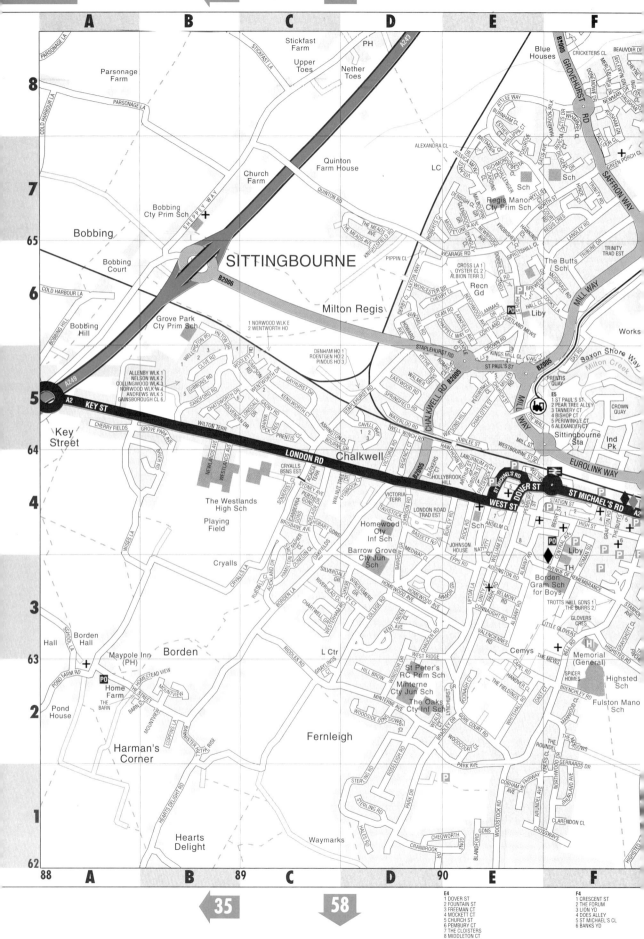

SITTINGBOURNE

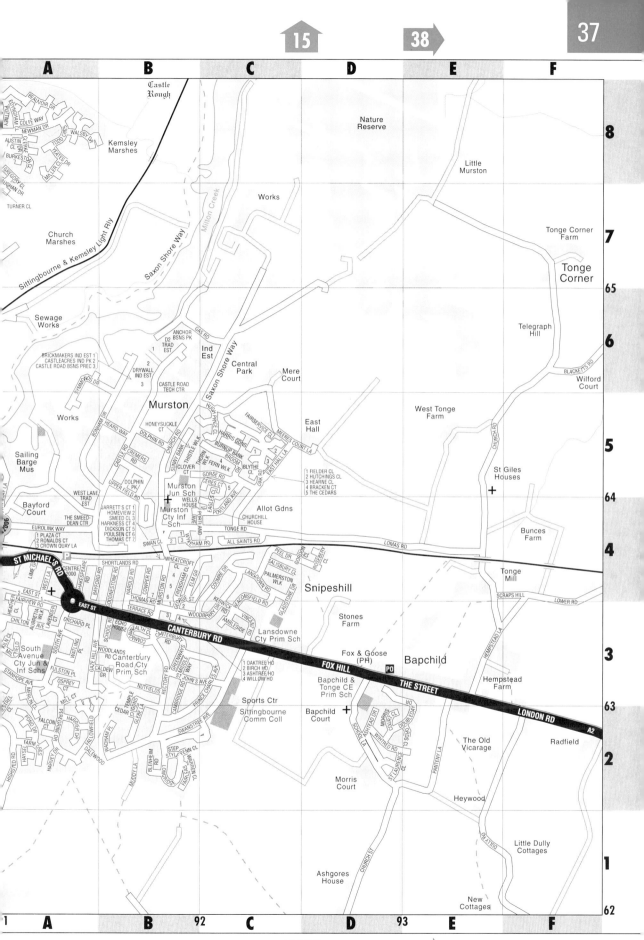

A B C D E F

8

Saxon Shore Way

The Swale

Wharf

Conyer Creek

Blacketts

7

BLACKETTS COTTS

Works

Saxon Shore Way

Rifle Range (dis)

65

BLACKETTS RD

Wilford Court Farm

Ship Inn (PH)

QUAY COTTS

1 COASTGUARD COTTS
2 BRUNSWICK COTTS

6

Cheke's Court

THE QUAY

Dock

1 2

EASTWOOD COTTS

THE MOORINGS

BRUNSWICK FIELD

Conyer

5

Stone Chimney Farm

Banks Farm

64

Bax

NEW COTTS

Teynham Street

Peete House

4

LC

Teynham Court

CONYER RD

Teynham Court Farm

+

Fair View

LOWER RD

LC

Sewage Works

Barrow Green

3

Frognal

CHURCHILL HO

Teynham Sta

STATION ROW

Railway Cotts

Osiers Farm

ORCHARD VIEW

MARY'S RD

THE CRESCENT

OSIER RD

LOWER RD

63

Little Radfield

Teynham

BAK CL

CHERRY TREE CL

ROPER RD

3

CLAXFIELD COTTS

HONEYBALL WLK

BROADARE

2

A2

Teynham Parochial CE Prim Sch

BELLE FRIDAY LA

MORELLO CL

RIVERS RD

AMBER CL

BRADFIELD AVE

FREDRICK'S ROW

1 ROUNDEL CL
2 TRIGG'S ROW
3 BRIDGE COTTS

2

Radfield

Depot

Comet Motel

FROGNAL

STATION RD

NUTBERRY CL

Whent's Farm

Liby

FROGNAL GDNS

DONALD MOOR AVE

NOBEL CL

P

PO

Claxfield Farm

CLAXFIELD RD

CHERRY GDNS RD

NEW GARDENS RD

LONDON RD

White Hall

+

LYNSTED LA

CELLAR HILL

NOLDS RD

SANDOWN COTTS

1

Cellarhill

Cellar Hill Farm

Orchard House

A2

VIGO TERR

62

A B C D E F

The Swale

Fowley
Island

South Deep

Saxon Shore Way

8

Rifle Range
(dis)

Luddenham Gut

7

65

Teynham Level

6

Little
Uplees

UPLEES
COTTS

UPLEES RD

Howletts

5

64

Luddenham
Marshes

Poplar
Hall

UP. S. R RD

4

Luddenham
Court

3

CHERRY TREE
DR

63

BROOK
COTTS

Elverton

Hawks & Beetles
Farm

Nash's
Farm

Deerton
Street

The
Mounted Rifleman
(PH)

2

The Old
Farmhouse

Wildmarsh

Lower
Newlands

THE ELMS

The
Old Rectory

Luddenham
Cty Prim Sch

LC

BYSING WOOD RD

LOWER RD

Mockbeggar

Bysing
Wood

1

Mockbeggar
Farm

LC

Stone
Farm

BYSING WOOD
COTTS

BYSING WOOD RD

62

7 A B 98 C D 99 E F

39
18

A B C D E F

8

The Ferry Inn (PH)

HARTY FERRY RD

The Swale

7

Uplees Marshes

65

6

Gate House Bungalow

Saxon Shore Way

Nature Reserve

Oare Marshes

Nagden Marshes

5

HARTY FERRY COTTS

64

UPLEES RD

4

Faversham Creek

Broomfield Farm

Court Lodge Farm

Norman's Hill

Shipwright's Arms (PH)

Hollowshore

UPLEES RD

CHURCH RD

+ Pheasant Farm

Oare Creek

Ham Marshes

3

Wharf

Works

Oare

RUSSELL PL

PO

PH

63

HARRISON TERR

COLEGATES CT

COLEGATES RD

MOUNT PLEASANT

THE STREET

Ham Farm

2

COLEGATES RD

B2045

JOHN HALL CL

Works

Gravel Works

Piggery

SEAGAR RD

WRIGHT CT

Windmill (dis)

ORE RD

Gate House

HAM RD

FAVERSHAM

WESTERN LINK

1

Works

The Brents

Saxon Shore Way

Faversham Creek

Sewage Works

MAITLAND CL

JOHNSON CL

CHURCH HILL

SHERWOOD CL

WELLS WAY

Davington Cty Prim Sch

GOLDFINCH CL

FOSTALL RD

SPRINGHEAD RD

LARKSFIELD RD

BROOK RD

UPPER BRENTS

BRENTS IND EST

Wharf

Works

ABBEY FIELDS

BLAXLAND CL

WILDISH RD

IVORY CL

BYSING WOOD RD

B2045

BYSING WOOD RD

62

00 A B 01 C D 02 E F

39
62

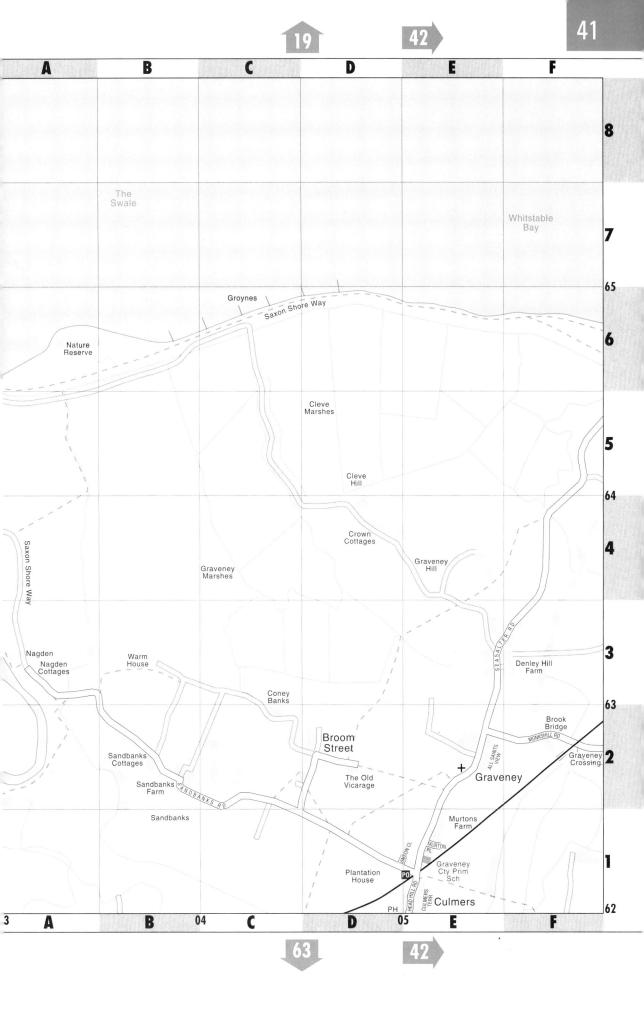

A   B   C   D   E   F

8

7

65

6

5

64

4

3

63

2

1

62

Whitstable Bay

Saxon Shore Way

FAVERSHAM RD

Caravan & Chalet Site

Blue Anchor (PH)

PRESTON PAR

BOWER RD
HODGSON RD
ST MARY'S GR
ALLAN RD
WALLDROKE RD
LUCERNE CT
KIMBERLEY GR
LUCERNE DR
ROBERTS RD
LADYSMITH GR
BEACONSFIELD

Caravan Park

Caravan Park

Caravan Parks

Ye Old Sportsman (Inn)

Graveney Marshes

Seasalter Level

Denly Hill

Mount Pleasant

SEASALTER LA

A299

Hern Hill Nursery

Brookdene Farm

Yorkletts

Brookhill Farm

Monkshill Farm

Ind Est

Waterham

MONKSHILL RD

HIGHSTREET RD

THANET WAY

HIGHSTREET RD

DARGATE RD

Highstreet

Horse Hill Farm

Waterham Farm

WATERHAM RD

Horse Hill

Brook Hall Farm

PLUMPUDDING LA

Lamberhurst Farm

A299

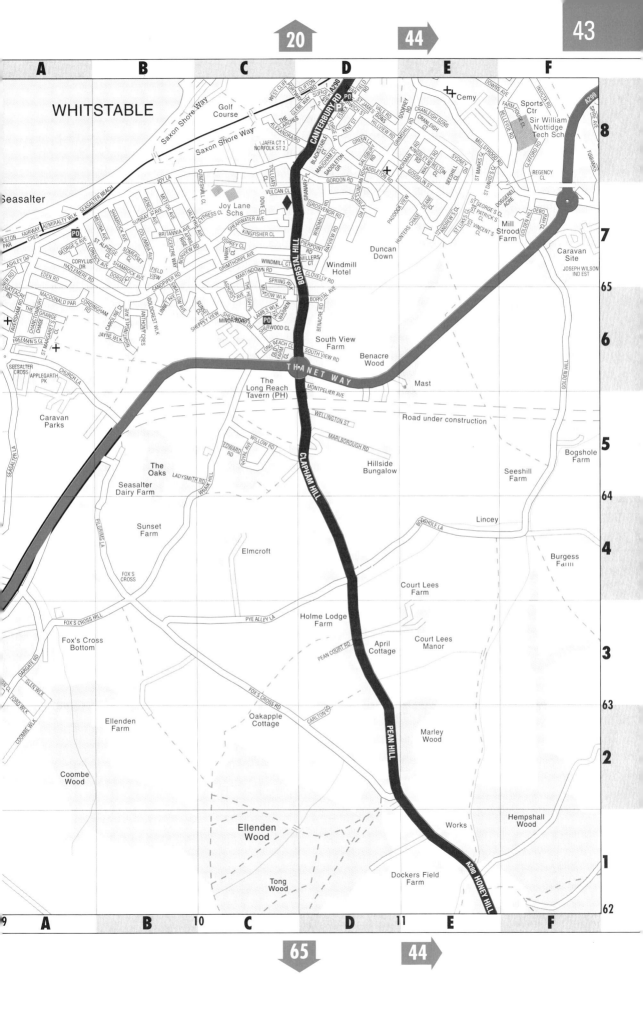

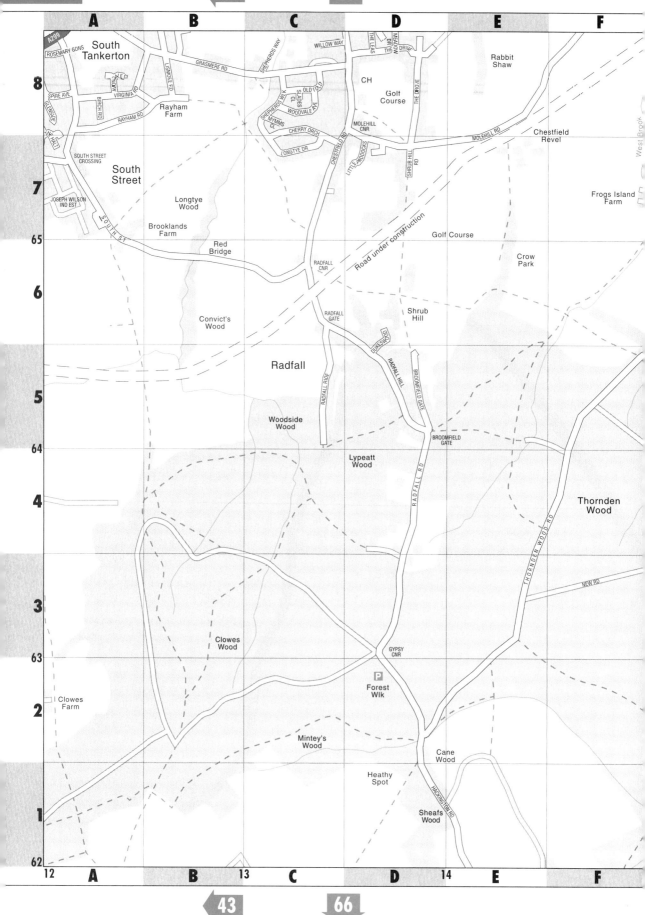

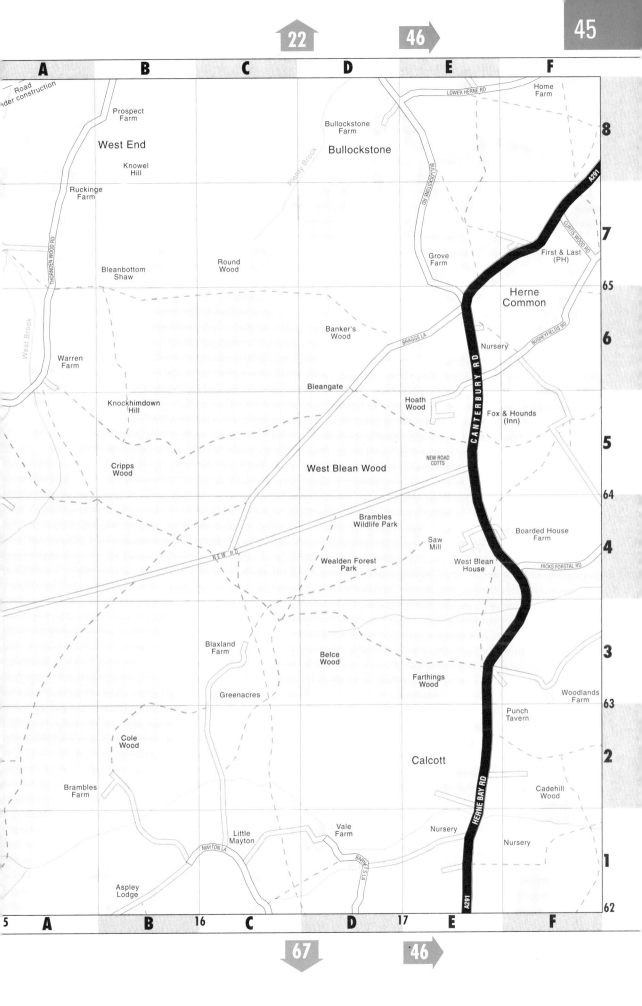

A B C D E F

Road under construction

Prospect Farm

West End

Knowel Hill

Ruckinge Farm

THORNDEN WOOD RD

Bleanbottom Shaw

Round Wood

West Brook

Warren Farm

Knockhimdown Hill

Cripps Wood

Rierly Brook

Bullockstone Farm

Bullockstone

BULLOCKSTONE RD

LOWER HERNE RD

Home Farm

Grove Farm

A291

CURTIS WOOD RD

First & Last (PH)

Herne Common

BUSHEYFIELDS RD

Nursery

Banker's Wood

BRAGGS LA

Bleangate

Hoath Wood

CANTERBURY RD

Fox & Hounds (Inn)

West Blean Wood

NEW ROAD COTTS

Brambles Wildlife Park

NEW RD

Wealden Forest Park

Saw Mill

Boarded House Farm

West Blean House

HICKS FORSTAL RD

Blaxland Farm

Belce Wood

Farthings Wood

Woodlands Farm

Greenacres

Punch Tavern

Cole Wood

Calcott

HERNE BAY RD

Cadehill Wood

Brambles Farm

Little Mayton

MAYTON LA

Vale Farm

BARNETS LA

Nursery

Nursery

Aspley Lodge

A291

45
23

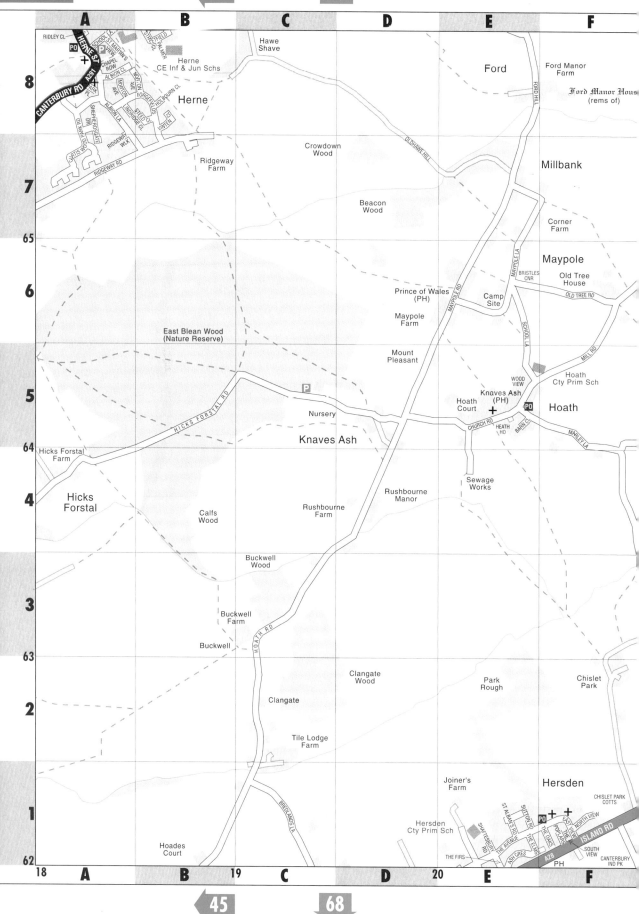

A B C D E F

Ford

Ford Manor
Farm

Ford Manor House
(rems of)

RIDLEY CL
PO
P
HERNE ST
SCHOOL LA
ST MARTIN'S
STREETFIELD
PALMER
Hawe
Shave

Herne
CE Inf & Jun Schs

CHAPEL
ROW
CANTERBURY RD
A291
ALBION CL
MORTON
AVE
FORGEFIELDS
HOLBURN CL
Herne

NORTON

Millbank

8

Crowdown
Wood

OLDHAWE HILL

Corner
Farm

SHEPHERDSGATE
DRI
MYRTIS WOOD RD
ALBION LA
RIDGEWAY WLK
STEEL CL
INGRIDGE CL
VINTEN

Ridgeway
Farm

Maypole

7

RIDGEWAY RD

Beacon
Wood

MAYPOLE LA
BRISTLES
CNR
Old Tree
House

OLD TREE RD

65

Prince of Wales
(PH)

MAYPOLE RD

SCHOOL LA

6

East Blean Wood
(Nature Reserve)

Maypole
Farm

Camp
Site

MILL RD

Mount
Pleasant

WOOD
VIEW
Hoath
Cty Prim Sch

P

HICKS FORSTAL RD

Nursery

Knaves Ash
(PH)

Hoath
Court
PO
A
Hoath

5

Knaves Ash

CHURCH RD
HEATH
HO
BARN CL
MARLEY LA

64

Hicks Forstal
Farm

Sewage
Works

Hicks
Forstal

Rushbourne
Manor

4

Calfs
Wood

Rushbourne
Farm

Buckwell
Wood

3

Buckwell
Farm

HOATH RD

Buckwell

63

Clangate
Wood

Park
Rough

Chislet
Park

Clangate

2

BREDLANDS LA

Tile Lodge
Farm

Joiner's
Farm

Hersden

Chislet Park
Cotts

1

Hersden
Cty Prim Sch

SHAFTESBURY RD
ST ALBAN'S RD
SUTTON RD
THE AVENUE
THE ELMS
PO
THE POPLARS
THE OAKS
EAST VIEW
NORTH VIEW
ISLAND RD
A28
SOUTH
VIEW
CANTERBURY
IND PK

Hoades
Court

THE FIRS
ASH CLOES
PH

62

18 A B 19 C D 20 E F

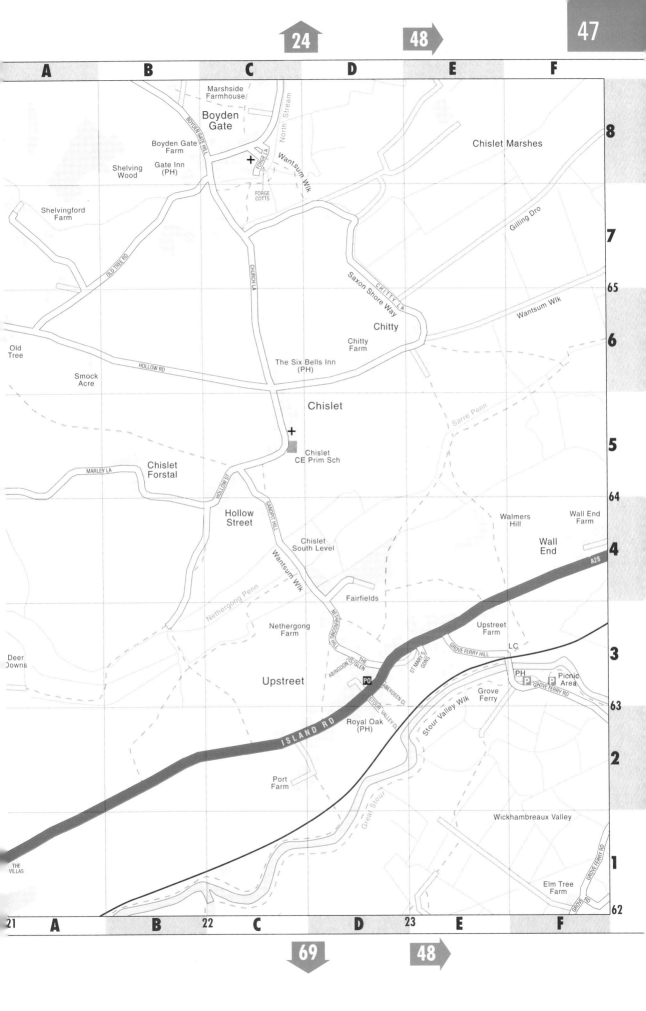

	A	B	C	D	E	F

8

Gilling Dro

Whitfield Sewer

Chislet Marshes

Wantsum Wlk

Wantsum Wlk

The Peak

A28

CANTERBURY RD

7

Sarre

Bolingbroke Farm

Crown Inn (PH)

Sarre Mill

PO

A253

65

A253

MILE RD

Sarre Penn

Sevenscore Dyke

SARRE CT

OSTLERS LA

Sarre Bridge

6

River Wantsum

LC

LC

SARRE WALL

ISLAND RD

LC

Cut End

5

Sarre Marshes

Great Stour

64

A28

4

Stourmouth Valley

Stour Bridge

Blood Point

Little Stour

Dog & Duck (PH)

Caravan Parks

3

Saxon Shore Way

Plucks Gutter

North Court Farm

63

Stour Valley Wlk

Russell Farm

BREWERY SQ

Stourmouth Stream

2

GROVE FERRY RD

Red Bridge

West Stourmouth

Dean Farm

Stonehall Farm

SCHOOL LA

Elmstone Valley

Rising Sun (PH)

THE STREET

1

NEWHOUSE CNR

Newhouse Farm

BEGGARS CNR

East Stourmouth

Blue Bridge

Preston Valley

Oast House Farm

PRESTON RD

Poulders Farm

SAXON LA

GROVE RD

62

ROOKSTON CNR

A   B   C   D   E   F

8

MANOR RD

A299

SEAMARK RD

Nature
Reserve

MONKTON
RDBT

A253

MILLERS LA

THE
GOLDINGS

PARSONAGE
FIELDS

VICARAGE GDN

COLLARDS
CL

WILLETTS HILL

Monkton

7

GORE
ST

MONKTON
MANOR

Monkton
Court
Farm

THE DROVE

SEAMARK CL

MONKTON ST

Monkton CE
Prim Sch

The
White Stag
(PH)

Walters Hall
Farm

Chipman's Way

Hoo Farm

Hoo

65

PO

THE
FOXHUNTER
PK

MONKTON RD

SOLIHULL
COTTS

Hoo Corner
Farm

6

Caravan
Park

SHERRIFFS COURT LA

Sherriffs
Court

LC

LC

LC

5

Monkton Marshes

Coxon's
Hill

64

Eastern Monkton Stream

Minster Stream

4

Docker Hill

Western Monkton Stream

Abbot's Wall

Minster Marshes

Abbot's Wall

3

River Stour

63

Saxon Shore Way

2

Corner Dro

Goldstone Dro

Westmarsh Dro

Ash Level

1

62

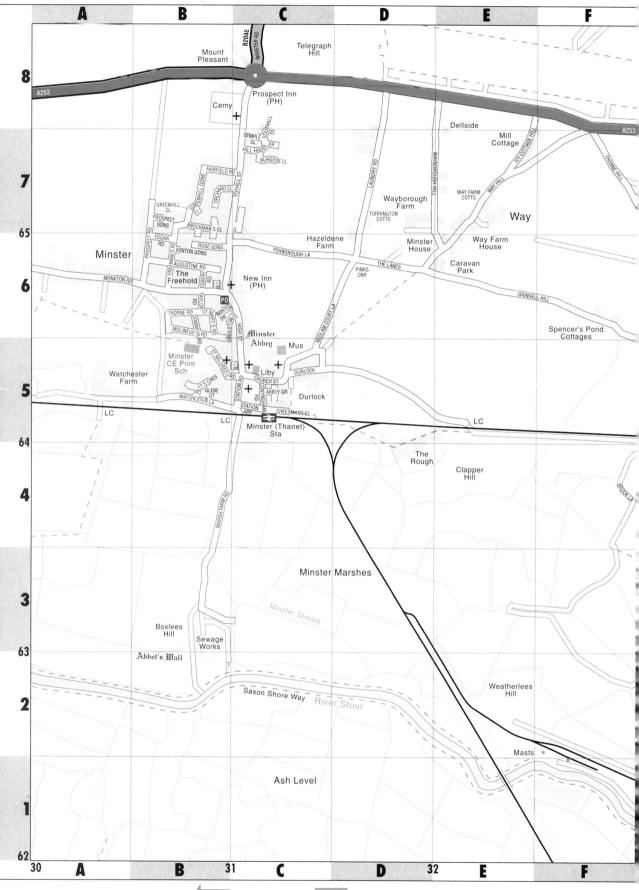

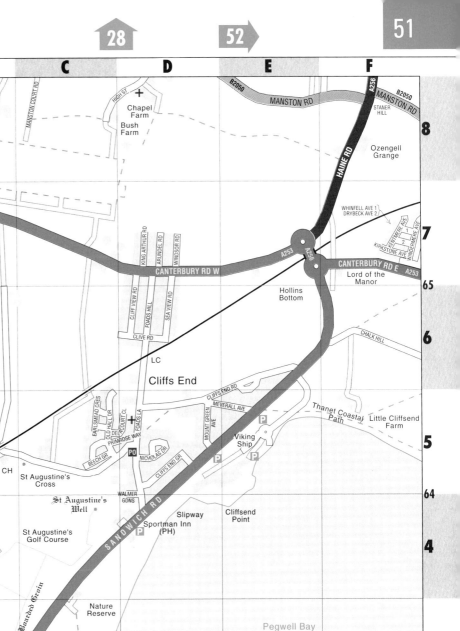

Manston Aerodrome

Chapel
Farm
Bush
Farm

HIGH ST

MANSTON COURT RD

B2050
MANSTON RD
B2050
MANSTON RD
STANER HILL

HAINE RD

Ozengell
Grange

WHINFELL AVE 1
DRYBECK AVE 2
CENTMERE AVE
WINDERMERE AVE

KIRKSTONE AVE
WINDERMERE AVE

A253

A256

CANTERBURY RD E A253

Lord of the
Manor

Chapel
House

THORNE HILL

Thorne
Farm

KING ARTHUR RD
ARUNDEL RD
WINDSOR RD
CLIFF VIEW RD
FOADS HILL
SEA VIEW RD

CANTERBURY RD W

CLIVE RD

Hollins
Bottom

CHALK HILL

Sevenscore

LC

Cliffs End

CLIFFS END RD

MEVERALL AVE

Thanet Coastal
Path

Little Cliffsend
Farm

SEVENSCORE FARM
COTTS

COTTINGTON RD

BARLSMEAD CRES
OLD HALL DR
COURT CL
OLD DELF
PRIMROSE WAY
FOADS LA
BEECH GR

PO

NICHOLAS DR

MOUNT GREEN AVE

CLIFFS END GR

P

P

Viking
Ship

P

Sevenscore
Crossing

CH

St Augustine's
Cross

SANDWICH RD

WALMER
GDNS

Slipway

Cliffsend
Point

St Augustine's
Well

PO

Sportman Inn
(PH)

P

Cliffsend
Point

St Augustine's
Golf Course

Cottington
Hill

Boarded Groin

Nature
Reserve

Pegwell Bay

EBBSFLEET LA

Minster Stream

Ebbsfleet
Farm

Ebbsfleet
(Traditional site of the
Landing of the Saxons 449
& St Augustine 597)

CH

Picnic Site

Water
Treatment
Wks

Golf
Course

Stonelees

Boarded Groin

River Stour

Shell
Ness

Stour Valley Wlk

Sandwich Bay

Richborough
Power Sta

Ebbsfleet
House

RAMSGATE RD

A256

Nature
Reserve

SEASIDE RD
NORTH RD
WEST RD
EAST RD

8
7
65
6
5
64
4
3
63
2
1
62

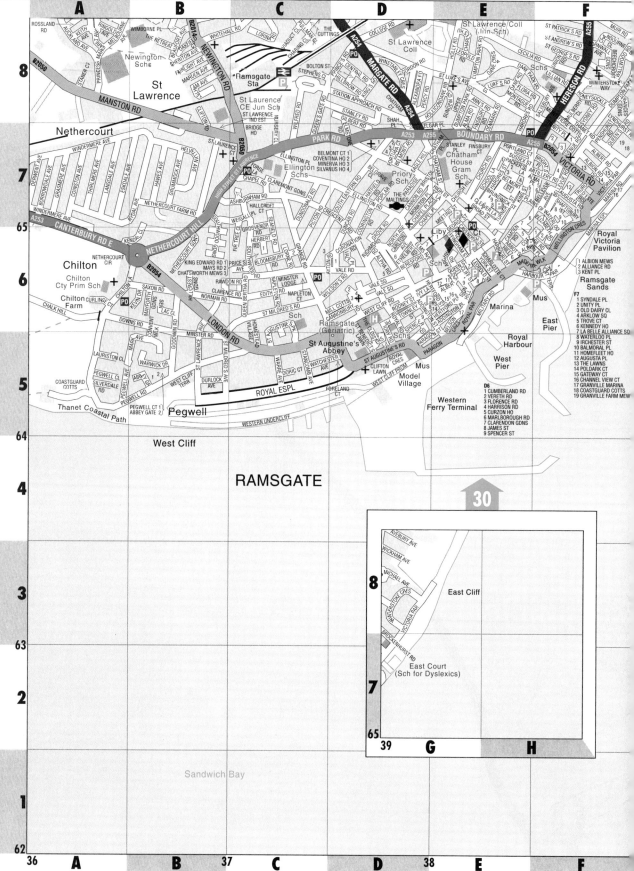

51
30

E6
1 GUILDFORD LAWN
2 CAVENDISH PL
3 COLEMAN S YD
4 KING'S PL
5 HIBERNIA ST
6 ALBION HILL

7 PRINCE'S ST
8 WEST CLIFF ARC
9 ROSE HILL
10 GRUNDY'S HILL
11 ST MICHAEL S ALLEY
12 CORNHILL
13 HARBOUR TWRS

14 HERTFORD HO
15 LIVERPOOL LAWN
16 ADELAIDE GDNS
17 PROSPECT TERR

E7
1 PEMBROKE CT
2 LOUGHBOROUGH CT

3 BRUNSWICK CT
4 DALTON CT
5 NEWCASTLE HILL
6 LA BELLE ALLIANCE SQ
7 CAMDEN SQ
8 STAFFORDSHIRE ST
9 UNION ST

1 ALBION MEWS
2 ALLIANCE RD
3 KENT PL

Ramsgate
Sands

F7
1 SYNDALE PL
2 UNITY PL
3 OLD DAIRY CL
4 ARKLOW SQ
5 TROVE CT
6 KENNEDY HO
7 LA BELLE ALLIANCE HO
8 WATERLOO PL
9 IRCHESTER ST
10 BALMORAL PL
11 HOMEFLEET HO
12 AUGUSTA PL
13 THE LAWNS
14 POLDARK CT
15 GATEWAY CT
16 CHANNEL VIEW CT
17 GRANVILLE MARINA
18 COASTGUARD COTTS
19 GRANVILLE FARM MEW

D6
1 CUMBERLAND RD
2 VERETH RD
3 FLORENCE RD
4 HARRISON RD
5 CURZON HO
6 MARLBOROUGH RD
7 CLARENDON GDNS
8 JAMES ST
9 SPENCER ST

RAMSGATE

St
Lawrence

Nethercourt

Chilton

Chilton Cty Prim Sch

Chilton Farm

Pegwell

Thanet Coastal Path

West Cliff

Sandwich Bay

Western Ferry Terminal

West Pier

Royal Harbour

East Pier

Marina

Mus

Royal Victoria Pavilion

East Cliff

East Court (Sch for Dyslexics)

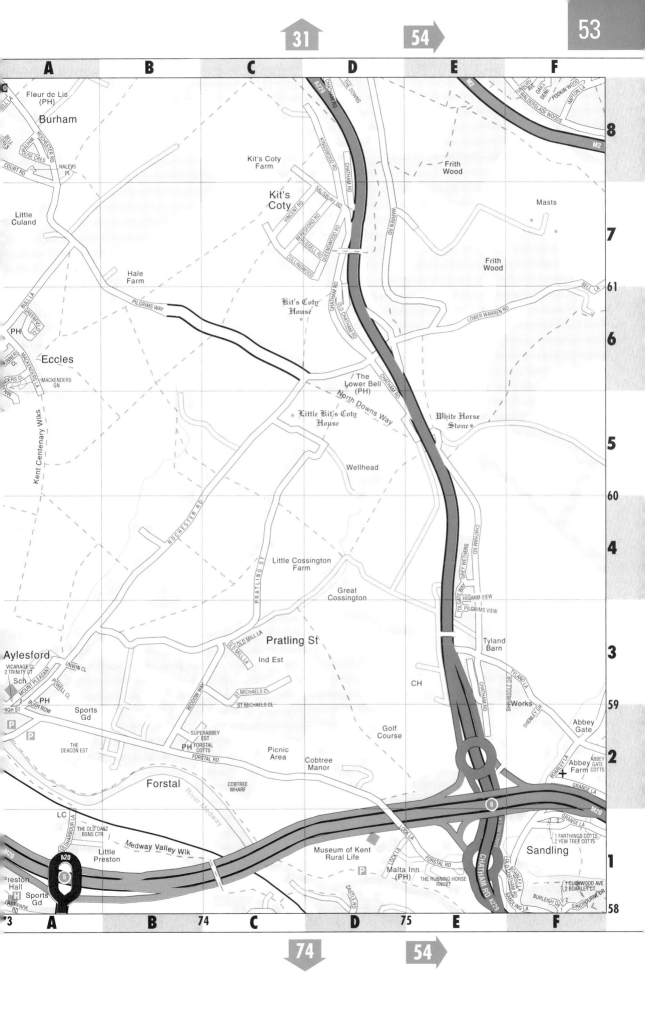

Fleur de Lis (PH)

Burham

Kit's Coty Farm

Kit's Coty

The Downs

Frith Wood

Masts

Little Culand

Hale Farm

PILGRIMS WAY

Kit's Coty House

Frith Wood

Eccles

PH

The Lower Bell (PH)

North Downs Way

Little Kit's Coty House

White Horse Stone

LOWER WARREN RD

Kent Centenary Wlks

MACKENDERS GN

Wellhead

Little Cossington Farm

Great Cossington

ROCHESTER RD

PRATLING ST

HIGHAM VIEW

PILGRIMS VIEW

Tyland Barn

Aylesford

VICARAGE CL
2 TRINITY CT
Sch

PH
BUSH ROW

Sports Gd

OLD MILL LA

Pratling St

Ind Est

ST MICHAELS CL
ST MICHAELS CL

CH

Works

Abbey Gate

59

SUPERABBEY EST

PH FORSTAL COTTS

FORSTAL RD

Picnic Area

Cobtree Manor

Golf Course

Abbey Farm

ABBEY GATE COTTS

GRANGE LA

Forstal

COBTREE WHARF

River Medway

LC

Medway Valley Wlk

Little Preston

Museum of Kent Rural Life

Malta Inn (PH)

THE RUNNING HORSE RNDBT

Sandling

1 FARTHINGS COTTS
2 YEW TREE COTTS

GRANGE LA

1 CUCKWOOD AVE
2 BOARLEY CT

BURLEIGH DR

A20

Preston Hall
H
Sports Gd

CHATHAM RD A229

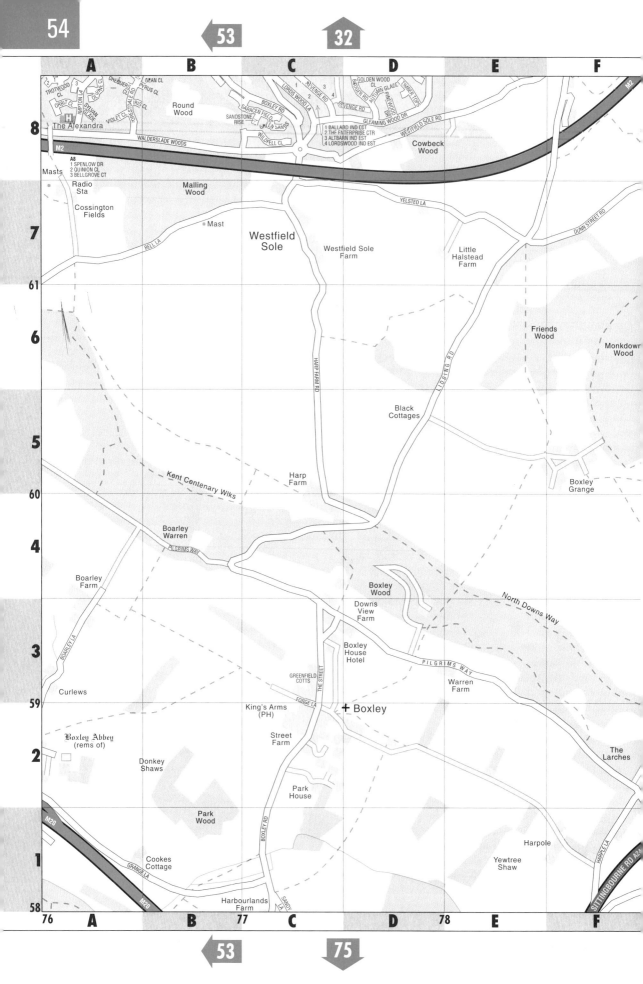

A   B   C   D   E   F

M2

TROTWOOD CL
ORBIT CL
HAMPTON LA
SYLVAN GLADE
CHERNE CL
IRIS CL
VIOLET CL
CHEQUERS
FORESTDALE RD
DEAN CL
PYRUS CL

8
The Alexandra

Round Wood

BOXLEY RD
SARACEN FIELD
SANDSTONE RISE
GREEN SAND
WILDFELL CL

LORDS WOOD LA
REVENGE RD
REVENGE RD

GOLDEN WOOD
BADGER RD
AUTUMN GLADE
PINEWOOD
TIMBER TOPS

GLEAMING WOOD DR
WESTFIELD SOLE RD

1 BALLARD IND EST
2 THE ENTERPRISE CTR
3 ALTBARN IND EST
4 LORDSWOOD IND EST

Cowbeck Wood

M2

WALDERSLADE WOODS

M2

A8
1 SPENLOW DR
2 QUINION CL
3 BELLGROVE CT

Masts

Radio Sta

Cossington Fields

Malling Wood

YELSTED LA

DUNN STREET RD

7
Mast

Westfield Sole

BELL LA

Westfield Sole Farm

Little Halstead Farm

61

Friends Wood

Monkdown Wood

6

HARP FARM RD

LIDSING RD

Black Cottages

5

Kent Centenary Wks

Harp Farm

Boxley Grange

60

Boarley Warren

PILGRIMS WAY

4

Boarley Farm

Boxley Wood

North Downs Way

BOARLEY LA

Downs View Farm

3

Boxley House Hotel

PILGRIMS WAY

Warren Farm

GREENFIELD COTTS

THE STREET

Curlews

FORGE LA

59

King's Arms (PH)

+ Boxley

Boxley Abbey
(rems of)

Street Farm

The Larches

2

Donkey Shaws

Park House

BOXLEY RD

Park Wood

Harpole

M20

1

Cookes Cottage

GRANGE LA

Yewtree Shaw

HARPLE LA

SITTINGBOURNE RD A24

M20

SANDY LA

58
Harbourlands Farm

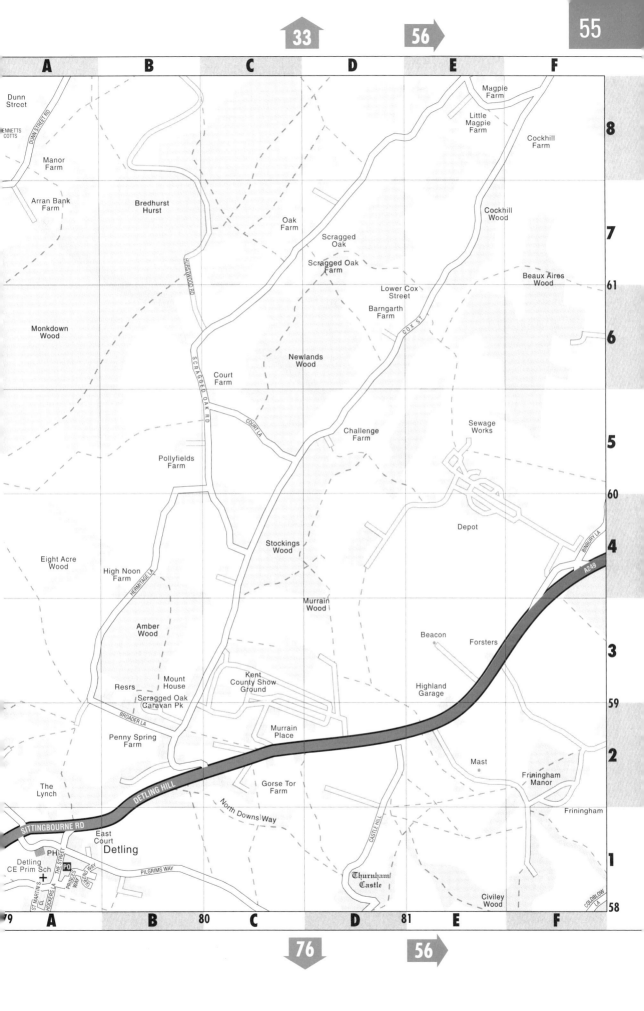

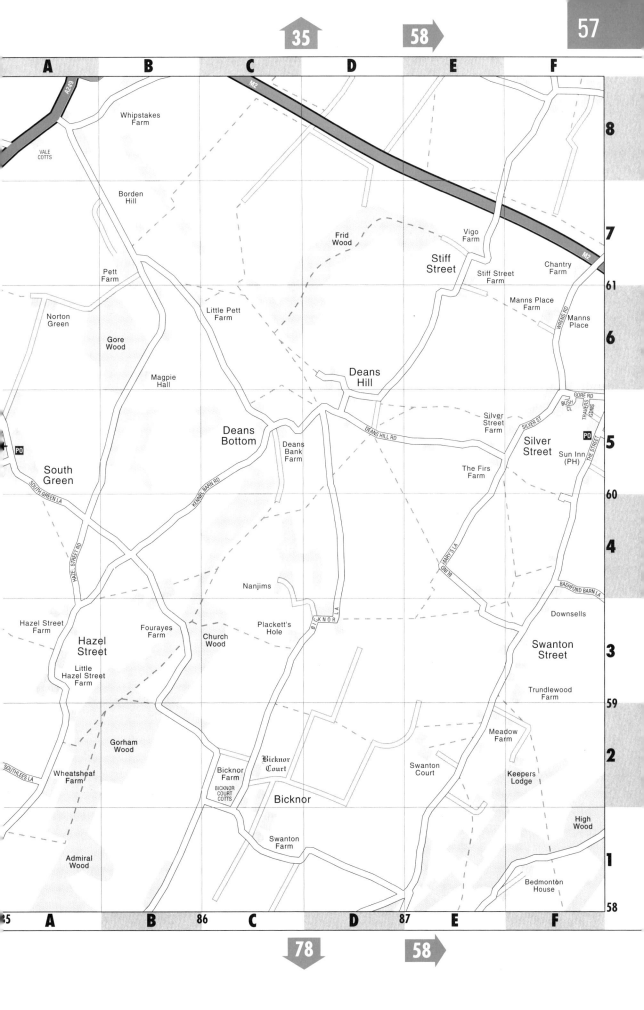

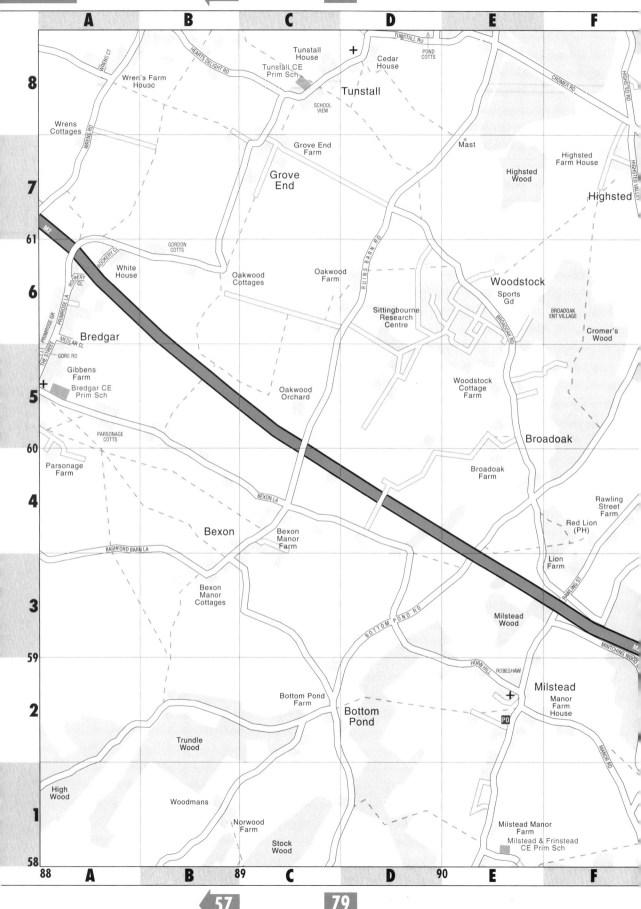

8

WRENS CT

Wren's Farm House

Wrens Cottages

WRENS RD

HEARTS DELIGHT RD

Tunstall House

Tunstall CE Prim Sch

TUNSTALL RD

Cedar House

POND COTTS

Tunstall

SCHOOL VIEW

Mast

CROMER RD

Highsted Farm House

HIGHSTED RD

Grove End Farm

Grove End

Highsted Wood

Highsted

7

61

M2

GORDON COTTS

ROOKERY CL

White House

ROOKERY CL

Oakwood Cottages

Oakwood Farm

RUINS BARN RD

Woodstock

Sports Gd

BROADOAK ENT VILLAGE

HIGHSTED VALLEY

6

PRIMROSE LA

PRIMROSE GR

Bredgar

MEDLAR CL

THE STREET

GORE RD

Gibbens Farm

Bredgar CE Prim Sch

Oakwood Orchard

Sittingbourne Research Centre

Woodstock Cottage Farm

BROADOAK RD

Cromer's Wood

5

PARSONAGE COTTS

Parsonage Farm

Broadoak Farm

Broadoak

60

BEXON LA

Rawling Street Farm

Red Lion (PH)

4

BASHFORD BARN LA

Bexon

Bexon Manor Farm

Lion Farm

RAWLING ST

Bexon Manor Cottages

BOTTOM POND RD

Milstead Wood

MINTCHING WOOD

M2

3

59

HORN HILL

ROBESHAW

Milstead

Manor Farm House

Bottom Pond Farm

Bottom Pond

PO

2

Trundle Wood

MANOR RD

High Wood

Woodmans

Norwood Farm

Milstead Manor Farm

Milstead & Frinstead CE Prim Sch

1

Stock Wood

58

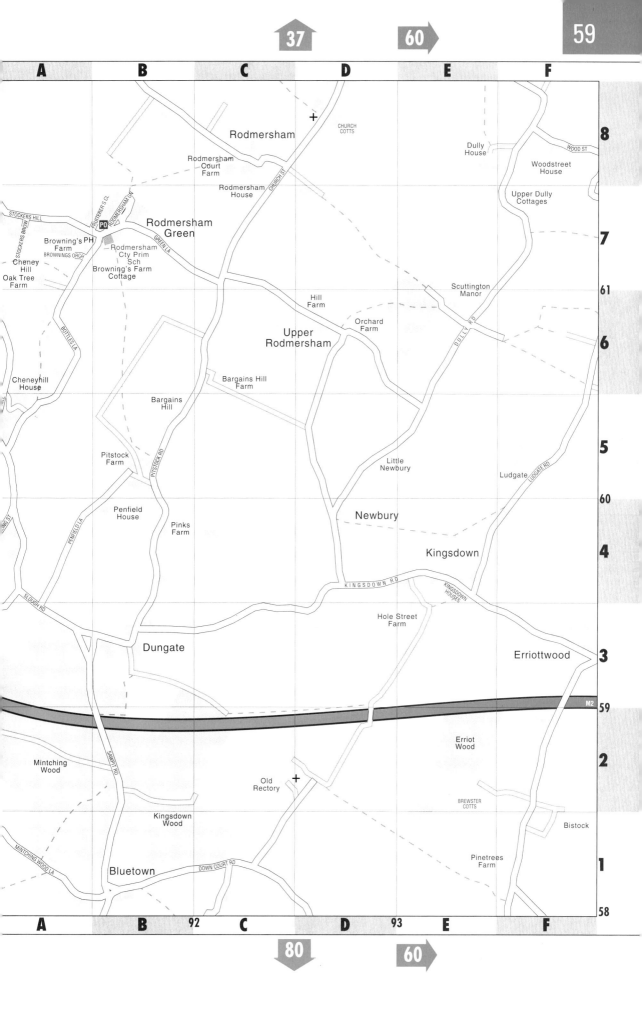

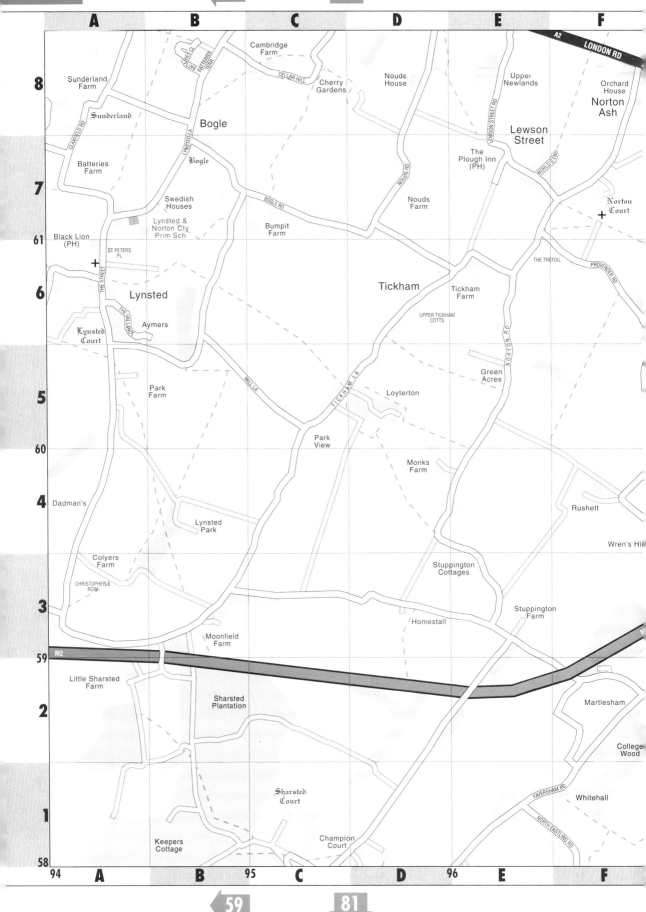

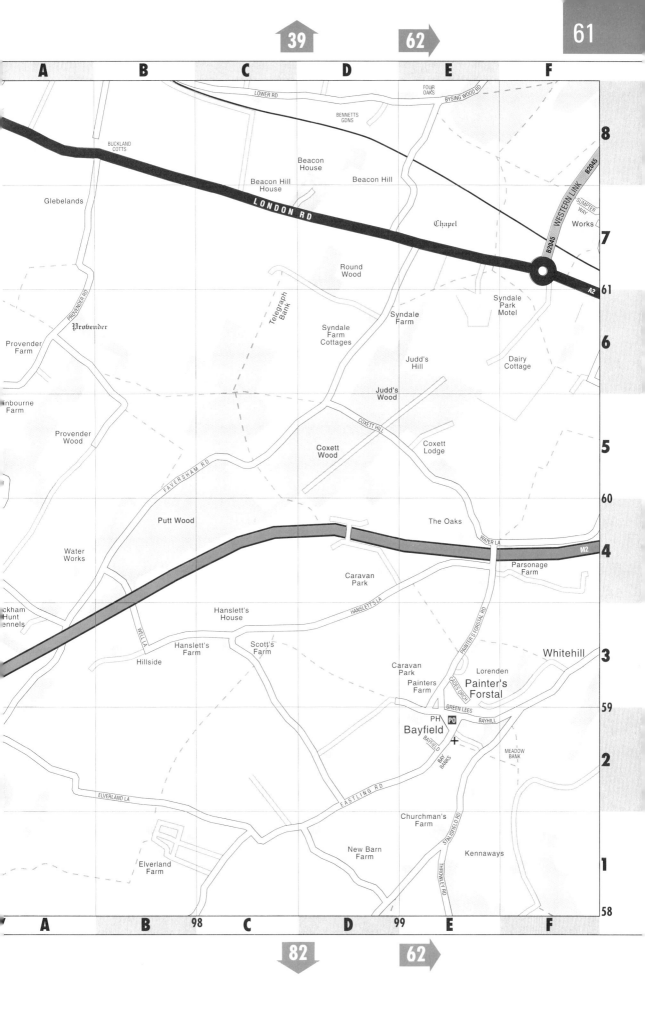

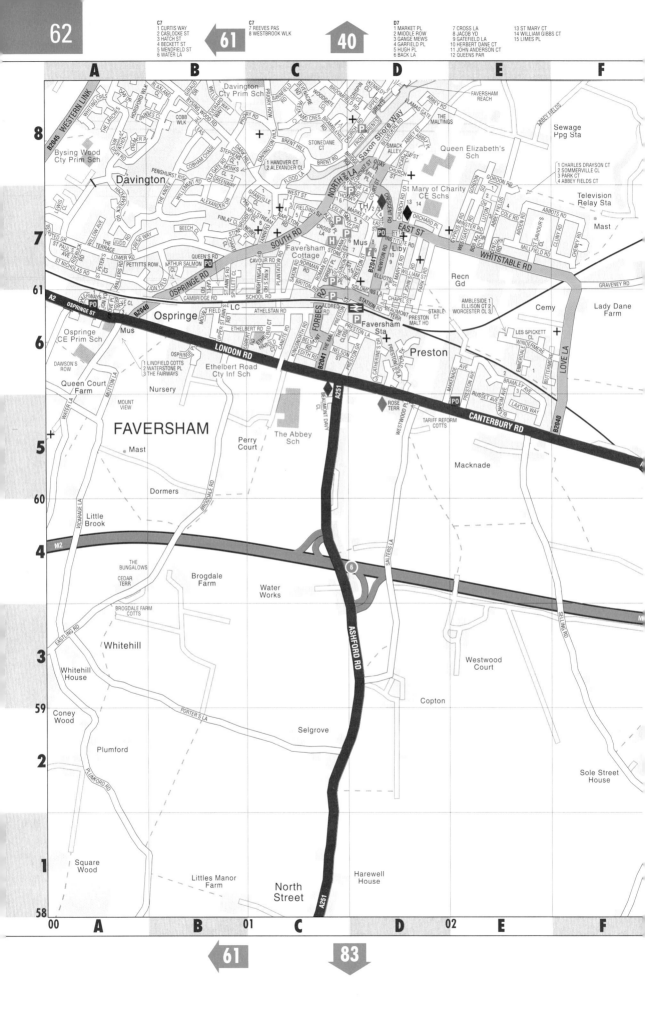

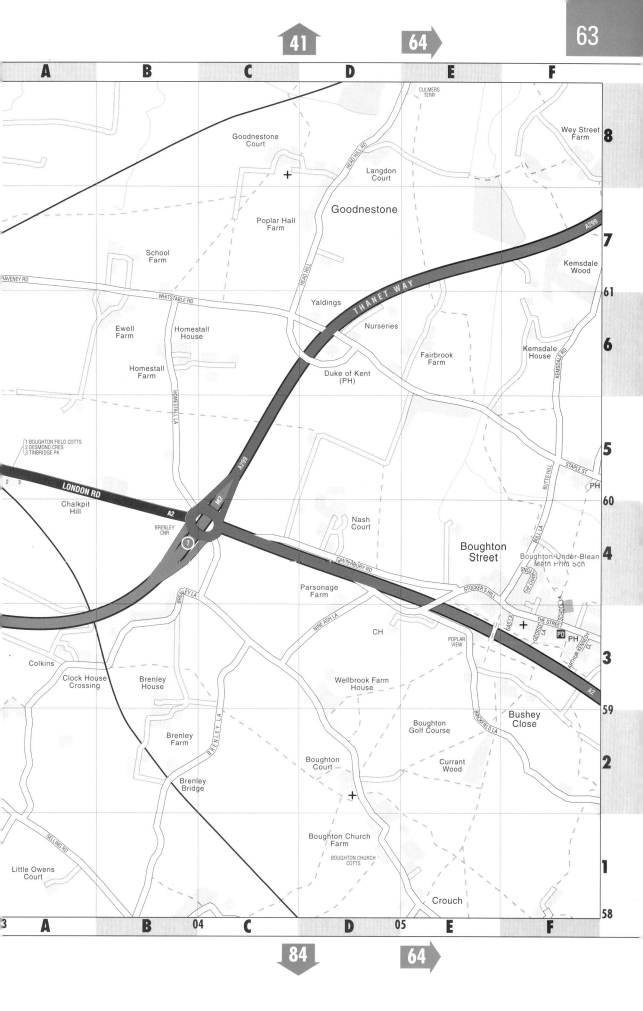

A   B   C   D   E   F

8

Lavender
Farm

A299

THANET WAY

Dargate
House

PO

PLUM PUDDING LA

OAST
COTTS

The Dove
(PH)

Dargate
Farm

Dargate

Wey Street
Farm

A299

Fostall

Beesborough
Farm

GODFREY'S
GRAVE

Dargate
Common

Belvedere
Farm

DARGATE RD

Summer
Lees

BUTLER'S HILL

WOODLANDS

7

61

Hernhill CE
Prim Sch

SWALE VIEW

Hernhill

MANOR
COTTS

CROCKHAM RD

Bradbourne
Cottages

Blean
Wood

Acorn
Cottage

6

Church
Farm

PH

CROCKHAM LA

Twr

Crockham
Wood

Holly
Hill

Holly
Hill
Farm

Firtree
Cottages

Slutshole

CHURCH HILL

Crockham
Farm

HOLLY HILL RD

RS1 RD

5

Staplestreet

Mount Ephraim
Wood

THREAD LA

COURTENAY RD

60

Mount
Ephraim

STAPLESTREET RD

Thread
Wood

DAWES RD

Courtenay
Farm

Bossenden
Wood

4

Clay Pits
Wood

Bossenden
Farm

BOUNDS LA

3

1 CHESTNUT CT
2 GROVE COURT

Boughton
Street

FARM

STONEY RD

BERKELEY CL

High
Wood

Dunkirk Cty
Prim Sch

Mast

Dunkirk

WHEATSHEAF

2

CLIFTON PL

THE STREET

OAK DR

THE RIDGEWAY

THE
CRESCENT

ST PAULS CRES

FERNLEIGH CL

HIGHWAY CL

BOUGHTON HILL

Caravan
Park

Red Lion
(PH)

Hospital
Wood

COLONEL ST LA

59

A2

LOACH
HO

BURNT OAST RD

ST PAUL'S
RD

ST PETER'S

DUNKIRK
RD

WOODSIDE

Boughton
Hill

CANTERBURY RD

A2

Horselees

2

HORSELEES RD

Hickmans
Green

DUNKIRK RD

Poundfall
Wood

Brotherhood
Woods

BRICKFIELD LA

Hurst
Wood

Arnolds
Wood

Forester's Lodge
Farm

Fishpond
Wood

1

Iron
Hill

58

06   A   B   07   C   D   08   E   F

A   B   C   D   E   F

8

Walnut Tree Farm

Well Court

Frog Hall

Timber Wood

Amery Court

Arbele House

Daw's Wood

The Radfall

7

Broadlands Ind Est

THE GAP

FRIEMAN CL

ROGERS CL YB

CHAPEL LA

LODGE CL

BOURNE CL

CHESTNUT AVE

SCHOOL LA

The Halt

Hothe Court Farm

TYLER HILL RD

FLEETS LA

SUNNY MEAD

JOHNS CL

CRES

HACKINGTON RD

SUMMER LA

IVY CT

LINK RD

PO

Honey Wood

Great Hall Wood

61

A290

BLEAN COMM

WESTFIELD

6

MOUNT PLEASANT

THE VILLAGE GREEN

LIME

VICARAGE LA

PO

Blean

Church Cottage

CALAIS HILL

Tyler Hill

PARK FARM CL

WOOD HILL

Little Hall Wood

BLEAN HILL

Hillside Farm

Hare & Hounds (Inn)

CANTERBURY HILL

5

Luckett's Farm

TILE KILN HILL

Brotherhood Wood

Little Hall Farm

Darwin Coll

60

Blean Cty Prim Sch

PURCHAS CT

LYEAT CT

Park Wood

1 CLOWES CT
2 HOMESTALL CT
3 GRIMSHILL CT
4 THORNDEN CT

Univ of Kent at Canterbury

Templeman Liby

GREEN DELL

LONG MEADOW

THE CLOSE

CROSSWAYS

UPLANDS

DOWNS RD

P

WHITSTABLE RD

ELLENDEN CT

BISHOPDEN CT

DENSTEAD CT

FARTHINGS CT

MARLEY CT

WILLOWS CT

WOODLAND WAY

GILES LA

BROTHERHOOD

Keynes Coll

Rutherford Coll

Eliot Coll

The Archbishop's CE Sec Sch

ST STEPHEN'S HILL

ORCHARD CL

MANWOOD AVE

THE CRESCENT

MOORFIELD

THE TERRACE

4

Masts

MOAT LA

OAKS PK

HIGHFIELD CL

UNIVERSITY RD

CRANBOURNE WLK

GADNAM CL

LYNDHURST CL

TYLER CL

HALES DR

P

Schs

PO

NEW RD

P

RAVENSCOURT RD

LOVELL RD

Kent Coll

St Edmund's Sch

Chaucer Coll

DAMERHAM CL

DURMFORD CL

KINGWOOD

BRACKENHURST

ST MICHAEL'S RD

ST STEPHEN'S GN

STEPHENSON

SHAFTESBURY RD

BEACONSFIELD RD

3

FIRTREE CL

ROSS AVE

Rough Common

Wtr Twr

THE CLOSE (ST EDMUNDS SCH)

ST THOMAS HILL

HARKNESS DR

BRAMSHAW RD

REDWOOD

VERWOOD CL

BIRCHWOOD WLK

PINE TREE AVE

CROWN RD

MANDEVILLE RD

BEVERLEY RD

HANGINGTON TERR

St Stephen's

NEW BEVERLEY HO

LC

59

STOCKWOOD CHASE

MALE CL

RNUGH COMMON RD

PO

Dog & Bear (PH)

CHURCH HILL

SYDNEY RD

COOPER RD

NEAL'S PLACE RD

GLEN IRIS AVE

GLEN IRIS CL

Neal's Place

RICHMOND ROAD

CHERRY AVE

CEDARVIEW

ROSELANDS GDNS

FENWOOD RD

LONG ACRE

NURSERY WLK

GREENHOUSE

HANSCOMB HO

ROPER RD

ROSLACRE CL

SHEPHERDS GATE

ST STEPHEN'S LODGE

VIKING CL

WACHEL CL ST STEPHEN'S RD

MALTHOUSE

ST STEPHEN'S FIELDS

Recn Ctr

2

WOODLAND CL

Stock Wood

GARDEN CL

ST MICHAELS CL

CHURCH COOPER

Hall Place

The Grove

HILLVIEW RD

MEADOW RD

HILLSIDE AVE

CARPO DR

HARCOURT DR

CLIFTON GDNS

St Dunstan's

COPPER GATE

STATION RD W

KIRBY'S LA

BECKET AVE

ST STEPHEN'S RD

NORTH HOLMES

DEANS MILL CT

1

PALMERS CROSS HILL

CHURCH HILL

CHANCEL CT 1

JOSEPH CONRAD HOUSE 2

RUNCIE PL 3

Cemy

BECKET RD

WESTGATE COURT AVE

BISHOPS WAY

TEMPLE RD

LONDON RD

ST DUNSTAN'S CL

ORCHARD

NEAL RD

ROSS RD

P

PO

WHITEHALL CHASE

LINDEN GROVE

POUND LA

ST PETER'S LA

THE FRIARS

A2B

58

A2050

FAULKNERS LA

Vernon Holme (Kent Coll Inf & Jun Sch)

ST NICHOLAS HOSPL

The Mint

HARBLEDOWN

SUMMER CT

LANE END CT

GINDS

SUMMER HILL

WHITGIFT

FISK RD

RHEIMS CT

A2050

RHEIMS WAY

QUEENS AVE

ST PETER'S PL

LC

12   A   B   13   C   D   14   E   F

E1
1 ROSIERS CT
2 CROSS ST
3 LIONARD HO

F1
1 RIVERSIDE CT
2 STOURSIDE STUDIOS
3 WESTGATE HALL RD
4 CHANTRY CT
5 BLACKFRIARS ST
6 ST ALPHEGE LA
7 THE CLOISTERS

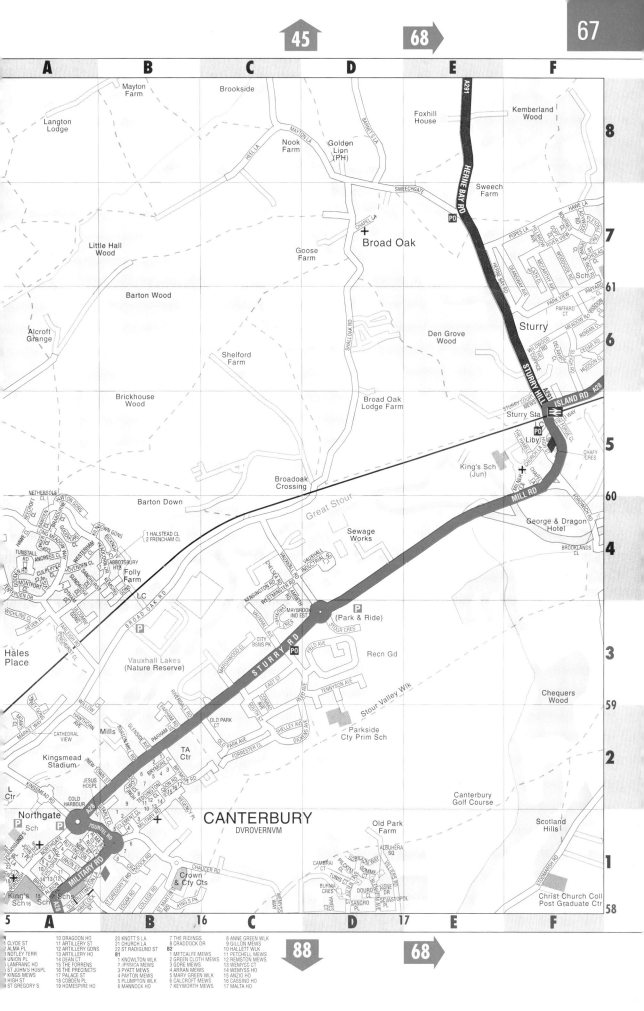

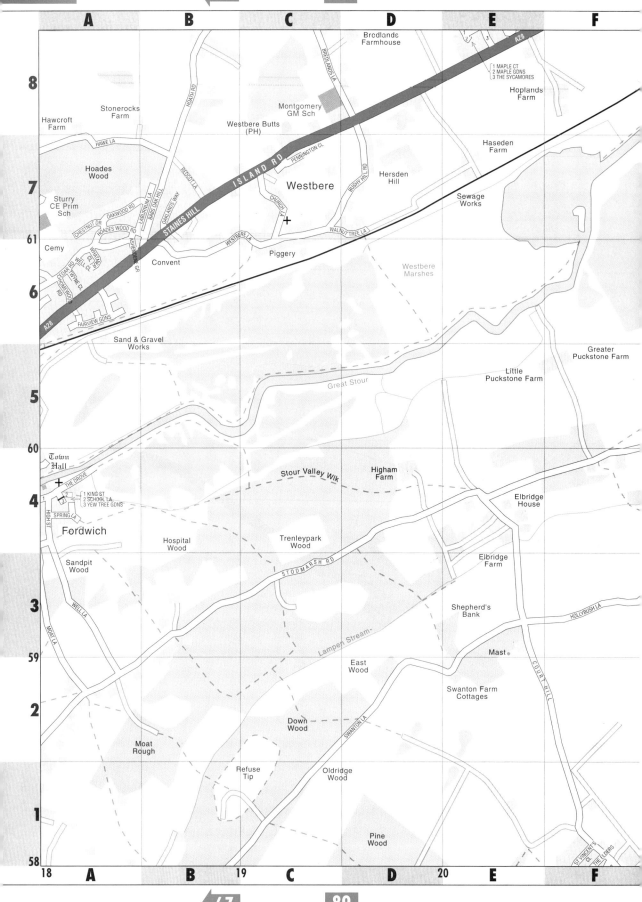

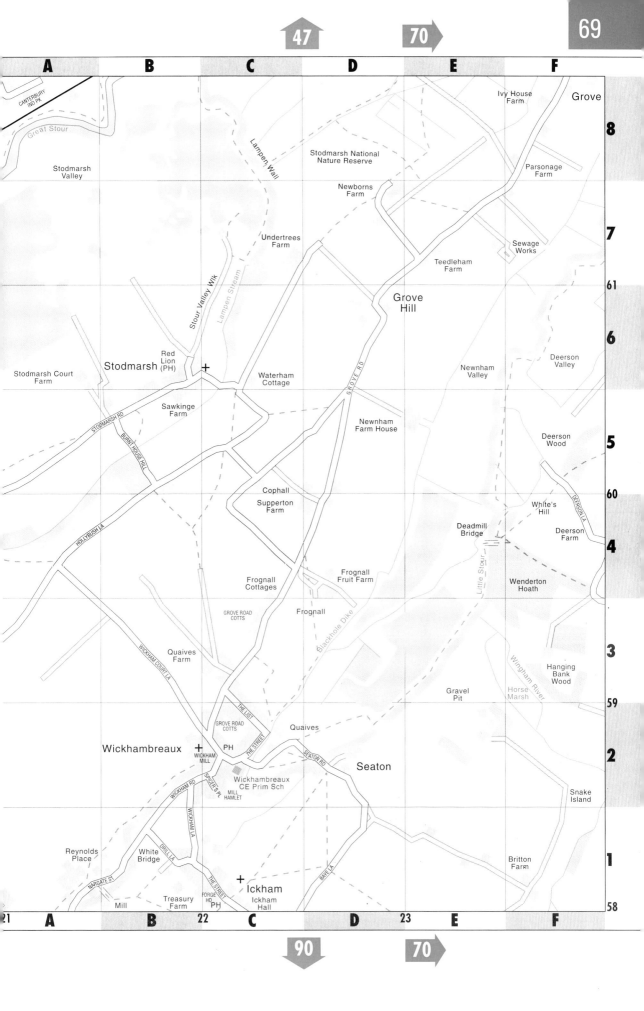

A B C D E F

Grove

Ivy House
Farm

8

Stodmarsh National
Nature Reserve

Parsonage
Farm

Stodmarsh
Valley

Lampen Wall

Newborns
Farm

7

Undertrees
Farm

Sewage
Works

Teedleham
Farm

61

Stour Valley Wlk

Lampen Stream

Grove
Hill

6

Red
Lion
(PH)

Stodmarsh

Stodmarsh Court
Farm

Waterham
Cottage

Newnham
Valley

Deerson
Valley

Sawkinge
Farm

STODMARSH RD

BURNT HOUSE HILL

Newnham
Farm House

Deerson
Wood

5

Cophall

Supperton
Farm

White's
Hill

60

BERRSON LA

Deadmill
Bridge

Deerson
Farm

4

HOLLYBUSH LA

Little Stour

Wenderton
Hoath

Frognall
Cottages

Frognall
Fruit Farm

GROVE ROAD
COTTS

Frognall

Blackhole Dike

Wingham River

Hanging
Bank
Wood

3

Quaives
Farm

WICKHAM COURT LA

Gravel
Pit

Horse
Marsh

59

THE LIST

GROVE ROAD
COTTS

Quaives

Wickhambreaux

PH

THE STREET

SEATON RD

Seaton

2

Snake
Island

WICKHAM
MILL

Wickhambreaux
CE Prim Sch

MILL
HAMLET

SPICER'S PL

WICKHAM RD

WICKHAM LA

DRILL LA

Reynolds
Place

White
Bridge

BAYE LA

Britton
Farm

1

NARGATE ST

THE STREET

FORGE
HO
PH

Ickham

Ickham
Hall

58

Mill

Treasury
Farm

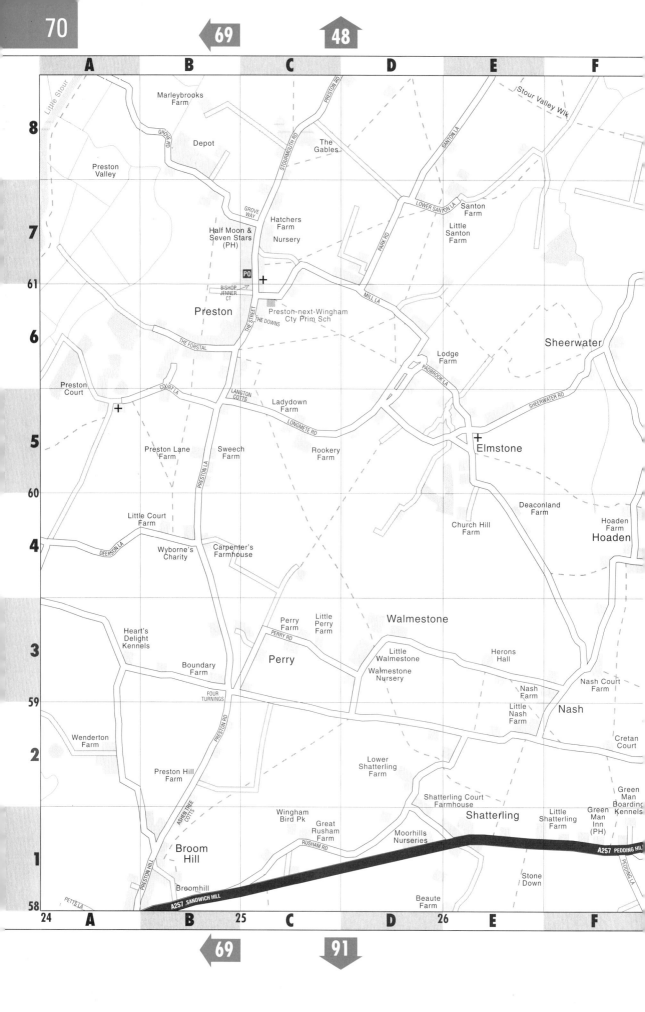

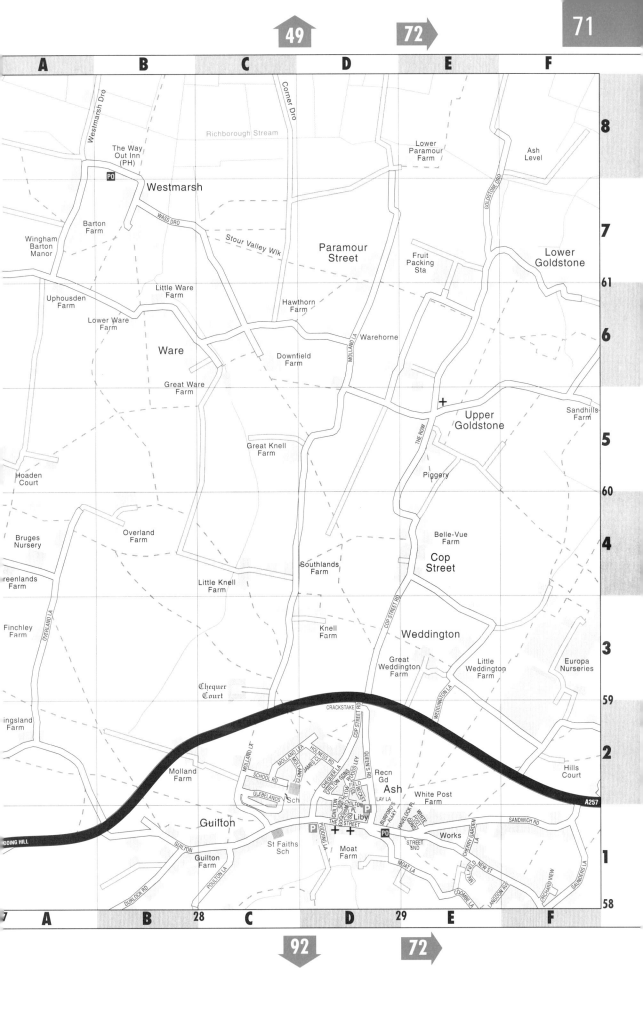

A   B   C   D   E   F

8

Westmarsh Dro

Corner Dro

Richborough Stream

The Way
Out Inn
(PH)

PO

Westmarsh

Lower
Paramour
Farm

Ash
Level

WASS DRO

Barton
Farm

7

Goldstone Dro

Wingham
Barton
Manor

Stour Valley Wlk

Paramour
Street

Fruit
Packing
Sta

Lower
Goldstone

61

Uphousden
Farm

Little Ware
Farm

Hawthorn
Farm

6

Lower Ware
Farm

Ware

Downfield
Farm

MOLLAND LA

Warehorne

Great Ware
Farm

+

Upper
Goldstone

Sandhills
Farm

5

Great Knell
Farm

THE ROW

Piggery

60

Hoaden
Court

Bruges
Nursery

Overland
Farm

Belle-Vue
Farm

4

OVERLAND LA

Southlands
Farm

Cop
Street

reenlands
Farm

Little Knell
Farm

Finchley
Farm

Knell
Farm

COP STREET RD

Weddington

3

Great
Weddington
Farm

Little
Weddington
Farm

Europa
Nurseries

WEDDINGTON LA

Chequer
Court

59

ingsland
Farm

CRACKSTAKE

COP STREET RD

2

Molland
Farm

MOLLAND LT

MOLLAND LEA

HOLNESS RD

JAMES CL

Recn
Gd

Ash

Hills
Court

SCHOOL RD

QUEEN'S RD

WOODS LEY

White Post
Farm

A257

GLEBELANDS

Sch

P

SANDWICH RD

Guilton

P

Liby

PO

Works

1

ODDING HILL

GUILTON

St Faiths
Sch

PUDDING LA

MOAT LA

Moat
Farm

NEW ST

Guilton
Farm

POULTON LA

LANGDON AVE

SAUNDERS LA

DURLOCK RD

58

A   B   28   C   D   29   E   F

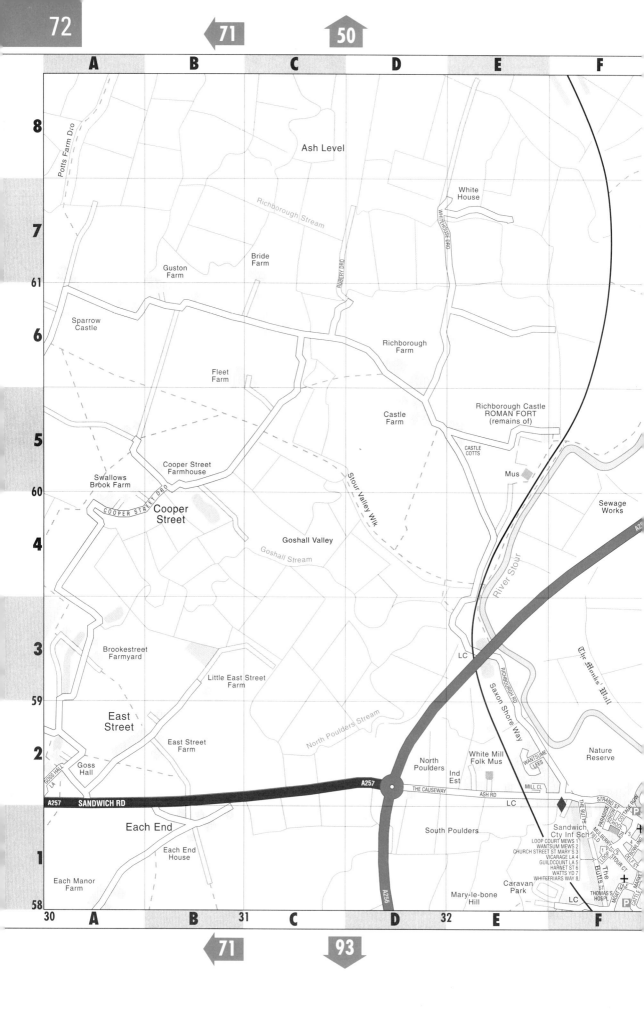

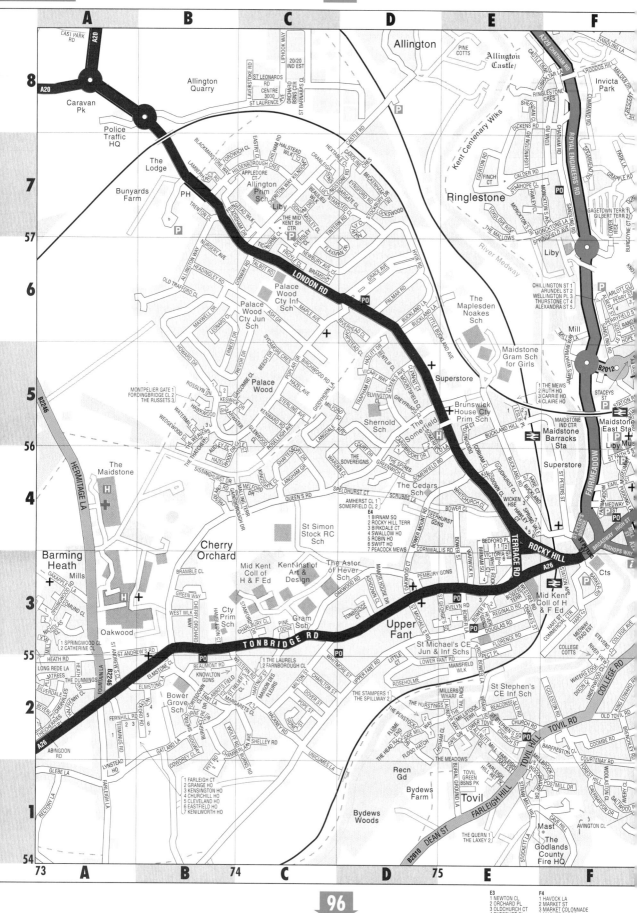

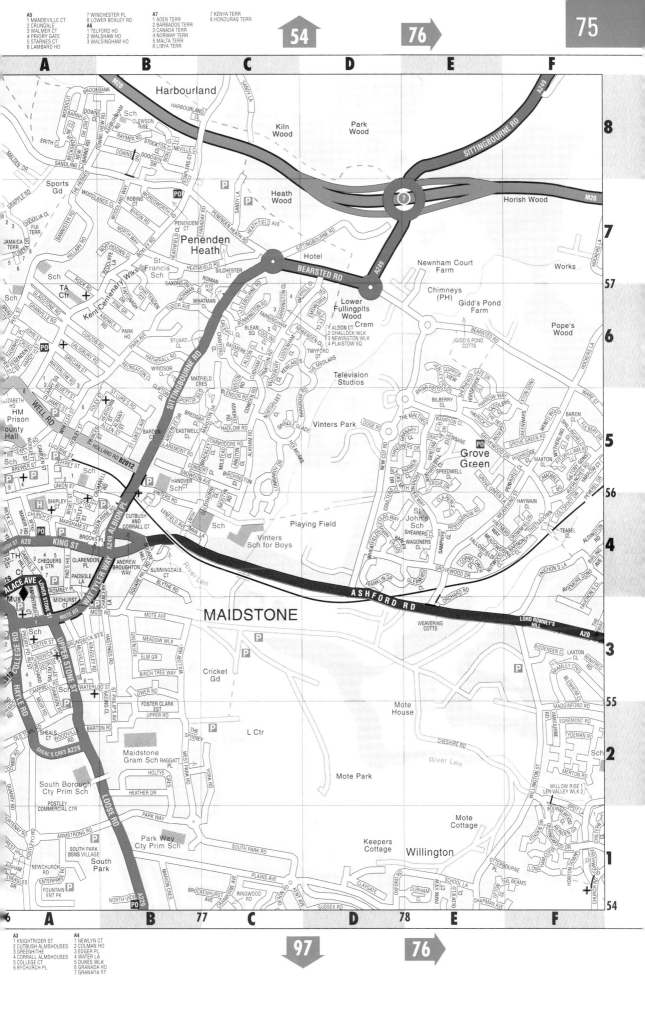

54

76

A	B	C	D	E	F

Harbourland

8

Kiln Wood

Park Wood

SITTINGBOURNE RD

Sports Gd

Heath Wood

Horish Wood

Works

7

Penenden Heath

Hotel

BEARSTED RD

Newnham Court Farm

57

TA Ctr

Kent Centenary Wks

Lower Fullingpits Wood
Crem
1 ALDON CT
2 CHALLOCK WLK
3 NEWINGTON WLK
4 PLAISTOW SQ

Chimneys (PH)

Gidd's Pond Farm

Pope's Wood

6

GIDD'S POND COTTS

Television Studios

SITTINGBOURNE RD

HM Prison

County Hall

Vinters Park

Grove Green

5

56

Vinters Sch for Boys

Playing Field

St John's Sch

KING ST

ALBION PL

WALTER TYLER WAY

ASHFORD RD

MAIDSTONE

4

River Len

Mote House

Weavering Cotts

Lord Romney's Hill

A20

3

Cricket Gd

Foster Clark Est

L Ctr

River Len

55

Maidstone Gram Sch

Mote Park

2

South Borough Cty Prim Sch

Postley Commercial Ctr

Park Way Cty Prim Sch

Keepers Cottage

Mote Cottage

Willington

1

South Park

Fountain Ent Pk

54

A	B	C	D	E	F

77

78

97

76

A B C D E F

8
Works
Detling
HOCKERS CL
HOCKERS LA

Black Horse (PH)
CASTLE HILL
Thurnham
North Downs Way
Fox Farm Cotts
COLDREUM LA

Thurnham Court
PILGRIMS WAY
ALDINGTON LA

M20
7
Court Farm
THURNHAM LA
Gorewood Farm
Thurnham Keep Farm
Cobham Manor Riding Centre

57
Honeyhills Wood

6
Gore Wood
The Lilk
WATER LA
Longham Wood

Golf Course
Clayswood

Birling House
Chapel Lane Farm

5
Ware Street
CH
FANCY ROW
1 BEARSTED GREEN BSNS CTR
2 INVICTA VILLAS
3 SMARTS COTTS
4 MATE HALL VILLAS
5 THE OASTS
6 OLIVERS COTTS
Bearsted & Thurnham Sta
Howe Court

PORT CL
AVERCONW
CREVE COEUR
DE
LONGFIELDS
PEVEREL
WARE ST
SHARP WAY
SANDY
SANDY LA
HOG HILL
PO
Liby
COLLEGATE DR
Bridge Farm

56
MAMIGNOT CL
MYTIN CRES
HILL BROW
MOUNT PLEASANT DR
WINDMILL CL
PIMPERNEL CL
BLAKENEY CL
MEREMANS RD
MALLINGS RD
MALLINGS DR
Barty Farm

4
HAMPSON WAY
BIRLING AVE
FULLERS CL
THE SPIES
THE ALMONDS
ROSEACRE LA
Roseacre Jun Sch
Eylesden Court Sch
THE STREET
CROSS KEYS
Bearsted
AMES
BIRLING CL
THE LANDWAY
SPDORNE
Thurnham CE Inf Sch
ST FAITH'S LA
THE ORCHARD
WHITEHEADS LA
MOUNT LA
CHURCH LA
TRAPFIELD LA
SUTTON ST
ROUNDWELL
CROMHILL RD

Roseacre
CLARENDON CL
COSSACRE GDNS
TOWER LA
TOWER RD
MANOR LA
MANOR RISE
DANEFIELD CT

PLANTATION LA
LITTERIDGE
NURSERY RD
MANOR CT
MANOR CL

THE GROVE
PO
3
A20
P
YEOMAN CT
LILK HILL
ASHFORD RD
Woodcut Farm

ROMNEY CL
SHIRLEY WAY
CATERBURY WAY
TASK
BIDSHAM
BUTTOLL LA
OTHAM LA
Tudor Park Hotel & Country Club

55
ROYSTON RD
MANSFIELD RD
MADGEFORD RD
COPSEWOOD WAY
GREENSIDE RD
Golf Course
FIRST LA
CARING LA
CROMHILL RD

MAIDSTONE
GREENSAND
YEOMAN WAY
River Len
Milgate Park
Milgate
Silver Hill
Mantle's

2
Liby
EGREMONT
RAGSTONE RD
Jun & Inf Schs
GAULT CL
RYAN DR
LENSIDE DR
Sewage Works
OTHAM ST
Nursery

COTSWOLD GDNS
CHEVIOT GDNS
PENNINE WAY
MALLARDS WAY
DEFINGWOOD DR
GORHAM DR
Orchard Spot (PH)
CARING DR

1
KIN ACRE
MONKDOWN
BRIDGEWOOD
MALHAM DR
GREEN HILL
Caring Farm
Caring
Fulling Mill Farm
OLD MILL RD

1 ELLENSWOOD CL
2 REDSELLS CL
3 RAVENS DANE CL

A20

54
79 A 80 B C 81 D E F

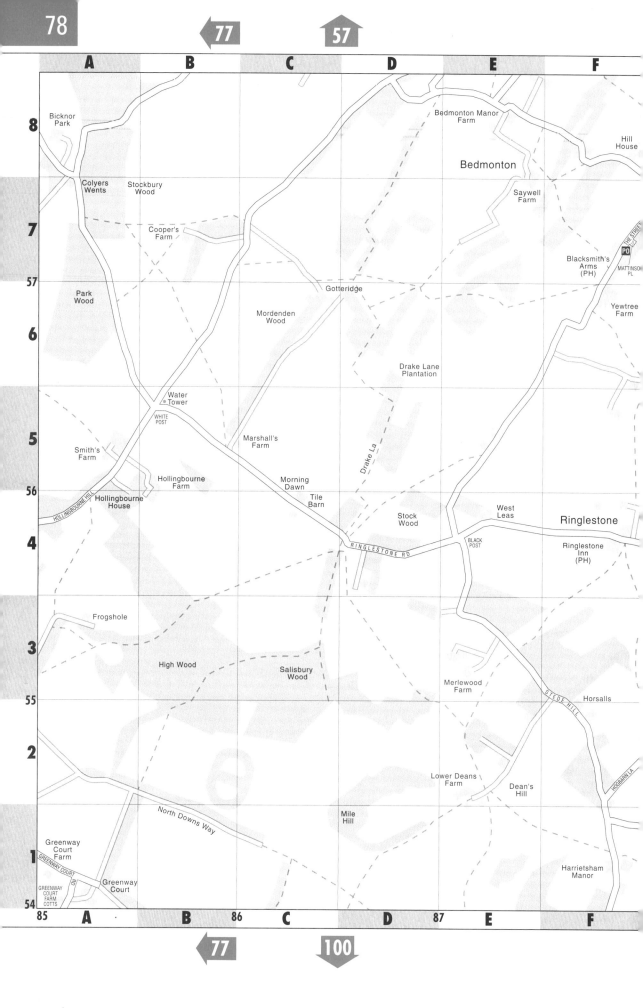

A   **B**   **C**   **D**   **E**   **F**

8

Bicknor Park

Bedmonton Manor Farm

Hill House

Bedmonton

Colyers Wents

Stockbury Wood

Saywell Farm

7

Cooper's Farm

THE STREET

PO

Blacksmith's Arms (PH)

MATTINSON PL

57

Park Wood

Gotteridge

Yewtree Farm

Mordenden Wood

6

Drake Lane Plantation

Water Tower

WHITE POST

Marshall's Farm

Drake La

5

Smith's Farm

Morning Dawn

HOLLINGBOURNE HILL

Hollingbourne Farm

Tile Barn

West Leas

Ringlestone

56

Hollingbourne House

Stock Wood

BLACK POST

Ringlestone Inn (PH)

4

RINGLESTONE RD

Frogshole

Merlewood Farm

Horsalls

3

High Wood

Salisbury Wood

STEDE HILL

55

Lower Deans Farm

Dean's Hill

HOGBARN LA

2

North Downs Way

Mile Hill

Harrietsham Manor

1

Greenway Court Farm

GREENWAY COURT RD

GREENWAY COURT FARM COTTS

Greenway Court

54

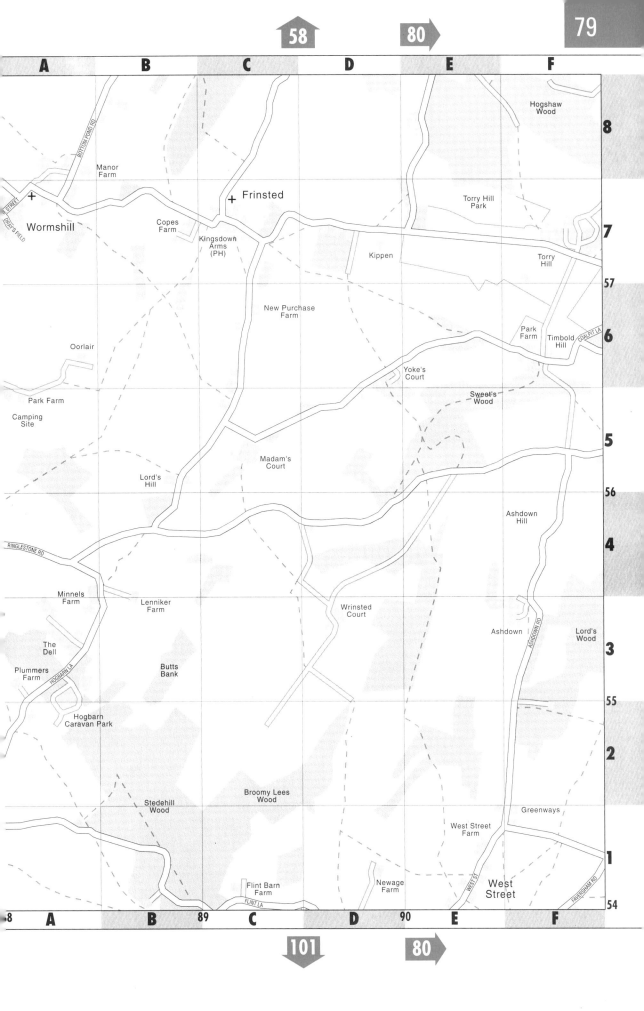

A   B   C   D   E   F

8

Hogshaw
Wood

Manor
Farm

+   Frinsted

Torry Hill
Park

7

Wormshill

Copes
Farm

Kingsdown
Arms
(PH)

Kippen

Torry
Hill

57

New Purchase
Farm

Park
Farm

Timbold
Hill

COALPIT LA

6

Oorlair

Yoke's
Court

Sweet's
Wood

Park Farm

Camping
Site

5

Madam's
Court

56

Lord's
Hill

Ashdown
Hill

RINGLESTONE RD

4

Minnels
Farm

Lenniker
Farm

Wrinsted
Court

Ashdown

ASHDOWN RD

Lord's
Wood

The
Dell

HOGBARN LA

3

Plummers
Farm

Butts
Bank

55

Hogbarn
Caravan Park

2

Stedehill
Wood

Broomy Lees
Wood

Greenways

West Street
Farm

West
Street

1

Flint Barn
Farm

FLINT LA

Newage
Farm

WEST ST

FAVERSHAM RD

54

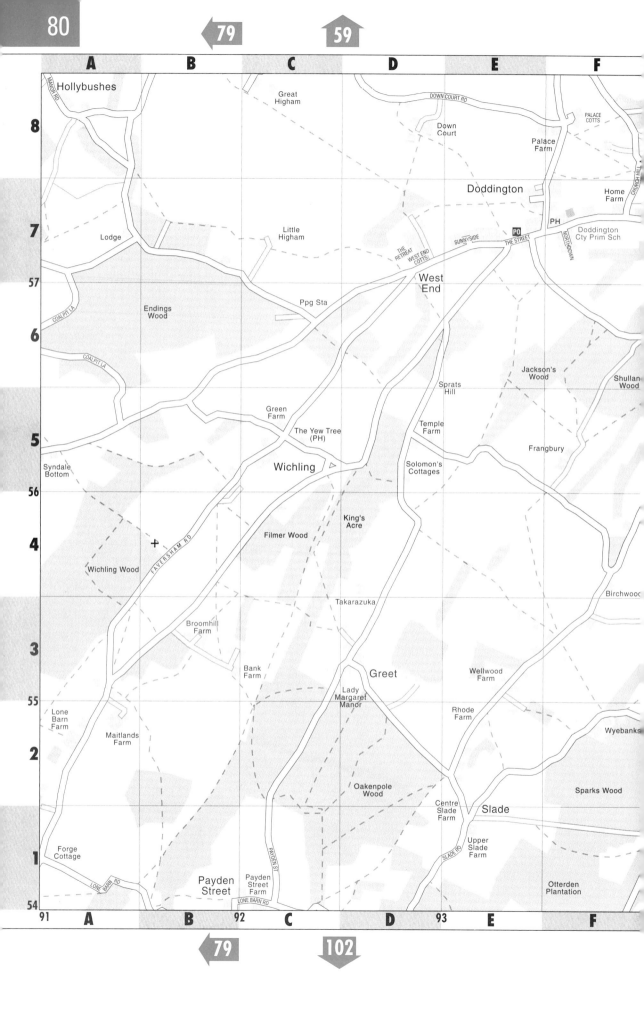

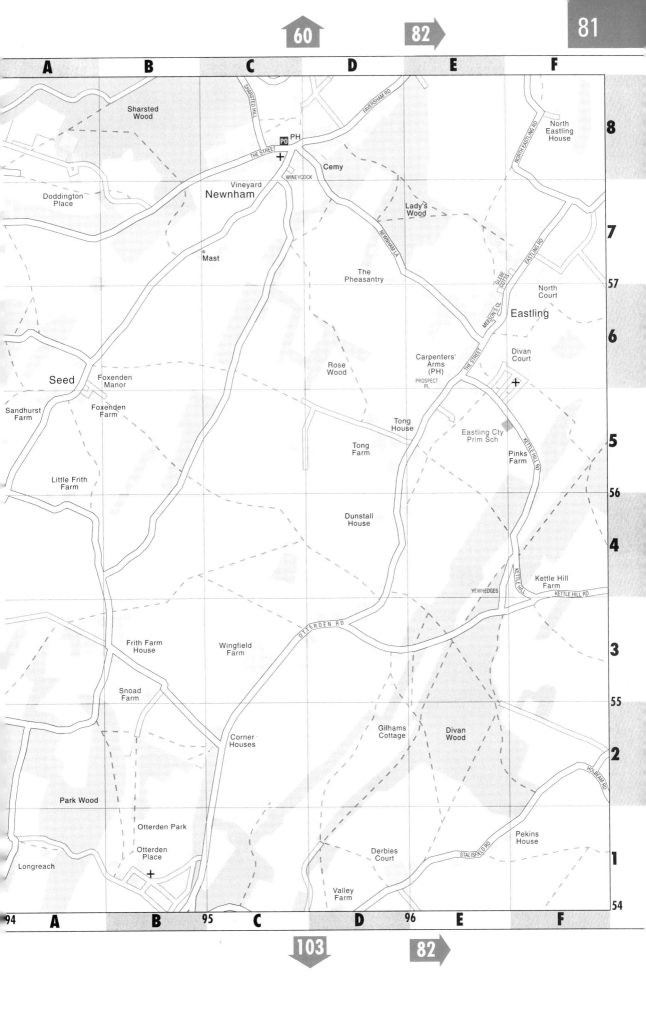

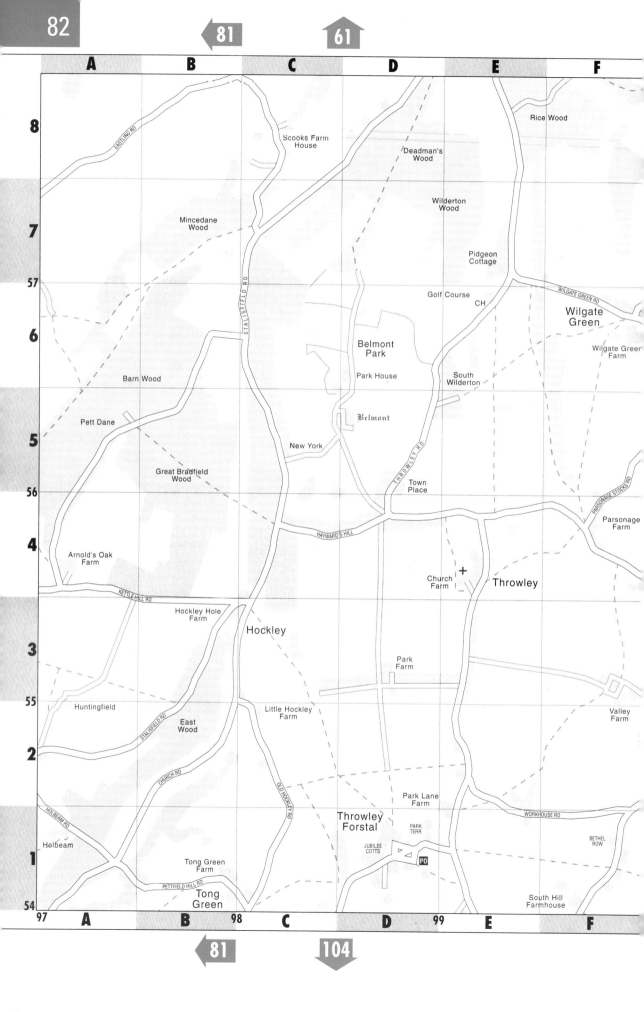

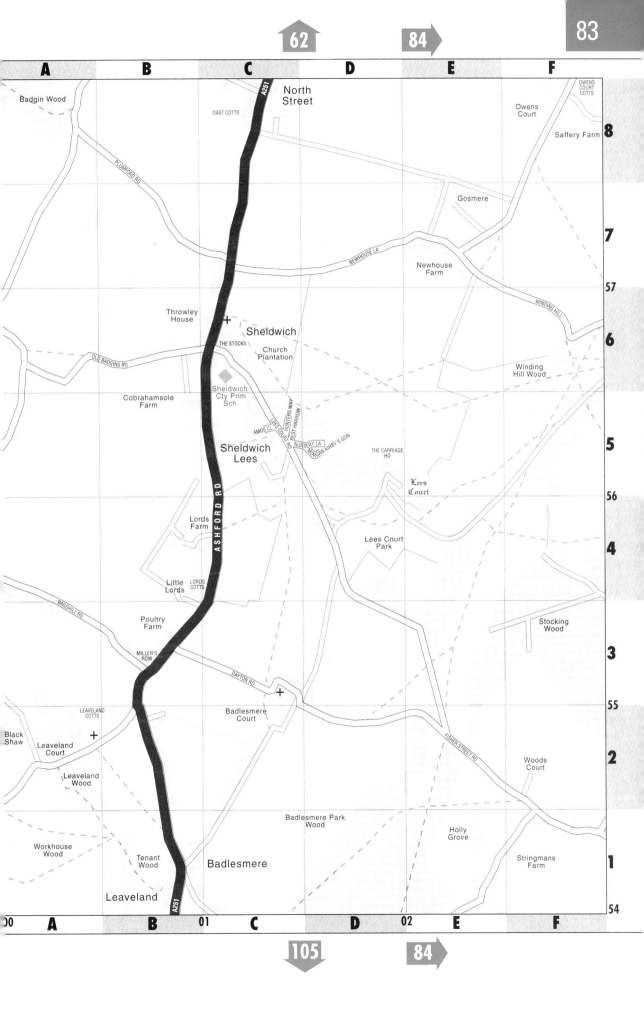

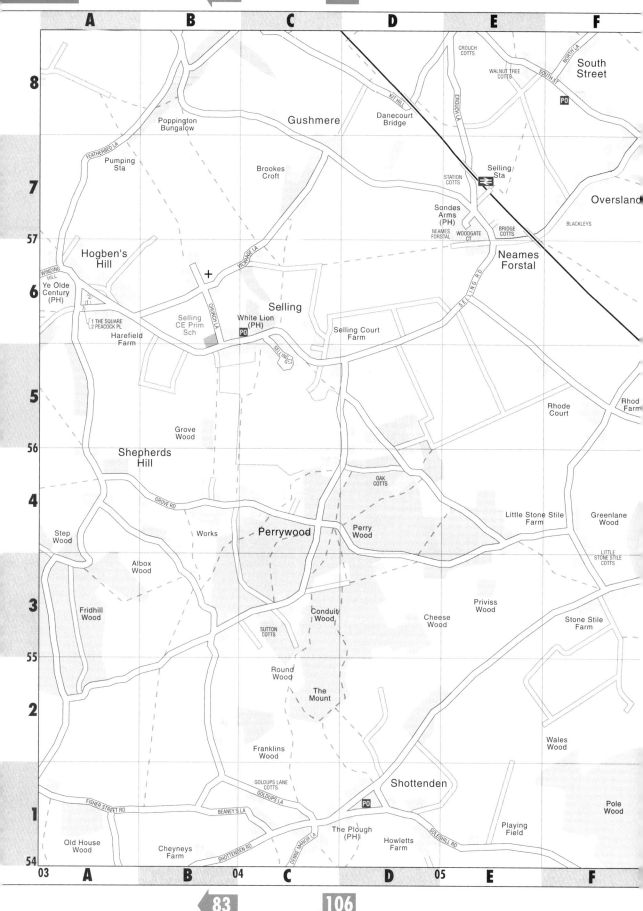

A B C D E F

8

Poppington
Bungalow

Gushmere

CROUCH
COTTS

WALNUT TREE
COTTS

NORTH LA

SOUTH ST

South
Street

PO

Danecourt
Bridge

KIT HILL

CROUCH LA

FEATHERBED LA

Pumping
Sta

Brookes
Croft

Selling
Sta

7

STATION
COTTS

Oversland

Sondes
Arms
(PH)

57

NEAMES
FORSTAL

WOODGATE
CT

BRIDGE
COTTS

BLACKLEYS

Hogben's
Hill

VICARAGE LA

+

Neames
Forstal

WINDING
HILL

Ye Olde
Century
(PH)

6

2
1

Selling

SELLING RD

1 THE SQUARE
2 PEACOCK PL

Selling
CE Prim
Sch

CHURCH LA

White Lion
(PH)

PO

Selling Court
Farm

Harefield
Farm

SELLING CT

5

Rhode
Court

Rhod
Farm

Grove
Wood

56

Shepherds
Hill

OAK
COTTS

4

GROVE RD

Little Stone Stile
Farm

Greenlane
Wood

Step
Wood

Works

Perrywood

Perry
Wood

LITTLE
STONE STILE
COTTS

Albox
Wood

3

Fridhill
Wood

Conduit
Wood

Priviss
Wood

Cheese
Wood

Stone Stile
Farm

SUTTON
COTTS

55

Round
Wood

2

The
Mount

Wales
Wood

Franklins
Wood

GOLDUPS LANE
COTTS

Shottenden

Pole
Wood

1

FISHER STREET RD

GOLDUPS LA

PO

BEANEY'S LA

Playing
Field

DENNE MANOR LA

The Plough
(PH)

Howletts
Farm

SOLESHILL RD

Old House
Wood

Cheyneys
Farm

SHOTTENDEN RD

54

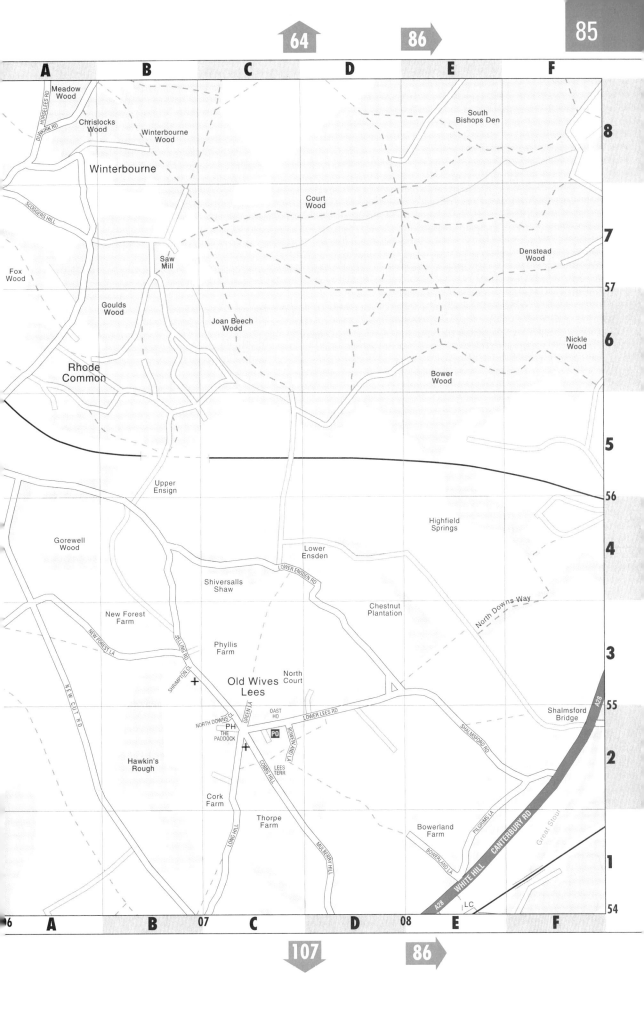

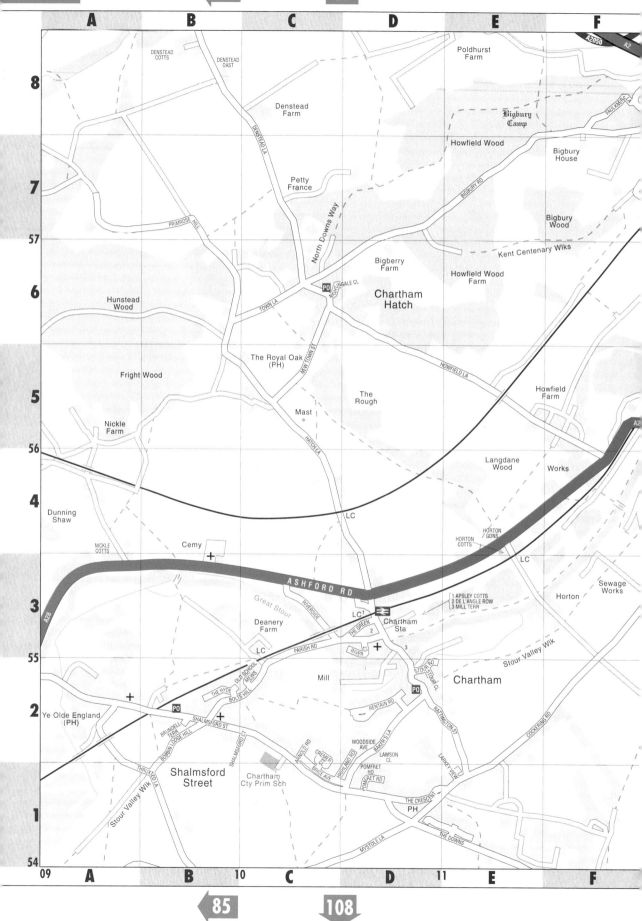

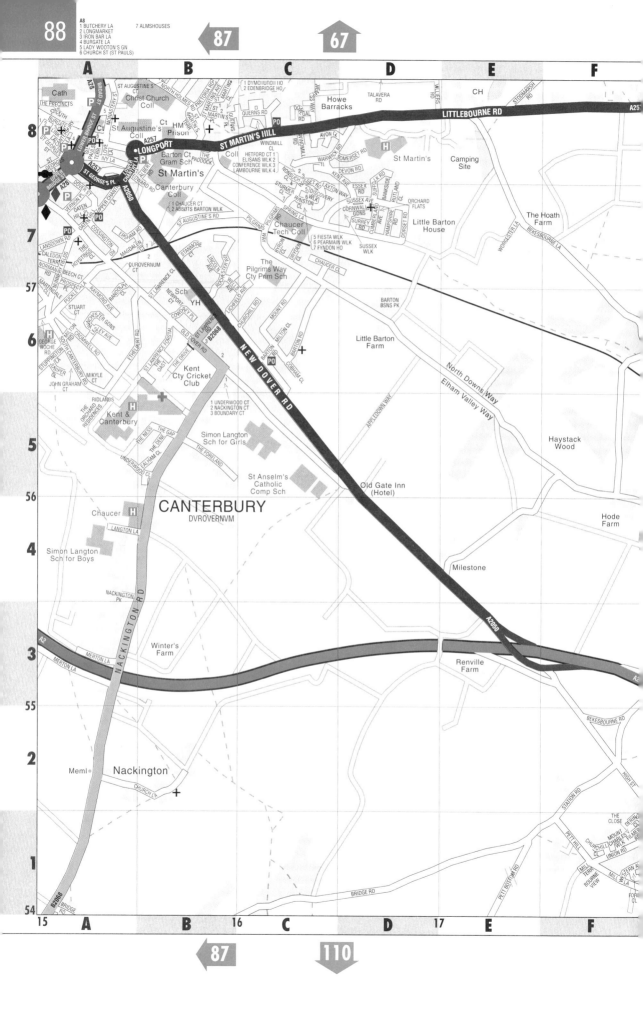

LITTLEBOURNE RD

CANTERBURY RD

Jacob's
Close

Fishpoolhill
Wood

Court
Wood

PINESIDE RD

HILLCREST RD

NEWHILL RD

EWING CL

Allot
Gdns

Littlebourne
CE Prim
Sch

COURT MEADOWS

COURT HILL

JUBILEE RD

THE HILL

Littlebourne

Recn
Gd

MARGATE ST

8

PO

HIGH ST A257

ROSE ACRE RD

ORCHARD CL

THE MALTINGS

THE GREEN

Farthings
Wood

Firdown
Wood

Ponds
Cottages

7

Silver Dike

57

Palmsted
Wood

Woolton
Farm

Howletts
Zoo Park

BEKESBOURNE LA

Lockenden
Cotts

BEKESBOURNE LA

Lower
Garrington
Farm

6

Conduit
Wood

BEKESBOURNE LA

Bekesbourne
Hill

Howletts
Farm

Upper Garrington
Farm

5

OAKLEIGH LA

BEKESBOURNE HILL

PH

UNICORN
COTTS

Howletts
Oast

Linces
Wood

56

Bekesbourne
Sta

SCHOOL LA

4

STATION RD

SCHOOL LA

Bekesbourne

LYSANDER
CL

BIFRONS HILL

BIFRONS RD

Patrixbourne

Ford

Nail Bourne

CHALKPIT HILL

AERODROME RD

3

THE STREET

BIFRONS
GDNS

Fords

ST MARY'S RD

Chalkpit
Farm
(Hop Farm)

DOWNSIDE

ADISHAM RD

55

Bifron's
Park

Elham Valley Way

PATRIXBOURNE RD

KEEPER'S HILL

BRAMLING RD

2

North Downs Way

Bridge & Patrixbourne
CE Prim Sch

CONYNGHAM LA

PO

HIGH ST

WESTERN AVE

SAXON GREEN

WINDMILL

MANSFIELD
CT

RIVERSIDE
MEWS

Recn
Gd

MEADOW CL

SHEPHERD'S CLOSE RD

Shepherd's
Close

1

BRIDGE HILL

BREWERY LA

LYNTON
PL

BRIDGEFORD
WAY

Ford

Bridge

54

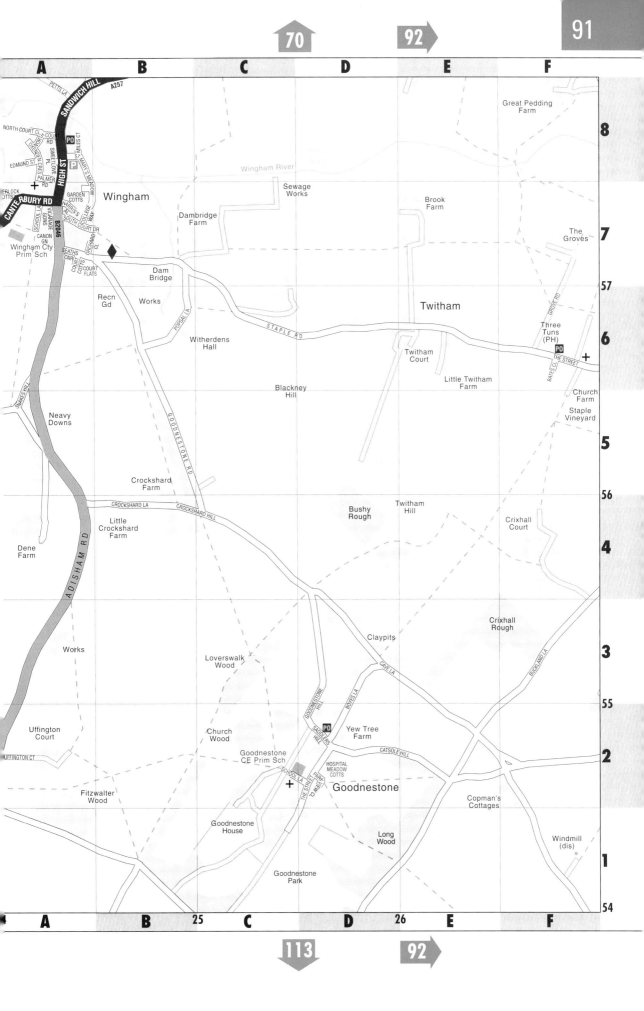

A B C D E F

Great Pedding Farm

PETTS LA
SANDWICH HILL A257
NORTH COURT CL
COURT RD
SWEETLOVE PL
DRENGEN CRES
EDMUND ST
HIGH ST
PALMER RD
CANTERBURY RD
SHERLOCK COTTS
CANON GN
Wingham Cty Prim Sch
Wingham
PO
P
ST MARY'S MEADOW
ST MILES CT
VICARAGE GDNS
GARDEN COTTS
HARRIS'S LA
COLLEGE WAY
SOUTH COURT DR
ORCHARD CL
SEATHS CNR
CNR COTTS COURT FLATS
B2046

Wingham River

Sewage Works

Brook Farm

The Groves

7

57

Dambridge Farm

Dam Bridge

POPSAL LA

Recn Gd

Works

Twitham

Three Tuns (PH)
PO
THE STREET
BATES CL
GROVE RD

6

Witherdens Hall

STAPLE RD

Twitham Court

Little Twitham Farm

Church Farm

Staple Vineyard

SNAKES HILL

Neavy Downs

GOODNESTONE RD

Blackney Hill

5

Crockshard Farm

Crockshard Hill

Bushy Rough

Twitham Hill

56

Crixhall Court

CROCKSHARD LA

Little Crockshard Farm

ADISHAM RD

Dene Farm

4

Crixhall Rough

BUCKLAND LA

Works

Loverswalk Wood

Claypits

CAVE LA

3

GOODNESTONE HILL

BOYES LA

55

Uffington Court

Church Wood

SADDLERS HILL
PO

Yew Tree Farm

CATSOLE HILL

2

UFFINGTON CT

Goodnestone CE Prim Sch

SCHOOL LA

THE STREET
PARK CL

HOSPITAL MEADOW COTTS

Goodnestone

Copman's Cottages

Fitzwalter Wood

Goodnestone House

Long Wood

Windmill (dis)

1

Goodnestone Park

54

A B C D E F
25 26

← 91
71

A B C D E F

8

PEDDING LA

Nursery

Durlock

Durlock
Bridge

DURLOCK RD

POULTON LA

Poulton
Farm

COOMBE LA

Ash Coombe
Vineyard

NEW ST

Coombe

Coombe
Farm

7

The
Rookery

Ringleton
Manor

Rad
St

57

Little
Flemings
Farm

Black Pond
Farm

Christian
Court

6

Staple
Farm

Nurseries

SCHOOL LA

CHURCH CT

1   2

3

1 THE OAST
2 THE OAST PADDOCK
3 THE COURTYARD

LOWER RD

Chapel
Farm

CHAPEL LA

FLEMING RD

Flemings

Ringlemere
Farm

DRAINLESS RD

THE STREET

Mill Road
Farm

Fernleigh

Barnsole

Flemings
House

Staple

MILL RD

PH

BARNSOLE RD

Gander
Court

Onionbeds

Mushroom
Farm

5

Nurseries

Chalk
Farm
Lodge

CHALK PIT LA

Hammill
Court

56

BUCKLAND LA

Summerfield
Farm

Summerfield Farm
(Eastry)
Pottery

Denne Court
Farm

4

Summerfield

Dix's
Farm

The Hammill
Brick Works

Hammill

Hammill
Farm

3

Green La

GREEN LA

55

Lower Rowling
Farm

Rowling
House

Upper Rowling
Farm

Great Tickenhurst
Farm

2

MEADOW
COTTS

Rowling
Court

Tickenhurst

1

Little Tickenhurst
Farm

Heronden

Middle Heronden
Farm

54

Tickenhurst
Shave

Heronden
Farm

HERONDEN RD

THORNTON

27   A   B   28   C   D   29   E   F

← 91
114 ▼

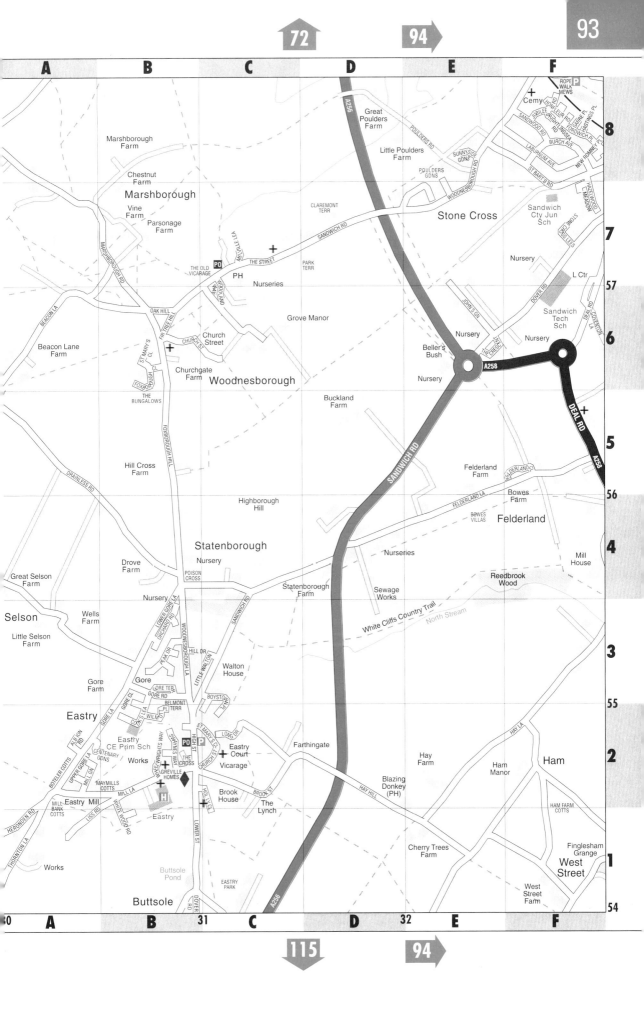

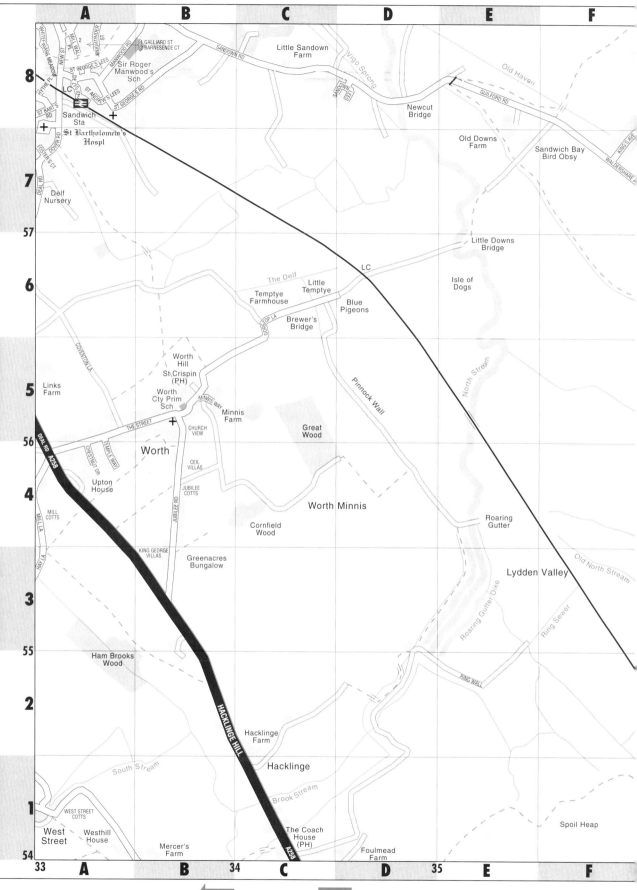

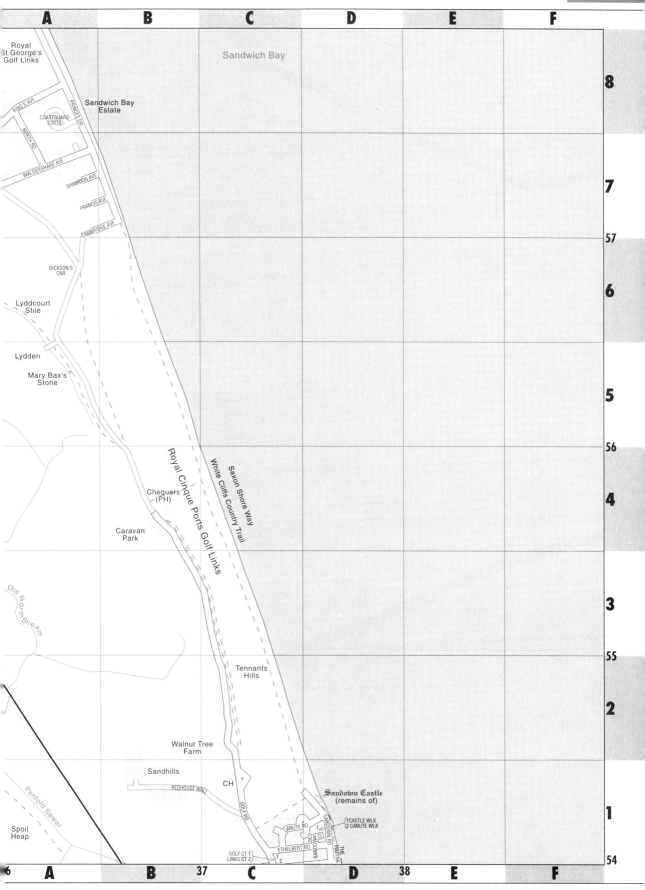

A B C D E F

Sandwich Bay

Royal
St George's
Golf Links

Sandwich Bay
Estate

KING'S AVE

PRINCES DR

COASTGUARD
COTTS

NORTH RD

WALDERSHARE AVE

SHAWDON AVE

FRANCIS AVE

CAMBRIDGE AVE

DICKSON'S
CNR

Lyddcourt
Stile

Lydden

Mary Bax's
Stone

Royal Cinque Ports Golf Links

White Cliffs Country Trail

Saxon Shore Way

Chequers
(PH)

Caravan
Park

Old North Stream

Tennants
Hills

Walnut Tree
Farm

Sandhills

REDHOUSE WAY

CH

GOLF RD

Sandown Castle
(remains of)

1 CASTLE WLK
2 CANUTE WLK

CANUTE RD

SANDOWN RD

THE MARINA

ETHELBERT RD

Pentold Sewer

Spoil
Heap

GOLF CT 1
LINKS CT 2

8

7

57

6

5

56

4

3

55

2

1

54

6   A   B   37   C   D   38   E   F

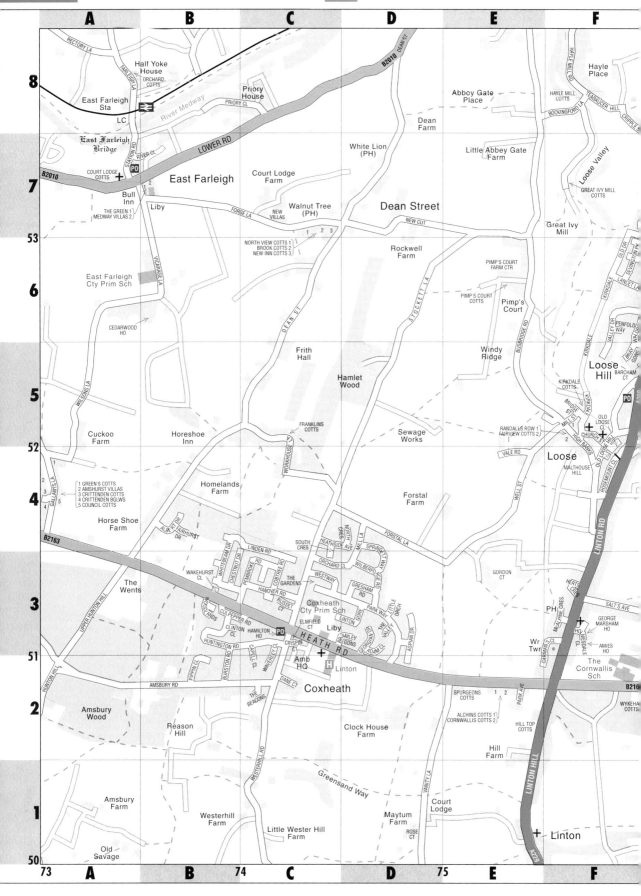

D7
1 ROCHESTER HO
2 CANTERBURY HO
3 CAMBRIDGE HO
4 WINCHESTER HO
5 SALISBURY HO

D8
1 MEDWAY HO
2 DARENTH HO
3 THAMES HO
4 STOUR HO
5 ROTHER HO

E7
1 SWALE HO
2 TRENT HO
3 SHROPSHIRE TERR
4 HUNTINGDON WLK
5 DERWENT HO
6 INVERNESS HO

7 GLASGOW HO
8 ABERDEEN HO
9 TEES HO
10 TYNE HO

E8
1 HARDWICK HO
2 NEATH CT

F5
1 CAPETOWN HO
2 JOHANNESBURG HO
3 HERON APARTMENTS
4 LIVINGSTONE WLK
5 NELSON HO
6 BALMORAL HO

F6
1 AINTREE HO
2 ASCOT HO
3 CHEPSTOW HO
4 FOLKSTONE HO
5 TITCHFIELD CL
6 FONTFIELD CL

7 DONCASTER CL
8 HAVANT WLK
9 PLUMPTON WLK
10 FAREHAM WLK
11 DENSTEAD WLK
12 ANDOVER WLK
13 GROOMBRIDGE SQ

75   **98**   **97**

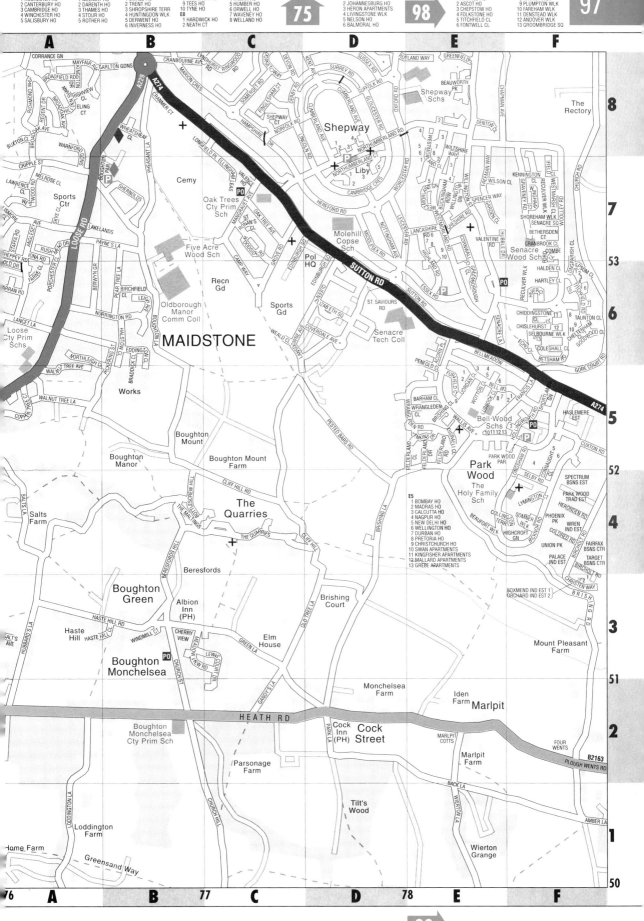

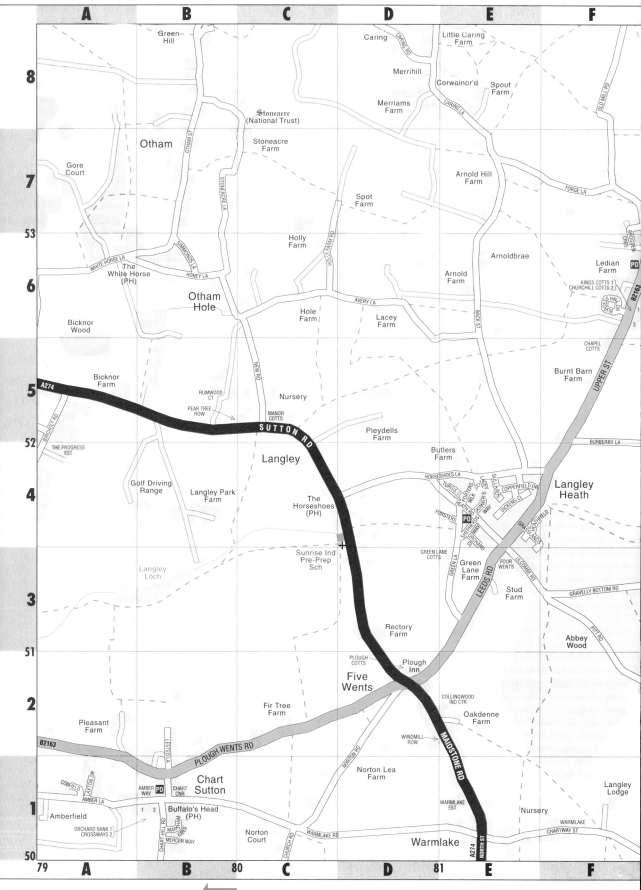

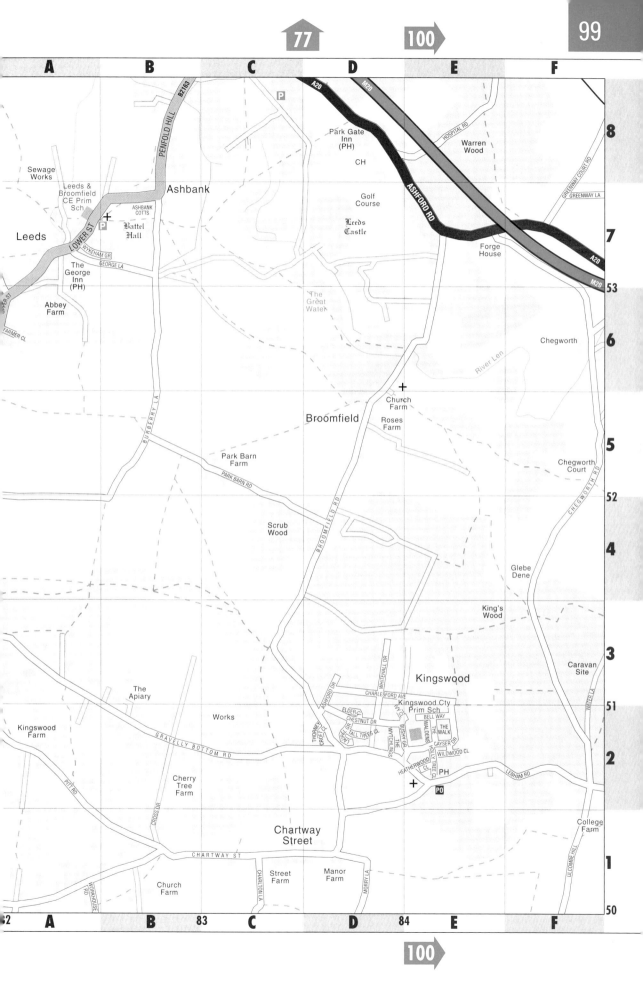

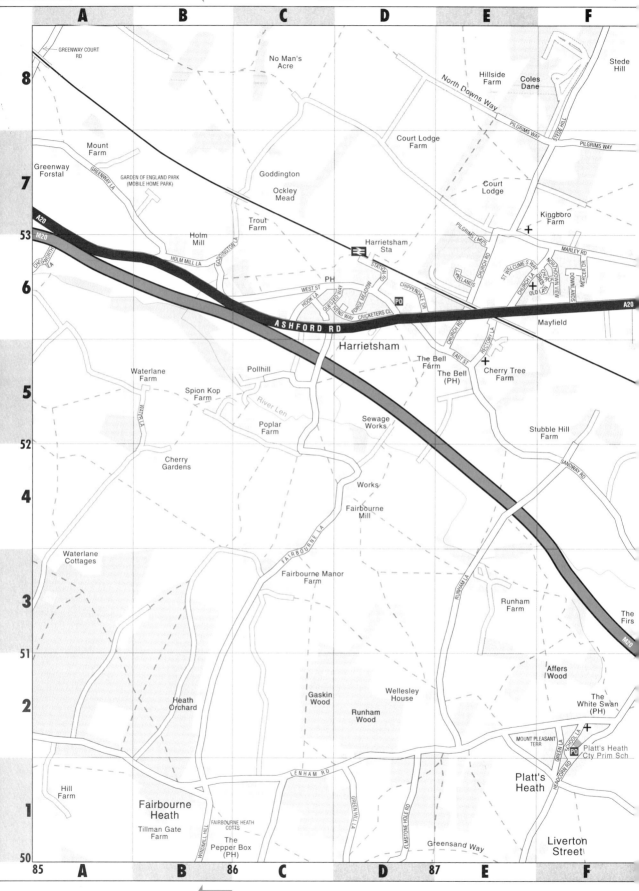

Greenway Court RD

No Man's Acre

Hillside Farm

Coles Dane

Stede Hill

North Downs Way

PILGRIMS WAY

PILGRIMS WAY

STEDE HILL

Mount Farm

Court Lodge Farm

Greenway Forstal

GREENWAY LA

Garden of England Park (MOBILE HOME PARK)

Goddington

Court Lodge

Kingboro Farm

A20

M20

Holm Mill

HOLM MILL LA

GODDINGTON LA

Ockley Mead

Trout Farm

Harrietsham Sta

PILGRIMS WAY

MARLEY RD

CHURCH RD

ST WELCUME'S WAY

NORTH DOWNS VIEW

CHURCH LA

MERCER DR

COMMON DR

PH

WEST ST

STATION RD

PO

CHIPPENDALE DR

YELANDS

OLD LA

CHEGWORTH LA

HOOK LA

QUEENS WAY

FORGE MEADOW

CRICKETERS CL

ASHFORD RD

A20

Harrietsham

CHURCH RD

EAST ST

RECTORY LA

Mayfield

Waterlane Farm

Pollhill

WATER LA

Spion Kop Farm

River Len

Sewage Works

The Bell Farm

The Bell (PH)

Cherry Tree Farm

Stubble Hill Farm

52

Poplar Farm

Cherry Gardens

Works

SANDWAY RD

Fairbourne Mill

Waterlane Cottages

FAIRBOURNE LA

Fairbourne Manor Farm

RUNHAM LA

Runham Farm

The Firs

M20

51

Affers Wood

Heath Orchard

Gaskin Wood

Wellesley House

Runham Wood

The White Swan (PH)

MOUNT PLEASANT TERR

GREEN LA

SCHOOL LA

HEADCORN RD

PO

Platt's Heath Cty Prim Sch

Hill Farm

LENHAM RD

Platt's Heath

Fairbourne Heath

Tillman Gate Farm

WINDMILL HILL

FAIRBOURNE HEATH COTTS

The Pepper Box (PH)

GREEN HILL LA

ELMSTONE HOLE RD

Greensand Way

Liverton Street

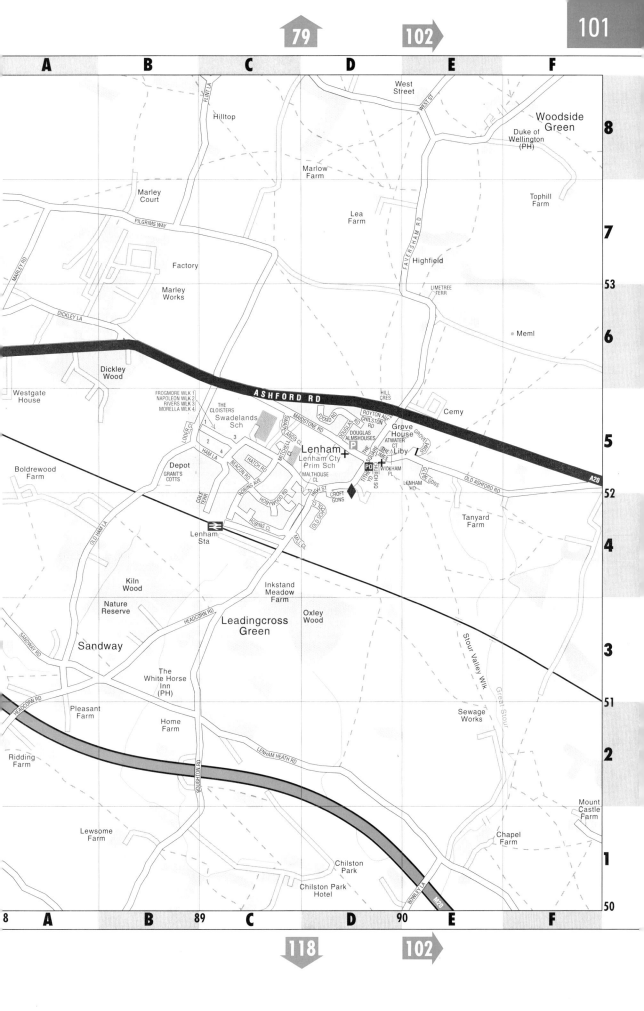

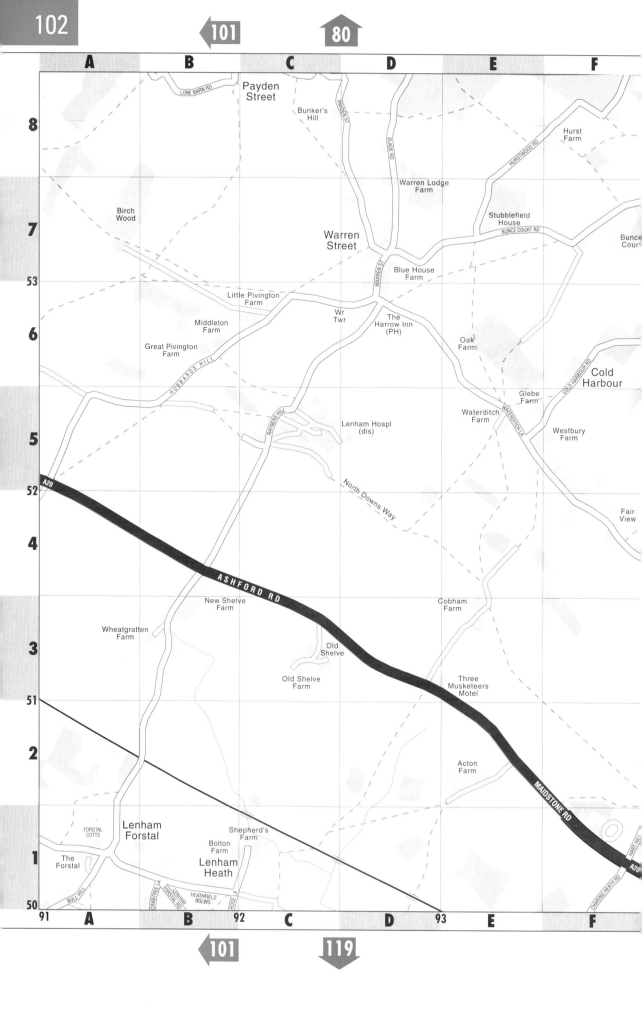

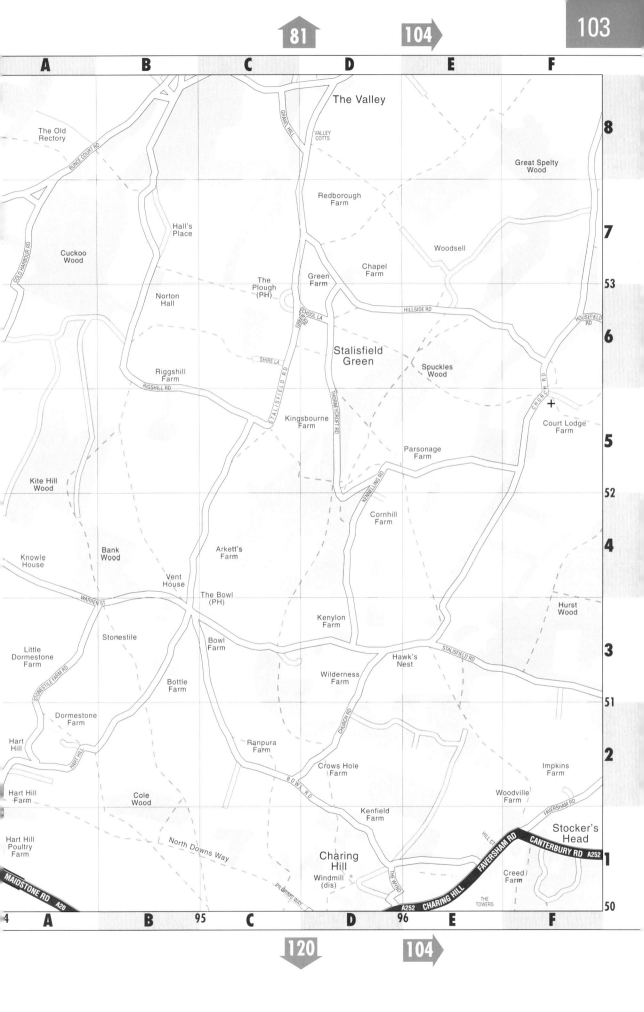

Tong Green

Dodds Willows

Hazel Wood

Bell's Forstal

CHURCH RD

HEEL RD

CROSS LA

ALMSHOUSE RD

LOOSE DOWN RD

Heel Farm

Cadman's Farm

Almhouse Cottages

OAST LA

HOUSEFIELD RD

Hurst Wood

Codling Wood

Rushmere Farm

Snoad Street Manor

Snoad Street Cottage

Newlands Farm

NEWLANDS FARM COTTS

Tir Beg

Landew's Farm

FAVERSHAM RD

Monkery Farm

Wagon & Horses (PH)

STALISFIELD RD

Longbeech Wood

MONKERY LA

Snoad Lodge

GREEN LA

Paddock

Brisley Farm

A252

CANTERBURY RD

A252

The Woodlands Inn (PH)

Cedar House Farm

Burnt Oak Farm

PATS LA

Great Paddock Fram

Beech Court

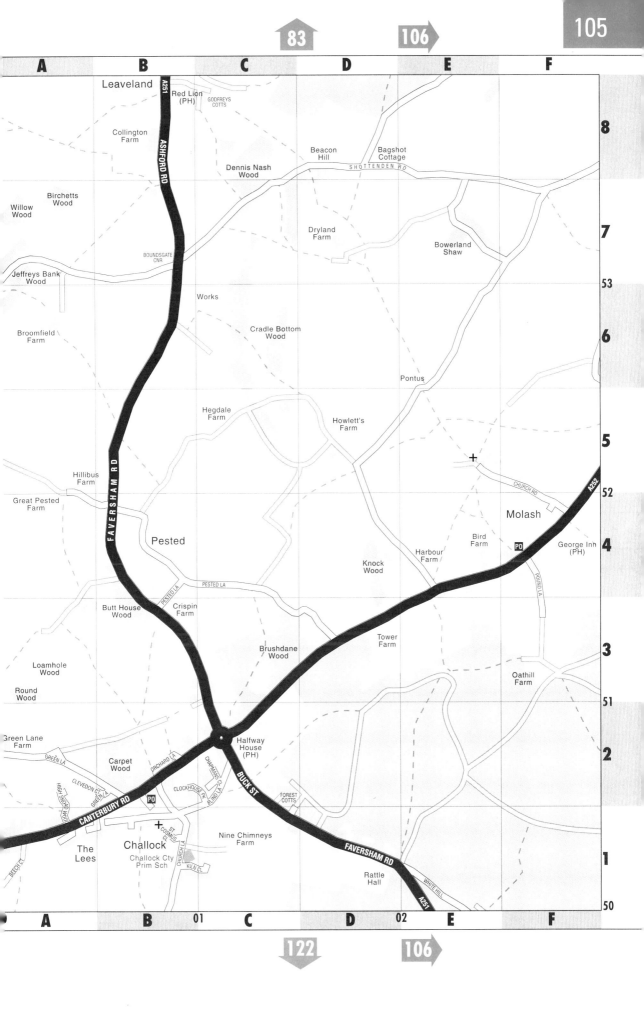

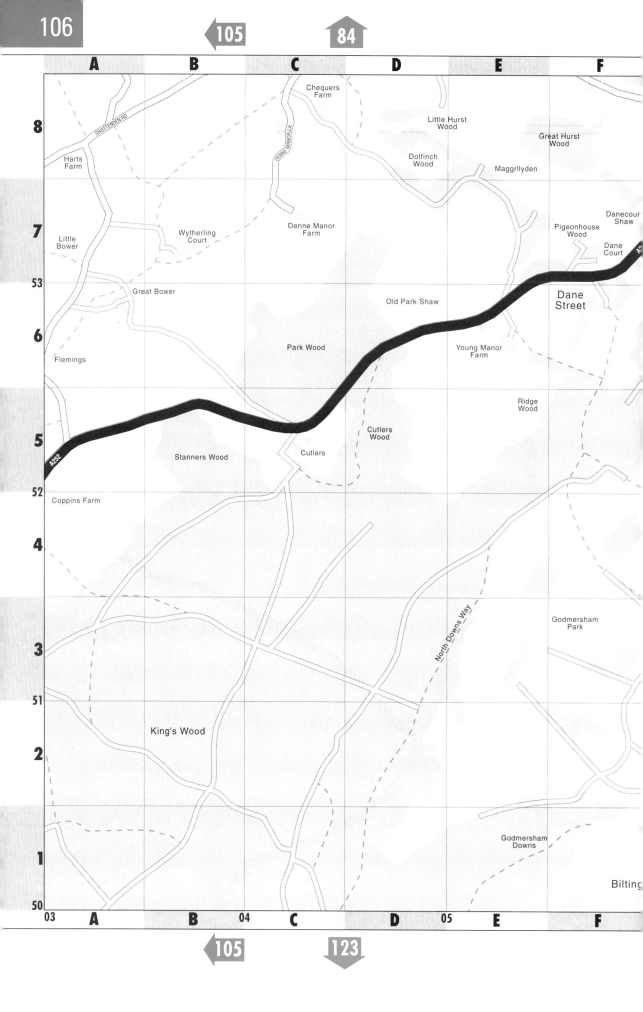

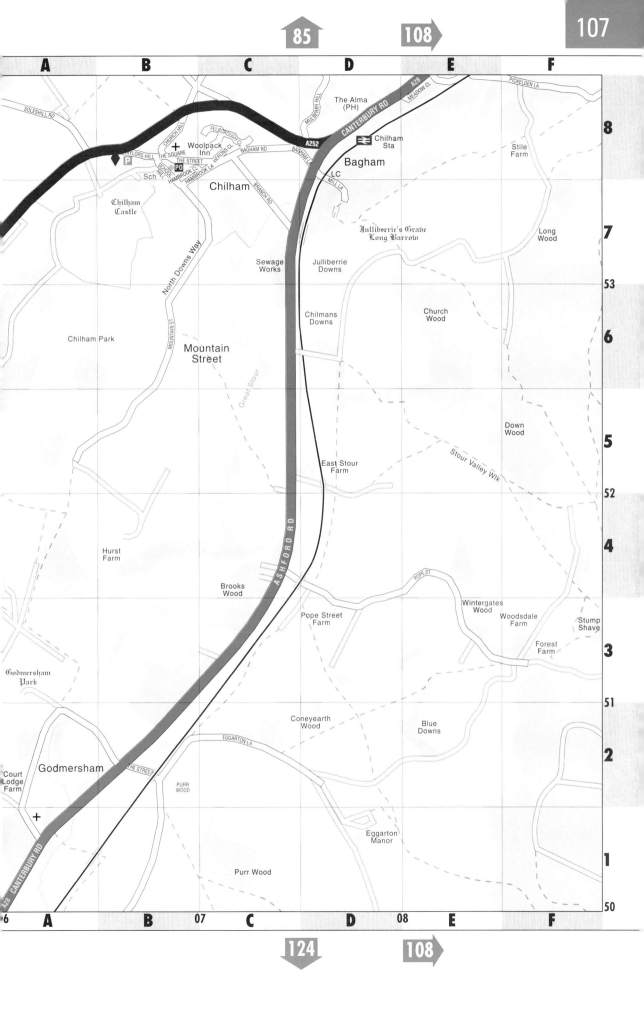

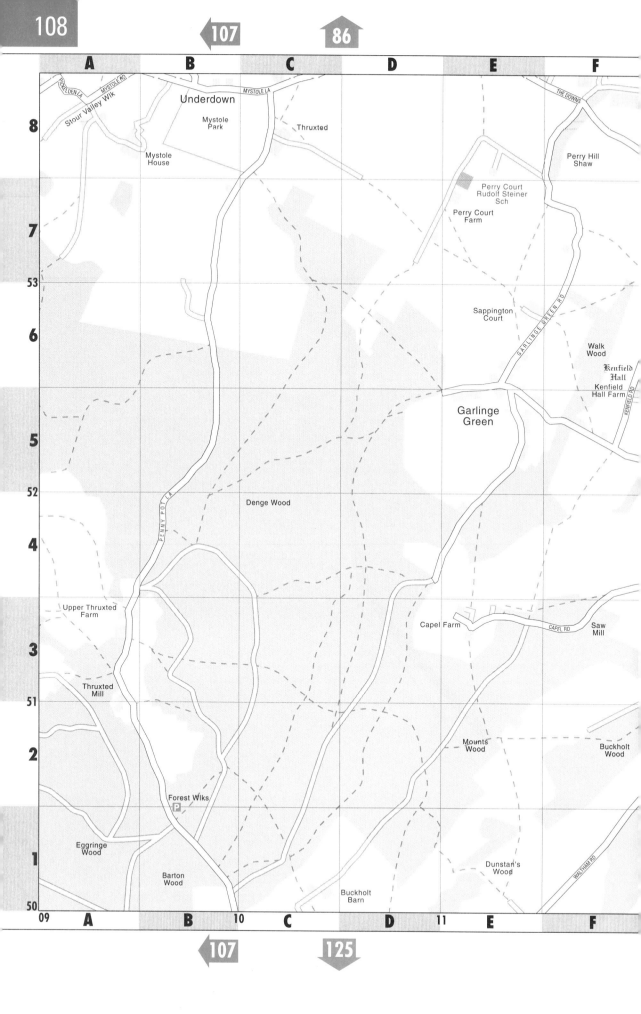

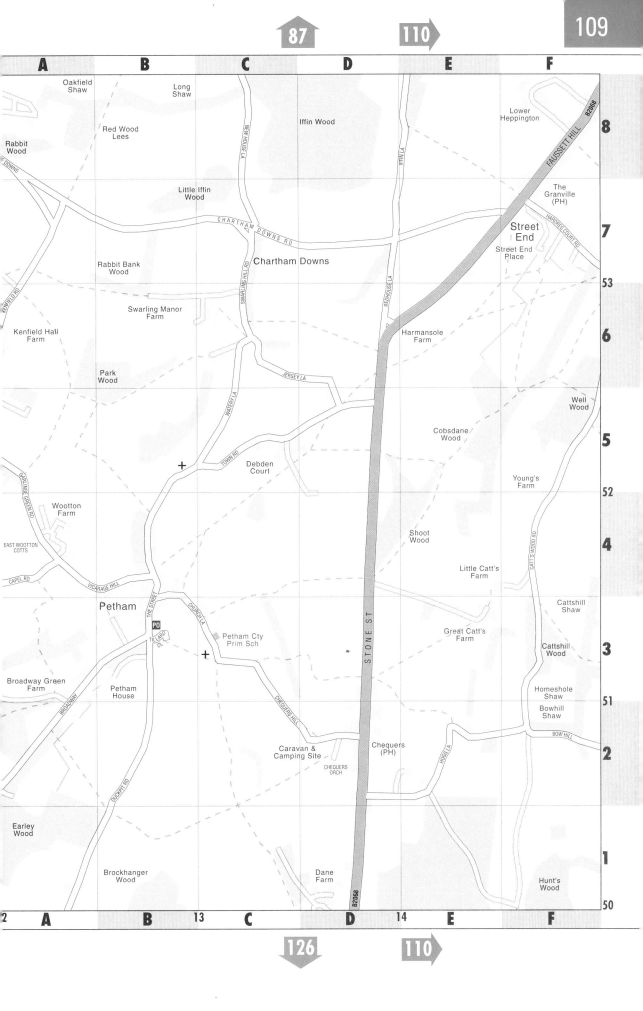

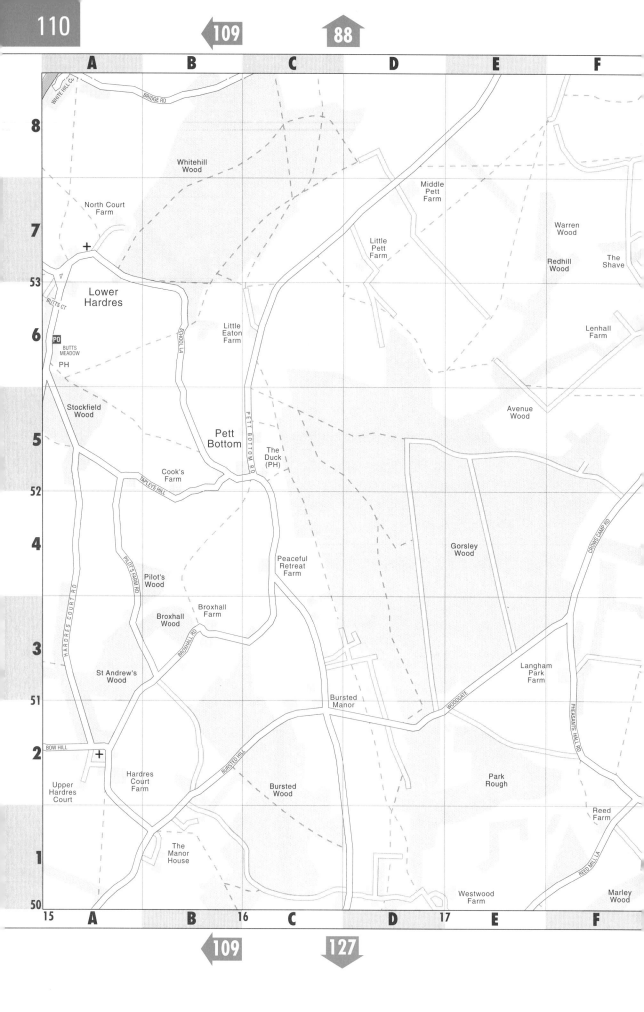

109
88

WHITEHILL CT
BRIDGE RD

Whitehill
Wood

North Court
Farm

Middle
Pett
Farm

Little
Pett
Farm

Warren
Wood

Lower
Hardres

Redhill
Wood

The
Shave

BUTTS CT

Little
Eaton
Farm

Lenhall
Farm

PO
BUTTS
MEADOW
PH

SCHOOL LA

Stockfield
Wood

Avenue
Wood

Pett
Bottom

The
Duck
(PH)

PETT BOTTOM RD

Cook's
Farm

TAPLEYS HILL

Gorsley
Wood

CROWS CAMP RD

Peaceful
Retreat
Farm

PILOT'S FARM RD

Pilot's
Wood

HARDRES COURT RD

Broxhall
Wood

Broxhall
Farm

BROXHALL RD

St Andrew's
Wood

Langham
Park
Farm

WOODGATE

Bursted
Manor

PHEASANTS HALL RD

BOW HILL

Hardres
Court
Farm

BURSTED HILL

Park
Rough

Upper
Hardres
Court

Bursted
Wood

Reed
Farm

The
Manor
House

REED MILL LA

Westwood
Farm

Marley
Wood

109
127

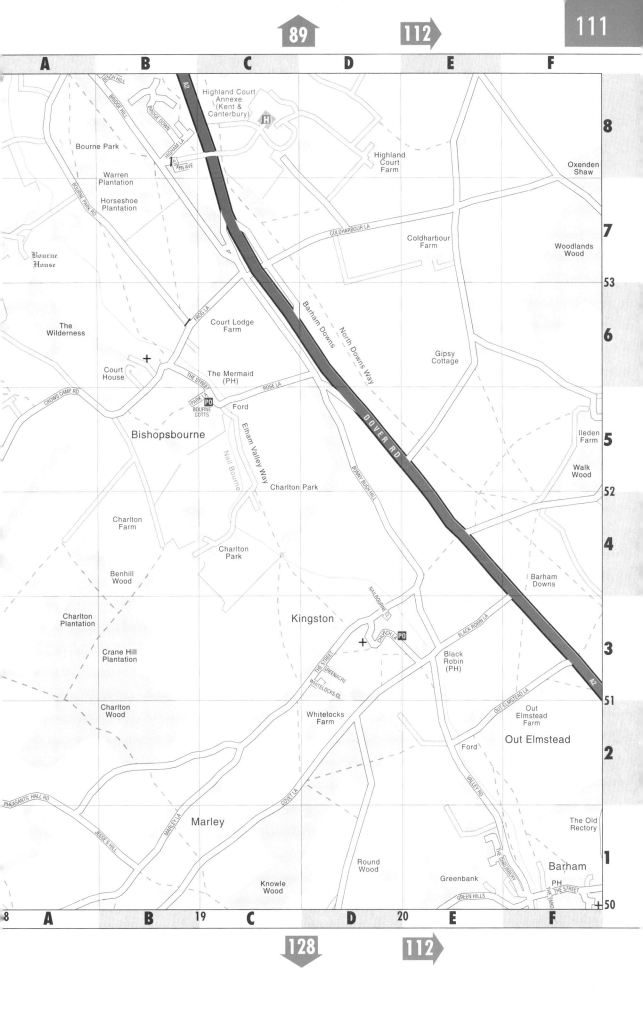

8

Bourne Park

Warren Plantation

Horseshoe Plantation

Bourne House Rd

Beech Hill

Bridge Hill

Bridge Down

Higham La

Pin Ave

A2

Highland Court Annexe (Kent & Canterbury)

H

Highland Court Farm

Oxenden Shaw

7

Coldharbour La

Coldharbour Farm

Woodlands Wood

53

The Wilderness

Bourne House

Frog La

Court Lodge Farm

Barham Downs

North Downs Way

Gipsy Cottage

6

Court House

+

The Street

The Mermaid (PH)

Rose La

Park La

PO

Bourne Cotts

Ford

Bishopsbourne

Crows Camp Rd

Nail Bourne

Elham Valley Way

Charlton Park

DOVER RD

Bonny Bush Hill

Ileden Farm

Walk Wood

5

52

Charlton Farm

Charlton Park

Benhill Wood

Charlton Plantation

Kingston

Mailbourne Cl

Church La

+

PO

Black Robin La

Barham Downs

4

Crane Hill Plantation

The Street

The Greenacre

Whitelocks Cl

Black Robin (PH)

A2

3

51

Charlton Wood

Whitelocks Farm

Out Elmstead La

Out Elmstead Farm

Out Elmstead

Pheasants Hall Rd

Marley La

Covet La

Ford

Valley Rd

The Old Rectory

2

Jesse's Hill

Marley

Round Wood

Greenbank

The Shrubbery

Barham

The Street

The Yard

PH

1

Knowle Wood

Green Hills

+

50

111
90

A B C D E F

8 7 53 6 5 52 4 3 51 2 1 50

Twelve Acre Shaw

Adisham CE Prim Sch

Adisham Sta

Bloodden

Ratling Court

Adisham

WOODLANDS RD

DONKEY LA

COOTING LA

THE STREET

Woodlands Manor

Oxenden Wood

Cooting Farm

STATION APP

B2046

Pitt Wood

TENNYSON GDNS
COLERIDGE GDNS
THIRLMERE GDNS
BUTTERMERE GDNS
WORDSWORTH GDNS
GRASMERE
CORNWALLIS AVE
KINGS RD
BURGESS RD
RATLING RD

Woodlands Wood

1 ULLSWATER GDNS
2 ENNERDALE GDNS

DORMAN AVE W

DERWENT WAY

WINDERMERE GDNS

Aylesham Cty Prim Sch

WOODLAND AVE

NEWMAN RD

Aylesham

Liby

Well Wood

VALE VIEW RD

WITLEE AVE

CRIPPS CL

SNOWDOWN CT

MARKET

PO

Queens RD

HYDE PL

Cooting Downs

ASH

HILL CRES

SYCAMORE

BEVAN

OAKSIDE RD

ELM RD

MILNER CRES

BOULEVARD COURRIERES

EASTRY CT

VICTORY

MARKET

CLARENDON RD

SPINNEY LA

Ileden Wood

CCY CL

WK

AVE

COOTING RD

WAY

HAWTHORN CL

Ind Est

Ackholt Wood

COVERT RD

SPINNEY LA

Aylesham Wood

AYLESHAM CNR

Barham Downs

Upper Digges Farm

Willow Wood

POND LA

Chalk Wood

A2

DOVER RD

ADISHAM RD

North Downs Way

Cemy

Well Wood

Nethersole Farm

RECTORY LA

DOVER RD

Aylesham Farm

CHURCH LA

THE STREET

Womenswold

Woodpeckers Country Hotel

Westmore Ho

Snow Down

B2046

OLD DOVER RD

GRAVEL CASTLE RD

A260

A2

PO

NETHERSOLE RD

POSTAL RD

THE PLACE

FIRS RD

Woolage Village

21 A 22 B C 22 D 23 E 23 F

A B C D E F

8

Chillenden

ORCHARD CT

Chillenden Court
Farm

Ratling

Nooketts
Wood

Ratling Farm
House

Old Court
Wood

Gooseberryhall
Wood

7

Goodnestone
Wood

Old Court
Farm

Gooseberryhall
Farm

CHERRYGARDEN LA

Park House
Farm

53

Great
Pinners
Wood

Pinners
Farm

SHELDON CL

LISTWAYS
COTTS

6

Highleas

Old Court
House

RATLING RD

St Alban's
Downs

ylesham
Sta

PINNERS HILL

OLD COURT HILL

SANDWICH RD

Home
Farm

ESS RD

ACKHOLT RD

St Joseph's
RC Prim Sch

PINNERS LA

BEAUCHAMPS LA

5

CHAPMANS HILL

White House
Farm

WHITE HOUSE
FARM CT

Nonington

HAMMOND CL

CHURCH ST

ST MARY'S CL

VICARAGE LA

Nonington
CE Prim Sch

EASOLE ST

BUTCHERS LA

52

PO

MILL LA

1 EASOLE HTS
2 PARK VIEW RISE

Royal
Oak
PH

4

BUTTER ST

Ackholt

HOLT ST

AYLESHAM RD

Fredville
Park

Beech
Plantation

SNOWDOWN
CARAVAN SITE

Summerhouse
Plantation

3

Snowdown

CRESCENT

THE

SOUTH AVE

Box
Wood

51

Snowdown
Sta

2

Spoil Heap

NIGHTINGALE LA

Cony
Wood

Oxney
Wood

Ruberries
Wood

Frogham

Barfrestone

Yew Tree
PH

1

BARFRESTONE RD

THE STREET

Frogham
Farm

Sole's
Farm

Soles Down
Plantation

Church
Farm

Barfrestone
Court

50

A   B   C   D   E   F

8

YEW TREE FARM

SHORT ST

Griffin's Head (PH)

War Meml

Home Wood

Knowlton

Home Farm

Knowlton Court

7

CUCKOLDS CNR

The Warren

Knowlton Park

Black La

THORNTON LA

53

The Grove

Manorial Earthworks

Shingleton Wood

SANDWICH RD

6

Dover Lodge Cottages

Shingleton Farm

Venson Farm

St Alban's Downs

Round Wood

Shingleton Cottages

Thorntonhill Cottages

5

Kelk Hill

Shingleton Cottages

Thornton Farm

Kittington Cottages

52

Garden Wood

Brown Pudding Plantation

The Downs

Thornton Wood

4

Kittington Farm

Dane Court

PIKE RD

SCHOOL RD

3

Beeches Farm

51

Craythorne Firs

2

Spoil Heap

POPLAR DR

CYPRESS GR

ASH GR

ROMAN WAY

SWEETBRIAR LA

BEECH DR

CHERRY GR

Works

BARVILLE RD

CHAUCER RD

ST JOHNS RD

OAK GR

Burgess Hill

PO

FAIRVIEW RD

LARCH RD

MILNER RD

MILNER CL

Elvington

ADELAIDE RD

TERRACE RD

1

BARFRESTONE RD

Sports Gd

ELMTON LA

WIGMORE LA

SANDWICH RD

50

27   A   B   28   C   D   29   E   F

A B C D E F

8
53
7
6
53
5
52
4
3
51
2
1
50

A 31 B C D 32 E F
0

DOVER RD

A256

Sangrado's Wood

Updown Farm

Updown House

Nursery

Lower Venson Farm

Betteshanger

Longlands

Scawsby

Northbourne Park Sch (Annexe)

HOME FARM COTTS

Northbourne Park Sch (Prep)

Home Farm

Northbourne CE Prim Sch

Mill House

New Park

Little Betteshanger

North Court Plantation

NORTH COURT LA

North Court

Lower Longlands

Admiral's Hole

Coldharbour

MILL LA

DOVES CNR

ST MARY'S GR

SCHOOL RD

UPPER ST

Tilmanstone

ST ANDREWS WAY

VICARAGE LA

CHAPEL RD

The Old Vicarage

LOWER ST

PH

WHITES HILL

SANDWICH RD

Telegraph Farm

Nine Acre Wood

Stoneheap Wood

Stoneheap Farm

Fairlight Bungalow

BARVILLE RD

Boys' Firs
Mast

Willow Wood

Pilgrim's Nook

Brighton Bungalow Farm

STONEHEAP RD

NORTHBOURNE RD

Barville Farm

115
94

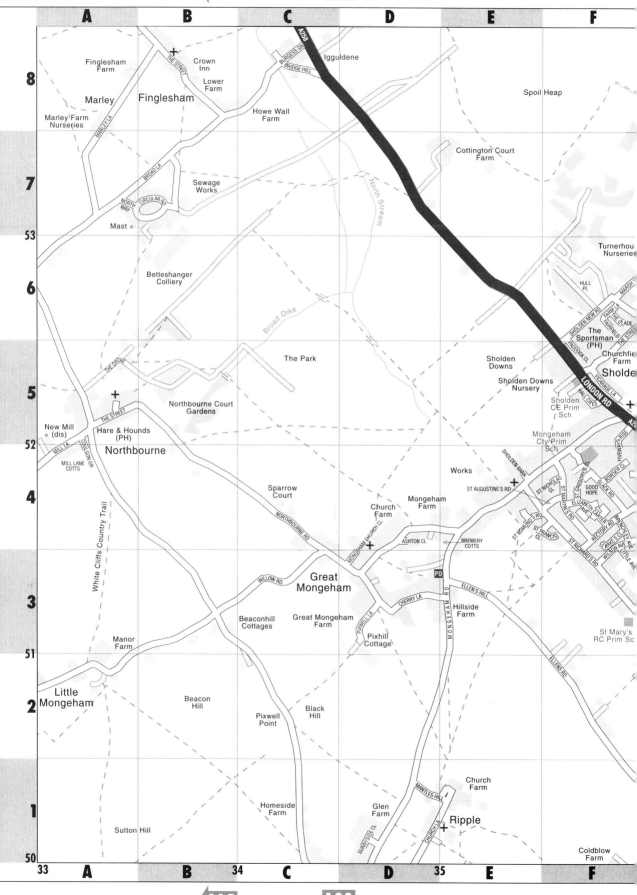

115
133

DEAL

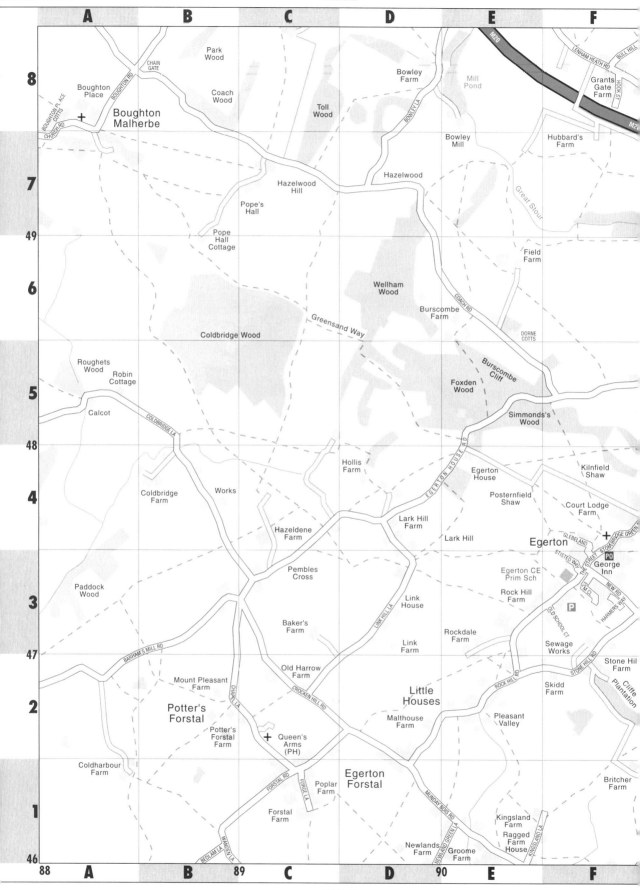

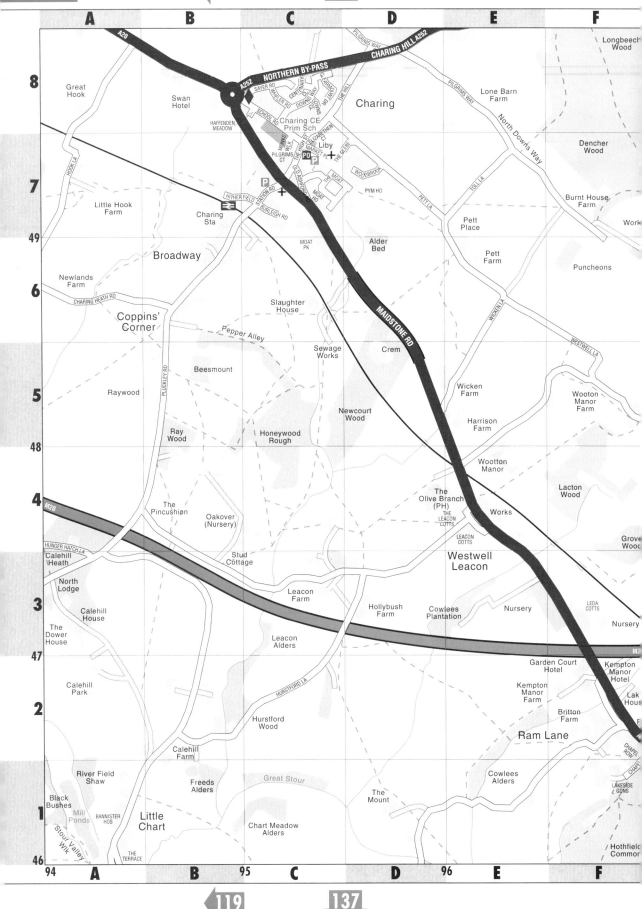

A20

Longbeech Wood

NORTHERN BY-PASS

CHARING HILL A252

PILGRIMS WAY

A252

8

Great Hook

Swan Hotel

SAYER RD

CENTNARY

DOWNS WAY

PEARMAN DR

THE HILL

Charing

Lone Barn Farm

Dencher Wood

HAFFENDEN MEADOW

Charing CE Prim Sch

MOONS WLK

ELIZABETHEN

MARKET PL

THE HIGH ST

Liby

THE GLEBE

WOODBROOK

North Downs Way

SCHOOL RD

WELER RD

PILGRIMS CT

OLD ASHFORD RD

P

PO

THE MOAT

Pilgrims Way

Burnt House Farm

7

Little Hook Farm

Charing Sta

STATION RD

BURLEIGH RD

HITHER FIELD

P

MOAT HO

PYM HO

PETT LA

TOLL LA

Pett Place

Work

49

Broadway

MOAT PK

Alder Bed

Pett Farm

Puncheons

Newlands Farm

CHARING HEATH RD

6

Coppins' Corner

Pepper Alley

Slaughter House

Sewage Works

Crem

MAIDSTONE RD

Wicken Farm

WICKEN LA

Wooton Manor Farm

WESTWELL LA

Beesmount

PLUCKLEY RD

5

Raywood

Ray Wood

Honeywood Rough

Newcourt Wood

Harrison Farm

Lacton Wood

48

Wootton Manor

4

M20

The Pincushion

Oakover (Nursery)

The Olive Branch (PH)

THE LEACON COTTS

Works

LEACON COTTS

Grove Wood

HUNGER HATCH LA

Calehill Heath

Stud Cottage

Westwell Leacon

North Lodge

3

Calehill House

Leacon Farm

Hollybush Farm

Cowlees Plantation

Nursery

LEDA COTTS

Nursery

The Dower House

Leacon Alders

Garden Court Hotel

Kempton Manor Hotel

47

Calehill Park

HURSTFORD LA

Kempton Manor Farm

Britton Farm

Lak Hous

2

Hurstford Wood

Ram Lane

CHAPEL ROW

Calehill Farm

River Field Shaw

Freeds Alders

Great Stour

The Mount

Cowlees Alders

LAKESIDE GDNS

CHAP

1

Black Bushes

Mill Ponds

BANNISTER HOS

Little Chart

Chart Meadow Alders

Hothfield Common

Stour Valley Wlk

THE TERRACE

46

A   B   C   D   E   F

8

Squids Gate

Squids Gate Farm

Catsdane Wood

Sunny Banks

7

Wrotham Wood

Foxbury Wood

The Willows

49

Stubyer's Wood

Camping Site

Carter's Firs

Giddyhorn Toll

6

Bourne Wood

Dean Court

Eastwell Park

Stubyer's Wood

Hanger Wood

5

Westwell Downs

North Downs Way

Dunn Street Farm

Dunn Street

Lacton Manor

PILGRIMS WAY

48

Digges Court

Squintels

4

WESTWELL LA

GOULD HILL

The Wheel Inn (PH)

Westwell

Skeats Wood

+

Westwell

Westwell Court

Parkhouse Farm

Cemy

3

Witchling Wood

The Downings

47

Roughets

DIGNASH

2

Sewage Works

Shottenden Manor

Tutt Hill Farm

GOTHIC COTTS

Tutt Hill

Parsonage Wood

Nash Court

Nash Court Cottages

Water Works

MAIDSTONE RD

Works

Grove Wood Farm

1

A20

Ripple Wood

Sunnybridge Farm

M20

46

A   **B**   **C**   **D**   **E**   **F**

A251

WHITE HILL

Ashes Wood

Well Wood

8

Brabourne Hill
Plantation

CHURCH LA

Brabourne Hill
Wood

Church Wood

Prickle
Down
Wood

Crow Down

7

Challock Manor

Round
Wood

Young's Plantation

49

Mount Ephraim

Coronation
Toll

6

Hayward's
Garden

Pear Tree
Toll

Yewtree
Toll

Jack's Hut Wood

Old Rook
Toll

Jackdaw Toll

FAVERSHAM RD

5

Round
Wood

Browns

48

Eastwell Park

Brewhouse

Home Farm

4

The
Beeches

Eastwell Park
(Hotel)

MALTHOUSE LA

The
Flying Horses
Inn

St Mary's Church
(rems of)

North Downs Way

SEATON COTTS

Boughton
Lees

3

MIDDLETON COTTS

EASTWELL TERR

ELM COTTS

PROSPECT COTTS

WYE RD

Aviary
Wood

Dogkennel
Plantation

47

Eastwell
Lake

Rook Toll

Tower Farm

THE OLD RECTORY

2

LENACRE ST

Rectory
Wood

Rectory
Plantation

Eastwell Court

Lake
Wood

1

Brookies
Lodge

Park Barn
Farm

Podberry
Wood

46

A251

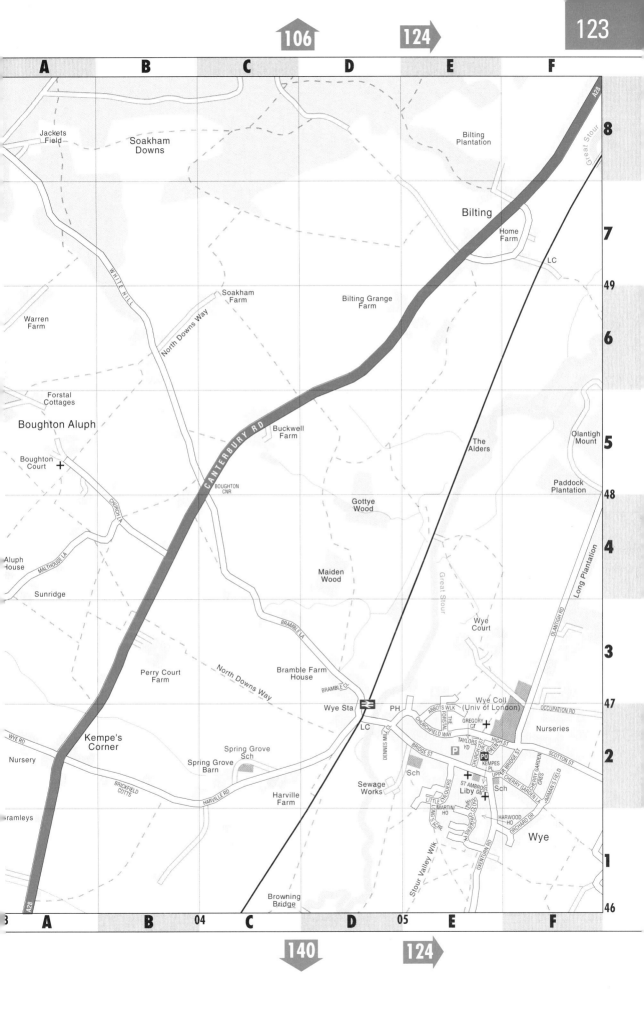

A B C D E F

8
7
49
6
5
48
4
3
47
2
1
46

Jackets Field

Soakham Downs

Bilting Plantation

Bilting

Home Farm

LC

A28

Great Stour

WHITE HILL

North Downs Way

Soakham Farm

Bilting Grange Farm

Warren Farm

Forstal Cottages

Boughton Aluph

Boughton Court

CANTERBURY RD

Buckwell Farm

Boughton CNR

The Alders

Olantigh Mount

Paddock Plantation

CHURCH LA

Gottye Wood

Long Plantation

OLANTIGH RD

Aluph House

MALTHOUSE LA

Sunridge

Maiden Wood

Great Stour

Wye Court

BRAMBLE LA

North Downs Way

Perry Court Farm

Bramble Farm House

BRAMBLE CL

Wye Sta

Wye Coll (Univ of London)

OCCUPATION RD

Nurseries

PH

LC

DENNES MILL CL

ABBOTS WLK

THE FORSTAL

CHURCHFIELD WAY

GREGORY CT

TAYLORS YD

HIGH ST

THE GREEN

SCOTTON ST

WYE RD

Kempe's Corner

Nursery

Spring Grove Sch

Spring Grove Barn

BRIDGE ST

P

PO

KEMPES PL

UPPER BRIDGE ST

CHURCH ST

CHERRY GARDEN LA

CHERRY GARDEN CRES

JARMAN'S FIELD

Sch

Sch

St Ambrose Liby Grn

BRICKFIELD COTTS

HARVILLE RD

Harville Farm

Sewage Works

LITTLE CHEQUERS

LONG'S ACRE

MARTIN HO

THE

MASERS CLOSE

ST AMBROSE CLOSE

HARWOOD HO

ORCHARD DR

Wye

Bramleys

A28

Stour Valley Wlk

OXENTURN RD

Browning Bridge

A B C D E F

04 05

A **B** **C** **D** **E** **F**

A28

Great Stour

8

Ripple
Farm

Trimworth
Manor

Little
Winchcombe

Works

Thornham
Lodge

Winchcombe
Farm

7

Tye
Wood

Crundale

Viney's
Wood

Great Stour

Glenwood
Farm

Oxen Lees
Wood

Fairisle
Farm

Church
Wood

49

Black Edge
Wood

Crundale
House

6

Little Olantigh
Farm

Crundale
Downs

Warren
Wood

OLANTIGH RD

Nursery

Marriage
Wood

5

Roughets

Round
Wood

48

Kidney
Clump

Marriage
Hill

4

Stour Valley Wlk

Marriage
Farm

Beech
Wood

Sheepfold

Pett Street
Farm

3

● Mast

HASSELL ST

47

North Downs Way

Down
Farm

Prout's
Spinney

2

Hurst
Wood

Scotton St

Meml
(Crown)

Woodmans
Arms
(PH)

COLDHARBOUR LA

Collyerhill
Wood

1
2
3

1 WITHERSDANE COTTS
2 BERNARD SUNLEY HALL
3 THE GARDEN HALL

Withersdane
Hall

Coldharbour
Farm

Coombe
Manor

Centre for
European
Agricultural
Studies

AMAGE ROAD
COTTS

AMAGE RD

1

Wye
Downs

Little
Combe

46

06 **A** **B** **07** **C** **D** **08** **E** **F**

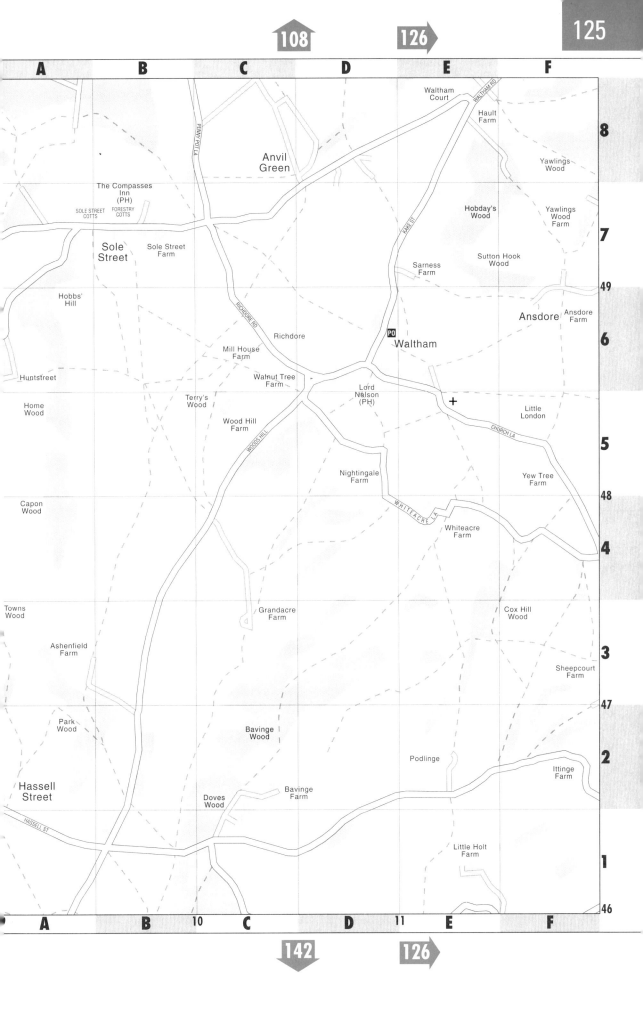

A   B   C   D   E   F

Waltham
Court

Hault
Farm

Anvil
Green

8

Yawlings
Wood

The Compasses
Inn
(PH)

SOLE STREET
COTTS   FORESTRY
COTTS

Hobday's
Wood

Yawlings
Wood
Farm

7

Sole
Street

Sole Street
Farm

KAKE ST

Sutton Hook
Wood

Sarness
Farm

49

Hobbs'
Hill

Ansdore

Ansdore
Farm

RICHDORE RD

Richdore

PO

Waltham

6

Mill House
Farm

Huntstreet

Walnut Tree
Farm

Lord
Nelson
(PH)

+

Little
London

CHURCH LA

Terry's
Wood

Home
Wood

WOODS HILL

Wood Hill
Farm

5

Nightingale
Farm

Yew Tree
Farm

48

Capon
Wood

WHITEACRE LA

Whiteacre
Farm

4

Towns
Wood

Grandacre
Farm

Cox Hill
Wood

Ashenfield
Farm

3

Sheepcourt
Farm

Park
Wood

47

Bavinge
Wood

Podlinge

2

Ittinge
Farm

Hassell
Street

Bavinge
Farm

Doves
Wood

HASSELL ST

Little Holt
Farm

1

46

A   B   10   C   D   11   E   F

A B C D E F

8

7

49

6

49

5

48

4

3

47

2

1

46

12 A B 13 C D 14 E F

New Barn Farm

Dane Chantry

Homestead Farm

B2068

Upper Hardres Wood

Rou Woo

Waddenhall Wood

Nursery

Stubb's Wood

Little Bossingham Farm

Dunlies Wood

The Hollies

DUCKPIT RD

Stelling Lodge Farm

Little Wadden Hall

Parkmead

HOMESIDE FAR

Yockletts Banks

HARDRES COURT R

WADDENHALL FARM

Stelling Minnis CE Prim Sch

Doghouse Farm

Wadden Hall Cottages

SPLIT LA

Syngate Wood

Syngate House

Church Wood

STONE ST

GOGWAY

48

Yockletts Farm

Cherry Garde Farm

WHITEACRE LA

Nature Reserve

Common

Holly Tree Farm

Butts Farm

Yewtree Farmhouse

Mead Farm

BOSSINGHAM RD

Westcroft Farm

North Leigh

Gaylees Farmhouse

Prim Farm

The Laurels

Malt Farm

Little Buckett Farm

CROWN LA

Rose & Crown (PH)

Stelling Minnis

DEAN HILL

PO

Chapel Farm

THORN LA

CURTIS LA

Thorn Farm

Knowler Farm

1 MINNIS GN
2 MINNIS FIELD

Little North Leigh Farm

MILL LA

Windmill (dis)

Dean Farm

Scarp's Farm

Great Dowles Farm

Courthope Farm

B2068

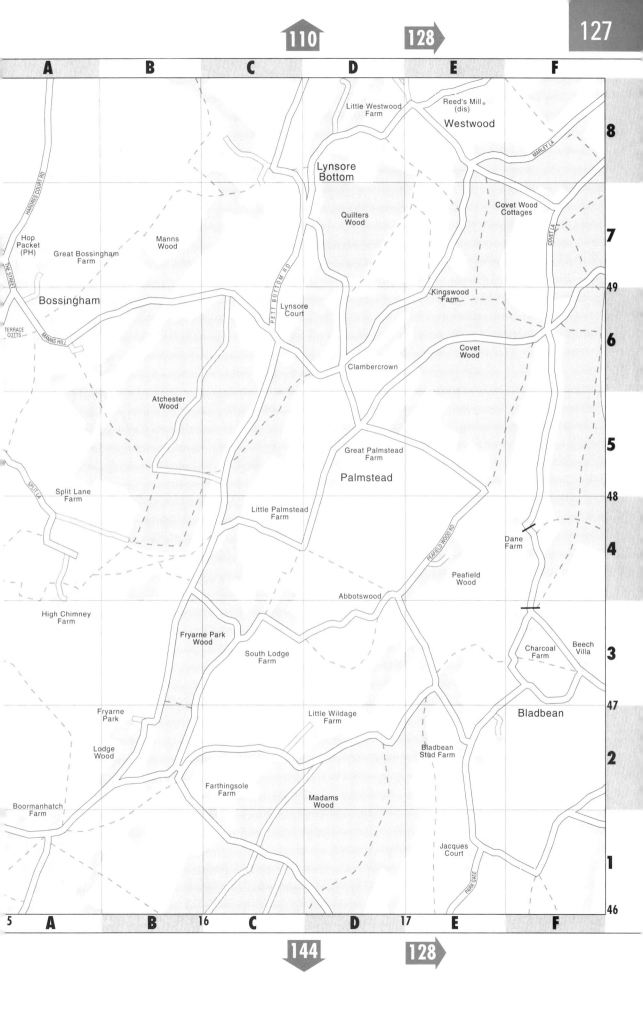

A B C D E F

8

Reed's Mill (dis)

Little Westwood Farm

Westwood

MARLEY LA

Covet Wood Cottages

7

Lynsore Bottom

Quilters Wood

COVET LA

Hop Packet (PH)

Great Bossingham Farm

Manns Wood

49

Kingswood Farm

THE STREET

Bossingham

Lynsore Court

PETT BOTTOM RD

6

Covet Wood

TERRACE COTTS

MANNS HILL

Clambercrown

Atchester Wood

SPLIT LA

Split Lane Farm

Great Palmstead Farm

5

Palmstead

48

Little Palmstead Farm

Dane Farm

4

PEAFIELD WOOD RD

Peafield Wood

High Chimney Farm

Abbotswood

Fryarne Park Wood

South Lodge Farm

Charcoal Farm

Beech Villa

3

47

Fryarne Park

Little Wildage Farm

Bladbean

Lodge Wood

Bladbean Stud Farm

2

Boormanhatch Farm

Farthingsole Farm

Madams Wood

Jacques Court

1

PARK GATE

46

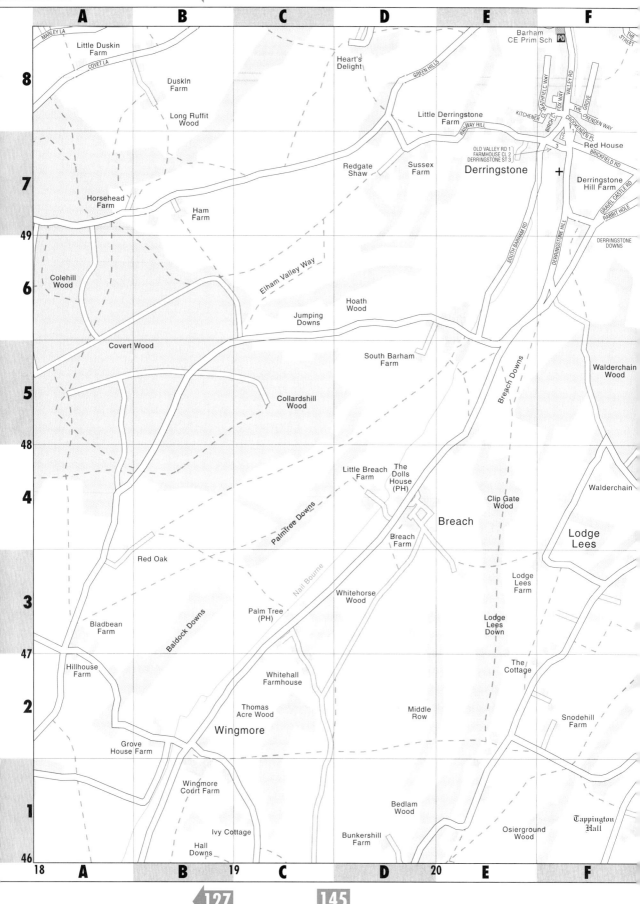

A   B   C   D   E   F

8

Little Duskin
Farm

MARLEY LA
COVET LA

Duskin
Farm

Long Ruffit
Wood

Heart's
Delight

GREEN HILLS

Barham
CE Prim Sch   PO

THE STREET

SPATHHILL WAY
KITCHENER
BIRCH CL
FOX WAY
VALLEY RD
CROOKENDEN PL
THE GROVE
OXENDEN WAY

Little Derringstone
Farm

RAILWAY HILL

Red House

7

Horsehead
Farm

Ham
Farm

Redgate
Shaw

Sussex
Farm

OLD VALLEY RD 1
FARMHOUSE CL 2
DERRINGSTONE ST 3

Derringstone

+

BRICKFIELD RD

Derringstone
Hill Farm

GRAVEL CASTLE RD
RABBIT HOLE

49

DERRINGSTONE
DOWNS

Colehill
Wood

SOUTH BARHAM RD
DERRINGSTONE HILL

6

Elham Valley Way

Hoath
Wood

Jumping
Downs

Covert Wood

South Barham
Farm

Breach Downs

Walderchain
Wood

5

Collardshill
Wood

48

Palmtree Downs

Little Breach
Farm

The
Dolls
House
(PH)

Clip Gate
Wood

Walderchain

4

Breach

Lodge
Lees

Red Oak

Breach
Farm

Nail Bourne

Whitehorse
Wood

Lodge
Lees Farm

3

Bladbean
Farm

Baldock Downs

Palm Tree
(PH)

Lodge
Lees
Down

47

Hillhouse
Farm

Whitehall
Farmhouse

The
Cottage

2

Thomas
Acre Wood

Middle
Row

Snodehill
Farm

Grove
House Farm

Wingmore

Wingmore
Court Farm

1

Ivy Cottage

Bedlam
Wood

Osierground
Wood

Tappington
Hall

Hall
Downs

Bunkershill
Farm

46

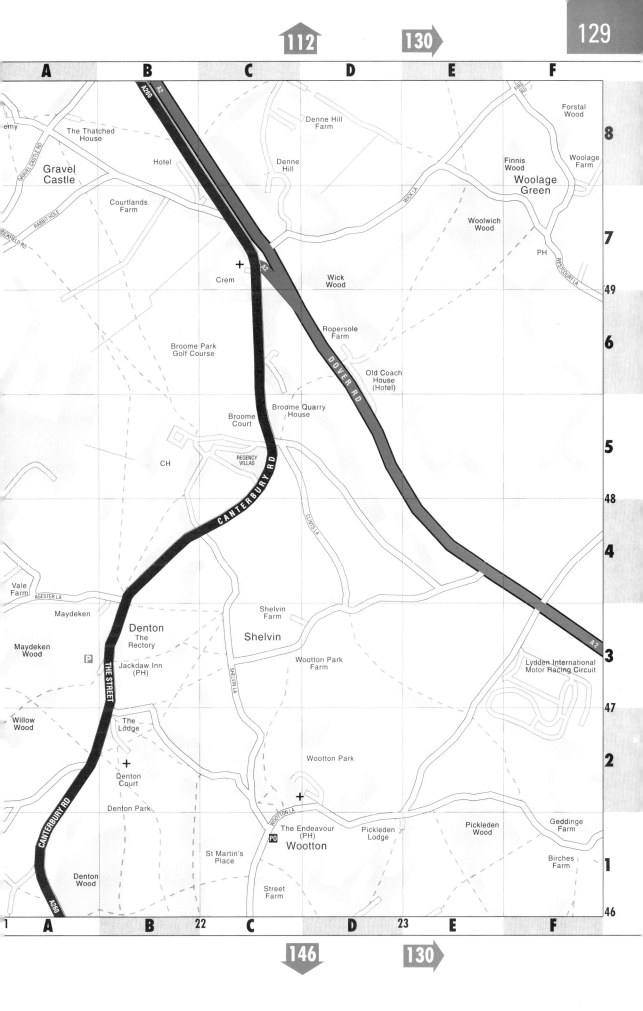

112
130

A　B　C　D　E　F

8

The Thatched
House

Gravel
Castle

Hotel

Denne Hill
Farm

Denne
Hill

Forstal
Wood

Finnis
Wood

Woolage
Farm

Woolage
Green

GRAVEL CASTLE RD

RABBIT HOLE

TICKFIELD RD

Courtlands
Farm

A260

A2

Wick LA

Woolwich
Wood

PH

WESTCOURT LA

FIRS RD

7

49

Crem

A2

Wick
Wood

Ropersole
Farm

Broome Park
Golf Course

DOVER RD

6

Old Coach
House
(Hotel)

Broome Quarry
House

Broome
Court

CH

REGENCY
VILLAS

CANTERBURY RD

5

CLINTS LA

48

4

Vale
Farm

AGESTER LA

Maydeken

Maydeken
Wood

Denton
The
Rectory

P

THE STREET

Jackdaw Inn
(PH)

Shelvin
Farm

Shelvin

SHELVIN LA

Wootton Park
Farm

Lydden International
Motor Racing Circuit

3

47

Willow
Wood

The
Lodge

Wootton Park

2

Denton
Court

Denton Park

WOOTTON LA

The Endeavour
(PH)

PO

Wootton

Pickleden
Lodge

Pickleden
Wood

Pickleden
Wood

Geddinge
Farm

A2

CANTERBURY RD

A260

Denton
Wood

St Martin's
Place

Street
Farm

Birches
Farm

1

46

1　A　B　22　C　D　23　E　F

146
130

← 129

↑ 113

A   **B**   **C**   **D**   **E**   **F**

8

Leighgate Bottom

Three Barrows Down

Lower Soles Wood

Stafflands Wood

LONG LA

7

North Downs Way

LONG LA

Golgotha

49

Long Lane Farm

West Court Downs

6

LC

Crossways

Shepherdswell or Sibertswold

THE GLEN

PENFOLD

GON LOOP

CYTHORNE RD

BETHNAL GDNS

MEADOW VIEW RD

SHEPHERDSWELL RD

WESTCOURT LA

Shepherds Well Sta

MOORSWELL DR

STATION RD

HILL AVE

MILL LA

HACKLING DANE

ST ANDREW'S GDNS

SIBERT S CL

5

THE GRANGE

THE TERRACE

APPROACH RD

Puckland Wood

West Court Farm

Bricklayers Arms (PH)

THE OAKLEYS

PO

MILL FIELDS

48

Botolph Street Farm

WHITTINGTON TERR

CHURCH HILL

4

MOORLAND RD

Sibertswold CE Prim Sch

MOON HILL

Upton Court Farm

Halfway Street

COLDRED RD

Coxhill Farm

Diamond Farm

CHURCH RD

3

A2

Hope Wood

COXHILL

Claysole Wood

Upton Wood

DOVER RD

47

2

Five Oaks

Lyddenhill Wood

LYDDEN HILL

A2

1

COLDRED HILL

CHURCH RD

46

A   **B**   **C**   **D**   **E**   **F**

24   25   26

← 129

↓ 147

A B C D E F

BARHESTONE RD
ADELAIDE RD
THANET VIEW
CHURCH HILL

The Rectory

Eythorne
Elvington Cty
Prim Sch

WIGMORE LA

East Kent Light Railway

Lower
Eythorne

VALLEY VIEW
LC

Eythorne

LC

SHOOTERS HILL

SANDWICH RD

NEW RD

EYTHORN
COURT
BARN

Eythorne
Sta

Eythorne
Court

SHEPHERDSWELL RD

LC

Upper
Eythorne

GREEN LA

GREEN ACRES

Eythorne
Green

PO

FLAX COURT LA

CHAPEL HILL

BEECH
GREEN CL

HAZEL CL

CHERRY
CL

PALM TREE
CL

WILLOW WAY
ROSE GDNS

MONKTON COURT LA

HAWTHORNE
CL

FORGE
CL

THE STREET

Malmains
Farm

The
Kennels

KENNEL HILL

A256

High and
Dry
(PH)

Haynes
Farm

COLDRED RD

OAK AVE

Malmains
Wood

Home
Farm

+

Little
Haynes

Waldershare
House

Poutty
Wood

SANDWICH RD

North Downs Way

Waldershare
Park

+
Coldred Court
Farm

The
Wilderness

Coldred

CHURCH RD

SINGLEDGE LA

Eastling Down
Farm

Carpenters' Arms
(PH)

Coldred
Street

Waddling
Wood

Parsonage
Farm

Chilli
Farm

Newsole
Farm

Caens
Wood

Captain's
Wood

Singledge
Wood

Wr
Twr

A2

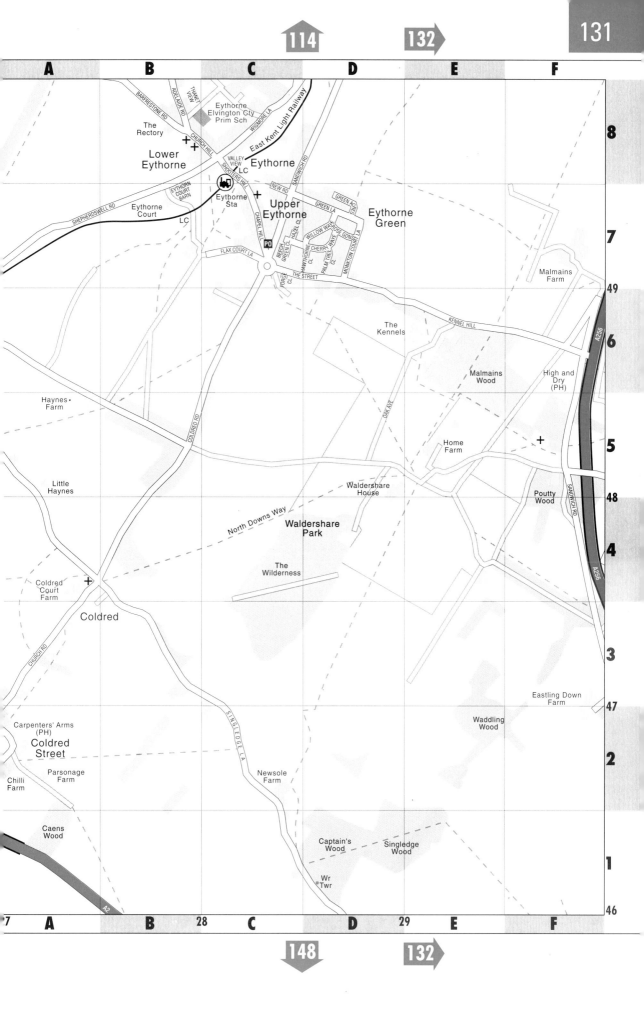

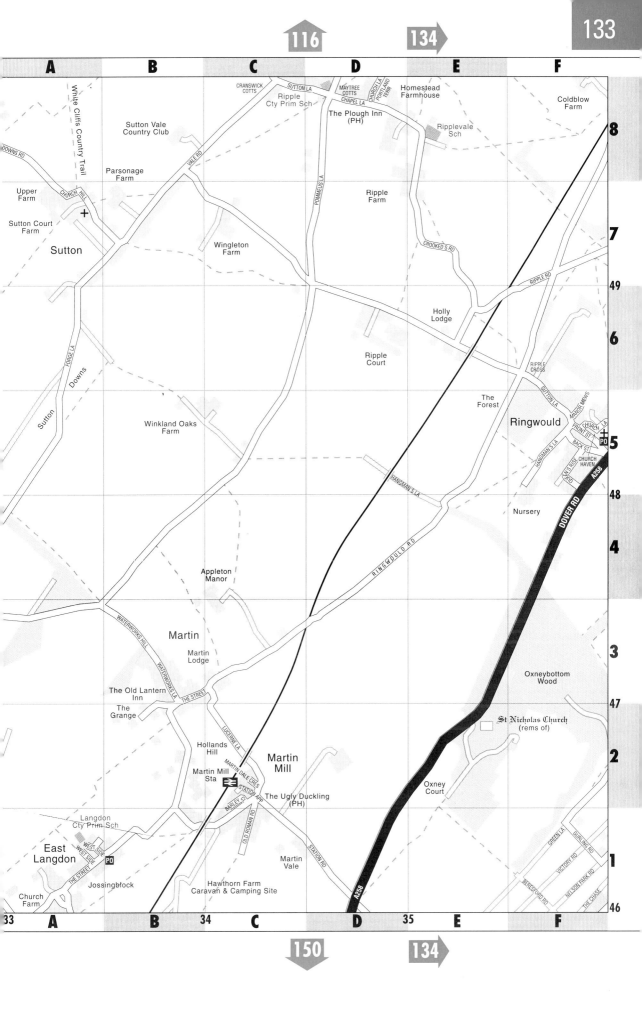

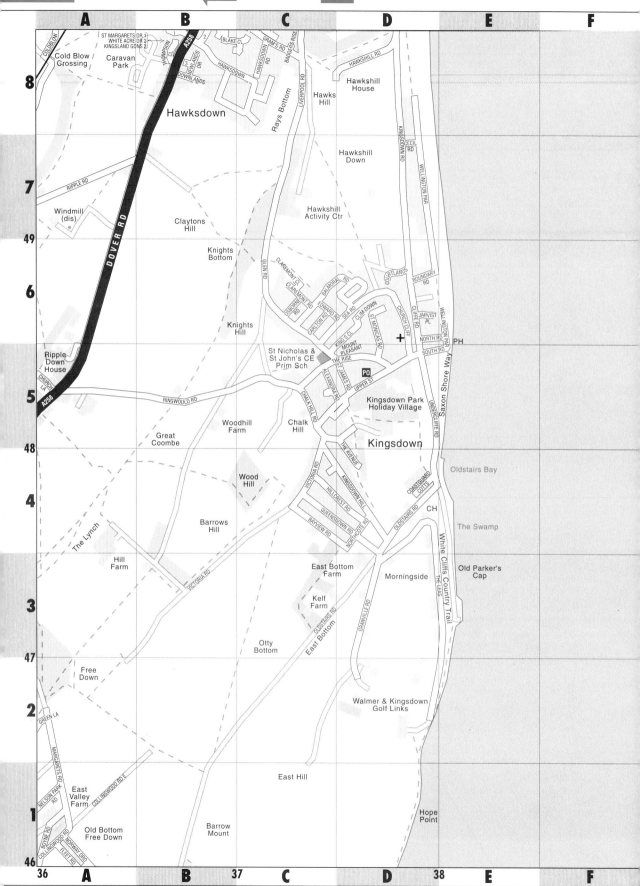

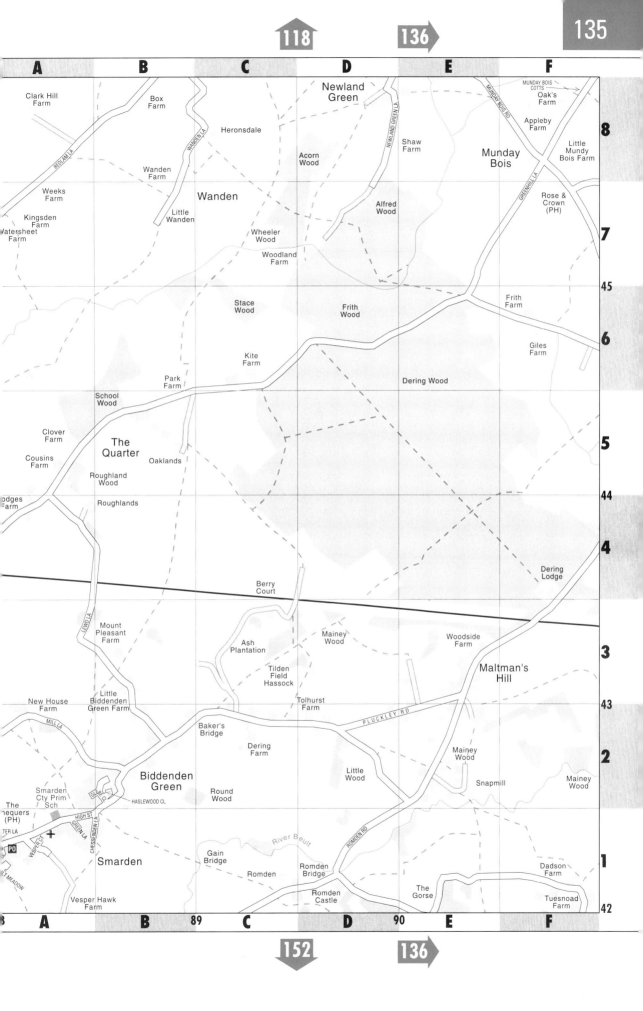

A   B   C   D   E   F

Clark Hill
Farm

Box
Farm

Heronsdale

Newland
Green

NEWLAND GREEN LA

MUNDAY BOIS RD

MUNDAY BOIS
COTTS

Oak's
Farm

8

BEDLAM LA

WANDEN LA

Wanden
Farm

Acorn
Wood

Shaw
Farm

Munday
Bois

Appleby
Farm

Little
Mundy
Bois Farm

Weeks
Farm

Wanden

Little
Wanden

Alfred
Wood

GREENHILL LA

Rose &
Crown
(PH)

7

Kingsden
Farm
Watersheet
Farm

Wheeler
Wood

Woodland
Farm

45

Stace
Wood

Frith
Wood

Frith
Farm

School
Wood

Kite
Farm

Dering Wood

Giles
Farm

6

Park
Farm

Clover
Farm

The
Quarter

Oaklands

5

Cousins
Farm

Roughland
Wood

44

odges
arm

Roughlands

4

LEWD LA

Berry
Court

Dering
Lodge

Mount
Pleasant
Farm

Ash
Plantation

Mainey
Wood

Woodside
Farm

3

New House
Farm

Little
Biddenden
Green Farm

Tilden
Field
Hassock

Maltman's
Hill

MILL LA

Tolhurst
Farm

PLUCKLEY RD

43

Baker's
Bridge

Mainey
Wood

2

Biddenden
Green

Dering
Farm

Little
Wood

Snapmill

Mainey
Wood

Smarden
Cty Prim
Sch

HASLEWOOD CL

Round
Wood

GLEB...

The
hequers
(PH)

HIGH ST

GREEN LA

CHESSENDEN LA

River Beult

ROMDEN RD

TER LA

PO

Smarden

Gain
Bridge

Romden

Romden
Bridge

The
Gorse

Dadson
Farm

1

LT MEADOW

Vesper Hawk
Farm

VESPER CT

Romden
Castle

Tuesnoad
Farm

42

B   A   B   89   C   D   90   E   F

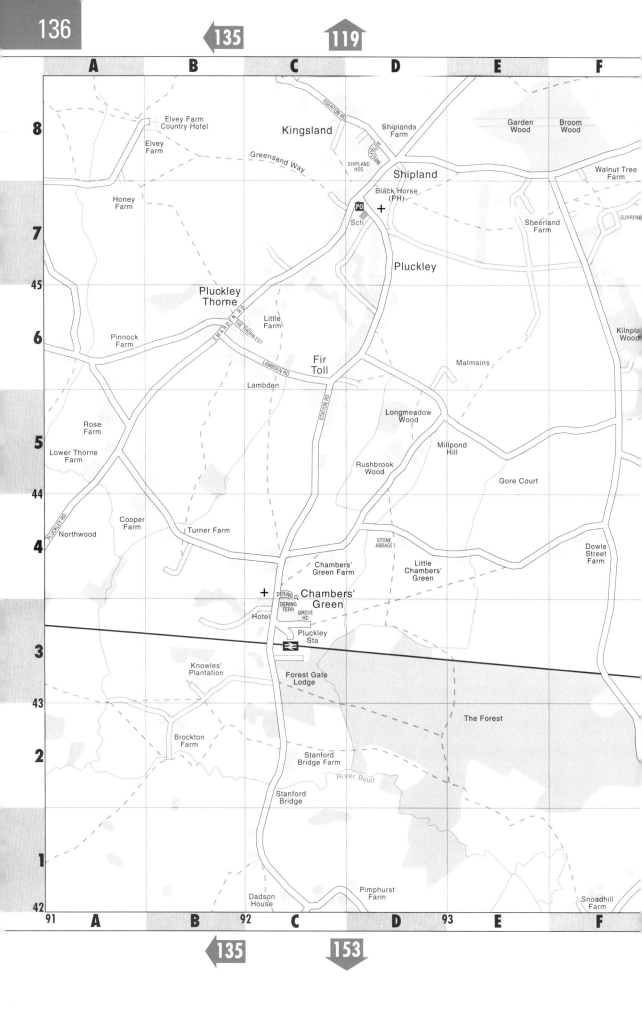

120
138

A **B** **C** **D** **E** **F**

Ford Mill

Swan Inn (PH)

Little Chart
Forstal

Greensand Way

RAM LA

Coldham
Wood

Hothfield Common
Nature Reserve

8

Oaks
Wood

Coldham
Acres

Hothfield
Bogs

Rooting Street
Farm

Brown
Mill

Sch

7

Brownmill
Bridge

Conyer
Wood

Turners

WEST ST

Rooting
Manor

Rooting
Alders

Brownmill
Spinney

45

Hall
Farm

Mitchell
Plantation

Thanet
Copse

THE STREET

6

Egg Hole

Knight's
Wood

Glebe
Shaw

Fred's
Spinney

THE
BUNGALOW

Stour Valley Wlk

Great Stour

Ash
Plantation

Bert's
Walk

5

Saracen's
Dairy

Benacre
Wood

Paddocks
Farm

Park
Spinney

44

PLUCKLEY RD

Benacre
Lodge

4

High
Ridge

Burntoak
Wood

Ripper's Cross
Farm

Hurst
Hill

Hurst Hill
Farm

BETHERSDEN RD

RIPPER'S CROSS

Worten
Wood

Worten House

March
Wood

Worten

BEAR'S LA

3

Newlands
Wood

Bear's Lane
Wood

43

Golf Driving
Range

Pumpfields

NINN LA

2

Dynes Farm

Bridge
Farm

Hoad's Wood

Brickhurst
Wood

GOLDWELL LA

South
Landing

Goldwell

Belmont Farm

BELMONT FARM
BSNS CTR

ETCHDEN RD

Etchden
Wood

Etchden

1

River Beult

Mill Land
Wood

42

A **B** **C** **D** **E** **F**

A B C D E F

97 A B 98 C D 99 E F

8
7
45
6
5
44
4
3
43
2
1
42

P

A20

Ripple
Court

Beechbrook
Farm

Beechbrook

Beechbrook
Wood

Foxenhill
Toll

Tollhill
Wood

Sch

COMMON
WAY

SCHOOL RD

PLANTATION CL

COACH DR

TUFTON
RD

SACKVILLE
CL

BEECH DR

PO

Hothfield

THANET
TERR

MEADOW VIEW

THE STREET

PARK DR

Home
Farm

Yonsea
Farm

Depot

MAIDSTONE RD

M20

Castle
Farm

Crouchers
Manor

Kingsland

SANDHURST LA

CH

WESTWELL LA

Mill
House

Woodside

PH

Potters
CNR

POTTERS

Potters
Corner

The
Larches

WATERALL RD

Mansion
Copse

Pigsbrook
Wood

Godinton
Plantation

GODINTON LA

Marble
Wood

Broomfield
Wood

Potters Corner
Wood

Eyesend
Plantation

Hoad's Wood

Nursery

The
Warre

ASHGROVE

ORCHARD HTS

FARRER RD

WARREN VIEW

M

Balls
Wood

Eyesend

Balls
Wood

West
Lodge

Petts
Hole

Godinton

Godinton
Park

Chestnut Tell
Plantation

Lodge
Wood

ORIEL
RD

ORCHARD DR

Worten
Mill

Swinford
Manor
Sch

Jubilee
Plantation

Greensand Way

LONG WLK

MANOR WAY

Worten Home
Farm

River
Spinney

Great Stour

Stour Valley Wlk

Loudon
Wood

Chimneys
(PH)

Godinton
Cty Prim
Sch

LOUDON PATH

LOUDON WAY

CEDAR CL

EAST LODGE RD

LIME CL

POPLAR CL

HORNBEAM

CHART RD

A20

Willow
Bed

Chart Ave

THE COPSE

SPRINGWOOD DR

MAPLE CL

ROWAN CL

LOCKHOLT CL

THE SPINNEY

YEW

THORNLEA

CYPRESS AVE

LABURNUM CL

JUNIPER CL

CHESTNUT CT

St GEORGE'S
BSNS CTR

HILTON RD

BRIDGE

BRUNSWICK RD

COBBS WOOD
IND EST

HANOVER CL

BRUNSWICK CL

Godinton
Park

NINN LA

Depot

Ninn Lodge
Farm

Bucksford
Manor

STAFFORD RD

Bucksford
Bridge

CHART RD

B2229

Buxford
Mill

BEAVER LA

POSTLING CL

MILLBROOK MEADOW

RIVERVIEW

LENCON CL

BROOKFIELD
IND PK

BROOKFIELD RD

B2229

Riverside
Sch

Montpelier
BSNS PK

FORD WAY

DENCORA

Great
Chart

PH

THE STREET

SINGLETON RD

CORONATION DR

THE PADDOCKS

DUKE CL

MIDDLE CL

Playing
Field

CHART RD

HOPPERS WAY

A28

Buxford
Lake

Singleton
Lake

COVERT 1
EGGRINGE 2
HONEYFIELD 3
SILECROFT CT 4
BROUGHTON CT 5
OAKENPOLE 6
HUNTSWOOD 7

BUCKSFORD LA

LONG BECH

STOUR CL

CYGNET WAY

COCKHOUSE LA

OAKLANDS

MILLBROOK LA

HILLBROW LA

BAILEYS FIELD

KNOLL

ARLINGTON

HAYMAKERS

CHESFIELD

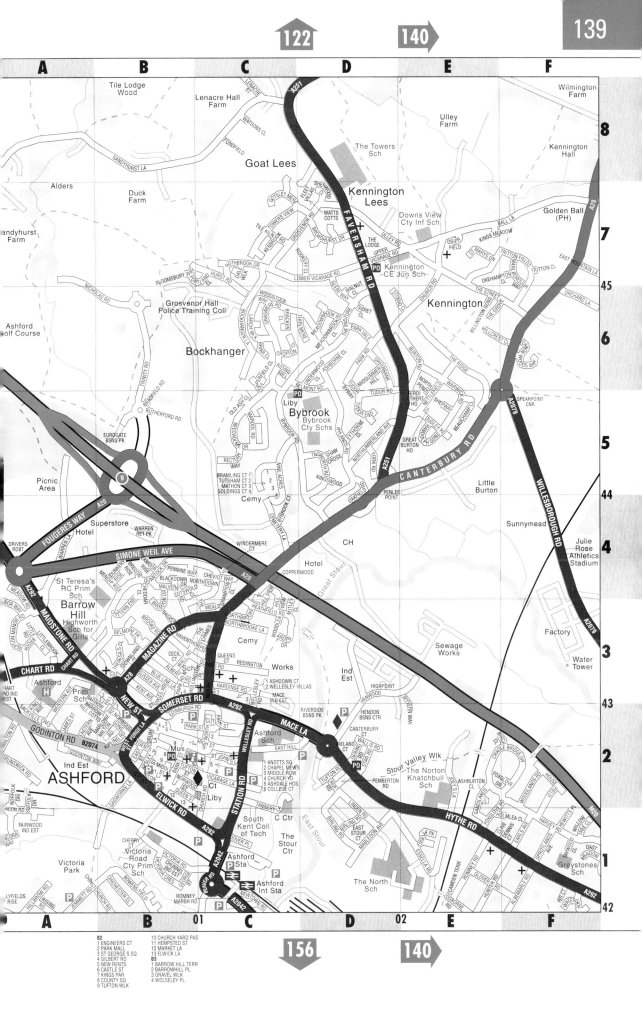

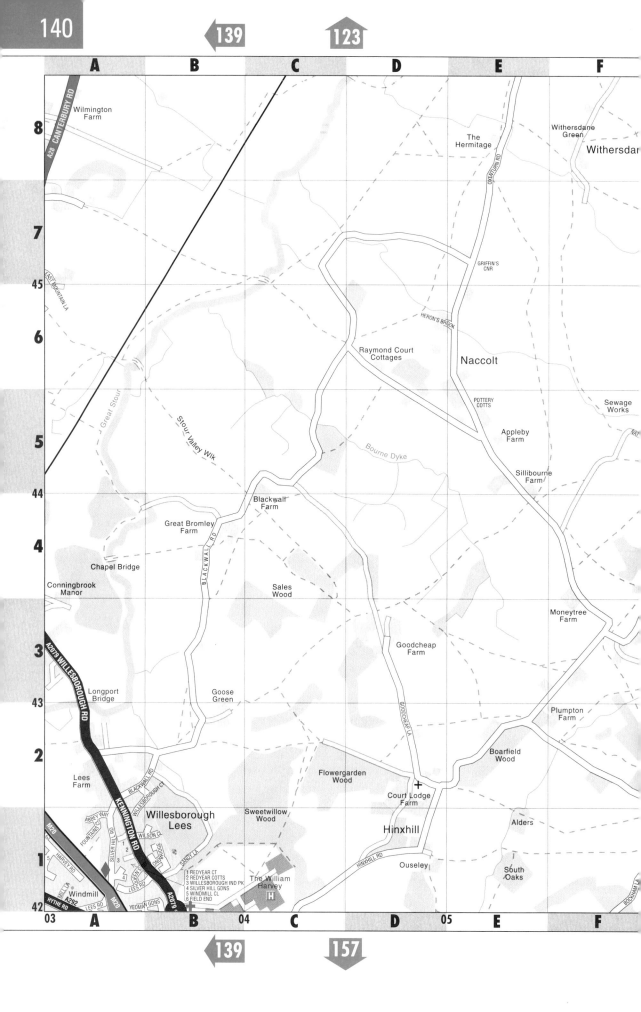

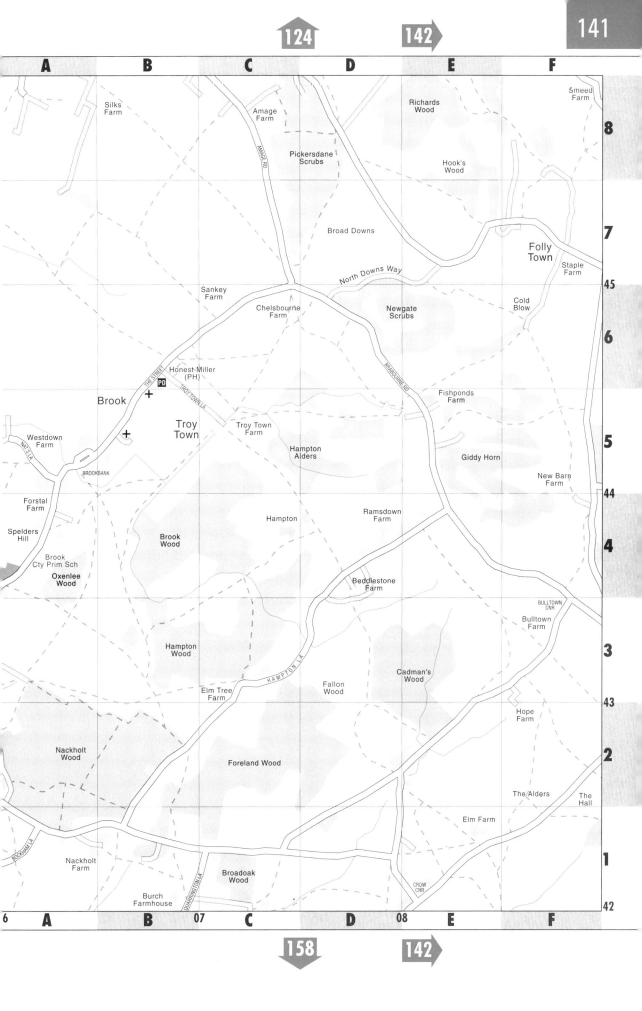

8

Lyddendane Farm

Shrub's Wood

Bodsham

COLLETT CL

Great Holt Farm

The Timber Batts Inn (PH)

Bodsham CE Prim Sch

West Down

Newlands Wood

Hill Street

Mast

Bow Lease

Mill Farm

Evington Park Farm

7

Malt House

Evington Pottery

45

BECKET'S CL

PO

THE STREET

Parsonage Farm

Bowl Inn (PH)

BOWL FIELD

Elmsted Court

6

Hastingleigh

Trinity Farm

Whatsole Street

Crabtree Farm

TAMLEY LA

Court Lodge

Dawlton Farm

5

Becks Wood

Whatsole Street Farm

44

South Hill Farm

Kingsmill Down

4

Dundas Park Farm

Pett Bottom

Dundas Farm

3

North Downs Way

Partridge Wood

43

Ten Acres

Brabourne Downs

2

Long Wood

BRABOURNE LA

Coomb Farm

Missingham Farm

North Downs Way

Combe Wood

1

CANTERBURY RD

42

143
127

A **B** **C** **D** **E** **F**

8

Elhampark Wood

Grimsacre

7

Clavertye Wood

Upper Park Gate Farm

Little Gate Farm

Maycroft

Park Gate

45

Hawes Farm

6

Clavertye Wood

Ash Ridge House

Beveridge Bottom Wood

Exted Farm

Works

5

Exted

Elham

HIGH ST

CHERRY

LIME VILLAS

44

Mountbottom

THE ROW

PO

PARK LA

FAIRFIELD

PH

COCK LA

CULLING'S HILL

East Kent Hunt Kennels

PROSPECT TERR 1
MANORFIELD 2
CHURCH WLK 3
ST MARY'S RD 4
THE SQUARE 5

OLD RD

NEW RD

VICARAGE LA

DUCK ST

WATER FARM

THE HALT

4

CHAPEL LA

Lower Mount Farm

Elham CE Prim Sch.

THE ORCHARDS

HOG GN

Collards Wood

COLLARDS LA

Cemy

Fir Tree Farm

MAGPIE LA

Tye

The Layn

Rhodes Minnis +

Tye Wood

CANTERBURY RD

Nail Bourne

3

WHITE HORSE LA

43

The Battle of Britain (PH)

Wenny Farm

Millhill Farm

Elham Valley Way

2

Home Farm

BOYKE LA

Bereforstal Farm

LONGAGE HILL

Ottinge

Ottinge Court Farm

Mill Dow

1

Stonebridge Farm

42

15 **A** **B** 16 **C** **D** 17 **E** **F**

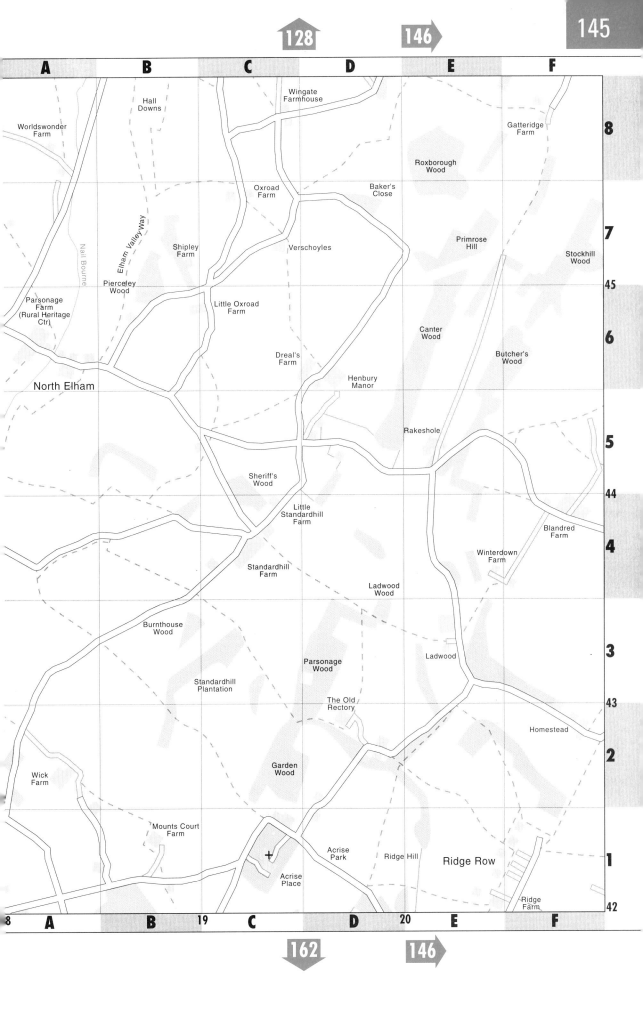

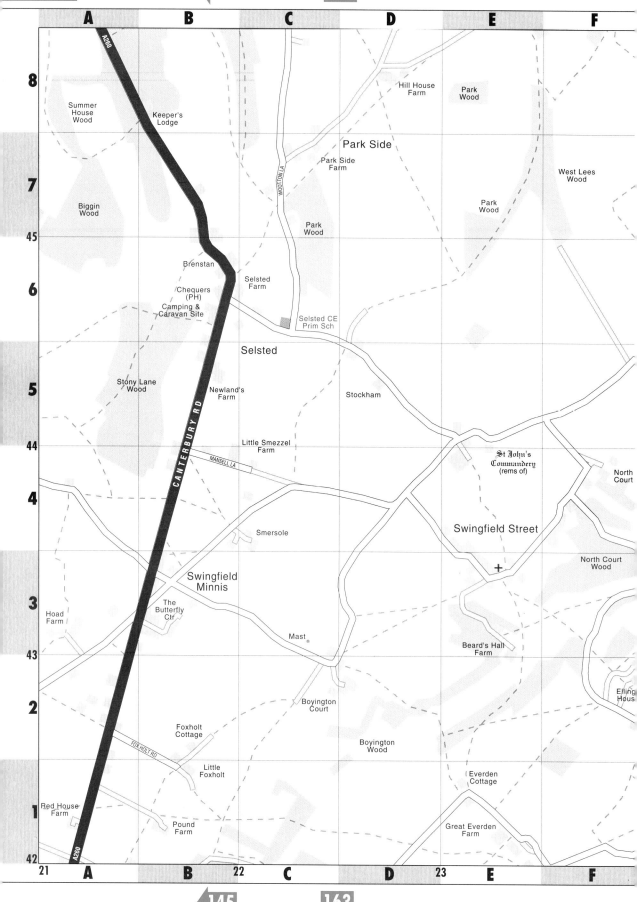

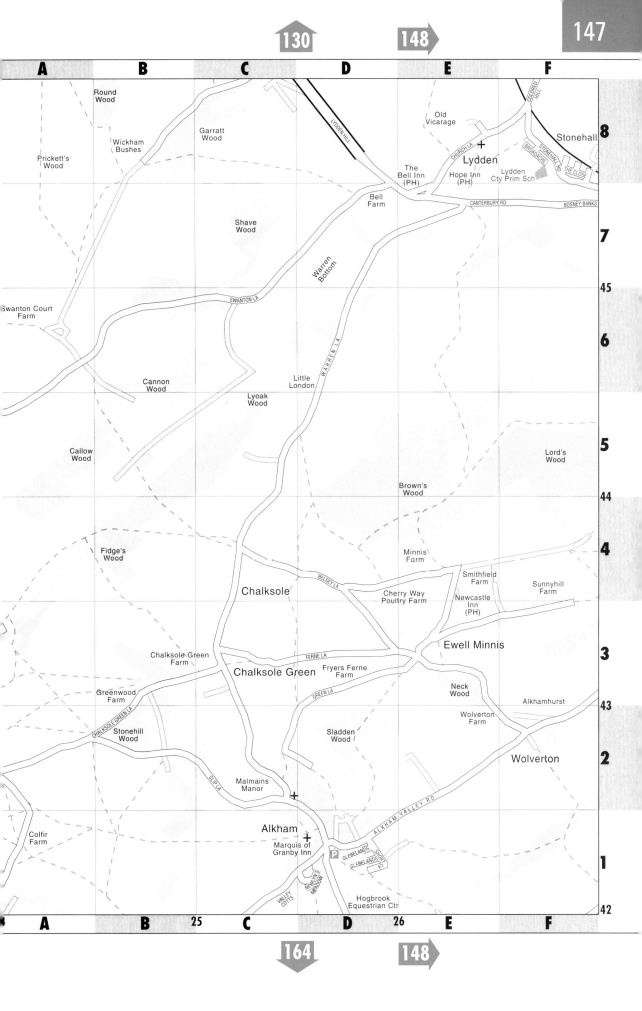

130
148

A B C D E F

8

Round
Wood

Prickett's
Wood

Wickham
Bushes

Garratt
Wood

COLRED HILL

Old
Vicarage

Stonehall

CHURCH LA

Lydden

BROADACRE

STONEHALL RD

THE CLOSE

Lydden
Cty Prim Sch

The
Bell Inn
(PH)

Hope Inn
(PH)

LYDDEN HILL

Bell
Farm

CANTERBURY RD

BOSNEY BANKS

Shave
Wood

7

Warren
Bottom

45

SWANTON LA

Swanton Court
Farm

6

Cannon
Wood

Lyoak
Wood

Little
London

WARREN LA

5

Callow
Wood

Lord's
Wood

Brown's
Wood

44

Fidge's
Wood

Minnis
Farm

4

BELSEY LA

Chalksole

Cherry Way
Poultry Farm

Smithfield
Farm

Newcastle
Inn
(PH)

Sunnyhill
Farm

Ewell Minnis

Chalksole Green
Farm

Chalksole Green

FERNE LA

Fryers Ferne
Farm

3

Neck
Wood

Alkhamhurst

43

Greenwood
Farm

GREEN LA

Wolverton
Farm

CHALKSOLE GREEN LA

Stonehill
Wood

Sladden
Wood

Wolverton

2

SLIP LA

Malmains
Manor

ALKHAM VALLEY RD

Colfir
Farm

Alkham

Marquis of
Granby Inn

P

GLEBELANDS

SHORT LA

GLEBELANDS

1

VALLEY COTTS

NEWBY'S MEADOW

Hogbrook
Equestrian Ctr

42

A 25 B C D 26 E F

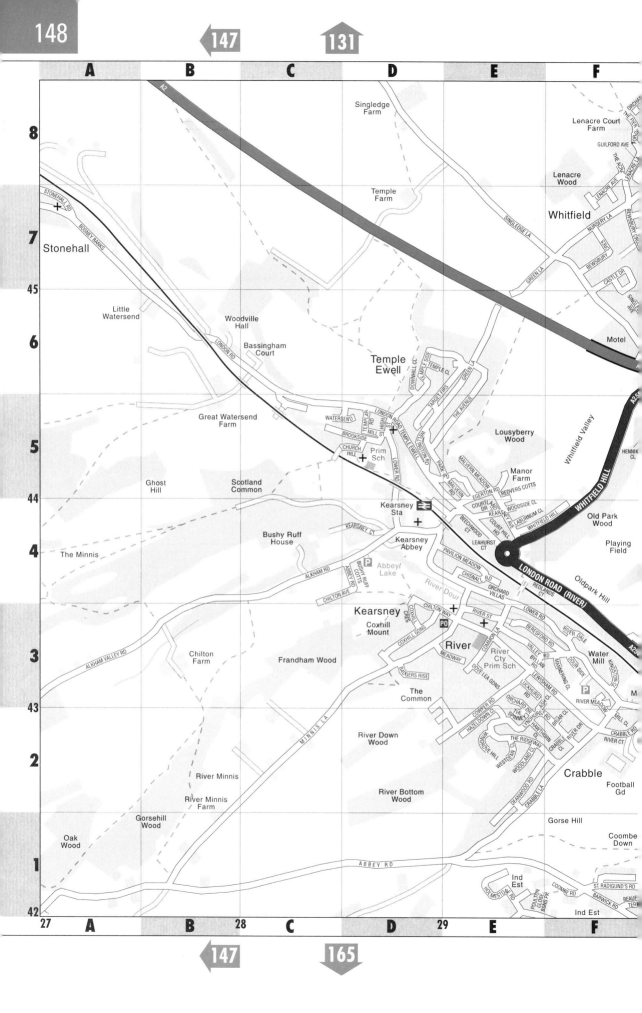

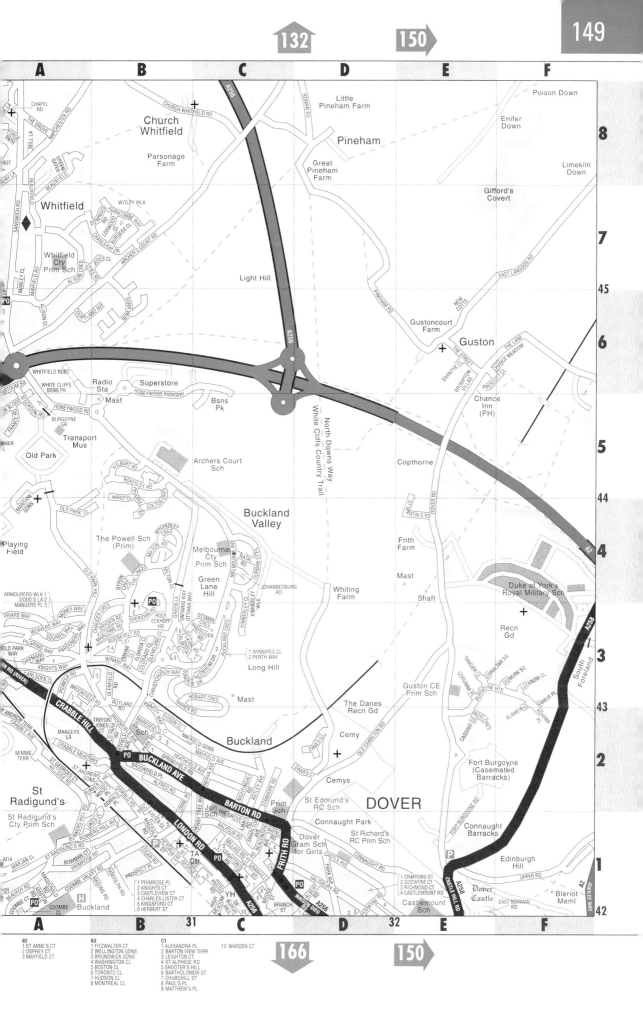

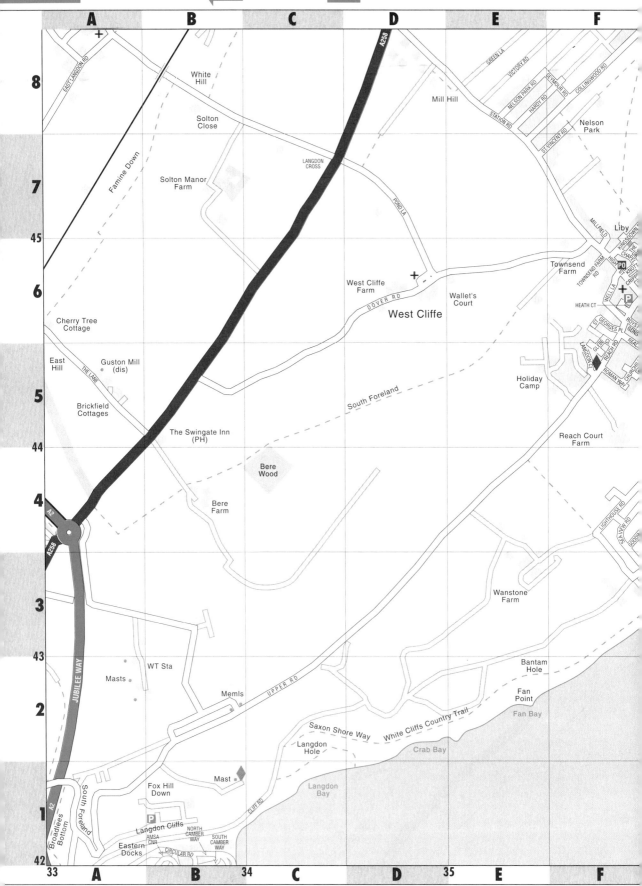

A B C D E F

8 White Hill

Solton Close

EAST LANGDON RD

Famine Down

LANGDON CROSS

7 Solton Manor Farm

Green La

Victory Rd

Nelson Park Rd

Hardy Rd

Seymour Rd

Collinwood Rd

Mill Hill

Station Rd

St Vincent Rd

Nelson Park

Millfield

Liby

Kingsdown

The Chapel

45

6 Cherry Tree Cottage

West Cliffe Farm

Wallet's Court

West Cliffe

Dover Rd

Pond La

Townsend Farm

Townsend Farm Rd

High St

Well La

PO

Heath Ct

St Georges Pl

East Hill

Guston Mill (dis)

The Lane

Roystl Gdns

Reach Rd

Globe

Langdon Cl

Roman Way

Real

Supple

5 Brickfield Cottages

South Foreland

Holiday Camp

44 The Swingate Inn (PH)

Reach Court Farm

Bere Wood

Bere Farm

4 A2

A258

Wanstone Farm

Lighthouse Rd

Sea View Rd

Goodw

3

43 Masts

WT Sta

Bantam Hole

Upper Rd

Fan Point

2 Memls

Saxon Shore Way

White Cliffs Country Trail

Fan Bay

Langdon Hole

Crab Bay

Mast

Fox Hill Down

Langdon Bay

1 P

Langdon Cliffs

North Camber Way

South Camber Way

A2

Boadlees Bottom

South Foreland

Eastern Docks

Circular Rd

Cliff Rd

Jubilee Way

42

33 A B 34 C D 35 E F

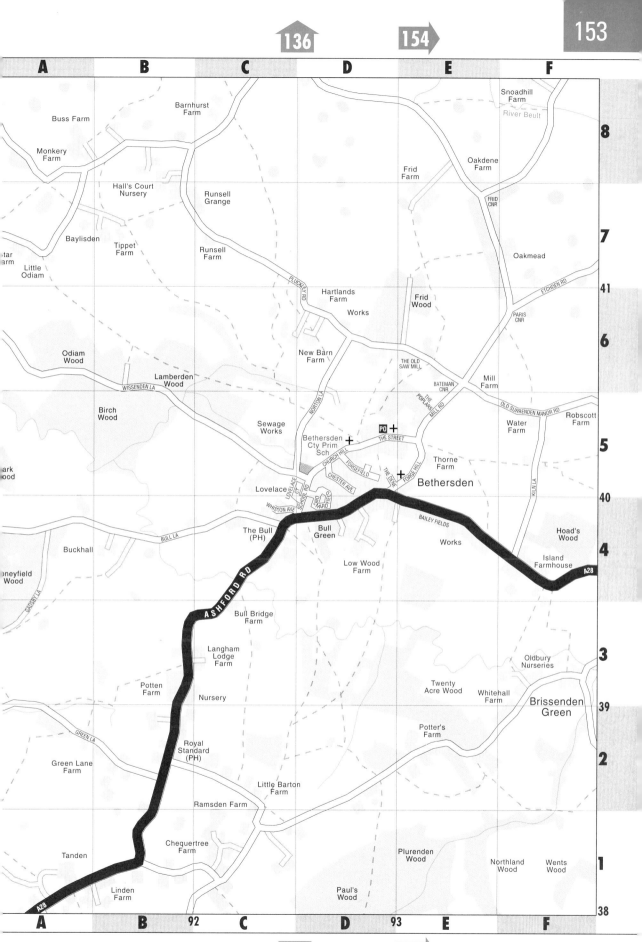

153
137

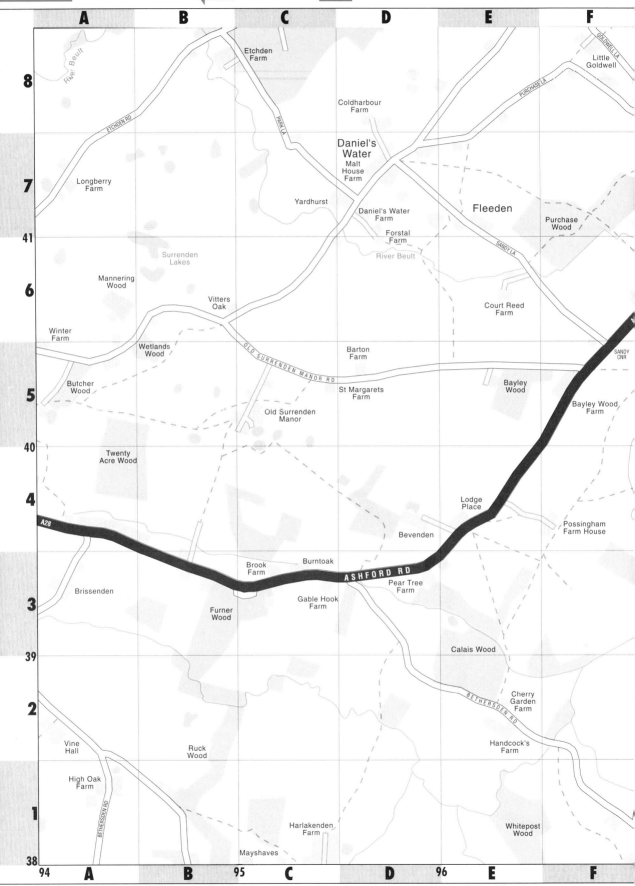

153
169

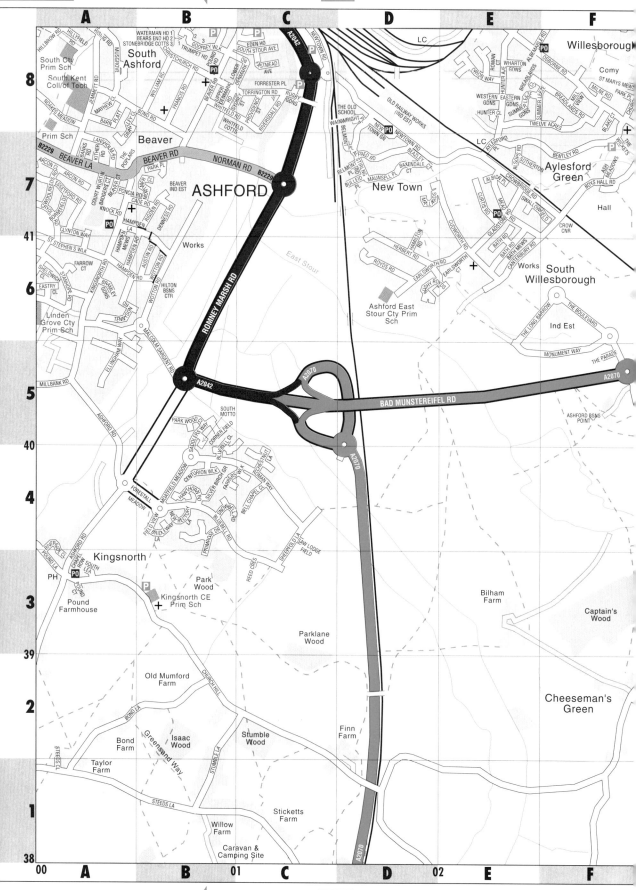

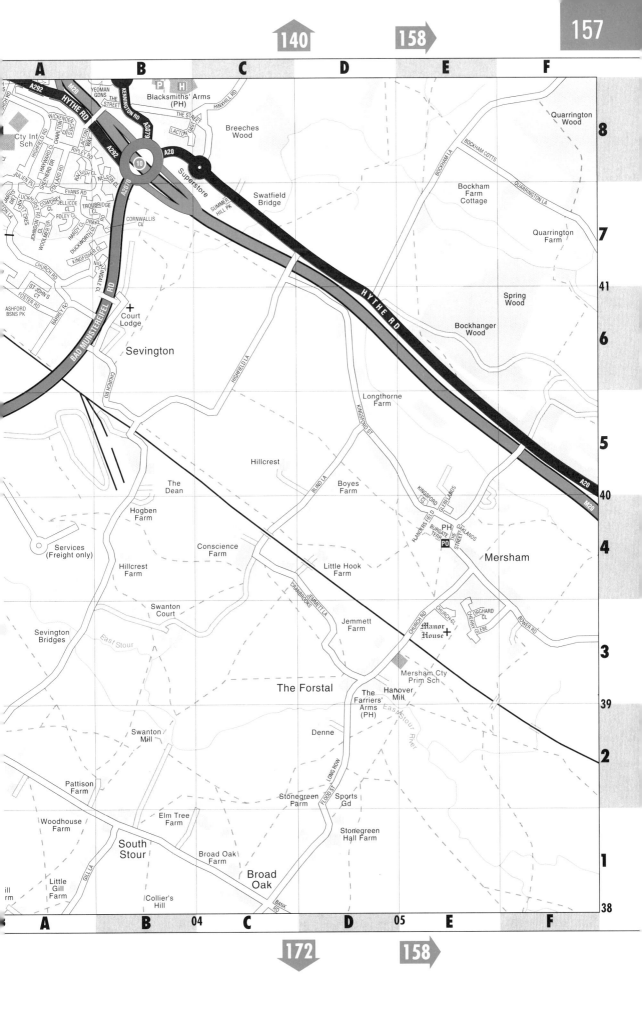

140
158

A292
HYTHE RD
M20
YEOMAN GDNS
THE STREET
KENNINGTON RD
A2070
P
H
Blacksmiths' Arms (PH)
THE STREET
HNXHILL RD
LACTON OAST
Breeches Wood

WICKENDEN RD
CHARLTON HILL
HIGHFIELD RD
RIPLEY CL
A292
A2070
10
A20
SUPERSTORE
LACTON WAY
SUMMER HILL PK
Swatfield Bridge

Quarrington Wood

BOCKHAM LA
BOCKHAM COTTS

Bockham Farm Cottage
QUARRINGTON LA

Cty Inf Sch

JULIEN PL
HAYWARD CL
SHEPHERD DR
ORCHARD RD
EVANS RD
JELLICOE CL
FOLEY CL
RALEIGH CL
NELSON CL
CORNWALLIS CL

Quarrington Farm

8

7

41

JARVIS
LUCKHURST RD
COWDREY CL
HARDY CL
DRAKE CL
DUCKWORTH CL
KINGFISHER CL
NIGHTINGALE CL

6

Spring Wood

Bockhanger Wood

CHURCH RD
ST JOHN'S CTY
FOSTER RD
BARREY RD

ASHFORD BSNS PK

BAD MUNSTEREIFEL RD

Court Lodge

Sevington

HIGHFIELD LA

HYTHE RD

A20

M20

5

40

KINGSFORD ST

Longthorne Farm

Services (Freight only)

Hillcrest Farm

The Dean

Hogben Farm

CHURCH RD

Hillcrest

BLIND LA

Boyes Farm

KINGSFORD CL
GLEBELANDS
OAKLANDS

FLANDERS FIELD
BURGATE TERR
THE STREET
PH
PO

Mersham

4

Conscience Farm

Little Hook Farm

CRAMBROOKS
JEMMETT LA

Swanton Court

Jemmett Farm

CHURCH RD
CHURCH CL
CHERRY GLEBE
ORCHARD CL
BOWER RD

Sevington Bridges

East Stour

Manor House

3

The Forstal

The Farriers' Arms (PH)

Hanover Mill

Mersham Cty Prim Sch

East Stour River

39

Swanton Mill

Denne

2

Pattison Farm

LONG ROW
FLOOD ST

Stonegreen Farm

Sports Gd

Woodhouse Farm

Elm Tree Farm

GILL LA

South Stour

Broad Oak Farm

Broad Oak

Stonegreen Hall Farm

1

Little Gill Farm

Collier's Hill

BANK RD

38

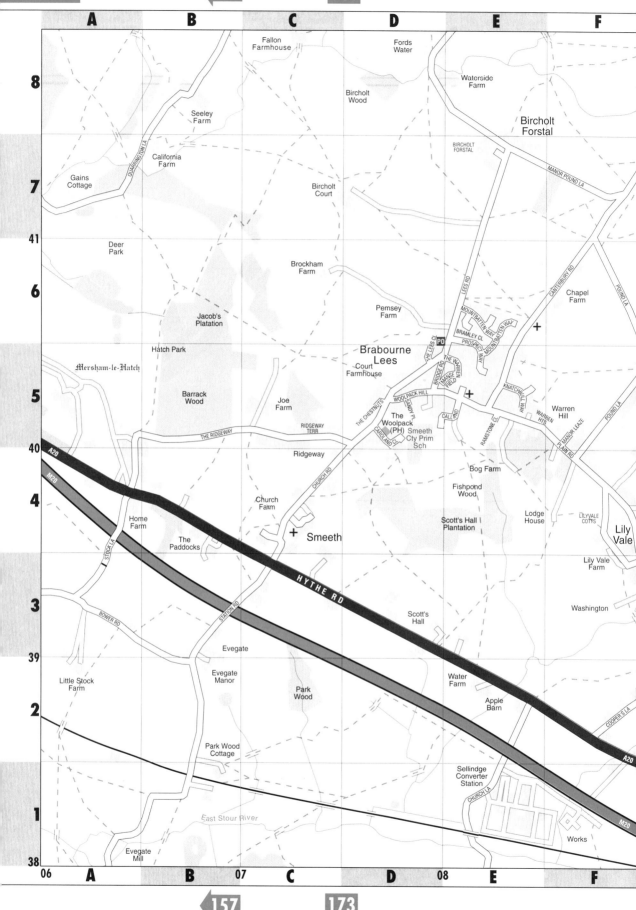

A B C D E F

Brabourne

Penstock
Hall

Five Bells
(PH)

Church
Farm

Parsonage
Farm

Brabourne CE
Prim Sch

CANTERBURY RD

THE STREET

CANTERBURY RD

PILGRIMS WAY

NORTH DOWNS WAY

Highfield
Farm

8

Stowting
Court

SCOTS LA

Field View
Farm

Woodlands
Farm

7

41

Forty Acre
Wood

Park
Farm

Horton View
Farm

FIDDLING LA

Mill
House

6

Water
Farm

The Pound
House

Upper Granary
Court

The Black Horse
(PH)

Broad
Street

5

GRANARY COURT RD

Little Granary
Court

Heminge
Farm

CHURCH LA

40

Coopers
Wood

Southenay
Farm

SOUTHENAY LA

Cock
Ash

Smeeds
Farm

4

PLAIN RD

The
Rookery

PRIORY LA

Lower Cock
Ash

Horton
Priory

Hyham
Hill

3

Priory
(rems of)

Great Priory
Wood

Home
Farm

39

Stone Hill

Hoddiford
Farm

MOORSTOCK LA

Ashley
House

STONE HILL

Hoddiford
Mill

Moorstock

Moorstock
Farm

GREENFIELDS

BROOK LA
COTTS

CHISLETT CL

SWAN LA

Craft Ctr

2

BROOK LA

Elm Tree
Farm

Sellindge

Gibbin's
Brook

Court Lodge
Farm

ASHFORD RD

Dukes Head
(PH)

Sellindge Cty
Prim Sch

SWAN GN

Gibbins Brook
Farm

1

HARRINGE LA

Potten
Farm

DOWNS WAY

A20

LEAFIELD

FORGE CL

WHITEHALL WAY

38

M20

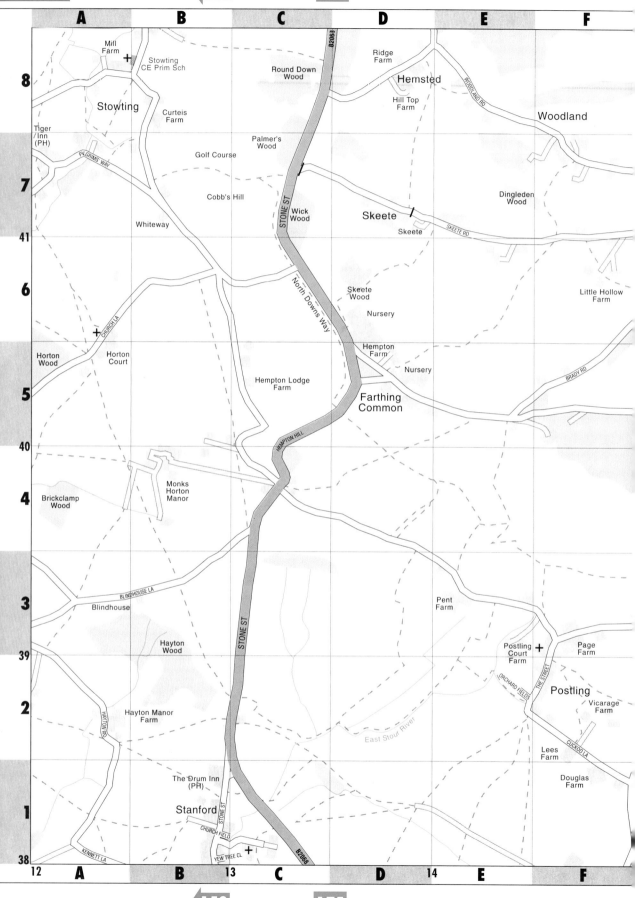

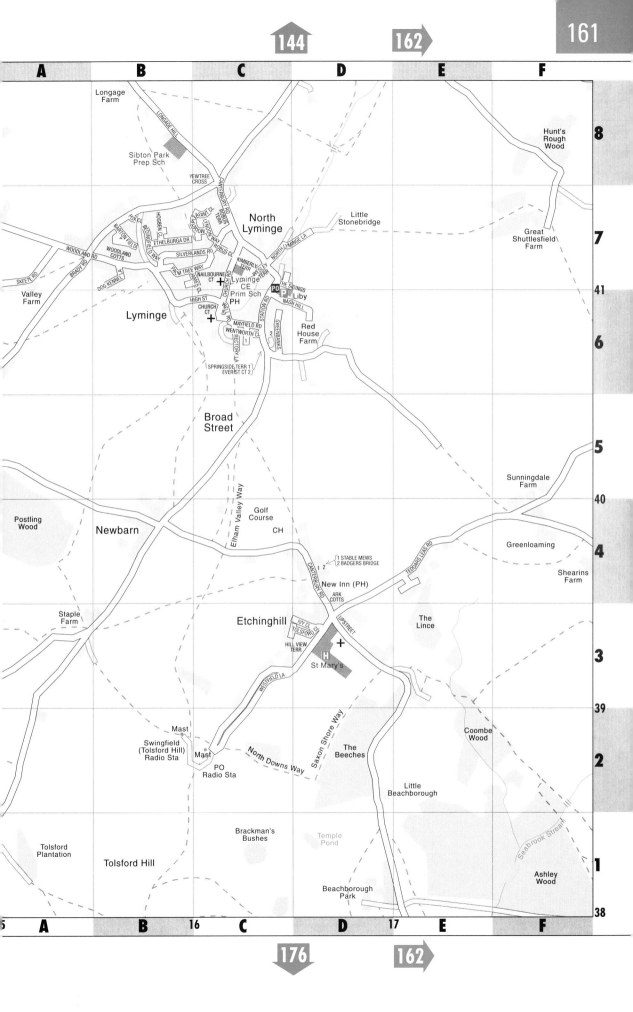

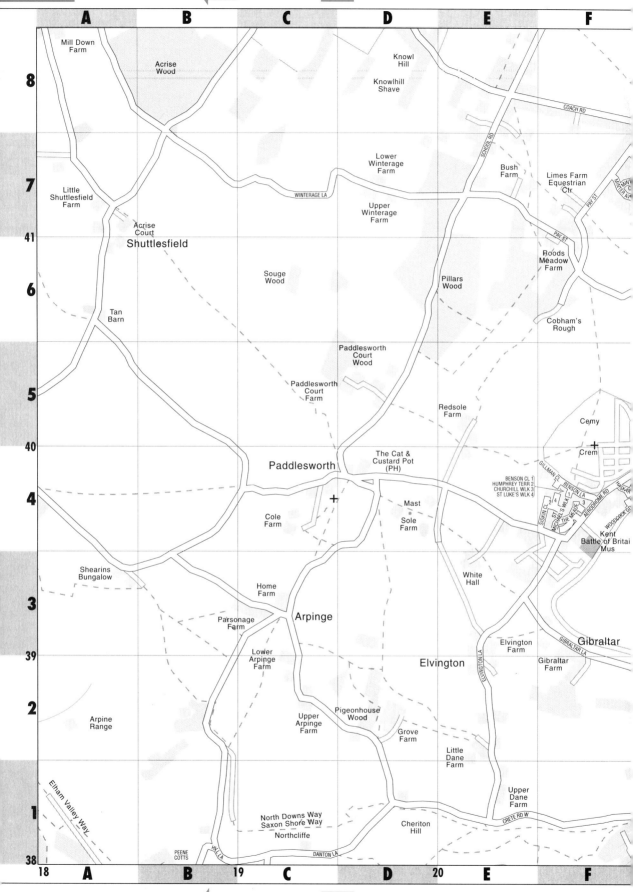

A   B   C   D   E   F

8

Mill Down
Farm

Acrise
Wood

Knowl
Hill

Knowlhill
Shave

COACH RD

7

Lower
Winterage
Farm

Bush
Farm

Limes Farm
Equestrian
Ctr

Little
Shuttlesfield
Farm

WINTERAGE LA

Upper
Winterage
Farm

SCHOOL RD

PAY ST

MILNER AV

41

Acrise
Court

Shuttlesfield

PAY ST

PAY ST

Roods
Meadow
Farm

6

Souge
Wood

Pillars
Wood

Tan
Barn

Cobham's
Rough

Paddlesworth
Court
Wood

Redsole
Farm

Cemy

5

Paddlesworth
Court
Farm

Crem

40

The Cat &
Custard Pot
(PH)

Paddlesworth

BENSON CL 1
HUMPHREY TERR 2
CHURCHILL WLK 3
ST LUKE'S WLK 4

GILLMAN CL

BENSON LA

4

Cole
Farm

Mast

Sole
Farm

SISKIN CL

MICHAEL'S
THE MEADE

AERODROME RD

HASKAR

WOODCOCK SQ

Kent
Battle of Britai
Mus

Shearins
Bungalow

Home
Farm

White
Hall

Gibraltar

GIBRALTAR LA

3

Parsonage
Farm

Arpinge

Elvington
Farm

Gibraltar
Farm

39

Lower
Arpinge
Farm

Elvington

ELVINGTON LA

2

Arpine
Range

Upper
Arpinge
Farm

Pigeonhouse
Wood

Grove
Farm

Little
Dane
Farm

Upper
Dane
Farm

1

Elham Valley Way

North Downs Way
Saxon Shore Way

Northcliffe

Cheriton
Hill

CRETE RD W

38

PEENE
COTTS

HVL LA

DANTON LA

18   A   B   19   C   D   20   E   F

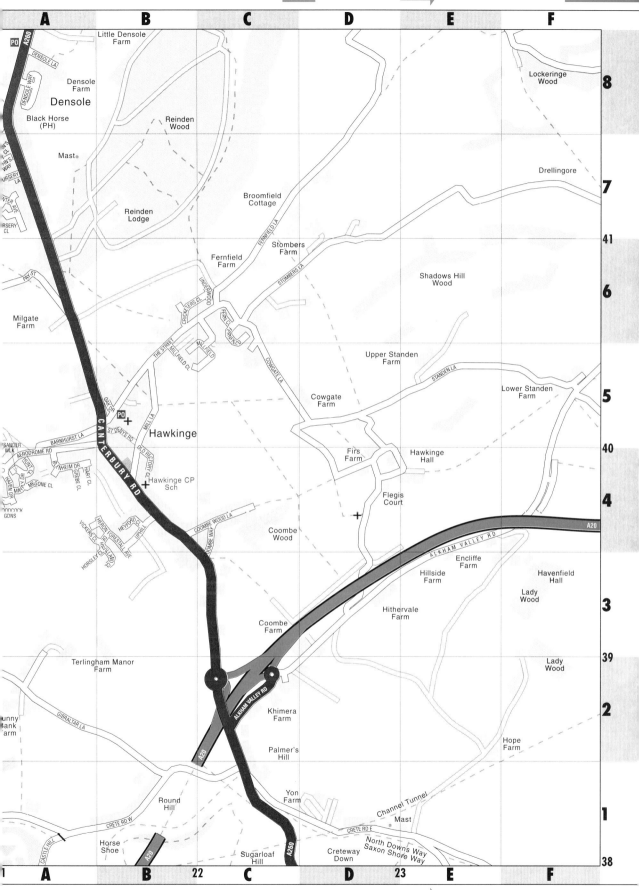

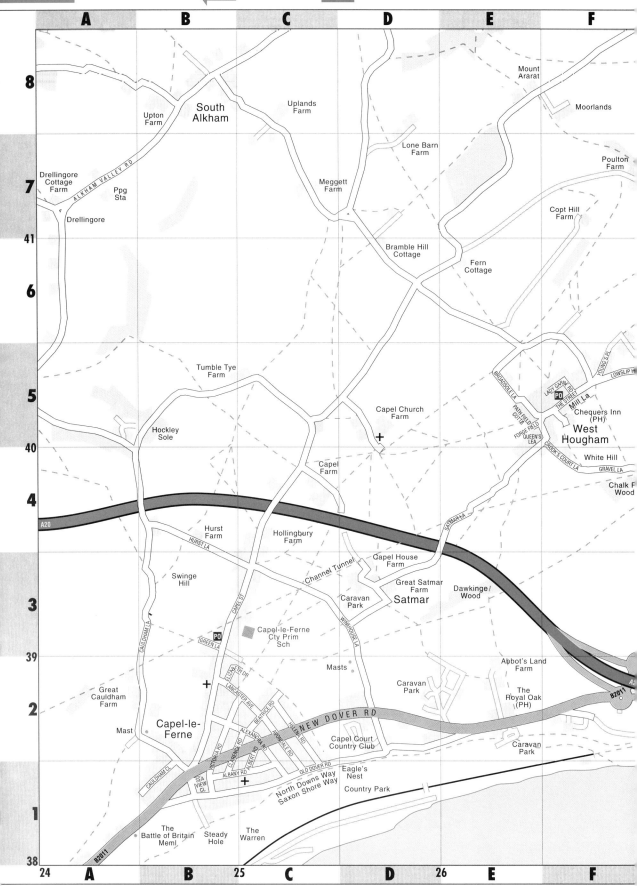

A B C D E F

8

South
Alkham

Upton
Farm

Uplands
Farm

Mount
Ararat

Moorlands

Lone Barn
Farm

Poulton
Farm

Drellingore
Cottage
Farm

7

Ppg
Sta

Meggett
Farm

ALKHAM VALLEY RD

Drellingore

Copt Hill
Farm

41

Bramble Hill
Cottage

Fern
Cottage

6

West
Hougham

LADY GARN RD

BROADSOLE LA

PATH FIELD

COTTS

QUEEN'S
LEA

FORGE
LEA

THE STREET

Mill La

Chequers Inn
(PH)

LOWSLIP H

YOUNGS PL

5

Tumble Tye
Farm

Capel Church
Farm

White Hill

CROOK'S COURT LA

40

Hockley
Sole

Capel
Farm

GRAVEL LA

Chalk F
Wood

4

A20

Hurst
Farm

HURST LA

Hollingbury
Farm

Capel House
Farm

SATMAR LA

Channel Tunnel

Swinge
Hill

Great Satmar
Farm

Satmar

Dawkinge
Wood

A2

B2011

3

CAULDHAM LA

CAPEL ST

GREEN LA

PO

Capel-le-Ferne
Cty Prim
Sch

Caravan
Park

WINGHOUSE LA

39

Great
Cauldham
Farm

ELIZABETH DR

Masts

Caravan
Park

Abbot's Land
Farm

The
Royal Oak
(PH)

B2011

2

Mast

Capel-le-
Ferne

LANCASTER AVE

ALEXANDRA RD

BEATRICE RD

HELENA RD

AVONDALE RD

NEW DOVER RD

Capel Court
Country Club

Caravan
Park

VICTORIA RD

CLARENCE RD

ALBERT RD

Old Dover Rd

Eagle's
Nest
Country Park

1

CAULDHAM CL

SEA
VIEW
CL

ALBANY RD

North Downs Way
Saxon Shore Way

The
Battle of Britain
Meml

Steady
Hole

The
Warren

B2011

38

24 A B 25 C D 26 E F

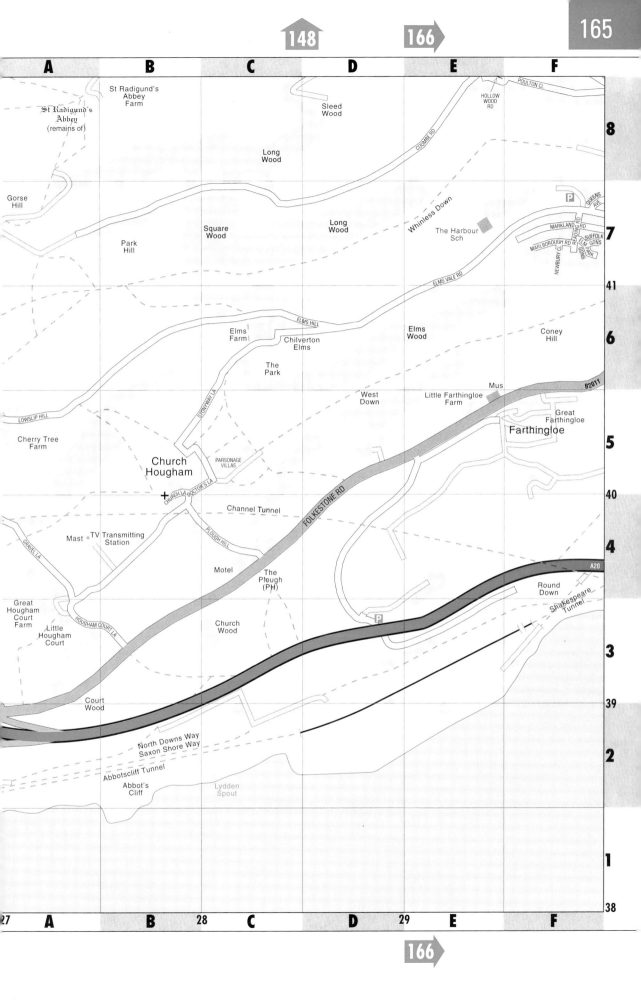

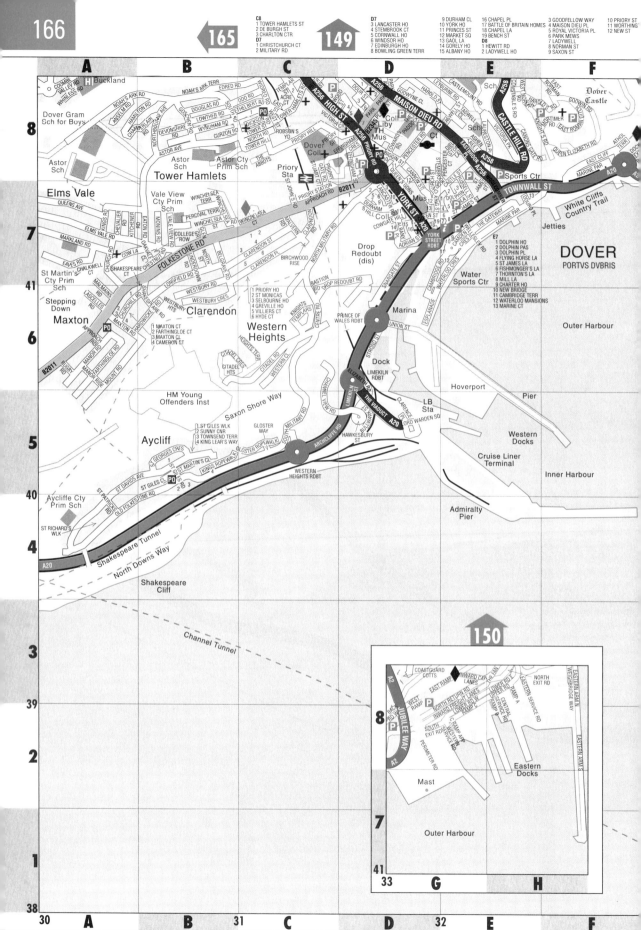

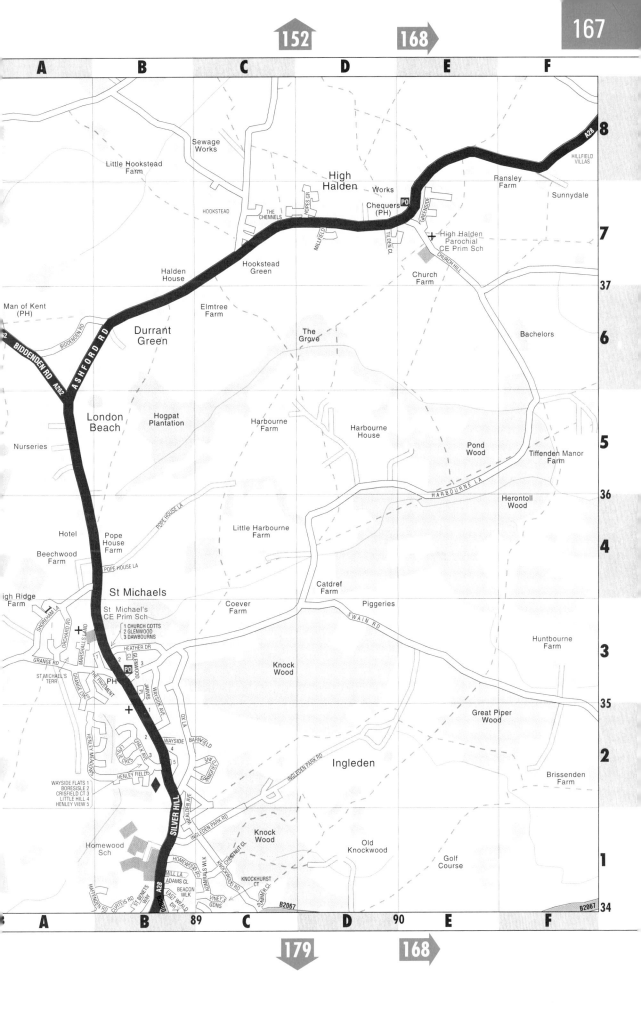

A   B   C   D   E   F

8

A28 ASHFORD RD A28
THE MARTINS
Brickyard
Farm

Marten
Farm

Mace View
Farm

Plurenden
Manor

Lyndhurst
Farm

PLURENDEN MANOR FARM COTTS

Oaktree
Farm

PLURENDEN RD

CUCKOLD'S
CNR

7

37

Brook
Wood

Coomb
Wood

6

Little
Tiffenden
Farm

Grove
Farm

Trottingale
Wood

Jarvis
Farm

REDBROOK ST

5

May Wood

Appleberry
Farm

Church Elms
Farm

King
Farm

36

Great Doney
Wood

Maywood
Farm

Butlers
Farm

4

Barn Wood

Boldshaves
Cottage

Boldshaves

Godfrey
Wood

Ghyll Wood
Farm

BRICKWALL
TERR
WEST
END

Brickwall
Farm

3

Susan's Hill
Farm

SUSAN'S HILL

35

SWAIN RD

Ruffets
Wood

2

Swain
Farm

Great
Robhurst
Farm

Little
Robhurst

Haycross
Wood

Maiden
Wood

Haycross
Farm

1

Cherry
Gardens

34

B2067   WOODCHURCH RD   B2067

91   A   92   B   C   92   D   93   E   F

A B C D E F

8

7

37

6

5

36

4

3

35

2

1

34

WOODCHURCH RD
RECTORY
BGLWS
CHURCH LA

Colebran
Wood

Great
Engeham
Manor

BLURENDEN RD

Harlakenden
Wood

Frightsbridge
Farm

Coleham
Green

Glebe
Farm

SHADOXHURST RD

DUCK LA

Kingsland's
Wood

Engeham
Farm

BETHERSDEN RD

Pound
Wood

Stone
Wood

Streetend
Wood

Shirkoak
Park

Gladwell
Farm

Hengherst

Post
Wood

Courthope
Wood West

Shirkoak

Orlestone
Wents

REDBROOK ST

Pond
Farm

COLDBLOW LA

Newhurst
Farm

Nurseries

Russett
Farm

May
Farm

Coldblow

unny Mead
Farm

PLACE LA

Windmill
(dis)

MILL VW

CHERRY ORCH

Caravan
Park

Cole Wood

Beacon
Farm

SUSAN'S

COPPICE

L

The
Six Bells Inn
(PH)

oodchurch
E Prim Sch

THE GREEN

BIG LANES

Court Lodge
Farm

PO

Mount Pleasant
Farm

Woodchurch

Hillside
Farm

ownland
Green

FRONT RD

KIRKWOOD AVE

LOWER RD

Sunnyside
Farm

Hatch

Barn Wood

Highlands
Farm

Highlands Farm
Rare Breeds
Ctr

Spring Place
Farm

PLUM TREE GDNS

Hunt's Wood

Kiln
Wood

95 96

A B C D E F

169
155

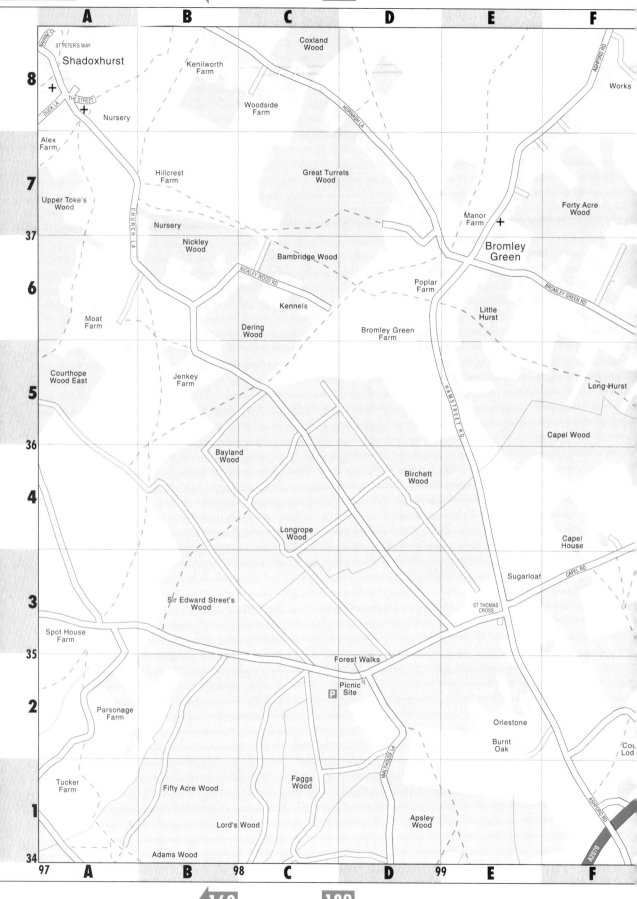

169
182

171
157

A B C D E F

8

7

Collier's Hill

Shelwyn

Walnut Farm

GILL LA

CHEQUERTREE

Chequer Tree Farm

John Cock Farm

Frithfield Farm

LANGS LA

BANK RD

Hande Farm

Bank Farm

Cla Hil

37

The Good Intent (PH)

Little Gains Farm

FRITH RD

PO

6

Frithgate

Aldington Frith

Beehive Cottage

Bourne Farm

BOURNE RD

Bourne Tap Plantation

Handen Wood

DICKSONS BOURNE

Poulton Wood

5

Tilelodge Wood

Park Wood

ROCKY BOURNE RD

Vale Farm

MILL LA

Barton Farm

NEW ROAD HILL

36

The Priory Home Farm

OAK CA KILN RD

EASTON'S CNR

HM Pris

4

Fagg's Farm

PRIORY RD

Priory Wood

Saxon Shore Way

May Cottage

CHERRY ORCHARD LA

BOAT LA

Goddard Farm

3

The Priory

The Park

Finch Wood

Yew Tree Farm

Bonnington Court

Bonnington

B20

Countryfields Wood

Pinn Farm

35

BONNINGTON CROSS

2

Crowhill Wood

Hill Farm

Gorsedown Farm

Parsonage Farm

PO

BILSINGTON CROSS

Marshland Sewer

St Rumwold's Church

1

Horn's Wood

COSWAY COTTS

White Horse (PH)

Mon

Court Lodge Farm

Bilsington

Royal Military Road

Herne Hill

B2067

Royal Military Canal (dis)

34

03 A B 04 C D 05 E F

171
184

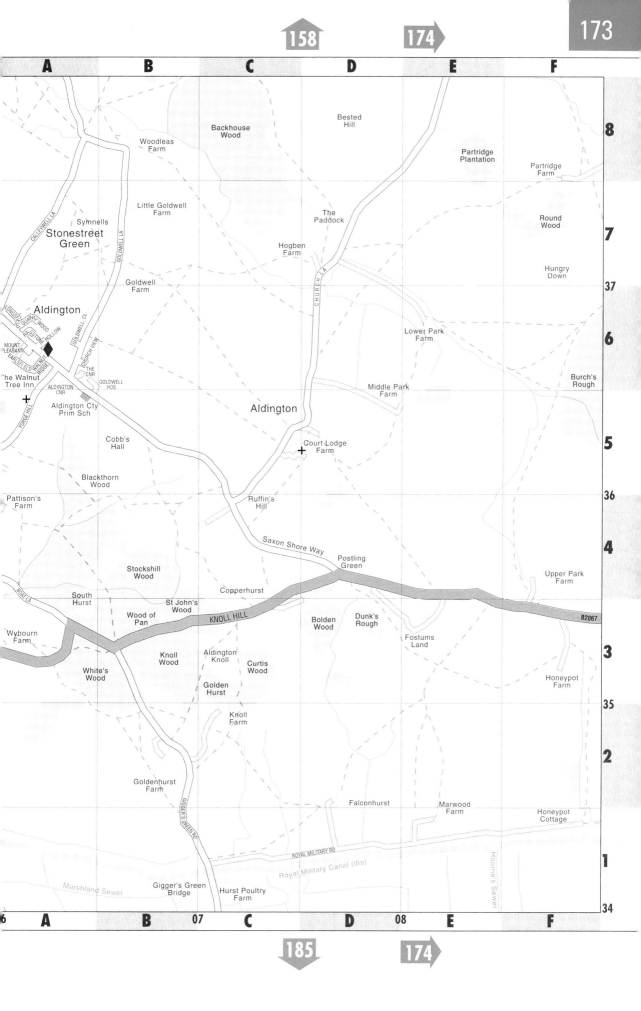

A B C D E F

8

Bested Hill

Backhouse Wood

Woodleas Farm

Partridge Plantation

Partridge Farm

Little Goldwell Farm

The Paddock

Round Wood

7

Symnells

Stonestreet Green

Hogben Farm

Hungry Down

37

Goldwell Farm

CHURCH LA

Lower Park Farm

6

Aldington

Burch's Rough

MOUNT PLEASANT

THE CNR

GOLDWELL HOS

Middle Park Farm

The Walnut Tree Inn

ALDINGTON CNR

Aldington

Aldington Cty Prim Sch

Cobb's Hall

Court Lodge Farm

5

Blackthorn Wood

Pattison's Farm

Ruffin's Hill

36

Saxon Shore Way

4

Stockshill Wood

Postling Green

Upper Park Farm

BOAT LA

South Hurst

Copperhurst

St John's Wood

Wood of Pan

KNOLL HILL

Bolden Wood

Dunk's Rough

B2067

Wybourn Farm

Knoll Wood

Aldington Knoll

Curtis Wood

Fostums Land

3

White's Wood

Golden Hurst

Honeypot Farm

35

Knoll Farm

2

Goldenhurst Farm

GIGGER'S GREEN RD

Falconhurst

Marwood Farm

Honeypot Cottage

Hoorne's Sewer

ROYAL MILITARY RD

1

Royal Military Canal (dis)

Marshland Sewer

Gigger's Green Bridge

Hurst Poultry Farm

34

A B C D E F

6 07 08

A   B   C   D   E   F

←173

M20

Harringe Bridge

Rotherwood Farm

SOMERFIELD BARN CT

PO

ASHFORD RD   A20

Brook Farm

PH   Grove Bridge

M20

8

Rabbit's Wood

East Stour River

MEADOW CR

BARROW HILL RISE

BARROW HILL

Barrowhill

7

Harringe Court

HARRINGE LA

Park Wood

OAK COTTAGES

Barrow Hill Farm

37

Springfield Wood

Mink Farm

Rose Cott

6

B2067

ASHFORD RD   A2...

BENHAM BSNS PK

Red House Farm

Otterpool Manor

Works

Benham Wate... Farm

Harringe Brooks Wood

Upper Otterpool

5

OTTERPOOL LA

36

Coldharbour Cott

Danehurst Wood

4

Welcome Stranger (PH)

Court-at-Street

B2067

Danehurst

LYMPNE IND EST

3

Ashden House

ALDINGTON RD

HARMAN...

TOURNEY CL

...ACON WA...

Aldergate Wood

Hill Hurst Wood

Port Lympne Zoo

REACH RD

Lympne Place

THE STREET

The County Members (PH)

35

French Ho

Coombe Farm

CASTLE...

2

Lympn... Castl...

Saxon Shore Way

ROYAL MILITARY RD

ALDERGATE LA

Aldergate Bridge

Royal Military Canal (dis)

Stutfall Castle (rems of)

1

34

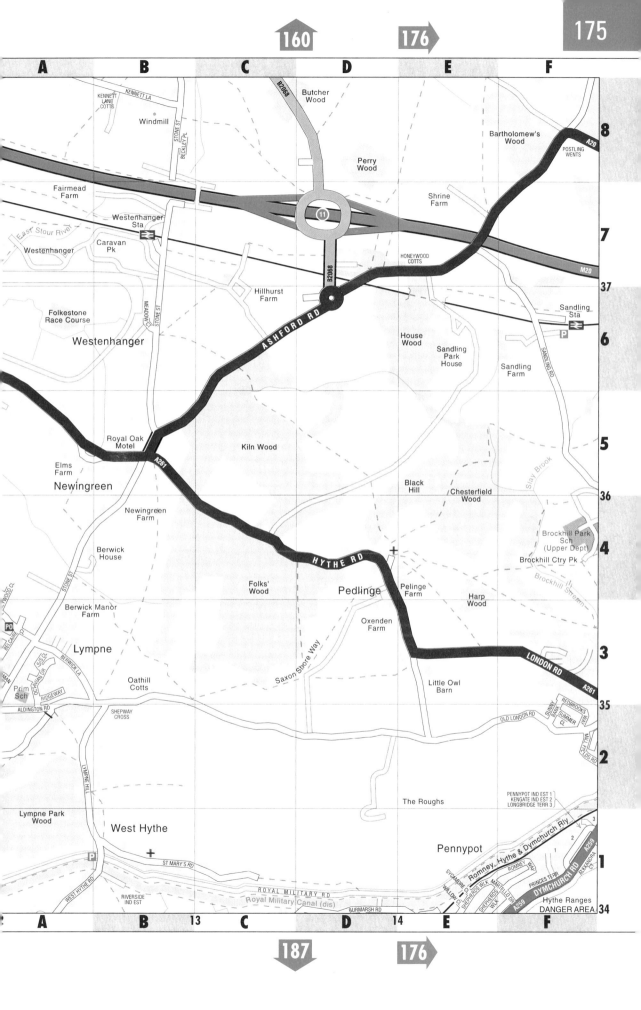

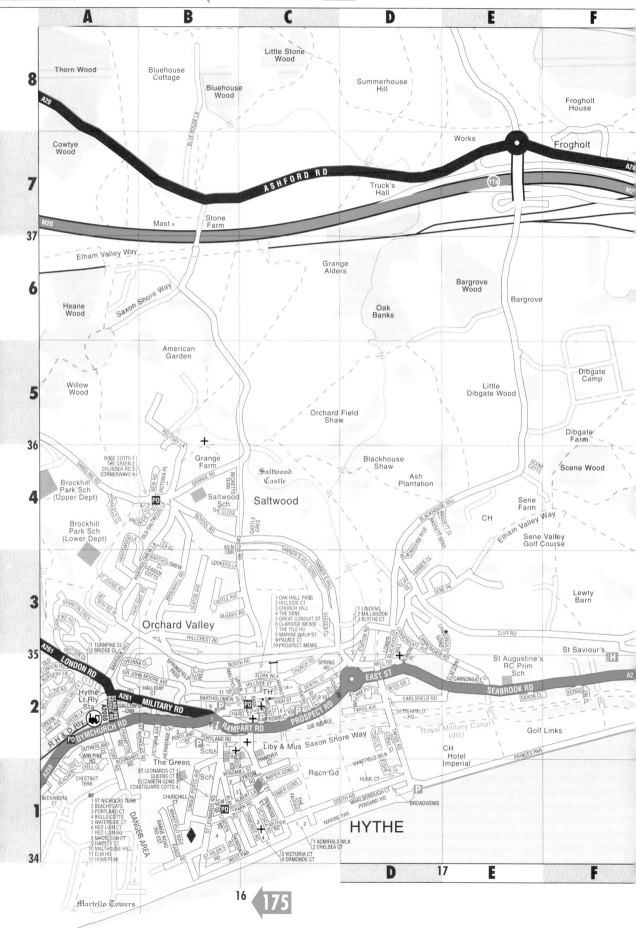

A B C D E F

8 Thorn Wood
Bluehouse Cottage
Little Stone Wood
Bluehouse Wood
Summerhouse Hill
Frogholt House

7 Cowtye Wood
Works
Frogholt
ASHFORD RD
Truck's Hall
11a

37 Mast
Stone Farm

Elham Valley Way

6 Heane Wood
Saxon Shore Way
Grange Alders
Bargrove Wood
Bargrove
Oak Banks

5 Willow Wood
American Garden
Orchard Field Shaw
Little Dibgate Wood
Dibgate Camp
Dibgate Farm

36 ROSE COTTS 1
THE GREEN 2
CYLINDER RD 3
CORNERWAYS 4
Grange Farm
Saltwood Castle
Blackhouse Shaw
Ash Plantation
Scene Wood
SCENE COTTS

4 Brockhill Park Sch (Upper Dept)
PO
Saltwood Sch
THE CLOSE
Saltwood
Sene Farm
CH
Sene Valley Golf Course
Elham Valley Way

Brockhill Park Sch (Lower Dept)
KILN CNR
CASTLE CRES
BLACKHOUSE HILL
BASSETT CL
BASSETT GDNS
BLACKHOUSE RISE

3 SPANTON CRES
Orchard Valley
1 OAK HALL PASS
2 HILLSIDE CT
3 CHURCH HILL
4 THE DENE
5 GREAT CONDUIT ST
6 CLARIDGE MEWS
7 THE TILE HO
8 MARINE WALK ST
9 PALACE CT
10 PROSPECT MEWS
1 LINDENS
2 MILLBROOK
3 BLYTHE CT
CLIFF CL
SENE PK
CLIFF RD
Lewty Barn

35 A261 LONDON RD
HILLCREST RD
ST AUGUSTINE'S RC PRIM SCH
St Saviour's
H
A2

Hythe Lt Rly Sta
MILITARY RD
EAST ST
SEABROOK RD

2 R H & D Rly
PO
DYMCHURCH RD
i RAMPART RD PROSPECT RD
Liby & Mus Saxon Shore Way
Royal Military Canal (dis)
Golf Links
CH Hotel Imperial

The Green
ST LEONARDS CT 1
QUEENS CT 2
ELIZABETH GDNS 3
COASTGUARD COTTS 4
Schs
Recn Gd

1 Alexandra Ct
B2
1 ST NICHOLAS TERR
2 BEACHFLATS
3 PORTLAND CT
4 BULLS COTTS
5 WATERSIDE CT
6 RED LION CT
7 RED LION SQ
8 MACKESON CT
9 FINDLEY CT
10 MALTHOUSE HILL
11 ELM HO
12 HOMEPEAK
DANGER AREA
Broadviews
HYTHE
1 ADMIRALS WLK
2 CHELSEA CT
3 VICTORIA CT
4 ORMONDE CT

34 Martello Towers

D 17 E F

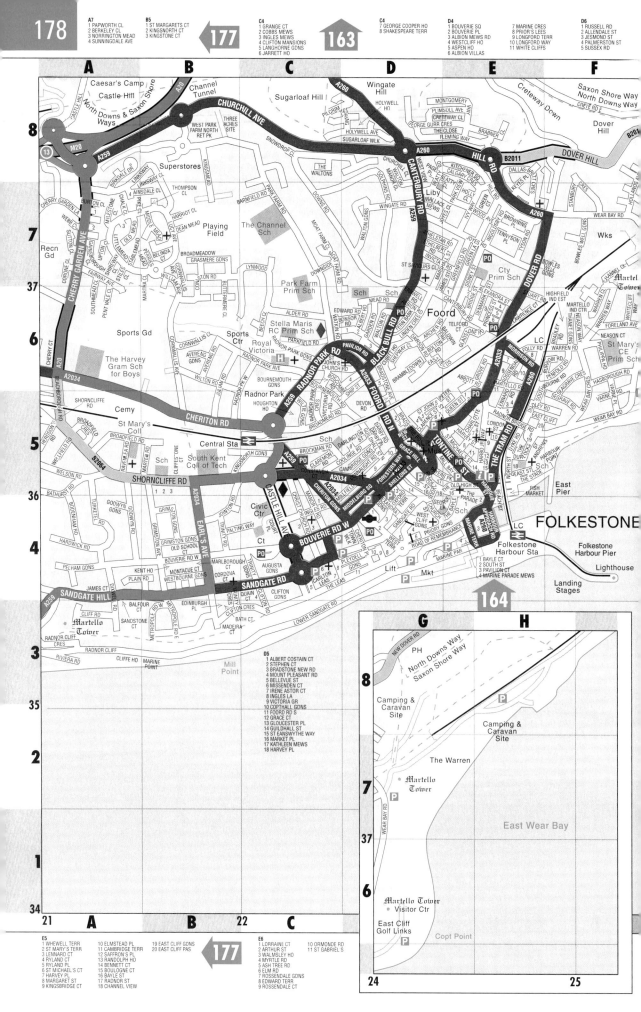

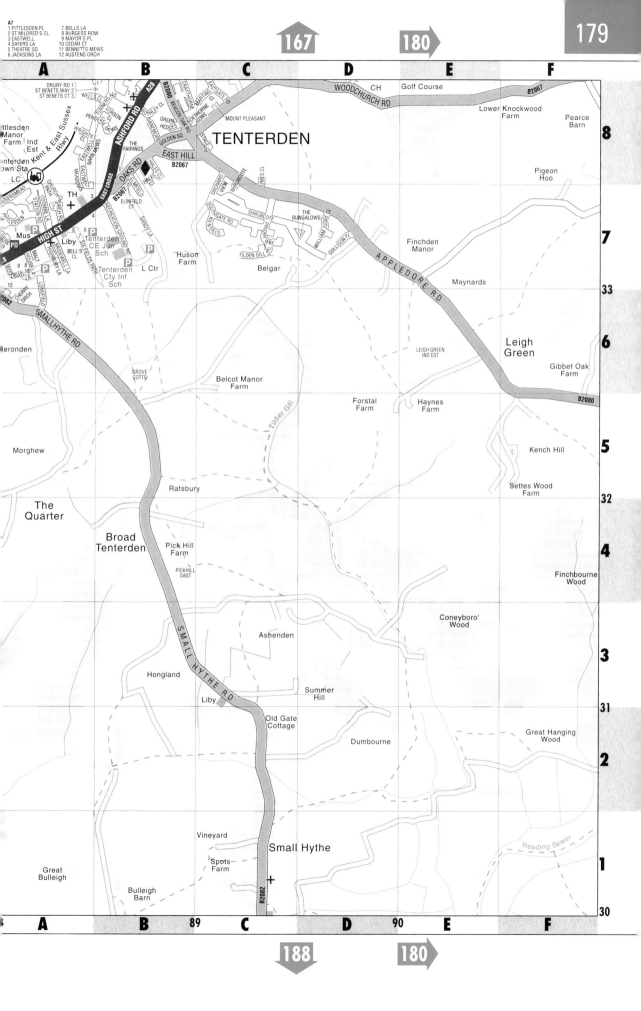

179
168

A **B** **C** **D** **E** **F**

The Dandy

Bourne
Farm

B2067

Cott
Farm

Bower Farm

Berridge
Farm

Oakhurst
Farm

Ditton
Farm

8

BROOK ST

Brook Street

B206

Diamond
House

Orange
Farm

Malt House
Farm

33

7

Glover
Farm

6

MOOR LA

Highbank
Farm

B2080

Nurseries

Shirley
Farm

Frenchay
Wood

Shirley Moor

5

Frenchay
Farm

Tenterden Sewer

New
Bridge

32

APPLEDORE RD

Fleet Petty Sewer

4

Finchbourne
Wood

Barrack
Farm

3

The Century
Farm

31

Little
Ramsden

2

Willow
Farm

Reading
Street

READING ST

Reading Sewer

Nurseries

TENTERDEN RD

Chapel Bank
Farm

Rother Levels

1

Redhill
Bridge

Red H

Barrowsland
Farm

B20

30

A **B** **C** **D** **E** **F**

91 92 93

179
189

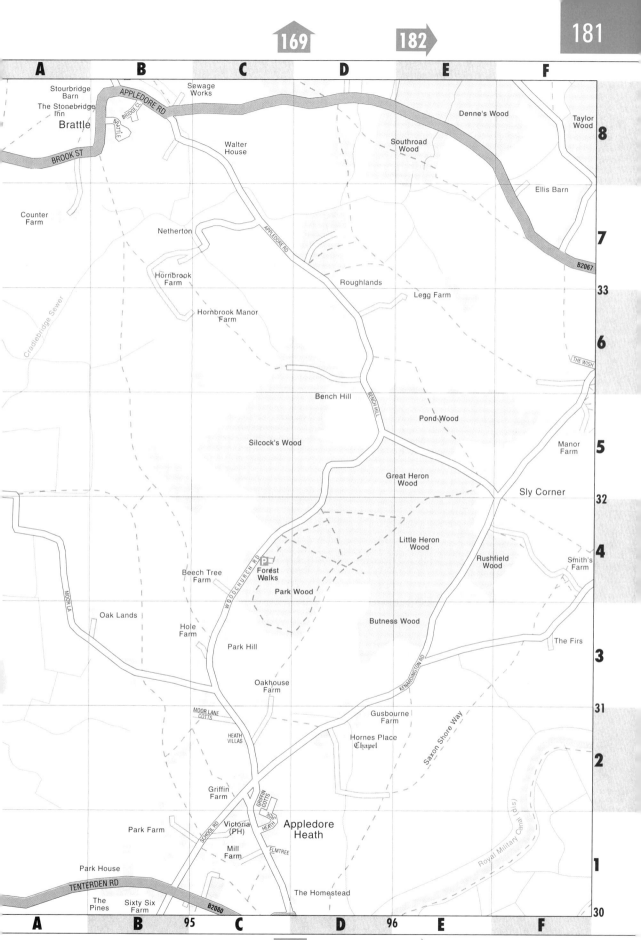

181
170

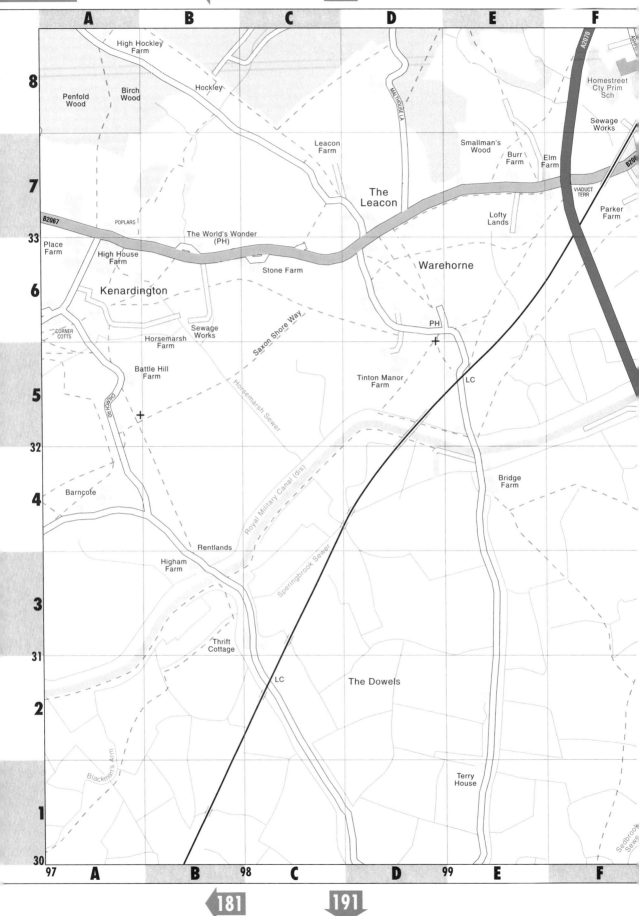

181
191

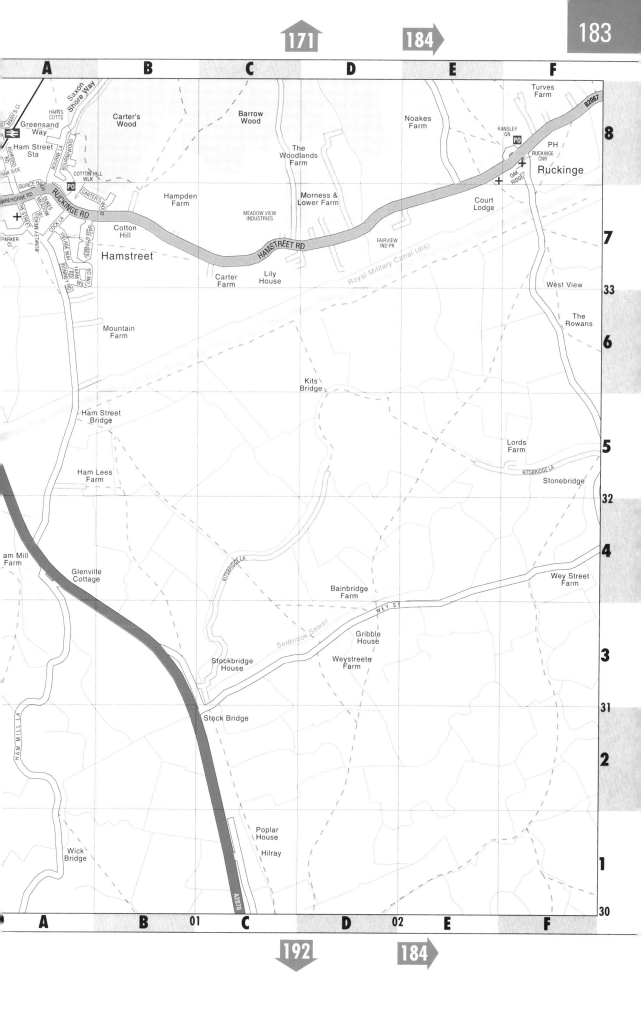

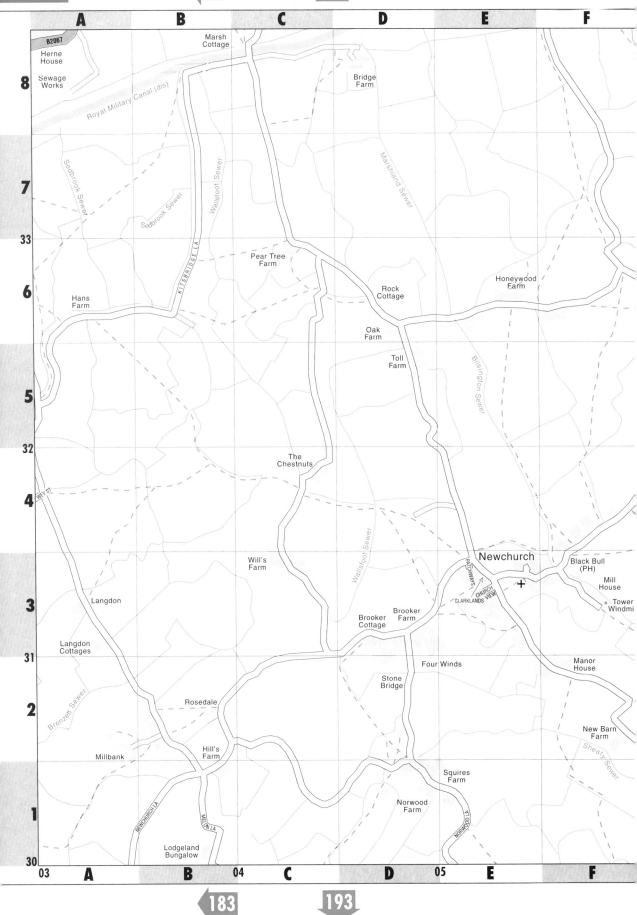

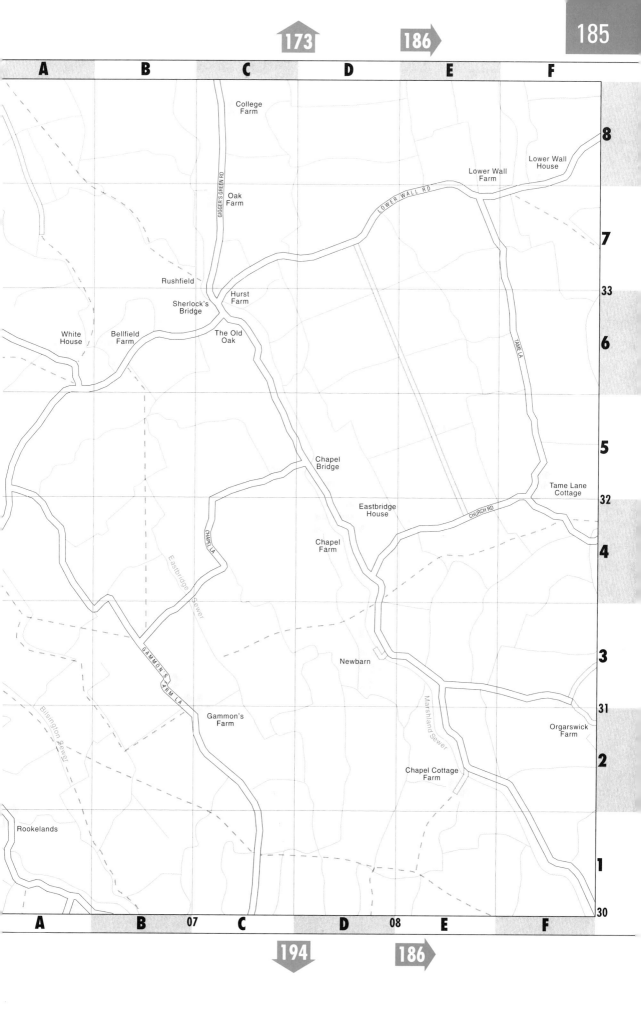

173
186
194
186

A B C D E F

8
7
33
6
5
32
4
3
31
2
1
30

College Farm

GIGGER'S GREEN RD

Oak Farm

LOWER WALL RD

Lower Wall Farm

Lower Wall House

Rushfield

Sherlock's Bridge

Hurst Farm

White House

Bellfield Farm

The Old Oak

TAME LA

CHAPEL LA

Eastbridge Sewer

Chapel Bridge

Tame Lane Cottage

Eastbridge House

CHURCH RD

Chapel Farm

GAMMON'S ARM LA

Newbarn

Marshland Sewer

Orgarswick Farm

Bilsington Sewer

Gammon's Farm

Chapel Cottage Farm

Rookelands

07 08

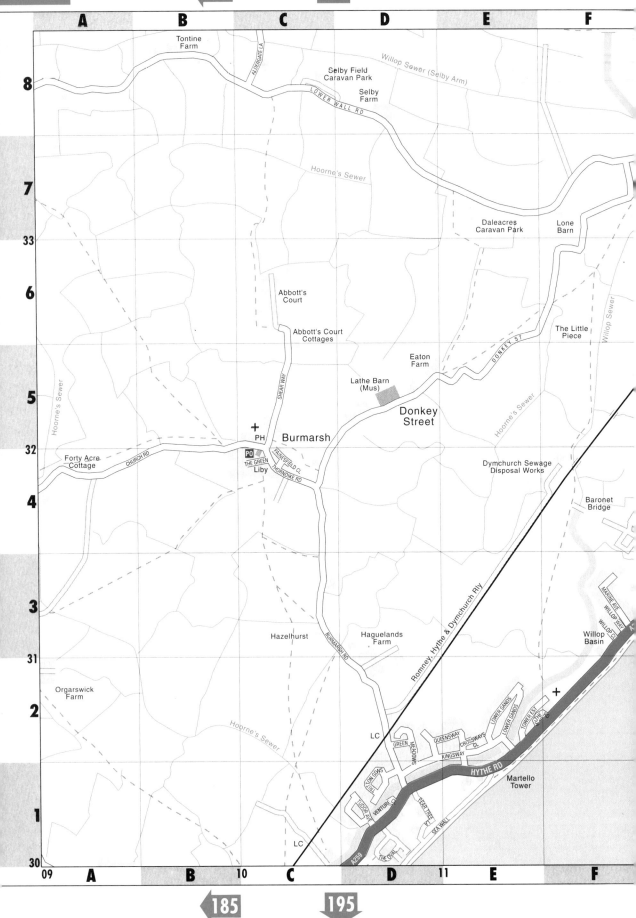

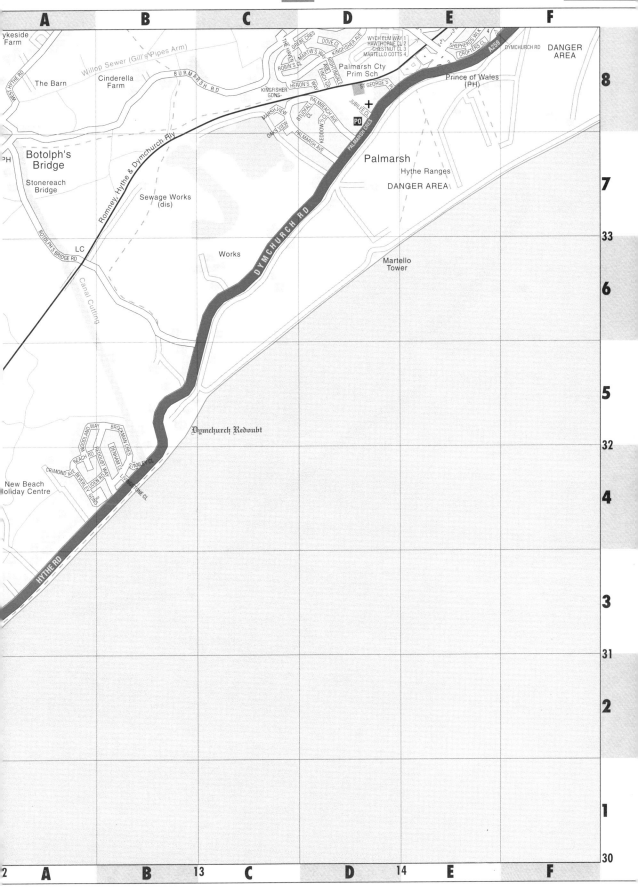

A   B   C   D   E   F

Dykeside Farm

Willop Sewer (Gill's Pipes Arm)

The Barn

Cinderella Farm

BURMARSH RD

Botolph's Bridge

Romney, Hythe & Dymchurch Rly

Stonereach Bridge

Botolph's Bridge Rd

LC

Canal Cutting

Sewage Works (dis)

Works

GREBE CRES
DOVE CL
KINGFISHER AVE
THE HAVEN
ST MARTIN'S WAY
NIGHTINGALE
PIED GLEN
ROBIN'S CL
HERON'S WAY
KINGFISHER GDNS
MARSH VIEW
STUDFALL CL
OAKS VIEW
PALMBEACH AVE
PALMARSH AVE
S. MEADOWS
JUBILEE CL
PALMARSH CRES

WYCH ELM WAY 1
HAWTHORNE CL 2
CHESTNUT CL 3
MARTELLO COTTS 4
SHEPHERDS WLK
CROFTERS CL
A259
DYMCHURCH RD
DANGER AREA

Palmarsh Cty Prim Sch
ST GEORGE'S
PO

Prince of Wales (PH)

Palmarsh

Hythe Ranges
DANGER AREA

DYMCHURCH RD

Martello Tower

Dymchurch Redoubt

WOODLAND WAY
BROCKMAN CRES
REDOUBT WAY
DENHAM CT
EUDEN RD
STANLEY CL
BEACH RD
CRIMOND AVE
BEVERLEY GDNS
LIVINGSTONE CL

New Beach Holiday Centre

HYTHE RD

8

7

33

6

5

32

4

3

31

2

1

30

179

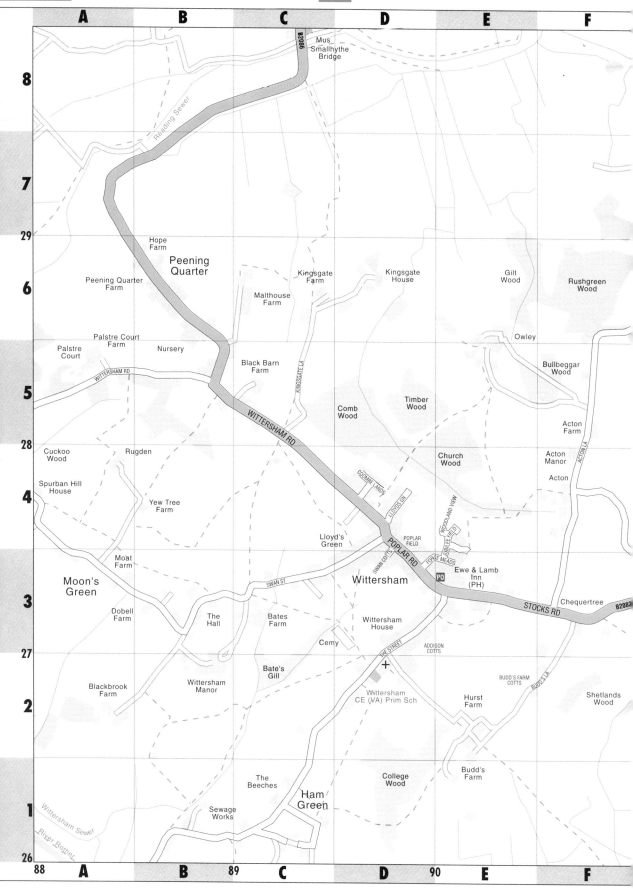

Smallhythe
Bridge

B2086

Mus

Reading Sewer

Hope
Farm

Peening
Quarter

Peening Quarter
Farm

Kingsgate
Farm

Kingsgate
House

Gilt
Wood

Rushgreen
Wood

Malthouse
Farm

Palstre Court
Farm

Nursery

Palstre
Court

Owley

Bullbeggar
Wood

WITTERSHAM RD

Black Barn
Farm

KINGSGATE LA

Comb
Wood

Timber
Wood

Acton
Farm

WITTERSHAM RD

ACTON LA

Cuckoo
Wood

Rugden

Church
Wood

Acton
Manor

Acton

Spurban Hill
House

Yew Tree
Farm

COOMBE LANDS

LLOYDS GN

WOODLAND VIEW

JUBILEE FIELD

Moat
Farm

Lloyd's
Green

POPLAR
FIELD

Ewe & Lamb
Inn
(PH)

Moon's
Green

SWAN ST

SWAN COTTS

Wittersham

POPLAR RD

FORGE MEADS

PO

STOCKS RD

Chequertree

B2082

Dobell
Farm

The
Hall

Bates
Farm

Wittersham
House

Blackbrook
Farm

Wittersham
Manor

Bate's
Gill

Cemy

THE STREET

ADDISON
COTTS

BUDD'S FARM
COTTS

BUDD'S LA

Shetlands
Wood

Wittersham
CE (VA) Prim Sch

Hurst
Farm

The
Beeches

College
Wood

Budd's
Farm

Ham
Green

Wittersham Sewer

River Rother

Sewage
Works

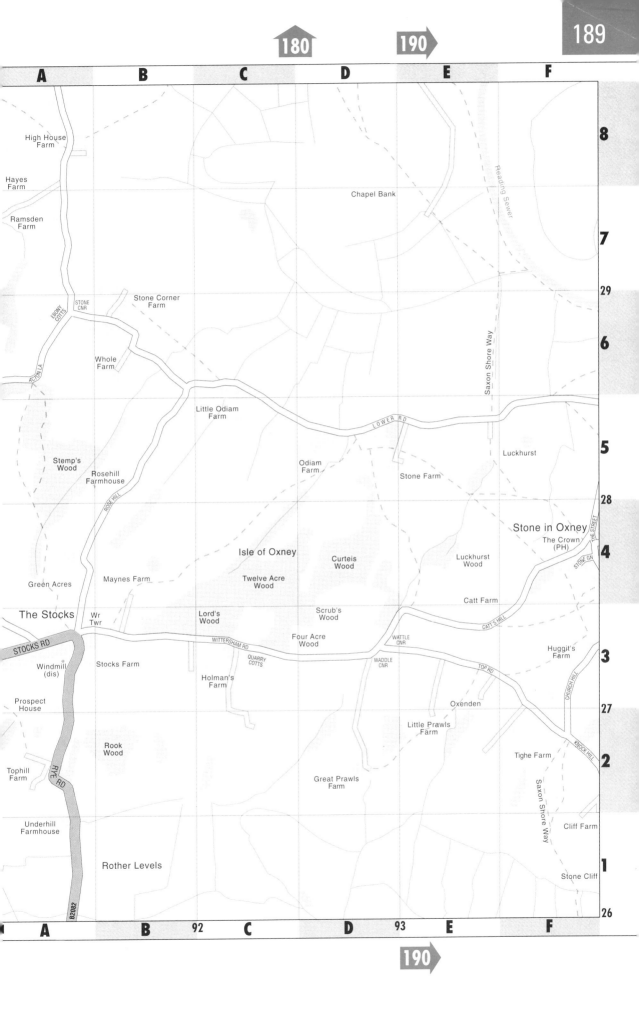

180
190

A B C D E F

8
7
29
6
5
28
4
27
3
2
1
26

High House Farm
Hayes Farm
Ramsden Farm

Chapel Bank

Reading Sewer

EBONY COTTS
STONE CNR
Stone Corner Farm

ACTON LA

Whole Farm

Saxon Shore Way

Little Odiam Farm

LOWER RD

Luckhurst

Stemp's Wood
Rosehill Farmhouse

ROSE HILL

Odiam Farm

Stone Farm

Stone in Oxney
The Crown (PH)

STONE GN
THE STREET

Isle of Oxney

Curteis Wood

Luckhurst Wood

Green Acres
Maynes Farm

Twelve Acre Wood

Catt Farm

Huggit's Farm

The Stocks
Wr Twr

Lord's Wood

Scrub's Wood

CATT'S HILL

STOCKS RD
WITTERSHAM RD
Four Acre Wood

WATTLE CNR

TOP RD

CHURCH HILL

Windmill (dis)
Stocks Farm

QUARRY COTTS

WADDLE CNR

Oxenden

Prospect House
Holman's Farm

Little Prawls Farm

27

Tighe Farm

RYE RD

Rook Wood

Tophill Farm

Great Prawls Farm

Saxon Shore Way

Cliff Farm

KNOCK HILL

Underhill Farmhouse

Rother Levels

Stone Cliff

B2082

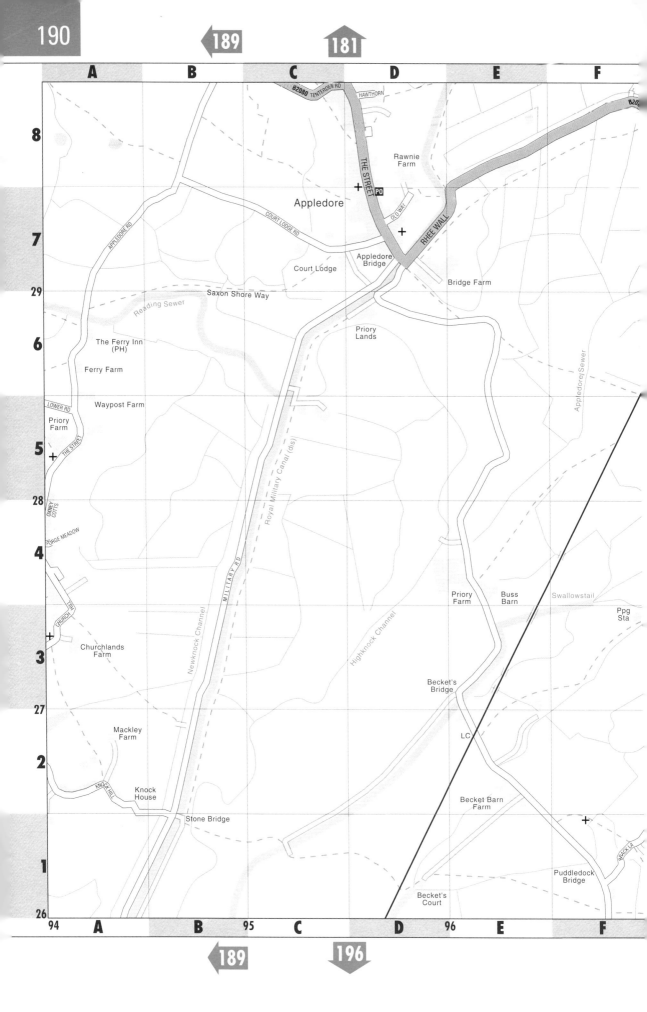

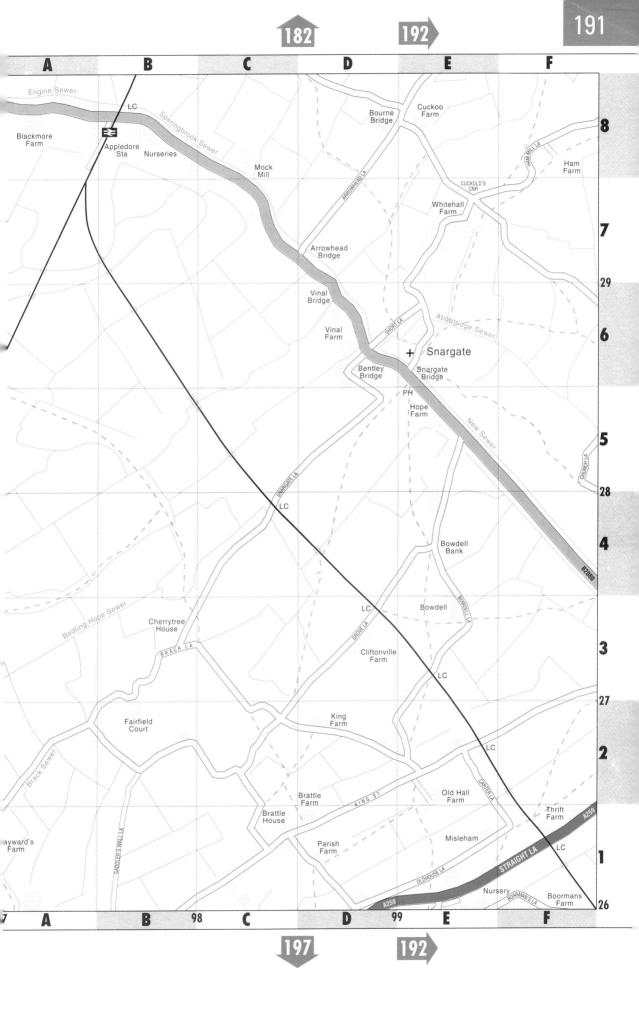

A B C D E F

Engine Sewer

LC

Blackmore
Farm

Appledore
Sta   Nurseries

Speringbrook Sewer

Mock
Mill

Bourne
Bridge

Cuckoo
Farm

HAM MILL LA

Ham
Farm

8

CUCKOLD'S
CNR

ARROWHEAD LA

Whitehall
Farm

7

Arrowhead
Bridge

29

Vinal
Bridge

SHORT LA

Abbatbridge Sewer

6

Vinal
Farm

+ Snargate

Bentley
Bridge

Snargate
Bridge

PH

Hope
Farm

New Sewer

5

SNARGATE LA

LC

28

Bowdell
Bank

4

B2080

Bedling Hope Sewer

Cherrytree
House

LC

Bowdell

BOWDELL LA

BRACK LA

Cliftonville
Farm

LC

3

GROVE LA

CHURCH LA

27

Fairfield
Court

King
Farm

LC

2

Brack Sewer

SADDLER'S WALL LA

Brattle
Farm

KING ST

Old Hall
Farm

CARTER LA

Thrift
Farm

A259

Brattle
House

Misleham

LC

Parish
Farm

STRAIGHT LA

1

ayward's
Farm

OLDHOUSE LA

Nursery

BOARMAN'S LA

Boormans
Farm

A259

26

7 A   B   98   C   D   99   E   F

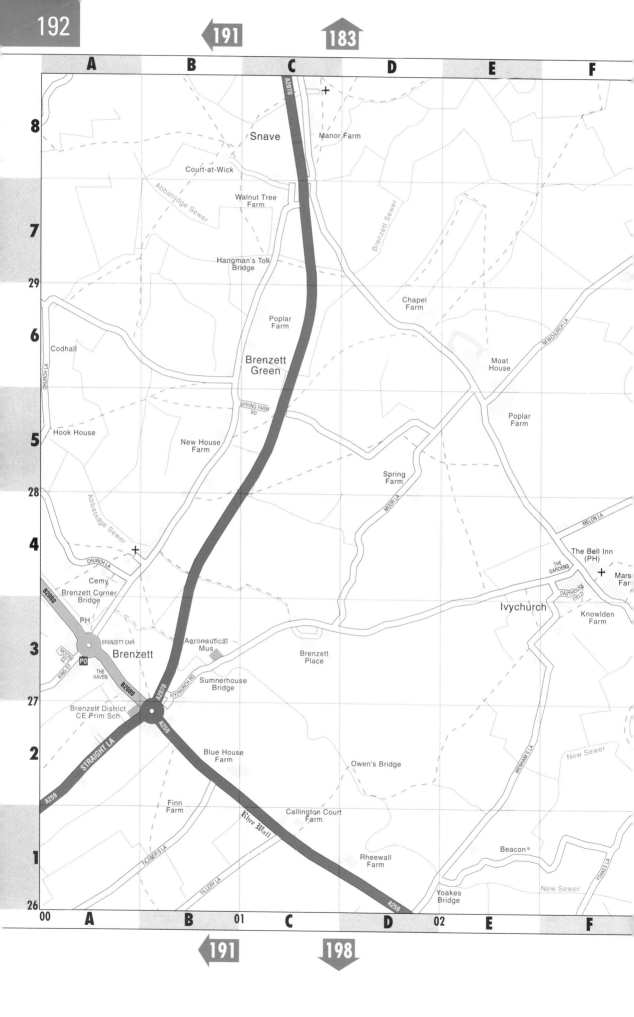

A B C D E F

8
29
7
6
5
28
4
3
27
2
1
26

00 01 02

A B C D E F

Snave

Manor Farm

Court-at-Wick

Walnut Tree Farm

Abbatridge Sewer

Brenzett Sewer

Hangman's Toll Bridge

Chapel Farm

Poplar Farm

Brenzett Green

Codhall

Moat House

CHURCH LA

NEWCHURCH LA

Poplar Farm

SPRING FARM RD

Hook House

New House Farm

Spring Farm

MOOR LA

MELON LA

Abbatridge Sewer

The Bell Inn (PH)

THE GARDENS

Mars Far

CHURCH LA

OASTHOUSE FIELD

Cemy

Brenzett Corner Bridge

Ivychurch

Knowlden Farm

B2080

PH

MOORE CL

Aeronautical Mus

Brenzett Place

KING ST

PO

THE HAVEN

BRENZETT CNR

Brenzett

SUMMERHOUSE BRIDGE

IVYCHURCH RD

A2070

B2080

Sumnerhouse Bridge

Brenzett District CE Prim Sch

A259

STRAIGHT LA

Blue House Farm

Owen's Bridge

WENHAM S LA

New Sewer

A259

Finn Farm

Rhee Wall

Callington Court Farm

TILLERY LA

Rheewall Farm

Beacon

New Sewer

YOAKES LA

A259

Yoakes Bridge

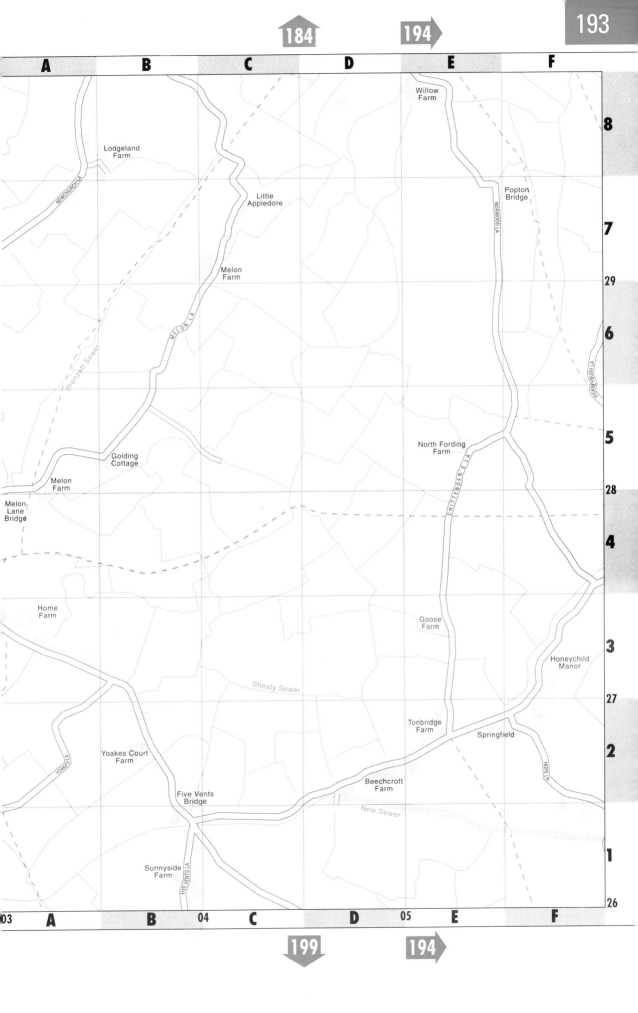

184
194

A B C D E F

8

7

29

6

5

28

4

3

27

2

1

26

Willow
Farm

Lodgeland
Farm

Little
Appledore

Popton
Bridge

NORWOOD LA

NEWCHURCH LA

Melon
Farm

Melon
Farm

Brenzett Sewer

MELON LA

FINN BUSH LA

Golding
Cottage

North Fording
Farm

CHITTENDEN'S LA

Melon
Farm

Melon
Lane
Bridge

Home
Farm

Goose
Farm

Honeychild
Manor

YOAKES LA

Sheaty Sewer

Tonbridge
Farm

Springfield

HOPE LA

Yoakes Court
Farm

Five Vents
Bridge

Beechcroft
Farm

New Sewer

Sunnyside
Farm

FIVE VENTS LA

A **B** **C** **D** **E** **F**

8

Oldhouse
Bridge

Blue House
Farm

Blackmanstone
Bridge

GAMMON'S FARM LA

Eastbridge Sewer

Pickneybush
Bridge

PICKNEY BUSH LA

Shealy Sewer

Tatnam
Farm

7

Pickney Bush
Farm

Clob sden Sewer

Tatnam
Bridge

Sellinge
Farm

Jefferstone Sewer

29

Pickney Bush
Farm Cotts

Marten
Farm

Swallowtail
Bridge

6

Turngates
Bridge

Wild
Refuge

ST MARY'S RD

5

PICKNEY BUSH LA

Haffenden
Farm

Shingle Hall
Farm

Sports
Gd

Golden Sands
Holiday Centre

28

RECTORY RD

WADES CL

Jefferstone
Lane
Sta

Jesson Court
Caravan Park

SEAWAY GDNS

SEAWAY
RD

Star
Inn

JEFFERSTONE LA

JEFFERSTONE GDNS

LC

MESSRP RD

SEAWAY CRES

St Mary in the Marsh

4

Jefferstone Sewer

OLD BAKERY
CL

PO

School
Farm

Brodnyx

LAUREL AVE

HOLLY RD

MAPLE DR

OAK DR

ASH TREE
CL

Romney, Hythe & Dymchurch Rly

ELM TREE RD

ASPEN

WILLOW DR

HAWTHORN DR

BEECHWOOD

ELM RD

FULMAR
CT

CEDAR CRES

3

New Sewer

Slinches

MEADS
WAY

TAYLOR'S CL

GRASSMERE

GAZEDOWN

BRIARS
RD

A259

27

NEW BRIDGE WAY

TAYLOR'S

JENNER'S WAY

FAIRWAY
CL

COAST DR

NEWLANDS

New Sewer

2

Winford
Bridge

DYMCHURCH RD

P

The
Warren

Littlestone
Golf Course

COAST RD

Paternosterford
Bridge

HOPE LA

1

Marlie Farm
Caravan & Camping Park

Brodynex
Farm

A259

Marlie
Farm

26

06 **A** **B** 07 **C** **D** 08 **E** **F**

A B C D E F

8

7

29

6

5

28

4

3

27

2

1

26

Marshall's Bridge

Sutton Farm

Dymchurch Cty Prim-Sch

Marshland Sewer

EASTBRIDGE RD

LC

Dymchurch Sta

Dunkirk End

Caravan Pks

ST MARY'S RD

LC

MARSHLANDS CL

MARSHLANDS CL

DUNKIRK CL

SUTTON RD

ST ANN'S RD

ORGARSWICK WAY

ORGARSWICK AVE

MILL RD

NEW INN RD

SEABOURNE RD

FISHER CL

Romney, Hythe & Dymchurch Rly

HIGHKNOCKE

Clobsden Sewer

DYMCHURCH RD

HYTHE RD

A259

New Hall CL

COUNTRY'S FIELD

LYNDHURST RD

MITCHAM RD

CHAPEL RD

HIGH ST

Dymchurch Wall

PAR LANE LA

WRAIGHTSFIELD

SARN CL

HIND CL

Ship CL

SEA WALL

INE CHARLES COBB CL

SYCAMORE GDNS

SYCAMORE CL

Mus

Dymchurch

Liby

PO

Martello Tower

Martello Tower

WINTON WAY

THE FAIRWAY

ST MARY'S GDNS

BROOKSIDE

DUNSTALL CL

DUNSTALL

DUNSTAL

ORCHARD RD

EDENS RD

RAYMOOR AVE

COBSDEN

COBSDEN RD

SPRING HOLLOW

WILLOWBANK CL

CRES

S MNS

KINGSLAND HOLLOW

HIGHLANDS CRES

St Mary's Bay

1 SHEARWATER HO
2 DUNLIN CT
3 TURNSTONE CT

190

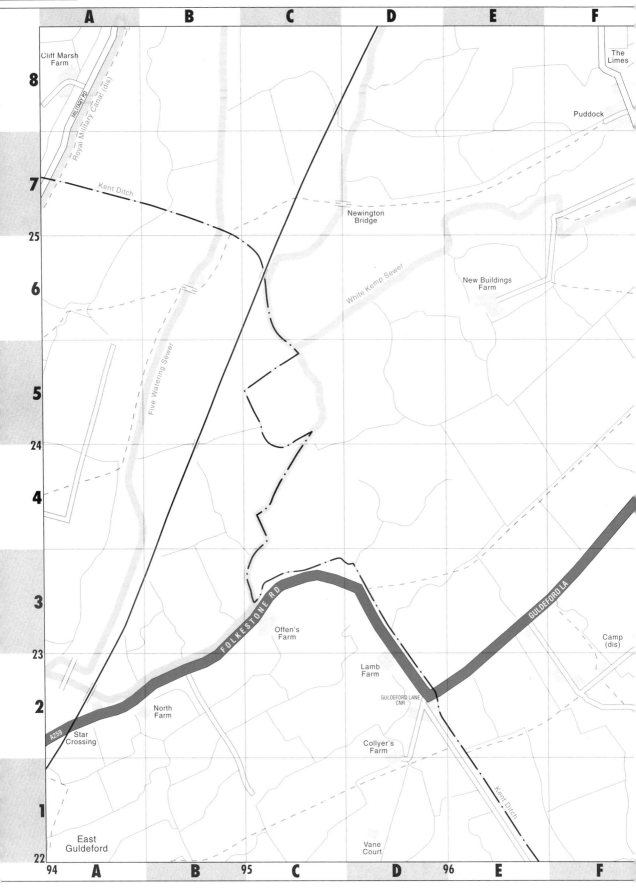

Cliff Marsh Farm

The Limes

Puddock

MILITARY RD

Royal Military Canal (dis)

Kent Ditch

Newington Bridge

White Kemp Sewer

New Buildings Farm

Five Watering Sewer

FOLKESTONE RD

GULDEFORD LA

Offen's Farm

Camp (dis)

Lamb Farm

North Farm

GULDEFORD LANE CNR

A259

Star Crossing

Collyer's Farm

Kent Ditch

East Guldeford

Vane Court

94   95   96

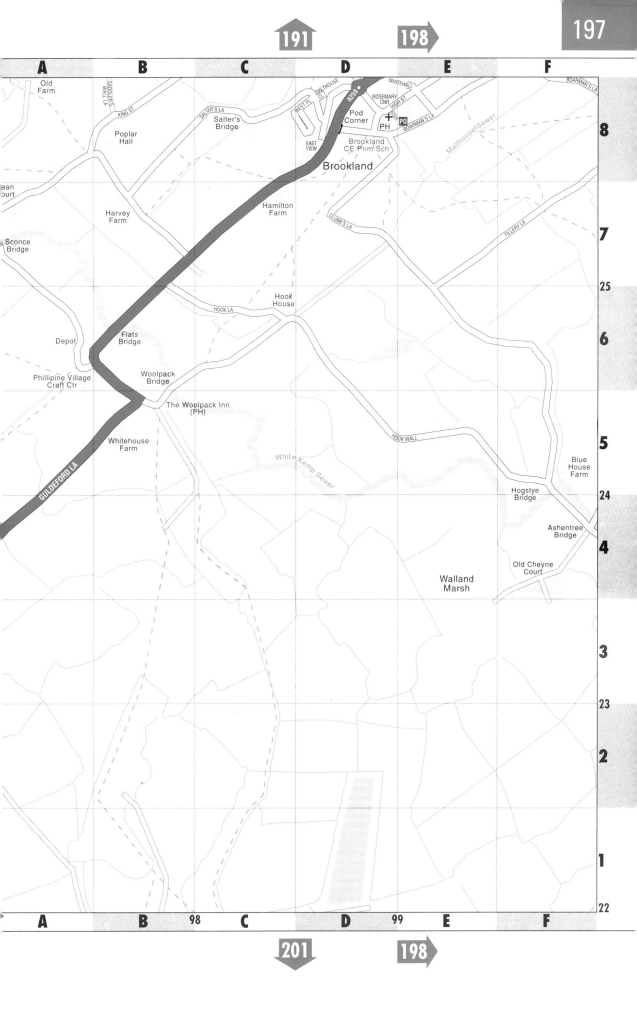

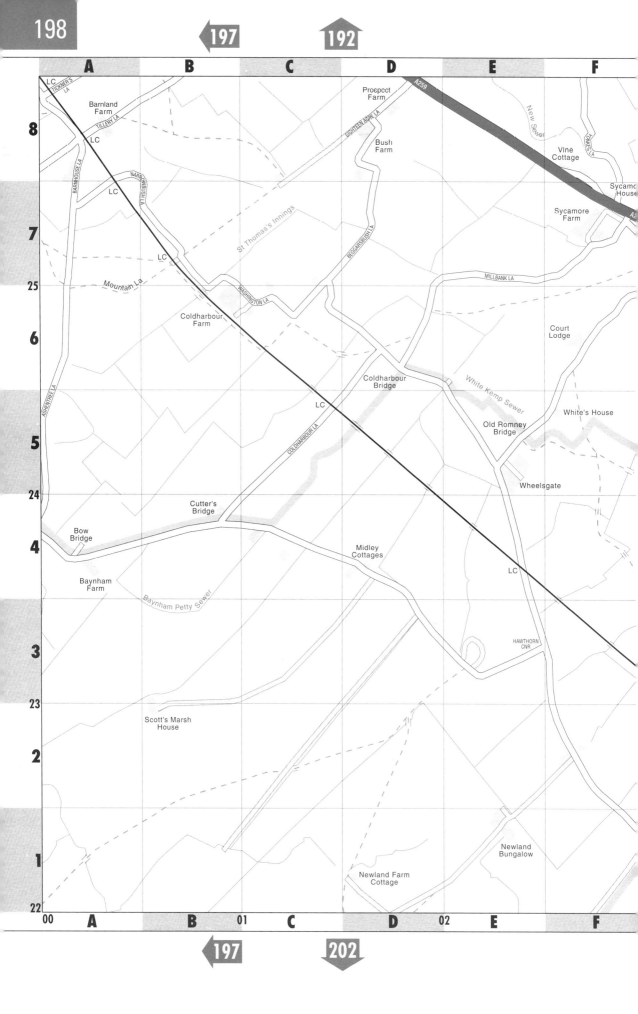

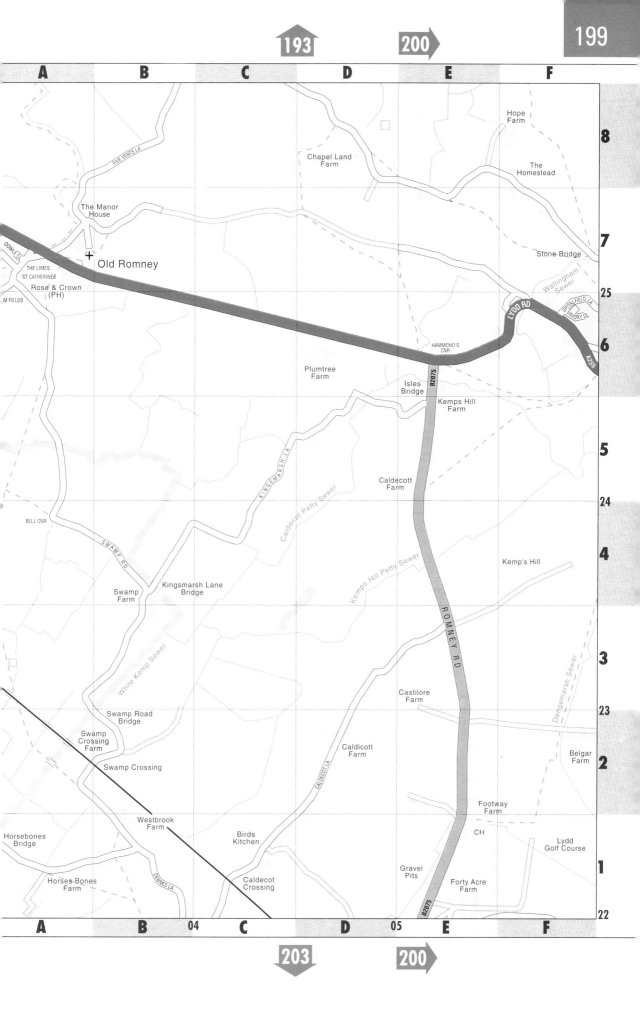

A B C D E F

8

Ellesmere Mews
Gloucester Mews
Clarendon Mews
St Mary's Rd
LOATHORNE CL
HAWKE
ELLIS DR
RICHMOND DR
BROADLANDS AVE
BROADLANDS CRES
BRISENDEN CL
A259
Warren House
DYMCHURCH RD
Warren Farm
Warren Inn (PH)
1 Melbury Mews
2 Pembroke Mews
3 Windsor Mews
4 Ryswick Mews
Littlestone Golf Course

7
New Romney Schs
COCKREED LA
WALNER GDNS
WALNER LA
FAIRFIELD RD
FAIRFIELD RD
IDLE LA
CRAFTHORNE LA
GEORGE LA
CANNON RD
PARK LODGE RD
Southlands Comm Comp Sch
New Romney Main Sewer
LANGPORT RD
Romney Warren Golf Course
Littlestone Tower
COAST RD
MARLBOROUGH CL
THE FAIRWAY
WARREN RD
MOUNTSIDE
CHERRY GDNS
ANNE ROYER CL
ORCHARD DR
MADEIRA RD
CH
CH

25
PRESCOTT HO
ASHFORD RD
MADDISON CL
Liby
B2071
STATION RD
Mountfield Row
PO
ST ANDREW'S RD
BLENHEIM RD
ST NICHOLAS RD

6
SPITALFIELD LA
SUSSEX RD
WEST ST
NORTH ST
HIGH ST
PO
TH
P
PO
THE CHURCH
SUTTON LA
THE CHURCHLANDS
MARSH CRES
ST MARTIN'S RD
HAYWARD RD
ENGLISH CL
DIMBERT RD
GREENLY WELLS CL
WELLS RD
MOUNTFIELD RD
Ind Est
New Romney Sta
WARREN RD
LINKS WAY
BLENHEIM RD
ST NICHOLAS RD
LITTLESTONE RD
B2071
Clovelly
Littlestone-on-Sea
SUSSEX RD
ST JOHN'S RD
A259 LYDD RD
CHURCH APP
CHURCH LA
TOOKEY RD
WILES AVE
CAREY RD
1 SPRINGWOOD CT
2 CHURCHLANDS HO
3 WILES HO
4 DERVILLE HO
5 ASHDOWN CRES
LEAROYD RD
STATION APP
QUEEN'S RD
NETHER AVE
ST NICHOLAS RD
THE SALTINGS
MARINE PAR
NO. 1

Cemy
1 GOLDEN SQ
2 MALTHOUSE COTTS
3 ROME HOUSE CNR
4 ROME RD
5 ST LAWRENCE CT
6 VICTORIA ST

NEW ROMNEY

VICTORIA RD W
VICTORIA CL
PARK RD
VICTORIA RD

5
THE APARTMENTS 1
GRAND CT 2
MULBERRY CT 3
Caravan Park
GRAND PAR
ARMADA CT

24
Caravan Park
CLARKE RD
CHANNEL WATCH
P
Sewage Works
MEEHAN RD

4
Romney Salts
Romney, Hythe & Dymchurch Railway
DUNES RD
ADIE RD N
ADIE RD
HARDY RD
COAST DR
IRB Sta

3
ALFRED RD
MEEHAN RD S

23
Jolly Fisherman (PH)
PO
P

2
MERRITT RD
THE PARADE

Greatstone Prim Sch
BALDWIN RD
LC

1
Northlade
Dengemarsh Sewer
Mockmill Sewer
ROBERTS RD
BALLARD RD
SEAVIEW RD
LC
Greatstone-on-Sea

22
06 A B 07 C D 08 E F

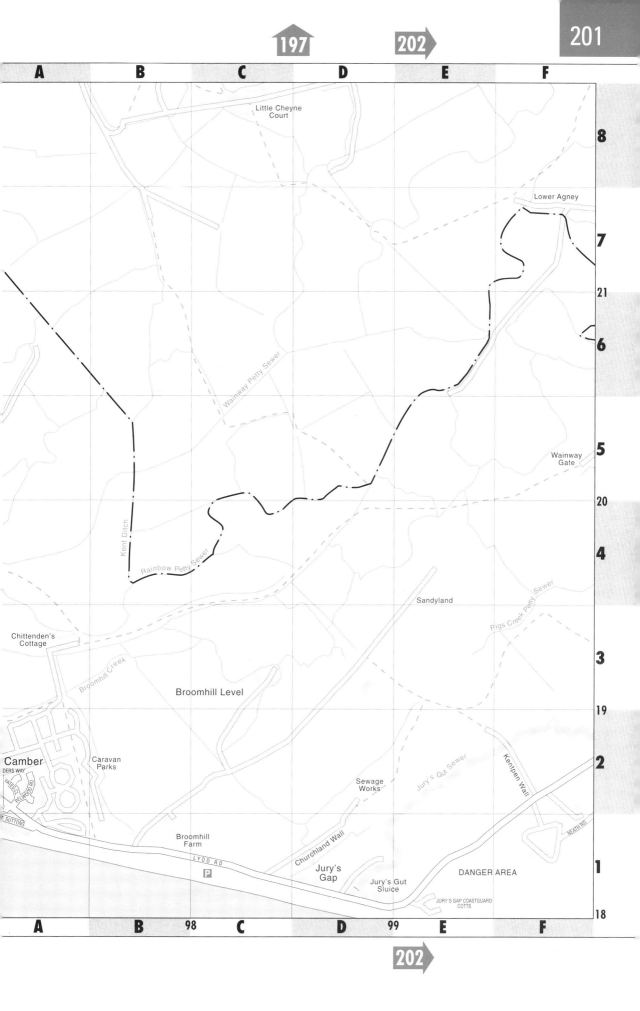

A B C D E F

8

Wainway Petty Sewer

Little
Scotney

Nod Wall

Tore Petty Sewer

Dering Petty Sewer

7

21

Tore Wall

6

Red
House

Scotney
Court
Farm

Burnthouse Wall

Sewage
Works

5

Oakhill Fleet

Scotney Bridge
North

Scotney

JURY'S GAP RD

DANGER ARE

20

Tore Wall

Scotney
Court

Jury's Gut Sewer

Scotney
Bridge South

4

3

The Forelands

Works

19

LC

Jury's Gap
Farm

Rosedale

DANGER AREA

2

NEATH RD

FERGUSON RD

Holmstone

LC

LC

SOUTH BROOKS RD

South
Brooks

Midrips

LC

LC

DANGER AREA

Lydd
Ranges

1

The
Wicks

18

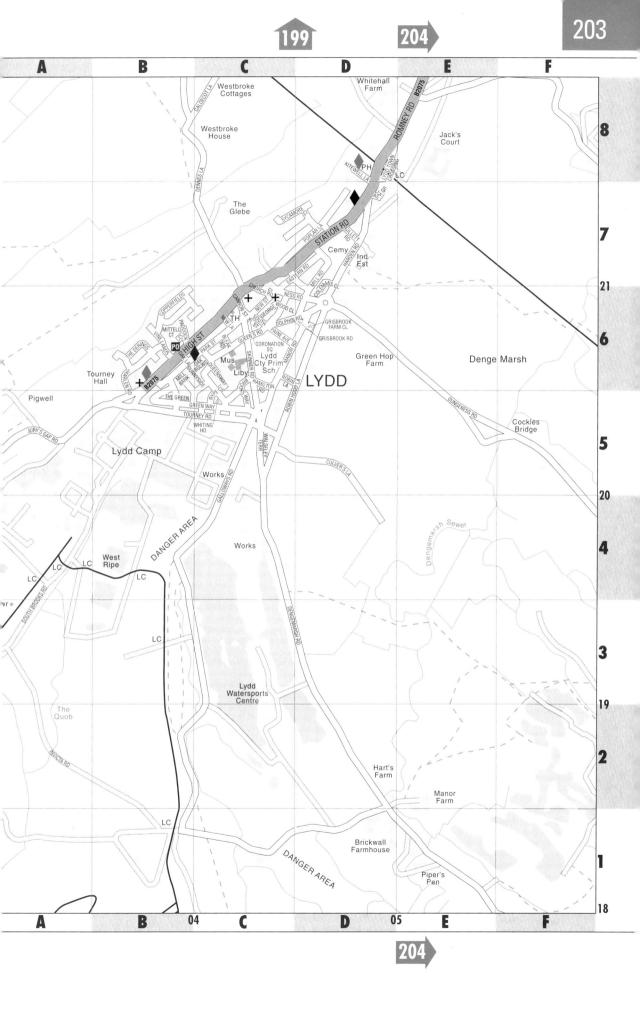

Westbroke Cottages

Whitehall Farm

ROMNEY RD

B2075

Jack's Court

8

Westbroke House

DENNESS LA

CALDECOT LA

PH

KITEWELL LA

LYDD TOWN CROSSING

LC

1ST GR

The Glebe

SYCAMORE

STATION RD

POPLAR LA

GILLET RD

7

HARGED RD

Cemy

Ind Est

COLEMAN'S CL

21

EASTERN RD

MILL RD

CHURCH RD

CANNON ST

NEW RD

NESS RD

WOOD CL

CORONATION SQ

DOLPHIN RD

GRISBROOK FARM CL

COPPERFIELDS

MITTELL CT

THE DERWICK

VINE YARDS

NEW LA

PLEAK RD

SOUTH

NEW RD

GEORGE

SKINNER RD

Mus

Liby

QUEEN'S RD

PAINE AVE

MANOR RD

GRISBROOK RD

6

TH

PO

HIGH ST

PARK RD

OVERSDWAY

Lydd Cty Prim Sch

HAMILTON

ROBIN LA

Green Hop Farm

Denge Marsh

Tourney Hall

KYRL GATE RD

B2075

MILL BANK

SUNNYSIDE

THE GREEN

RYPE

COMB WAY

WALSSLEY TERR

LYDD

Pigwell

GREEN WAY

TOURNEY RD

WHITING HO

DUNGENESS RD

Cockles Bridge

5

Lydd Camp

GALLOWAY'S RD

Works

CULVER'S LA

20

Dengemarsh Sewer

DANGER AREA

Works

4

LC

LC

LC

West Ripe

LC

SOUTH BROOKS RD

DENGEMARSH RD

LC

3

LC

Lydd Watersports Centre

19

The Quob

INVICTA RD

Hart's Farm

2

Manor Farm

LC

Brickwall Farmhouse

DANGER AREA

Piper's Pen

1

18

A   B   C   D   E   F

8

Romney Sands
Holiday Village

LC

Romney Sands
Sta

Caravan
Park   1
        2
        3

LA ROCCO 1
LA TAUSCO 2
LA GALAMINA 3

BEACHMONT CL

PRIOR RD

CHANNON RD

THE PARADE

DERVILLE RD

7

Lydd
Airport

Mockmill Sewer

WALLER RD

LEONARD RD

COLEVILLE CRES

BEATRICE
MEWS

21

HULL RD
TIDY RD

The Ship
(PH)

LCs

P

6

TAYLOR RD

FORT CL

LADE FORT
COTTS

LC

Lade

FORT CRES

LYDD CL

LE FORT CL SOUTH

WILLIAMSON RD

SAXTON RD

PLEASANCE RD N

Romney, Hythe & Dymchurch Railway

5

COAST DR

20

Works

Boulderwall
Farm

4

PLEASANCE ROAD CENTRAL

Conveyor

3

DUNGENESS RD

KERTON RD

Lydd-on-Sea

19

Halfway
Bush

2

Mast

BATTE

Denge
Marsh

Coastguard
Cottages

1

Walkers Outland
(RSPB Reserve)

18

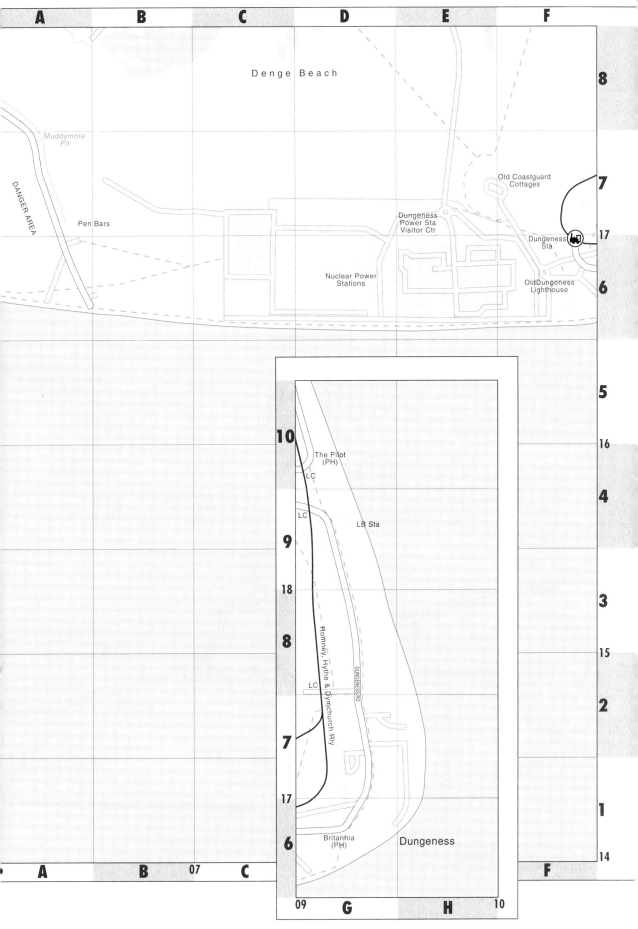

A　B　C　D　E　F

8

Denge Beach

Muddymore
Pit

DANGER AREA

7

Pen Bars

Old Coastguard
Cottages

17

Dungeness
Power Sta
Visitor Ctr

Dungeness
Sta

Nuclear Power
Stations

OldDungeness
Lighthouse

6

5

10

The Pilot
(PH)

16

LC

LC

4

LC

LB Sta

9

18

Romney, Hythe & Dymchurch Rly

3

8

DUNGENESS RD

15

LC

LC

2

7

17

1

6

Britannia
(PH)

Dungeness

14

A　B　07　C　F

09　G　H　10

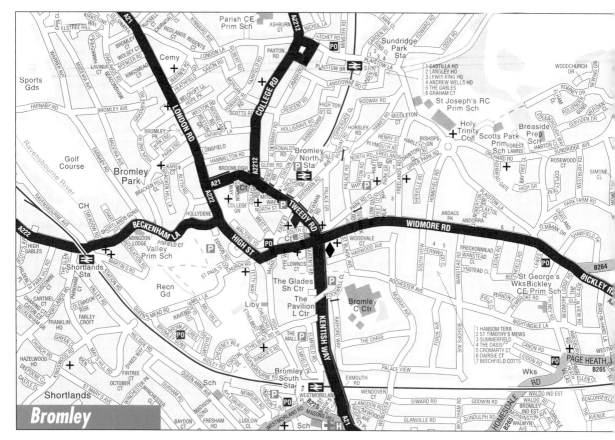

Bromley

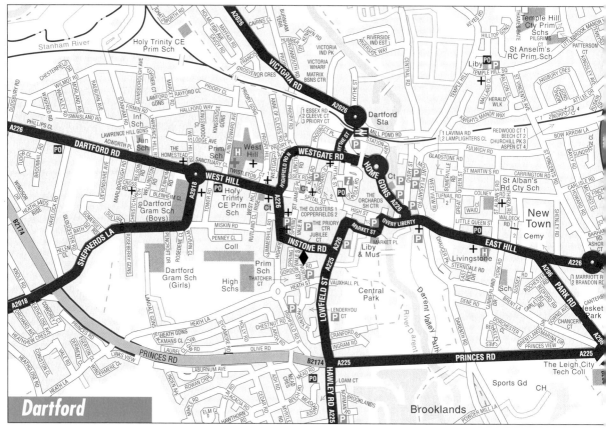

Dartford

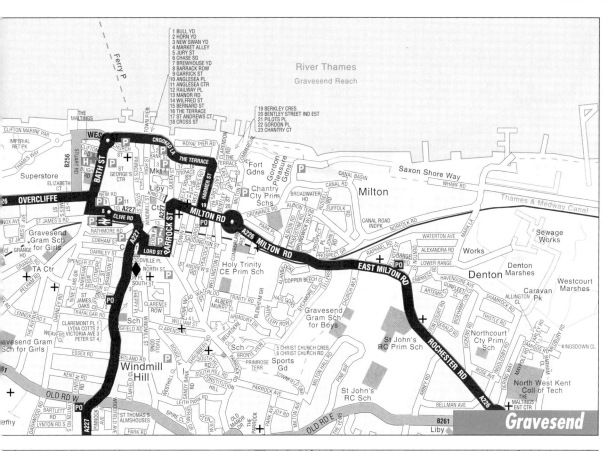

1 BULL YD
2 HORN YD
3 NEW SWAN YD
4 MARKET ALLEY
5 JURY ST
6 CHASE SQ
7 BREWHOUSE YD
8 BARRACK ROW
9 GARRICK ST
10 ANGLESEA PL
11 ANGLESEA CTR
12 RAILWAY PL
13 MANOR RD
14 WILFRED ST
15 BERNARD ST
16 THE TERRACE
17 ST ANDREWS CT
18 CROSS ST

19 BERKLEY CRES
20 BENTLEY STREET IND EST
21 PILOTS PL
22 GORDON PL
23 CHANTRY CT

Gravesend

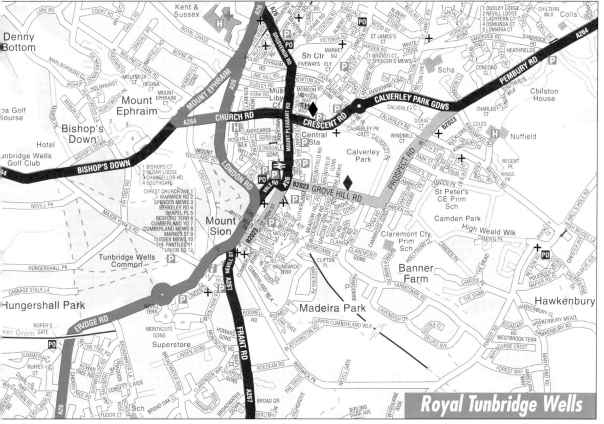

1 BISHOPS CT
2 GEDAR LODGE
3 CHANCELLOR HO
4 SOUTHGATE

CHRIST CHURCH AVE 1
WARWICK RD 2
SPENCER MEWS 3
BERKELEY RD 4
CHAPEL PL 5
BEDFORD TERR 6
CUMBERLAND YD 7
CUMBERLAND MEWS 8
MARKET 9
SUSSEX MEWS 10
THE PANTILES 11
UNION SQ 12

1 DUDLEY LODGE
2 NEVILL LODGE
3 LADYFERN CT
4 OSMUNDA CT
5 LOMARIA CT

1 GROVEN CT
2 SPENCER'S MEWS

Royal Tunbridge Wells

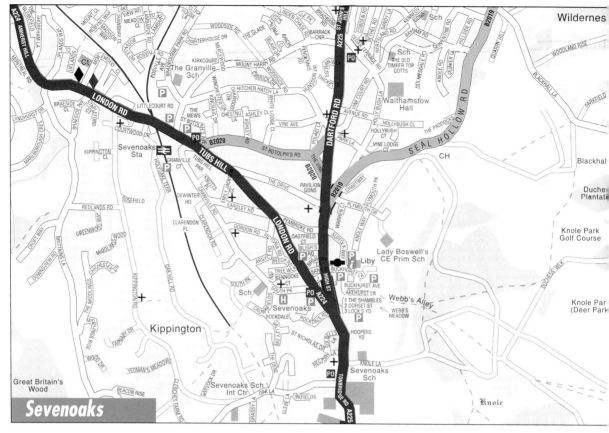

Sevenoaks

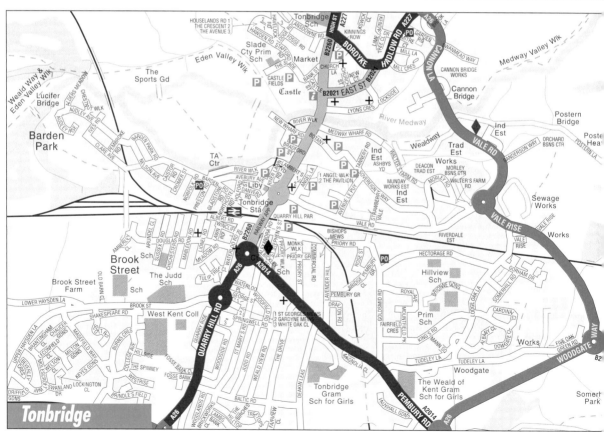

Tonbridge

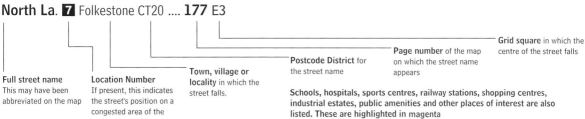

Street names are listed alphabetically and show the locality, the Postcode District, the page number and a reference to the square in which the name falls on the map page

North La. 7 Folkestone CT20 .... 177 E3

Full street name This may have been abbreviated on the map

Location Number If present, this indicates the street's position on a congested area of the map instead of the name

Town, village or locality in which the street falls.

Postcode District for the street name

Page number of the map on which the street name appears

Grid square in which the centre of the street falls

Schools, hospitals, sports centres, railway stations, shopping centres, industrial estates, public amenities and other places of interest are also listed. These are highlighted in magenta

Abbreviations used in the index

App	Approach	Cl	Close	Espl	Esplanade	N	North	S	South
Arc	Arcade	Comm	Common	Est	Estate	Orch	Orchard	Sq	Square
Ave	Avenue	Cnr	Corner	Gdns	Gardens	Par	Parade	Strs	Stairs
Bvd	Boulevard	Cotts	Cottages	Gn	Green	Pk	Park	Stps	Steps
Bldgs	Buildings	Ct	Court	Gr	Grove	Pas	Passage	St	Street, Saint
Bsns Pk	Business Park	Ctyd	Courtyard	Hts	Heights	Pl	Place	Terr	Terrace
Bsns Ctr	Business Centre	Cres	Crescent	Ho	House	Prec	Precinct	Trad Est	Trading Estate
Bglws	Bungalows	Dr	Drive	Ind Est	Industrial Estate	Prom	Promenade	Wlk	Walk
Cswy	Causeway	Dro	Drove	Intc	Interchange	Ret Pk	Retail Park	W	West
Ctr	Centre	E	East	Junc	Junction	Rd	Road	Yd	Yard
Cir	Circus	Emb	Embankment	La	Lane	Rdbt	Roundabout		

20/20 Ind Est. ME16 74 C8
Abbeville Ho. ME1 9 C4
Abbey Cl. Deal CT14 117 A5
Abbey Cl. Minster ME12 4 D6
Abbey Fields. ME13 62 E7
Abbey Fields Ct. ME13 62 E7
Abbey Gate. CT11 52 B5
Abbey Gate Cotts. ME20 53 F2
Abbey Gdns. CT2 67 A2
Abbey Gr. Minster, Thanet CT12 50 C5
Abbey Gr. Ramsgate CT11 52 B5
Abbey Pl. ME13 62 D8
Abbey Rd. Faversham ME13 62 D8
Abbey Rd. Gillingham ME8 11 A2
Abbey Rd. Kearsney CT16 148 D4
Abbey Rd. River CT15 & CT17 148 D1
Abbey Sch The. CT8 27 E8
Abbey St. ME13 62 D8
Abbey Way. TN24 140 A1
Abbeyview Dr. ME12 4 B6
Abbot's Hill. CT11 52 E6
Abbots Barton Wlk. CT1 88 B7
Abbots Field. ME16 74 B2
Abbots Pl. CT1 66 F1
Abbots Rd. ME13 62 F7
Abbots The. CT17 166 C8
Abbots Wlk. TN25 123 E2
Abbotsbury Hts. CT2 67 B4
Abbott Rd. CT20 178 E6
Abbotts Cl. ME1 9 B3
Aberdeen Cl. CT3 47 D3
Aberdeen Ho. 8 ME15 97 E7
Abigail Cres. ME5 32 A1
Abingdon Gr. CT3 47 D3
Abingdon Rd. ME16 74 A2
Abinger Dr. ME5 32 D2
Absalam Ct. ME8 11 C2
Acacia Ho. ME12 1 C2
Acacia Terr. ME10 36 C4
Academy Dr. ME7 10 F1
Achilles Rd. ME5 32 C2
Ackerey Ct. TN23 155 F6
Ackholt Rd. CT3 113 A5
Acol Hill. CT7 27 B4
Acorn Pl. ME15 97 E6
Acorn Rd. ME7 10 F4
Acorn St. ME12 1 D1
Acre Cl. ME4 9 E1
Acre Ct. CT17 166 C8
Acre The. CT16 148 F8
Acton La. TN30 188 F4
Acton Rd. CT5 20 D2
Ada Rd. CT1 87 D6
Adam Cl. ME17 96 D3
Adam Ct. 1 CT9 8 B2
Adams Cl. TN30 167 B1
Adbert Dr. ME15 96 B4
Addelam Cl. CT14 117 A4
Addelam Rd. CT14 117 A4
Addington Pl. CT11 52 E6
Addington Rd. Margate CT9 7 J2
Addington Rd. Sittingbourne ME10 36 E3
Addington Sq. CT9 7 J2
Addington St. Margate CT9 7 J2
Addington St. Ramsgate CT11 52 D6
Addiscombe Gdns. CT9 7 J1
Addiscombe Rd. CT9 8 A1
Addison Cotts. TN30 188 D3
Adelaide Dr. ME10 36 C4
Adelaide Gdns. Halfway Houses ME12 3 E6
Adelaide Gdns. 16 Ramsgate CT11 52 E6
Adelaide Pl. CT1 87 F8
Adelaide Rd. Elvington CT15 114 B1
Adelaide Rd. Gillingham ME7 10 C4
Aden Terr. 1 ME14 75 A7
Adie Rd. TN28 200 D3
Adie Rd N. TN28 200 D4
Adisham CE Prim Sch. CT3 112 D8
Adisham Downs Rd. CT3 & CT4 90 B2
Adisham Dr. ME16 74 B7
Adisham Gn. ME10 36 F8
Adisham Rd. Bekesbourne CT4 89 E3
Adisham Rd. Wingham CT3 91 A4
Adisham Rd. Womenswold CT3 & CT4 112 C2
Adisham Sta. CT3 112 E8
Adisham Way. CT9 8 C1
Admiral's Wlk. ME4 9 F7
Admirals Wlk. Chatham ME5 32 B3
Admirals Wlk. Halfway Houses ME12 3 E6
Admirals Wlk. Hythe CT21 176 C1
Admirals Wlk. Tenterden TN30 167 C1
Admiralty Terr. 1 ME4 10 A7
Admiralty Wlk. CT5 43 A7
Adrian Mews. CT8 7 D1
Adrian Sq. CT8 7 D1
Adrian St. CT16 & CT17 166 D7
Aerodrome Rd. Bekesbourne CT3 & CT4 89 E3
Aerodrome Rd. Hawkinge CT18 163 A4
Afghan Rd. Broadstairs CT10 29 F8
Afghan Rd. Chatham ME4 9 E4
Agester La. CT4 129 A4
Ainsdale Cl. CT19 178 B7
Aintree Ho. 1 ME15 97 F6
Aintree Rd. ME5 32 C3
Airedale Cl. CT9 8 A1
Airfield View. ME12 17 C8
Aisne Dr. CT1 67 D1
Ajax Rd. ME1 31 C8
Alamein Ave. ME5 31 F7
Alamein Cl. CT16 149 F3
Albany Dr. CT6 22 D4
Albany Ho. 15 CT17 166 D7
Albany Pl. CT17 166 D7
Albany Rd. Capel-le-F CT18 164 C1
Albany Rd. Chatham ME4 10 B2
Albany Rd. Gillingham ME7 10 D4
Albany Rd. Rochester ME1 9 C4
Albany Rd. Sittingbourne ME10 36 E3
Albany St. ME14 75 B5
Albany Terr. Chatham ME4 9 E4
Albany Terr. Gillingham ME7 10 D4
Albemarle Rd. Ashford TN24 139 F1
Albemarle Rd. Chatham ME5 32 C2
Albert Costain Ct. 1 CT20 178 D5
Albert Ct. 16 CT5 20 D2
Albert La. CT21 176 C1
Albert Manor. ME7 10 B5
Albert Pl. ME2 9 B7
Albert Rd. Ashford TN24 139 B3
Albert Rd. Broadstairs CT10 29 E8
Albert Rd. Canterbury CT1 88 B8
Albert Rd. Capel-le-F CT18 164 C2
Albert Rd. Chatham ME4 10 A3
Albert Rd. Deal CT14 117 C6
Albert Rd. Dover CT16 149 D1
Albert Rd. Folkestone CT19 178 D6
Albert Rd. Gillingham ME7 10 C4
Albert Rd. Hythe CT21 176 B1
Albert Rd. Margate CT9 7 H2
Albert Rd. Ramsgate CT11 52 F7
Albert Rd. Rochester ME1 9 C3
Albert St. Maidstone ME14 74 F6
Albert St. Ramsgate CT11 52 E6
Albert St. Whitstable CT5 20 D2
Albert Terr. Margate CT9 7 I2
Albert Terr. Minster ME12 5 A5
Alberta Cl. CT16 149 B3
Albion Cl. CT6 46 A8
Albion Hill. 6 CT11 52 E6
Albion La. CT6 46 A8
Albion Mews. CT11 52 F6
Albion Mews Rd. 3 CT20 178 D4
Albion Pl. Ashford TN24 156 E7
Albion Pl. Canterbury CT1 67 A1
Albion Pl. Faversham ME13 62 C7
Albion Pl. Hythe CT21 176 D2
Albion Pl. Maidstone ME14 75 B4
Albion Pl. Newington ME9 35 B6
Albion Pl. Ramsgate CT11 52 E6
Albion Pl. Sheerness ME12 1 D2
Albion Rd. Birchington CT7 27 A7
Albion Rd. Broadstairs CT10 29 F6
Albion Rd. Chatham ME5 32 B2
Albion Rd. Deal CT14 117 D8
Albion Rd. Eastry CT13 93 A2
Albion Rd. Folkestone CT19 178 D6
Albion Rd. Margate CT9 8 B3
Albion Rd. Ramsgate CT11 52 F7
Albion St. CT10 30 B4
Albion Terr. ME10 36 E6
Albion Villas. 6 CT20 178 D4
Albuhera Sq. CT1 67 D1
Albury Cl. ME5 32 D2
Alchins Cotts. ME17 96 E2
Alder Cl. ME12 3 A8
Alder Rd. CT19 178 C6
Aldergate La. CT21 & TN29 174 C1
Alderney Gdns. CT10 29 E5
Aldershot Rd. ME5 32 A7
Aldington Cl. ME5 32 B5
Aldington Cnr. TN25 173 A6
Aldington Cty Prim Sch. TN25 173 A5
Aldington La. ME14 76 D8
Aldington Rd. Lympne CT21 174 E3
Aldington Rd. Maidstone ME14 75 F4
Aldon Cl. ME14 75 C6
Aldon Ct. ME14 75 C6
Aldred Rd. ME13 62 C6
Aldridge Cl. CT6 22 B3
Alexander Cl. ME13 62 B8
Alexander Ct. Rochester ME2 9 B8
Alexander Ct. 6 Sittingbourne ME10 36 E5
Alexander Dr. ME13 62 B7
Alexandra Ave. ME7 10 E4
Alexandra Cl. ME10 36 E7
Alexandra Ct. CT21 176 A1
Alexandra Gdns. CT20 178 D4
Alexandra Glen. ME5 32 A1
Alexandra Homes. CT9 7 I1
Alexandra Hospl The. ME5 54 A8
Alexandra Pl. 1 CT16 149 C1
Alexandra Rd. Birchington CT7 27 A5
Alexandra Rd. Broadstairs CT10 30 B4
Alexandra Rd. Capel-le-F CT18 164 C2
Alexandra Rd. Chatham ME4 10 B2
Alexandra Rd. Deal CT14 117 D2
Alexandra Rd. Kingsdown CT14 134 C5
Alexandra Rd. Margate CT9 28 E8
Alexandra Rd. Ramsgate CT11 52 D8
Alexandra Rd. Sheerness ME12 1 E2
Alexandra Rd. Whitstable CT5 43 C8
Alexandra St. Folkestone CT19 178 E6
Alexandra St. Maidstone ME14 74 F6
Alexandra Terr. CT9 7 I1
Alexandria Dr. CT6 22 C5
Alfred Cl. Canterbury CT1 87 C6
Alfred Cl. Chatham ME4 10 B2
Alfred Cotts. CT11 52 E7
Alfred Rd. Ashford TN24 156 D7
Alfred Rd. Birchington CT7 26 D8
Alfred Rd. Canterbury CT1 87 C6
Alfred Rd. Dover CT16 149 B2
Alfred Rd. Littlestone-on-S TN28 200 D3
Alfred Rd. Margate CT9 8 B1
Alfred Row. CT14 117 D7
Alfred Sq. CT14 117 D7
Alicia Ave. CT9 28 A8
Alison Cl. Birchington CT7 27 B8
Alison Cl. Whitfield CT16 149 A6
Alison Cres. CT16 149 A7
Alkham Cl. CT9 8 F2
Alkham Rd. Maidstone ME14 75 C5
Alkham Rd. Temple Ewell CT15 & CT16 148 C4
Alkham Valley Rd. Alkham CT15 147 E1
Alkham Valley Rd. Hawkinge CT18 & CT15 163 E4
All Saints' Ave. CT9 7 H1
All Saints' CE Prim Sch. Chatham ME4 10 A3
All Saints CE Prim Sch. Maidstone ME15 75 A3
All Saints' Cl. CT5 20 F1
All Saints Hospl. ME4 10 A2
All Saints Ind Est. CT9 7 I1
All Saints La. 2 CT1 87 F8
All Saints Rd. ME10 37 C4
All Saints View. ME13 41 E2
All Souls CE Prim Sch. CT19 177 E6
Allan Rd. CT5 42 E6
Alland Grange La. CT12 27 E2
Allen Ave. CT8 27 D7
Allen Cl. ME5 32 C6
Allen Ct. ME12 4 A5
Allen Field. TN23 155 F8
Allen St. ME14 75 B5
Allenby Ave. CT14 117 B5
Allenby Rd. CT12 29 C2
Allenby Wlk. ME10 36 B5
Allendale St. 2 CT19 178 D6
Alliance Rd. CT11 52 F6
Allington Prim Sch. ME16 74 C7
Allington Rd. ME8 11 A3
Allington Way. ME16 74 B6
Allison Ave. ME7 10 E1
Allnutt Mill Cl. ME15 74 E2
Allsworth Cl. ME9 35 B6
Alma Pl. 2 Canterbury CT1 67 A1
Alma Pl. Ramsgate CT11 52 E7
Alma Pl. Rochester ME2 9 A7
Alma Rd. Folkestone CT20 177 D5
Alma Rd. Herne Bay CT6 23 C5
Alma Rd. Margate CT9 7 J1
Alma Rd. Ramsgate CT11 52 E8
Alma Rd. Sheerness ME12 1 D2
Alma St. Canterbury CT1 67 A1
Alma St. Sheerness ME12 1 E2
Alma Street Pas. ME12 1 E2
Almon Pl. ME1 9 D5
Almond Cl. Ashford TN23 138 F5
Almond Cl. Broadstairs CT10 29 C4
Almond Cl. Whitstable CT5 21 D1
Almond Gr. ME7 33 A4
Almond Tree Cl. ME12 3 A8
Almonds The. ME14 76 A4
Almshouse Rd. ME13 104 C7
Almshouses. 7 CT1 88 A8
Alpha Rd. Birchington CT7 27 A7
Alpha Rd. Ramsgate CT11 52 D6
Alsager Ave. ME11 2 F3
Alsops Rd. TN24 156 E7
Alston Cl. ME12 4 C7
Altbarn Ind Est. ME5 54 C8
Alvis Ave. CT6 22 A4
Amage Rd. TN25 141 C8
Amage Road Cotts. TN25 124 B1
Amanda Cl. ME5 31 F3
Amber Cl. ME9 38 D2

Amber La. ME17 .... 98 A1
Amber Way. ME17 .... 98 B1
Ambleside. Faversham ME13 .. 62 E6
Ambleside. Sittingbourne ME10 .. 37 C3
Ambley Gn. ME7 .... 33 A8
Ambley Rd. ME7 .... 33 B8
Ambrose Hill. ME4 & ME5 .. 10 C2
Amels Hill. ME9 .... 56 F8
Ames Ave. ME14 .... 76 A4
Amethyst Ave. ME5 .... 31 E6
Amherst Cl. Maidstone ME16 .. 74 D4
Amherst Cl. Margate CT9 .. 8 C1
Amherst Hill. ME4 .... 10 A6
Amherst Rd. ME1 .... 9 D3
Amherst Redoubt. ME4 .. 10 A5
Amies Ho. ME15 .... 96 F3
Amos. Herne Bay CT6 .. 23 C3
Amos Cl. Sheldwich ME13 .. 83 C5
Amsa Cnr. CT16 .... 150 B1
Amsbury Rd. ME17 .... 96 B2
Amshurst Villas. ME15 .. 96 A4
Anchor Bsns Pk. ME10 .. 37 B6
Anchor Hill. 4 CT9 .... 7 J2
Anchor La. Deal CT14 .. 117 C6
Anchor La. Sheerness ME12 .. 1 B3
Anchor Rd. ME1 .... 9 C1
Ancress Cl. CT2 .... 67 A4
Andover Wlk. 12 ME15 .. 97 F6
Andrew Broughton Way.
ME14 .... 75 B4
Andrew Manor. ME7 .. 10 C6
Andrews Wlk. ME10 .. 36 B5
Anerley Cl. ME16 .... 74 D7
Angel Cotts. ME8 .... 12 A4
Anglesey Ave. ME15 .. 97 A7
Anglesey Cl. ME5 .... 32 B7
Ann's Rd. CT11 .... 52 E8
Anna Pk. CT7 .... 26 F8
Anne Boleyn Cl. ME12 .. 5 E3
Anne Cl. CT7 .... 27 B7
Anne Green Wlk. 8 CT1 .. 67 B2
Anne Roper Cl. TN28 .. 200 E6
Anne's Rd. CT10 .... 30 C7
Ansell Ave. ME4 .... 10 A1
Anselm Ave. ME10 .... 36 E4
Anselm Rd. CT17 .... 166 A8
Anson Cl. Broadstairs CT10 .. 29 D3
Anson Cl. Chatham ME5 .. 32 C6
Anstee Rd. CT16 & CT17 .. 149 C1
Anthony Cres. CT5 .... 43 B6
Anthonys Way. ME2 .... 9 E8
Anvil Cl. CT7 .... 27 A6
Anzio Cres. CT16 .... 149 E2
Anzio Ho. 15 CT1 .... 67 B2
Apartments The. TN28 .. 200 A6
Apollo Ho. ME5 .... 32 A6
Appleby Cl. ME1 .... 31 D7
Appledore Ave. ME12 .. 3 B8
Appledore Cl. CT9 .... 8 C1
Appledore Cres. CT19 .. 177 D7
Appledore Ct. ME16 .. 74 C7
Appledore Rd.
Appledore TN26 & TN30 .. 190 A7
Appledore Rd. Brattle TN26 .. 181 B8
Appledore Rd.
Brattle TN26 & TN30 .. 181 C7
Appledore Rd. Gillingham ME8 .. 11 A3
Appledore Rd. Tenterden TN30 .. 179 E7
Appledown Way. CT1 .. 88 D5
Appleford Dr. ME12 .. 3 F7
Applegarth Pk. CT5 .. 43 A6
Approach Rd. Broadstairs CT10 .. 30 A4
Approach Rd. Dover CT17 .. 166 A6
Approach Rd. Margate CT9 .. 8 A2
Approach Rd.
Shepherdswell CT15 .. 130 D5
April Rise. Birchington CT7 .. 26 D8
April Rise. Whitstable CT5 .. 43 B7
Apsley Cotts. CT4 .... 86 D3
Apsley Rd. TN23 .... 139 B2
Aragon Cl. TN23 .... 155 E7
Archbishop's
CE Sec Sch The. CT2 .. 66 C5
Archcliffe Rd. CT17 .... 166 C5
Archer Rd. Chatham ME5 .. 32 B6
Archer Rd. Folkestone CT19 .. 178 D6
Archer's Court Rd.
CT15 & CT16 .... 149 B7
Archers Court Sch. CT16 .. 149 B5
Archery Sq. CT17 .... 117 D3
Archway Ct. 1 ME2 .... 9 B8
Archway Rd. Ramsgate CT11 .. 52 E6
Archway Rd. Sheerness ME12 .. 1 B3
Arcon Cl. TN23 .... 156 A7
Arcon Rd. TN23 .... 156 A7
Arden Bsns Pk. ME2 .. 9 E8
Arden Cty Jun Sch. ME7 .. 10 D6
Arden Dr. TN24 .... 139 C3
Arden Rd. Faversham ME13 .. 62 E7
Arden Rd. Herne Bay CT6 .. 23 C2
Arden St. ME7 .... 10 C6
Ardenlee Dr. ME14 .. 75 B5
Arethusa Rd. ME1 .... 31 C8
Argent Bsns Pk. ME11 .. 3 A3
Argent Rd. ME11 .... 3 A2
Argyle Ave. CT9 .... 7 G1
Argyle Cl. ME1 .... 31 E8
Argyle Gdns. CT9 .... 7 G1
Argyle Rd. CT5 .... 20 D1
Argyll Dr. CT10 & CT11 .. 29 D7
Ark Cotts. CT18 .... 161 D4
Ark La. CT14 .... 117 D7
Arkley Rd. CT6 .... 22 F4
Arklow Sq. 4 CT11 .. 52 F7
Arlington. TN23 .... 155 F8

Arlington Gdns. CT9 .... 29 C8
Arlington Ho. CT9 .... 7 H2
Arlington Sq. CT9 .... 7 H2
Arlott Cl. ME14 .... 74 F6
Armada Cl. TN28 .... 200 E5
Armada Ct. ME4 .... 9 E1
Armada Way. ME4 .... 9 F3
Armourers Wlk. CT16 .. 149 A3
Armstrong Rd. ME15 .. 75 A1
Armstrong Sq. CT6 .. 22 A3
Arnhem Dr. ME5 .... 31 F7
Arnold Rd. Chartham CT4 .. 86 C2
Arnold Rd. 5 Margate CT9 .. 7 J1
Arnolde Cl. ME2 .... 9 E7
Arran Mews. 4 CT1 .. 67 B2
Arran Rd. ME15 .... 97 A6
Arrowhead La. TN26 .. 191 D7
Arthur Kennedy Cl. ME13 .. 63 F3
Arthur Rd. Birchington CT7 .. 26 D8
Arthur Rd. Deal CT14 .. 117 A3
Arthur Rd. Gillingham ME8 .. 33 E7
Arthur Rd. Hythe CT21 .. 176 C1
Arthur Rd. Margate CT9 .. 8 A3
Arthur Rd. Rochester ME1 .. 9 D3
Arthur Salmon Cl. ME13 .. 62 B7
Arthur St. 2 Folkestone CT19 .. 178 E6
Arthur St. Sittingbourne ME10 .. 36 E4
Artillery Gdns. 12 CT1 .. 67 A1
Artillery Ho. 13 CT1 .. 67 A1
Artillery Rd. CT11 .... 52 F7
Artillery St. 11 CT1 .. 67 A1
Arundel Ave. ME10 .... 36 E1
Arundel Cl. ME5 .... 32 D1
Arundel Rd. Cliffs End CT12 .. 51 D7
Arundel Rd. Margate CT9 .. 8 B2
Arundel St. ME14 .... 74 F6
Ascot Ave. ME5 .... 32 C2
Ascot Gdns. CT8 .... 27 E7
Ascot Ho. 2 ME15 .... 97 F6
Ash Cl. Ashford TN23 .. 138 E3
Ash Cl. Broadstairs CT10 .. 29 C4
Ash Cl. Chatham ME5 .. 10 C1
Ash Cl. Gillingham ME8 .. 11 B3
Ash Cl. Herne Bay CT6 .. 22 F1
Ash Cl. River CT17 .... 148 E3
Ash Cres. CT3 .... 46 E1
Ash Gr. Elvington CT15 .. 114 B2
Ash Gr. Lydd TN29 .... 203 D7
Ash Gr. Maidstone ME16 .. 74 C6
Ash Meadows. TN24 .. 156 F7
Ash Rd. Aylesham CT3 .. 112 E5
Ash Rd. Sandwich CT13 .. 72 E2
Ash Tree Cl. TN29 .... 194 F3
Ash Tree La. ME5 .... 10 D1
Ash Tree Rd. 5 CT19 .. 178 E6
Ashbank Cotts. ME17 .. 99 B7
Ashbee Gdns. CT6 .... 23 C5
Ashborne Cl. TN24 .. 139 D6
Ashburn Gdns. CT6 .. 23 C5
Ashburnham Rd.
Maidstone ME14 .... 75 B8
Ashburnham Rd.
Ramsgate CT11 .... 52 C7
Ashburton Cl. TN24 .. 139 E2
Ashdale Ho. TN23 .... 139 C2
Ashdown Cl. Herne Bay CT6 .. 23 B2
Ashdown Cl. Maidstone ME16 .. 74 D3
Ashdown Cres. TN28 .. 200 B6
Ashdown Ct. TN24 .. 139 C3
Ashdown Rd. ME17 & ME9 .. 79 F3
Ashen Tree Cotts. CT3 .. 70 B1
Ashen Tree La. CT16 .. 166 E8
Ashenden Cl. CT1 .... 87 C5
Ashendene Gr. ME15 .. 68 A6
Ashentree La. TN29 .. 198 A5
Ashford Bsns Pk. TN24 .. 157 A6
Ashford Bsns Point. TN24 .. 156 F5
Ashford Dr. ME17 .... 99 D3
Ashford East Stour
Cty Prim Sch. TN24 .. 156 D6
Ashford Golf Course. TN24 .. 139 A6
Ashford Hospl. TN23 .. 139 A3
Ashford Int Sta. TN23 .. 139 C1
Ashford Rd.
Bethersden TN26 & TN23 .. 153 C4
Ashford Rd.
Chartham CT4 & CT1 .. 86 C3
Ashford Rd.
Folkestone CT18 & CT19 .. 177 B7
Ashford Rd. Godmersham CT4 .. 107 C4
Ashford Rd. Great Chart TN23 .. 155 B8
Ashford Rd. Hamstreet TN26 .. 170 F1
Ashford Rd.
Harrietsham ME17 .... 100 C6
Ashford Rd.
Kingsnorth TN23 & TN26 .. 156 A4
Ashford Rd. Maidstone,Grove Green
ME14 & ME15 .... 75 D4
Ashford Rd.
Maidstone,Silver Hill ME14 .. 76 D3
Ashford Rd.
New Romney TN28 .... 200 A6
Ashford Rd. Sellindge TN25 .. 159 B1
Ashford Rd. Sheldwich ME13 .. 83 C4
Ashford Rd. Tenterden TN30 .. 179 B8
Ashford Rd.
Westenhanger TN25 .. 174 E6
Ashford Rd.Westenhanger
CT21 & TN25 & CT18 .. 175 C6
Ashford Sch. TN23 .. 139 C2
Ashford Sta. TN23 .... 139 C1
Ashgrove. TN23 .... 138 F5
Ashington Cl. ME10 .. 36 C5
Ashley Ave. CT19 .... 177 E6
Ashley Cl. Ramsgate CT12 .. 29 B2
Ashley Dr. CT5 .... 43 A7
Ashley Ho. CT19 .... 177 E6

Ashley Mill Cotts. CT19 .. 177 E7
Ashley Rd. ME8 .... 11 C2
Ashmead Cl. ME5 .... 32 C3
Ashstead Dr. ME9 .... 37 D2
Ashton Cl. CT14 .... 116 D4
Ashtree Ho. ME10 .... 37 B3
Ashtrees. L16 .... 23 B3
Ashurst Ave. CT5 .... 43 C6
Ashurst Gdns. CT9 .... 8 E3
Ashurst Rd. ME14 .... 75 C5
Askes Ct. TN23 .... 155 D8
Aspen Cl. TN29 .... 194 F3
Aspen Ho. 5 CT20 .... 178 D4
Aspen Way. 2 ME5 .... 31 E4
Aspian Dr. ME17 .... 96 D3
Asquith Rd. ME8 .... 33 C6
Association Wlk. ME1 .. 31 C7
Astley Ave. CT16 .... 149 C2
Astley St. ME14 .... 75 A4
Aston Cl. ME5 .... 32 A2
Astor Ave. CT17 .... 166 B8
Astor Cty Prim Sch. CT17 .. 166 B8
Astor Dr. CT14 .... 117 C5
Astor of Hever Sch The. ME16 .. 74 C3
Astor Rd. CT10 .... 29 F8
Astor Sch. Dover CT16 .. 166 A8
Astor Sch. Dover CT16 .. 166 B8
Astrid Rd. CT14 .... 117 A2
Athelstan Gn. ME17 .. 77 C2
Athelstan Pl. CT14 .. 117 C8
Athelstan Rd. Canterbury CT1 .. 87 C5
Athelstan Rd. Chatham ME4 .. 9 F2
Athelstan Rd. Faversham ME13 .. 62 C6
Athelstan Rd.
Folkestone CT19 .... 178 D7
Athelstan Rd. Margate CT9 .. 8 A3
Athol Pl. ME13 .... 62 A8
Athol Rd. Ashford TN23 .. 155 F7
Athol Rd. Whitstable CT5 .. 20 F2
Athol Terr. CT16 .... 166 F8
Atlanta Cl. ME1 .... 9 D3
Attlee Ave. CT3 .... 112 E5
Attlee Way. ME10 .... 36 E8
Atwater Ct. ME17 .... 101 D5
Aubretia Wlk. ME10 .. 37 A3
Auckland Ave. CT12 .. 52 A8
Auckland Cres. CT13 .. 149 C3
Auckland Dr. ME10 .. 36 C3
Audley Ave. Gillingham ME7 .. 10 E1
Audley Ave. Margate CT9 .. 7 E1
Audley Cl. ME16 .... 74 B5
Audley Rd. CT20 .... 177 F5
Augusta Cl. 1 ME7 .... 10 C2
Augusta Gdns. CT20 .. 178 C4
Augusta Pl. 12 CT11 .. 52 F7
Augusta Rd. CT11 .... 52 F7
Augustine Rd. Minster ME12 .. 4 B8
Augustine Rd. Minster, Minster
CT12 .... 50 B6
Austell Manor. ME7 .. 10 C6
Austens Orch. 12 TN30 .. 179 A7
Austin Ave. CT6 .... 21 F4
Austin Cl.
Gillingham ME5 & ME7 .. 10 E2
Austin Cl. Sittingbourne ME10 .. 37 A8
Austin Rd. TN23 .... 156 B6
Austins La. 4 CT13 .. 73 A1
Autumn Glade. ME14 .. 54 D8
Avebury Ave. CT11 .. 52 G8
Aveling Ct. 2 ME2 .... 9 B7
Avenue Gdns. CT9 .... 8 C3
Avenue of Remembrance.
ME10 .... 36 F3
Avenue Rd. Dover CT16 .. 149 C1
Avenue Rd. Herne Bay CT6 .. 22 E5
Avenue Rd. Ramsgate CT11 .. 52 F7
Avenue The. Deal CT14 .. 117 C7
Avenue The. Hersden CT3 .. 46 E1
Avenue The. Hythe CT21 .. 176 C2
Avenue The.
Kingsdown CT14 .... 134 D4
Avenue The. Margate CT9 .. 8 A1
Avenue The.
St Margaret's at Cliffe CT15 .. 150 F6
Avenue The.
Temple Ewell CT16 .... 148 E5
Averenches Rd. ME14 .. 75 F5
Avereng Gdns. CT19 .. 178 B6
Avereng Rd. CT19 .... 178 B6
Avery Cl. ME15 .... 74 F1
Avery La. ME15 .... 98 D6
Aviemore Gdns. ME14 .. 75 F4
Avington Cl. ME15 .. 74 F1
Avocet Wlk. ME5 .... 32 D2
Avon Cl. CT1 .... 88 C8
Avondale Cl. CT5 .... 44 A8
Avondale Rd. Capel-le-F CT18 .. 164 C2
Avondale Rd. Gillingham ME7 .. 10 D5
Axford Cl. ME8 .... 34 A8
Aycliffe Cty Prim Sch. CT17 .. 166 A4
Aylesford Cres. ME8 .. 11 B4
Aylesford Pl. TN24 .. 156 F7
Aylesham Cnr. CT3 .. 112 D3
Aylesham Cty Prim Sch. CT3 .. 112 E5
Aylesham Rd. CT15 & CT3 .. 113 A4
Aylesham Sta. CT3 .. 113 A5
Aylewyn Gn. ME10 .. 36 F8
Aynsley Cl. 1 CT13 .. 73 A1
Ayton Rd. CT11 .... 52 C6
Babs Oak Hill. CT2 & CT3 .. 68 B7
Back La. 6 Faversham ME13 .. 62 D7
Back La. Marlpit ME7 .. 97 E1
Back La. Minster ME12 .. 4 D6
Back Rd W. CT6 .... 166 G8
Back St. Langley Heath ME17 .. 98 E6
Back St. Ringwould CT14 .. 133 F5
Backfields. ME1 .... 9 B4

Bad Munstereifel Rd.
TN23 & TN24 .... 156 D5
Baddlesmere Rd. CT5 .. 21 A2
Bader Cres. ME5 .... 32 A7
Badger Rd. ME7 .... 10 D7
Badgers Bridge. CT18 .. 161 D4
Badgers Cl. CT2 .... 66 A7
Badgers Cl. TN23 .... 156 A7
Badgers Oak. TN23 .. 155 D8
Badgers Rise. Deal CT14 .. 134 C8
Badgers Rise. River CT17 .. 148 D3
Badlesmere Cl. TN23 .. 155 E6
Baffin Cl. ME4 .... 9 F2
Bagham La. CT4 .... 107 D8
Bagham Rd. CT4 .... 107 C8
Bagshill Rd. ME13 .. 83 A3
Bailey Dr. ME7 .... 11 A1
Bailey Fields. TN26 .. 153 E4
Baileys Field. TN23 .. 138 F1
Baird's Hill. CT10 .... 29 F6
Bairdsley Cl. CT10 .. 29 F6
Bakenham Ho. 1 ME1 .. 9 C1
Baker Cl. ME9 .... 38 C2
Baker Rd. ME19 .... 177 E6
Baker St. ME1 .... 9 C6
Baker's La. CT4 .... 86 D2
Baker's Wlk. ME1 .... 9 C6
Bakers Cl. CT2 .... 87 C7
Balcomb Cres. CT9 .. 29 C8
Baldric Rd. CT20 .... 177 F5
Baldwin Rd.
Greatstone-on-S TN28 .. 200 D1
Baldwin Rd. Minster ME12 .. 4 D7
Baldwin Terr. CT19 .. 178 D6
Balfour Cl. CT20 .... 178 B3
Balfour Cty Inf Sch. ME4 .. 9 E1
Balfour Cty Jun Sch. ME4 .. 9 E2
Balfour Rd. Chatham ME4 .. 9 E2
Balfour Rd. Deal CT14 .. 117 C2
Balfour Rd. Dover CT16 .. 149 C1
Baliol Rd. CT5 .... 20 E2
Balliol Rd. CT10 .... 29 F8
Balmer Cl. ME8 .... 33 D7
Balmoral Ho. 6 ME15 .. 97 F5
Balmoral Pl. 10 CT11 .. 52 F7
Balmoral Rd. Gillingham ME7 .. 10 D5
Balmoral Rd. Kingsdown CT14 .. 134 C6
Balmoral Rd. 4 Margate CT9 .. 28 B8
Bamford Way. CT14 .. 117 C4
Bank Cotts. ME17 .... 77 E3
Bank Rd. TN25 .... 172 E8
Bank Side. TN26 .... 183 A8
Bank St. Chatham ME4 .. 10 B3
Bank St. Faversham ME13 .. 62 C7
Bank St. Herne Bay CT6 .. 22 F5
Bank St. Hythe CT21 .. 176 C2
Bank St.
Maidstone ME14 & ME15 .. 75 A4
Banks Rd. Ashford TN23 .. 156 A7
Banks Rd. Rochester ME2 .. 9 C8
Banks The. CT10 .... 29 F6
Banks Rd. 6 ME10 .... 36 F4
Bankside. Canterbury CT1 .. 88 D7
Bankside. Chatham ME5 .. 32 B8
Banky Fields Cl. ME8 .. 12 B1
Banner Way. ME12 .... 3 E6
Banning St. ME2 .... 9 B8
Banningbrook Cl. CT14 .. 117 D4
Bannister Hill. ME9 .. 36 B2
Bannister Hos. TN26 .. 120 A1
Bannister Rd. ME14 .. 75 A7
Bapchild & Tonge
CE Prim Sch. ME10 .. 37 A7
Barbados Terr. 2 ME14 .. 75 A7
Barberry Ave. ME5 .. 31 E5
Barcham Cl. ME15 .. 96 F5
Barclay Ct. CT7 .... 7 C1
Bardell Terr. ME1 .... 9 D5
Barden Ct. ME14 .... 75 B5
Barfleur Manor. 8 ME4 .. 10 A6
Barfreston Cl. ME15 .. 74 F2
Barfrestone Rd. CT15 .. 114 A1
Bargates. TN23 .... 155 E6
Bargrove Rd. ME14 .. 75 C5
Barham CE Prim Sch. CT4 .. 128 F8
Barham Cl. ME15 .... 97 E5
Barham's Mill Rd. TN27 .. 118 B3
Barker Rd. ME16 .... 74 F3
Barkers Cl. ME10 .... 36 D4
Barkis Cl. ME1 .... 31 D7
Barler Pl. ME11 .... 3 A5
Barley Cl. Herne Bay CT6 .. 23 D2
Barley Cl. Martin Mill CT15 .. 133 C2
Barley Fields. ME14 .. 75 F6
Barleycorn Dr. ME8 .. 33 E6
Barleymow Cl. ME7 .. 10 D5
Barling Cl. ME5 .... 31 D1
Barlow Cl. ME8 .... 33 E5
Barn Cl. Borden ME9 .. 36 A2
Barn Cl. Hoath CT3 .. 46 E5
Barn Cl. Yorklets CT5 .. 43 A3
Barn Cres. CT7 .... 7 F1
Barn Platt. TN23 .... 156 A6
Barn The. ME9 .... 36 A2
Barnaby Terr. ME1 .... 9 D2
Barnard Ct. ME4 .... 10 A2
Barnberry Cl. TN23 .. 155 E8
Barncroft Cl. ME14 .. 76 F6
Barncroft Dr. ME7 .. 32 F4
Barnes Ave. CT9 .... 7 F1
Barnes Cl. ME13 .... 62 B8

Barnes Ct. CT1 .... 87 D6
Barnesende Ct. CT14 .. 94 A8
Barnet's La. CT2 .... 67 D8
Barnett Cl. CT12 .... 29 B1
Barnett Field. TN23 .. 155 F8
Barnfield. Chatham ME5 .. 32 A8
Barnfield. Herne Bay CT6 .. 22 C2
Barnfield. St Michaels TN30 .. 167 C2
Barnfield Rd. Faversham ME13 .. 62 C8
Barnfield Rd. Folkestone CT19 .. 178 C7
Barnhouse La. ME29 .. 198 A8
Barnhurst La. CT18 .. 163 A5
Barnhurst Rd. ME14 .. 75 A8
Barnsley Cl. ME12 .... 1 F2
Barnsole Cty Inf Sch. ME7 .. 10 E4
Barnsole Cty Jun Sch. ME7 .. 10 E4
Barnsole Rd. Gillingham ME7 .. 10 E3
Barnsole Rd. Staple CT3 .. 92 B5
Barntye Cl. CT15 .... 149 E6
Barnwood Cl. ME1 .. 31 B8
Baron Cl. Gillingham ME7 .. 10 C7
Baron Cl. Maidstone ME14 .. 75 F5
Barrack Hill. CT21 .. 176 A2
Barrack Rd. ME4 .... 10 B8
Barrey Rd. TN24 .... 157 A6
Barrier Rd. ME4 .... 9 F5
Barrington Cl. ME5 .. 31 F5
Barrington Cres. CT7 .. 27 B7
Barrow Gr. ME10 .... 36 D3
Barrow Grove Cty Jun Sch.
ME10 .... 36 D3
Barrow Hill.
Ashford TN23 & TN24 .. 139 B2
Barrow Hill. Sellindge TN25 .. 174 D7
Barrow Hill Cotts. TN23 .. 139 A2
Barrow Hill Rise. TN25 .. 174 D7
Barrow Hill Terr. 1 TN23 .. 139 B3
Barrowfields. ME15 .. 32 D1
Barrowhill Pl. 2 TN23 .. 139 B3
Barrows Cl. CT7 .... 27 A6
Bartholomew Cl. CT21 .. 176 B3
Bartholomew La. CT21 .. 176 B3
Bartholomew St. 6
Dover CT16 .... 149 C1
Bartholomew St. Hythe CT21 .. 176 B2
Bartlett Cl. ME15 .... 32 C1
Bartlett Dr. CT5 .... 21 A1
Bartletts Cl. ME12 .... 3 C5
Barton Bsns Pk. CT1 .. 88 B6
Barton Court Gram Sch. CT1 .. 88 B8
Barton Cty Jun Sch. CT16 .. 149 C2
Barton Field. CT18 .. 161 B7
Barton Hill Dr. ME12 .. 4 A5
Barton Mill Rd. CT1 .. 67 B2
Barton Rd. Canterbury CT1 .. 88 C6
Barton Rd. Dover CT16 .. 149 C2
Barton Rd. Maidstone ME15 .. 75 A2
Barton Rd. Rochester ME2 .. 9 A7
Barton View Terr. 2 CT16 .. 149 C1
Barton's Point
Recn Ctr. ME12 .... 1 F2
Barville Rd. CT15 .... 114 E2
Barwick Rd. CT17 .... 148 F1
Bashford Barn La. ME9 .. 58 A4
Basing Cl. ME15 .... 75 B3
Baskerville. TN24 .... 139 B3
Basmere Cl. ME14 .. 75 C6
Bassett Cl. CT21 .... 176 E4
Bassett Gdns. CT21 .. 176 D4
Bassett Rd. ME10 .... 36 C4
Bastion Rd. CT17 .... 166 C6
Batchelor St. ME4 .. 10 A4
Bateman Cnr. TN26 .. 153 E6
Bates Cl. CT3 .... 91 F6
Bath Ct. CT20 .... 178 B3
Bath Hard. ME1 .... 9 D5
Bath Mews. TN24 .... 156 E6
Bath Pl. CT9 .... 7 J2
Bath Rd. Ashford TN24 .. 156 E6
Bath Rd. Margate CT9 .. 7 J2
Bathurst Cl. CT12 .... 29 B1
Bathurst Rd. CT20 .... 178 A5
Batteries Cl. ME9 .... 60 B8
Batteries Terr. ME9 .. 60 B8
Battery Point. CT17 .. 177 B2
Battery Rd. TN29 .... 204 F2
Battle of Britain Homes. 17
CT16 .... 166 D7
Bawden Cl. CT12 .... 67 A4
Baxendale Ct. TN24 .. 156 D7
Bay Banks. ME13 .... 61 E2
Bay Cotts. CT15 .... 151 C6
Bay Hill. CT15 .... 151 B6
Bay Hill CT15 .... 151 A5
Bay Mus The. CT15 .. 151 B5
Bay View Gdns. ME12 .. 6 D2
Bay View Hts. CT7 .. 26 E8
Bay View Rd. CT10 .. 30 A2
Baye La. CT3 .... 69 D1
Bayfield. ME13 .... 61 E2
Bayford Rd. ME10 .. 37 A4
Bayhill. ME13 .... 61 E2
Bayle Ct. CT20 .... 178 E4
Bayle St. 16 CT20 .. 178 E5
Bayle The. CT20 .... 178 E4
Bayswater Dr. ME8 .. 33 E4
Bayview Rd. Kingsdown CT14 .. 134 C4
Bayview Rd. Whitstable CT5 .. 43 D7
Beach Alley. 9 CT5 .. 20 D2
Beach App. ME12 .... 6 E3
Beach Ave. CT7 .... 26 F8
Beach Flats. 2 CT21 .. 176 B2
Beach Ho's. CT7 .... 7 G2
Beach House Mews. CT8 .. 7 D1
Beach Marine. CT20 .. 177 F3
Beach Rd.
Dymchurch TN29 .... 187 A4
Beach Rd.
St Margaret's at Cliffe CT15 .. 151 B6

Beach Rd. Westgate-on-S CT8 & CT9 ..... 7 D1
Beach Rise. CT9 ..... 7 D1
Beach St. Deal CT14 ..... 117 D6
Beach St. Folkestone CT20 ..... 178 E4
Beach St. Herne Bay CT6 ..... 22 F5
Beach St. Sheerness ME12 ..... 1 C3
Beach Terr. ME12 ..... 1 C2
Beach The. CT14 ..... 117 D3
Beach Wlk. CT5 ..... 20 E3
Beachborough Rd. CT19 & CT20 ..... 178 A5
Beachfield Lodge. ME12 ..... 1 D2
Beachmont Cl. TN29 ..... 204 E8
Beacon Ave. CT6 ..... 23 B5
Beacon Cl. ME8 ..... 33 D7
Beacon Hill. Chatham ME5 ..... 10 D2
Beacon Hill. Herne Bay CT6 ..... 23 B5
Beacon La. CT13 ..... 93 A6
Beacon Oak Rd. TN30 ..... 179 B8
Beacon Rd. Broadstairs CT10 ..... 29 F7
Beacon Rd. Chatham ME5 ..... 10 C2
Beacon Rd. Herne Bay CT6 ..... 23 A5
Beacon Rd. Lenham ME17 ..... 101 C5
Beacon Way. CT21 ..... 174 F3
Beacon Wlk. Herne Bay CT6 ..... 23 A5
Beacon Wlk. Tenterden TN30 ..... 167 B1
Beacons The. ME17 ..... 96 C2
Beaconsfield. CT5 ..... 42 F6
Beaconsfield Ave. Dover CT16 ..... 149 C1
Beaconsfield Ave. Gillingham ME7 ..... 10 E5
Beaconsfield Gdns. CT10 ..... 29 F5
Beaconsfield Rd. Canterbury CT2 ..... 66 F2
Beaconsfield Rd. Chatham ME4 ..... 9 F3
Beaconsfield Rd. Deal CT14 ..... 117 D5
Beaconsfield Rd. Dover CT16 ..... 149 C1
Beaconsfield Rd. Maidstone ME15 ..... 74 E2
Beaconsfield Rd. Sittingbourne ME10 ..... 37 C4
Beamont Cl. CT12 ..... 27 F2
Beams The. ME15 ..... 75 F1
Bean Cl. TN23 ..... 138 C1
Beaney Inst (Liby & Mus). CT1 ..... 87 F8
Beaney's La. CT4 & ME13 ..... 84 C1
Bear's La. TN26 ..... 137 E3
Bears End Ho. TN23 ..... 156 B8
Bearsted Cl. ME8 ..... 11 B3
Bearsted Green Bsns Ctr. ME14 ..... 76 C4
Bearsted Rd. ME14 ..... 75 E6
Bearsted & Thurnham Sta. ME14 ..... 76 B5
Beatrice Mews. TN28 ..... 204 E7
Beatrice Rd. Capel-le-F CT18 ..... 164 C2
Beatrice Rd. Margate CT9 ..... 28 E8
Beatty Ave. ME7 ..... 10 F4
Beatty Cl. CT19 ..... 178 E8
Beatty Rd. Chatham ME1 ..... 31 D8
Beatty Rd. Folkestone CT19 ..... 178 D8
Beauchamp Ave. CT14 ..... 117 A3
Beauchamp Cl. TN24 ..... 139 E5
Beauchamps La. CT15 ..... 113 D5
Beaufort Ave. CT12 ..... 52 B8
Beaufort Ct. ME2 ..... 9 E6
Beaufort Wlk. ME15 ..... 97 E4
Beaufoy Rd. CT17 ..... 149 A1
Beaufoy Terr. CT17 ..... 148 F1
Beauherne Cty Prim Sch. CT2 ..... 87 D8
Beaulieu Rise. ME1 ..... 9 D1
Beaulieu Wlk. ME16 ..... 74 C7
Beaumanor. CT6 ..... 23 A3
Beaumont Davy Cl. ME13 ..... 62 C5
Beaumont Rd. ME16 ..... 74 B2
Beaumont St. CT6 ..... 22 C4
Beaumont Terr. ME13 ..... 62 D6
Beauvoir Dr. ME10 ..... 37 A8
Beauworth Pk. ME15 ..... 97 E8
Beauxfield. CT16 ..... 149 A7
Beaver Ct. TN23 ..... 156 A7
Beaver Green Cty Inf Sch. TN23 ..... 155 E7
Beaver Ind Est. TN23 ..... 156 B7
Beaver La. Ashford TN23 ..... 138 E1
Beaver La. Ashford, Beaver TN23 ..... 156 A7
Beaver Rd. TN23 ..... 156 B8
Beazley Ct. TN24 ..... 156 D7
Beckenham Dr. ME16 ..... 74 D7
Becket Ave. CT2 ..... 66 D1
Becket Cl. Ash CT3 ..... 71 D2
Becket Cl. Deal CT14 ..... 117 C8
Becket Cl. Whitstable CT5 ..... 21 B1
Becket Mews. CT2 ..... 66 F1
Becket's Cl. TN25 ..... 142 B6
Beckett St. 4 ME13 ..... 62 C7
Becketts Terr. CT21 ..... 176 B4
Beckley Mews. ME5 ..... 31 F5
Beckley Pl. TN25 ..... 175 B8
Beckley Rd. ME12 ..... 1 F2
Becksbourne Cl. ME14 ..... 75 A8
Beckwith Gn. CT20 ..... 177 E5
Beddow Way. ME20 ..... 53 B3
Bede Ho. CT14 ..... 117 D8
Bedford Ave. ME8 ..... 11 D1
Bedford Pl. ME16 ..... 74 E4
Bedford Sq. CT12 ..... 29 B2
Bedford Way. CT7 ..... 25 F1
Bedgebury Cl. Chatham ME1 ..... 31 D8
Bedgebury Cl. Maidstone ME14 ..... 75 C6
Bedingfield Way. CT18 ..... 161 B7
Bedlam Court La. CT12 ..... 50 C6
Bedlam La. TN12 ..... 135 A8
Bedson Wlk. ME8 ..... 12 B1
Bedwin Cl. ME1 ..... 31 D7
Beech Cl. Faversham ME13 ..... 62 B7
Beech Cl. Folkestone CT19 ..... 178 C6
Beech Ct. Canterbury CT1 ..... 88 A7
Beech Ct. Challock TN25 ..... 105 A1
Beech Dr. Broadstairs CT10 ..... 29 D4
Beech Dr. Elvington CT15 ..... 114 B2
Beech Dr. Hothfield TN26 ..... 138 A7
Beech Dr. Maidstone ME16 ..... 74 C5
Beech Gr. CT12 ..... 51 C5
Beech Green Cl. CT15 ..... 131 C7
Beech Hill. CT4 ..... 111 B8
Beechcroft. CT5 ..... 21 D1
Beechcroft Gdns. CT11 ..... 52 F8
Beechen Bank Rd. ME5 ..... 32 A1
Beeches The. ME5 ..... 32 A4
Beeching Rd. ME5 ..... 32 B3
Beechings Gn. ME8 ..... 11 C3
Beechings Way. ME8 ..... 11 C3
Beechmore Dr. ME5 ..... 32 A2
Beecholme Dr. TN24 ..... 139 C5
Beechwood Ave. Chatham ME5 ..... 10 D2
Beechwood Ave. Deal CT14 ..... 117 C5
Beechwood Ave. Sittingbourne ME10 ..... 36 E6
Beechwood Cl. St Mary's Bay TN29 ..... 194 F3
Beechwood Cl. Whitfield CT16 ..... 132 A1
Beechwood Ct. CT16 ..... 148 E4
Beecroft Cl. CT2 ..... 67 A4
Beer Cart La. CT1 ..... 87 F8
Beggars Cnr. CT3 ..... 48 D1
Beggarsbush La. TN29 ..... 198 D7
Begonia Ave. ME8 ..... 11 C2
Beke Rd. ME8 ..... 33 D4
Bekesbourne Hill. CT4 ..... 89 B5
Bekesbourne La. Bekesbourne CT3 & CT4 ..... 89 E6
Bekesbourne La. Canterbury CT1 & CT3 & CT4 ..... 88 F7
Bekesbourne La. Littlebourne CT3 ..... 89 F6
Bekesbourne Rd. CT4 ..... 88 F2
Bekesbourne Sta. CT4 ..... 89 B5
Belcaire Cl. CT21 ..... 175 A3
Belgrave Cl. CT11 ..... 52 D7
Belgrave Rd. Dover CT17 ..... 166 B7
Belgrave Rd. Halfway Houses ME12 ..... 3 C5
Belgrave Rd. Margate CT9 ..... 7 I2
Belinda Ct. CT19 ..... 178 B7
Bell Chapel Cl. TN23 ..... 156 C4
Bell Cnr. TN29 ..... 199 A4
Bell Cres. ME1 ..... 53 A8
Bell Farm La. ME12 ..... 5 A6
Bell Gr. CT3 ..... 113 A5
Bell La. Burham ME1 ..... 53 A8
Bell La. Maidstone ME14 ..... 76 A5
Bell La. Sandwich CT13 ..... 73 A1
Bell La. Westfield Sole ME14 ..... 54 B2
Bell Rd. Park Wood ME15 ..... 97 E5
Bell Rd. Sittingbourne ME10 ..... 36 F3
Bell Way. ME17 ..... 99 E2
Bell Wood Cty Inf Sch. ME15 ..... 97 E5
Bell Wood Cty Jun Sch. ME15 ..... 97 E5
Bell's Cl. TN30 ..... 179 A7
Bell-Davies Dr. CT12 ..... 28 A1
Belle Friday Cl. ME9 ..... 38 C2
Belle Vue Rd. CT6 ..... 23 B5
Bellevue Ave. CT11 ..... 52 F7
Bellevue Rd. Minster ME12 ..... 4 C6
Bellevue Rd. Ramsgate CT11 ..... 52 F7
Bellevue Rd. Whitstable CT5 ..... 43 F8
Bellevue St. 5 CT20 ..... 178 D5
Bellgrove Ct. ME5 ..... 54 A8
Bellmeadow. ME15 ..... 97 E6
Bells La. 7 TN30 ..... 179 A7
Belmont. CT14 ..... 117 B1
Belmont Ct. CT11 ..... 52 D7
Belmont Farm Bsns Ctr. TN26 ..... 137 A1
Belmont Pl. TN24 ..... 156 D7
Belmont Rd. Ashford TN24 ..... 139 D6
Belmont Rd. Broadstairs CT10 ..... 30 A4
Belmont Rd. Faversham ME13 ..... 62 C6
Belmont Rd. Gillingham ME7 ..... 10 C4
Belmont Rd. Halfway Houses ME12 ..... 3 E6
Belmont Rd. Ramsgate CT11 ..... 52 D7
Belmont Rd. Sittingbourne ME10 ..... 36 E3
Belmont Rd. Westgate-on-S CT8 ..... 27 F8
Belmont Rd. Whitstable CT5 ..... 20 D1
Belmont St. CT11 ..... 52 E7
Belmont Terr. CT13 ..... 93 B3
Belmore Pk. TN24 ..... 139 B3
Belnor Ave. ME9 ..... 13 F1
Belsey La. CT15 ..... 147 D4
Belting Dr. CT6 ..... 23 E5
Beltinge Rd. CT6 ..... 23 B5
Belton Cl. CT5 ..... 43 E8
Belvedere Rd. Broadstairs CT10 ..... 30 B4
Belvedere Rd. Faversham ME13 ..... 62 D8
Benacre Rd. CT5 ..... 43 D6
Bench Hill. TN30 ..... 181 D5
Bench St. 19 CT16 ..... 166 D7
Bendon Way. ME8 ..... 33 D8
Benenden Manor. ME8 ..... 11 B3
Bengal Rd. CT12 ..... 29 A1
Benham Bsns Pk. TN25 ..... 174 F5
Bennells Ave. CT5 ..... 21 B3
Bennett Ct. 14 CT20 ..... 178 E5
Bennetts Cotts. ME7 ..... 55 A8
Bennetts Gdns. ME13 ..... 61 D8
Bennetts Mews. 11 TN30 ..... 179 A7
Benson Cl. CT18 ..... 162 F4
Benson La. CT18 ..... 162 F4
Bensted. TN23 ..... 155 F5
Bensted Gr. ME13 ..... 62 A7
Benstede Cl. CT6 ..... 23 A1
Bentham Sq. ME12 ..... 1 B3
Bentley Ave. CT6 ..... 22 B4
Bentley Cl. ME5 ..... 32 D2
Bentley Rd. TN24 ..... 156 F7
Bentlif Cl. ME16 ..... 74 D5
Berber Rd. ME2 ..... 9 B8
Berengrave La. ME8 ..... 11 F2
Berengrave Lane Chalk Pit (Nature Reserve). ME8 ..... 12 A3
Beresford Ave. ME4 ..... 9 E2
Beresford Gap. CT7 ..... 26 F8
Beresford Gdns. CT9 ..... 8 C3
Beresford Rd. Gillingham ME7 ..... 10 D4
Beresford Rd. Kit's Coty ME20 ..... 53 D7
Beresford Rd. Ramsgate CT11 ..... 52 D6
Beresford Rd. River CT17 ..... 148 E3
Beresford Rd. St Margaret's at Cliffe CT15 ..... 133 F1
Beresford Rd. Whitstable CT5 ..... 20 D1
Beresfords Hill. ME17 ..... 97 B4
Bergland Pk. ME2 ..... 9 D8
Berkeley Cl. Boughton Street ME13 ..... 64 B3
Berkeley Cl. Chatham ME1 ..... 31 D8
Berkeley Cl. 2 Folkestone CT19 ..... 178 A7
Berkeley Ct. ME10 ..... 36 D3
Berkeley Mount. 1 ME4 ..... 9 F4
Berkeley Rd. CT7 ..... 26 F8
Berkshire Cl. ME5 ..... 32 C8
Bernard Sunley Hall. TN25 ..... 124 A2
Bernards Gdns. CT15 ..... 130 E5
Berridge Rd. ME12 ..... 1 D2
Berry St. ME10 ..... 36 F4
Berwick La. CT21 ..... 175 A3
Berwyn Gr. ME15 ..... 97 A6
Best La. CT1 ..... 87 F8
Best St. ME4 ..... 9 F4
Bethel Row. ME13 ..... 82 F1
Bethersden Ct. ME15 ..... 97 F7
Bethersden Cty Prim Sch. TN26 ..... 153 D5
Bethersden Rd. Bethersden TN27 & TN26 ..... 152 C5
Bethersden Rd. Hothfield TN26 ..... 137 D4
Bethersden Rd. Shadoxhurst TN26 ..... 154 E2
Bethersden Rd. Woodchurch TN26 ..... 169 A6
Betony Gdns. ME14 ..... 75 F5
Betsham Rd. ME15 ..... 97 F6
Bettescombe Rd. ME8 ..... 33 E7
Betty Shelvey Ct. CT14 ..... 117 D4
Beult Meadow. TN27 ..... 135 A1
Bevan Way. CT3 ..... 112 E5
Beverley Cl. ME8 ..... 33 F8
Beverley Gdns. TN29 ..... 187 A4
Beverley Rd. Canterbury CT2 ..... 66 E2
Beverley Rd. Maidstone ME16 ..... 74 A1
Beverley Way. CT12 ..... 29 C1
Beverly Cl. CT7 ..... 27 B8
Bewsbury Cres. CT16 ..... 148 F7
Bewsbury Cross La. CT16 ..... 148 F7
Bexley St. CT5 ..... 20 D2
Bexon La. ME9 ..... 58 C4
Bicknor Cl. CT2 ..... 67 B4
Bicknor Court Cotts. ME9 ..... 57 C2
Bicknor La. ME9 ..... 57 D3
Bicknor Rd. ME15 ..... 97 F4
Biddenden Cl. Maidstone ME15 ..... 75 F3
Biddenden Cl. Margate CT9 ..... 8 C1
Biddenden Rd. TN26 ..... 167 A6
Bierce Ct. CT7 ..... 26 F7
Bifrons Gdns. CT4 ..... 89 B3
Bifrons Hill. CT4 ..... 89 B4
Bifrons Rd. CT4 ..... 89 B4
Bigbury Rd. CT2 & CT4 ..... 86 E7
Biggin St. CT16 ..... 166 D8
Biggins Wood Rd. CT19 ..... 177 E7
Bilberry Cl. ME14 ..... 75 E5
Bill Street Rd. ME2 ..... 9 C8
Billington Gdns. TN24 ..... 139 E6
Bilsington Cl. ME5 ..... 32 B5
Bilsington Cross. TN25 ..... 172 C1
Binbury La. ME14 ..... 56 A5
Bindon Blood Rd. CT16 ..... 149 A5
Bingley Rd. ME1 ..... 9 E4
Binland Gr. ME5 ..... 31 D5
Binnacle Rd. ME1 ..... 31 C8
Binnie Cl. CT10 ..... 29 F2
Birch Cl. Ashford TN24 ..... 139 F2
Birch Cl. Broadstairs CT10 ..... 29 C3
Birch Ct. CT4 ..... 128 F8
Birch Dr. ME5 ..... 32 D1
Birch Gr. ME7 ..... 33 A5
Birch Hill Ct. CT7 ..... 27 B7
Birch Ho. Sheerness ME12 ..... 1 C2
Birch Ho. Sittingbourne ME10 ..... 37 B3
Birch Rd. CT5 ..... 44 A8
Birch Tree Way. ME15 ..... 75 B3
Birches The. CT7 ..... 27 B7
Birchett. TN23 ..... 138 E1
Birchfield Cl. ME15 ..... 97 B6
Birchfields. ME5 ..... 32 A3
Birchington CE Prim Sch. CT7 ..... 27 A6
Birchington Cl. ME14 ..... 75 C5
Birchington-on-Sea Sta. CT7 ..... 26 F7
Bircholt Forstal. TN25 ..... 158 E7
Bircholt Rd. ME15 ..... 97 F4
Birchwood Rd. ME16 ..... 74 C5
Birchwood Rise. CT17 ..... 166 C7
Birchwood Wlk. CT2 ..... 66 E2
Bird Farm. CT4 ..... 105 E4
Birds Ave. CT9 ..... 28 B7
Birdwood Ave. CT14 ..... 117 A5
Birkdale Ct. 3 ME16 ..... 74 E4
Birkdale Dr. CT19 ..... 178 A8
Birkdale Gdns. CT6 ..... 22 D2
Birkhall Cl. ME5 ..... 32 A5
Birling Ave. Gillingham ME8 ..... 11 E1
Birling Ave. Maidstone ME14 ..... 76 A4
Birling Cl. ME14 ..... 76 A4
Birling Rd. TN24 ..... 139 D1
Birnam Sq. 1 ME16 ..... 74 E4
Bishop Ct. 4 ME10 ..... 36 E5
Bishop Jenner Ct. CT3 ..... 70 C6
Bishop La. ME9 ..... 12 E3
Bishop's Ave. CT10 ..... 30 B6
Bishopbourne Gn. ME8 ..... 11 B4
Bishopden Ct. CT2 ..... 66 C4
Bishops Gn. TN23 ..... 155 E7
Bishops Way. Canterbury CT2 ..... 66 D1
Bishops Way. Maidstone ME15 ..... 74 F4
Bishops Wlk. ME1 ..... 9 C5
Bishopstone Dr. CT6 ..... 23 F6
Bishopstone La. CT6 ..... 23 F5
Black Bull Rd. CT19 ..... 178 D6
Black Griffin La. CT1 ..... 87 F8
Black Post. ME17 ..... 78 E4
Black Robin La. CT4 ..... 111 E3
Black Rock Gdns. ME7 ..... 33 B4
Blackburn Rd. CT6 ..... 22 B2
Blackdown Dr. TN24 ..... 139 B4
Blacketts Cotts. ME9 ..... 38 B7
Blacketts Rd. ME9 ..... 38 A6
Blackfriars St. 5 CT1 ..... 66 F1
Blackhouse Hill. CT18 & CT21 ..... 176 D4
Blackhouse Rise. CT21 ..... 176 D3
Blackleys. ME13 ..... 84 F7
Blackmanstone Way. ME16 ..... 74 B7
Blacksmith Dr. ME14 ..... 75 D5
Blackstable Ct. CT5 ..... 43 D8
Blackthorn Ave. ME5 ..... 32 A3
Blackthorne Rd. ME8 ..... 34 B8
Blackwall Rd. TN24 & TN25 ..... 140 B4
Blake Cl. CT14 ..... 134 C8
Blake Ct. TN24 ..... 156 F8
Blakeney Cl. ME14 ..... 76 B4
Blaker Ave. ME1 ..... 9 E1
Blandford Gdns. ME10 ..... 36 E1
Blatcher Cl. ME12 ..... 4 B6
Blaxland Cl. ME13 ..... 62 B8
Bleak Ho. CT10 ..... 30 B4
Bleak Rd. TN29 ..... 203 C6
Bleakwood Rd. ME5 ..... 31 F4
Blean Bird Pk. CT2 ..... 65 F8
Blean Comm. CT2 ..... 66 A6
Blean Cty Prim Sch. CT2 ..... 66 B4
Blean Hill. CT2 ..... 66 A5
Blean Rd. ME8 ..... 11 C2
Blean Sq. ME14 ..... 75 C6
Blean View Rd. CT6 ..... 22 B2
Blendon Rd. ME14 ..... 75 C5
Blenheim Ave. Canterbury CT1 ..... 67 D1
Blenheim Ave. Chatham ME1 & ME4 ..... 9 E2
Blenheim Ave. Faversham ME13 ..... 62 E5
Blenheim Cl. Broadstairs CT10 ..... 29 D3
Blenheim Cl. Herne Bay CT6 ..... 23 A1
Blenheim Cl. Maidstone ME15 ..... 75 F3
Blenheim Dr. Dover CT16 ..... 149 C3
Blenheim Dr. Hawkinge CT18 ..... 163 A4
Blenheim Pl. CT20 ..... 177 F4
Blenheim Rd. Deal CT14 ..... 117 D5
Blenheim Rd. Littlestone-on-S TN28 ..... 200 D6
Blenheim Rd. Sittingbourne ME10 ..... 37 B2
Bleriot Meml. CT16 ..... 149 F1
Bliby Cnr. TN25 ..... 171 F8
Blind La. Bredhurst ME7 ..... 33 A1
Blind La. Challock TN25 ..... 105 C2
Blind La. Lidsing ME7 ..... 32 F1
Blind La. Mersham TN24 & TN25 ..... 157 D5
Blind Mary's La. ME9 ..... 57 E4
Blindgrooms La. TN26 ..... 155 C1
Blindhouse La. TN25 ..... 160 B3
Blockmakers Ct. ME4 ..... 10 B1
Bloomsbury Rd. CT11 ..... 52 C6
Bloomsbury Way. TN24 ..... 139 B7
Bloors La. Gillingham ME8 ..... 11 D1
Bloors La. Gillingham ME8 ..... 11 E3
Bloors Wharf Rd. ME7 ..... 11 F4
Blowers Grove Wood. ME7 ..... 33 B3
Blue Boar La. ME1 ..... 9 D5
Blue House La. CT21 ..... 176 B8
Blue Line La. TN24 ..... 139 B3
Bluebell Cl. Gillingham ME7 ..... 10 F6
Bluebell Cl. Kingsnorth TN23 ..... 156 B4
Bluebell Rd. TN23 ..... 156 B4
Bluett St. ME14 ..... 75 A5
Blythe Cl. ME10 ..... 37 C5
Blythe Ct. CT21 ..... 176 D2
Blythe Rd. ME15 ..... 75 B4
Boarley Ct. ME14 ..... 53 F1
Boarley La. ME14 ..... 53 F2
Boarman's La. TN29 ..... 197 E8
Boat La. TN25 ..... 173 A4
Boathouse Rd. ME12 ..... 1 A3
Bob Amor Cl. ME13 ..... 62 E7
Bobbin Lodge Hill. CT4 ..... 86 B2
Bobbing Cty Prim Sch. ME10 ..... 36 B7
Bobbing Hill. ME10 & ME9 ..... 36 A6
Bockham Cotts. TN25 ..... 157 E8
Bockham La. Hinxhill TN25 ..... 141 A1
Bockham La. Mersham TN24 & TN25 ..... 157 E8
Bockhanger La. TN24 ..... 139 C6
Bockingford La. ME15 ..... 96 F8
Bodenham Rd. CT20 ..... 178 A4
Bodiam Cl. ME8 ..... 11 C3
Bodsham CE Prim Sch. TN25 ..... 142 E8
Bodsham Cres. ME15 ..... 76 B3
Bogle Rd. ME9 ..... 60 C7
Bognor Dr. CT6 ..... 22 D4
Bogshole La. Herne Bay CT6 ..... 23 D3
Bogshole La. Whitstable CT5 ..... 43 E4
Boley Hill. ME1 ..... 9 C6
Boleyn Ave. CT9 ..... 7 E1
Bolner Cl. ME5 ..... 31 F2
Bolton Rd. CT19 ..... 178 D6
Bolton St. CT11 ..... 52 D8
Bolts Hill. CT4 ..... 86 C2
Bombay Ho. 1 ME15 ..... 97 E5
Bond La. TN23 ..... 156 A2
Bond Rd. Ashford TN23 ..... 156 B8
Bond Rd. Gillingham ME8 ..... 33 E5
Bonetta Ct. ME12 ..... 3 B8
Bonham Dr. ME10 ..... 37 B5
Bonners Alley. 13 CT5 ..... 20 D2
Bonnington Cross. TN25 ..... 172 E3
Bonnington Gn. ME8 ..... 11 C3
Bonnington Rd. ME14 ..... 75 C6
Bonny Bush Hill. CT4 ..... 111 D5
Bonsor Rd. CT19 ..... 178 D6
Booth Pl. CT9 ..... 7 J3
Booth Rd. ME4 ..... 9 F2
Borden CE Cty Prim Sch. ME9 ..... 35 F3
Borden Gram Sch for Boys. ME10 ..... 36 F3
Borden La. ME10 & ME9 ..... 36 C3
Boresisle. TN30 ..... 167 B2
Bornefields. TN23 ..... 156 A7
Borough. CT1 ..... 67 A1
Borough Rd. Gillingham ME7 ..... 10 D4
Borough Rd. Queenborough ME11 ..... 3 B4
Borrowdale Ave. CT11 ..... 52 A7
Borstal Ave. CT5 ..... 43 D6
Borstal Hill. CT5 ..... 43 D7
Borstal HM Prison & Youth Custody Ctr. ME1 ..... 9 B1
Borstal Rd. ME1 ..... 9 B3
Borstal St. ME1 ..... 9 A2
Boscombe Rd. CT19 ..... 178 C6
Bosney Banks. CT15 ..... 148 A7
Bossingham Rd. CT4 ..... 126 F3
Bossington Rd. CT3 ..... 90 E1
Boston Cl. 5 CT16 ..... 149 B3
Boston Gdns. ME8 ..... 11 C1
Boston Rd. ME5 ..... 32 C2
Botany Cl. ME12 ..... 1 C1
Botany Rd. CT10 & CT9 ..... 8 F2
Boteler Cotts. CT13 ..... 93 A2
Botolph's Bridge Rd. CT21 ..... 187 A6
Bottles La. ME9 ..... 59 A6
Bottlescrew Hill. ME17 ..... 97 B4
Bottom Pond Rd. ME9 ..... 58 D3
Boughton Ave. CT10 ..... 30 A2
Boughton Church Cotts. ME13 ..... 63 D1
Boughton Cl. ME8 ..... 11 B3
Boughton Cnr. TN25 ..... 123 C5
Boughton Field Cotts. ME13 ..... 63 A5
Boughton Golf Course. ME13 ..... 63 E2
Boughton Hill. ME13 ..... 64 C3
Boughton La. ME15 ..... 97 B6
Boughton Monchelsea Cty Prim Sch. ME17 ..... 97 B2
Boughton Par. ME15 ..... 97 A7
Boughton Place Cotts. ME17 ..... 118 A8
Boughton Rd. ME17 ..... 101 B2
Boulevard Courrieres. CT3 ..... 112 E5
Boulevard The. TN24 ..... 156 F6
Boulogne Ct. 15 CT20 ..... 178 E5
Boundary Cl. ME12 ..... 4 E6
Boundary Ct. CT1 ..... 88 B6
Boundary Rd. Chatham ME1 & ME4 ..... 9 E3
Boundary Rd. Hythe CT21 ..... 176 A2
Boundary Rd. Kingsdown CT14 ..... 134 D6
Boundary Rd. Ramsgate CT11 ..... 52 E7
Boundary The. CT1 ..... 87 D7
Bounds La. ME13 ..... 64 A3
Boundsgate Cnr. ME13 ..... 105 B7
Bourne. CT2 ..... 66 A7
Bourne Cotts. CT4 ..... 111 C5
Bourne Gr. ME10 ..... 36 C5
Bourne La. TN26 ..... 183 A8
Bourne Park Rd. CT4 ..... 111 A7
Bourne Pk. TN25 ..... 172 D5
Bourne View. CT4 ..... 88 F1
Bournemouth Dr. CT6 ..... 22 D4
Bournemouth Gdns. CT19 ..... 178 C6
Bournemouth Rd. CT19 ..... 178 C5
Bournes Cl. CT2 ..... 67 F7
Bournes Pl. TN26 ..... 169 A2
Bourneside Terr. ME17 ..... 77 D2
Bournewood. TN26 ..... 183 A8
Bournewood Cl. ME15 ..... 75 F1
Bournville Ave. ME4 ..... 9 F1
Bouverie Pl. 2 CT20 ..... 178 D4
Bouverie Rd. CT20 ..... 178 D4
Bouverie Rd W. CT20 ..... 178 C4
Bouverie Sq. 1 CT20 ..... 178 D4
Bow Hill. CT4 ..... 109 F2
Bowdell La. TN29 ..... 191 E3
Bowden Cres. CT20 ..... 177 C6
Bowen Rd. CT19 ..... 177 E6

Bowens Field. TN23 ...... 139 B1
Bower Cl. ME16 ...... 74 E4
Bower Gr. ME5 ...... 32 C1
Bower Grove Sch. ME16 ...... 74 B2
Bower La. Maidstone ME16 ...... 74 E2
Bower La. Maidstone ME16 ...... 74 E3
Bower Mount Rd. ME16 ...... 74 D4
Bower Pl. ME16 ...... 74 E3
Bower Rd. TN25 ...... 158 A3
Bower St. ME16 ...... 74 E4
Bower Terr. ME16 ...... 74 E4
Bowerland La. Chilham CT4 ...... 85 E1
Bowerland La.
    Old Wives Lees CT4 ...... 85 C2
Bowers Ho. ME7 ...... 10 E7
Bowes Ave. CT9 ...... 7 E1
Bowes La. CT6 ...... 23 A2
Bowes La. CT6 ...... 23 A3
Bowes Rd. ME2 ...... 9 B8
Bowes Villas. ME14 ...... 93 E4
Bowl Field. TN25 ...... 142 B6
Bowl Rd. TN27 ...... 103 D2
Bowland Cl. CT6 ...... 23 C2
Bowles Well Gdns. CT19 ...... 178 F7
Bowley La. ME17 ...... 118 D8
Bowling Green La. CT14 ...... 117 B5
Bowling Green Terr. 8 CT17 ...... 166 D7
Bowling St. CT13 ...... 72 F1
Bowman Cl. ME5 ...... 32 C5
Bowman Ct. CT17 ...... 149 A1
Bowser Cl. CT14 ...... 116 F4
Bowyer Rd. CT5 ...... 42 F7
Boxley. TN23 ...... 155 F8
Boxley Cl. Maidstone ME14 ...... 75 B8
Boxley Cl. West Minster ME12 ...... 3 B7
Boxley Rd. Chatham ME5 ...... 32 B2
Boxley Rd. Maidstone ME14 ...... 75 B7
Boxmend Ind Est. ME15 ...... 97 F3
Boxted La. ME9 ...... 13 A1
Boyces Hill. ME9 ...... 35 D6
Boyden Gate Hill. CT3 ...... 47 B8
Boyes La. CT3 ...... 91 D3
Boyke La. CT4 ...... 144 C2
Boyne Rd. CT15 ...... 134 A1
Boys Hall Rd. TN24 ...... 156 F7
Boystown Pl. CT13 ...... 93 C3
Brabazon Rd. ME12 ...... 5 C1
Brabner Cl. CT17 ...... 178 E8
Brabourne Ave. ME8 ...... 11 C3
Brabourne
    CE Prim Sch. TN25 ...... 159 A8
Brabourne Cl. CT2 ...... 67 A4
Brabourne Gdns. CT20 ...... 177 E5
Brabourne La. TN25 ...... 142 F2
Brabourne Rd. TN25 ...... 141 D6
Brack La. TN29 ...... 191 B3
Bracken Cl. TN24 ...... 139 C6
Bracken Ct. Broadstairs CT10 ...... 29 E5
Bracken Ct. Sittingbourne ME10 .. 37 C5
Bracken Hill. ME5 ...... 32 A1
Bracken Lea. ME5 ...... 10 C1
Brackley Cl. ME14 ...... 75 C5
Brackwood Cl. ME8 ...... 33 D5
Bradbridge Gn. TN23 ...... 155 D8
Braddick Cl. ME15 ...... 97 B6
Bradfield Ave. ME9 ...... 38 D2
Bradfield Rd. TN24 ...... 139 B5
Bradfields Ave. ME5 ...... 31 F5
Bradfields Ave W. ME5 ...... 31 F5
Bradfields Sch. ME5 ...... 32 A6
Bradley Dr. ME10 ...... 36 E2
Bradley Rd. Folkestone CT19 ...... 178 F6
Bradley Rd. Ramsgate CT12 ...... 29 C1
Bradshaw Cl. ME9 ...... 12 E3
Bradstone Ave. CT19 ...... 178 D6
Bradstone New Rd. 3 CT20 .. 178 D5
Bradstone Rd. CT20 ...... 178 D5
Bradstow Way. CT10 ...... 30 A5
Brady Rd. CT18 ...... 161 A7
Braeside. CT10 ...... 30 B3
Braggs La. CT6 ...... 45 E6
Brake Ave. ME5 ...... 31 E5
Bramble Cl. Maidstone ME16 ...... 74 B3
Bramble Cl. Wye TN25 ...... 123 D3
Bramble La. TN25 ...... 123 C3
Brambledown. Chatham ME5 ...... 32 B8
Brambledown.
    Folkestone CT19 ...... 178 D6
Bramblefield La. ME10 ...... 14 E1
Bramblefields Cl. CT3 ...... 23 B2
Bramblehill Rd. ME13 ...... 62 C8
Brambles Wildlife Pk.
    CT2 &CT6 ...... 45 D4
Bramley Cres. CT20 ...... 177 E5
Bramley Ave. Canterbury CT1 ...... 87 C6
Bramley Ave. Faversham ME13 ... 62 E6
Bramley Cl.
    Brabourne Lees TN25 ...... 158 E6
Bramley Cl. Eastchurch ME12 ...... 5 D3
Bramley Cl. Gillingham ME8 ...... 34 B8
Bramley Cres. ME15 ...... 75 F3
Bramley Gdns. Ashford TN23 ... 156 A6
Bramley Gdns. Coxheath ME17 ... 96 C3
Bramley Way. ME15 ...... 5 D3
Bramling Gap. CT3 ...... 90 C3
Bramling Rd. CT3 & CT4 ...... 90 B4
Bramshaw Rd. CT2 ...... 66 E2
Bramshott Cl. ME16 ...... 74 C6
Bramston Rd. ME12 ...... 4 C6
Branch Cl. CT4 ...... 107 C2
Branch St. CT16 ...... 149 C1
Brandon Rd. CT12 ...... 29 A1
Brandon Way. CT7 ...... 27 B6
Bransgore Cl. ME8 ...... 33 D7
Brasenose Rd. ME7 ...... 10 E4

Brasier Ct. ME12 ...... 4 A5
Brassey Ave. CT10 ...... 29 F3
Brattle. TN26 ...... 181 B8
Bray Gdns. ME15 ...... 96 F5
Breach La. ME9 ...... 13 A2
Breadlands Cl. TN24 ...... 156 E8
Breadlands Rd. TN24 ...... 156 F8
Brecon Chase. ME12 ...... 4 C7
Brecon Rise. TN24 ...... 139 B4
Brecon Sq. CT12 ...... 29 A1
Bredgar CE Prim Sch. ME9 .... 58 A5
Bredgar Cl. Ashford TN23 ...... 155 F6
Bredgar Cl. Maidstone MC14 .... 75 C5
Bredgar Rd. ME8 ...... 11 B4
Bredhurst CE Prim Sch. ME7 .. 33 B1
Bredhurst Cl. ME12 ...... 3 B7
Bredhurst Rd. Gillingham ME8 ... 33 B4
Bredhurst Rd. Gillingham ME8 ... 33 C5
Bredlands La. CT3 & CT2 ...... 46 C1
Brenchley Ave. CT14 ...... 116 F4
Brenchley Cl. Ashford TN23 ...... 155 E6
Brenchley Cl. Chatham ME1 ...... 9 D2
Brenchley Rd. Gillingham ME8 ... 11 B2
Brenchley Rd. Maidstone ME15 .. 74 F2
Brenchley Rd.
    Sittingbourne ME10 ...... 36 F2
Brendon Ave. ME5 ...... 32 A3
Brendon Dr. TN24 ...... 139 B3
Brenley Cnr. ME13 ...... 63 B4
Brenley La. ME13 ...... 63 C2
Brent Cl. ME5 ...... 31 E5
Brent Hill. ME13 ...... 62 C8
Brent Rd. ME13 ...... 62 C8
Brents Ind Est. ME13 ...... 40 D1
Brentwood. TN23 ...... 155 F5
Brenzett Cl. ME5 ...... 32 B5
Brenzett Cnr. TN29 ...... 192 A3
Brenzett District
    CE Prim Sch. TN29 ...... 192 A2
Breton Rd. ME1 ...... 9 C2
Brett Wlk. ME8 ...... 33 D4
Brewer St. Deal CT14 ...... 117 D6
Brewer St. Maidstone ME14 ...... 75 A5
Brewer's Hill. CT20 ...... 177 D3
Brewery Cotts. CT14 ...... 116 E4
Brewery La. ME14 ...... 89 A1
Brewery Rd. ME10 ...... 36 E6
Brewery Sq. CT3 ...... 48 D2
Brewster Cotts. ME9 ...... 59 E2
Brian Roberts Ho. CT6 ...... 22 F5
Briar Cl. Ashford TN24 ...... 139 C6
Briar Cl. River CT17 ...... 148 F2
Briar Fields. ME14 ...... 75 E5
Briars Rd. TN29 ...... 194 F3
Briars Wlk. CT10 ...... 29 F3
Briary Cl. CT9 ...... 28 A8
Brice Ave. CT4 ...... 86 C1
Brices Alley. CT5 ...... 20 D2
Brickfield Cotts. TN25 ...... 123 B2
Brickfield La. ME13 ...... 63 E2
Brickfield Rd. CT14 ...... 128 F7
Brickmakers Ind Est. ME10 .... 37 B6
Brickwall Terr. TN26 ...... 168 F3
Bridewell La. TN30 ...... 179 A7
Bridewell Pk. CT5 ...... 21 A1
Bridge App The. CT5 ...... 20 F1
Bridge Cl. Hythe CT21 ...... 176 A3
Bridge Cl. Woodchurch TN26 ...... 181 B8
Bridge Cotts. Selling ME13 ...... 84 E7
Bridge Cotts. Teynham ME9 ...... 38 D2
Bridge Down. CT4 ...... 111 B8
Bridge Hill. Bridge CT4 ...... 111 B8
Bridge Hill. Finglesham CT14 .... 116 C8
Bridge Ho. CT11 ...... 52 C7
Bridge Mill Way. ME15 ...... 74 D2
Bridge & Patrixbourne
    CE Prim Sch. CT4 ...... 89 A2
Bridge Rd. Ashford TN23 ...... 138 F2
Bridge Rd.
    Brabourne Lees TN25 ...... 158 D5
Bridge Rd. Bridge CT4 ...... 88 D1
Bridge Rd. Deal CT14 ...... 117 D7
Bridge Rd. Faversham ME13 ...... 62 D8
Bridge Rd. Gillingham ME7 ...... 10 C7
Bridge Rd. Margate CT9 ...... 7 E1
Bridge Rd. Rochester ME1 ...... 9 C2
Bridge Rd. Sheerness ME12 ...... 1 C3
Bridge St. Dover CT16 ...... 149 C1
Bridge St. Folkestone CT19 ...... 178 E6
Bridge St. Loose ME15 ...... 96 F5
Bridge St. Wye TN25 ...... 123 E2
Bridge View Ind Est. ME11 ...... 3 A2
Bridgefield Rd. CT5 ...... 21 B3
Bridgeford Way. CT4 ...... 89 A1
Bridges Cl. CT17 ...... 25 E2
Bridgeside. CT14 ...... 117 C6
Bridgewater Rd. ME12 ...... 3 B8
Bridgeway. CT5 ...... 20 F2
Bridle Way. CT21 ...... 177 A3
Bridleway Gdns. CT10 ...... 29 E3
Bridleway La. TN23 ...... 156 B4
Brielle Way.
    Queenborough ME11 & ME12 ... 3 A6
Brielle Way. Sheerness ME12 ...... 1 B2
Brier Cl. ME5 ...... 32 C8
Brier Rd. ME10 & ME9 ...... 36 B4
Bright Rd. ME4 ...... 10 B2
Bright's Pl. CT11 ...... 52 F7
Brightlingsea Rd. CT13 ...... 93 F8
Brindle Way. ME5 ...... 32 C1
Brinklow Terr. TN26 ...... 155 A1
Brisbane Ave. ME10 ...... 36 C4
Brisbane Dr. CT12 ...... 29 A1
Brisbane Rd. ME4 ...... 10 A3
Brishing Cl. ME15 ...... 97 E5
Brishing La. ME15 ...... 97 E5
Brishing Rd. ME15 & ME17 ...... 97 F3
Brissenden Cl. TN28 ...... 200 B8

Bristles Cnr. CT3 ...... 46 E6
Bristol Pl. CT11 ...... 52 D7
Bristol Rd. CT1 ...... 87 F6
Britannia Ave. CT5 ...... 43 B7
Britannia Cl. ME10 ...... 36 F7
Britannia Rd. CT14 ...... 117 D8
Briton Ct. ME12 ...... 3 B8
Briton Rd. ME13 ...... 62 C7
Britten Cl. CT21 ...... 176 A3
Britton St. ME7 ...... 10 B5
Broad La. CT14 ...... 116 B7
Broad Oak Rd. CT2 ...... 67 B3
Broad St. Canterbury CT1 ...... 67 A1
Broad St. Canterbury CT1 ...... 88 A8
Broad St. Deal CT14 ...... 117 D6
Broad St. Margate CT9 ...... 7 I3
Broad St. Ramsgate CT11 ...... 52 E7
Broad St. Sheerness ME12 ...... 1 C2
Broad Street Hill.
    ME14 & ME17 ...... 77 D7
Broadacre. Lydden CT15 ...... 147 F8
Broadacre. Teynham ME9 ...... 38 D2
Broader La. ME14 ...... 55 B2
Broadfield Cres. CT20 ...... 178 A5
Broadfield Rd.
    Folkestone CT20 ...... 178 A5
Broadfield Rd.
    Maidstone ME15 ...... 97 A8
Broadhurst Dr. TN24 ...... 139 D7
Broadlands Ave. TN28 ...... 200 B8
Broadlands Cres. TN28 ...... 200 B8
Broadlands Dr. ME5 ...... 32 B4
Broadlands Ind Est. CT2 ...... 66 A7
Broadley Ave. CT7 ...... 26 F5
Broadley Rd. CT9 ...... 29 C7
Broadmead. TN23 ...... 155 E6
Broadmead Rd. CT19 ...... 178 C5
Broadmeadow. CT19 ...... 178 B7
Broadoak Ave. ME5 ...... 97 A8
Broadoak Rd. ME9 ...... 58 F6
Broadsole La. CT15 ...... 164 E5
Broadstairs Rd. CT10 ...... 29 E5
Broadstairs Sta. CT10 ...... 30 A4
Broadview. CT20 ...... 177 C6
Broadview Ave. ME8 ...... 33 E8
Broadviews. CT21 ...... 176 D1
Broadway. Gillingham ME8 ...... 11 A3
Broadway. Maidstone ME16 ...... 74 F4
Broadway. Petham CT4 ...... 109 A2
Broadway. Sheerness ME12 ...... 1 D1
Broadway The.
    Broadstairs CT10 ...... 30 A4
Broadway The. Herne Bay CT6 .. 22 C5
Broadway The. Minster ME12 ...... 4 B7
Brockenhurst Ave. ME15 ...... 75 C1
Brockenhurst Cl.
    Canterbury CT2 ...... 66 E2
Brockenhurst Cl.
    Gillingham ME8 ...... 33 C7
Brockenhurst Rd. CT11 ...... 52 G8
Brockhill Ctry Pk. CT21 ...... 175 F4
Brockhill Park Sch
    (Lower Dept) CT21 ...... 176 A3
Brockhill Park Sch
    (Upper Dept) CT21 ...... 175 F4
Brockhill Rd. CT21 ...... 176 B3
Brockley Rd. CT9 ...... 8 A2
Brockman Cres. TN29 ...... 187 B4
Brockman Rd. CT20 ...... 178 C5
Brockman's Cl. CT12 ...... 50 B7
Brogdale Farm Cotts. ME13 ...... 62 A3
Brogdale Rd. ME13 ...... 62 B5
Brogden Cres. ME17 ...... 98 F7
Bromley Cl. Chatham ME5 ...... 32 B4
Bromley Cl. Newington ME9 ...... 35 A5
Bromley Green Rd. TN26 ...... 171 A5
Brompton Hill. ME4 ...... 9 F6
Brompton La. ME2 ...... 9 A8
Brompton Rd. ME7 ...... 10 B6
Brompton Villas. CT13 ...... 149 E6
Brompton-Westbrook
    Cty Prim Sch. ME7 ...... 10 A5
Bromstone
    Cty Prim Sch. CT10 ...... 29 D3
Bromstone Mews. CT10 ...... 29 E3
Bromstone Rd. CT10 ...... 29 E3
Bronington Cl. ME5 ...... 32 A5
Brook. ME4 ...... 10 A4
Brook Cl. Herne Bay CT6 ...... 22 C3
Brook Cl. Hythe CT21 ...... 177 B3
Brook Cotts. Dean Street ME15 .. 96 C7
Brook Cotts. Teynham ME9 ...... 39 A2
Brook Cty Prim Sch. TN25 ..... 141 A4
Brook La. Cliffs End CT12 ...... 50 F4
Brook La. Reculver CT6 ...... 24 B5
Brook La. Sellindge TN25 ...... 159 E2
Brook La Cotts. TN25 ...... 159 E2
Brook Rd. Faversham ME13 ...... 40 D1
Brook Rd. Whitstable CT5 ...... 21 C3
Brook St. Eastry CT13 ...... 93 C2
Brook St. Woodchurch TN26 .... 180 D8
Brookbank. Brook TN25 ...... 141 A5
Brookbank. Maidstone ME14 ...... 75 A8
Brooke Ave. CT9 ...... 28 B7
Brooke Rd. TN24 ...... 139 B3
Brookes Pl. ME9 ...... 35 B6
Brookfield Ave. CT16 ...... 149 B2
Brookfield Ct. TN23 ...... 155 F8
Brookfield Ind Pk. TN23 ...... 138 F1
Brookfield Pl. CT16 ...... 149 B2
Brookfield Rd. Ashford TN23 .... 155 F8
Brookfield Rd. Dover CT16 ...... 149 A3
Brookland
    CE Prim Sch. TN29 ...... 197 D8
Brooklands Cl. CT4 ...... 67 A4
Brooklyn Paddock. ME7 ...... 10 D6
Brooks Pl. ME14 ...... 75 A4

Brooks Way. TN29 ...... 203 C5
Brookside. St Mary's Bay TN29 .. 195 A5
Brookside. Temple Ewell CT16 .. 148 D5
Broom Rd. ME10 ...... 37 C5
Broomcroft Rd. ME8 ...... 11 F2
Broome Park Golf Course.
    CT4 ...... 129 B6
Broomfield Cres. CT9 ...... 8 F2
Broomfield Gate. CT5 ...... 44 D5
Broomfield Rd.
    Broomfield MF17 ...... 99 D4
Broomfield Rd
    Faversham ME13 ...... 62 C8
Broomfield Rd.
    Folkestone CT19 ...... 177 E6
Broomfield Rd. Herne Bay CT6 .. 23 C2
Brotherhood Cl. CT2 ...... 66 D4
Broughton St. TN23 ...... 138 E1
Brown St. ME8 ...... 11 F1
Brownelow Copse. ME5 ...... 32 B1
Brownhill Cl. ME5 ...... 32 A4
Browning Pl. CT19 ...... 178 E7
Browning Orch. ME9 ...... 59 A7
Broxhall Rd. CT4 ...... 110 B3
Bruce Cl. CT14 ...... 117 B4
Bruges Ct. ME10 ...... 14 F1
Brundell Terr. CT4 ...... 86 B2
Brunel Way. ME4 ...... 10 A7
Brunswick Cotts. ME9 ...... 38 E6
Brunswick Cl. 3 CT11 ...... 52 E7
Brunswick Field. ME9 ...... 38 E6
Brunswick Gdns. 3 CT16 ...... 149 B3
Brunswick House
    Cty Prim Sch. ME16 ...... 74 E5
Brunswick Ind Ctr. TN23 ...... 138 F2
Brunswick Rd. Ashford TN23 .... 138 F2
Brunswick Rd. Birchington CT7 ... 27 A5
Brunswick Sq. CT6 ...... 22 E5
Brunswick St. Maidstone ME15 ... 75 A3
Brunswick St. Ramsgate CT11 ... 52 E7
Brunswick St E. ME15 ...... 75 A3
Bryant Rd. ME2 ...... 9 A7
Bryant St. ME4 ...... 10 A3
Brymore Cl. CT1 ...... 67 B2
Brymore Rd. CT1 ...... 67 B2
Bryony Sch (private). ME8 ...... 33 F5
Buck Cl. TN25 ...... 105 C2
Buckhurst Dr. CT9 ...... 8 F2
Buckingham Rd. 14
    Broadstairs CT10 ...... 30 B4
Buckingham Rd.
    Gillingham ME7 ...... 10 D5
Buckingham Rd. Margate CT9 .... 7 I1
Buckingham Rd.
    Whitstable CT5 ...... 21 B2
Buckingham Row. ME15 ...... 97 E7
Buckland Ave. CT16 ...... 149 B2
Buckland Cl. ME5 ...... 32 A2
Buckland Cotts. ME13 ...... 61 B8
Buckland Hill. ME16 ...... 74 D6
Buckland Hospl. CT17 ...... 149 A1
Buckland La. Maidstone ME16 ... 74 D6
Buckland La. Staple CT3 ...... 92 A4
Buckland Pl. ME16 ...... 74 E4
Buckland Rd. ME16 ...... 74 E4
Bucklers Cl. ME12 ...... 6 E4
Buckmore Park
    (Scout Camp). ME5 ...... 31 C3
Bucksford La. TN23 ...... 155 C7
Buckthorn Cl. CT14 ...... 117 C7
Budd's Farm Cotts. TN30 ...... 188 F2
Budd's La. TN30 ...... 188 F2
Buenos Ayres. CT9 ...... 7 H2
Buffs Ave. CT20 ...... 177 B6
Builders Sq. CT3 ...... 90 A8
Bull Hill. ME17 ...... 102 A1
Bull La. Bethersden TN26 ...... 153 B4
Bull La. Boughton Street ME13 ... 63 F4
Bull La. Eccles ME20 ...... 53 A6
Bull La. Stockbury ME9 ...... 34 E2
Bulldog Rd. ME5 ...... 31 C3
Bulleid Pl. TN24 ...... 156 D7
Buller Rd. ME4 ...... 9 F2
Buller's Ave. CT6 ...... 22 E4
Bullockstone Rd. CT6 ...... 45 E7
Bulls Cl. 4 CT21 ...... 176 B2
Bulltown Cnr. TN25 ...... 141 F3
Bullwark St. CT17 ...... 166 D5
Bulrush Cl. ME5 ...... 31 F3
Bulrushes The. TN23 ...... 155 D8
Bulwark Rd. CT14 ...... 117 D7
Bumbles Cl. ME1 ...... 31 D7
Bunce Court Rd.
    ME13 & ME17 ...... 102 E7
Bungalow The. TN26 ...... 137 F5
Bungalows The.
    Faversham ME13 ...... 62 A4
Bungalows The.
    Tenterden TN30 ...... 179 D7
Bungalows The.
    Woodnesborough CT13 ...... 93 B5
Bunker's Hill. CT17 ...... 149 B2
Bunkers Hill Cl. CT17 ...... 149 B1
Bunkers Hill Rd. CT17 ...... 149 A1
Bunkley Meadow. TN26 ...... 183 A7
Burberry La. ME17 ...... 99 B5
Burch Ave. CT13 ...... 93 F8
Burford's Alley. CT3 ...... 71 D1
Burgate. CT1 ...... 88 A8
Burgate La. 4 CT1 ...... 88 A8
Burgate Terr. TN25 ...... 157 E4
Burgess Cl. Minster,Thanet CT12 . 50 C7
Burgess Cl. Whitfield CT16 ...... 149 B7
Burgess Hall Dr. ME17 ...... 98 F6
Burgess Rd. Aylesham CT3 ...... 112 F6
Burgess Rd. Rochester ME2 ...... 9 B7
Burgess Row. 8 TN30 ...... 179 A7

Burghclere Dr. ME16 ...... 74 B2
Burgoyne Ct. ME14 ...... 74 F7
Burgoyne Gr. CT16 ...... 149 A5
Burgoyne Hts. CT16 ...... 149 E3
Burial Ground La. ME15 ...... 74 F7
Burkeston Cl. ME10 ...... 37 A8
Burleigh Dr. ME14 ...... 53 F1
Burleigh Rd. TN27 ...... 120 C7
Burley Rd. ME10 ...... 36 E4
Burlington Dr. CT6 ...... 23 D5
Burlington Gdns.
    Gillingham ME8 ...... 33 E4
Burlington Gdns. Margate CT9 ... 28 C8
Burma Cl. CT1 ...... 67 D1
Burma Way. ME5 ...... 31 F6
Burmarsh Cl. ME5 ...... 32 B5
Burmarsh Rd. Burmarsh TN29 .. 186 C3
Burmarsh Rd. Hythe CT21 ...... 187 C8
Burn's Rd. ME7 ...... 10 C7
Burnan Rd. CT5 ...... 21 C2
Burnham Cl. ME10 ...... 36 E8
Burnham Wlk. ME8 ...... 33 E3
Burns Rd. ME16 ...... 74 C2
Burnt House Hill. CT3 ...... 69 B5
Burnt Oak Terr. ME7 ...... 10 D6
Burnt Oast Rd. ME13 ...... 64 A3
Burntwick Dr. ME9 ...... 13 B3
Burnup Bank. ME10 ...... 37 C5
Burrow Rd. CT19 ...... 178 F6
Burrs The. ME10 ...... 36 F3
Burrstock Way. ME8 ...... 12 B2
Bursill Cres. CT12 ...... 29 B3
Bursted Hill. CT4 ...... 110 B2
Burston Rd. ME17 ...... 96 B2
Burton Cl. CT19 ...... 178 A7
Burton Fields. CT6 ...... 23 B4
Burton Rd. TN24 ...... 139 E6
Busbridge Rd. ME15 ...... 96 E6
Bush Ave. CT12 ...... 29 B3
Bush Cl. ME9 ...... 57 F5
Bush Row. ME20 ...... 53 A3
Bushey Cl. ME13 ...... 63 F3
Busheyfields Rd. CT6 ...... 45 F6
Bushmeadow Rd. ME8 ...... 11 F2
Bushy Gr. ME17 ...... 99 D2
Bushy Hill Rd. CT2 ...... 68 D7
Bushy Royds. TN24 ...... 156 D6
Bushy Ruff Cotts. CT16 ...... 148 D4
Butchers La. CT15 ...... 113 E8
Butchery La. 1 CT1 ...... 88 A8
Butchery The. 2 CT13 ...... 73 A1
Butler's Hill. ME13 ...... 64 D7
Butt Field Rd. TN23 ...... 155 E2
Butter St. CT15 ...... 113 C4
Butterfly Ctr The. CT15 ...... 146 B3
Buttermere. ME13 ...... 62 C6
Buttermere Cl.
    Folkestone CT19 ...... 178 B6
Buttermere Cl. Gillingham ME7 .. 11 A5
Buttermere Gdns. CT3 ...... 112 F6
Button La. ME15 ...... 76 B2
Butts Ct. CT4 ...... 110 A6
Butts Cty Prim Inf Sch The.
    ME10 ...... 36 E6
Butts Hill. ME13 ...... 63 F5
Butts Meadow. CT4 ...... 110 A6
Butts The. Sandwich CT13 ...... 72 F1
Butts The. Sittingbourne ME10 .. 36 F4
Buxton Cl. Chatham ME5 ...... 32 D3
Buxton Cl. Maidstone ME15 ...... 97 A8
Buxton Rd. CT12 ...... 29 B2
Bybrook Ct. TN24 ...... 139 C4
Bybrook Cty Inf Sch. TN24 .... 139 B3
Bybrook Cty Jun Sch. TN24 ... 139 C3
Bybrook Field. CT3 ...... 177 E3
Bybrook Rd. TN24 ...... 139 C3
Bybrook Way. CT20 ...... 177 E4
Bychurch Pl. 6 ME15 ...... 75 A3
Byllan Rd. CT17 ...... 148 E1
Byron Ave. CT9 ...... 7 J1
Byron Cl. CT1 ...... 88 C2
Byron Cres. CT16 ...... 149 B6
Byron Cty Prim Sch. ME7 ...... 10 C3
Byron Rd. Gillingham ME7 ...... 10 C3
Byron Rd. Maidstone ME14 ...... 75 B4
Bysing Wood Cotts. ME13 ...... 39 F3
Bysing Wood Cty Prim Sch.
    ME13 ...... 62 A8
Bysing Wood Rd. ME13 ...... 39 F3
Bythorne Ct. ME8 ...... 12 B2

C Ramp App. CT16 ...... 166 D5
Cade Rd. TN23 ...... 156 B2
Cades Orch. ME13 ...... 61 E5
Cadnam Cl. CT2 ...... 66 E2
Caernarvon Dr. ME15 ...... 74 F2
Caesar's Way. CT19 ...... 177 E2
Cage La. TN2 ...... 135 A7
Calais Hill. CT2 ...... 66 A4
Calcroft Mews. 6 CT1 ...... 67 B2
Calcutta Ho. 3 ME15 ...... 97 E8
Caldecot La. TN29 ...... 199 D2
Caldecote Cl. ME8 ...... 12 B1
Calder Rd. ME14 ...... 74 E1
Caldew Ave. ME8 ...... 11 C2
Caldew Gr. ME10 ...... 37 A2
Caledon Terr. CT1 ...... 88 A2
Caledonian Ct. ME8 ...... 33 E4
Calehill Cl. ME14 ...... 75 C6
Calgary Cres. CT19 ...... 178 A6
California Row. CT3 ...... 90 E6
Callams Cl. ME8 ...... 33 D6
Calland. TN25 ...... 158 E1
Callaways La. ME9 ...... 35 B6
Calleywell La. TN25 ...... 173 A4
Callis Court Rd. CT10 ...... 29 F6
Callis Grange
    Cty Inf Sch. CT10 ...... 29 F6

Calverden Rd. CT12 ...... 29 A1
Camborne Manor. ME7 ...... 10 C6
Cambourne Ave. CT8 ...... 27 D8
Cambrai Ct. CT1 ...... 67 D1
Cambridge Ave. CT13 ...... 95 B1
Cambridge Cl. CT17 ...... 27 B7
Cambridge Cres. ME15 ...... 97 D7
Cambridge Gdns. CT20 ...... 178 D5
Cambridge Ho. 3 ME15 ...... 97 D7
Cambridge Rd. Canterbury CT1 .. 87 F6
Cambridge Rd. Deal CT14 ...... 117 D3
Cambridge Rd.
  Dover CT16 & CT17 ...... 166 D7
Cambridge Rd.
  Faversham ME13 ...... 62 B6
Cambridge Rd. Gillingham ME8 .. 33 C6
Cambridge Rd. Rochester ME2 .. 9 A8
Cambridge Rd.
  Sittingbourne ME10 ...... 37 B3
Cambridge Terr. Chatham ME4 ... 9 F4
Cambridge Terr. 11
  Dover CT16 ...... 166 E7
Cambridge Terr. 11
  Folkestone CT20 ...... 178 E5
Cambridge Terr. Margate CT9 ...... 8 B1
Cambridge Way. CT1 ...... 87 F6
Camden Cl. ME5 ...... 32 B5
Camden Cres. CT16 ...... 166 E7
Camden Rd. Broadstairs CT10 ..... 29 E7
Camden Rd. Gillingham ME7 ...... 10 D7
Camden Rd. Ramsgate CT11 ...... 52 E6
Camden Sq. 7 CT11 ...... 52 E7
Camden St. ME14 ...... 75 A5
Camden Terr. TN24 ...... 139 E1
Camellia Cl. Gillingham ME8 ...... 33 D7
Camellia Cl. 2 Margate CT9 ...... 28 B8
Cameron Cl. ME5 ...... 32 B8
Cameron Ct. CT17 ...... 166 A6
Camomile Dr. ME14 ...... 75 F5
Camp Way. ME15 ...... 97 C6
Campbell Cl. CT6 ...... 23 C3
Campbell Rd. Deal CT14 ...... 117 D4
Campbell Rd. Maidstone ME15 ... 75 A3
Campion Cl. ME5 ...... 31 E3
Campleshon Rd. ME8 ...... 33 D5
Campus Way. ME7 ...... 33 A8
Canada Cl. CT18 & CT19 ...... 177 C6
Canada Rd. CT14 ...... 117 D3
Canada Terr. 3 ME14 ...... 75 A7
Canadian Ave. ME7 ...... 10 F4
Canal Rd. ME2 ...... 9 C7
Canberra Gdns. ME10 ...... 36 C4
Canning St. ME14 ...... 75 A6
Cannon Appleton Ct. CT1 ...... 87 E7
Cannon Rd. CT11 ...... 52 D7
Cannon St. Deal CT14 ...... 117 C4
Cannon St. Dover CT16 ...... 166 D8
Cannon St. Lydd TN29 ...... 203 D1
Cannon St. New Romney TN28 ... 200 B7
Cannonbury Rd. CT11 ...... 52 D6
Cannongate Ave. CT21 ...... 176 D3
Cannongate Cl. CT21 ...... 176 E2
Cannongate Gdns. CT21 ...... 176 E3
Cannongate Rd. CT21 ...... 176 D3
Canon Cl. ME1 ...... 9 B2
Canon Gn. CT3 ...... 91 A7
Canon Woods Way. TN24 ...... 139 F6
Canons Gate Rd. CT16 ...... 166 E8
Canterbury Cl. CT10 ...... 29 D5
Canterbury Ct. TN24 ...... 139 D2
Canterbury East Sta. CT1 ...... 87 F7
Canterbury
  Equestrian Ctr. CT6 ...... 22 D3
Canterbury Golf Course. CT2 .. 67 E2
Canterbury
  High Sch The. CT2 ...... 87 D8
Canterbury Hill. CT2 ...... 66 E5
Canterbury Ho. 2 ME15 ...... 97 D7
Canterbury Ind Pk. CT3 ...... 69 A8
Canterbury La.
  Gillingham ME8 & ME9 ...... 12 C1
Canterbury Rd.
  Ashford, Bybrook TN24 ...... 139 E5
Canterbury Rd.
  Ashford, S Willesborough TN24 .. 156 E6
Canterbury Rd. Barham CT4 ...... 129 C5
Canterbury Rd. Boughton Aluph
  CT4 & TN25 & TN24 ...... 123 C5
Canterbury Rd.
  Boughton Street ME13 ...... 63 D4
Canterbury Rd.
  Brabourne TN25 ...... 159 C8
Canterbury Rd.
  Brabourne Lees TN25 ...... 158 F6
Canterbury Rd.
  Challock TN25 & TN27 ...... 104 C1
Canterbury Rd. Chilham CT4 ...... 85 E1
Canterbury Rd. Denton CT4 ...... 129 A1
Canterbury Rd. Dunkirk ME13 ... 64 E2
Canterbury Rd. Elham CT4 ...... 144 E3
Canterbury Rd.
  Etchinghill CT18 ...... 161 D4
Canterbury Rd.
  Faversham ME13 ...... 62 E5
Canterbury Rd.
  Folkestone CT19 ...... 178 D7
Canterbury Rd.
  Folkestone, Foord CT19 ...... 178 E6
Canterbury Rd. Hawkinge
  CT18 & CT19 & CT15 & CT4 ...... 163 B4
Canterbury Rd. Herne CT3 & CT6 45 E5
Canterbury Rd. Herne Bay CT6 .. 23 A3
Canterbury Rd. Littlebourne CT3 89 E8
Canterbury Rd. Lydden CT15 .. 147 E7
Canterbury Rd. Lyminge CT18 .. 161 C7
Canterbury Rd. Sarre CT7 ...... 48 E7

Canterbury Rd.
  Sittingbourne ME10 ...... 37 B3
Canterbury Rd. Whitstable CT5 .. 43 D8
Canterbury Rd E. CT11 & CT12 .. 52 A6
Canterbury Rd W. CT12 ...... 51 D7
Canterbury Road Birchington.
  CT7 ...... 27 B7
Canterbury Road Cty Prim Sch.
  ME10 ...... 37 B3
Canterbury Road Margate.
  CT9 ...... 7 G1
Canterbury Road Westgate.
  CT8 & CT9 ...... 27 E8
Canterbury West Sta. CT2 ...... 66 F1
Canute Rd. Birchington CT7 ...... 26 D7
Canute Rd. Deal CT14 ...... 95 C1
Canute Rd. Faversham ME13 .. 62 C6
Capel Cl. Broadstairs CT10 ...... 8 F1
Capel Cl. Gillingham ME8 ...... 33 D4
Capel Rd. Faversham ME13 ...... 62 B7
Capel Rd. Petham CT4 ...... 108 F3
Capel Rd.
  Ruckinge TN25 & TN26 ...... 171 B4
Capel Rd. Sittingbourne ME10 .. 36 E2
Capel St. CT18 ...... 164 B3
Capel-le-Ferne Cty Prim Sch.
  CT18 ...... 164 C3
Capell Cl. ME17 ...... 96 C3
Capetown Ho. 1 ME15 ...... 97 F5
Capstan Row. CT14 ...... 117 A3
Capstone Farm Country Pk.
  ME7 ...... 32 D5
Capstone Rd. Chatham ME5 ...... 10 D1
Capstone Rd. Gillingham ME7 ... 32 B8
Cardine Cl. ME10 ...... 36 E7
Carey Cl. TN28 ...... 200 B6
Carey Ho. 5 CT1 ...... 87 F7
Caring La. ME15 ...... 76 E1
Caring La. ME15 ...... 76 C1
Carisbrooke Dr. ME16 ...... 74 D4
Carlsden Cl. CT16 ...... 149 A3
Carlton Ave. Broadstairs CT10 .. 30 A5
Carlton Ave. Gillingham ME7 ..... 10 E4
Carlton Ave. Ramsgate CT11 .... 52 D6
Carlton Ave. Sheerness ME12 .... 1 C1
Carlton Cres. ME5 ...... 32 D8
Carlton Gdns. ME15 ...... 97 B8
Carlton Hill. CT6 ...... 22 C4
Carlton Leas. CT20 ...... 178 C4
Carlton Mansions. CT10 ...... 8 A2
Carlton Rd. Ashford TN23 ...... 139 A2
Carlton Rd. Kingsdown CT14 .... 134 C6
Carlton Rd. Whitstable CT5 ...... 43 D2
Carlton Rd E. CT8 ...... 27 D8
Carlton Rd W. CT8 ...... 27 D8
Carlton Rise. CT8 ...... 27 C8
Carman's St. ME15 & ME17 ...... 96 F3
Carmel Ct. 2 CT7 ...... 26 F8
Caroland Cl. TN25 ...... 158 D5
Caroline Cl. CT5 ...... 43 B6
Caroline Cres. Broadstairs CT10 . 29 E6
Caroline Cres. Maidstone ME16 .. 74 D7
Caroline Sq. CT9 ...... 7 J3
Carpeaux Cl. ME4 ...... 10 A4
Carpenters Cl. ME4 ...... 9 E2
Carpinus Cl. ME5 ...... 32 B1
Carriage Ho The. ME13 ...... 83 D5
Carriage Mus. ME15 ...... 75 A3
Carrie Ho. ME16 ...... 74 E5
Carroway's Pl. CT9 ...... 7 J2
Carter La. TN29 ...... 191 E2
Carter's Rd. CT20 ...... 177 F5
Carter's Wood. TN26 ...... 183 B7
Carton Cl. ME1 ...... 9 D2
Cartwright & Kelsey
  CE Prim Sch The. CT3 ...... 71 C2
Carvoran Way. ME8 ...... 33 C5
Caslocke St. 2 ME13 ...... 62 C7
Cassino Ho. 16 CT1 ...... 67 B2
Cassino Sq. CT16 ...... 149 E2
Castalla Cotts. CT14 ...... 117 C3
Castle Ave. Broadstairs CT10 .... 30 B6
Castle Ave. Dover CT16 ...... 149 D1
Castle Ave. Hythe CT21 ...... 176 B3
Castle Ave. Rochester ME1 ...... 9 C4
Castle Bay. CT20 ...... 177 D3
Castle Cl. 4 Folkestone CT20 .... 177 F3
Castle Cl. Lympne CT21 ...... 174 F2
Castle Comm Sch. CT14 ...... 117 C4
Castle Cotts. CT13 ...... 72 E5
Castle Cres. CT21 ...... 176 C4
Castle Dene. ME14 ...... 74 F8
Castle Dr. CT16 ...... 148 F7
Castle Hill.
  Folkestone CT19 & CT18 ...... 178 A8
Castle Hill. Rochester ME1 ...... 9 C6
Castle Hill. Thurnham ME14 ...... 55 D1
Castle Hill Ave. CT20 ...... 178 C4
Castle Hill Rd. CT16 ...... 166 E8
Castle Mayne Ave. CT7 ...... 27 F3
Castle Mews. CT14 ...... 117 A4
Castle Rd. Chatham ME4 ...... 10 B2
Castle Rd. Folkestone CT20 ...... 177 F3
Castle Rd. Hythe CT21 ...... 176 B2
Castle Rd. Maidstone ME16 ...... 74 D7
Castle Rd. Sittingbourne ME10 .. 37 B5
Castle Rd. Whitstable CT5 ...... 20 F2
Castle Road Bsns Prec. ME10 .. 37 B6
Castle Road Tech Ctr. ME10 .... 37 B6
Castle Rough La. ME10 ...... 14 F1
Castle Row. CT1 ...... 87 F7
Castle St. 6 Ashford TN23 ...... 139 B2
Castle St. Canterbury CT1 ...... 87 F7
Castle St. Queenborough ME11 .. 3 A5
Castle View Rd. ME2 ...... 9 A7

Castle Wlk. CT14 ...... 95 D1
Castleacres Ind Pk. ME10 ...... 37 B6
Castlemaine Ave. ME7 ...... 10 F6
Castlemere Ave. ME11 ...... 3 B5
Castlemount Rd. CT16 ...... 149 C1
Castlemount Sch. CT16 ...... 149 E1
Castleview Ct. CT17 ...... 149 B1
Cathedral View. CT2 ...... 67 A2
Catherine Cl. ME16 ...... 74 A3
Catherine St. ME1 ...... 9 D3
Catherine Way. CT10 ...... 30 A6
Catkin Cl. ME5 ...... 31 F1
Catsole Hill. CT3 ...... 91 D2
Catt's Hill. TN30 ...... 189 E3
Catt's Wood Rd. CT4 ...... 109 F4
Catterick Rd. ME5 ...... 32 D2
Cattle Market. CT13 ...... 72 F1
Cauldham Cl. CT18 ...... 164 B1
Cauldham La. CT18 ...... 164 B3
Causeway The. Canterbury CT2 .. 66 F1
Causeway The. Sandwich CT13 .. 72 D2
Cavalry Ct. CT20 ...... 177 D5
Cave Hill. ME15 ...... 74 F1
Cave La. CT3 ...... 91 D3
Cavell Sq. CT14 ...... 117 A3
Cavell Way. CT10 ...... 36 D5
Cavenagh Rd. CT15 ...... 151 B6
Cavendish Ave. ME7 ...... 10 E6
Cavendish Ct. CT6 ...... 23 A5
Cavendish Pl. 2 CT11 ...... 52 E6
Cavendish Rd. Herne Bay CT6 .. 23 A5
Cavendish Rd. Rochester ME1 ... 9 D3
Cavendish St. CT11 ...... 52 E6
Cavendish Way. ME15 ...... 76 B3
Caversham Cl. ME8 ...... 11 F1
Cavour Rd. Faversham ME13 .. 62 C7
Cavour Rd. Sheerness ME12 ...... 1 D2
Caxton Rd. CT9 ...... 28 C8
Cayser Dr. ME17 ...... 99 E2
Cazeneuve St. ME1 ...... 9 C5
Cecil Ave. Gillingham ME8 ...... 11 A2
Cecil Ave. Rochester ME2 ...... 9 B8
Cecil Ave. Sheerness ME12 ...... 1 C1
Cecil Ct. Ashford TN24 ...... 139 B3
Cecil Ct. Herne Bay CT6 ...... 23 A4
Cecil Pk. CT6 ...... 23 A4
Cecil Rd. Kingsdown CT14 ...... 134 D7
Cecil Rd. Rochester ME1 ...... 9 C3
Cecil Sq. CT9 ...... 7 I2
Cecil St. CT9 ...... 7 I2
Cecilia Gr. CT10 ...... 29 F6
Cecilia Rd. CT11 ...... 52 E8
Cedar Cl. Ashford TN23 ...... 138 E3
Cedar Cl. Broadstairs CT10 ...... 29 F7
Cedar Cl. Margate CT9 ...... 29 B4
Cedar Cl. Sittingbourne ME10 ... 37 B2
Cedar Cres. TN29 ...... 194 F3
Cedar Ct. Folkestone CT20 ...... 177 E5
Cedar Ct. 10 Tenterden TN30 .... 179 A7
Cedar Gdns. ME9 ...... 56 E8
Cedar Gr. ME7 ...... 33 A5
Cedar Ho. ME12 ...... 1 C2
Cedar Rd. CT2 ...... 68 A6
Cedar Terr. ME13 ...... 62 A4
Cedars Sch The.
  Maidstone ME16 ...... 74 D4
Cedars Sch The.
  Rochester ME1 ...... 9 C4
Cedars The. ME10 ...... 37 C5
Cedarview. CT2 ...... 66 C1
Cedarwood Ho. ME15 ...... 96 B6
Cedric Rd. CT6 ...... 7 C1
Ceil Villas. CT14 ...... 94 B4
Celestine Cl. ME5 ...... 32 A1
Celtic Rd. CT14 ...... 117 A2
Cemetery La. TN24 ...... 139 C4
Centenary Cl. TN27 ...... 120 C8
Centenary Gdns. CT13 ...... 93 A2
Central Ave. Gillingham ME4 .... 10 B8
Central Ave. Herne Bay CT6 ..... 22 D4
Central Ave. Sittingbourne ME10 . 36 F4
Central Bsns Pk. ME2 ...... 9 E7
Central Par. Herne Bay CT6 ..... 22 E5
Central Par. Rochester ME1 ...... 9 D2
Central Park Gdns. ME1 ...... 9 E2
Central Rd. Ramsgate CT11 ...... 52 D8
Central Rd. Rochester ME2 ...... 9 A7
Central Service Rd. CT16 ...... 166 H8
Central Sta. CT19 ...... 178 C5
Centre 2000. Maidstone ME16 .. 74 C8
Centre 2000.
  Sittingbourne ME10 ...... 37 A4
Centre Ct. ME2 ...... 9 E7
Centre Rd. CT17 ...... 166 C6
Centre The. Margate CT9 ...... 7 I2
Centre The. Ramsgate CT12 ..... 29 A1
Centurion Cl. ME7 ...... 10 F1
Centurion Wlk. TN23 ...... 156 B4
Century Ct. Faversham ME13 .... 62 E7
Century Rd. Gillingham ME8 .... 33 D8
Century Wlk. CT14 ...... 117 C6
Ceres Rd. ME10 ...... 37 C5
Chada Ave. ME7 ...... 10 E3
Chaffe's La. ME9 ...... 12 E3
Chaffes Terr. ME4 ...... 12 E2
Chaffinch Cl. ME5 ...... 32 A7
Chafy Cres. CT2 ...... 67 F5
Chain Gate. TN27 ...... 118 A8
Chain The. 6 CT13 ...... 73 A1
Chalcroft Rd. CT20 ...... 177 E4
Chalfont Dr. Gillingham ME8 .... 33 D6
Chalfont Dr. Herne Bay CT6 ..... 22 D3
Chalk Ave. TN30 ...... 167 B2
Chalk Cl. CT9 ...... 178 A7
Chalk Hill. CT11 & CT12 ...... 51 F6
Chalk Hill Rd. CT14 ...... 134 C5
Chalk Pit Hill. ME4 ...... 10 A7

Chalk Pit La. CT13 & CT3 ...... 92 C5
Chalk Rd. ME11 ...... 3 A5
Chalkenden Ave. ME8 ...... 11 A2
Chalkpit Hill. CT4 ...... 89 D3
Chalksole Green La. CT15 ...... 147 B2
Chalkwell Ct. CT17 ...... 166 A7
Chalkwell Rd. ME10 ...... 36 D5
Chalky Bank Rd. ME8 ...... 11 F2
Chalky Rd. ME9 ...... 56 C6
Challenger Cl. ME10 ...... 36 E7
Challock Ct. CT9 ...... 8 F2
Challock
  Cty Prim Sch. TN25 ...... 105 B1
Challock Wlk. ME14 ...... 75 C6
Chamberlain Ave. ME16 ...... 74 C2
Chamberlain Cl. ME8 ...... 33 B5
Chamberlain Dr. CT6 ...... 22 B4
Chamberlain Rd.
  Chatham ME4 ...... 10 B2
Chamberlain Rd. Dover CT17 ... 166 B8
Chance Meadow. CT15 ...... 149 E6
Chancel Ct. CT2 ...... 66 D1
Chancery La. ME15 ...... 75 B3
Chanctonbury Chase. CT5 ...... 43 A6
Chandos Rd. 18 CT10 ...... 30 B4
Chandos Sq. 15 CT10 ...... 30 B4
Channel Cl. CT19 ...... 178 F7
Channel Lea. CT14 ...... 117 C1
Channel Rd. CT19 ...... 29 A6
Channel Sch The. CT19 ...... 178 C7
Channel Tunnel Terminal.
  CT18 ...... 177 B8
Channel View. 13 CT19 ...... 178 E5
Channel View Ct. 16 CT11 ...... 52 F7
Channel View Rd. CT17 ...... 166 C5
Channel Watch. TN28 ...... 200 E4
Channon Rd. TN29 ...... 204 E2
Chantry Ct. 4 CT1 ...... 66 F1
Chapel Cotts. ME17 ...... 98 F5
Chapel Hill. Eythorne CT15 ...... 131 C7
Chapel Hill. Margate CT9 ...... 29 A6
Chapel Hill Cl. ME17 ...... 28 F7
Chapel La. Blean CT2 ...... 66 A7
Chapel La. Broad Oak CT2 ...... 67 D7
Chapel La. 18 Dover CT16 ...... 166 D7
Chapel La. East Studdal CT15 ... 132 C6
Chapel La.
  Gillingham,Hempstead ME7 ...... 33 A4
Chapel La.
  Gillingham,Lidsing ME7 ...... 33 A2
Chapel La. Maidstone ME14 ..... 76 A5
Chapel La. Newchurch TN29 .... 185 C4
Chapel La.
  Potter's Forstal TN27 ...... 118 B2
Chapel La. Rhodes Minnis CT4 ... 144 B4
Chapel La. Ripple CT14 ...... 133 D8
Chapel La.
  St Margaret's at Cliffe CT15 .... 150 F6
Chapel La. Staple CT3 ...... 92 B6
Chapel La. Sturry CT3 ...... 67 F5
Chapel Mews. TN23 ...... 139 C2
Chapel Pl. 16
  Dover CT16 & CT17 ...... 166 D7
Chapel Pl. Ramsgate CT11 ...... 52 D7
Chapel Place La. CT11 ...... 52 D7
Chapel Rd. Dymchurch TN29 ... 195 C2
Chapel Rd. Ram Lane TN26 .... 120 F1
Chapel Rd. Ramsgate CT11 ..... 52 C7
Chapel Rd. Tilmanstone CT14 ... 115 A3
Chapel Rd. Whitfield CT16 ...... 149 A8
Chapel Row. Herne CT6 ...... 46 A8
Chapel Row. Kingsnorth TN23 ... 156 A3
Chapel Row. Ram Lane TN26 .... 120 F2
Chapel St. Deal CT14 ...... 117 D6
Chapel St. Faversham ME13 ..... 62 D6
Chapel St. Herne Bay CT6 ...... 23 A5
Chapel St. Hythe CT21 ...... 176 B2
Chapel St. Minster ME12 ...... 4 D6
Chapel St. Sheerness ME12 ...... 1 B2
Chapman Ave. ME15 ...... 97 F8
Chapman Ho. CT14 ...... 117 B3
Chapmans Cl. TN25 ...... 105 C2
Chapmans Hill. CT15 & CT3 .... 113 B5
Chappell Way. ME10 ...... 36 E6
Charing CE Prim Sch. TN27 ... 120 C8
Charing Cl. CT12 ...... 52 C8
Charing Ct. CT8 ...... 27 D7
Charing Heath Rd.
  Charing TN27 ...... 119 F8
Charing Heath Rd.
  Coppins Corner TN27 ...... 120 A6
Charing Hill. TN27 ...... 103 E1
Charing Rd. ME8 ...... 11 B3
Charing St. TN27 ...... 120 B7
Charlbury Cl. ME16 ...... 74 C3
Charlecote Ct. ME8 ...... 33 D8
Charles Cobb Cl. TN29 ...... 195 D8
Charles Cres. CT19 ...... 177 E2
Charles Ct. CT8 ...... 27 F8
Charles Dickens
  High Sch The. CT10 ...... 29 E4
Charles Drayson Ct. ME13 ...... 62 E7
Charles Ho. CT14 ...... 117 B3
Charles Lister Ct. CT17 ...... 149 B1
Charles Rd. Deal CT14 ...... 117 B4
Charles Rd. Ramsgate CT11 ..... 52 E8
Charles St. Chatham ME4 ...... 9 E3
Charles St. Herne Bay CT6 ...... 23 A5
Charles St. Maidstone ME16 ..... 74 E3
Charles St. Rochester ME2 ...... 9 A7
Charles St. Sheerness ME12 ...... 1 B3
Charlesford Ave. ME17 ...... 99 D3
Charleston Cl. CT10 ...... 30 B3
Charlesworth Dr. CT7 ...... 27 B7
Charlotte Cl. ME5 ...... 32 B6
Charlotte Ct. CT11 ...... 52 E6
Charlotte Dr. ME8 ...... 11 C1
Charlotte Pl. 2 CT9 ...... 7 J1

Charlotte Sq. 8 CT9 ...... 7 J2
Charlotte St. 13
  Broadstairs CT10 ...... 30 B4
Charlotte St. Folkestone CT20 .. 178 E5
Charlotte St.
  Sittingbourne ME10 ...... 36 E5
Charlton Ave. CT16 ...... 149 C1
Charlton CE Prim Sch. CT16 ... 149 C1
Charlton Cl. Ashford TN24 ...... 157 A8
Charlton Cl. Ramsgate CT12 .... 29 B2
Charlton Ctr. 3 CT17 ...... 166 C8
Charlton Gn. CT16 ...... 149 C1
Charlton La. ME17 ...... 99 C1
Charlton Manor. ME7 ...... 10 B5
Charlton St. ME16 ...... 74 C2
Charltons The. ME13 ...... 63 F4
Charminster. TN23 ...... 155 E6
Charnwood. CT5 ...... 21 D1
Charnwood Rd. CT6 ...... 23 B1
Chart Cl. ME13 ...... 62 B7
Chart Cnr. ME17 ...... 98 B1
Chart Hill Rd. ME17 ...... 98 B1
Chart Pl. ME8 ...... 33 C3
Chart Rd. Ashford TN23 ...... 138 D1
Chart Rd. Ashford TN23 ...... 155 D6
Chart Rd.
  Ashford, Godinton Park TN23 ... 138 F2
Chart Rd. Folkestone CT19 ...... 177 F6
Chart Road Ind Est. TN23 ...... 139 A3
Charter Ho. 9 CT16 ...... 166 E7
Charter St. Chatham ME4 ...... 9 F2
Charter St. Gillingham ME7 ...... 10 C7
Chartham Cty Prim Sch. CT4 .. 86 C1
Chartham Downs Rd. CT4 ...... 109 C7
Chartham Sta. CT4 ...... 86 D3
Chartway St. ME17 ...... 99 C1
Chartwell Ave. CT6 ...... 23 D4
Chartwell Gr. ME10 ...... 36 C3
Chase The. Chatham ME1 ...... 9 D2
Chase The. Gillingham ME8 ..... 11 A2
Chase The.
  St Margaret's at Cliffe CT15 .... 133 F1
Chater Cl. CT14 ...... 117 C4
Chatham Ct. CT11 ...... 52 D8
Chatham Gr. ME4 ...... 9 F1
Chatham Gram Sch for Boys.
  ME4 ...... 31 F8
Chatham Gram Sch for Girls.
  ME5 ...... 10 C2
Chatham Hill. ME4 ...... 10 B3
Chatham Historic Dockyard.
  ME4 ...... 10 A7
Chatham House
  Gram Sch for Boys. CT11 .... 52 E7
Chatham Pl. CT11 ...... 52 E7
Chatham Rd. Chatham ME20 .... 53 D8
Chatham Rd. Kit's Coty ME20 ... 53 D6
Chatham Rd. Kit's Coty ME20 ... 53 D7
Chatham Rd. Maidstone ME14 ... 53 E4
Chatham Rd. Sandling ME14 .... 53 E4
Chatham Ski Ctr. ME7 ...... 32 A7
Chatham South Sec Sch. ME4 .. 31 F8
Chatham St. CT11 ...... 52 E7
Chatham Sta. ME4 ...... 9 E4
Chatsworth Dr. ME10 ...... 36 B5
Chatsworth Mews. CT11 ...... 52 C6
Chatsworth Rd. ME7 ...... 10 C6
Chattenden Ct. ME14 ...... 75 B6
Chaucer Ave. CT5 ...... 21 B1
Chaucer Cl. Canterbury CT1 ..... 88 C7
Chaucer Cl. Rochester ME2 ...... 9 E8
Chaucer Coll. CT2 ...... 66 D3
Chaucer Cres. CT16 ...... 149 B3
Chaucer Ct. CT1 ...... 88 B7
Chaucer Hospl. CT1 ...... 88 A4
Chaucer Rd. Broadstairs CT10 ... 30 A3
Chaucer Rd. Canterbury CT1 .... 67 C1
Chaucer Rd. Elvington CT15 .... 114 B2
Chaucer Rd. Gillingham ME7 .... 10 D3
Chaucer Rd. Sittingbourne ME10 . 36 D3
Chaucer Tech Coll. CT1 ...... 88 C7
Cheddar Cl. TN24 ...... 139 B4
Cheesmans Cl. CT12 ...... 50 C5
Cheffins Ho. ME7 ...... 10 E7
Chegwell Dr. ME5 ...... 32 B4
Chegworth Gdns. ME10 ...... 36 E1
Chegworth La. ME17 ...... 100 A6
Chegworth Rd. ME17 ...... 99 F5
Chelmar Rd. ME7 ...... 10 B4
Chelsea Ct. CT21 ...... 176 C1
Chelsea Rd. CT11 ...... 67 C4
Cheltenham Cl. ME15 ...... 97 F6
Cheney Cl. ME8 ...... 33 D5
Cheney Hill. ME9 ...... 59 A5
Cheney Rd. ME13 ...... 62 F7
Chennels The. TN26 ...... 167 C7
Chepstow Ho. 3 ME15 ...... 97 F6
Chequer La. CT3 ...... 71 D2
Chequer's Terr. ME12 ...... 5 A5
Chequers Cl. ME5 ...... 54 A8
Chequers Ctr. ME15 ...... 75 A4
Chequers Hill. CT4 ...... 109 C2
Chequers Orch. CT4 ...... 109 D2
Chequers Pk. TN25 ...... 123 E1
Chequers Rd. ME12 ...... 4 E6
Chequertree. TN25 ...... 172 A7
Cherbourg Cres. ME5 ...... 31 F7
Cheriton Ave. CT12 ...... 52 B8
Cheriton Court Rd. CT20 ...... 177 C6
Cheriton Cty Prim Sch. CT18 . 177 C6
Cheriton Gdns. CT20 ...... 178 C4
Cheriton High St.
  CT18 & CT19 & CT20 ...... 177 D6
Cheriton Interchange. CT19 ... 177 C6
Cheriton Pl. Deal CT14 ...... 117 D4

Cheriton Pl. Folkestone CT20 ...... **178** D4
Cheriton Rd. Deal CT14 ...... **117** D4
Cheriton Rd.
　Folkestone CT19 & CT20 ...... **178** B5
Cheriton Rd.
　Folkestone, Morehall CT19 ...... **177** F6
Cheriton Rd. Gillingham ME8 ...... **33** D8
Cheriton Way. ME16 ...... **74** C7
Cheriton Wood Ho. CT19 ...... **177** D7
Cherries The. ME1b **74** A2
Cherry Amber Cl. ME8 ...... **33** F8
Cherry Ave. CT2 ...... **66** D2
Cherry Cl. ME10 ...... **36** D6
Cherry Ct. Ashford TN23 ...... **139** B1
Cherry Ct. Folkestone CT19 ...... **178** A6
Cherry Dr. CT2 ...... **66** D2
Cherry Fields. ME10 ...... **36** A5
Cherry Garden Ave. CT19 ...... **178** A4
Cherry Garden Cres. TN25 ...... **123** F2
Cherry Garden La. Ash CT3 ...... **71** E1
Cherry Garden La.
　Folkestone CT19 ...... **177** F7
Cherry Garden La. Wye TN25 ...... **123** F2
Cherry Garden Rd. CT2 ...... **66** D2
Cherry Gdns. Broadstairs CT10 ...... **29** C3
Cherry Gdns. Elham CT4 ...... **144** F5
Cherry Gdns. Herne Bay CT6 ...... **22** F4
Cherry Gdns.
　Littlebourne-on-S TN28 ...... **200** D6
Cherry Gdns. Teynham ME9 ...... **38** C2
Cherry Glebe. TN25 ...... **157** E3
Cherry Gr. CT15 ...... **114** B2
Cherry Hill Ct. ME9 ...... **35** B6
Cherry La. CT14 ...... **116** D3
Cherry Orch. Tenterden TN30 ...... **179** A6
Cherry Orch. Whitstable CT5 ...... **44** C8
Cherry Orch. Woodchurch TN26 ...... **169** A3
Cherry Orchard La. TN25 ...... **172** E4
Cherry Orchard Way. ME16 ...... **74** B3
Cherry Tree Ave. CT16 ...... **149** C1
Cherry Tree Cl. Teynham ME9 ...... **38** C2
Cherry Tree Cl.
　West Minster ME12 ...... **3** A8
Cherry Tree Dr. ME12 ...... **1** E2
Cherry Tree Gdns. CT12 ...... **29** B3
Cherry Tree Rd.
　Charing Heath TN27 ...... **119** E7
Cherry Tree Rd. Gillingham ME8 ...... **33** F8
Cherry View. ME17 ...... **97** B3
Cherry Way. CT15 ...... **131** D7
Cherrybrook Rd. CT20 ...... **177** D6
Cherrygarden La. CT15 & CT3 ...... **113** E7
Cherville La. CT3 ...... **90** C7
Chervilles. ME16 ...... **74** A2
Chesham Dr. ME8 ...... **33** E6
Cheshire Rd.
　Maidstone,Shepway ME15 ...... **97** E7
Cheshire Rd.
　Maidstone,Willington ME15 ...... **75** E2
Chessenden La. TN27 ...... **135** A1
Chester Ave. TN26 ...... **153** D5
Chester Rd. Gillingham ME7 ...... **10** D2
Chester Rd. Westgate-on-S CT8 ...... **27** F8
Chestfield Cl. ME8 ...... **11** E2
Chestfield Rd. CT5 ...... **44** C7
Chestfield & Swalecliffe Sta.
　CT5 ...... **21** D2
Chestnut Ave. Blean CT2 ...... **66** A7
Chestnut Ave. Chatham ME5 ...... **31** F3
Chestnut Cl. Ashford TN23 ...... **138** E3
Chestnut Cl. Hythe CT21 ...... **187** E8
Chestnut Cl. Tenterden TN30 ...... **167** C1
Chestnut Cl. Whitfield CT16 ...... **149** A8
Chestnut Cl. ME13 ...... **64** A3
Chestnut Dr. Broadstairs CT10 ...... **29** D4
Chestnut Dr. Coxheath ME17 ...... **96** B3
Chestnut Dr. Herne Bay CT6 ...... **22** D3
Chestnut Dr. Kingswood ME17 ...... **99** D2
Chestnut Dr. Sturry CT2 ...... **68** A7
Chestnut Dr. Worth CT14 ...... **94** A4
Chestnut La. TN23 ...... **156** C4
Chestnut Rd. CT17 ...... **166** B7
Chestnut St. ME9 ...... **35** E4
Chestnut Terr. CT21 ...... **176** A1
Chestnut Wood La. ME9 ...... **35** E3
Chestnuts The. TN25 ...... **158** D5
Chevalier Rd. CT17 ...... **166** A4
Chevening Cl. ME5 ...... **32** A5
Cheviot Cl. CT10 ...... **30** B5
Cheviot Gdns. ME15 ...... **76** A1
Cheviot Way. TN24 ...... **139** C4
Cheyne Cl. ME10 ...... **36** F8
Cheyne Mid Sch The. ME12 ...... **1** E2
Cheyne Rd. ME12 ...... **5** D3
Chicago Ave. ME7 ...... **10** F5
Chichester Cl. Ashford TN23 ...... **139** B1
Chichester Cl. Gillingham ME8 ...... **34** A8
Chichester Rd.
　Folkestone CT20 ...... **177** E4
Chichester Rd. Ramsgate CT12 ...... **29** B1
Chickfield Gdns. ME5 ...... **10** C2
Chiddingfold Cl. ME12 ...... **4** D6
Chiddingstone Cl. ME15 ...... **97** F6
Chieftain Cl. ME7 ...... **11** B1
Childscroft Rd. ME8 ...... **11** F2
Chilham Ave. CT6 ...... **27** D7
Chilham Castle. CT4 ...... **107** B7
Chilham Cl. Chatham ME4 ...... **9** E3
Chilham Cl. West Minster ME12 ...... **3** B8
Chilham Rd. Folkestone CT19 ...... **177** E6
Chilham Rd. Gillingham ME8 ...... **11** A3
Chilham Rd. Maidstone ME16 ...... **74** C7
Chilham Sta. CT4 ...... **107** D8
Chillington St. ME14 ...... **74** F6
Chilston Rd. ME17 ...... **101** D5

Chiltern Cl. ME15 ...... **75** F1
Chiltern End. TN24 ...... **139** B3
Chilton Ave. Kearsney CT16 ...... **148** C4
Chilton Ave.
　Sittingbourne ME10 ...... **37** A3
Chilton Ct. ME8 ...... **11** E1
Chilton Cty Prim Sch. CT11 ...... **52** A6
Chilton Field. CT3 ...... **71** D2
Chilton Gdns. CT3 ...... **71** D2
Chilton La. CT11 ...... **52** A6
Chilton Pl. CT3 ...... **71** D2
Chilton Sq. CT3 ...... **71** D2
Chilton Way. CT17 ...... **148** D3
Chimes The. Ashford TN24 ...... **139** C3
Chimes The. Rochester ME1 ...... **9** C5
Chippendale Cl. ME5 ...... **31** F1
Chippendale Dr. ME17 ...... **100** D6
Chipstead Cl. ME16 ...... **74** D6
Chipstead Rd. ME8 ...... **33** D4
Chislehurst Cl. ME15 ...... **97** F6
Chislet CE Prim Sch. CT3 ...... **47** C5
Chislet Ct. CT6 ...... **22** E5
Chislet Park Cotts. CT3 ...... **46** F1
Chislet Wlk. ME8 ...... **33** D5
Chislett Cl. TN25 ...... **159** E2
Chisnall Rd. CT17 ...... **148** E4
Chittenden's La. TN29 ...... **193** E5
Chitty La. CT3 ...... **47** D6
Christ Church Cath. CT1 ...... **88** A8
Christ Church CE High Sch.
　TN23 ...... **155** F5
Christ Church CE Jun Sch.
　Ramsgate CT11 ...... **52** C6
Christ Church CE Jun Sch.
　Ramsgate CT11 ...... **52** D6
Christ Church CE Prim Sch.
　CT20 ...... **178** C5
Christ Church Coll. CT1 ...... **88** B8
Christ Church Coll
　Post Graduate Ctr. CT2 ...... **67** F1
Christ Church Ct. ■
　Dover CT17 ...... **166** D7
Christchurch Ho. ⑨ ME15 ...... **97** E5
Christchurch Rd. TN23 ...... **156** B8
Christchurch Way. CT16 ...... **149** B3
Christen Way. ME15 & ME17 ...... **97** F3
Christie Cl. ME5 ...... **32** B6
Christmas St. ME7 ...... **10** E7
Christopher's Row. ME9 ...... **60** A3
Chrysler Ave. CT6 ...... **22** B4
Chunnel Ind Est. TN23 ...... **139** B1
Church App. TN28 ...... **200** A6
Church Cl. Mersham TN25 ...... **157** E3
Church Cl. New Romney TN28 ...... **200** B6
Church Cliff. CT14 ...... **134** C6
Church Cotts.
　Rodmersham ME9 ...... **59** D8
Church Cotts.
　St Michaels TN30 ...... **167** B3
Church Court Gr. CT10 ...... **29** E6
Church Cres. ME17 ...... **100** F6
Church Ct. CT18 ...... **161** C6
Church Farm Rd. ME9 ...... **12** E3
Church Field. TN25 ...... **160** B1
Church Gn. ME2 ...... **9** C8
Church Haven. CT14 ...... **133** F5
Church Hill. Bethersden TN26 .. **153** D5
Church Hill.
　Boughton Street ME13 ...... **64** A5
Church Hill. Canterbury CT2 ...... **66** C1
Church Hill.
　Charing Heath ME17 & TN27 .. **119** C7
Church Hill. Chatham ME5 ...... **10** C2
Church Hill. Chilham CT4 ...... **107** B8
Church Hill. Doddington ME9 ...... **80** F8
Church Hill. Eythorne CT15 ...... **131** B4
Church Hill. High Halden TN26 .. **167** E7
Church Hill. Hythe CT21 ...... **176** C2
Church Hill.
　Kingsnorth TN23 & TN25 ...... **156** B2
Church Hill. Ramsgate CT11 ...... **52** E7
Church Hill.
　Shepherdswell CT15 ...... **130** D4
Church Hill. Stockbury ME9 ...... **56** F7
Church Hill.
　Stone in Oxney TN30 ...... **189** F3
Church Hill. Sutton CT15 ...... **133** A7
Church Hill. Temple Ewell CT16 ... **148** D5
Church Ho. CT14 ...... **117** C7
Church La. Adisham CT3 ...... **90** D1
Church La. Aldington TN25 ...... **173** D7
Church La.
　Boughton Aluph TN25 ...... **123** B4
Church La. Boyden Gate CT3 ...... **47** C7
Church La. Brenzett TN29 ...... **192** A4
Church La. Brenzett TN29 ...... **192** A5
Church La. 21 Canterbury CT1 ... **67** A1
Church La. Canterbury CT1 ...... **87** F8
Church La. Challock TN25 ...... **122** B8
Church La. Chatham ME4 ...... **9** F6
Church La.
　Church Hougham TN25 ...... **165** B5
Church La. Deal CT14 ...... **117** B6
Church La. Harrietsham ME17 ... **100** E6
Church La. Kingston CT4 ...... **111** D3
Church La. Lower Hardres CT4 ... **88** B2
Church La. Lydden CT15 ...... **147** E8
Church La. Maidstone ME14 ...... **76** B4
Church La. New Romney TN28 ... **200** B5
Church La. Newington ME9 ...... **35** B6
Church La. Petham CT4 ...... **109** C3
Church La. Ringwould CT14 ...... **133** F5
Church La. Ripple CT14 ...... **116** D1
Church La. Selling ME13 ...... **84** B5
Church La. Shadoxhurst TN26 ... **170** A7
Church La. Stockbury ME9 ...... **56** E8

Church La. Stowting TN25 ...... **160** A6
Church La. Sturry CT2 ...... **67** F5
Church La. Waltham CT4 ...... **125** F5
Church La. Westbere CT2 ...... **68** C7
Church La. Whitstable CT5 ...... **43** A6
Church La. Womenswold CT4 ... **112** D2
Church Meadows. CT14 ...... **117** A6
Church Mews. ME8 ...... **33** F8
Church Path. Deal CT14 ...... **117** B5
Church Path. Gillingham ME7 ...... **10** E6
Church Rd. Ashford TN23 ...... **139** C2
Church Rd. Ashford TN24 ...... **157** A8
Church Rd.
　Ashford, Kennington TN24 ...... **139** C6
Church Rd.
　Boughton Malherbe ME17 ...... **118** A8
Church Rd. ■
　Broadstairs CT10 ...... **30** B4
Church Rd. Burmarsh TN29 ...... **185** E4
Church Rd. Charing TN27 ...... **103** D2
Church Rd. Chart Sutton ME17 ... **98** C1
Church Rd. Coldred CT15 ...... **131** A3
Church Rd.
　Coldred Street CT15 ...... **130** F2
Church Rd. Dover CT17 ...... **166** A7
Church Rd. Eastchurch ME12 ...... **5** D1
Church Rd. Eastling ME13 ...... **82** B2
Church Rd. Faversham ME13 ...... **62** D7
Church Rd. Faversham ME13 ...... **62** D8
Church Rd. Folkestone CT20 ...... **177** C6
Church Rd. Harrietsham ME17 ... **100** A6
Church Rd. Hoath CT3 ...... **46** E5
Church Rd. Hucking ME17 ...... **56** E1
Church Rd. Hythe CT21 ...... **176** C2
Church Rd. Kenardington TN26 .. **182** A5
Church Rd. Littlebourne CT3 ...... **90** A8
Church Rd. Lydd TN29 ...... **203** C6
Church Rd. Lyminge CT18 ...... **161** C7
Church Rd.
　Maidstone,Shepway ME15 ...... **97** F7
Church Rd.
　Maidstone,Tovil ME15 ...... **74** E2
Church Rd. Margate CT9 ...... **7** J1
Church Rd. Mersham TN25 ...... **157** E3
Church Rd. Molash CT4 ...... **105** F5
Church Rd. New Romney TN28 .. **200** A6
Church Rd. Oare ME13 ...... **40** B3
Church Rd. Ramsgate CT11 ...... **52** E7
Church Rd. Sevington TN24 ...... **157** A7
Church Rd. Sevington TN24 ...... **157** B6
Church Rd. Sittingbourne ME9 ... **37** E5
Church Rd.
　Sittingbourne, Murston ME10 ... **37** B5
Church Rd. Smeeth TN25 ...... **158** C4
Church Rd.
　Stalisfield Green ME13 ...... **103** B3
Church Rd. Tenterden TN30 ...... **179** A7
Church Sq. ②
　Broadstairs CT10 ...... **30** B4
Church Sq. Lenham ME17 ...... **101** D5
Church St.
　Boughton Monchelsea ME17 ...... **97** B2
Church St. Broadstairs CT10 ...... **29** E6
Church St. Canterbury CT1 ...... **66** E1
Church St. Chatham ME4 ...... **10** A4
Church St. Deal CT14 ...... **117** B1
Church St. Dover CT16 ...... **166** D7
Church St. Eastry CT13 ...... **93** C2
Church St. Faversham ME13 ...... **62** D8
Church St. Folkestone CT20 ...... **178** D4
Church St. Gillingham ME7 ...... **10** E6
Church St. Loose ME15 ...... **96** F5
Church St. Maidstone ME14 ...... **75** A4
Church St.
　Maidstone,Tovil ME15 ...... **74** E2
Church St. Margate CT9 ...... **7** J1
Church St. Minster,Thanet CT12 .. **50** C5
Church St. Nonington CT15 ...... **113** C5
Church St. Rochester ME1 ...... **9** D4
Church St. Rodmersham ME9 ...... **59** C8
Church St. ⑦ Sandwich CT13 ... **73** A1
Church St. ⑤
　Sittingbourne ME10 ...... **36** E4
Church St. Sittingbourne ME10 ... **36** E5
Church St. Whitstable CT5 ...... **20** F1
Church St.
　Woodnesborough CT13 ...... **93** B6
Church St. Wye TN25 ...... **123** E2
Church Street St Mary's.
　CT13 ...... **72** F1
Church Street (St Pauls). ⑥
　CT1 ...... **88** A8
Church Terr. ME5 ...... **10** C2
Church View. Aldington TN25 .... **173** A6
Church View. Herne Bay CT6 ...... **23** C4
Church View. Newchurch TN29 .. **184** E3
Church View. Worth CT14 ...... **94** B5
Church Way. CT5 ...... **21** D3
Church Whitfield Rd. CT15 ...... **149** B8
Church Wlk. CT14 ...... **144** F4
Church Wood Cl. CT2 ...... **66** B2
Church Yard Pas. ⑩ TN23 ...... **139** B2
Church Yd. TN23 ...... **139** C2
Churchfield Pl. CT9 ...... **7** I2
Churchfield Way. TN25 ...... **123** E2
Churchfields. Broadstairs CT10 ... **29** F7
Churchfields. Margate CT9 ...... **7** J1
Churchfields Terr. ME1 ...... **9** B4
Churchill Ave. Chatham ME5 ...... **32** A7
Churchill Ave. Deal CT14 ...... **117** C2
Churchill Ave. Folkestone CT19 .. **178** C8
Churchill Ave. Herne Bay CT6 ...... **23** D4
Churchill Cl. Bridge CT4 ...... **88** F1
Churchill Cl. Folkestone CT19 .. **178** D8
Churchill Cl.
　St Margaret's at Cliffe CT15 ...... **150** F5
Churchill Cotts. ME17 ...... **98** F6
Churchill Ct. CT21 ...... **176** B1

Churchill Ho. ②
　Folkestone CT20 ...... **177** F5
Churchill Ho. Maidstone ME16 .... **74** B2
Churchill Ho.
　Sittingbourne ME10 ...... **37** C4
Churchill Rd. Teynham ME9 ...... **38** C3
Churchill Rd. Canterbury CT1 ...... **88** C6
Churchill Rd. Dover CT17 ...... **166** A6
Churchill Rd. Minster ME12 ...... **4** B6
Churchill St. ⑦ CT16 ...... **149** C1
Churchill Way. ME13 ...... **40** B1
Churchill Wlk. CT18 ...... **162** F4
Churchlands The. TN28 ...... **200** B6
Churchlands The. TN28 ...... **200** B6
Churchwood Dr. CT5 ...... **21** D1
Chute Cl. ME8 ...... **33** D4
Cinder Path. CT10 ...... **30** A4
Cinnabar Cl. ME5 ...... **32** A1
Cinque Ports Ave. CT21 ...... **176** B1
Circular Rd. Dover CT16 ...... **150** B1
Circular Rd. Finglesham CT14 ... **116** B7
Circus The. CT6 ...... **22** E4
Citadel Cres. CT17 ...... **166** B6
Citadel Hts. CT17 ...... **166** B6
Citadel Rd. CT17 ...... **166** B6
Citroen Cl. CT6 ...... **22** B4
City Bsns Pk. CT1 ...... **67** C3
City View. ME1 ...... **87** C8
City Way. ME1 ...... **9** D2
Claire Ct. Birchington CT7 ...... **26** F7
Claire Ct. Broadstairs CT10 ...... **30** B5
Claire Ho. ME16 ...... **74** E5
Clandon Rd. ME5 ...... **32** D2
Clanwilliam Rd. CT14 ...... **117** D5
Clapham Hill. CT5 ...... **43** D5
Clapton Cl. ME8 ...... **33** D8
Clare Dr. CT6 ...... **22** C2
Clare Rd. CT5 ...... **20** E2
Claremont Cl. CT14 ...... **134** C6
Claremont Gdns. CT11 ...... **52** C7
Claremont Pl. CT1 ...... **87** F7
Claremont Rd. Deal CT14 ...... **117** B5
Claremont Rd.
　Folkestone CT20 ...... **178** C5
Claremont Rd.
　Kingsdown CT14 ...... **134** C6
Claremont Rd.
　Maidstone ME14 ...... **75** B5
Claremont St. CT6 ...... **22** E4
Claremont Terr. CT13 ...... **93** D7
Clarence Ave. CT9 ...... **8** D2
Clarence Ave. Rochester ME1 ...... **9** E4
Clarence Ct. ME14 ...... **75** E4
Clarence Gdns. ME12 ...... **6** E3
Clarence Pl. Deal CT14 ...... **117** D3
Clarence Pl. Dover CT17 ...... **166** D5
Clarence Rd. Capel-le-F CT18 ... **164** B2
Clarence Rd. Chatham ME4 ...... **10** B2
Clarence Rd. Deal CT14 ...... **117** D3
Clarence Rd. Herne Bay CT6 ...... **22** D5
Clarence Rd. Ramsgate CT11 ...... **52** C6
Clarence Row. ME12 ...... **1** C2
Clarence St. Folkestone CT20 ... **178** D5
Clarence St. Herne Bay CT6 ...... **22** E5
Clarendon Cl. Maidstone ME14 ... **76** A4
Clarendon Cl.
　Sittingbourne ME10 ...... **36** F1
Clarendon Gdns. ⑦ CT11 ...... **52** D6
Clarendon House Gram Sch.
　CT11 ...... **52** E6
Clarendon Mews.
　Broadstairs CT10 ...... **30** A4
Clarendon Mews.
　New Romney TN28 ...... **200** C8
Clarendon Pl. Dover CT17 ...... **166** C7
Clarendon Pl. Maidstone ME14 ... **75** A4
Clarendon Rd. Aylesham CT3 ...... **112** F5
Clarendon Rd.
　Broadstairs CT10 ...... **30** A4
Clarendon Rd. Dover CT17 ...... **166** C7
Clarendon Rd. Margate CT9 ...... **8** A2
Clarendon St. Dover CT17 ...... **166** C7
Clarendon St. Herne Bay CT6 ...... **22** C4
Claridge Cl. ME7 ...... **32** F4
Claridge Mews. CT21 ...... **176** C2
Clarke Rd. TN28 ...... **200** E4
Clarke's Cl. CT14 ...... **116** F4
Clarklands. TN29 ...... **184** E3
Clavell Cl. ME8 ...... **33** C5
Claxfield Cotts. ME9 ...... **38** A2
Claxfield Rd. ME9 ...... **60** A8
Claygate. Ashford TN23 ...... **155** F5
Claygate. Maidstone ME15 ...... **75** D1
Clearmount Dr. TN27 ...... **120** C8
Cleave Rd. ME7 ...... **10** E3
Cleaver La. CT11 ...... **52** E7
Clematis Ave. ME8 ...... **33** B5
Clement Cl. CT1 ...... **67** B1
Clement Ho. ME16 ...... **74** D5
Clement's Rd. CT12 ...... **29** C2
Clementine Cl. CT6 ...... **23** D4
Clerke Dr. ME10 ...... **37** A8
Clermont Cl. ME7 ...... **33** A4
Clevedon Ct. TN25 ...... **105** B2
Cleveland Cl. CT16 ...... **149** B3
Cleveland Ho. ME16 ...... **74** B2
Cleveland Rd. ME7 ...... **10** D6
Cleveley Lodge. CT11 ...... **29** C2
Cleves Way. TN23 ...... **155** E8
Clewson Rise. ME14 ...... **75** B8
Cliff Ave. CT6 ...... **23** C5
Cliff Dr. Herne Bay CT6 ...... **22** F2
Cliff Dr. Warden ME12 ...... **6** E4
Cliff Field. CT8 ...... **27** C8
Cliff Gdns. ME12 ...... **4** E7
Cliff Hill. ME17 ...... **97** D4

Cliff Hill Rd. ME17 ...... **97** C4
Cliff Prom. CT10 ...... **30** C7
Cliff Rd. Birchington CT7 ...... **26** F8
Cliff Rd. Broadstairs CT10 ...... **30** B7
Cliff Rd. Dover CT15 & CT16 ... **150** C1
Cliff Rd. Folkestone CT20 ...... **178** A3
Cliff Rd. Hythe CT21 ...... **176** B3
Cliff Rd. Whitstable CT5 ...... **20** F3
Cliff Sea Gr. CT6 ...... **22** C4
Cliff St. CT11 ...... **52** E6
Cliff Terr. CT9 ...... **7** J3
Cliff View Gdns.
　Leysdown-on-S ME12 ...... **6** D1
Cliff View Gdns. Warden ME12 ... **6** D1
Cliff View Rd. CT12 ...... **51** D6
Cliffe Ave. CT9 ...... **7** F1
Cliffe Ho. CT20 ...... **178** A3
Cliffe Rd. Kingsdown CT14 ...... **134** D6
Cliffe Rd. Rochester ME2 ...... **9** B8
Cliffestone Ct. CT20 ...... **178** B5
Clifford Gdns. CT14 ...... **117** B2
Clifford Rd. CT5 ...... **43** F8
Cliffs End Gr. CT12 ...... **51** D5
Cliffs End Rd. CT12 ...... **51** E5
Cliffside Dr. CT10 ...... **30** A1
Clifftown Gdns. CT6 ...... **22** B4
Clifton Cl. ME14 ...... **75** B5
Clifton Cres. CT20 ...... **178** B3
Clifton Gdns. Canterbury CT2 ...... **66** C2
Clifton Gdns. Folkestone CT20 .. **178** C4
Clifton Gdns. Margate CT9 ...... **7** J3
Clifton Lawn. CT11 ...... **52** D5
Clifton Mansions. ④ CT20 ... **178** C4
Clifton Pl. CT9 ...... **8** A2
Clifton Rd. Folkestone CT20 ...... **178** C4
Clifton Rd. Gillingham ME7 ...... **10** C7
Clifton Rd. Margate CT9 ...... **8** A2
Clifton Rd. Ramsgate CT11 ...... **52** B8
Clifton Rd. Whitstable CT5 ...... **20** D1
Clifton St. CT9 ...... **7** J3
Cliftonville Ave. Margate CT9 ...... **8** A2
Cliftonville Ave. Ramsgate CT12 .. **29** B1
Cliftonville Ct. CT9 ...... **8** A4
Cliftonville Cty Prim Sch. CT9 .. **8** C2
Cliftonville Mews. CT9 ...... **8** A4
Clim Down. CT14 ...... **134** D6
Clinton Cl. ME17 ...... **96** B3
Clints La. CT4 ...... **129** D4
Clipper Cl. ME2 ...... **9** E7
Clipper Ct. ME2 ...... **9** E7
Clive Dennis Ct. TN24 ...... **139** E1
Clive Rd. Cliffs End CT12 ...... **51** D6
Clive Rd. Margate CT9 ...... **29** A5
Clive Rd. Rochester ME1 ...... **9** C3
Clive Rd. Sittingbourne ME10 ... **36** B5
Clockhouse. TN23 ...... **138** F1
Clockhouse Pk. TN25 ...... **105** C2
Cloisterham Rd. ME1 ...... **31** D7
Cloisters The. ⑦
　Canterbury CT1 ...... **66** F1
Cloisters The. Lenham ME17 ...... **101** C5
Cloisters The. Ramsgate CT11 ... **52** D5
Cloisters The. ⑦
　Sittingbourne ME10 ...... **36** E4
Close The. Ashford TN23 ...... **155** F7
Close The. Bridge CT4 ...... **88** F1
Close The. Canterbury CT2 ...... **66** F4
Close The. Faversham ME13 ...... **62** C6
Close The. Folkestone CT19 ...... **178** E8
Close The. Hythe CT21 ...... **176** B4
Close The. Lydden CT15 ...... **147** F1
Close The. Rochester ME1 ...... **9** C4
Close The. Wye TN25 ...... **123** C2
Close The (St Edmunds Sch).
　CT2 ...... **66** C2
Cloudesley Cl. ME1 ...... **9** B1
Clovelly. TN28 ...... **200** E6
Clovelly Dr. ME12 ...... **4** B8
Clovelly Rd. CT5 ...... **43** D7
Clover Bank View. ME5 ...... **32** B6
Clover Ct. ME10 ...... **37** B5
Clover Rise. CT5 ...... **21** B1
Clover St. ME4 ...... **9** F4
Clowes Ct. CT2 ...... **66** C4
Clubb's La. TN29 ...... **197** D2
Cluny Rd. ME13 ...... **62** F7
Clyde Cotts. ME12 ...... **1** E2
Clyde St. ■ Canterbury CT1 ...... **67** A1
Clyde St. Sheerness ME12 ...... **1** E1
Clynton Way. TN23 ...... **156** A7
Coach Dr. TN26 ...... **138** A2
Coach Rd. Densole CT18 ...... **162** F4
Coach Rd. Egerton TN27 ...... **118** E6
Coalpit La. ME9 ...... **80** A6
Coast Dr.
　Littlebourne-on-S TN28 ...... **200** E3
Coast Dr. Lydd-on-S TN29 ...... **204** F4
Coast Rd. St Mary's Bay TN29 .. **194** F2
Coast Rd. TN28 & TN29 ...... **200** F7
Coastguard Alley. CT5 ...... **20** C1
Coastguard Cotts.
　Conyer ME9 ...... **38** E6
Coastguard Cotts.
　Dover CT16 ...... **166** G8
Coastguard Cotts.
　Herne Bay CT6 ...... **21** F4
Coastguard Cotts. Hythe CT21 .. **176** B1
Coastguard Cotts.
　Kingsdown CT14 ...... **134** D4
Coastguard Cotts.
　Leysdown-on-S ME12 ...... **19** E4
Coastguard Cotts. Minster ME12 .. **5** C5
Coastguard Cotts.
　Ramsgate CT11 ...... **52** F2
Coastguard Cotts. ⑱
　Ramsgate CT11 ...... **52** F7
Coastguard Cotts.
　Sandwich CT13 ...... **95** B7

Coastguard Cotts The. ME12 .... 1 I1
Coastguard Hos. ME12 .... 6 C5
Coats Ave. ME12 .... 3 A8
Cobay Cl. CT21 .... 176 D2
Cobb Ct. CT9 .... 7 I3
Cobb Wlk. ME13 .... 62 B8
Cobblers Bridge Rd. CT6 .... 22 D3
Cobblestones. ME7 .... 32 F5
Cobbs Hill. CT4 .... 85 C2
Cobbs Mews. 2 CT20 .... 178 C4
Cobbs Pl. CT9 .... 7 I3
Cobbs Wood Ind Est. TN23 ..... 138 F2
Cobden Pl. 18 CT1 .... 67 A1
Cobden Rd. CT21 .... 176 B1
Cobdown Gr. ME8 .... 12 A2
Cobfield. ME17 .... 98 A1
Cobham Ave. ME10 .... 36 E1
Cobham Chase. ME13 .... 62 B8
Cobham Cl. Canterbury CT1 ...... 88 C6
Cobham Cl. Maidstone ME16 .... 74 E4
Cobsden Cl. TN29 .... 195 A4
Cobsden Rd. TN29 .... 195 A4
Cobtree Cl. ME5 .... 32 C8
Cobtree Rd. ME17 .... 96 C3
Cobtree Wharf. ME20 .... 53 C2
Cock La. Elham CT4 .... 144 F4
Cock La. Hamstreet TN26 .... 183 A4
Cockering Rd. CT1 & CT4 .... 87 B4
Cockreed La. TN28 .... 200 B7
Codrington Rd. CT11 .... 52 D7
Cogans Terr. CT1 .... 87 E6
Coggan Ho. 7 CT1 .... 87 F7
Coinston Ave. CT11 .... 52 A7
Colburn Rd. CT10 .... 30 A2
Colchester Cl. ME5 .... 32 A7
Cold Harbour. CT1 .... 67 A2
Cold Harbour La. ME9 .... 35 F6
Cold Harbour Rd.
ME13 & ME17 .... 103 A7
Coldblow. CT14 .... 117 A1
Coldblow La. Thurnham ME14 ... 56 A2
Coldblow La.
Woodchurch TN26 .... 169 D4
Coldbridge La. TN27 .... 118 B5
Coldharbour La.
Aylesford ME20 .... 53 A1
Coldharbour La.
Bekesbourne CT4 .... 111 D7
Coldharbour La. Hucking ME14 .. 56 B1
Coldharbour La.
Old Romney TN29 .... 198 C5
Coldharbour La.
Sittingbourne ME10 .... 14 F1
Coldharbour La. Wye TN25 ...... 124 A2
Coldred Hill. CT15 .... 130 F1
Coldred Rd. Coldred CT15 .... 131 B5
Coldred Rd. Park Wood ME15 ... 97 F4
Coldred Rd.
Shepherdswell CT15 .... 130 E3
Coldswood Rd. CT12 .... 28 F2
Cole Rd. ME13 .... 62 E7
Cole Terr. ME17 .... 101 C4
Colegate Dr. ME14 .... 76 C4
Colegates Cl. ME13 .... 40 B2
Colegates Ct. ME13 .... 40 B2
Colegates Rd. ME13 .... 40 A2
Coleman Cres. CT12 .... 29 C1
Coleman's Stairs Rd. CT7 .... 27 A8
Coleman's Yd. 3 CT11 .... 52 E6
Colemans. CT20 .... 203 D7
Coleridge Gdns. CT3 .... 112 F6
Coleshall Cl. ME15 .... 97 F6
Coleshall Cotts. ME9 .... 14 D3
Colette. CT10 .... 8 G2
Coleville Cres. CT20 .... 204 E7
Colewood Rd. CT5 .... 21 E3
Colfe Way. ME10 .... 37 A8
Colin's Way. CT21 .... 177 A3
Collard Ct. CT6 .... 23 A4
Collard Rd. TN24 .... 157 A8
Collards Cl. CT12 .... 49 D7
Collards La. CT4 .... 144 E3
College Ave. Gillingham ME7 ... 10 B4
College Ave. Maidstone ME15 ... 74 F3
College Cotts. ME16 .... 74 F3
College Ct. Ashford TN23 .... 139 C2
College Ct. 5 Maidstone ME15 .. 75 A3
College Rd. Canterbury CT1 ...... 67 B1
College Rd. Chatham ME4 .... 10 A7
College Rd. Deal CT14 .... 117 D8
College Rd. Maidstone ME15 .... 74 F2
College Rd. Margate CT9 .... 8 A1
College Rd. Margate CT9 .... 28 F8
College Rd. Ramsgate CT11 ...... 29 E1
College Rd.
Sittingbourne ME10 .... 36 D3
College Row. CT17 .... 166 B7
College Sq. 2 CT9 .... 7 J2
College Way. CT3 .... 91 A7
College Wlk. 3 CT9 .... 7 J2
College Yd. ME1 .... 9 C6
Collett Wlk. ME8 .... 33 D4
Collett. TN25 .... 142 D8
Collingbourne. TN23 .... 155 E6
Collings Wlk. ME8 .... 33 D4
Collington Terr. ME15 .... 97 E4
Collingwood Cl.
Broadstairs CT10 .... 29 E4
Collingwood Cl.
Westgate-on-S CT8 .... 27 D7
Collingwood Ct. CT20 .... 177 E5
Collingwood Ind Ctr. ME17 ...... 98 E2
Collingwood Rd.
Kit's Coty ME20 .... 53 C7
Collingwood Rd.
St Margaret's at Cliffe CT15 .. 150 F8
Collingwood Rd.
Whitstable CT5 .... 20 C1

Collingwood Rd E.
CT14 & CT15 .... 134 A1
Collingwood Rise. CT20 .... 177 E5
Collingwood Wlk. ME10 .... 36 B5
Collins Rd. CT6 .... 22 C2
Collis St. ME2 .... 9 A8
Collison Pl. TN30 .... 179 D7
Colman Ho. 2 ME14 .... 75 A4
Colombo Sq. CT12 .... 29 A1
Colonel's La. ME13 .... 64 A3
Colorado Cl. CT16 .... 149 B3
Colton Cres. CT16 .... 149 B4
Columbia Ave. CT15 .... 43 B7
Command Rd. ME14 .... 74 F8
Commercial Rd. ME2 .... 9 A7
Commissioner's Rd. ME2 .... 9 C8
Commodore Rd. ME14 .... 75 C5
Common La. CT17 .... 148 E3
Common Rd. ME1 .... 31 B1
Common The. ME1 .... 9 C6
Common Way. TN26 .... 138 A3
Commonwealth Cl. ME10 .... 37 B3
Compass Cl. ME1 .... 9 C1
Compass Ctr. ME4 .... 10 B8
Compton Cl. ME5 .... 32 D2
Concord Ave. ME5 .... 31 E5
Conduit St. ME13 .... 62 D8
Conference Wlk. CT1 .... 88 C8
Conifer Ct. CT8 .... 7 D1
Conifer Dr. ME5 .... 32 D1
Coniston Cl. ME7 .... 11 A6
Coniston Dr. CT3 .... 112 F6
Coniston Rd. CT19 .... 178 B7
Connaught Barracks. CT16 ...... 149 E1
Connaught Cl. ME15 .... 97 F4
Connaught Gdns. 9 CT9 .... 7 J1
Connaught Mews. CT1 .... 67 A3
Connaught Rd. Chatham ME4 ... 10 C2
Connaught Rd. Dover CT16 .... 149 D1
Connaught Rd.
Folkestone CT20 .... 178 C4
Connaught Rd. Gillingham ME7 .. 10 D5
Connaught Rd. Margate CT9 ...... 7 J1
Connaught Rd.
Sittingbourne ME10 .... 36 E3
Conquest Ind Est. ME2 .... 9 A6
Conrad Ave. CT1 .... 67 C3
Conrad Cl. ME8 .... 33 D4
Consort Cl. ME14 .... 75 B5
Constable Rd. CT7 .... 27 A8
Constable's Rd. CT16 .... 166 E8
Constancia Ct. CT20 .... 178 C5
Constitution Hill. ME4 .... 10 B3
Constitution Rd. ME4 .... 10 C1
Consul Cl. CT6 .... 22 B4
Continental App. CT9 .... 28 F6
Convent Cl. CT15 .... 151 B6
Convent Rd. CT10 .... 8 G1
Convent Wlk. CT11 .... 52 E5
Conway Cl. CT7 .... 26 E7
Conway Mews. ME7 .... 10 A6
Conway Rd. ME16 .... 74 C6
Conyer Rd. ME9 .... 38 F4
Conyngham Cl. CT12 .... 29 B2
Conyngham La. CT4 .... 89 A2
Conyngham Rd. Herne Bay CT6 . 23 D5
Conyngham Rd. Minster, Thanet
CT12 .... 50 C5
Cooden Cl. ME8 .... 12 A2
Cook Cl. ME5 .... 32 C6
Cook's Lea. CT13 .... 93 B2
Cookham Hill. ME1 .... 9 A2
Cookham Wood Rd. ME1 .... 31 B8
Cooks La. ME10 .... 36 F6
Cooling Cl. ME14 .... 75 C6
Coolinge La. CT20 .... 177 F4
Coolinge Rd. CT20 .... 178 D5
Coombe Cl. Chatham ME5 .... 32 B3
Coombe Cl. Dover CT17 .... 149 A1
Coombe Ct. CT17 .... 149 A1
Coombe Dr. ME10 .... 37 C4
Coombe La. Ash CT3 .... 92 E8
Coombe La. Tenterden TN30 ... 179 A7
Coombe Lands. TN30 .... 188 D4
Coombe Rd. Dover CT17 .... 148 F1
Coombe Rd. Dover CT15 , CT17 . 165 E8
Coombe Rd. Folkestone CT19 . 177 F6
Coombe Rd. Maidstone ME15 ... 74 F2
Coombe Valley Rd. CT17 .... 149 A1
Coombe Way. CT18 .... 163 C4
Coombe Wlk. CT5 .... 43 A2
Coombe Wood La. CT18 .... 163 C4
Cooper Rd. ME5 .... 32 B3
Cooper Street Dro. CT3 .... 72 B4
Cooper's Hill. CT6 .... 22 F5
Cooper's La. TN25 .... 158 F2
Coopers La. CT1 .... 87 E7
Cooting La. CT3 .... 112 D8
Cooting Rd. CT3 .... 112 E4
Cop Street Rd. CT3 .... 71 D3
Copenhagen Rd. ME7 .... 10 C4
Copinger Cl. CT2 .... 67 A4
Copland Ave. ME12 .... 4 C6
Copper Tree Ct. ME15 .... 97 A5
Copper Tree Wlk. ME5 .... 32 C1
Copperfield. ME12 .... 5 F6
Copperfield Cl. TN24 .... 139 C6
Copperfield Cl. CT10 .... 30 B5
Copperfield Dr. ME17 .... 98 E4
Copperfield Ho. ME4 .... 10 A4
Copperfield Rd. ME1 .... 9 C2
Copperfields. TN29 .... 203 B6
Copperfields The. ME1 .... 9 C2
Coppergate. Canterbury CT2 .... 66 E2
Coppergate. Gillingham ME7 .... 32 F5
Copperhouse La. ME7 .... 11 B6

Copperhurst Wlk. CT9 .... 8 F2
Copperwood. TN24 .... 139 C4
Coppice Cl. ME7 .... 33 B4
Coppice Rd. ME5 .... 32 C2
Coppice The. CT2 .... 67 F6
Coppice View. ME14 .... 75 E6
Coppin St. CT14 .... 117 D6
Coppins La. ME9 .... 36 B2
Copse The. TN23 .... 138 D3
Copsewood Way. ME15 .... 76 A3
Copt Cl. CT2 .... 67 F7
Copthall Gdns. 10 CT20 .... 178 D5
Cordingham Rd. CT5 .... 43 A6
Cordova Ct. CT20 .... 178 B4
Corkwell St. ME4 .... 9 E3
Corner Cotts. TN26 .... 182 A6
Corner Field. TN23 .... 156 B5
Corner The. TN25 .... 173 A6
Cornerways. CT21 .... 176 B4
Cornflower Cl. ME14 .... 75 E4
Cornford Rd. CT7 .... 27 A7
Cornhill. 12 CT11 .... 52 E6
Corniche The. CT20 .... 177 C3
Cornwall Ave. CT11 .... 52 F8
Cornwall Cl. ME15 .... 97 E7
Cornwall Gdns.
Canterbury CT1 .... 88 D7
Cornwall Gdns. Margate CT9 ..... 8 B3
Cornwall Ho. Deal CT14 .... 117 A5
Cornwall Ho. 5 Dover CT17 ... 166 D7
Cornwall Rd. Deal CT14 .... 117 C3
Cornwall Rd. Gillingham ME7 ... 10 D6
Cornwall Rd. Herne Bay CT6 .... 22 B2
Cornwall Rd. Rochester ME1 ...... 9 C3
Cornwallis Ave.
Aylesham CT3 .... 112 F6
Cornwallis Ave. Herne Bay CT6 . 23 C3
Cornwallis Circ. CT5 .... 20 D1
Cornwallis Cl. Ashford TN24 ... 157 B7
Cornwallis Cl. Folkestone CT19 178 B6
Cornwallis Cotts. ME17 .... 96 E2
Cornwallis Gdns. CT10 .... 30 A6
Cornwallis Rd. ME16 .... 74 D4
Cornwallis Sch The. ME15 .... 96 F2
Coronation Cl. CT10 .... 29 E7
Coronation Cotts. CT19 .... 177 D6
Coronation Cres. Margate CT9 .. 28 B8
Coronation Cres.
Queenborough ME11 .... 2 F5
Coronation Dr. Bay View ME12 ... 6 D2
Coronation Dr.
Great Chart TN23 .... 138 C1
Coronation Flats. 2 ME4 .... 9 F3
Coronation Rd. Chatham ME5 ... 10 C2
Coronation Rd. Ramsgate CT11 . 52 D6
Coronation Rd.
Sheerness ME12 .... 1 E1
Coronation Sq. TN29 .... 203 C6
Corone Cl. CT19 .... 178 A7
Corporation Rd. ME7 .... 10 D7
Corporation St. ME1 .... 9 C6
Corral Cl. ME5 .... 10 D2
Corrall Almshouses. 4 ME15 .... 75 A3
Corrance Gn. ME15 .... 97 A8
Corsican Wlk. CT6 .... 23 C3
Cortland Cl. ME10 .... 36 E6
Cortland Mews. ME10 .... 36 E6
Corunna Cl. CT21 .... 176 A2
Corunna Pl. CT16 .... 149 E3
Corylus Dr. CT5 .... 43 A7
Cossack St. ME1 .... 9 D3
Cossington Rd. Canterbury CT1 .. 88 A7
Cossington Rd. Chatham ME5 ... 32 B1
Cosway Cotts. TN25 .... 172 C1
Cotswold Cl. TN24 .... 139 B4
Cotswold Gdns. ME15 .... 76 A2
Cottage Rd. Chatham ME4 .... 9 F6
Cottage Rd. Ramsgate CT11 ..... 52 E6
Cottage Row. CT13 .... 72 F1
Cottall Ave. ME4 .... 9 F2
Cottington Rd. CT12 .... 51 B5
Cotton Hill Wlk. TN26 .... 183 A7
Cotton Rd. CT1 .... 87 F7
Coulman St. ME7 .... 10 D5
Coulson Gr. ME4 .... 116 A5
Coulter Rd. CT6 .... 22 B2
Coulters Cl. ME5 .... 75 D5
Council Cotts. ME15 .... 96 A4
Countess Mountbatten Ct.
CT8 .... 27 E8
Country's Field. TN29 .... 195 C8
County Rd. ME14 .... 75 A5
County Sq. 8 TN23 .... 139 B2
Court Cotts. CT7 .... 25 E2
Court Dr. ME16 .... 74 D4
Court Flats. CT3 .... 91 A7
Court Hall. ME11 .... 2 F5
Court Hill. CT3 .... 68 E2
Court Hill Ho. CT16 .... 148 E4
Court House Farm. CT15 .... 113 E5
Court La. Detling ME14 .... 55 C5
Court La. Preston CT3 .... 70 B6
Court Lodge Cotts. ME15 .... 96 A7
Court Lodge Rd.
Appledore TN26 .... 190 C7
Court Lodge Rd.
Gillingham ME7 .... 10 F6
Court Meadow. ME8 .... 11 B2
Court Meadows. CT3 .... 89 F8
Court Pl. CT20 .... 178 C4
Court Rd. Deal CT14 .... 117 B1
Court Rd. Eccles ME1 .... 53 A6
Court Rd. Sittingbourne ME10 ... 36 F7

Court Rd.
St Nicholas at Wade CT7 .... 25 E2
Court St. ME13 .... 62 D7
Court Wurtin. TN23 .... 156 A7
Courtenay Rd.
Boughton Street CT2 & ME13 .. 64 E5
Courtenay Rd. Deal CT14 .... 117 C8
Courtenay Rd. Maidstone ME15 . 74 F2
Courteney Rd. Gillingham ME8 .. 33 B8
Courtfield Ave. ME5 .... 32 B3
Courtland Ave. CT16 .... 149 A6
Courtland Dr. CT16 .... 148 E4
Courtlands. Herne Bay CT6 .... 23 B3
Courtlands. Kingsdown CT14 ... 134 D6
Courtlands Way. CT8 .... 7 D1
Courts The. CT9 .... 7 E1
Courtyard The. Gillingham ME7 .. 33 A8
Courtyard The. Staple CT3 .... 92 A6
Coventina Ho. CT11 .... 52 D7
Coventon La. CT13 & CT14 .... 94 A5
Coventry Gdns. CT6 .... 23 E5
Coverdale Ave. ME15 .... 97 D6
Coverdale Cl. ME5 .... 32 B7
Covert. TN23 .... 138 E1
Covert Rd. CT3 .... 112 E4
Covert The. ME5 .... 32 B1
Covet La. CT4 .... 111 C2
Cow La. Canterbury CT1 .... 87 D7
Cow La. Dover CT17 .... 166 A7
Cowbeck Cl. ME8 .... 33 D6
Cowden Rd. ME14 .... 75 C5
Cowdray Rd. CT14 .... 117 A3
Cowdray Sq. CT14 .... 117 A3
Cowdrey Cl. Ashford TN24 ..... 157 A7
Cowdrey Cl. Maidstone ME16 ... 74 B2
Cowdrey Cl. Rochester ME1 .... 9 B2
Cowdrey Pl. CT1 .... 88 B6
Cowgate Hill. CT16 & CT17 ... 166 D7
Cowgate La. CT18 .... 163 C5
Cowley Rise. CT9 .... 29 C8
Cowper Cl. CT5 .... 21 D3
Cowper Rd. Deal CT14 .... 117 C5
Cowper Rd. Gillingham ME7 ..... 10 D3
Cowper Rd. Margate CT9 .... 7 J1
Cowper Rd. River CT17 .... 148 E3
Cowper Rd. Sittingbourne ME10 . 37 B4
Cowstead Rd. ME9 .... 34 D2
Cox St. ME14 .... 55 E6
Coxes Ave. CT10 .... 29 B3
Coxes La. CT12 .... 29 B3
Coxett Hill. ME13 .... 61 D5
Coxheath Cty Prim Sch. ME17 .. 96 C3
Coxhill. CT15 .... 130 C3
Coxhill Cres. CT17 .... 148 D3
Coxhill Gdns. CT17 .... 148 D3
Cozenton Cl. ME8 .... 11 E1
Crabble Ave. CT17 .... 149 A2
Crabble Cl. CT17 .... 148 F2
Crabble Hill. CT16 & CT17 .... 149 A2
Crabble La. CT15 & CT17 ...... 148 E2
Crabble Meadows. CT17 .... 149 A2
Crabble Rd. CT17 .... 149 A3
Crabble Water Mill. CT17 ...... 148 F3
Crabtree La. ME17 .... 119 B8
Crabtree Rd. ME8 .... 33 D8
Crackstake. CT3 .... 71 D2
Craddock Dr. 8 CT1 .... 67 B1
Craddock Rd. CT1 .... 67 B2
Craddock Way. ME8 .... 33 D5
Cradle Bridge Dr. TN24 .... 139 F2
Cradles Rd. ME9 .... 34 C2
Crafford St. CT16 .... 149 D1
Cragie Wlk. ME8 .... 33 E4
Crampton Ct. CT10 .... 30 A4
Cranborne Ave. ME15 .... 75 C1
Cranborne Ave. ME15 .... 97 B8
Cranbourne Cl. CT11 .... 52 F8
Cranbourne Wlk. CT2 .... 66 E3
Cranbrook Cl. Gillingham ME8 ... 11 C3
Cranbrook Cl. Maidstone ME15 . 97 F7
Cranbrook Cl. Margate CT9 .... 8 E1
Cranbrook Dr. ME10 .... 36 D1
Cranbrooks. TN25 .... 157 D4
Cranford Cl. ME8 .... 11 D1
Cranleigh Dr. CT16 .... 149 B7
Cranleigh Gdns. Chatham ME1 .. 9 D3
Cranleigh Gdns.
Maidstone ME16 .... 74 C7
Cranleigh Gdns.
Whitstable CT5 .... 43 E8
Cranmer Cl. ME15 .... 97 B8
Cranswick Cotts. CT14 .... 133 C8
Craufurd Gn. CT20 .... 177 D5
Craven Cl. CT9 .... 28 C8
Crawford Gdns. CT9 .... 8 B2
Crawford Rd. CT10 .... 29 F5
Crayford Cl. ME14 .... 75 C6
Craythorne. TN30 .... 179 B8
Craythorne Cl. Hythe CT21 .... 177 B4
Craythorne Cl.
New Romney TN28 .... 200 B8
Craythorne La. TN28 .... 200 B7
Cremer Cl. CT4 .... 86 C1
Cremer Pl. ME13 .... 62 A8
Cremers Rd. ME13 .... 62 B8
Crescent Rd. Birchington CT7 ... 27 A7
Crescent Rd. Broadstairs CT10 .. 30 C8
Crescent Rd. Faversham ME13 ... 62 D7
Crescent Rd. Margate CT9 .... 7 H2
Crescent Rd. Ramsgate CT11 ... 52 D7
Crescent St. 1 ME10 .... 36 F4
Crescent The. Aylesham CT15 .. 113 A3
Crescent The.
Boughton Street ME13 .... 64 A3
Crescent The. Canterbury CT2 ... 66 E1
Crescent The. Chartham CT4 .... 86 D1
Crescent The.
Folkestone CT20 .... 177 C3

Crescent The.
Halfway Houses ME12 .... 3 E6
Crescent The.
Lower Halstow ME9 .... 13 C3
Crescent The. Maidstone ME14 .. 74 F8
Crescent The. Sandwich CT13 ... 93 E6
Crescent The. Sheerness ME12 ... 1 D2
Crescent The.
Sittingbourne ME10 .... 15 A1
Crescent The.
St Margaret's at Cliffe CT15 .. 151 A5
Crescent The. Teynham ME9 ..... 38 D3
Crescent Way. ME5 .... 31 D5
Cress Way. ME13 .... 62 A7
Cressey Ct. ME4 .... 9 E4
Cressfield. TN23 .... 138 F1
Crest Rd. ME1 .... 9 C1
Cresta Cl. CT6 .... 21 F4
Crestway. ME5 .... 32 B8
Crete Rd E. CT18 & CT19 .... 163 D1
Crete Rd W. CT18 .... 163 B1
Creteway Cl. CT19 .... 178 E8
Creve Coeur Cl. ME14 .... 76 A5
Cricketers Cl.
Harrietsham ME17 .... 100 D6
Cricketers Cl. Hawkinge CT18 . 163 B6
Cricketers Cl.
Sittingbourne ME10 .... 36 F8
Crimond Ave. TN29 .... 187 A4
Criol La. TN26 .... 155 A2
Cripple Hill. TN26 .... 152 D1
Cripple St. ME15 .... 97 A7
Cripps Cl. CT3 .... 112 E5
Cripps' La. CT15 .... 150 F6
Crisfield Ct. TN30 .... 167 B2
Crismill La. ME14 .... 76 F4
Crismill Rd. ME14 .... 76 F3
Crispe Cl. ME8 .... 33 D4
Crispe Rd. CT7 .... 27 A3
Crispin Cl. ME13 .... 62 D8
Crispin Ct. ME17 .... 96 C3
Crittenden Bglws. ME15 .... 96 A4
Crittenden Cotts. ME15 .... 96 A4
Crocken Hill Rd. TN27 .... 118 C2
Crockham La. ME13 .... 64 B6
Crockham Rd. ME13 .... 64 C6
Crockshard Hill. CT3 .... 91 B4
Crockshard La. CT3 .... 91 B4
Croft Cl. ME5 .... 32 C1
Croft Gdns. ME17 .... 101 D4
Croft La. CT20 .... 177 F5
Croft Rd. TN24 .... 139 D2
Croft's Pl. 8 CT10 .... 30 B4
Crofters Cl. CT21 .... 187 E8
Crofters The. ME8 .... 33 F7
Crofton Cl. TN24 .... 139 C6
Crofton Rd. CT8 .... 27 E7
Croftwood. TN23 .... 155 D6
Croidene Ct. ME12 .... 4 A6
Cromer Rd. Rochester ME2 .... 9 B8
Cromer Rd. Sittingbourne ME10 . 58 F8
Cromwell Park Pl. CT20 .... 177 D4
Cromwell Rd. Canterbury CT1 ... 88 A6
Cromwell Rd. Maidstone ME14 ... 75 B5
Cromwell Rd.
West Minster ME11 & ME12 ..... 2 F7
Cromwell Rd. Whitstable CT5 ... 20 E1
Cromwell Terr. ME4 .... 10 A3
Crook's Court La. CT15 .... 164 F4
Crooked S Rd. CT14 .... 133 E7
Crookenden Pl. CT4 .... 128 F8
Crosier Ct. ME9 .... 12 E3
Crosley Rd. ME7 .... 10 D3
Cross Dr. ME17 .... 99 B1
Cross Keys. ME14 .... 76 C4
Cross La. Faversham ME13 .... 62 C7
Cross La. 7 Faversham ME13 ... 62 D7
Cross La. Sittingbourne ME10 ... 36 E6
Cross La.
Throwley Forstal ME13 .... 104 C7
Cross Rd. Birchington CT7 .... 27 B8
Cross Rd. Deal CT14 .... 117 A2
Cross Rd.
St Margaret's at Cliffe CT15 .. 151 A4
Cross St. 2 Canterbury CT2 .... 66 E1
Cross St. Chatham ME4 .... 10 A4
Cross St. Gillingham ME7 .... 10 C6
Cross St. Herne Bay CT6 .... 22 D3
Cross St. Maidstone ME14 .... 75 A6
Cross St. Rochester ME2 .... 9 B8
Cross St. Sheerness ME12 .... 1 C2
Cross Stile. TN23 .... 155 F8
Cross The. CT13 .... 93 B2
Cross Way. ME1 .... 9 C3
Crossley Ave. CT6 .... 21 F4
Crossway. ME5 .... 31 E6
Crossways. Canterbury CT2 ...... 66 E4
Crossways. Chart Sutton ME17 .. 98 B1
Crossways. Sittingbourne ME10 . 36 F1
Crossways Ave. CT9 .... 29 A5
Crossways Cl. TN29 .... 186 E2
Crouch Cotts. ME15 .... 84 E8
Crouch Hill Ct. ME9 .... 13 C3
Crouch La. ME13 .... 84 E8
Crow Cnr. Ashford TN24 .... 156 F7
Crow Cnr. Brabourne TN25 .... 141 E1
Crow Cnr. Rochester ME1 .... 9 C5
Crow Hill. CT10 .... 30 B5
Crow Hill Rd. CT9 .... 28 B8
Crow La. ME1 .... 9 C5
Crowbridge Rd. TN24 .... 156 E7
Crown Ct. CT14 .... 117 D6
Crown Gdns. CT2 .... 66 E1
Crown Hill Rd. CT6 .... 22 C4
Crown La. CT4 .... 126 E3

Crown Quay. ME10 .... 36 F5
Crown Quay La. ME10 .... 37 A4
Crown Rd. ME10 .... 36 E6
Crown St. ME7 .... 10 D6
Crownfield Rd. TN23 .... 155 F8
Crownfields. ME14 .... 75 F4
Crows Camp Rd. CT4 .... 111 A5
Croydon Cl. ME5 .... 32 C4
Cruise Liner Terminal. CT17 .. 166 E4
Crundale. **2** ME14 .... 75 A5
Crundale Cl. TN23 .... 155 F6
Crundale Rd. ME8 .... 11 C3
Crundale Way. CT10 & CT9 ... 8 E1
Crusader Cl. ME7 .... 33 B8
Cryalls Bsns Est. ME10 .... 36 C4
Cryalls La. ME10 & ME9 ...... 36 C3
Cryol Rd. TN23 .... 156 A7
Crystal Bsns Ctr. CT13 .... 73 B2
Ctr for European Agricucultural
  Studies. TN25 .... 124 A1
Cubitt Ho. CT10 .... 178 D6
Cuckmere Ho. **3** ME15 ...... 97 E8
Cuckold's Cnr.
  High Halden TN26 .... 168 B7
Cuckold's Cnr. Snargate TN29 .. 191 E7
Cuckolds Cnr. CT3 .... 114 A7
Cuckoo La. Ashford TN23 .... 155 D6
Cuckoo La. Ashford TN23 .... 155 E7
Cuckoo La. Postling CT21 ... 160 F2
Cuckoowood Ave. ME14 ...... 53 F1
Cudham Cl. ME14 .... 75 C6
Cudham Gdns. CT9 .... 8 E2
Cudworth Rd. TN24 .... 156 E7
Cullens Hill. CT4 .... 144 F4
Cullet Dr. ME11 .... 3 A3
Culling's Hill. CT4 .... 144 F4
Culmers Terr. ME13 .... 41 E1
Culpeper Cl.
  Hollingbourne ME17 .... 77 E2
Culpeper Cl. Rochester ME2 .... 9 E6
Culpepper Cl. CT2 .... 67 A4
Culpepper Rd. Coxheath ME17 .. 96 B3
Culpepper Rd. Gillingham ME8 .. 33 D4
Culter Field. TN23 .... 155 E8
Culver's La. TN29 .... 203 D5
Cumberland Ave.
  Broadstairs CT10 .... 30 A5
Cumberland Ave.
  Canterbury CT1 .... 88 D7
Cumberland Ave.
  Maidstone ME15 .... 97 D8
Cumberland Dr. ME9 .... 13 C3
Cumberland Rd.
  Gillingham ME4 & ME7 ..... 10 B7
Cumberland Rd.
  Gillingham ME7 .... 10 C7
Cumberland Rd. Margate CT9 .. 8 B3
Cumberland Rd. **1**
  Ramsgate CT11 .... 52 D6
Cundishall Cl. CT5 .... 43 C8
Cunningham Cres.
  Birchington CT7 .... 26 E7
Cunningham Cres.
  Chatham ME5 .... 32 A8
Cunningham Ho. ME1 .... 9 B4
Curlew Ave. ME9 .... 13 B3
Curlew Cl. CT6 .... 23 C2
Curlinge Cl. CT1 .... 52 A6
Curteis Rd. TN30 .... 167 B1
Curtis La. CT4 .... 126 D2
Curtis Rd. TN24 .... 156 E7
Curtis Way. **1** ME13 .... 62 C7
Curtis Wood Park Rd. CT6 ... 46 A7
Curtis Wood Rd. CT6 .... 45 F7
Curzon Cl. CT14 .... 117 C3
Curzon Ho. **5** CT11 .... 52 D6
Curzon Rd. Chatham ME4 ..... 9 F3
Curzon Rd. Dover CT17 ..... 166 B8
Curzon Rd. Maidstone ME14 .. 75 A6
Cushman Rd. CT1 .... 87 E7
Cutbush Almshouses. **2**
  ME15 .... 75 A3
Cutbush and Corrall Ct. ME14 .. 75 B4
Cuthbert Rd. CT8 .... 27 E8
Cuttings The. CT12 .... 52 C8
Cuxton Rd. Park Wood ME15 .. 97 F5
Cuxton Rd. Rochester ME2 ..... 9 A7
Cygnet Rd. ME5 .... 32 C2
Cygnet Way. TN23 .... 138 F1
Cylinder Rd. CT21 .... 176 B4
Cypress Ave. TN23 .... 138 E2
Cypress Cl. CT5 .... 43 C7
Cypress Ct. ME7 .... 10 F6
Cypress Gr. CT15 .... 114 B2
Cyprus Rd. ME13 .... 62 E7

D'este Rd. CT11 .... 52 F7
D2 Trad Est. ME10 .... 37 B6
Daglish Cl. TN28 .... 200 B6
Dagmar Rd. ME4 .... 10 B2
Daimler Ave. CT6 .... 22 B3
Dalby Rd. CT9 .... 8 A3
Dalby Sq. CT9 .... 8 A3
Dale Rd. ME1 .... 9 C3
Dale St. ME4 .... 9 E2
Dale Wlk. TN24 .... 139 C7
Dalewood. ME10 .... 37 A2
Dallas-Brett Cres. CT19 ..... 178 A8
Dallinger Rd. **1** CT7 .... 26 F8
Dalmatia Ct. CT17 .... 149 A1
Dalmeny Ave. CT9 .... 8 D1
Dalton Cl. **4** CT11 .... 52 E7
Dalton St. ME7 .... 10 C6
Dame Janet
  Cty Inf Sch. CT12 .... 29 B2

Dame Janet
  Cty Jun Sch. CT12 .... 29 B2
Damerham Cl. CT2 .... 66 E3
Damiem Cl. ME4 .... 10 A2
Dan Dr. ME13 .... 62 A8
Danaway Cotts. ME9 .... 35 C3
Dane Cl. Chatham ME5 .... 32 C2
Dane Cl. Hartlip ME9 .... 34 D6
Dane Court Gdns. CT10 ..... 29 D5
Dane Court Gram Sch. CT10 .. 29 E4
Dane Court Rd. CT10 & CT9 .. 29 C6
Dane Cres. CT11 .... 52 E8
Dane Ct. ME17 .... 96 C2
Dane End Rd. CT8 .... 27 D8
Dane Gdns. CT9 .... 29 B8
Dane Hill. CT9 .... 7 J3
Dane Hill Gr. CT9 .... 7 J2
Dane Hill Row. CT9 .... 7 J2
Dane John Ct. **3** CT1 ...... 87 F7
Dane John Mews. **1** CT1 ... 87 F7
Dane La. ME9 .... 34 D6
Dane Mount. CT9 .... 29 C8
Dane Park Rd. Margate CT9 .... 7 J2
Dane Park Rd. Ramsgate CT11 .. 52 E8
Dane Rd. Birchington CT7 ... 26 D7
Dane Rd. Margate CT9 .... 8 A2
Dane Rd. Ramsgate CT11 ..... 52 E8
Dane Valley Rd. CT10 & CT9 .. 29 C8
Danecourt Sch The. ME8 ..... 11 A2
Danedale Ave. ME12 .... 4 F6
Danefield Ct. ME14 .... 76 B4
Danehurst. CT7 .... 7 C1
Danemore. TN30 .... 179 B8
Danes Ct. CT16 .... 149 D2
Danes Dr. ME12 .... 6 D2
Danes Hill. ME7 .... 11 A6
Danes Mead. ME10 .... 14 F1
Danesmead Terr. CT9 .... 7 J2
Daniels Cl. CT5 .... 20 C1
Danley Mid Sch. ME12 .... 3 E7
Danley Rd. ME12 .... 3 E7
Danson Way. ME8 .... 11 D2
Danton La. CT18 & CT19 ... 162 C1
Darby Pl. CT20 .... 178 D5
Darby Rd. CT20 .... 178 D5
Darenth Cl. CT6 .... 23 B3
Darenth Ho. **2** ME15 ...... 97 D8
Darenth Rise. ME5 .... 32 B3
Dargate Cl. ME16 .... 74 D7
Dargate Rd.
  Dargate CT2 & ME13 .... 64 F7
Dargate Rd. Yorklets CT5 .... 43 A3
Dargets Rd. ME5 .... 32 A3
Dark Hill. ME13 .... 62 C8
Darland Ave. ME7 .... 10 E1
Darlinghurst Rd. CT19 ...... 177 E7
Darlington Dr. ME2 .... 4 A6
Darlington St. CT20 .... 178 D5
Darnley Cl. Broadstairs CT10 .. 30 B3
Darnley Cl. Folkestone CT20 .. 177 F4
Darnley Rd. ME2 .... 9 A6
Darracott Cl. CT14 .... 117 B5
Darrell Cl. CT6 .... 22 C3
Darren Gdns. CT10 .... 29 F2
Darwin Coll. CT2 .... 66 E5
Darwin Rd. CT7 .... 26 F8
Daryngton Ave. CT7 .... 26 C7
Davenport Ave. ME7 .... 10 E7
David Ave. CT9 .... 8 D2
Davids Cl. CT10 .... 30 B3
Davidson Rd. CT2 .... 66 D1
Davie Cl. ME12 .... 3 B8
Davis Ave. CT14 .... 117 A4
Dawbourns. TN30 .... 167 B3
Dawes Rd. CT2 & ME13 ...... 64 C4
Dawes St. ME7 .... 10 F5
Dawn Rise. ME12 .... 5 F6
Dawson Rd. CT19 .... 178 D6
Dawson's Row. ME13 .... 62 A6
Dayton Rd. ME13 .... 83 C3
Daytona Way. CT6 .... 22 A4
De Burgh Hill. CT17 .... 149 C1
De Burgh St. **2** CT17 ...... 166 C8
De Havilland Cl. CT18 ...... 163 B4
De L'angle Row. CT4 .... 86 D3
De Mere Cl. ME8 .... 33 D6
Deacon Est The. ME20 .... 53 A2
Deacon Trad Ctr. ME2 .... 9 A6
Deal Castle. CT14 .... 117 D5
Deal Castle Rd. CT14 ...... 117 D5
Deal Parochial
  CE Prim Sch. CT14 .... 117 C5
Deal Rd. CT13 & CT14 .... 93 F5
Deal Sta. CT14 .... 117 C6
Dean Croft. CT6 .... 23 B2
Dean Ct. **14** CT1 .... 67 A1
Dean Hill. CT4 & TN25 ..... 126 B2
Dean Mead. CT19 .... 178 B7
Dean Rd. ME10 .... 36 E6
Dean St. ME15 .... 96 C6
Dean Wood
  Cty Prim Inf Sch. ME8 .... 33 D3
Dean Wood
  Cty Prim Jun Sch. ME8 ... 33 D4
Dean's Wlk. TN23 .... 155 F7
Deane Cl. CT5 .... 43 E7
Deans Hill Rd. ME9 .... 57 D5
Deans Mill Ct. CT2 .... 66 F1
Deansway Ave. CT2 .... 66 F3
Deanwood Cl. ME8 .... 33 D6
Deanwood Dr. ME8 .... 33 D6
Deanwood Rd. CT17 .... 148 E2
Deborah Cl. CT5 .... 43 F7
Deedes Cl. CT21 .... 176 C3

Deerhurst Gdns. ME16 .... 74 D4
Deerson La. CT3 .... 70 A4
Defiant Cl. ME5 .... 32 B6
Delce Cl. ME5 .... 32 B6
Delacourt Cl. CT12 .... 51 D5
Delamark Rd. ME12 .... 1 D2
Delane Rd. CT14 .... 117 A5
Delaware Cl. CT12 .... 67 F6
Delce Cty Inf Sch. ME1 .... 9 D2
Delce Cty Jun Sch. ME1 .... 9 C2
Delce Rd. ME1 .... 9 D4
Delf St. CT13 .... 72 F1
Delfside. CT13 .... 94 A8
Delmaney Cl. CT10 .... 30 B5
Delmar Cl. CT5 .... 21 D3
Denbigh Ave. ME8 .... 11 D1
Denbigh Cl. ME10 .... 36 E7
Denbigh Rd. CT12 .... 29 A1
Dence Cl. CT6 .... 23 B5
Dencora Way. TN23 .... 139 A1
Dene The. Bethersden TN26 .. 153 D5
Dene The. Canterbury CT1 ... 88 B5
Dene The. Hythe CT21 ..... 176 C2
Dene Wlk. CT9 .... 28 F7
Dengemarsh Rd. TN29 ...... 203 C3
Denham Cl. ME10 .... 36 D5
Denham Ho. ME10 .... 36 D5
Denham Rd. ME9 .... 35 B7
Denmark Rd. CT11 .... 52 E8
Denmark St. CT19 .... 178 E6
Denne Cl. CT2 .... 67 F7
Denne Manor La. CT4 ...... 106 C8
Dennes La. TN29 .... 203 C8
Dennes Mill Cl. TN25 ...... 123 D2
Denness Rd. TN23 .... 156 B7
Dennis Way. CT19 .... 177 E7
Dennis Willocks Cl. ME9 .... 35 B6
Densole Cl. CT18 .... 163 A8
Densole Way. CT18 .... 163 A8
Denstead Cotts. CT4 .... 86 B8
Denstead Ct. CT2 .... 66 C4
Denstead La. CT4 & ME13 .. 86 C7
Denstead Oast. CT4 .... 86 B8
Denstead Wlk. **11** ME15 .. 97 F6
Denstroude La. CT2 .... 65 D8
Dent-De Lion Ct. CT9 .... 28 A8
Dent-De-Lion Rd.
  Margate CT9 .... 28 A8
Dent-De-Lion Rd.
  Westgate-on-S CT8 .... 7 C1
Dental St. CT21 .... 176 C2
Denton Cl. ME15 .... 97 E8
Denton Way. CT9 .... 8 C1
Derby Rd. ME10 .... 36 D6
Derby Rd. Chatham ME5 .... 10 E2
Derby Rd. Gillingham ME5 .. 10 E2
Derby Rd. Maidstone ME15 .. 97 C8
Dering Cl. Bridge CT4 .... 88 F1
Dering Cl.
  Chamber's Green TN27 ... 136 C4
Dering Rd. Ashford TN24 ... 139 D2
Dering Rd. Bridge CT4 .... 89 A1
Dering Rd. Herne Bay CT6 ... 22 F4
Dering Terr. TN27 .... 136 C3
Derings The. TN29 .... 203 B6
Deringwood Dr. ME15 .... 75 F1
Derringstone Downs. CT4 .. 128 F6
Derringstone Hill. CT4 ..... 128 F6
Derringstone St. CT4 ...... 128 F7
Derville Ho. TN28 .... 200 B6
Derville Rd. TN29 .... 204 C7
Derwent Ave. CT14 .... 117 A4
Derwent Cl. Chatham ME5 ... 32 C7
Derwent Ho. **5** ME15 ..... 97 E7
Derwent Way. Aylesham CT3 .. 112 F6
Derwent Way. Gillingham ME8 .. 33 D8
Desmond Cres. ME13 .... 63 A5
Detling Ave. ME10 .... 30 A1
Detling CE Prim Sch. ME14 .. 55 A1
Detling Cl. Gillingham ME8 .. 11 C2
Detling Cl. West Minster ME12 .. 3 B7
Detling Hill. ME14 .... 55 B2
Devon Ave. CT14 .... 117 C3
Devon Cl. Chatham ME5 ..... 32 C7
Devon Cl. Gillingham ME8 ... 11 F1
Devon Ct. CT12 .... 29 B2
Devon Gdns. CT7 .... 26 F7
Devon Rd. Canterbury CT1 .. 88 D8
Devon Rd. Folkestone CT19 .. 178 D5
Devon Rd. Maidstone ME15 .. 97 C8
Devonshire Gdns. CT9 .... 8 C3
Devonshire Rd. Dover CT17 .. 166 B8
Devonshire Rd. Gillingham ME7 .. 10 D7
Devonshire Terr. CT10 ...... 30 B5
Dhekelia Cl. ME14 .... 75 A7
Dial Cl. ME7 .... 10 F6
Dial Rd. ME7 .... 10 F6
Diamond Ct. ME12 .... 1 C1
Diamond Rd. CT5 .... 20 E2
Diana Gdns. CT14 .... 117 A5
Dibdin Rd. CT14 .... 117 D7
Dickens Ave. CT2 .... 67 D2
Dickens Cl. ME17 .... 98 E4
Dickens Ct. ME2 .... 9 D8
Dickens Rd. Broadstairs CT10 .. 30 B5
Dickens Rd. Maidstone ME14 .. 74 E8
Dickens Rd. Rochester ME1 .. 9 C2
Dickens Wlk. CT10 .... 30 B4
Dickley La. ME17 .... 101 A6
Dickson Cl. ME10 .... 37 B4
Dickson Rd. CT17 .... 166 C8
Dickson's Cnr. CT13 .... 95 A6
Dicksons Bourne. TN25 .... 172 F6
Dieu Stone La. CT16 .... 166 E8
Digby Rd. CT20 .... 177 E5
Dignals Cl. ME8 .... 11 F2
Dignash. TN25 .... 121 E2
Diligent Dr. ME10 .... 36 F7

Diocesan & Payne Smith
  CE Prim Sch. CT1 .... 67 A1
Discovery Wlk. CT1 .... 88 C7
Disraeli Cl. ME15 .... 97 E5
Dixon Cl. ME5 .... 74 F2
Dixwell Cl. MF8 .... 33 D5
Dixwell Rd. CT20 .... 178 A4
Dobbie Cl. ME10 .... 36 E6
Dock Exit Rd. CT16 .... 166 F8
Dock Head Rd. ME4 .... 10 A8
Dock Rd. Chatham ME4 .... 9 F6
Duck Rd. Gillingham ME4 ... 10 A7
Doctor's La. CT15 .... 165 B5
Dodd's La. CT16 .... 149 A3
Doddington Ct. ME16 ...... 74 E5
Doddington
  Cty Prim Sch. ME9 .... 80 F7
Doddington Rd. ME8 .... 11 D3
Dodes Alley. **4** ME9 ...... 36 F4
Dog Kennel La. CT18 ...... 161 B7
Doggerel Acre. CT5 .... 43 F7
Doggett's Sq. ME2 .... 9 C7
Dogwood Cl. ME5 .... 32 D1
Dola Ave. CT14 .... 117 B6
Dolphin Cl. CT10 .... 8 G3
Dolphin Dr. ME8 .... 33 E5
Dolphin Ho. **1** CT16 ..... 166 E7
Dolphin La. CT16 .... 166 E7
Dolphin Pas. **2** CT16 .... 166 E7
Dolphin Pk. CT16 .... 37 B5
Dolphin Pl. **3** CT16 ..... 166 E7
Dolphin Rd. Lydd TN29 .... 203 C6
Dolphin Rd.
  Sittingbourne ME10 .... 37 B5
Dolphin St. Deal CT14 ..... 117 D7
Dolphin St. Herne Bay CT6 .. 22 E5
Dolphins Rd. CT19 .... 178 D5
Dombey Cl. ME1 .... 9 C3
Domneva Rd. Minster, Thanet
  CT12 .... 50 B6
Domneva Rd.
  Westgate-on-S CT8 .... 27 D8
Donald Moor Ave. ME9 ...... 38 C2
Doncaster Cl. **7** ME15 ... 97 F6
Donegal Rd. CT1 .... 88 C8
Donemowe Dr. ME10 .... 36 F8
Donet Cl. ME8 .... 33 C5
Dongola Rd. ME2 .... 9 A8
Donkey La. CT3 .... 112 C8
Donkey St. CT21 & TN29 ... 186 E5
Donnahay Rd. CT12 .... 29 C3
Donnithorne Ho. CT6 .... 22 E5
Dorcas Gdns. CT10 .... 30 A6
Doric Ct. CT11 .... 52 C5
Dorman Ave N. CT3 .... 112 E6
Dorman Ave S. CT3 .... 112 F5
Dornden Gdns. ME5 .... 32 B2
Dorne Cotts. TN27 .... 118 E6
Dorothy Dr. CT12 .... 29 C2
Dorrit Way. ME1 .... 9 D2
Dorset Cl. CT5 .... 43 B7
Dorset Ct. Deal CT14 ...... 117 D7
Dorset Ct. Ramsgate CT12 .. 29 B2
Dorset Gdns. Birchington CT7 .. 26 F7
Dorset Gdns. Deal CT14 .... 117 C2
Dorset Pl. ME13 .... 62 C7
Dorset Rd. Canterbury CT1 .. 88 D7
Dorset Rd. West Minster ME12 .. 3 A8
Dorset Sq. ME8 .... 11 D1
Dorset Way. ME15 .... 97 C8
Dossett Ct. CT14 .... 117 A2
Dotterel Cl. ME5 .... 32 D2
Doubleday Dr. ME9 .... 37 F4
Douglas Almshouses. ME17 .. 101 D5
Douglas Ave. Hythe CT21 .. 176 C2
Douglas Ave. Whitstable CT5 .. 20 E1
Douglas Bglws. CT15 ...... 132 E8
Douglas Cl. CT10 .... 29 E5
Douglas Rd. Deal CT14 .... 117 A3
Douglas Rd. Dover CT17 ... 166 B8
Douglas Rd. Herne Bay CT6 .. 23 A4
Douglas Rd. Lenham ME17 .. 101 D5
Douglas Rd. Maidstone ME16 .. 74 E3
Douglas Terr. CT14 .... 117 D5
Dour Side. CT17 .... 148 F3
Dour St. CT16 .... 166 D8
Dour Cl. CT1 .... 67 D1
Douro Pl. CT16 .... 166 E7
Dove Cl. Chatham ME5 ...... 32 B6
Dove Cl. Hythe CT21 ...... 187 D8
Dove Cl. Whitstable CT5 .... 43 C7
Dove Lea Gdns. CT17 ..... 148 E3
Dovedale Cl. CT17 .... 27 B7
Dovedale Ct. CT17 .... 27 B7
Dover Castle. CT16 .... 166 F8
Dover Coll. CT17 .... 166 C8
Dover Coll. Dover CT16 ... 166 D7
Dover Gram Sch for Boys.
  CT17 .... 166 A8
Dover Gram Sch for Girls.
  CT16 .... 149 C1
Dover Hill. CT19 .... 178 F8
Dover Pl. TN23 .... 139 C1
Dover Rd. Barham CT4 ..... 112 A1
Dover Rd. Bishopsbourne CT4 .. 111 D5
Dover Rd.
  Folkestone CT19 & CT20 .. 178 E7
Dover Rd. Guston CT15 ... 149 E4
Dover Rd.
  Ringwould CT14 & CT15 .. 134 A6
Dover Rd. Sandwich CT13 .. 93 F6
Dover Rd.
  St Margaret's at Cliffe CT15 .. 150 D6
Dover Rd.
  Tilmanstone CT13 & CT14 .. 115 B5
Dover St.
  Woolage Green CT4 & CT15 .. 129 D6
Dover St. Canterbury CT1 ... 88 A7

Dover St. Maidstone ME16 .... 74 C2
Dover St. **1**
  Sittingbourne ME10 .... 36 E4
Doves Cnr. CT14 .... 115 A4
Dowle Cl. TN29 .... 199 A7
Down Barton Rd. CT7 .... 25 E1
Down Ct. TN23 .... 155 E5
Downer Ct. ME4 .... 31 E8
Downhill Cl. CT16 .... 148 D6
Downings The. CT6 .... 23 A2
Downland Ct. TN24 .... 139 B3
Downlands. Deal CT14 ..... 134 B8
Downlands.
  Harrietsham ME17 .... 100 F6
Downs Ave. CT5 .... 20 E1
Downs
  CE Prim Sch The. CT14 .. 117 B2
Downs Cl. Charing TN27 ... 120 C8
Downs Cl. East Studdal CT15 .. 132 D8
Downs Cl. Maidstone ME14 .. 75 D8
Downs Cl. Sittingbourne ME10 .. 36 D2
Downs Pk. CT6 .... 23 A5
Downs Rd. Canterbury CT2 .. 66 F4
Downs Rd. Deal CT14 ..... 117 C3
Downs Rd. East Studdal CT15 .. 132 E8
Downs Rd. Folkestone CT19 .. 178 C7
Downs Rd. Maidstone ME14 .. 75 B8
Downs Rd. Ramsgate CT11 .. 52 B6
Downs The. Chartham CT4 .. 86 E1
Downs The. Chatham ME5 ... 31 D1
Downs The. Preston CT3 .... 70 C6
Downs View
  Cty Inf Sch. TN24 .... 139 C7
Downs View Rd. ME14 ..... 75 B8
Downs Way. Charing TN27 .. 120 C8
Downs Way. Sellindge TN25 .. 159 C1
Downside. Bekesbourne CT4 .. 89 E3
Downside. Folkestone CT19 .. 178 C7
Downside. Rochester ME2 ..... 9 A7
Downside.
  St Margaret's at Cliffe CT15 .. 151 A4
Downside Rd. CT16 .... 149 B7
Downsview. ME5 .... 32 C8
Dragonfly Cl. TN23 .... 155 D8
Dragoon Ho. **10** CT1 ..... 67 A1
Drainless Rd. CT13 .... 93 A5
Drake Ave. ME12 .... 4 D5
Drake Rd. TN24 .... 157 B7
Drakes Cl. ME5 .... 12 E2
Drapers Almshouses. CT9 .. 29 A8
Drapers Ave. CT9 .... 28 F8
Drapers Cl. CT9 .... 29 A8
Drapers Mills
  Cty Prim Sch. CT9 .... 29 A8
Drapers Windmill (dis). CT9 .... 8 A1
Dray's Field. ME9 .... 79 A7
Dreadnought Ave. ME12 ...... 4 B6
Drew La. CT14 .... 117 C4
Drewery Dr. ME8 .... 33 C5
Drill La. CT3 .... 69 B1
Drive The. Canterbury CT1 .. 88 B6
Drive The. Whitstable CT5 .. 44 D8
Drivers Rdbt. TN24 .... 139 A4
Drop Redoubt Rd. CT17 ... 166 D7
Drove Rd. ME12 .... 3 E7
Drove The. Fordwich CT2 ... 68 A4
Drove The. Monkton CT12 .. 49 B6
Drove The. Northbourne CT14 .. 116 A5
Drove The. Whitfield CT16 .. 149 A8
Drove The. Whitstable CT5 .. 44 D8
Droveway Gdns. CT15 ..... 151 A6
Droveway The. CT15 .... 151 B6
Drum La. TN23 .... 139 B2
Drury Rd. TN30 .... 179 B8
Drybeck Ave. CT11 .... 51 F7
Dryden Cl. CT1 .... 88 C7
Dryden Rd. CT16 .... 149 B3
Drywall Ind Est. ME10 ...... 37 B6
Duchess Of Kent Dr. ME5 ... 32 B3
Duck La. Canterbury CT1 .... 67 A1
Duck La. Shadoxhurst TN26 .. 169 F7
Duck St. CT4 .... 144 F4
Duckpit Rd. CT4 .... 126 A6
Duckworth Cl. TN24 ...... 157 B7
Dudley Ave. CT8 .... 27 C8
Dudley Rd. Ashford TN24 .. 139 E5
Dudley Rd. Folkestone CT19 .. 178 C5
Duke of Clarence
  Trad Est The. ME12 .... 1 B3
Duke of York's
  Royal Military Sch. CT15 .. 149 F4
Duke St. Deal CT14 .... 117 D7
Duke St. Margate CT9 .... 7 13
Dukes Meadow. TN26 ...... 183 A7
Dukes Meadow Dr. ME7 ..... 32 F6
Dukes Wlk. **5** ME15 ..... 75 A4
Dukeswood. CT5 .... 44 D6
Dully Rd. ME9 .... 59 E6
Dumergue Ave. ME11 .... 3 B5
Dumpton Gap Rd. CT10 .... 30 A2
Dumpton La. CT11 .... 29 E1
Dumpton Park Dr.
  CT10 & CT11 .... 30 A2
Dumpton Park Rd. CT11 ... 52 E8
Dumpton Park Sta. CT11 ... 29 F1
Duncan Dr. CT7 .... 26 E8
Duncan Rd. Gillingham ME7 .. 10 D5
Duncan Rd. Ramsgate CT11 .. 52 D7
Duncan Rd. Whitstable CT5 .. 43 D7
Dundein Dr. CT16 .... 149 B3
Dundonald Rd. **11**
  Broadstairs CT10 .... 30 B4
Dundonald Rd. Ramsgate CT11 .. 52 C7
Dunedin Cl. ME10 .... 36 C3
Dunedin Rd. CT12 .... 29 A1
Dunera Dr. ME14 .... 75 A7
Duncs Rd. TN28 .... 200 D3

Dungeness Power Sta
Visitor Ctr. TN29 ..... 205 E6
Dungeness Rd. TN29 ..... 204 C3
Dungeness Sta. TN29 ..... 205 F6
Dunkery Rise. TN24 ..... 139 B4
Dunkirk Cl. TN29 ..... 195 B7
Dunkirk Cty Prim Sch. ME13 ..... 64 D2
Dunkirk Dr. ME5 ..... 31 F6
Dunkirk Rd.
  Boughton Street ME13 ..... 64 B1
Dunkirk Rd.
  Boughton Street ME13 ..... 64 B2
Dunkirk Sq. CT16 ..... 149 F3
Dunlin Ct. TN29 ..... 195 A3
Dunn Street Rd. ME7 ..... 55 A8
Dunnett Rd. CT19 ..... 177 E6
Dunning's La. ME1 ..... 9 C4
Dunnings The. ME16 ..... 74 A2
Dunoon Ct. CT11 ..... 29 F1
Dunstall Cl. TN29 ..... 195 A5
Dunstall Gdns. TN29 ..... 195 A5
Dunstall La. TN29 ..... 195 A5
Dunstan Ave. CT8 ..... 27 D7
Dunston Cl. CT2 ..... 66 E1
Dunston Ho. CT14 ..... 117 D8
Durban Cl. CT12 ..... 29 A2
Durban Cres. CT16 ..... 149 C4
Durban Ho. **7** ME15 ..... 97 E5
Durban Rd. CT9 ..... 8 A1
Durham Cl. Canterbury CT1 ..... 87 F6
Durham Cl. **9** Dover CT17 ..... 166 B7
Durham Cl. Maidstone ME15 ..... 75 E1
Durham Hill. CT16 & CT17 ..... 166 D7
Durham Rd. ME8 ..... 33 C7
Durling Cl. ME8 ..... 12 A1
Durlock. CT12 ..... 50 C5
Durlock Ave. CT11 ..... 52 B5
Durlock Rd. CT3 ..... 92 B7
Durlocks The. CT19 ..... 178 E5
Durnford Cl. CT2 ..... 66 E2
Durovernum Ct. CT1 ..... 88 A7
Durrell Gdns. ME5 ..... 10 C1
Duval Dr. ME1 ..... 31 E8
Duvard's Pl. ME9 ..... 35 F1
Dyke Rd. CT19 ..... 178 E5
Dymchurch
  Cty Prim Sch. TN29 ..... 195 C8
Dymchurch Ho. CT1 ..... 88 B8
Dymchurch Rd. Hythe CT21 ..... 176 A2
Dymchurch Rd.
  Hythe CT21 & TN29 ..... 187 C6
Dymchurch Rd.
  St Mary's Bay TN29 & TN28 ..... 195 A5
Dymchurch Sta. TN29 ..... 195 B7
Dyngley Cl. ME10 ..... 36 E6

Eagle Hill. CT11 ..... 52 D7
Eagles Cl. ME10 ..... 37 C4
Ealham Cl. Ashford TN24 ..... 157 A8
Ealham Cl. Canterbury CT1 ..... 88 B5
Ealing Cl. ME5 ..... 32 C4
Earl Cl. ME5 ..... 32 B4
Earl St. ME14 ..... 74 F4
Earl's Ave. CT20 ..... 178 B4
Earls Ave. TN24 ..... 139 F1
Earlsfield. TN25 ..... 173 A6
Earlsfield Rd. CT21 ..... 176 D2
Earlsmead Cres. CT12 ..... 51 C5
Earlsworth Ct. TN24 ..... 156 E6
Earlsworth Rd. TN24 ..... 156 D6
Easole Hts. CT15 ..... 113 D5
Easole St. CT15 ..... 113 D5
East Borough
  Cty Prim Sch ME14 ..... 75 B5
East Cliff. Dover CT16 ..... 166 F8
East Cliff. Folkestone CT19 ..... 178 F6
East Cliff Gdns. **19** CT19 ..... 178 E5
East Cliff Golf Links. CT19 ..... 178 G6
East Cliff Par. CT14 ..... 23 A5
East Cliff Pas. **20** CT19 ..... 178 E5
East Court
  (Sch for Dyslexics). CT11 ..... 52 G7
East Cross. TN30 ..... 179 B7
East Farleigh
  Cty Prim Sch. ME15 ..... 96 B6
East Farleigh Sta. ME16 ..... 96 B8
East Gn. ME10 ..... 15 A1
East Hall La. ME10 ..... 37 C5
East Hill. Ashford TN23 & TN24 ..... 139 C2
East Hill. Tenterden TN30 ..... 179 B8
East Kent Light Railway.
  CT15 ..... 131 C8
East La. ME12 ..... 1 B2
East Langdon Rd. CT15 ..... 149 F7
East Lodge Rd. TN23 ..... 138 F3
East Mountain La. TN24 ..... 139 F7
East Norman Rd. CT16 ..... 149 E1
East Northdown Cl. CT9 ..... 8 E1
East Park Rd. ME20 ..... 74 A8
East Ramp. CT16 ..... 166 G8
East Rd. Chatham ME4 ..... 10 A7
East Rd. Folkestone CT20 ..... 177 D4
East Rd. Gillingham ME4 ..... 10 A8
East Rd. Sandwich CT12 & CT13 ..... 73 A8
East Rise. CT12 ..... 29 B1
East Roman Ditch. CT16 ..... 166 F8
East Row. ME1 ..... 9 C5
East St. Ashford TN23 ..... 139 B2
East St. Canterbury CT1 ..... 67 C3
East St. Chatham ME4 ..... 10 A3
East St. Dover CT17 ..... 166 C8
East St. Faversham ME13 ..... 62 D7
East St. Folkestone CT19 ..... 178 E5
East St. Gillingham ME7 ..... 10 D6
East St. Harrietsham ME17 ..... 100 C5
East St. Herne Bay CT6 ..... 23 A5
East St. Hythe CT21 ..... 176 D2
East St. Sittingbourne ME10 ..... 37 A4

East Stour Ct. TN24 ..... 139 D1
East View. Brookland TN29 ..... 197 D8
East View. Hersden CT3 ..... 46 F1
East Weald Dr. TN30 ..... 167 B1
East Wootton Cotts. CT4 ..... 109 A4
Eastbridge Rd. TN29 ..... 195 B8
Eastbrook Pl. CT16 ..... 166 E8
Eastchurch
  CE Prim Sch. ME12 ..... 5 D3
Eastchurch Rd. Margate CT9 ..... 8 E3
Eastchurch Rd. Minster ME12 ..... 5 B5
Eastcourt Gn. ME8 ..... 11 B4
Eastcourt La. Gillingham ME8 ..... 11 B3
Eastcourt La. Gillingham,
  Lower Twydall ME7 & ME8 ..... 11 B4
Eastern Arm N. CT16 ..... 166 H8
Eastern Arm S. CT16 ..... 166 H8
Eastern Ave. Ashford TN23 ..... 139 A2
Eastern Ave.
  Halfway Houses ME12 ..... 3 D6
Eastern Ave.
  Queenborough ME11 ..... 3 B4
Eastern Espl. Broadstairs CT10 ..... 30 B5
Eastern Espl. Margate CT9 ..... 8 B3
Eastern Gdns. TN24 ..... 156 E8
Eastern Rd. Gillingham ME7 ..... 10 F6
Eastern Rd.
  Leysdown-on-S ME12 ..... 6 G2
Eastern Rd. Lydd TN29 ..... 203 D7
Eastern Service Rd. CT16 ..... 166 H8
Eastfield Rd. ME16 ..... 74 B2
Eastfield Rd. CT7 ..... 27 A7
Eastfields. CT19 ..... 178 D6
Eastgate. ME1 ..... 9 D5
Eastgate Cl. CT6 ..... 23 B3
Eastgate Ct. ME1 ..... 9 C5
Eastgate Rd. TN30 ..... 179 C8
Eastgate Terr. ME1 ..... 9 C5
Eastling Cl. ME8 ..... 11 D3
Eastling Cty Prim Sch. ME13 ..... 81 F5
Eastling Rd. Bayfield ME13 ..... 61 D2
Eastling Rd. Eastling ME13 ..... 81 F7
Eastmead Ave. TN23 ..... 156 C8
Easton's Cnr. TN25 ..... 172 F4
Eastry CE Prim Sch. CT13 ..... 93 B2
Eastry Cl. Ashford TN23 ..... 156 A6
Eastry Cl. Maidstone ME16 ..... 74 C7
Eastry Ct. CT3 ..... 112 C5
Eastry Hospl. CT13 ..... 93 B2
Eastry Park. CT13 ..... 93 C1
Eastwell. **3** TN30 ..... 179 A8
Eastwell Barn Mews. TN30 ..... 179 A8
Eastwell Cl. Maidstone ME14 ..... 75 C5
Eastwell Cl. Shadoxhurst TN26 ..... 155 B1
Eastwell Meadows. TN30 ..... 179 A8
Eastwell Terr. TN25 ..... 122 E3
Eastwood Cotts. ME9 ..... 38 E6
Eastwood Rd. ME10 ..... 36 D5
Eaton Hill. CT9 ..... 7 I2
Eaton Rd. Dover CT17 ..... 166 A7
Eaton Rd. Margate CT9 ..... 7 I1
Eaves Rd. CT17 ..... 166 A7
Ebbsfleet La. CT12 ..... 51 A3
Ebony Cotts. TN30 ..... 189 A6
Eccleston Rd. ME15 ..... 74 F2
Echo Cl. ME15 ..... 97 F6
Echo Ho. ME10 ..... 37 B3
Echo Wlk. ME10 ..... 4 D6
Eddington Cl. ME15 ..... 97 B6
Eddington La. CT6 ..... 22 F3
Eddington Way. CT6 ..... 22 E3
Eden Ave. ME5 ..... 32 A7
Eden Ho. TN23 ..... 156 C8
Edenbridge Dr. ME12 ..... 3 B8
Edenbridge Ho. CT1 ..... 88 B8
Edenfield. CT7 ..... 27 B7
Edgar Cl. CT5 ..... 21 D3
Edgar Ho. CT14 ..... 117 B3
Edgar Rd. Canterbury CT1 ..... 67 B1
Edgar Rd. Dover CT17 ..... 149 B1
Edgar Rd. Margate CT9 ..... 8 A3
Edgar Rd. Minster, Thanet CT12 ..... 50 B6
Edge End Rd. CT10 ..... 29 F4
Edgehill Cl. CT20 ..... 177 D4
Edger Pl. **3** ME15 ..... 75 A4
Edinburgh Rd.
  Ashford TN23 & TN24 ..... 139 B2
Edinburgh Rd. Chatham ME4 ..... 10 C2
Edinburgh Rd. Gillingham ME7 ..... 10 D5
Edinburgh Rd. Margate CT9 ..... 28 B8
Edinburgh Sq. Maidstone ME15 ..... 97 C7
Edinburgh Wlk. **5** CT9 ..... 28 B8
Edith Rd. Faversham ME13 ..... 62 D6
Edith Rd. Ramsgate CT11 ..... 52 C6
Edith Rd. Westgate-on-S CT8 ..... 7 D1
Edmanson Ave. CT9 ..... 7 E1
Edmund Cl. ME16 ..... 74 A3
Edmund St. CT3 ..... 91 A8
Edna Rd. ME14 ..... 74 F8
Edred Rd. CT17 ..... 166 B8
Edward Ct. ME5 ..... 10 C1
Edward Dr. CT7 ..... 26 F4
Edward Rd. Canterbury CT1 ..... 88 A8
Edward Rd. Folkestone CT19 ..... 178 D6
Edward Rd. Kingsdown CT14 ..... 134 C6
Edward Rd.
  Queenborough ME11 ..... 3 B5
Edward Rd. Whitstable CT5 ..... 43 C5
Edward St. Chatham ME4 ..... 10 A3
Edward St. Rochester ME2 ..... 9 B7
Edward Terr. **8** CT20 ..... 178 E6
Edwards Cl. ME8 ..... 33 C5
Edwards Rd. CT16 ..... 166 D8

Edwin Rd. ME8 ..... 33 C8
Edwina Ave. ME12 ..... 4 A7
Edwina Pl. ME9 ..... 35 C7
Edyngham Cl. ME10 ..... 37 A8
Effingham Cres. CT16 & CT17 ..... 166 D8
Effingham St. Dover CT17 ..... 166 D8
Effingham St. Ramsgate CT11 ..... 52 E6
Egbert Rd. Birchington CT7 ..... 26 D8
Egbert Rd. Faversham ME13 ..... 62 C6
Egbert Rd. Minster, Thanet CT12 ..... 50 B6
Egbert Rd. Westgate-on-S CT8 ..... 7 C1
Egerton CE Prim Sch. TN27 ..... 118 F3
Egerton Dr. CT9 ..... 8 E2
Egerton House Rd. TN27 ..... 118 E4
Egerton Rd. Maidstone ME14 ..... 74 E7
Egerton Rd. Pluckley TN27 ..... 119 B1
Egerton Rd. Temple Ewell CT16 ..... 148 E5
Eggarton La. CT4 ..... 107 C2
Eggringe. TN23 ..... 138 E1
Egremont Rd. ME15 ..... 75 F2
Eighteen Acre La. TN29 ..... 198 D8
Elder Cl. ME17 ..... 99 D2
Elder Cl. ME8 ..... 33 B6
Elders The. CT3 ..... 68 F1
Eldon Pl. **4** CT10 ..... 30 B4
Eldon St. ME4 ..... 10 A4
Elfrida Cl. CT9 ..... 29 C8
Elgar Pl. **1** CT17 ..... 52 D7
Elham CE Prim Sch. CT4 ..... 144 F4
Elham Cl. Gillingham ME8 ..... 11 B3
Elham Cl. Margate CT9 ..... 8 C1
Elham Rd. CT1 ..... 87 E6
Elham Way. CT10 ..... 30 A2
Eling Ct. ME15 ..... 97 A8
Eliot Coll. CT2 ..... 66 E4
Elisans Wlk. CT1 ..... 88 C8
Elizabeth Carter Ave. CT14 ..... 116 F4
Elizabeth Cl. Broadstairs CT10 ..... 30 B6
Elizabeth Cl. Chatham ME5 ..... 32 A7
Elizabeth Ct. Gillingham ME8 ..... 11 C1
Elizabeth Ct. Herne Bay CT6 ..... 22 F5
Elizabeth Dr. CT18 ..... 164 B2
Elizabeth Gdns. CT21 ..... 176 B1
Elizabeth Ho. ME14 ..... 75 A6
Elizabeth Kemp Ct. CT12 ..... 29 C1
Elizabeth Rd. Dover CT17 ..... 166 D6
Elizabeth Rd. Ramsgate CT11 ..... 52 F6
Elizabeth Way. CT6 ..... 23 B3
Elizabethen Ct. TN27 ..... 120 C7
Ellen Ave. CT11 ..... 29 E2
Ellen's Hill. CT14 ..... 116 E3
Ellen's Pl. ME9 ..... 35 C6
Ellenden Ct. CT2 ..... 66 C4
Ellens Rd. CT14 ..... 116 F2
Ellenswood Cl. ME15 ..... 76 A1
Ellesmere Mews. TN28 ..... 200 C8
Ellingham Leas. ME15 ..... 97 C7
Ellingham Way. ME23 ..... 156 A5
Ellington Ave. CT9 ..... 28 B8
Ellington Cty Inf Sch. CT11 ..... 52 C7
Ellington High Sch. CT11 ..... 52 C7
Ellington Pl. CT11 ..... 52 C7
Ellington Rd. CT11 ..... 52 D7
Elliots Pl. ME13 ..... 62 D7
Elliott Park Sch. ME12 ..... 4 A7
Ellis Dr. TN28 ..... 200 C8
Ellis Rd. CT5 ..... 21 A3
Ellis Way. CT6 ..... 23 C2
Ellison Cl. CT5 ..... 21 C1
Ellison Cl. ME13 ..... 62 E6
Ellison Way. ME8 ..... 12 A2
Elm Ave. ME4 ..... 9 E1
Elm Cl. TN27 ..... 118 F3
Elm Cotts. TN25 ..... 122 E3
Elm Court Ind Est. ME7 ..... 32 E3
Elm Ct. CT8 ..... 27 E8
Elm Fields. TN29 ..... 199 A6
Elm Gdns. CT21 ..... 176 E2
Elm Gr. Maidstone ME15 ..... 75 B3
Elm Gr. Sittingbourne ME10 ..... 37 B4
Elm Gr. Westgate-on-S CT8 ..... 27 E8
Elm Ho. **11** CT21 ..... 176 B2
Elm La. ME12 ..... 4 E5
Elm Park Gdns. CT17 ..... 165 F7
Elm Pl. TN23 ..... 155 F7
Elm Rd. Aylesham CT3 ..... 112 E5
Elm Rd. **6** Folkestone CT19 ..... 178 E6
Elm Rd. Gillingham ME7 ..... 10 E6
Elm Rd. St Mary's Bay TN29 ..... 194 F3
Elm Tree Dr. ME1 ..... 9 A2
Elm Wood Cl. CT5 ..... 21 C2
Elm Wood W. CT5 ..... 21 C2
Elmfield. Gillingham ME8 ..... 11 A3
Elmfield. Tenterden TN30 ..... 179 B8
Elmfield Ct. Coxheath ME17 ..... 96 C3
Elmfield Ct. Tenterden TN30 ..... 179 B8
Elmhurst Gdns. ME1 ..... 9 E3
Elmleigh Rd. CT3 ..... 90 A8
Elmley Cl. ME12 ..... 3 A6
Elmley Rd. ME12 ..... 4 D3
Elmley Way. CT9 ..... 28 F6
Elms Ave. CT11 ..... 52 D6
Elms Hill. CT15 ..... 165 D6
Elms The. Hersden CT3 ..... 46 E1
Elms The. Teynham ME9 ..... 39 A2
Elms Vale Rd. CT15 & CT17 ..... 165 E7
Elmstead Pl. **10** CT20 ..... 178 E5
Elmstone Cl. ME16 ..... 74 B2
Elmstone Gdns. CT9 ..... 8 E2
Elmstone Hole Rd. ME17 ..... 100 D1
Elmstone La. ME16 ..... 74 B2
Elmstone Rd. Gillingham ME8 ..... 33 D7
Elmstone Rd. Ramsgate CT11 ..... 52 D7
Elmton La. CT15 ..... 114 C1
Elmtree. TN26 ..... 181 C1
Elmway. ME12 ..... 5 F6
Elmwood Ave. CT10 ..... 30 A8
Elmwood Cl. CT10 ..... 30 A7

Elventon Cl. CT19 ..... 177 E7
Elverland La. TN13 & ME9 ..... 61 B2
Elvington Cl. ME16 ..... 74 D5
Elvington La. CT18 ..... 162 E2
Elwick La. **13** TN23 ..... 139 B2
Elwick Rd. TN23 ..... 139 B2
Ely Cl. ME5 ..... 11 E2
Embassy Cl. ME7 ..... 10 F1
Emerald Cl. ME1 ..... 31 D7
Emerald View. ME12 ..... 6 E4
Emily Rd. ME5 ..... 32 B6
Emmerson Gdns. CT5 ..... 21 D3
Empire Terr. CT9 ..... 28 E8
Empress Gdns. ME14 ..... 6 D4
Emsworth Gr. ME14 ..... 75 D6
Enbrook Rd. CT20 ..... 177 E4
Enbrook Valley. CT20 ..... 177 E5
Encombe. CT20 ..... 177 D7
Enfield Rd. CT14 ..... 117 D7
Engineers Ct. **1** TN23 ..... 139 B2
English Martyrs'
  RC Prim Sch. ME2 ..... 9 B8
Ennerdale. ME13 ..... 62 E6
Ennerdale Gdns. CT3 ..... 112 F6
Enterprise Bsns Est. ME2 ..... 9 E7
Enterprise Cl. ME2 ..... 9 D8
Enterprise Ctr The. ME5 ..... 54 C8
Enterprise Rd. Maidstone ME15 ..... 75 A1
Enterprise Rd. Margate CT9 ..... 29 A6
Enticott Cl. CT5 ..... 21 A1
Epaul La. ME1 ..... 9 C6
Epping Cl. CT5 ..... 23 B2
Epple Bay Ave. CT7 ..... 27 B8
Epple Bay Rd. CT7 ..... 27 A8
Epple Rd. CT7 ..... 27 B8
Epps Rd. ME10 ..... 36 E3
Epsom Cl. ME15 ..... 97 F6
Eric Rd. CT17 ..... 149 B2
Erith Cl. ME14 ..... 75 A8
Erith St. CT17 ..... 149 B1
Ernest Dr. ME16 ..... 74 B5
Ernest Rd. ME4 ..... 10 A3
Ernwell Rd. CT19 ..... 178 D6
Ersham Rd. CT1 ..... 88 A7
Eskdale Ave. CT11 ..... 52 A7
Esmonde Dr. CT12 ..... 27 F2
Esplanade. Dover CT17 ..... 166 D6
Esplanade. Rochester ME1 ..... 9 B5
Esplanade.
  Westgate-on-S CT8 & CT9 ..... 7 C1
Essella Pk. CT19 ..... 139 E1
Essella Rd. TN24 ..... 139 E1
Essetford Rd. TN23 ..... 156 A7
Essex Ave. CT6 ..... 22 B4
Essex Gdns. CT7 ..... 26 F6
Essex Rd. Canterbury CT1 ..... 88 D7
Essex Rd. Maidstone ME15 ..... 97 E6
Essex Rd. Westgate-on-S CT8 ..... 27 F8
Essex St. CT5 ..... 43 D8
Estelle Cl. ME1 ..... 31 D7
Esther Cl. ME10 ..... 36 E8
Estuary Rd. ME12 ..... 1 C1
Etchden Rd. TN26 ..... 154 A8
Ethel Rd. CT10 ..... 29 F5
Ethel-Maud Ct. ME7 ..... 10 D7
Ethelbert Cres. CT9 ..... 8 A3
Ethelbert Gdns. CT9 ..... 7 J3
Ethelbert Rd. Birchington CT7 ..... 26 D8
Ethelbert Rd. Canterbury CT1 ..... 88 B6
Ethelbert Rd. Deal CT14 ..... 95 C1
Ethelbert Rd. Dover CT17 ..... 166 C8
Ethelbert Rd. Faversham ME13 ..... 62 C6
Ethelbert Rd.
  Folkestone CT19 ..... 178 D7
Ethelbert Rd. Margate CT9 ..... 7 J3
Ethelbert Rd. Ramsgate CT11 ..... 52 D6
Ethelbert Rd. Rochester ME1 ..... 9 C4
Ethelbert Road Cty Inf Sch.
  ME13 ..... 62 C6
Ethelbert Sq. CT8 ..... 7 C1
Ethelbert Terr. Margate CT9 ..... 8 A3
Ethelbert Terr.
  Westgate-on-S CT8 ..... 7 C1
Ethelburga Dr. CT18 ..... 161 B7
Ethelred Rd. ME13 ..... 62 C6
Ethelred Rd. CT8 ..... 7 C1
Eton Cl. ME5 ..... 31 F4
Eurogate Bsns Pk. TN24 ..... 139 B5
Eurolink Way. ME10 ..... 36 F4
Eva Rd. ME7 ..... 10 D3
Evans Rd. TN24 ..... 157 A7
Evelings Alley. **12** CT5 ..... 20 D2
Evelyn Ct. CT21 ..... 177 A2
Evelyn Rd. ME16 ..... 74 E3
Evenhill Rd. CT3 ..... 89 E8
Everard Way. ME13 ..... 62 B8
Everglades The. ME7 ..... 32 F6
Evergreen Cl. Gillingham ME7 ..... 33 A5
Evergreen Cl. Iwade ME9 ..... 14 D4
Everist Ct. CT18 ..... 161 C6
Eversley Cl. ME16 ..... 74 C6
Eversley Coll. CT20 ..... 177 B3
Eversley Rd. CT21 ..... 177 B3
Eversley Way. CT20 ..... 177 F5
Evison Cl. CT16 ..... 149 B2
Ewart Rd. ME4 ..... 9 E1
Exchange St. CT14 ..... 117 D7
Exeter Cl. CT19 ..... 177 D6
Exeter St. ME5 ..... 8 E2
Exmoor Rise. TN24 ..... 139 B4
Exmouth Rd. ME7 ..... 10 C7
Exton Gdns. ME14 ..... 75 F5
Eyhorne St. ME17 ..... 77 D2
Eylesden Court Sch. ME14 ..... 76 B4
Eynsford Cl. CT9 ..... 8 F2
Eynsford Rd. ME16 ..... 74 D7
Eythorn Court Barn. CT15 ..... 131 B7

Eythorne Cl. TN24 ..... 139 D5
Eythorne Elvington
  Cty Prim Sch. CT15 ..... 131 C8
Eythorne Rd. CT15 ..... 130 C6
Eythorne Sta. CT15 ..... 131 C8

Fagus Cl. ME5 ..... 32 B1
Fair St. CT10 ..... 29 G4
Fair View Jun & Inf Schs. ME8 ..... 33 C5
Fairacre. CT10 ..... 29 E4
Fairacres Cl. CT6 ..... 23 C4
Fairbourne Heath Cotts.
  ME17 ..... 100 B1
Fairbourne La. ME17 ..... 100 C4
Fairfax Bsns Ctr. ME15 ..... 97 F4
Fairfax Cl. Folkestone CT20 ..... 177 D5
Fairfax Cl. Gillingham ME8 ..... 33 D5
Fairfax Dr. CT6 ..... 23 F5
Fairfield. Deal CT14 ..... 116 F6
Fairfield. Elham CT4 ..... 144 F5
Fairfield Cl. TN28 ..... 200 B7
Fairfield Pk. CT10 ..... 29 E4
Fairfield Rd. Broadstairs CT10 ..... 29 E4
Fairfield Rd. Minster, Thanet
  CT12 ..... 50 B7
Fairfield Rd.
  New Romney TN28 ..... 200 B7
Fairfield Rd. Ramsgate CT11 ..... 29 E2
Fairfield Terr. TN26 ..... 183 A7
Fairhurst Dr. ME15 ..... 96 B4
Fairings The. TN30 ..... 179 B8
Fairlawn. CT5 ..... 21 D1
Fairlawn Rd. CT10 & CT12 ..... 29 B3
Fairlead Rd. ME1 ..... 9 D1
Fairleas. ME10 ..... 37 B2
Fairlight Ave. CT12 ..... 52 B8
Fairlight Rd. CT21 ..... 176 A3
Fairmeadow. ME14 ..... 74 F4
Fairoaks. CT6 ..... 23 B3
Fairservice Cl. ME10 ..... 37 C5
Fairview Ave. ME8 ..... 33 B5
Fairview Cl. CT9 ..... 8 A2
Fairview Cotts. ME15 ..... 96 F5
Fairview Gdns. Deal CT14 ..... 117 A4
Fairview Gdns. Sturry CT2 ..... 68 A6
Fairview Ind Pk. TN24 ..... 183 D7
Fairview Rd. Elvington CT15 ..... 114 B1
Fairview Rd.
  Sittingbourne ME10 ..... 37 A3
Fairway Ave. CT19 ..... 178 A2
Fairway Cl. Rochester ME1 ..... 9 C1
Fairway Cl. St Mary's Bay TN29 ..... 194 F3
Fairway Cres. CT5 ..... 43 A7
Fairway The. Deal CT14 ..... 117 C8
Fairway The. Herne Bay CT6 ..... 22 D2
Fairway The. Hythe CT21 ..... 176 C1
Fairway The.
  Littlestone-on-S TN28 ..... 200 D6
Fairway The. Rochester ME1 ..... 9 C1
Fairway The.
  Sittingbourne ME10 ..... 36 E1
Fairway The.
  St Mary's Bay TN29 ..... 195 A5
Fairways The. ME13 ..... 62 A6
Fairwood Ind Est. TN23 ..... 139 A1
Falcon Ct. ME10 ..... 37 A2
Falcon Gdns. ME12 ..... 4 D7
Falcon Way. TN23 ..... 155 E7
Falkland Pl. ME5 ..... 31 E1
Fallowfield. Chatham ME5 ..... 32 B8
Fallowfield. Sittingbourne ME10 ..... 37 A2
Fallowfield Cl. ME14 ..... 75 A4
Fan The. CT16 ..... 166 H8
Fanconi Rd. ME5 ..... 32 B3
Fancy Row. ME14 ..... 76 C5
Fane Way. ME8 ..... 33 D4
Fans La. ME9 ..... 14 D4
Fant La. ME16 ..... 74 B2
Faraday Rd. ME14 ..... 75 C7
Fareham Wlk. **10** ME15 ..... 97 A8
Farleigh Cl. ME8 ..... 74 A2
Farleigh Hill. ME15 ..... 74 E1
Farleigh Hill Ret Pk. ME15 ..... 74 E1
Farleigh La. ME16 ..... 74 A1
Farleigh Rd. CT2 ..... 67 A3
Farleigh Trad Est. ME15 ..... 74 E1
Farley Cl. Chatham ME5 ..... 32 D2
Farley Cl. Shadoxhurst TN26 ..... 155 A1
Farley Rd. CT9 ..... 28 F7
Farm Cl. TN23 ..... 155 E7
Farm Cres. ME10 ..... 37 A2
Farm House Cl. CT5 ..... 43 F8
Farm La. CT14 ..... 116 F6
Farm Rd. Chatham ME5 ..... 31 E3
Farm Rd. Hamstreet TN26 ..... 183 A7
Farmer Cl. Hythe TN26 ..... 176 D3
Farmer Cl. Leeds ME17 ..... 99 A6
Farmhouse Cl. CT4 ..... 128 F7
Farnborough Cl. ME16 ..... 74 C2
Farncombe Way. CT16 ..... 149 B8
Farne Cl. ME15 ..... 97 A6
Farnham Cl. ME8 ..... 12 B2
Farningham Cl. ME14 ..... 75 C6
Farraday Cl. ME1 ..... 31 D8
Farrar Rd. CT7 ..... 27 A6
Farrers Wlk. TN23 ..... 156 B4
Farrier Cl. Ashford TN23 ..... 138 F5
Farrier Cl. Maidstone ME14 ..... 75 E5
Farrier St. CT14 ..... 117 C7
Farriers Ct. ME8 ..... 34 C8
Farrow Ct. TN23 ..... 156 A6
Farthing Cnr. ME9 ..... 33 E3
Farthingloe Ct. CT17 ..... 166 A6
Farthingloe Rd. CT17 ..... 166 A6
Farthings Cotts. ME14 ..... 53 F1

Farthings Ct. CT2 .... 66 C4
Fauchon's Cl. ME14 .... 75 F3
Fauchon's La. ME14 .... 75 F4
Faulkners La. CT2 .... 66 A1
Faussett Hill. CT4 .... 109 F8
Faversham Cottage Hospl.
ME13 .... 62 C7
Faversham Rd.
Boughton Lees TN24 & TN25 ...... 122 E5
Faversham Rd. Charing TN27 ... 103 E1
Faversham Rd.
Faversham MC13 & ME9 .... 61 B5
Faversham Rd. Lenham ME17 ... 101 E7
Faversham Rd.
Paddock ME13 & TN25 & TN27 ... 104 C3
Faversham Rd.
Pested CT4 & ME13 & TN25 ... 105 B4
Faversham Rd. Whitstable CT5 ... 42 C6
Faversham Rd.
Wichling ME17 & ME9 .... 80 B4
Faversham Reach. ME13 ... 62 D8
Faversham Sta. ME13 .... 62 D6
Fawley Cl. ME14 .... 74 E7
Featherbed La. Selling ME13 ... 84 A7
Featherbed La.
Sittingbourne ME9 .... 14 E2
Featherby
Cty Prim Inf Sch. ME8 ..... 11 A3
Featherby Jun Sch. ME8 ... 11 A3
Featherby Rd.
Gillingham,Lower Twydall ME7 ... 11 A5
Featherby Rd.
Gillingham,Twydall ME8 ..... 11 A3
Felborough Cl. CT4 .... 107 C8
Felderland Cl.
Park Wood ME17 .... 97 E5
Felderland Cl. Sandwich CT14 ... 93 F5
Felderland Dr. ME17 .... 97 E5
Felderland La. CT13 & CT14 ... 93 E4
Felderland Rd. ME17 .... 97 E5
Feldspar Cl. ME5 .... 32 A1
Fellows Cl. ME8 .... 33 B6
Fenner Cl. CT20 .... 177 E4
Fenoulhet Way. CT6 .... 23 A5
Ferdi Lethert Ho. TN24 ... 139 E5
Ferguson Cl. CT21 .... 176 F2
Ferguson Rd. TN29 .... 202 D2
Fern Bank Cres. CT19 ...... 178 D6
Fern Cl. Hawkinge CT18 ... 163 C6
Fern Cl. Whitstable CT5 ..... 21 C1
Fern Ct. CT10 .... 30 B5
Fern Wlk. ME10 .... 37 C5
Fernbank Cl. ME5 .... 31 F2
Fernbank Ct. CT7 .... 27 A6
Ferndale Cl. ME12 .... 3 D6
Ferndale Ct. CT7 .... 27 A6
Ferndale Rd. ME7 .... 10 E5
Ferndown. CT7 .... 26 D8
Ferndown Cl. ME7 .... 33 A5
Ferne La. CT15 .... 147 D3
Ferne Way. CT20 .... 177 E6
Fernfield. CT18 .... 163 C6
Fernfield La. CT18 .... 163 C7
Fernhill Rd. ME16 .... 74 A2
Fernlea Ave. CT6 .... 22 E4
Fernleigh Cl. ME13 .... 64 B3
Ferrier Cl. ME8 .... 33 E4
Ferry Rd. Iwade ME7 .... 14 E4
Ferry Rd.
Queenborough ME11 & ME12 ...... 3 D1
Ferry View. ME11 .... 2 F3
Fiddling La. TN25 .... 159 E6
Field Ave. CT1 .... 67 D3
Field Cl. ME5 .... 31 E6
Field End. TN24 .... 140 A1
Field End Pl. ME13 .... 64 A3
Field Mill Rd. TN27 .... 119 B5
Field View. Kingsnorth TN23 ... 156 B4
Field View. Whitstable CT5 ... 43 B7
Field View Cl. ME12 .... 3 C6
Field Way. CT2 .... 67 F5
Fielder Cl. ME10 .... 37 C5
Fielding St. ME13 .... 62 C7
Fieldings The. ME10 .... 36 E2
Fieldworks Rd. ME4 & ME7 ... 10 A7
Fiesta Wlk. CT1 .... 88 C7
Fife Rd. CT6 .... 22 B3
Fifth Ave. CT9 .... 8 B3
Fig Tree Rd. CT10 .... 29 F7
Fiji Terr. ME14 .... 75 A7
Filer Rd. ME12 .... 3 E7
Filmer Rd. CT4 .... 88 F1
Finch Ct. ME14 .... 74 E7
Finch Gr. CT21 .... 187 D8
Finch Mews. CT14 .... 117 C4
Finches The.
Sittingbourne ME10 .... 36 F3
Finches The.
St Nicholas at Wade CT7 ... 25 E2
Findlay Cl. ME8 .... 33 D6
Findley Ct. CT21 .... 176 B2
Finglesham Ct. ME15 .... 97 C8
Finlay Cl. ME13 .... 62 B7
Finsbury Ct. CT11 .... 52 E8
Finsbury Rd. CT11 .... 52 E8
Fintonagh Dr. ME14 .... 75 B6
Finwell Rd. ME8 .... 12 A2
Fir Ct. TN24 .... 139 F1
Fir Tree Cl. CT11 .... 52 C6
Fir Tree Gr. Bredhurst ME7 ... 33 B1
Fir Tree Gr. Chatham ME5 ... 32 D1
Fir Tree Hill. CT13 .... 93 B6
Firbank Gdns. CT9 .... 28 D7
Firbanks. CT5 .... 43 F8
Firethorn Cl. ME7 .... 10 E6
Firs Cl. CT19 .... 177 D7

Firs La. CT19 .... 177 D7
Firs Rd. CT4 .... 112 F1
Firs The. Deal CT14 .... 117 C8
Firs The. Hersden CT3 .... 46 E1
First Ave. Broadstairs CT10 ... 8 F2
First Ave. Chatham ME4 ..... 10 C2
First Ave. Eastchurch ME12 ... 5 E5
First Ave. Gillingham ME7 ... 10 E3
First Ave. Margate CT9 .... 8 B3
First Ave. Rushenden ME11 ... 2 F3
First Ave. Sheerness ME12 ... 1 D1
First La. ME13 .... 76 E2
Firtree Cl. CT2 .... 66 B3
Fish Market. CT19 .... 178 E5
Fisher Cl. CT21 .... 176 D1
Fisher Rd. Canterbury CT2 ... 66 D1
Fisher Rd. Chatham ME5 ..... 32 B7
Fisher St. Maidstone ME14 ... 75 A6
Fisher St. Sandwich CT13 ... 73 A1
Fisher Street Rd. ME13 ..... 83 E2
Fitzgerald Ave. CT6 .... 22 C4
Fitzmary Ave. CT9 .... 7 E1
Fitzroy Ave. Broadstairs CT10 ... 8 G2
Fitzroy Ave. Margate CT9 ..... 8 B1
Fitzroy Ave. Ramsgate CT12 ... 29 B2
Fitzroy Rd. CT5 .... 20 F2
Fitzthorold Ho. ME7 .... 10 E7
Fitzwalter Ct. █ CT16 ...... 149 B3
Fitzwilliam Rd. ME14 .... 75 F5
Five Acre Wood Sch. ME15 ... 97 B7
Five Bells La. ME1 .... 9 D4
Five Vents La. TN29 .... 199 B8
Fiveways L Ctr. ME4 .... 10 A4
Fiveways Rise. CT14 .... 116 F5
Flamingo Cl. ME5 .... 32 A7
Flanders Cl. ME10 .... 14 F1
Flanders Field. TN25 ...... 157 E4
Flax Court La. CT15 .... 131 C7
Flaxman Ct. █ ME7 .... 10 A6
Flaxman Dr. ME16 .... 74 C6
Flaxpond Rd. TN23 .... 155 F7
Fleet Ave. ME12 .... 1 C1
Fleet Rd. Rochester ME1 ..... 9 D1
Fleet Rd.
St Margarets' at cliffe CT15 ... 134 A1
Fleet Villas. TN24 .... 139 D7
Fleets La. CT2 .... 66 D7
Fleetwood Ave. CT6 .... 22 D4
Fleetwood Cl. ME12 .... 4 B6
Fleming Rd. CT13 & CT3 ..... 92 D6
Fleming Way. CT19 .... 178 E8
Fletcher Rd. CT5 .... 21 B1
Flete Rd. CT9 .... 28 D5
Flimwell. TN23 .... 155 D6
Flint Gn. ME5 .... 32 C3
Flint La. ME17 .... 79 C1
Flood Hatch. ME15 .... 74 D2
Flood La. ME13 .... 62 C8
Flood St. TN25 .... 157 D2
Flora Rd. CT11 .... 52 E8
Florence Ave. CT5 .... 43 B7
Florence Ct. CT9 .... 8 B3
Florence Rd. Maidstone ME16 ... 74 E3
Florence Rd. █ Ramsgate CT11 ... 52 D6
Florence St. ME2 .... 9 B8
Florida Cl. CT16 .... 149 B3
Flower Rise. ME14 .... 74 E7
Flume End. ME14 .... 74 D2
Flying Horse La. █ CT16 ... 166 E7
Foads Hill. CT12 .... 51 D6
Foads La. CT12 .... 51 D5
Fodbury Ct. CT8 .... 7 C1
Foley Cl. TN24 .... 157 A7
Foley St. ME14 .... 75 A5
Folkestone Harbour Sta.
.... 178 E4
Folkestone Race Course.
TN25 .... 175 A6
Folkestone Rd.
Church Hougham CT15 ...... 165 D4
Folkestone Rd.
Dover CT17 & CT15 .... 166 B7
Folkestone Rd.
East Guldeford TN31 .... 196 C3
Folkestone
Sch for Girls. CT20 .... 177 F4
Folkestone West Sta. CT18 ... 177 F5
Folkstone Ho. █ ME15 .... 97 F6
Folly Rd. CT20 .... 178 E6
Fonblanque Rd. ME12 .... 1 D2
Fontwell Cl. █ ME5 .... 97 F6
Foord Almshouses. ME1 ...... 9 B3
Foord Rd. ME17 .... 101 D5
Foord Rd N. CT19 & CT20 ... 178 D5
Foord Rd S. █ CT20 .... 178 D5
Foord St. ME1 .... 9 D4
Forbes Rd. ME13 .... 62 C6
Ford Cl. Bridge CT4 .... 88 F1
Ford Cl. Herne Bay CT6 ...... 22 A4
Ford Hill. CT3 .... 46 E8
Ford Way. TN23 .... 138 F1
Ford Wlk. CT5 .... 43 A3
Fordcombe Cl. ME4 .... 97 F7
Fordingbridge Cl. ME16 ..... 74 B5
Fordoun Rd. CT10 .... 29 F5
Fordwich Cl. ME16 .... 74 B7
Fordwich Gn. ME8 .... 11 C3
Fordwich Pl. CT13 .... 93 F8
Fordwich Rd. CT2 .... 67 F4
Foreland Ave.
Folkestone CT19 .... 178 F6
Foreland Ave. Margate CT9 ... 8 D1
Foreland Ct.
St Margaret's at Cliffe CT15 ... 151 A5

Foreland Park Ho. CT10 ...... 30 B7
Foreland Rd. CT15 .... 151 A4
Foreland Sch The. CT10 ...... 30 A6
Foreland The. CT1 .... 88 B5
Forelands Sq. CT14 .... 117 B3
Foreness Cl. CT10 & CT9 ...... 8 G3
Forest Cotts. TN25 .... 105 C2
Forest Dr. ME5 .... 31 F2
Forest Hill. ME5 .... 74 F1
Forestall Meadow. TN23 ... 156 B4
Forestdale Rd. ME5 .... 54 A8
Foresters Cl. ME5 .... 31 F2
Foresters Way. CT20 ...... 178 D5
Forestry Cutts. C14 .... 125 B7
Forge Cl. Eythorne CT15 ... 131 C7
Forge Cl. Sellindge TN25 ... 159 D1
Forge Cl. Sturry CT2 .... 67 F5
Forge Cotts. CT3 .... 47 C8
Forge Field. CT15 .... 164 E5
Forge Hill. Aldington TN25 ... 173 A5
Forge Hill. Bethersden ME9 ... 153 E5
Forge Ho. Canterbury CT1 ... 87 E6
Forge Ho. Ickham CT3 .... 69 C1
Forge La. Ashford TN23 ..... 139 B2
Forge La. Boxley ME14 .... 54 C2
Forge La. Boyden Gate CT3 ... 47 C8
Forge La. Bredhurst ME7 ..... 33 A1
Forge La. Dean Street ME15 ... 96 C7
Forge La. Egerton Forstal TN27 ... 118 C1
Forge La. Gillingham ME7 .... 10 E7
Forge La. Leeds ME17 .... 98 F7
Forge La. Ramsgate CT12 .... 52 C7
Forge La. Sutton CT15 ...... 133 A6
Forge La. Upchurch ME9 ..... 12 F3
Forge La. Whitfield CT15 ... 149 A8
Forge La. Whitstable CT5 .... 43 D8
Forge Lane Cty Inf Sch. ME7 ... 10 E6
Forge Meadow.
Harrietsham ME17 .... 100 D6
Forge Meadow.
Stone in Oxney TN30 .... 190 A4
Forge Meads. TN30 .... 188 E3
Forge Path. CT16 .... 149 A8
Forge Rd. ME10 .... 36 E6
Forgefield. TN26 .... 153 D5
Forgefields. CT6 .... 46 B8
Forrens The. █ CT1 .... 67 A1
Forrester Cl. CT2 .... 67 C2
Forson Cl. TN30 .... 179 B8
Forstal Cotts.
Lenham Heath ME17 .... 102 A1
Forstal Cotts.
Pratling Street ME20 .... 53 B2
Forstal La. ME17 .... 96 D4
Forstal Rd.
Egerton Forstal TN27 .... 118 C1
Forstal Rd. Forstal ME20 ... 53 C2
Forstal Rd.
Woolage Village CT4 .... 112 E1
Forstal The. Preston CT3 .... 70 B6
Forstal The. Wye TN25 ..... 123 E2
Forsters. ME17 .... 98 E4
Fort Burgoyne (Casemated
Barracks). CT16 .... 149 E2
Fort Burgoyne Rd. CT16 ... 149 E1
Fort Cl. TN29 .... 204 E6
Fort Cres. CT9 .... 7 J3
Fort Hill. CT9 .... 7 J3
Fort Lower Prom. CT9 .... 7 J3
Fort Luton (Mus). ME4 ...... 10 A1
Fort Paragon. CT9 .... 7 J3
Fort Pitt Gram Sch. ME1 ..... 9 E4
Fort Pitt Hill. ME1 & ME4 .... 9 E4
Fort Pitt St. ME4 .... 9 E3
Fort Prom. CT9 .... 7 J3
Fort Rd. Broadstairs CT10 ... 30 B4
Fort Rd. Hythe CT21 .... 176 A2
Fort Rd. Margate CT9 .... 7 I3
Fort St. ME1 .... 9 D4
Fortuna Ct. CT11 .... 52 D7
Forty Acres Hill. ME12 .... 4 C4
Forty Acres Rd. CT2 .... 66 E2
Forum The. █ ME10 .... 36 F4
Fostall Gn. TN23 .... 155 F7
Fostall Rd. ME13 .... 40 C1
Foster Cl. CT19 .... 177 E7
Foster Clark Est. ME15 ...... 75 B2
Foster Rd. TN24 .... 157 A6
Foster St. ME15 .... 75 A3
Foster Way. CT14 .... 117 B5
Foster's Ave. CT10 .... 29 E7
Foster's Cl. CT13 .... 94 A7
Fostington Way. ME5 .... 31 F1
Foulds Cl. ME8 .... 33 B5
Fountain Ent Pk. ME15 ...... 75 A1
Fountain Inn Cl. CT9 .... 7 I3
Fountain La. ME16 .... 74 A2
Fountain St. █
Sittingbourne ME10 .... 36 E4
Fountain St. █ Whitstable CT5 ... 20 D2
Fountains Cl. TN24 .... 140 A1
Four Oaks. ME13 .... 61 E8
Four Turnings. CT3 .... 70 B3
Four Wents.
Langley Heath ME17 .... 98 E3
Four Wents. Marlpit ME17 ... 97 F2
Fouracre Cotts. ME9 .... 34 F6
Fourth Ave. Eastchurch ME12 ... 5 F5
Fourth Ave. Gillingham ME7 ... 10 E4
Fowey Cl. ME5 .... 32 C5
Fowler Cl. ME8 .... 33 C3
Fox Cl. CT18 .... 161 B7
Fox Hill. ME10 & ME9 .... 37 D3
Fox Holt Rd. CT15 .... 146 B2
Fox St. ME7 .... 10 C6
Fox Way. CT4 .... 128 F8
Fox's Cross. CT5 .... 43 B4
Fox's Cross Hill. CT5 .... 43 A3

Fox's Cross Rd. CT5 .... 43 C3
Foxborough Cl. CT13 .... 93 B6
Foxborough Hill. CT13 ...... 93 B5
Foxborough La. CT12 .... 50 C6
Foxburrow Cl. ME8 .... 33 D5
Foxden Dr. ME15 .... 75 F1
Foxdown Cl. CT14 .... 116 C2
Foxglove Cres. ME5 .... 31 E4
Foxglove Gn. TN23 .... 139 E2
Foxglove Gn. TN24 .... 139 E1
Foxglove Rise. ME14 .... 74 E7
Foxgrove. MF10 .... 36 E7
Foxhunter Pk The. CT12 ..... 49 D6
Foxley Rd. ME11 .... 3 A5
Frampton Rd. CT21 .... 176 A2
France Rd. CT16 .... 149 A5
Frances Gdns. CT11 .... 52 F8
Francis Ave. CT13 .... 95 B7
Francis Dr. ME5 .... 32 A2
Francis Rd. Ashford TN23 ... 156 B8
Francis Rd. Broadstairs CT10 ... 30 B7
Frank Walters
Bsns Pk The. CT10 .... 29 D3
Frankapps Cl. ME9 .... 35 B6
Franklin Dr. ME14 .... 75 D4
Franklin Rd. ME7 .... 10 D5
Franklins Cotts. ME15 .... 96 C5
Franklyn Rd. CT2 .... 87 C8
Franks Ct. ME8 .... 11 B2
Freda Cl. CT10 .... 29 F1
Frederick Rd. Deal CT14 ... 117 A3
Frederick Rd. Gillingham ME7 ... 10 C4
Fredville Rd. CT15 .... 131 C7
Freedown The. CT15 .... 151 A7
Freeman Cl. █ ME10 .... 36 E4
Freeman Gdns. ME4 .... 9 F2
Freeman Way. ME15 .... 97 E7
Freeman's Cl. CT5 .... 43 A6
Freeman's Rd. CT12 .... 50 B6
Freemen's Way. CT14 ...... 117 B3
Freesia Cl. ME7 .... 10 F6
Fremantle Rd. CT20 .... 177 E5
Fremlins Rd. ME14 .... 76 C4
French's Row. ME9 .... 38 D2
Frencham Cl. CT2 .... 67 A4
Frensham Cl. CT12 .... 37 B4
Frensham Wlk. ME5 .... 31 F1
Freshfield Cl. CT21 .... 176 B4
Freshland Rd. ME16 .... 74 B4
Freshlands. CT6 .... 23 E5
Freshwater Rd. ME5 .... 32 B7
Friars Ave. ME5 .... 31 F2
Friars Cl. CT5 .... 21 A1
Friars Sch. TN23 .... 155 B8
Friars The. CT1 .... 66 F1
Friars Way. CT16 .... 149 A3
Friary Pl. █ ME2 .... 9 B7
Friary Prec. ME2 .... 9 B7
Friary Way. CT2 .... 66 D2
Frid Cnr. TN27 .... 153 E7
Friendly Cl. CT9 .... 8 D1
Friends Ave. CT9 .... 29 D8
Frindsbury Rd. ME2 .... 9 B8
Frinstead Wlk. ME16 .... 74 B7
Frinsted Cl. ME8 .... 11 C3
Friston Way. ME1 .... 31 D8
Frith Rd. Aldington TN25 ... 172 C6
Frith Rd. Dover CT16 .... 149 C1
Frithwood Cl. ME15 .... 75 F1
Frittenden Cl. TN23 .... 155 E6
Frobisher Cl. ME10 .... 36 E7
Frobisher Gdns. ME1 .... 9 C2
Frog Farm Cotts. ME9 .... 13 A4
Frog La. CT4 .... 111 C6
Frogmore Wlk. ME17 .... 101 C5
Frognal Cl. ME9 .... 38 B2
Frognal Gdns. ME9 .... 38 C2
Frognal La. ME9 .... 38 B2
Front Brents. ME13 .... 62 D8
Front Rd. TN26 .... 169 A1
Front St. CT14 .... 133 F5
Front The. CT15 .... 151 A4
Frost Cres. ME5 .... 32 A7
Froyle Cl. ME8 .... 74 C6
Fruiterer's Cl. ME9 .... 59 B7
Fulbert Dr. ME14 .... 75 F5
Fulbert Rd. CT16 .... 149 B5
Fulham Ave. CT9 .... 28 C7
Fullers Cl. ME14 .... 76 A4
Fulmar Cl. TN29 .... 194 F3
Fulsam Pl. CT9 .... 7 H1
Fulston Manor Sch. ME10 ... 36 F2
Fulston Pl. ME10 .... 37 A3
Furfield Cl. ME17 .... 97 E5
Furrell's Rd. ME1 .... 9 D5
Furze Hill Cres. ME12 .... 3 E6
Fusilier Ave. CT20 .... 177 B5
Fyndon Ho. CT1 .... 88 C7

Gabriel's Hill. ME14 & ME15 ... 75 A4
Gadby Rd. ME10 .... 36 C5
Gads Hill. ME7 .... 10 F6
Gadsby La. TN26 .... 153 A3
Gagetown Terr. ME14 .... 74 F7
Gainsboro Rd. █ CT7 .... 26 C2
Gainsborough Cl.
Folkestone CT19 .... 178 A7
Gainsborough Cl.
Gillingham ME8 .... 33 D6
Gainsborough Cl.
Sittingbourne ME10 .... 36 B5
Gainsborough Dr.
Herne Bay CT6 .... 23 E5
Gainsborough Dr.
Maidstone ME16 .... 74 B4
Gainsborough Ho. ME1 .... 9 D5

Galena Cl. ME5 .... 32 A1
Gallants La. ME15 .... 96 A4
Galleon Cl. ME1 .... 31 C8
Galliard St. CT13 .... 94 A8
Gallow's Cnr. CT21 .... 176 A2
Galloways Rd. TN29 .... 203 C5
Gallwey Ave. CT7 .... 26 E7
Galway Rd. ME12 .... 1 D1
Gammon's Farm La. TN29 ... 185 B3
Gandy's La. ME7 .... 97 C2
Gange Mews. █ ME13 .... 62 D7
Gann Rd. CT5 .... 20 F2
Gaol La. █ CT16 .... 166 D7
Gap House Sch. CT10 .... 30 B2
Gap The. Blean CT2 .... 66 A7
Gap The. Canterbury CT1 .... 88 B5
Garden Cl. Maidstone ME15 ... 97 E7
Garden Cl. Rough Common CT2 ... 66 A2
Garden Cotts. CT3 .... 91 A7
Garden Hall The. TN25 ..... 124 C1
Garden of England Pk
(Mobile Home Pk) ME17 ... 100 B7
Garden Rd. CT19 .... 178 D6
Garden St. ME7 .... 10 A6
Gardens The. Coxheath ME17 ... 96 C3
Gardens The. Ivychurch TN29 ... 192 F4
Gardiner St. ME7 .... 10 C6
Garfield Pl. █ ME13 .... 62 D7
Garfield Rd. Gillingham ME7 ... 10 C6
Garfield Rd. Margate CT9 ..... 7 H2
Garlinge Cty Inf Sch. CT9 ... 28 C8
Garlinge Cty Jun Sch. CT9 ... 28 C8
Garlinge Green Rd. CT4 ... 108 E6
Garrard Ave. CT9 .... 28 B8
Garrington Cl. ME14 .... 75 C6
Garrison Rd. ME12 .... 1 B3
Gas House Rd. ME1 .... 9 C6
Gas La. ME13 .... 63 F3
Gas Rd. Sittingbourne ME10 ... 36 F5
Gas Rd. Sittingbourne ME10 ... 37 C6
Gas St. CT1 .... 87 F7
Gasworks La. TN23 .... 139 B2
Gatcombe Cl. Chatham ME5 ... 32 A5
Gatcombe Cl. Maidstone ME16 ... 74 B5
Gateacre Rd. CT5 .... 43 A6
Gatefield La. █ ME13 .... 62 D7
Gateway Ct. █ CT11 .... 52 F7
Gateway The. CT16 .... 166 E7
Gatland La. ME16 .... 74 B2
Gault Cl. ME15 .... 76 A2
Gaunt's Cl. CT14 .... 117 A4
Gayhurst Cl. ME8 .... 33 D6
Gayhurst Dr. ME10 .... 36 C5
Gaze Hill Ave. ME10 .... 37 A3
Gazedown. TN29 .... 194 F3
Gean Cl. ME5 .... 54 A8
Genesta Ave. CT5 .... 43 B7
Genesta Cl. ME10 .... 36 E7
Geneva Ave. ME8 .... 11 A2
Gentian Cl. █ Chatham ME5 ... 31 E4
Gentian Cl. Maidstone ME14 ... 75 E5
Geoffrey Ct. CT7 .... 27 A7
George Alley. CT14 .... 117 D6
George Cooper Ho. █ CT20 ... 178 C4
George Gurr Cres. CT19 ... 178 D8
George Hill Rd. CT10 .... 29 F8
George La.
Boughton Street ME13 ...... 63 F3
George La. Folkestone CT20 ... 178 C4
George La. Leeds ME17 ...... 99 B7
George La. New Romney TN28 ... 200 B3
George La. Rochester ME1 ..... 9 C6
George Marsham Ho. ME15 ... 96 F3
George Parris Ct. ME12 ...... 4 C6
George Roche Rd. CT1 .... 88 A6
George Spurgen
Cty Prim Sch. CT19 .... 178 E7
George St. Ashford TN23 ... 139 B1
George St. Deal CT14 ...... 117 D7
George St. Dover CT17 .... 149 C1
George St. Maidstone ME15 ... 75 A4
George St. Ramsgate CT11 ... 52 E7
George St. Sittingbourne ME10 ... 37 B4
George Summers Cl. ME2 ..... 9 E8
George V Ave. CT9 .... 28 C8
George Warren Cl. █ CT9 ..... 7 J1
George Wood Cl. TN29 ..... 203 C6
George's Ave. CT5 .... 43 A4
Georgian Cl. ME11 .... 3 A3
Georgian Dr. ME17 .... 96 D3
Georgian Way. ME8 .... 33 C4
Gerald Ave. ME4 .... 9 F2
Gerald Palmby Ct. CT14 ... 117 C7
Geraldine Rd. CT19 .... 177 F6
Gerrard Ave. ME1 .... 31 E8
Gerrards Dr. ME10 .... 36 F2
Gibbons Rd. ME10 .... 36 B5
Gibraltar Ave. ME7 .... 10 B7
Gibraltar Hill. ME4 .... 9 F4
Gibraltar La. Hawkinge CT18 ... 163 A2
Gibraltar La. Maidstone ME14 ... 74 F8
Gibraltar Sq. CT16 .... 149 C3
Gibson St. ME10 .... 36 E4
Gidd's Pond Cotts. ME14 ... 75 E6
Giddyhorn La. ME16 .... 74 C5
Gifford Cl. ME8 .... 11 C3
Gigger's Green Rd. TN25 ... 185 C7
Gilbert St. ME7 .... 33 A5
Gilbert Rd. █ Ashford TN23 ... 139 B2
Gilbert Rd. Ramsgate CT11 ... 52 D8
Gilbert Terr. ME14 .... 74 F7
Gilchrist Ave. CT6 .... 22 C2
Giles Gdns. CT9 .... 28 F8
Giles La. CT2 .... 66 D4
Gilford Rd. CT14 .... 117 B4
Gilham Gr. CT14 .... 117 B4
Gill La. Mersham TN25 ...... 172 A8
Gill La. Ruckinge TN26 ..... 171 C2

Gillett Rd. TN29 .... 203 D7
Gillingham Gn. ME7 .... 10 E6
Gillingham Rd. ME7 .... 10 D5
Gillingham Sta. ME7 .... 10 D5
Gilman Cl. CT18 .... 162 F4
Gillon Mews. **9** CT1 .... 67 B2
Gills Terr. ME8 .... 12 C3
Ginsbury Cl. ME2 .... 9 E6
Giraud Dr. ME13 .... 62 B8
Glack Rd. CT14 .... 116 F4
Glade The. Chatham ME5 .... 32 A2
Glade The. Deal CT14 .... 116 F6
Gladstone Dr. ME10 .... 37 C4
Gladstone Rd. Ashford TN24 .... 156 E7
Gladstone Rd. Broadstairs CT10 .. 29 F4
Gladstone Rd. Chatham ME4 .... 9 E2
Gladstone Rd. Deal CT14 .... 117 C4
Gladstone Rd. Folkestone CT19 .. 178 E6
Gladstone Rd. Maidstone ME14 ... 75 A6
Gladstone Rd. Margate CT9 .... 7 I1
Gladstone Rd. Whitstable CT5 ... 20 D2
Gladwyn Cl. ME8 .... 33 D4
Glamis Cl. ME5 .... 32 A5
Glanville Rd. Gillingham ME7 .... 10 D5
Glanville Rd. Rochester ME2 .... 9 A8
Glasgow Ho. **7** ME15 .... 97 E7
Gleaming Wood Dr. ME5 .... 54 D8
Gleaners Cl. ME14 .... 75 E4
Glebe Cl. Biddenden Green TN27 . 135 B2
Glebe Cl.
  St Margaret's at Cliffe CT15 .. 150 F6
Glebe Cotts. ME13 .... 81 E7
Glebe Ct. CT12 .... 50 B5
Glebe Gdns. Lenham ME17 ...... 101 E5
Glebe Gdns. **6** Margate CT9 .... 28 B8
Glebe La. Maidstone ME16 .... 74 A1
Glebe La. Sittingbourne ME10 .... 37 B2
Glebe Rd. Gillingham ME7 .... 10 E3
Glebe Rd. Margate CT9 .... 28 B8
Glebe The. TN27 .... 120 D7
Glebe Way. Ashford TN24 .... 139 D6
Glebe Way. Whitstable CT5 .... 43 D8
Glebeland. TN27 .... 118 F4
Glebelands. Alkham CT15 .... 147 D1
Glebelands. Ash CT3 .... 71 C2
Glebelands. Mersham TN25 ..... 157 E4
Glemsford Cotts. CT2 .... 65 E1
Glen Ave. CT6 .... 23 C5
Glen Gr. CT17 .... 166 B7
Glen Iris Ave. CT2 .... 66 C2
Glen Iris Cl. CT2 .... 66 C2
Glen Rd. CT14 .... 134 C6
Glen The. Minster ME12 .... 4 B7
Glen The. Minster ME12 .... 4 C7
Glen The. Shepherdswell CT15 .. 130 D5
Glen The. Upstreet CT3 .... 47 D3
Glen Wlk. CT5 .... 43 A3
Glenavon Ho. CT10 .... 30 B7
Glenbervie Dr. CT6 .... 23 E5
Glenbrook Cl. CT6 .... 23 D5
Glenbrook Gr. ME10 .... 36 E7
Glencoe Cty Inf Sch. ME4 .... 10 A2
Glencoe Cty Prim Sch. ME4 ..... 10 A2
Glencoe Rd. Chatham ME4 .... 10 A2
Glencoe Rd. Margate CT9 .... 8 A1
Glendale Rd. ME12 .... 4 B7
Gleneagles Ct. ME5 .... 31 F2
Gleneagles Dr. ME15 .... 75 A1
Glenfield Rd. CT16 .... 149 B3
Glenside. CT5 .... 44 A8
Glenside Ave. CT1 .... 67 B2
Glenwood. TN30 .... 167 B3
Glenwood Cl. Chatham ME5 .... 10 C1
Glenwood Cl. Gillingham ME7 .... 33 A7
Glenwood Cl. Maidstone ME16 ... 74 C5
Glenwood Cl. St Michaels TN30 . 167 B3
Glenwood Dr. ME12 .... 4 C6
Glistening Glade. ME8 .... 33 E6
Globe La. ME4 .... 9 F5
Gloster Ropewalk. CT17 .... 166 C5
Gloster Way. CT17 .... 166 C5
Gloucester Ave.
  Broadstairs CT10 .... 29 F3
Gloucester Ave. Margate CT9 ..... 8 D2
Gloucester Cl. ME8 .... 34 A8
Gloucester Mews. TN28 .... 200 C8
Gloucester Pl. **13** CT20 ...... 178 D5
Gloucester Rd.
  Maidstone ME15 .... 97 D8
Gloucester Rd. Whitstable CT5 ... 20 F2
Glover Rd. TN24 .... 139 E1
Glovers Cres. ME10 .... 36 F3
Goad Ave. ME5 .... 32 B3
Godden Rd. CT2 .... 67 A4
Goddings Dr. ME1 .... 9 A3
Goddington La. ME17 .... 100 B6
Goddington Rd. ME2 .... 9 B8
Godfrey Ho. CT5 .... 43 E8
Godfrey Wlk. TN23 .... 156 B8
Godfrey's Grave. ME13 .... 64 B7
Godfreys Cotts. ME13 .... 105 C8
Godinton
  Cty Prim Sch. TN23 .... 138 D3
Godinton La. TN23 & TN26 ..... 138 D5
Godinton Park. TN23 .... 138 C4
Godinton Rd. TN23 .... 139 A2
Godinton Way. TN23 .... 139 A2
Godwin Bglws. CT9 .... 8 B3
Godwin Cl. ME10 .... 14 F1
Godwin Cotts. CT9 .... 8 A3
Godwin Rd. Canterbury CT1 ...... 87 C6
Godwin Rd. Dover CT16 .... 166 F8
Godwin Rd. Margate CT9 .... 8 A3
Godwyn Gdns. CT20 .... 178 A4
Godwyn Rd. Deal CT14 .... 117 C8
Godwyn Rd. Folkestone CT20 .. 178 A4
Godwyne Cl. CT16 .... 166 D8
Godwyne Ct. CT16 .... 149 D1

Godwyne Rd. CT16 .... 149 D1
Gogway. CT4 .... 126 B4
Gold Hill. TN25 .... 121 D4
Goldcrest Wlk. CT5 .... 43 B6
Golden Acre La. CT8 .... 27 D7
Golden Cl. CT8 .... 27 D7
Golden Hill. CT5 .... 43 F6
Golden Sq. New Romney TN28 .. 200 A6
Golden Sq. Tenterden TN30 .... 179 B8
Golden St. CT17 .... 117 D7
Golden Wood Cl. ME5 .... 54 D8
Goldfinch Cl. Faversham ME13 .. 40 C1
Goldfinch Cl. Herne Bay CT6 .... 23 C2
Goldings The. Gillingham ME8 ... 33 C8
Goldings The. Monkton CT12 .... 49 C7
Goldsmith Rd. ME8 .... 33 E5
Goldstone Dro. CT3 .... 71 E7
Goldstone Wlk. ME5 .... 32 A1
Goldthorne Cl. ME14 .... 75 C5
Goldups La. CT4 & ME13 .... 84 C1
Goldups Lane Cotts. CT4 .... 84 C1
Goldwell Cl. TN25 .... 173 A6
Goldwell Hos. TN25 .... 173 A6
Goldwell La. Aldington TN25 .... 173 B7
Goldwell La.
  Great Chart TN23 & TN26 ..... 154 F8
Golf Cl. CT14 .... 95 C1
Golf Rd. CT14 .... 117 C8
Golf Road Pl. CT14 .... 117 C8
Good Hope. CT14 .... 116 F4
Good Intent Cotts. TN27 .... 119 A5
Goodall Cl. ME8 .... 33 E5
Goodban Sq. CT3 .... 71 D1
Goodcheap La. TN24 & TN25 .. 140 D2
Goodfellow Way. **3** CT16 .... 166 D8
Goodnestone
  CE Prim Sch. CT3 .... 91 C2
Goodnestone Hill. CT3 .... 91 C2
Goodnestone Ho. CT3 .... 91 C1
Goodnestone Rd.
  Sittingbourne ME10 .... 37 B4
Goodnestone Rd. Wingham CT3 .. 91 B5
Goodwin Ave. CT5 .... 21 E2
Goodwin Dr. ME14 .... 75 B8
Goodwin Rd. Ramsgate CT11 .... 52 B5
Goodwin Rd.
  St Margaret's at Cliffe CT15 .. 151 A4
Goodwood Cl. ME15 .... 97 F6
Goose Cl. ME5 .... 32 A7
Gordon Ave. ME11 .... 3 A4
Gordon Cl. ME10 .... 37 C4
Gordon Cotts. ME9 .... 58 B6
Gordon Cott. ME7 .... 96 E3
Gordon Cty Jun Sch. ME2 .... 9 A8
Gordon Gr. CT8 .... 27 D7
Gordon Rd. Canterbury CT1 ..... 87 F7
Gordon Rd. Faversham ME13 .... 62 B8
Gordon Rd. Folkestone CT20 ... 177 D6
Gordon Rd. Gillingham ME7 ..... 10 E5
Gordon Rd.
  Gillingham,Brompton ME7 ...... 9 C4
Gordon Rd. Herne Bay CT6 ...... 22 F4
Gordon Rd. Margate CT9 .... 8 A3
Gordon Rd.
  Margate, Westwood CT9 .... 29 A5
Gordon Rd. Ramsgate CT11 ...... 52 D8
Gordon Rd. Rochester ME2 .... 9 A8
Gordon Rd. Whitfield CT16 ..... 149 A5
Gordon Rd. Whitstable CT5 ...... 43 D8
Gordon Sq. Birchington CT7 ..... 26 F7
Gordon Sq. Faversham ME13 .... 62 E7
Gordon Terr. ME1 .... 9 C4
Gore Cl. CT13 .... 93 B3
Gore Cotts. ME9 .... 12 E1
Gore Court Rd.
  Park Wood ME15 .... 97 F5
Gore Court Rd.
  Sittingbourne ME10 .... 36 E2
Gore End Cl. CT7 .... 26 F7
Gore La. CT13 .... 93 B2
Gore Mews. **3** CT1 .... 67 B2
Gore Rd. Eastry CT13 .... 93 B3
Gore Rd. Silver Street ME9 ...... 57 F5
Gore St. CT12 .... 49 A7
Gore Terr. CT13 .... 93 B3
Gorely Ho. **14** CT17 .... 166 D7
Goretop La. CT14 .... 94 C6
Gorham Dr. ME15 .... 76 A1
Gorrell Rd. CT5 .... 20 E1
Gorse Ave. ME5 .... 31 F5
Gorse La. CT6 .... 23 C2
Gorse Mead. TN23 .... 155 F8
Gorse Rd. ME10 .... 37 C5
Goschen Rd. CT17 .... 166 B8
Gosfield Rd. CT6 .... 23 A4
Goss Hall La. CT3 .... 72 A2
Gosselin St. CT5 .... 43 E8
Goteley Mere. TN24 .... 139 C7
Gothic Cl. CT14 .... 117 B1
Gothic Cotts. TN25 .... 121 A1
Goudhurst Cl. Canterbury CT2 ... 67 A4
Goudhurst Cl. Maidstone ME16 .. 74 E4
Goudhurst Rd. ME8 .... 11 B3
Gough Rd. CT20 .... 177 E3
Gould Rd. ME5 .... 32 B3
Grace Ave. ME16 .... 74 D6
Grace Ct. **12** CT20 .... 178 D5
Grace Hill. CT20 .... 178 D5
Grace Meadow. CT16 .... 149 A7
Grace Rd. ME12 .... 1 B1
Grace Wlk. CT14 .... 117 A5
Grafton Ave. ME1 .... 31 E8
Grafton Rd. Broadstairs CT10 .... 29 E4
Grafton Rd. Sittingbourne ME10 . 36 F4
Grafton Rise. CT6 .... 22 C4
Grain Rd. ME8 .... 33 C3
Grainey Field. ME9 .... 34 E4

Gram's Rd. CT14 .... 134 C8
Grampian Way. ME15 .... 76 A1
Grampion Cl. TN24 .... 139 C4
Granada Ho. **6** ME15 .... 75 A4
Granada St. **7** ME15 .... 75 A4
Granary Cl. Gillingham ME8 ..... 11 F1
Granary Cl. Maidstone ME14 ... 75 E5
Granary Court Rd. TN25 .... 159 A4
Granary Pl. CT5 .... 43 D8
Grand Ct. TN28 .... 200 E5
Grand Dr. CT6 .... 22 C4
Grand Par. TN28 .... 200 E5
Grange Cres. TN30 .... 167 A3
Grange Ct. **1** CT20 .... 178 C4
Grange Hill. ME4 .... 10 B3
Grange Ho. ME16 .... 74 A2
Grange La. ME5 .... 54 A1
Grange Rd. Broadstairs CT10 .... 29 F6
Grange Rd. Deal CT14 .... 117 B5
Grange Rd. Gillingham ME7 ...... 11 B5
Grange Rd. Herne Bay CT6 .... 23 C4
Grange Rd. Hythe CT21 .... 176 B4
Grange Rd. Ramsgate CT11 ...... 52 C6
Grange Rd. Rochester ME2 .... 9 B7
Grange Rd. St Michaels TN30 .. 167 A3
Grange The.
  Shepherdswell CT15 .... 130 D5
Grange The. Whitstable CT5 ..... 43 A6
Grange Way. Broadstairs CT10 .. 29 F2
Grange Way. Rochester ME1 ...... 9 C3
Grant Cl. Broadstairs CT10 ...... 29 E6
Grant Cl. Gillingham ME7 .... 11 B1
Grant's Cotts. ME17 .... 101 B5
Grantham Ave. CT14 .... 117 A5
Grantley Cl. TN23 .... 156 A8
Granville Ave. Broadstairs CT10 . 30 B3
Granville Ave. Ramsgate CT12 ... 29 B1
Granville Cl. ME13 .... 62 C7
Granville Dr. CT6 .... 22 B2
Granville Farm Mews. **15** CT11 52 F7
Granville Marina. **17** CT11 ... 52 F7
Granville Par. CT20 .... 177 E3
Granville Pl. ME12 .... 1 C1
Granville Rd. Broadstairs CT10 .. 30 B3
Granville Rd. Deal CT14 .... 117 C2
Granville Rd. Gillingham ME7 .... 10 E5
Granville Rd. Kingsdown CT14 . 134 D3
Granville Rd. Maidstone ME14 .. 75 A6
Granville Rd. Sheerness ME12 .... 1 D2
Granville Rd.
  St Margaret's at Cliffe CT15 .. 151 B6
Granville Rd E. CT20 .... 177 F3
Granville St. Deal CT14 .... 117 D5
Granville St. Dover CT16 .... 149 C1
Grapple Rd. ME14 .... 75 A7
Grasmere Ave. CT11 .... 52 A7
Grasmere Gdns. CT19 .... 178 B7
Grasmere Rd. Ashford TN24 ... 139 C6
Grasmere Rd. Whitstable CT5 ... 44 B8
Grasmere Way. CT3 .... 112 F6
Grasslands. Ashford TN23 ..... 155 D7
Grasslands.
  Langley Heath ME17 .... 98 E4
Grassmere. TN29 .... 194 E3
Grassy Glade. ME7 .... 33 B6
Gravel Castle Rd. CT4 .... 129 A8
Gravel Hill. ME13 .... 103 C3
Gravel La. CT15 .... 165 A4
Gravel Wlk. **3** Ashford TN23 139 B3
Gravel Wlk. **12** Canterbury CT1 87 F8
Gravel Wlk. Rochester ME1 .... 9 D5
Gravelly Bottom Rd. ME17 ...... 99 B2
Graveney Cty Prim Sch. ME13 .. 41 E1
Graveney Rd. Faversham ME13 .. 62 F7
Graveney Rd. Maidstone ME15 .. 97 F7
Graylings Cl. ME10 .... 36 C2
Grays Way. CT1 .... 87 B6
Grayshott Cl. ME10 .... 36 F3
Graystone Rd. CT5 .... 21 A2
Great Basin Rd. ME12 .... 1 A2
Great Burton Ho. TN24 .... 139 C5
Great Chart
  Cty Prim Sch. TN23 .... 155 D8
Great Conduit St. CT21 .... 176 C2
Great Ivy Mill Cotts. ME15 ..... 96 F7
Great Lines. ME7 .... 10 B5
Great South Ave. ME4 .... 10 A1
Greatstone Halt. TN28 .... 200 D3
Greatstone Prim Sch. TN28 ... 200 D2
Grebe Apartments. **13** ME15 . 97 E5
Grebe Cl. CT18 .... 163 A4
Grebe Cres. CT21 .... 187 C8
Grecian St. ME14 .... 75 A6
Green Acres Cl. CT14 .... 131 D7
Green Acres Cl. CT6 .... 23 B3
Green Bank ME7 .... 33 A5
Green Cl. ME1 .... 9 D2
Green Cloth Mews. **2** CT1 .... 67 B2
Green Ct. Bridge CT4 .... 89 A1
Green Ct. Folkestone CT19 .... 178 E7
Green Dell. CT2 .... 66 F4
Green Gates. CT16 .... 149 A8
Green Hedges. TN30 .... 179 B8
Green Hill. ME15 .... 76 B1
Green Hill La. ME17 .... 100 D1
Green Hills. CT4 .... 128 D8
Green La. Ashford TN23 .... 155 C5
Green La. Bethersden TN26 .... 153 A2
Green La.
  Boughton Monchelsea ME17 ... 97 C3
Green La. Broadstairs CT10 ...... 29 E5
Green La. Capel-le-F CT18 ..... 164 B3
Green La. Challock TN25 .... 105 A2
Green La. Chilham CT4 .... 85 C2
Green La. Deal CT14 .... 117 B1
Green La. Dover CT16 .... 149 B3
Green La. Ewell Minnis CT15 .. 147 D3

Green La. Eythorne CT15 ...... 131 D7
Green La. Folkestone CT19 .... 178 C8
Green La. Goodnestone CT3 ..... 92 B3
Green La. Hythe CT21 .... 176 A2
Green La. Langley Heath ME17 .. 98 E3
Green La. Margate CT9 .... 29 E8
Green La. Platt's Heath ME17 .. 100 F2
Green La. Rhodes Minnis CT4 .. 143 C2
Green La. Rodmersham ME9 ..... 59 E3
Green La. Smarden TN27 .... 135 A1
Green La.
  St Margaret's at Cliffe CT15 .. 133 F1
Green La. Stockbury ME9 .... 34 F1
Green La. Temple Ewell CT16 .. 148 E6
Green La. Whitfield CT16 ...... 148 E7
Green La. Whitstable CT5 .... 43 D8
Green Lane Ave. CT21 .... 176 A2
Green Lane Cotts. ME17 .... 98 E3
Green Leas. CT5 .... 21 D1
Green Lees. ME13 .... 61 E2
Green Meadows. TN29 .... 186 D2
Green Porch Cl. ME10 .... 36 F7
Green Rd. Birchington CT7 ...... 26 F8
Green Rd.
  Stalisfield Green ME13 .... 103 C6
Green Sands. ME14 .... 54 C8
Green St. ME7 .... 10 C5
Green The. Blean CT2 .... 66 A6
Green The. Burmarsh ME29 ... 186 C4
Green The. Chartham CT4 .... 86 D3
Green The. East Farleigh ME15 .. 96 B7
Green The. Harbledown CT2 ..... 65 E1
Green The. Hythe CT21 .... 176 B4
Green The. Littlebourne CT3 .... 89 F7
Green The. Lower Halstow ME9 .. 13 B3
Green The. Lydd TN29 .... 203 B5
Green The. Manston CT12 .... 28 D1
Green The. Sheerness ME12 ...... 1 I1
Green The. Woodchurch TN26 .. 169 A2
Green The. Wye TN25 .... 123 E2
Green Way. Lydd TN29 .... 203 C5
Green Way. Maidstone ME16 .... 74 B3
Green's Cotts. ME15 .... 96 A4
Greenacre. CT14 .... 111 D3
Greenacre Cl. ME5 .... 32 A5
Greenacre Dr. CT14 .... 117 C1
Greenacre Sch. ME5 .... 31 F5
Greenbank. Ashford TN24 ..... 139 D6
Greenbank. Chatham ME5 .... 32 B8
Greenbanks. CT18 .... 161 C6
Greenborough Cl. ME15 .... 97 E6
Greencroft. TN23 .... 155 E6
Greenfield Cl. ME20 .... 53 A6
Greenfield Cotts. Boxley ME14 . 54 C3
Greenfield Cotts. **10**
  Canterbury CT1 .... 87 F7
Greenfield Rd.
  Folkestone CT19 .... 178 E7
Greenfield Rd. Gillingham ME7 .. 10 D6
Greenfield Rd. Ramsgate CT12 .. 29 C2
Greenfields. Maidstone ME15 ... 97 E8
Greenfields. Sellindge TN25 ... 159 F2
Greenfinches. ME7 .... 32 F6
Greenhill Bridge Rd. CT6 .... 22 D3
Greenhill Cl. CT12 .... 50 B7
Greenhill Gdns. Herne Bay CT6 . 22 D3
Greenhill Gdns.
  Minster CT12 .... 50 B7
Greenhill La. TN27 .... 135 F8
Greenhill Rd. CT6 .... 22 C2
Greenhithe. **3** ME15 .... 75 A3
Greenhouse La. CT2 .... 66 E2
Greenland Rd. ME15 .... 75 A3
Greenly Way. TN28 .... 200 C6
Greensand Rd. ME15 .... 76 A2
Greenside. High Halden ME26 . 167 E7
Greenside. Maidstone ME15 ..... 75 B2
Greenvale Gdns. ME8 .... 11 B2
Greenview Wlk. ME8 .... 11 A4
Greenway. Chatham ME5 .... 31 D6
Greenway. Faversham ME13 .... 62 B8
Greenway Court Farm Cotts.
  ME17 .... 78 A1
Greenway Court Rd. ME17 ..... 78 A1
Greenway La. ME17 .... 100 A7
Greenways. Lower Halstow ME9 . 13 B3
Greenways. Maidstone ME14 ... 75 F5
Greenways. Sittingbourne ME10 . 37 B3
Greenwich Cl. Chatham ME5 .... 32 B4
Greenwich Cl. Maidstone ME16 . 74 D4
Gregory Cl. Gillingham ME8 ..... 33 E4
Gregory Ct. Sittingbourne ME10 . 37 A8
Gregory Ct. TN25 .... 123 E2
Grenham Bay Ave. CT7 .... 26 E8
Grenham Rd. CT7 .... 26 F8
Grenville Gdns. CT7 .... 26 B8
Grenville Way. CT10 .... 29 E4
Gresham Ave. CT9 .... 7 E1
Gresham Rd. ME17 .... 96 D3
Greville Homes. CT13 .... 93 B2
Grey Friars Cotts. **8** CT1 .... 87 F8
Grey Wethers. ME15 .... 53 E4
Grey Willow Gdns. TN23 ...... 155 C8
Greyfriars Cl. ME16 .... 74 D5
Greyfriars Ct. CT10 .... 8 F1
Greystones Rd. ME15 .... 76 A2
Greystones Sch. TN24 .... 139 F1
Grieveson Ho. ME4 .... 10 A4
Griffin Cotts. TN26 .... 181 C2
Griffin St. CT14 .... 117 D7
Griffin's Cnr. TN25 .... 140 E7
Grimshill Cl. CT2 .... 66 C4
Grimshill Rd. CT5 .... 43 E8
Grimston Ave. CT20 .... 178 B4
Grimston Gdns. CT20 .... 178 B4
Grimthorpe Ave. CT5 .... 43 C7
Grinsell Hill. CT12 .... 50 B6
Grisbrook Farm Cl. TN29 ...... 203 D6
Grisbrook Rd. TN29 .... 203 D6

Grizedale Cl. ME1 .... 31 D8
Groombridge Sq. **13** ME15 .. 97 F6
Grosvenor Ave. ME1 & ME4 ...... 9 E3
Grosvenor Gdns. CT9 .... 7 I1
Grosvenor Hill. CT9 .... 7 I2
Grosvenor Pl. CT9 .... 7 I2
Grosvenor Rd. Ashford TN24 .. 139 D7
Grosvenor Rd. Broadstairs CT10 . 30 A4
Grosvenor Rd. Gillingham ME7 .. 11 A1
Grosvenor Rd. Ramsgate CT11 .. 52 C7
Grosvenor Rd. Whitstable CT5 ... 43 D7
Grotto Gdns. CT9 .... 7 J2
Grotto Hill. CT9 .... 7 J2
Grotto Rd. **5** CT9 .... 7 J2
Grove Ave. ME12 .... 6 G2
Grove Cl. ME13 .... 62 A6
Grove Cotts. TN30 .... 179 B6
Grove Court Farm. ME13 .... 64 A3
Grove Ferry Hill. CT3 .... 47 E3
Grove Ferry Rd. CT3 .... 48 A2
Grove Gdns. **6** CT9 .... 7 G1
Grove Green La. ME14 .... 75 E5
Grove Green Rd. ME14 .... 75 F5
Grove Ho. TN27 .... 136 C3
Grove La. TN29 .... 191 D3
Grove Park Ave. ME10 .... 36 B5
Grove Park
  Cty Prim Sch. ME10 .... 36 B6
Grove Pl. ME13 .... 62 A6
Grove Rd. Chatham ME4 .... 10 B2
Grove Rd. Deal CT14 .... 117 D3
Grove Rd. Folkestone CT20 .... 178 E6
Grove Rd. Gillingham ME7 .... 11 A6
Grove Rd. Maidstone ME15 ...... 97 C7
Grove Rd. Preston CT3 .... 70 B8
Grove Rd. Ramsgate CT11 .... 52 D6
Grove Rd. Rochester ME2 .... 9 B8
Grove Rd. Selling ME13 .... 84 B4
Grove Rd. Staple CT3 .... 91 F6
Grove Rd. Wickhambreaux CT3 . 69 D6
Grove Road Cotts.
  Wickhambreaux CT3 .... 69 C2
Grove Road Cotts.
  Wickhambreaux CT3 .... 69 C3
Grove Terr. CT1 .... 87 E7
Grove The. Ashford TN24 ...... 139 E6
Grove The. Barham CT4 .... 128 F8
Grove The. Deal CT14 .... 117 C6
Grove The. Dover CT16 .... 149 C1
Grove The. Herne Bay CT6 ...... 22 C2
Grove The. Maidstone ME14 .... 76 A3
Grove The. Westgate-on-S CT8 .. 27 F8
Grove Way. CT3 .... 70 C7
Grovehurst Ave. ME10 .... 14 F1
Grovehurst Rd. ME10 & ME9 ... 14 E2
Grovelands. ME17 .... 101 E5
Groveway. ME12 .... 6 F2
Grovewood Dr. ME14 .... 75 E4
Grummock Ave. CT11 .... 52 B7
Grundy's Hill. **10** CT11 ...... 52 E6
Guardian Ct. ME8 .... 11 C1
Guildcount La. CT13 .... 72 F1
Guildford Ave. CT8 .... 27 E8
Guildford Lawn. **1** CT11 .... 52 E6
Guildford Rd. CT13 .... 87 F6
Guildhall St. **4** Canterbury CT1 . 87 F8
Guildhall St. **14**
  Folkestone CT20 .... 178 D5
Guildhall St N. CT19 & CT20 .. 178 D5
Guilford Ave. CT16 .... 149 A8
Guilford Ct. CT14 .... 117 D2
Guilford Rd. CT13 .... 94 E8
Guilton. CT3 .... 71 B1
Guldeford La. TN29 & TN31 ... 196 F3
Guldeford Lane Cnr. TN31 .... 196 D2
Gullands. ME17 .... 98 E4
Gun La. ME2 .... 9 B7
Gundulph Rd. ME1 & ME4 .... 9 E4
Gundulph Sq. ME1 .... 9 C6
Gunnis Cl. ME8 .... 33 D4
Gurling Rd. CT15 .... 133 F1
Guston CE Prim Sch. CT16 .... 149 E3
Guston Rd. ME14 .... 75 C6
Guy Cl. CT10 .... 30 A7
Gwyn Rd. CT12 .... 29 C2
Gypsy Cnr. CT2 .... 44 D3

Hackfield. TN23 .... 138 F1
Hackington Cl. CT2 .... 66 E4
Hackington Pl. CT2 .... 66 F2
Hackington Rd. CT2 .... 66 E7
Hackington Terr. CT2 .... 66 F2
Hacklinge Hill. CT14 .... 94 B2
Hackney Rd. ME16 .... 74 C2
Haddon Dene Sch. CT10 .... 29 F4
Hadleigh Ct. ME7 .... 33 B3
Hadleigh Gdns. CT6 .... 23 B5
Hadley Gdns. ME17 .... 77 E2
Hadlow Coll of Agriculture &
  Horticulture (Horticultural
  Unit). CT1 .... 88 B2
Hadlow Dr. CT9 .... 8 E2
Hadlow Rd. ME14 .... 75 C5
Haffenden Meadow. TN27 .... 120 C8
Haffenden Rd. TN30 .... 167 B1
Haig Ave. Chatham ME1 .... 9 D1
Haig Ave. Chatham,Luton ME4 .. 10 A2
Haig Ave. Gillingham ME7 .... 10 E4
Haine Hospl. CT12 .... 29 A4
Haine Ind Est. CT12 .... 28 F1
Haine Rd. CT12 & CT10 .... 28 F2
Halden Cl. ME15 .... 97 F6
Hales Cl. TN30 .... 179 B8
Hales St. TN30 .... 179 B8
Hales Dr. CT2 .... 66 F3

Hales Rd. ME10 .... 36 D1
Haleys Pl. ME1 .... 53 A8
Halfmile Ride. CT9 .... 28 E6
Halford Cl. CT6 .... 23 B2
Halfpenny Cl. ME16 .... 74 A7
Halfway Houses
  Prim Sch. ME12 .... 3 D6
Halfway Rd. ME12 .... 3 D8
Halifax Cl. ME5 .... 32 B6
Hall Cl. ME10 .... 36 E6
Hall Cres. CT14 .... 116 F5
Hall Rd. ME5 .... 32 C3
Hallcroft Ct. CT11 .... 52 C7
Hallett Wlk. 10 CT1 .... 67 B2
Halliday Ct. CT21 .... 176 A2
Hallsfield Rd. ME5 .... 31 D2
Hallwood Cl. ME8 .... 33 D5
Hallwood Ho. ME5 .... 32 C2
Halstatt Rd. CT14 .... 117 A3
Halstead Cl. CT2 .... 67 B4
Halstead Gdns. CT9 .... 8 F3
Halstead Wlk. ME16 .... 74 C7
Halstow Cl. ME15 .... 97 B6
Halstow Way. TN23 .... 155 F8
Halt The. Elham CT14 .... 144 F4
Halt The. Whitstable CT5 .... 44 A7
Ham Farm Cotts. CT14 .... 93 F2
Ham La. Gillingham ME5 .... 32 E3
Ham La. Lenham ME17 .... 101 C5
Ham Mill La. Snargate TN29 .... 191 F8
Ham Mill La.
  Warehorne TN26 & TN29 .... 183 A2
Ham Rd. ME13 .... 40 C1
Ham Shades La. CT5 .... 21 A1
Ham Street Sta. TN26 .... 183 A8
Hambledon Cl. ME16 .... 74 B3
Hambrook Cl. CT4 .... 107 B8
Hambrook La. CT4 .... 107 C8
Hambrook Wlk. ME10 .... 36 F8
Hamele The. CT2 .... 67 F5
Hamelin Rd. ME7 .... 32 F8
Hamilton Cl. CT12 .... 29 B1
Hamilton Cres. ME10 .... 36 C3
Hamilton Ho. ME17 .... 96 C3
Hamilton Rd. Ashford TN24 .... 156 D6
Hamilton Rd. Deal CT14 .... 117 C4
Hamilton Rd. Dover CT17 .... 166 B8
Hamilton Rd. Gillingham ME7 .... 10 D7
Hamilton Rd. Lydd TN29 .... 203 C6
Hamilton Rd. Whitstable CT5 .... 20 D1
Hammond Cl. CT15 .... 113 E5
Hammond's Cnr. TN29 .... 199 E6
Hammond's Rd. CT20 .... 177 E5
Hamond Hill. ME4 .... 9 E4
Hampden La. ME15 .... 156 A7
Hampden Mews. TN23 .... 156 A7
Hampden Rd. TN23 .... 156 A6
Hampshire Cl. ME5 .... 32 C7
Hampshire Dr. ME15 .... 97 C8
Hampshire Rd. CT1 .... 88 D7
Hampson Way. ME14 .... 76 A4
Hampton Cl. Chatham ME5 .... 32 A5
Hampton Cl. Herne Bay CT6 .... 22 A3
Hampton Cty Prim Sch
  (Jun & Inf). CT6 .... 22 C4
Hampton Gdns. CT6 .... 22 A3
Hampton La. TN25 .... 141 C3
Hampton Pier Ave. CT6 .... 22 B4
Hampton Rd. ME14 .... 75 C6
Hampton Vale. CT21 .... 177 B4
Hamstreet Rd.
  Bromley Green TN26 .... 170 E5
Hamstreet Rd.
  Hamstreet TN25 & TN26 .... 183 C7
Hamwick Gn. ME5 .... 32 C1
Hancocks Field. CT14 .... 117 A5
Hangman's La.
  Ringwould CT14 .... 133 F5
Hangman's La. Ripple CT14 .... 133 D5
Hanover Cl. Ashford TN23 .... 138 F2
Hanover Cl. Deal CT14 .... 117 D2
Hanover Cl. Margate CT9 .... 8 E2
Hanover Cl. Sittingbourne ME10 .... 36 E2
Hanover Cl. Faversham ME13 .... 62 B8
Hanover Ct. Hythe CT21 .... 176 C1
Hanover Ct. Maidstone ME14 .... 75 B5
Hanover Dr. ME8 .... 33 C4
Hanover Pl. CT2 .... 66 F2
Hanover Rd. ME17 .... 96 C3
Hanover Sq. CT6 .... 22 F5
Hanover St. CT6 .... 22 F5
Hanscomb Ho. CT2 .... 66 E2
Hanslett's La. ME13 .... 61 D3
Hanway. ME8 .... 11 A2
Harbledown Gdns. CT9 .... 8 E3
Harbledown Manor. ME8 .... 11 B3
Harbledown Pk. CT2 .... 66 C1
Harbour Approach Rd. CT20 .... 178 E4
Harbour Par. CT11 .... 52 E6
Harbour Point. CT19 .... 178 F5
Harbour Sch The. CT15 .... 165 E7
Harbour St. Broadstairs CT10 .... 30 B4
Harbour St. Folkestone CT20 .... 178 E5
Harbour St. Ramsgate CT11 .... 52 E6
Harbour St. Whitstable CT5 .... 20 D2
Harbour Twrs. 13 CT11 .... 52 E6
Harbour Way. CT20 .... 178 E5
Harbourland Cl. ME14 .... 75 B8
Harbourne La. TN26 & TN30 .... 167 E5
Harcourt Dr. Canterbury CT2 .... 66 D2
Harcourt Dr. Herne Bay CT6 .... 22 B5
Harcourt Gdns. ME8 .... 33 E4
Harcourt Prim Sch. CT19 .... 177 E7
Harcourt Rd. CT19 .... 177 F7
Harden Rd. TN29 .... 203 D7

Hardinge Cl. ME8 .... 33 D4
Hardinge Rd. TN24 .... 139 C3
Hardres Court Rd.
  Lower Hardres CT4 .... 110 A3
Hardres Court Rd.
  Stelling Minnis CT4 .... 126 F6
Hardres Rd. CT11 .... 52 E8
Hardres St. CT11 .... 52 E7
Hards Town. ME4 .... 10 A4
Hardwick Ho. 1 ME15 .... 97 B8
Hardwick Rd. CT20 .... 178 A4
Hardwicke Rd. CT17 .... 166 B6
Hardy Cl. Ashford TN24 .... 157 A7
Hardy Cl. Canterbury CT2 .... 66 C1
Hardy Cl. Chatham ME5 .... 32 B6
Hardy Rd.
  Littlestone-on-S TN28 .... 200 D3
Hardy Rd.
  St Margaret's at Cliffe CT15 .... 150 E8
Hardy St. ME14 .... 75 A6
Hare St. 2 ME4 .... 10 B3
Harebell Cl. 3 Chatham ME5 .... 31 F4
Harebell Cl. Maidstone ME14 .... 75 E5
Haredale Cl. ME1 .... 31 D7
Harkness Ct. ME10 .... 37 B4
Harkness Dr. CT2 .... 66 E2
Harman Ave. CT21 .... 174 F3
Harman Ct. ME5 .... 32 B3
Harmers Way. TN27 .... 118 F3
Harmsworth Gdns. CT10 .... 30 A5
Harnet St. CT13 .... 72 F1
Harold Ave. Gillingham ME7 .... 10 E4
Harold Ave. Westgate-on-S CT8 .... 27 E8
Harold Cl. ME13 .... 62 C6
Harold Rd. Birchington CT7 .... 26 E8
Harold Rd. Deal CT14 .... 117 D8
Harold Rd. Margate CT9 .... 8 B3
Harold Rd. Sittingbourne ME10 .... 37 B4
Harold St. Dover CT16 .... 166 D8
Harold St. Queenborough ME11 .... 3 A4
Harold's Rd. CT16 .... 166 E8
Harp Farm Rd. ME14 .... 54 C6
Harper Rd. TN23 .... 155 F8
Harple La. ME14 .... 54 F1
Harps Ave. CT7 .... 4 C6
Harpswood La. ME17 .... 77 F1
Harpswood La. CT21 .... 176 A4
Harptree Dr. ME5 .... 31 F5
Harrier Dr. ME10 .... 37 A2
Harrietsham Sta. ME17 .... 100 D6
Harringe La. TN25 .... 174 A6
Harriot Cl. CT19 .... 178 B7
Harris Gdns. ME10 .... 37 C5
Harris Rd. ME12 .... 1 D2
Harris's Alley. CT3 .... 91 A7
Harrison Rd. 4 CT11 .... 52 D6
Harrison Terr. ME13 .... 40 A2
Harrow Ct. Chatham ME5 .... 32 C4
Harrow Ct. Stockbury ME9 .... 56 D8
Harrow Dene. CT10 .... 29 E6
Harrow Rd. ME7 .... 32 F6
Harrow Way. ME14 .... 75 E5
Harry Wells Rd. CT6 .... 22 B3
Harrys Rd. ME9 .... 38 D3
Hart Cl. CT18 .... 163 A4
Hart Hill. TN27 .... 103 A2
Hart St. ME16 .... 74 F3
Hart St Commercial Ctr. ME16 .... 74 F3
Hartington St. ME4 .... 10 A3
Hartley Cl. ME15 .... 97 F6
Hartlip Cl. ME12 .... 3 B7
Hartlip Endowed
  CE Prim Sch. ME9 .... 34 D5
Hartlip Hill. ME9 .... 34 F7
Hartnup St. ME16 .... 74 C2
Hartpiece Cl. ME8 .... 11 F2
Harts Cotts. TN26 .... 183 A8
Harts La. 6 CT5 .... 20 D2
Hartsdown Rd. CT9 .... 28 D8
Hartsdown Sch. CT9 .... 28 D8
Harty Ave. ME8 .... 33 C3
Harty Ferry Cotts. ME13 .... 40 C5
Harty Ferry Rd. ME12 .... 18 E4
Harty Terr. ME12 .... 5 A5
Harvest Way. TN23 .... 155 D7
Harvesters Cl. ME8 .... 33 E7
Harvesters Way. ME14 .... 75 D4
Harvey Dr. Sittingbourne ME10 .... 37 A2
Harvey Dr. Whitstable CT5 .... 21 B1
Harvey Gram Sch
  for Boys The. CT19 .... 178 B6
Harvey Pl. 18 Folkestone CT20 .... 178 D5
Harvey Pl. 7 Folkestone CT20 .... 178 E5
Harvey Rd. Ashford TN24 .... 139 F1
Harvey Rd. Gillingham ME8 .... 33 E8
Harvey St. CT20 .... 178 E5
Harville Rd. TN25 .... 123 C2
Harwich St. CT5 .... 43 D8
Harwick Dr. TN28 .... 200 C8
Harwood Ho. TN25 .... 123 E1
Harwood Rd. Gillingham ME8 .... 11 B4
Hasborough Rd. CT19 .... 178 F6
Haskard Cl. CT18 .... 162 F4
Haslemere Est. ME15 .... 97 F5
Haslewood Cl. TN27 .... 135 B2
Hassall Reach. CT1 .... 87 B6
Hassell St. CT4 & TN25 .... 124 F2
Haste Hill Cl. ME17 .... 97 B3
Haste Hill Rd. ME17 .... 97 B3
Hasted Dr. ME9 .... 35 B7
Hasteds. ME17 .... 77 D2
Hastings Ave. CT9 .... 8 A1
Hastings Pl. CT13 .... 93 F8
Hastings Rd. ME15 .... 75 D3
Hatch La. CT4 .... 86 C5
Hatch Rd. ME17 .... 101 C5
Hatch St. 3 ME13 .... 62 C7
Hatfield Rd. Margate CT9 .... 7 G2

Hatfield Rd. Ramsgate CT11 .... 52 D7
Hatfield Rd. Rochester ME2 .... 9 A8
Hathaway Ct. Gillingham ME8 .... 33 D8
Hathaway Ct. Rochester ME1 .... 9 B5
Hatherall Rd. ME14 .... 75 B6
Hatherley Ct. CT9 .... 8 A3
Hatton Rd. ME5 .... 32 C3
Havant Wlk. 8 ME15 .... 97 F6
Havelock Pl. CT3 .... 71 E1
Havelock Rd. CT14 .... 117 C3
Havelock St. CT1 .... 67 A1
Haven Cl. ME1 .... 9 C2
Haven Dr. Hawkinge CT18 .... 163 A4
Haven Dr. Herne Bay CT6 .... 23 F6
Haven The. Ashford TN23 .... 155 F5
Haven The. Brenzett TN29 .... 192 A3
Haven The. Hythe CT21 .... 187 C8
Haventhorpe. TN24 .... 139 C3
Havisham Cl. ME1 .... 9 D2
Havock La. 1 ME14 .... 74 F4
Hawbeck Rd. ME8 .... 33 C3
Hawe Cl. CT2 .... 67 A4
Hawe Farm Way. CT6 .... 23 B2
Hawe La. CT2 & CT3 .... 68 A7
Hawes Ave. CT11 .... 52 B7
Hawk St. CT5 .... 43 C7
Hawk's La. CT1 .... 87 F8
Hawkesbury St. CT17 .... 166 D5
Hawkhurst Cl. CT7 .... 27 B8
Hawkhurst Rd. ME8 .... 11 B3
Hawkhurst Way. CT10 .... 30 A2
Hawkinge CP Sch. CT18 .... 163 B4
Hawkins Cl. Chatham ME4 .... 10 A6
Hawkins Cl. Sittingbourne ME10 .... 36 E7
Hawkins Rd. CT19 .... 177 D6
Hawks Rd. CT6 .... 22 B2
Hawks Way. TN23 .... 155 E7
Hawksdown. CT14 .... 134 B8
Hawksdown Rd. CT14 .... 134 C8
Hawkshill Activity Ctr. CT14 .... 134 C7
Hawkshill Rd. CT14 .... 134 D8
Hawkwood. ME16 .... 74 B5
Hawkwood Cl. ME1 .... 9 D5
Hawley Cl. ME16 .... 74 E4
Hawley Sq. CT9 .... 7 J2
Hawley Sq. CT9 .... 7 I2
Hawser Rd. ME1 .... 9 C1
Hawthorn. TN26 .... 190 D8
Hawthorn Ave. Canterbury CT2 .... 67 A2
Hawthorn Ave.
  West Minster ME12 .... 3 A8
Hawthorn Cl. Hythe CT21 .... 187 E8
Hawthorn Cl. Ramsgate CT11 .... 29 E1
Hawthorn Cl. River CT17 .... 148 E2
Hawthorn Cl.
  St Mary's Bay TN29 .... 194 F3
Hawthorn Cl.
  Womenswold CT3 .... 112 E4
Hawthorn Cnr. Herne Bay CT6 .... 24 A3
Hawthorn Cnr.
  Old Romney CT29 .... 198 E3
Hawthorn Ho. 5 ME5 .... 31 F5
Hawthorn Rd.
  Sittingbourne ME10 .... 36 E4
Hawthorne Ave. ME8 .... 11 C2
Hawthorne Cl. CT15 .... 131 D7
Hawthorns. ME5 .... 31 F1
Hawthorns The. CT10 .... 29 C4
Hay Hill. CT13 & CT14 .... 93 D2
Hay La. CT14 .... 93 F2
Hayes Alley. 11 CT5 .... 20 D2
Hayes La. ME5 .... 56 F6
Hayfields. ME5 .... 32 D2
Hayle Mill Cotts. ME15 .... 96 F8
Hayle Mill Rd. ME15 .... 96 F8
Hayle Rd. ME15 .... 75 A3
Haymakers La. TN23 .... 155 D8
Haymen St. ME4 .... 9 E3
Hayrick Cl. ME14 .... 75 E5
Haysel. ME10 .... 37 A2
Hayton Rd. TN25 .... 160 A2
Haywain Cl. ME14 .... 75 F4
Hayward Ave. ME2 .... 9 B8
Hayward Cl. Ashford TN24 .... 157 A8
Hayward Cl. Deal CT14 .... 117 A4
Hayward's Cl. TN28 .... 200 B6
Hayward's Hill. ME13 .... 82 C4
Hazebrouck Rd. ME13 .... 62 A7
Hazel Ave. ME16 .... 74 C5
Hazel Cl. CT15 .... 131 C7
Hazel Gr. Chatham ME5 .... 32 B8
Hazel Gr. Sheerness ME12 .... 1 H1
Hazel Street Rd. ME9 .... 57 A4
Hazel Wlk. CT10 .... 29 C4
Hazeldene. ME12 .... 5 F6
Hazeldown Cl. CT17 .... 148 E2
Hazelmere Dr. CT6 .... 23 D5
Hazels The. ME8 .... 33 B5
Hazelwood Dr. ME16 .... 74 B4
Hazelwood Meadow. CT13 .... 93 F7
Hazlemere Dr. ME7 .... 11 A5
Hazlemere Rd. CT5 .... 43 A7
Hazling Dane. CT15 .... 130 F5
Hazlitt Dr. ME16 .... 74 D5
Head Hill. ME13 .... 63 D7
Head Hill Rd. ME13 .... 63 D8
Head Race The. ME15 .... 74 D2
Headcorn Dr. CT2 .... 67 B4
Headcorn Gdns. CT9 .... 8 E2
Headcorn Rd. Gillingham ME8 .... 11 B4
Headcorn Rd. Sandway ME17 .... 101 A2
Headingley Rd. ME16 .... 74 B6
Heard Way. ME10 .... 37 B5
Heart In Hand Cnr. CT6 .... 23 F2
Heart In Hand Rd. CT6 .... 23 F2
Hearts Delight Rd. ME9 .... 36 B1
Heath Cl. CT2 .... 67 F7

Heath Ct. CT15 .... 150 F6
Heath Gr. ME16 .... 74 A2
Heath Ho. CT3 .... 46 E5
Heath Rd. Coxheath ME17 .... 96 C3
Heath Rd. Langley Heath ME17 .... 98 E4
Heath Rd. Maidstone ME16 .... 74 A2
Heath Thc. CT5 .... 21 B1
Heath Villas. TN26 .... 181 C2
Heather Cl. Chatham ME5 .... 31 F4
Heather Cl. Margate CT9 .... 28 C8
Heather Cl. Sittingbourne ME10 .... 37 A3
Heather Dr. Maidstone ME15 .... 75 B2
Heather Dr. St Michaels TN30 .... 167 B3
Heatherwood Cl. ME17 .... 99 E2
Heathfield Ave.
  Maidstone ME14 .... 75 C7
Heathfield Bglws. ME17 .... 102 B1
Heathfield Cl. Chatham ME5 .... 32 B7
Heathfield Cl. Maidstone ME14 .... 75 B7
Heathfield Rd. Ashford TN24 .... 139 C3
Heathfield Rd. Maidstone ME14 .... 75 C7
Heathfield Way. CT4 .... 128 F8
Heathorn St. ME14 .... 75 B5
Heathside. TN26 .... 181 C1
Heathside Ave. ME17 .... 96 C4
Heathwood Dr. CT11 .... 29 E1
Heaton Rd. CT1 .... 87 F6
Hedgend Ind Est. CT7 .... 25 F3
Hedgerow The. ME14 .... 75 E5
Hedgerows. TN23 .... 155 D7
Hedges The. ME14 .... 75 A5
Hedley St. ME14 .... 75 A5
Heel La. CT2 .... 67 C8
Heel Rd. ME13 .... 104 B7
Heights Terr. CT17 .... 166 C6
Heights The. CT5 .... 43 C6
Helding Cl. CT6 .... 23 B2
Helena Ave. CT9 .... 28 E8
Helena Corniche. CT20 .... 177 C3
Helena Rd. CT18 .... 164 C2
Helmdon Cl. CT12 .... 29 C2
Helvellyn Ave. CT11 .... 52 B7
Hempstead Cty Jun Sch. ME7 .... 33 A5
Hempstead
  Cty Prim Sch. ME7 .... 33 A5
Hempstead La. ME9 .... 37 E3
Hempstead Rd. Gillingham ME7 .... 33 A5
Hempstead Rd. Gillingham ME7 .... 33 B6
Hempstead Valley Dr. ME7 .... 33 A4
Hempstead Valley
  Sh Ctr. ME7 .... 33 A3
Hempsted St. 11 TN23 .... 139 B2
Henbane Cl. ME14 .... 75 E5
Hendon Bsns Ctr. TN24 .... 139 D2
Hengest Rd. CT14 .... 117 D7
Hengist Ave. CT9 .... 8 B1
Hengist Rd. Birchington CT7 .... 26 C7
Hengist Rd. Westgate-on-S CT8 .... 27 E8
Henley Bsns Pk. ME2 .... 9 D7
Henley Cl. Chatham ME5 .... 32 A6
Henley Cl. Gillingham ME8 .... 33 D8
Henley Fields. Maidstone ME14 .... 75 E6
Henley Fields.
  St Michaels TN30 .... 167 B2
Henley Meadows. TN30 .... 167 A2
Henley View. TN30 .... 167 B2
Henniker Cl. CT16 .... 149 A5
Henry Ct. 9 CT1 .... 87 F7
Henry Rd. CT1 .... 87 F7
Henry St. Chatham ME4 .... 10 B3
Henry St. Gillingham ME8 .... 12 A1
Henwood. TN24 .... 139 D3
Hera Ho. ME12 .... 1 C2
Herbert Dane Ct. 10 ME13 .... 62 D7
Herbert Rd. Ashford TN24 .... 156 D6
Herbert Rd. Chatham ME4 .... 10 A6
Herbert Rd. Gillingham ME8 .... 33 E8
Herbert Rd. Ramsgate CT11 .... 52 C6
Herbert St. CT17 .... 149 B1
Herdson Rd. CT20 .... 178 A5
Hereford Cl. ME8 .... 11 D2
Hereford Gdns. CT7 .... 26 F6
Hereford Rd. ME15 .... 97 D7
Hereson Rd. CT11 .... 52 F8
Hereson Sch The. CT11 .... 52 F8
Hereward Ave. CT7 .... 26 E8
Heritage Dr. ME7 .... 10 F1
Heritage Rd. Chatham ME5 .... 32 A6
Heritage Rd. Folkestone CT20 .... 177 D6
Herman Terr. ME4 .... 10 A3
Hermitage Cl. CT21 .... 176 B2
Hermitage La. Detling ME14 .... 55 B4
Hermitage La. Maidstone ME16 .... 74 A4
Herne Ave. CT6 .... 23 A4
Herne Bay
  Cty Prim & Inf Sch. CT6 .... 22 F4
Herne Bay Golf Course. CT6 .... 22 F2
Herne Bay High Sch. CT6 .... 22 D3
Herne Bay Jun Sch. CT6 .... 22 F4
Herne Bay Rd.
  Calcott CT3 & CT2 .... 45 E2
Herne Bay Rd. Whitstable CT5 .... 21 C3
Herne Bay Sta. CT6 .... 22 F2
Herne CE Inf Sch. CT6 .... 46 B8
Herne CE Jun Sch. CT6 .... 46 A8
Herne Ct. CT9 .... 177 C6
Herne Dr. CT6 .... 22 C2
Herne Rd. ME8 .... 11 C2
Herne St. CT6 .... 46 A8
Herneville Gdns. CT6 .... 23 B5
Hernhill CE Prim Sch. ME13 .... 64 B6
Hero Wlk. ME1 .... 31 C7
Heron Apartments. 3 ME15 .... 97 F5
Heron Cl. ME9 .... 13 B3
Heron Forestall Ave. CT18 .... 163 B4
Heron Way. ME5 .... 32 B7

Heron Wlk. TN23 .... 155 E8
Heron's Brook. TN25 .... 140 E6
Heron's Way. CT21 .... 187 D8
Heronden. Eastry CT13 .... 92 F1
Heronden Rd. Park Wood ME15 .... 97 F4
Herons Cl. CT4 .... 107 C8
Herschell Rd. CT7 .... 26 F8
Herschell Rd E. CT14 .... 117 C3
Herschell Rd W. CT14 .... 117 C3
Herschell Sq. CT14 .... 117 C3
Hersden Cty Prim Sch. CT3 .... 46 E1
Hertford Ho. Herne Bay CT6 .... 23 A5
Hertford Ho. 14 Ramsgate CT11 .... 52 E6
Hertford Pl. CT11 .... 52 E6
Hertford St. CT9 .... 29 C8
Hertford St. CT11 .... 52 E6
Herts Cres. ME15 .... 96 F3
Hetford Ct. CT1 .... 88 C8
Hever Cl. ME15 .... 97 F6
Hever Gdns. ME16 .... 74 E3
Hever Pl. CT2 .... 67 A3
Hewitt Cl. ME7 .... 10 F6
Hewitt Rd. 1 CT16 .... 166 D8
Hewitts Pl. TN24 .... 139 F1
Hextable Cl. Ashford TN23 .... 155 E6
Hextable Cl. Maidstone ME16 .... 74 D7
Heyford Cl. CT18 .... 163 B4
Hibernia St. 5 CT11 .... 52 E6
Hickory Dell. ME7 .... 33 A5
Hicks Forstal Rd. CT3 & CT6 .... 46 B5
Higgins' La. ME4 .... 9 F5
High Banks. Loose ME15 .... 96 F5
High Banks. Rochester ME1 .... 9 D2
High Dewar Rd. ME8 .... 34 A8
High Elms. ME8 .... 11 E1
High Halden Parochial
  CE Prim Sch. TN26 .... 167 E7
High Knocke. TN29 .... 195 B6
High Meadow. CT17 .... 149 C1
High Minnis. CT4 .... 143 F8
High Oak Hill. ME9 .... 13 C1
High Snoad Wood. TN25 .... 105 A1
High St. Ashford TN23 .... 139 C2
High St. Aylesford ME20 .... 53 A2
High St. Bridge CT4 .... 89 A1
High St. Broadstairs CT10 .... 29 B8
High St.
  Broadstairs, St Peter's CT10 .... 30 A4
High St. Brookland TN29 .... 197 E8
High St. 8 Canterbury CT1 .... 67 A1
High St. Canterbury CT1 .... 87 F8
High St. Chatham ME4 .... 9 E4
High St. Chatham ME4 .... 10 A4
High St. Deal CT14 .... 117 D6
High St. Dover CT16 & CT17 .... 166 C8
High St. Dymchurch TN29 .... 195 C8
High St. Eastchurch ME12 .... 5 D3
High St. Eastry CT13 .... 93 B2
High St. Elham CT4 .... 144 F5
High St. Fordwich CT2 .... 68 A4
High St. Gillingham ME7 .... 10 B6
High St. Gillingham ME8 .... 10 C5
High St.
  Gillingham,Brompton ME4 .... 10 A6
High St. Gillingham,Rainham ME8 .... 33 F8
High St. Herne Bay CT6 .... 22 F5
High St. Hythe CT21 .... 176 C2
High St. Lenham ME17 .... 101 D5
High St. Littlebourne CT3 .... 89 F7
High St. Lydd TN29 .... 203 B6
High St. Lyminge CT18 .... 161 C6
High St. Maidstone ME14 .... 74 F4
High St. Manston CT12 .... 51 B8
High St. Margate CT9 .... 7 I2
High St. Margate CT9 .... 7 J1
High St. Margate, Garlinge CT9 .... 28 B7
High St. Minster, Thanet ME12 .... 4 D6
High St. Minster CT12 .... 50 C6
High St. New Romney TN28 .... 200 B6
High St. Newington ME9 .... 35 C6
High St. Queenborough ME11 .... 2 F5
High St. Ramsgate CT11 .... 52 D7
High St. Rochester ME1 .... 9 A6
High St. Rochester ME1 .... 9 C6
High St. Rochester ME4 .... 9 A5
High St. Sandwich CT13 .... 73 A1
High St. Sheerness ME12 .... 1 B3
High St. Sheerness ME12 .... 1 D1
High St. Sittingbourne ME10 .... 36 E6
High St. Sittingbourne ME10 .... 36 F4
High St. Smarden TN27 .... 135 A1
High St.
  St Margaret's at Cliffe CT15 .... 150 F6
High St. Sturry CT2 .... 67 F5
High St. Temple Ewell CT16 .... 148 D5
High St. Tenterden TN30 .... 179 A7
High St. Whitstable CT5 .... 20 D2
High St. Wingham CT3 .... 91 A8
High St. Wye TN25 .... 123 C3
High St The. TN30 .... 120 C7
High Street St Lawrence.
  CT11 .... 52 B7
High Trees. 1 TN24 .... 157 A8
High View Ave. CT6 .... 22 B5
Higham Cl. ME15 .... 74 E2
Higham La. CT4 .... 111 B8
Higham View. ME14 .... 53 E4
Highbury Gdns. CT12 .... 29 B3
Highbury La. TN30 .... 179 A7
Highbury Wlk. CT12 .... 29 B2
Highcroft Gn. ME15 .... 97 F4
Highfield Cl. Gillingham ME8 .... 33 D7
Highfield Cl. Hythe CT21 .... 176 A4
Highfield Cl. Ramsgate CT12 .... 29 B3
Highfield Cl. Rough Common CT2 .... 66 B3
Highfield Ct. 5 Margate CT9 .... 8 B2
Highfield Ct. Ramsgate CT12 .... 29 B3
Highfield Gdns. CT9 .... 7 H1

Highfield Ind Est. CT19 .... 178 F6
Highfield La. TN24 .... 157 C6
Highfield Rd. Ashford TN24 ...... 157 A8
Highfield Rd. Gillingham ME8 .... 33 D7
Highfield Rd.
  Halfway Houses ME12 .... 3 E6
Highfield Rd. Ramsgate CT12 .... 29 B3
Highfields Ave. CT6 .... 23 D4
Highfields View. CT6 .... 23 C4
Highgate Rd. CT5 .... 21 B1
Highgrove Rd. ME5 .... 32 A5
Highland Ct. CT20 .... 177 F4
Highland Court Annexe (Kent &
  Canterbury Hospl). CT4 ...... 111 C8
Highland Rd. Chartham CT4 ...... 86 D1
Highland Rd. Maidstone ME15 .... 97 E6
Highlands Cres. TN29 .... 195 A4
Highlands Farm
  Rare Breeds Ctr. TN26 .... 169 D1
Highpoint. TN24 .... 139 D3
Highridge. Gillingham ME7 .... 10 F1
Highridge. Hythe CT21 .... 177 A3
Highridge Cl. ME14 .... 75 F5
Highsted Rd. ME9 &10 .... 36 F1
Highsted Sch. ME10 .... 36 F2
Highsted Valley. ME9 .... 58 F7
Highstreet Rd. Waterham ME13 . 42 D2
Highstreet Rd.
  Yorklets CT5 & ME13 .... 42 E2
Highview Cl.
  Boughton Street ME13 .... 64 B3
Highview Cl. Maidstone ME15 .... 97 A8
Highview Dr. ME5 .... 31 D5
Highview Rd. ME12 .... 4 C7
Highview Sch. CT19 .... 178 D6
Highworth
  Gram Sch for Girls. TN24 .... 139 A3
Hilary Cl. CT6 .... 23 C4
Hilda Rd. Chatham ME4 .... 10 A3
Hilda Rd. Halfway Houses ME12 .. 3 D6
Hildenborough Cres. ME16 ...... 74 C7
Hildersham Cl. CT10 .... 29 E5
Hill Ave. CT15 .... 130 E5
Hill Brow. Maidstone ME14 ...... 76 A5
Hill Brow. Sittingbourne ME10 .. 36 D2
Hill Chase. ME5 .... 31 E3
Hill Cres. Aylesham CT3 .... 112 E5
Hill Cres. Lenham ME17 .... 101 D5
Hill Crest. TN23 .... 155 B8
Hill Ct. TN27 .... 103 E1
Hill Dr. CT13 .... 93 B3
Hill Green Rd. ME9 .... 56 D8
Hill House Dr. CT12 .... 50 C7
Hill La. CT18 .... 162 B1
Hill Rd. Chatham ME1 .... 31 A3
Hill Rd. Folkestone CT19 .... 178 E7
Hill Rd. Folkestone CT19 .... 178 E8
Hill Rd. Rochester ME1 .... 9 A2
Hill The. Charing TN27 .... 120 D8
Hill The. Littlebourne CT3 .... 89 F8
Hill Top Cotts. ME17 .... 96 E2
Hill Top Rd. CT6 .... 23 B5
Hill View. Ashford TN24 .... 139 C3
Hill View. Margate CT9 .... 28 D7
Hill View Terr. CT18 .... 161 D3
Hill View Way. ME5 .... 31 E5
Hill's Terr. ME4 .... 9 F3
Hillary Rd. ME14 .... 75 A7
Hillborough Dr. CT6 .... 23 F5
Hillborough Gr. ME5 .... 32 A3
Hillborough Rd. CT6 .... 23 B5
Hillbrow Ave. Herne Bay CT6 .... 23 B2
Hillbrow Ave. Sturry CT2 .... 67 F7
Hillbrow La. TN23 .... 138 F1
Hillbrow Rd. Ashford TN24 ..... 139 A1
Hillbrow Rd. Ramsgate CT11 .... 52 D8
Hillcrest Cl. TN24 .... 139 E6
Hillcrest Gdns. Deal CT14 .... 117 A2
Hillcrest Gdns. Ramsgate CT11 . 52 B6
Hillcrest Rd. Chatham ME4 .... 9 F2
Hillcrest Rd. Hythe CT21 .... 176 B3
Hillcrest Rd. Kingsdown CT14 . 134 D4
Hillcrest Rd. Littlebourne CT3 .. 89 E8
Hillcroft Rd. CT6 .... 23 B3
Hilden Shaw. ME15 .... 97 A8
Hiller Cl. CT10 .... 30 A6
Hillfield Villas. TN26 .... 167 F8
Hillman Ave. CT6 .... 22 A4
Hillside. 1 CT20 .... 177 E3
Hillside Ave. Canterbury CT2 .... 66 C2
Hillside Ave. Rochester ME2 ...... 9 B8
Hillside Ave. Rushenden ME11 .... 2 F3
Hillside Ct. Hythe CT21 .... 176 C2
Hillside Ct. 1 Rochester ME2 ..... 9 A7
Hillside Ind Est. CT20 .... 177 E4
Hillside Rd. Chatham ME4 .... 10 A4
Hillside Rd. Dover CT17 .... 149 A2
Hillside Rd. Minster ME12 .... 4 B7
Hillside Rd.
  Stalisfield Green ME13 .... 103 C6
Hillside Rd. Whitstable CT5 ...... 21 A1
Hillside St. CT21 .... 176 C2
Hilltop Rd. ME12 .... 4 A5
Hillview Rd. Canterbury CT2 ..... 66 C2
Hillview Rd. Whitstable CT5 ...... 43 D8
Hillyfield Rd. TN23 .... 156 A8
Hillyfields Cty Jun Sch. ME7 .... 10 E6
Hillyfields Rise. TN23 .... 139 A1
Hilton Bsns Ctr. TN23 .... 156 B6
Hilton Dr. ME10 .... 36 B6
Hilton Rd. TN23 .... 138 F2
Hinchliffe Way. CT9 .... 29 D8
Hind Cl. TN29 .... 195 C8
Hinde Cl. ME10 .... 36 F7
Hines Terr. ME4 .... 10 C1
Hinton Cres. ME7 .... 33 A6
Hinxhill Rd. TN24 & TN25 ...... 140 D1
Hirst Cl. CT16 .... 149 B4

Hither Field. TN27 .... 120 C7
Hoades Wood Rd. CT2 .... 68 A7
Hoath Cl. ME7 .... 33 B7
Hoath Cty Prim Sch. CT3 .... 46 E5
Hoath La. ME8 .... 33 B7
Hoath Rd. CT3 .... 46 C3
Hoath Way. ME7 & ME8 .... 33 B5
Hobart Ct. CT16 .... 149 C3
Hobart Gdns. ME10 .... 36 C4
Hobart Rd. CT12 .... 52 A2
Hockeredge Gdns. CT8 & CT9 ... 27 F8
Hockers Cl. ME14 .... 76 A8
Hockers La. ME14 .... 76 A7
Hodge's Gap. CT9 .... 8 C3
Hodgson Rd. CT5 .... 42 F7
Hog Gn. CT4 .... 144 F4
Hog Hill. ME14 .... 76 B5
Hogarth Cl. CT6 .... 23 E5
Hogben La. ME17 .... 79 A3
Hogben Cl. CT18 .... 161 B7
Hogg La. CT4 .... 109 E2
Holbeam Rd. ME13 .... 82 A1
Holborn La. ME4 .... 9 F5
Holbourn Cl. CT6 .... 46 B8
Holbrook Dr. CT12 .... 29 B1
Holcombe Rd. Chatham ME4 .... 9 F2
Holcombe Rd. Rochester ME1 ...... 9 C3
Holdenhurst. TN23 .... 155 E6
Holder Cl. ME5 .... 32 C6
Holding St. ME8 .... 11 F1
Holland Cl. Broadstairs CT10 ..... 8 G2
Holland Cl. Sheerness ME12 .... 1 C1
Holland Ho. ME1 .... 9 D5
Holland Rd. Chatham ME5 .... 31 E4
Holland Rd. Maidstone ME14 ..... 75 B5
Hollands Ave. CT19 .... 178 F7
Hollicondane Rd. CT11 .... 52 E8
Hollingbourne
  Cty Prim Sch. ME17 .... 77 E2
Hollingbourne Hill. ME17 .... 77 F4
Hollingbourne Rd. ME8 .... 11 C2
Hollingbourne Sta. ME17 .... 77 C3
Hollingworth Rd. ME15 .... 97 F5
Hollow La. Canterbury CT1 .... 87 E5
Hollow La. Hartlip ME9 .... 34 E5
Hollow Rd. CT3 .... 47 B6
Hollow St. CT3 .... 47 C5
Hollow Wood Rd. CT17 .... 165 E8
Hollowmede. CT1 .... 87 E6
Holly Cl. Broadstairs CT10 .... 29 C4
Holly Cl. Chatham ME5 .... 32 C8
Holly Cl. Eastry CT13 .... 93 B2
Holly Cl. Folkestone CT19 ...... 178 E7
Holly Cl. Gillingham ME7 .... 10 E6
Holly Farm Rd. ME15 .... 98 C6
Holly Gdns. CT9 .... 8 C2
Holly Hill Rd. ME13 .... 64 D5
Holly Ho. ME12 .... 1 C2
Holly La. CT9 .... 8 C2
Holly Rd. Ramsgate CT11 .... 52 E8
Holly Rd. St Mary's Bay TN29 .. 194 F4
Holly Tree Cl. ME17 .... 99 E2
Hollybrook Hill. ME10 .... 36 D4
Hollybush Cnr. CT4 .... 90 A3
Hollybush La. CT3 .... 69 A4
Holm Mill La. ME17 .... 100 B6
Holm Oak Cl. CT1 .... 87 F6
Holm Oak Gdns. CT10 .... 29 F4
Holmesdale Cl. ME15 .... 96 F3
Holmestone Rd. CT15 & CT17 .. 148 E1
Holmlea Cl. TN24 .... 139 E1
Holmoaks. Gillingham ME8 .... 11 E2
Holmoaks. Maidstone ME14 ...... 75 C5
Holmscroft Rd. CT6 .... 23 D5
Holmside. ME7 .... 10 E3
Holmside Ave. ME12 .... 3 D6
Holmwood Rd. TN23 .... 155 E7
Holness Rd. CT3 .... 71 D2
Holt St. CT15 .... 113 C4
Holton Cl. CT7 .... 27 A6
Holtwood Cl. ME8 .... 33 D6
Holtye Cres. ME15 .... 75 B2
Holy Cross
  RC High Sch The. CT10 .... 30 A3
Holy Family
  RC Prim Sch The. ME15 .... 97 F4
Holy Trinity
  CE Prim Sch. CT10 .... 30 A1
Holy Trinity & St John's
  CE Prim Sch. CT9 .... 7 J2
Holyrood Dr. ME12 .... 4 A5
Holywell Ave. CT19 .... 178 D8
Holywell Cty Prim Sch. ME9 .... 12 F3
Holywell Ho. CT19 .... 178 D8
Holywell La. ME9 .... 12 F2
Home Farm Cotts. CT14 .... 115 E6
Homebirch Rd. 6 CT7 .... 26 F8
Homefern Ho. CT9 .... 7 I3
Homefield Ave. CT14 .... 117 B6
Homefield Row. CT14 .... 117 B6
Homefleet Ho. 11 CT11 .... 52 F7
Homeleigh Rd. CT12 .... 29 B3
Homepeak. 12 CT12 .... 176 B2
Homeside Farm. CT4 .... 126 F6
Homespire Ho. 10 CT1 .... 67 A1
Homestall Ct. CT2 .... 66 C4
Homestall La. ME13 .... 63 B5
Homestead. TN23 .... 155 D8
Homestead Cl. 7 CT9 .... 7 J1
Homestead La. CT15 .... 132 C7
Homestead View. ME9 .... 36 B2
Homestead Village. CT11 .... 52 C5
Homestreet
  Cty Prim Sch. TN26 .... 182 F8
Homevale Ho. 3 CT20 .... 177 E3
Homeview. ME10 .... 37 B4

Homewood Ave. ME10 .... 36 D3
Homewood Cty Inf Sch. ME10 .. 36 D4
Homewood Rd. Sturry CT2 .... 68 A6
Homewood Rd.
  Tenterden TN30 .... 167 B1
Homewood Sch. TN30 .... 167 B1
Honduras Terr. 8 ME14 .... 75 A7
Hone St. ME2 .... 9 B8
Honey Bee Glade. ME8 .... 33 E6
Honey Cl. ME7 .... 33 A5
Honey Hill. CT2 & CT5 .... 65 F8
Honey La. ME15 .... 98 B6
Honeyball Wlk. ME9 .... 38 C2
Honeycrock Hill. ME9 .... 56 F8
Honeyfield. TN23 .... 138 E1
Honeypot Cl. ME2 .... 9 B8
Honeysuckle Cl. 8
  Chatham ME5 .... 31 E4
Honeysuckle Cl. Gillingham ME7 32 E4
Honeysuckle Cl. Margate CT9 .... 28 C8
Honeysuckle Cl. ME10 .... 37 B5
Honeysuckle Rd. CT11 .... 52 F8
Honeysuckle Way. CT6 .... 23 D2
Honeywood Cl. Canterbury CT1 . 67 B2
Honeywood Cl. Lympne CT21 .. 175 A4
Honeywood Parkway. CT15 ..... 149 B5
Honeywood Rd. CT15 & CT16 .. 149 A5
Honfleur Rd. CT13 .... 93 F8
Honiton House Sch. CT9 .... 8 B2
Honywood Rd. ME17 .... 101 C4
Hook Cl. Chatham ME5 .... 31 E5
Hook Cl. Folkestone CT20 ...... 177 F5
Hook La. Brookland TN29 .... 197 C6
Hook La. Charing TN27 .... 120 A7
Hook La. Harrietsham ME17 .... 100 C6
Hook St. ME17 .... 118 F8
Hook Wall. TN29 .... 197 E5
Hookstead. TN30 .... 167 C7
Hooper's Pl. ME1 .... 9 C4
Hooper's Rd. ME1 .... 9 C4
Hoopers La. CT6 .... 23 D3
Hop Garden Way. CT1 .... 87 E6
Hope La. New Romney TN28 .... 200 A8
Hope La. St Mary in the Marsh
  TN28 & TN29 .... 193 F2
Hope Rd. CT14 .... 117 D5
Hope St. Chatham ME4 .... 10 A3
Hope St. Maidstone ME14 .... 74 F6
Hope St. Sheerness ME12 .... 1 C2
Hope's La. CT12 .... 29 C3
Hopes Gr. TN26 .... 167 D7
Hopeville Ave. CT10 .... 29 E6
Hopewell Dr. ME5 .... 32 C8
Hopewell Sch. TN23 .... 155 B7
Hoppers Way. TN23 .... 155 D8
Hopsons Pl. ME12 .... 4 C5
Horn Hill. ME9 .... 58 E2
Horn St. CT19 & CT20 & CT21 . 177 B4
Hornash La. TN26 .... 170 D8
Hornbeam Ave. ME5 .... 32 B2
Hornbeam Cl. TN23 .... 138 F3
Hornes Place Chapel. TN26 .... 181 D2
Hornet Cl. CT17 .... 29 D3
Horsa Rd. Birchington CT7 .... 26 D7
Horsa Rd. ME5 .... 117 D8
Horsebridge Rd. CT5 .... 20 D2
Horseshoe Cl. Gillingham ME7 .. 32 F5
Horseshoe Cl. Maidstone ME14 . 75 E5
Horseshoes La. ME17 .... 98 E4
Horsewash La. ME1 .... 9 C4
Horsford Wlk. ME13 .... 62 A8
Horsham Hill. ME8 & ME9 .... 12 E4
Horsham La. ME8 .... 12 D3
Horshams The. CT6 .... 23 D5
Horsley Cl. CT18 .... 163 B4
Horsley Rd. ME1 .... 9 B4
Horsted Ave. ME4 .... 9 E1
Horsted Cty Inf Sch. ME4 .... 31 D5
Horsted Cty Jun Sch. ME5 .... 31 D5
Horsted Way. ME1 .... 31 D7
Horton Cotts. ME4 .... 86 E4
Horton Downs. ME15 .... 75 F1
Horton Gdns. CT4 .... 86 E4
Horwood Cl. ME1 .... 31 B8
Hoser Gdns. CT7 .... 27 A7
Hospital Hill. CT20 & CT21 .... 177 C3
Hospital La. Canterbury CT1 ..... 87 F8
Hospital La. Chatham ME4 .... 10 A3
Hospital Meadow Cotts. CT3 .... 91 D2
Hospital Rd. ME17 .... 99 E8
Hotel Rd. Gillingham ME8 .... 11 A2
Hotel Rd.
  St Margaret's at Cliffe CT15 . 151 B6
Hothfield Common
  Nature Reserve. TN26 .... 137 F8
Hothfield
  Cty Prim Sch. TN26 .... 138 A7
Hothfield Rd. ME8 .... 11 F1
Hougham Court La. CT15 .... 165 A3
Houghton Ave. ME7 .... 33 B3
Houghton Ho. CT19 .... 178 C5
House Field. TN24 .... 139 F2
Housefield Rd. ME13 .... 104 C6
Hovenden Cl. CT2 .... 67 A4
Howard Ave. Rochester ME1 ...... 9 C3
Howard Ave. Sittingbourne ME10 36 D6
Howard Cl. ME12 .... 4 C7
Howard Dr. ME16 .... 74 B5
Howard Rd. ME10 .... 30 A3
Howard Sch The. ME8 .... 33 D8
Howbury Wlk. ME8 .... 33 D4
Howfield La. CT4 .... 86 E5
Howletts Oast. CT4 .... 89 C5
Howletts Zoo Pk. CT4 .... 89 D7
Hoxton Cl. TN23 .... 155 D8
Hoystings Cl The. CT1 .... 88 A7
Hubbard's La. ME15 .... 97 A3

Hubbards Cotts. ME8 .... 12 C2
Hubbards Hill. ME17 .... 102 B6
Hubble Dr. ME15 .... 97 E7
Hubert Way. CT10 .... 29 E6
Huckleberry Cl. ME5 .... 32 B3
Hudson Cl. 7 Dover CT16 .... 149 B3
Hudson Cl. Gillingham ME8 ...... 11 C1
Hudson Cl. Sturry CT2 .... 67 F6
Hudson Rd. CT1 .... 67 B2
Hugh Pl. 5 ME13 .... 62 D7
Hugh Price Cl. ME10 .... 37 C5
Hugin Ave. CT10 .... 29 E7
Hull Pl. CT14 .... 116 F6
Hull Rd. TN29 .... 204 E6
Humber Ave. CT6 .... 21 F4
Humber Ho. 5 ME15 .... 97 E8
Hume Ct. CT21 .... 176 D1
Humphrey Terr. TN18 .... 162 F4
Hundreds Cl. CT7 .... 27 D7
Hunger Hatch La. TN27 .... 119 F4
Hunstanton Cl. ME8 .... 33 E3
Hunt Cl. CT18 .... 163 A4
Hunter Ave. TN24 .... 156 E8
Hunter Cl. TN24 .... 156 E8
Hunter Rd. TN24 .... 139 E1
Hunters Chase. Herne Bay CT6 .. 23 C2
Hunters Chase. Whitstable CT5 .. 43 E7
Hunters Ct. 4 ME7 .... 10 C7
Hunters Forstal Rd. CT6 .... 23 C2
Hunters Way. Gillingham ME7 .. 10 E1
Hunters Way. Sheldwich ME13 .. 83 C5
Hunters Way W. ME5 & ME7 .... 10 E1
Hunters Wlk. CT16 .... 117 B6
Huntersfield Cl. ME5 .... 32 C1
Hunting Gate. CT7 .... 26 F8
Hunting Rd. CT7 .... 26 F7
Huntingdon Wlk. 4 ME15 .... 97 E7
Huntington Rd. ME17 .... 96 B3
Hunton Gdns. CT2 .... 67 A4
Hunton Rd. ME15 .... 96 A2
Huntsfield Ind Est. CT20 .... 177 D4
Huntsman Cl. ME4 .... 75 B4
Huntsman's Cnr. ME4 .... 31 E8
Huntsmans Cl. ME4 .... 9 E1
Huntswood. TN23 .... 138 E1
Hurst Cl. ME5 .... 31 E6
Hurst Gr. CT12 .... 29 C1
Hurst Hill. ME5 .... 31 E2
Hurst La. Capel-le-F CT18 ...... 164 B4
Hurst La. Charing Heath TN27 . 119 C6
Hurst La. Sittingbourne ME10 .. 14 F1
Hurst Pl. ME8 .... 33 F8
Hurst Rd. TN24 .... 139 C7
Hurstford La. TN26 & TN27 .... 120 C2
Hurstings The. ME16 .... 74 D2
Hurstwood. ME5 .... 31 E4
Hurstwood Rd. Bredhurst ME7 .. 33 B1
Hurstwood Rd. Detling ME14 .... 55 B7
Hurstwood Rd.
  Warren Street ME13 & ME17 . 102 E8
Hutchings Cl. ME10 .... 37 C5
Hutsford Cl. ME8 .... 33 D5
Huxley Cl. ME1 .... 9 D4
Hyde Ct. CT17 .... 166 C7
Hyde Pl. CT3 .... 112 F5
Hyde Rd. ME16 .... 74 D6
Hyde The. CT4 .... 86 B2
Hythe. CT20 .... 177 F5
Hythe Cty Inf Sch. CT21 .... 176 B1
Hythe Light Railway
  Sta. CT21 .... 176 A2
Hythe Pl. CT13 .... 94 A8
Hythe Rd. Ashford TN24 .... 139 E1
Hythe Rd. Dymchurch TN29 .... 186 E1
Hythe Rd. Pedlinge CT21 .... 175 D4
Hythe Rd. Sittingbourne ME10 . 36 D5
Hythe Rd. Smeeth TN25 & TN24 . 158 C3

Ian's Wlk. CT21 .... 177 A3
Iden La. TN27 .... 119 B4
Idenwood Cl. ME8 .... 33 D6
Iffin La. CT1 & CT4 .... 87 E2
Ifield Cl. ME15 .... 97 F7
Ilex Rd. CT19 .... 177 F6
Illustrious Cl. ME5 .... 32 A6
Imbert Cl. TN28 .... 200 C6
Imperial Ave. ME12 .... 4 D7
Imperial Dr. ME12 .... 4 C3
Imperial Rd. ME7 .... 10 C3
Impton La. ME5 .... 32 A1
Ince Rd. CT2 .... 67 F7
Ingle Rd. ME4 .... 9 F2
Ingleden Cl. ME10 .... 36 F8
Ingleden Park Rd. TN30 .... 167 C1
Ingles La. CT20 .... 178 D5
Ingles Mews. 3 CT20 .... 178 C4
Ingles Rd. CT20 .... 178 C4
Ingoldsby Rd. Birchington CT7 .. 26 E7
Ingoldsby Rd. Canterbury CT1 .. 87 D6
Ingoldsby Rd. Folkestone CT19 . 178 E7
Ingram Rd. ME7 .... 10 E6
Institute Rd. Chatham ME4 ...... 10 A4
Institute Rd. Faversham ME13 ... 62 D7
Inverary Ct. CT11 .... 29 E1
Inverness Ho. 6 ME15 .... 97 E7
Inverness Terr. CT10 .... 30 A3
Invicta Ct. ME10 .... 36 F7
Invicta Gram Sch for Girls.
  ME14 .... 75 C4
Invicta Ho. Canterbury CT1 ...... 87 F7
Invicta Ho. Margate CT9 .... 8 C1
Invicta Rd. Folkestone CT19 .... 178 D8
Invicta Rd. Lydd TN29 .... 203 A2
Invicta Rd. Margate CT9 .... 29 B8
Invicta Rd. Sheerness ME12 ...... 1 D2
Invicta Rd. Whitstable CT5 .... 43 F8

Invicta Villas. ME14 .... 76 C4
Inward Car Lanes. CT16 .... 166 G8
Inward Freight Lanes. CT16 .... 166 G8
Iona Cl. ME5 .... 32 C1
Iona Rd. ME15 .... 97 A7
Irchester St. 9 CT11 .... 52 F7
Ireland Ct. TN24 .... 139 D2
Irene Astor Ct. 7 CT20 .... 178 D5
Iris Cl. ME5 .... 54 A8
Iron Bar La. 3 CT1 .... 88 A8
Ironside Cl. ME5 .... 32 A8
Irvine Dr. CT9 .... 29 C8
Isis Cl. CT21 .... 175 A3
Island Rd. Upstreet CT3 & CT7 .. 47 D2
Island Rd. Westbere CT2 & CT3 . 68 C7
Island Wall. CT5 .... 20 C1
Ivanhoe Rd. Herne Bay CT6 ...... 23 A4
Ivanhoe Rd. Westgate-on-S CT8 .. 7 C1
Ivens Way. ME17 .... 100 D6
Iversgate Cl. ME8 .... 11 F2
Ivory Cl. ME13 .... 40 A1
Ivy Cl. Etchinghill CT18 .... 161 D3
Ivy Cl. Kingswood ME17 .... 99 D2
Ivy Cottage Hill. CT12 .... 50 E7
Ivy Cotts. TN23 .... 155 C8
Ivy Ct. CT2 .... 66 E6
Ivy House Rd. CT5 .... 20 F1
Ivy La. Canterbury CT1 .... 88 A8
Ivy La. Ramsgate CT11 .... 52 D6
Ivy Pl. Canterbury CT1 .... 87 E7
Ivy Pl. Deal CT14 .... 117 D7
Ivy St. ME8 .... 33 F8
Ivy Way. CT19 .... 178 E7
Ivychurch Gdns. CT9 .... 8 E2
Ivychurch Rd. TN29 .... 192 B3
Iwade Cty Prim Sch. ME9 .... 14 E2

Jaarlen Rd. TN29 .... 203 B6
Jacklin Cl. ME5 .... 31 F2
Jackson Ave. ME1 .... 31 B8
Jackson Cl. ME8 .... 11 C1
Jackson Rd. CT1 .... 87 E7
Jacksons La. 6 TN30 .... 179 A7
Jacob Cl. CT9 .... 28 E7
Jacob Yd. 8 ME13 .... 62 D7
Jacobs Ho. ME12 .... 1 D2
Jaffa Ct. CT5 .... 43 D8
Jamaica Terr. ME14 .... 75 A7
James Cl. Ash CT3 .... 71 D2
James Cl. Lyminge CT18 .... 161 C7
James Ct. Folkestone CT20 ..... 178 A4
James Ct. 2 Margate CT9 .... 8 B2
James Hall Gdns. CT14 .... 117 C3
James Morris Ct. 3 CT20 .... 177 F3
James St. Ashford TN23 .... 139 A2
James St. Chatham ME4 .... 9 F4
James St. Folkestone CT19 ..... 178 D6
James St. Gillingham ME7 .... 10 C6
James St. Maidstone ME14 .... 75 A5
James St. 8 Ramsgate CT11 .... 52 D6
James St. Rochester ME1 .... 9 C4
James St. Sheerness ME12 .... 1 E2
James Whatman Way. ME14 .... 74 F5
Japonica Cl. ME5 .... 32 C2
Jarman's Field. TN25 .... 123 F2
Jarrett Ho. 6 CT20 .... 178 C4
Jarrett's Ct. ME10 .... 37 B4
Jarvis Dr. TN24 .... 157 A7
Jarvis Pl. TN24 .... 167 B3
Jarvist Pl. CT14 .... 134 D6
Jasmine Cl. 2 ME5 .... 31 F4
Jasper Ave. ME1 .... 9 D2
Jayne Wlk. CT5 .... 43 B6
Jefferson Cl. TN23 .... 138 F1
Jefferson Dr. ME8 .... 11 C1
Jefferson Rd. ME12 .... 1 E2
Jefferstone Gdns. TN29 .... 194 E4
Jefferstone La. TN29 .... 194 E4
Jefferstone Lane Sta. TN29 .... 194 F4
Jeffery St. ME7 .... 10 C6
Jeffrey St. ME14 .... 75 A5
Jellicoe Cl. TN24 .... 157 A7
Jemmett La. TN25 .... 157 D3
Jemmett Rd. TN23 .... 156 A8
Jenkins' Dale. ME4 .... 9 F3
Jenkins Dr. ME15 .... 97 E5
Jenner Rd. ME1 .... 9 C4
Jenner's Way. TN29 .... 194 F3
Jennifer Gdns. CT9 .... 29 C8
Jersey Cl. CT4 .... 109 C6
Jersey Rd. ME2 .... 9 A8
Jesmond St. 3 CT19 .... 178 D6
Jesse's Hill. CT4 .... 111 B1
Jessica Mews. 2
  Canterbury CT1 .... 67 C1
Jessica Mews.
  Sittingbourne ME10 .... 36 E7
Jesuit Cl. CT2 .... 67 A4
Jesus Hospl. CT1 .... 67 A1
Jetty Rd. Sheerness ME12 .... 1 B3
Jetty Rd. Warden ME12 .... 6 E4
Jewry La. CT1 .... 87 F8
Jeyes Rd. ME7 .... 10 C4
Jezreels Rd. ME7 .... 10 D3
Jillian Way. TN23 .... 155 E7
Jiniwin Rd. ME1 .... 31 D7
Joey's La. TN24 .... 139 E2
Johannesburg Ho. 2 ME15 ..... 97 F5
Johannesburg Rd. CT16 .... 149 C4
John Anderson Ct. 11 ME13 .... 62 D7
John Bowley Ho. CT19 .... 177 F6
John Graham Ct. CT1 .... 88 A6
John Hall Cl. ME13 .... 40 B2
John St. Broadstairs CT10 .... 30 B4
John St. Maidstone ME14 .... 75 A6

John St. Rochester ME1 ... 9 C4
John Tapping Cl. CT14 ... 117 B1
John Wilson Bsns Pk. CT5 ... 21 B1
John's Gn. CT13 ... 93 E6
Johnson Ave. ME7 ... 10 C7
Johnson Cl. TN24 ... 157 A7
Johnson Cl. ME13 ... 40 B1
Johnson Rd. ME10 ... 36 D4
Johnson Way. ME12 ... 4 A7
Joiners Ct. ME4 ... 10 B2
Jointon Rd. CT20 ... 178 B4
Jordan Cl. ME15 ... 97 E5
Joseph Conrad Ho. CT20 ... 66 D1
Joseph Wilson Ind Est. CT5 ... 44 A7
Joss Gap Rd. CT10 ... 8 H1
Joy La. CT5 ... 43 B8
Joy Lane
  Cty Prim Inf Sch. CT5 ... 43 C7
Joy Lane
  Cty Prim Jun Sch. CT5 ... 43 C7
Joyes Cl. Folkestone CT19 ... 178 E4
Joyes Cl. Whitfield CT16 ... 149 B7
Joyes Rd. Folkestone CT19 ... 178 E4
Joyes Rd. Whitfield CT16 ... 149 B7
Jubilee Cl. CT21 ... 187 D8
Jubilee Cotts. Throwley ME13 ... 82 D1
Jubilee Cotts. Worth CT14 ... 94 B4
Jubilee Cres. ME11 ... 2 F5
Jubilee Ct. **18** CT10 ... 30 B4
Jubilee Field. TN30 ... 188 E4
Jubilee Rd. Littlebourne CT3 ... 89 F8
Jubilee Rd. Sandwich CT13 ... 93 F8
Jubilee Rd. Worth CT14 ... 94 B4
Jubilee St. ME10 ... 36 E5
Jubilee Terr. ME7 ... 10 C6
Jubilee Way. Dover CT16 ... 166 G8
Jubilee Way.
  Guston CT15 & CT16 ... 150 A2
Judd Rd. ME13 ... 62 A7
Judkins Cl. ME5 ... 32 C6
Julian Rd. CT19 ... 178 B6
Julie Cl. CT10 ... 30 A7
Julien Pl. TN24 ... 157 A8
Junction Rd. Gillingham ME7 ... 10 D4
Junction Rd. Herne Bay CT6 ... 22 C2
Juniper Cl. Ashford TN24 ... 138 E2
Juniper Cl. Canterbury CT1 ... 88 A6
Juniper Cl. Chatham ME5 ... 32 A4
Juniper Cl. Whitstable CT5 ... 20 F1
Jury's Gap Coastguard Cotts.
  TN31 ... 201 E1
Jury's Gap Rd. TN29 ... 203 A5

Kake St. CT4 ... 125 E7
Katherine Ct. ME5 ... 32 B2
Kathleen Mews. **17** CT20 ... 178 D5
Kearsney Abbey. CT16 ... 148 D4
Kearsney Ave. CT16 ... 148 E4
Kearsney Ct. CT16 ... 148 D4
Kearsney Sta. CT16 ... 148 D4
Keat Farm Cl. CT6 ... 23 F5
Keddow's Cl. CT21 ... 187 D8
Keefe Cl. ME5 ... 31 D1
Keeper's Hill. CT4 ... 89 D2
Keith Ave. CT12 ... 52 A8
Kellaway Rd. ME5 ... 32 A2
Kelly Dr. ME7 ... 10 C7
Kelly Ho. ME1 ... 31 C7
Kelvedon Rd. CT14 ... 117 C2
Kemp Alley. **2** CT5 ... 20 D1
Kemp Cl. ME5 ... 31 E4
Kemp Rd. CT5 ... 21 C2
Kempes Pl. TN25 ... 123 E2
Kempton Cl. ME5 ... 32 C2
Kemsdale Rd. ME13 ... 63 F6
Kemsing Gdns. CT2 ... 67 B4
Kemsley Halt. ME10 ... 14 E1
Kemsley Street Rd. ME14 ... 33 C1
Kenardington Rd. TN26 ... 181 E3
Kenbrook. TN24 ... 139 C7
Kendal Cl. CT11 ... 52 B6
Kendal Rise. CT10 ... 30 A5
Kendal Way. ME8 ... 33 D8
Kendon Bsns Pk. ME2 ... 9 D8
Kenfield Rd. CT4 ... 109 A6
Kengate Ind Est. CT21 ... 175 F1
Kenilworth Cl. CT15 ... 151 A6
Kenilworth Ct. ME10 ... 36 C5
Kenilworth Dr. ME8 ... 33 D6
Kenilworth Gdns. ME8 ... 33 D7
Kenilworth Ho. ME16 ... 74 B2
Kennedy Cl. ME13 ... 62 D8
Kennedy Dr. CT14 ... 117 B2
Kennedy Ho. **6** CT11 ... 52 F7
Kennel Barn Rd. ME9 ... 57 C5
Kennel Hill. CT15 ... 131 E6
Kennelling Rd. ME13 & TN27 ... 103 D5
Kennett Dr. CT14 ... 117 A2
Kennett La. TN25 ... 175 B8
Kennett Lane Cotts. TN25 ... 175 B8
Kennington
  CE Jun Sch. TN24 ... 139 E7
Kennington Cl. Gillingham ME8 ... 11 B4
Kennington Cl.
  Maidstone ME15 ... 97 F7
Kennington Rd. TN24 ... 140 A1
Kensington Ho. ME16 ... 74 A2
Kensinton Rd. CT1 ... 67 C4
Kent Ave. Ashford TN24 ... 139 B3
Kent Ave. Canterbury CT1 ... 88 D8
Kent Ave. Maidstone ME15 ... 75 C1
Kent Ave. Minster ME12 ... 4 B6
Kent Ave. Sittingbourne ME10 ... 36 D3
Kent Battle of Britain Mus.
  CT18 ... 162 F4

Kent & Canterbury Hospl. CT1 ... 88 A5
Kent Cl. ME1 ... 31 C8
Kent Coll. CT2 ... 66 C3
Kent County Optholmic
  & Aural Hospl. ME14 ... 75 A4
Kent County Show Gd. ME14 ... 55 C3
Kent Gdns. CT7 ... 26 F7
Kent Ho. CT20 ... 178 B4
Kent Inst of Art & Design.
  Chatham ME1 ... 9 E4
Kent Inst of Art & Design.
  Maidstone ME16 ... 74 C3
Kent Int Bsns Pk. CT12 ... 27 D2
Kent International Airport.
  CT12 ... 28 B1
Kent Music Sch. CT2 ... 66 F1
Kent Pl. CT11 ... 52 F6
Kent Rd. Folkestone CT19 ... 177 E2
Kent Rd. Margate CT9 ... 29 B8
Kent Rd. Sheerness ME12 ... 1 C1
Kent St. CT5 ... 43 D8
Kent Terr. Gillingham ME8 ... 12 C2
Kent Terr. Ramsgate CT11 ... 52 F6
Kent View Dr. ME12 ... 5 D1
Kentmere Ave. CT11 & CT12 ... 51 F7
Kenton Gdns. CT12 ... 50 B6
Kenward Rd. ME16 ... 74 C5
Kenwood Ave. ME5 ... 32 A4
Kenya Terr. **7** ME14 ... 75 A7
Kenyon Wlk. ME8 ... 33 B3
Kerton Rd. TN29 ... 204 F3
Kestrel Cl. ME14 ... 37 A2
Kestrel Ho. **8** ME7 ... 10 B6
Kestrel Rd. ME5 ... 32 C2
Keswick Dr. ME16 ... 74 B5
Keswick Rd. ME10 ... 37 C3
Kettle Hill. ME13 ... 81 F5
Kettle Hill Rd. Eastling ME13 ... 81 F5
Kettle Hill Rd. Hockley ME13 ... 82 A4
Kevin Dr. CT11 ... 52 B6
Kewlands. ME14 ... 75 C6
Key St. ME10 ... 36 A5
Keycol Hill.
  Key Street ME10 & ME9 ... 36 A5
Keycol Hill. Sittingbourne ME9 ... 35 F5
Keycol Hospl. ME9 ... 35 E6
Keyes Ave. ME4 ... 9 F2
Keyes Pl. CT19 ... 178 E7
Keynes Coll. CT2 ... 66 D4
Keyworth Mews. **7** CT1 ... 67 B2
Khartoum Rd. Chatham ME4 ... 9 F1
Khartoum Rd. Gillingham ME4 ... 10 A6
Khartoum Sq. CT16 ... 149 A6
Khyber Rd. ME4 & ME7 ... 10 B7
Kilbride Ct. CT11 ... 29 F1
Kiln Cl. Challock TN25 ... 105 B1
Kiln Cl. Sittingbourne ME10 ... 37 A3
Kiln Cnr. CT21 ... 176 B4
Kiln Field. TN30 ... 179 C7
Kiln La. TN26 ... 153 F5
Kiln Rd. TN25 ... 172 F4
Kilndown Cl. Ashford TN23 ... 155 E6
Kilndown Cl. Maidstone ME16 ... 74 C7
Kilndown Gdns. Canterbury CT2 ... 67 A4
Kilndown Gdns. Margate CT9 ... 8 E2
Kimberley Cl. CT16 ... 149 C3
Kimberley Cnr. CT10 ... 29 F8
Kimberley Ct. CT7 ... 7 C1
Kimberley Gr. CT5 ... 42 F6
Kimberley Rd. Gillingham ME7 ... 10 D3
Kimberley Rd. Ramsgate CT12 ... 29 A1
Kimberly Terr. CT18 ... 161 C7
King Arthur Rd. CT12 ... 51 D7
King Charles Ct. CT14 ... 117 D2
King Edward Ave.
  Broadstairs CT10 ... 30 A4
King Edward Ave.
  Herne Bay CT6 ... 23 B4
King Edward Ct. CT6 ... 23 B4
King Edward Rd.
  Birchington CT7 ... 27 A5
King Edward Rd. Chatham ME4 ... 9 F2
King Edward Rd. Deal CT14 ... 117 D8
King Edward Rd.
  Gillingham ME7 ... 10 F6
King Edward Rd.
  Maidstone ME15 ... 74 F2
King Edward Rd.
  Ramsgate CT11 ... 52 C6
King Edward Rd. Rochester ME1 ... 9 C5
King Ethelbert Sch The. CT7 ... 27 C7
King George Rd. ME5 ... 31 E4
King George V Meml Hos.
  ME8 ... 11 C2
King George Villas. CT14 ... 94 B3
King Lear's Way. CT17 ... 166 B5
King St. Brookland TN29 ... 191 D2
King St. Canterbury CT1 ... 66 F1
King St. Chatham ME4 ... 10 A4
King St. Deal CT14 ... 117 D6
King St. Deal, Walmer CT14 ... 117 D3
King St. Dover CT16 ... 166 D7
King St. Fordwich CT2 ... 68 A4
King St. Gillingham ME7 ... 10 C6
King St. Maidstone ME14 & ME15 ... 75 A4
King St. Margate CT9 ... 7 J3
King St. Ramsgate CT11 ... 52 E7
King St. Rochester ME1 ... 9 B8
King St. Sandwich CT13 ... 73 A1
King St. Sheerness ME12 ... 1 B2
King St. Sittingbourne ME10 ... 36 E5
King William Rd. **5** ME7 ... 10 C7
King's Ave. Ashford TN23 ... 139 B2
King's Ave. Birchington CT7 ... 26 D7
King's Ave. Broadstairs CT10 ... 30 B4
King's Ave. Ramsgate CT12 ... 29 B1
King's Ave. Rochester ME1 ... 9 C3

King's Ave. Sandwich CT13 ... 95 A8
King's Ave. Whitstable CT5 ... 20 E1
King's Bastion. ME7 ... 10 A5
King's Cl. CT14 ... 134 D6
King's Head Alley. ME12 ... 1 B3
King's Orch. ME1 ... 9 C5
King's Pk. CT1 ... 67 B1
King's Pl. **4** CT11 ... 52 E6
King's Rd. Birchington CT7 ... 27 A6
King's Rd. Chatham ME5 ... 10 D1
King's Rd. Faversham ME13 ... 62 C7
King's Rd. Herne Bay CT6 ... 22 F5
King's Rd. Ramsgate CT11 ... 52 D8
King's Sch. Canterbury CT1 ... 67 A1
King's Sch. Rochester ME1 ... 9 C5
King's Sch (Jun). CT1 ... 67 E5
Kingfisher Apartments. **11**
  ME15 ... 97 E5
Kingfisher Ave. CT21 ... 187 D8
Kingfisher Cl. Margate CT9 ... 28 B8
Kingfisher Cl. Sevington TN24 ... 157 A7
Kingfisher Cl. Whitstable CT5 ... 43 C7
Kingfisher Ct. CT6 ... 22 D3
Kingfisher Dr. ME5 ... 32 C7
Kingfisher Drive
  Cty Prim Sch. ME5 ... 32 B7
Kingfisher Gdns. CT21 ... 187 C8
Kingfisher Wlk. CT10 ... 29 F5
Kings Acre. ME15 ... 76 A1
Kings Cotts. ME17 ... 98 F6
Kings Ct. CT14 ... 117 D3
Kings Meadow. TN24 ... 139 E7
Kings Mews. **7** CT1 ... 67 A1
Kings Mill Cl. ME10 ... 36 E5
Kings Par. **7** TN23 ... 139 B2
Kings Rd. Dover CT17 ... 166 A7
Kings Rd. Folkestone CT20 ... 177 D6
Kings Rd. Minster ME12 ... 4 D7
Kings Ropewalk. CT17 ... 166 B5
Kingsbridge Ct. **9** CT20 ... 178 E5
Kingsdale Sch. ME5 ... 10 C1
Kingsdown Cl. Gillingham ME7 ... 33 B4
Kingsdown Cl. Maidstone ME16 ... 74 B4
Kingsdown Hill. CT14 ... 134 D4
Kingsdown Hos. ME9 ... 59 E4
Kingsdown Pk. CT5 ... 20 F2
Kingsdown Rd.
  Erriottwood ME9 ... 59 D4
Kingsdown Rd.
  Kingsdown CT14 ... 134 D7
Kingsdown Rd.
  St Margaret's at Cliffe CT15 ... 151 A7
Kingsfield Rd. CT6 ... 23 B2
Kingsford Cl. TN25 ... 157 E4
Kingsford Ct. CT17 ... 149 B1
Kingsford St. TN24 & TN25 ... 157 D5
Kingsgate Ave. CT10 ... 8 F1
Kingsgate Bay Rd. CT10 ... 8 H2
Kingsgate Cl. ME16 ... 74 C4
Kingsgate Coll. CT10 ... 30 A8
Kingsgate La. TN30 ... 188 C5
Kingsland Gdns. CT14 ... 134 B8
Kingsland Hollow. TN29 ... 195 A4
Kingsland La. TN27 ... 118 C1
Kingsley Rd. Maidstone ME15 ... 75 A3
Kingsley Rd. Whitstable CT5 ... 43 E8
Kingsmarsh La. TN29 ... 199 C5
Kingsmead
  Cty Prim Sch. CT1 ... 67 A1
Kingsmead Rd. CT1 & CT2 ... 67 A2
Kingsmead Stadium. CT1 ... 67 A2
Kingsnorth
  CE Prim Sch. TN23 ... 156 B3
Kingsnorth Ct. **2** CT20 ... 178 B5
Kingsnorth Gdns. CT20 ... 178 C5
Kingsnorth Rd. Ashford TN23 ... 156 A6
Kingsnorth Rd.
  Faversham ME13 ... 62 C6
Kingsnorth Rd. Gillingham ME8 ... 11 C4
Kingston Ave. CT9 ... 28 C7
Kingston Cl. Herne Bay CT6 ... 23 F5
Kingston Cl. Ramsgate CT12 ... 29 B2
Kingston Cl. River CT17 ... 148 F3
Kingston Cres. ME5 ... 32 C4
Kingston Dr. ME5 ... 97 A8
Kingstone Ct. **3** CT20 ... 178 B5
Kingsway. Chatham ME5 ... 10 D1
Kingsway. Dymchurch TN29 ... 186 E2
Kingsway. Gillingham ME7 ... 10 E1
Kingswood. TN24 ... 139 D5
Kingswood Ave. ME4 ... 9 F2
Kingswood
  Cty Prim Sch. ME17 ... 99 E2
Kingswood Rd. Gillingham ME7 ... 10 D6
Kingswood Rd.
  Kit's Coty ME1 & ME20 ... 53 D8
Kinross Ct. ME5 ... 32 B7
Kipling Rd. TN23 ... 139 B2
Kirby's La. CT2 ... 66 F1
Kirk Gdns. CT14 ... 117 B2
Kirkdale. ME15 ... 96 F5
Kirkdale Cl. ME5 ... 32 D1
Kirkdale Cotts. ME5 ... 96 F5
Kirkdale Rd. ME15 ... 96 F6
Kirkstone Ave. CT11 ... 51 F7
Kirkwood Ave. TN26 ... 169 A1
Kit Hill. ME13 ... 84 D8
Kit Hill Ave. ME5 ... 31 E3
Kit's Coty Ho. ME20 ... 53 C6
Kitchener Ave. ME4 ... 10 A1
Kitchener Cl. CT4 ... 128 F8
Kitchener Rd. Dover CT17 ... 166 A7
Kitchener Rd. Rochester ME2 ... 9 A8
Kitchener Sq. CT19 ... 178 E8
Kite Farm. CT5 ... 21 D3
Kitewell La. TN29 ... 203 D8

Kither Rd. TN23 ... 156 A7
Kitsbridge La.
  Hamstreet TN26 ... 183 C4
Kitsbridge La. Ruckinge TN26 ... 183 F5
Kitsbridge La.
  Ruckinge TN25 & TN26 ... 184 B6
Klondyke Ind Est. ME11 ... 2 F4
Knatchbull Way. TN25 ... 158 E5
Knavesacre Ct. ME8 ... 33 D5
Knight Ave. Canterbury CT2 ... 87 D8
Knight Ave. Gillingham ME7 ... 10 D7
Knight Rd. ME2 ... 9 A6
Knight's Ave. CT10 ... 30 B6
Knight's Rd. CT16 ... 166 E8
Knightrider Ct. ME15 ... 75 A3
Knightrider St. **1**
  Maidstone ME15 ... 75 A3
Knightrider St. Sandwich CT13 ... 73 A1
Knights Alley. **14** CT5 ... 20 D2
Knights Ct. CT17 ... 149 B1
Knights Pk. ME2 ... 9 A6
Knights Templars. CT17 ... 166 C6
Knights Way. CT16 ... 149 A3
Knightsfield Rd. ME10 ... 36 D7
Knock Hill. TN30 ... 190 A2
Knock Rd. TN23 ... 156 A7
Knockhill Rd. CT9 ... 8 F3
Knockhurst Ct. TN30 ... 167 C1
Knockwood Rd. TN30 ... 167 C1
Knold Pk. CT9 ... 28 E8
Knole Pk. ME5 ... 32 C3
Knole The. ME13 ... 62 B7
Knoll Hill. TN25 ... 173 C3
Knoll La. TN23 ... 155 E7
Knoll Pl. CT14 ... 117 C2
Knoll Way. ME12 ... 6 D4
Knott Cres. TN24 ... 157 A7
Knott Ct. ME14 ... 74 F6
Knott's La. **20** CT1 ... 67 A1
Knotts La. CT15 ... 150 F6
Knotts Sq. TN23 ... 139 C2
Knowler Way. CT6 ... 23 C5
Knowlton Gdns. ME16 ... 74 B2
Knowlton Wlk. **1** CT1 ... 67 B1
Kohima Pl. CT16 ... 149 F2
Kyetop Wlk. ME8 ... 33 D6
Kymbeline Ct. CT14 ... 117 B4

La Belle Alliance Sq. **6**
  Ramsgate CT11 ... 52 E7
La Belle Alliance Sq. **7**
  Ramsgate CT11 ... 52 F7
La Galamina. TN28 ... 204 E8
La Rocco. TN28 ... 204 E8
La Tausco. TN28 ... 204 D8
La-Tene. CT14 ... 117 B2
Laburnum Ave. CT13 ... 93 F8
Laburnum Cl. CT16 ... 148 E4
Laburnum Gr. ME12 ... 1 I1
Laburnum Ho. ME12 ... 62 A8
Laburnum La. CT2 ... 68 B7
Laburnum Pl. ME10 ... 36 E6
Labworth Cl. ME12 ... 3 E6
Lacey Cl. ME17 ... 98 E4
Lachlan Way. **2** CT20 ... 177 F3
Lacton Oast. TN24 ... 157 B8
Lacton Way. TN24 ... 157 A8
Ladds Cnr. ME7 ... 11 B5
Lade Fort Cotts. TN28 ... 204 E6
Lade Fort Cres. TN29 ... 204 E6
Lady Garne Rd. CT15 ... 164 F5
Lady J Thornhill's Endowed
  Prim Sch. TN25 ... 123 E2
Lady Wootton's Gn. **5** CT1 ... 88 A8
Ladyfields. Chatham ME5 ... 32 D2
Ladyfields. Herne Bay CT6 ... 23 C7
Ladysmith Gr. CT5 ... 42 F6
Ladysmith Rd. CT5 ... 43 C5
Ladywell. **7** CT16 ... 166 D8
Ladywood Ho. **2** CT16 ... 166 D8
Ladywood Rd. CT2 ... 67 F7
Lagos Ave. CT12 ... 29 A1
Lakelands. Harrietsham ME17 ... 100 E6
Lakelands. Maidstone ME15 ... 97 A7
Lakemead. TN23 ... 155 E8
Lakeside. TN23 ... 155 E8
Lakeside Gdns. TN26 ... 120 F1
Lakeside Pk. ME2 ... 9 E7
Lakewood Dr. ME8 ... 33 C6
Laking Ave. CT10 ... 30 B7
Laleham Gdns. CT9 ... 8 B2
Laleham Rd. CT9 ... 8 B1
Laleham Wlk. CT9 ... 8 B1
Lamb's Wlk. CT5 ... 43 C6
Lambard Ho. **6** ME14 ... 75 A5
Lambden Rd. TN27 ... 136 C6
Lamberhurst Gn. ME8 ... 11 C3
Lamberhurst Rd. ME16 ... 74 B7
Lamberhurst Way. CT9 ... 8 F3
Lambert Ho. CT14 ... 117 B3
Lambeth Cl. ME5 ... 32 B4
Lambeth Rd. CT1 ... 66 D3
Lambourn Way. ME5 ... 32 C2
Lambourne Pl. ME8 ... 12 A2
Lambourne Rd. ME15 ... 75 B7
Lambourne Way. CT1 ... 88 C8
Lambsfrith Gr. ME7 ... 33 B3
Lambton Rd. CT17 ... 149 A1
Laming Rd. CT7 ... 27 A6
Lammas Dr. ME10 ... 36 E6
Lamplighters Cl. ME7 ... 10 D7
Lancashire Rd. ME15 ... 97 E7
Lancaster Ave. CT18 ... 164 C6
Lancaster Cl. CT12 ... 29 B1
Lancaster Ct. ME5 ... 33 C7

Lancaster Gdns.
  Birchington CT7 ... 26 F6
Lancaster Gdns.
  Herne Bay CT6 ... 23 D5
Lancaster Ho. Deal CT14 ... 117 A5
Lancaster Ho. **8** Dover CT17 ... 166 D7
Lancaster Rd. Canterbury CT1 ... 87 F6
Lancaster Rd. Dover CT17 ... 166 D7
Lancet La. ME15 ... 97 A6
Lanchester Cl. CT6 ... 22 A3
Landbury Wlk. TN23 ... 138 F4
Landon Rd. CT6 ... 23 C4
Landor Ct. ME7 ... 33 A3
Landrail Rd. ME9 ... 13 B3
Landway The. ME14 ... 76 A4
Lane End. CT15 ... 22 D5
Lane The. CT15 ... 149 F6
Lane's Wlk. CT5 ... 20 E2
Lanes The. CT12 ... 50 D6
Lanfranc Gdns. CT2 ... 66 C1
Lanfranc Ho. **5** CT1 ... 67 A1
Lang Ct. CT5 ... 21 C3
Langdale. TN23 ... 155 E8
Langdale Ave. CT11 ... 52 A7
Langdale Cl. ME8 ... 11 D1
Langdale Rise. ME16 ... 74 C5
Langdon Ave. CT3 ... 71 F1
Langdon Cl. CT15 ... 150 F5
Langdon Cross. CT15 ... 150 C7
Langdon Cty Prim Sch. CT15 ... 133 A1
Langdon Rd. Folkestone CT17 ... 177 D7
Langdon Rd. Rochester ME1 ... 9 C4
Langham Ct. CT9 ... 7 F1
Langham Gr. ME16 ... 74 C4
Langholm Rd. TN23 ... 156 A7
Langhorne Gdns. **5** CT20 ... 178 C4
Langley Gdns. CT9 ... 8 E3
Langley Rd. ME10 ... 36 F7
Langney Dr. TN23 ... 155 E8
Langport Rd. TN28 ... 200 C6
Langton Cl. ME14 ... 75 C5
Langton Cotts. CT3 ... 70 B5
Langton La. CT1 ... 88 A4
Lankester Parker Rd. ME1 ... 31 C6
Lansdown Rd. Canterbury CT1 ... 88 A7
Lansdown Rd.
  Sittingbourne ME10 ... 37 C4
Lansdowne Ave. ME15 ... 97 C6
Lansdowne Ct. **2** ME4 ... 9 F4
Lansdowne
  Cty Prim Sch. ME10 ... 37 C3
Lansdowne Rd. ME4 ... 9 E2
Lanthorne Rd. CT10 ... 30 A6
Lapwing Dr. ME9 ... 13 B3
Larch Cl. CT10 ... 29 D4
Larch Rd. CT5 ... 114 B1
Larch Terr. ME12 ... 3 A8
Larch Wlk. TN24 ... 139 C6
Larch Wood Cl. ME5 ... 32 D1
Larchcroft. ME5 ... 32 A4
Larches The. Faversham ME13 ... 64 B7
Larches The. Whitstable CT5 ... 43 C8
Larkey View. CT4 ... 86 E1
Larkfield Ave. Gillingham ME7 ... 10 E4
Larkfield Ave.
  Sittingbourne ME10 ... 36 F6
Larksfield Rd. ME13 ... 40 C1
Larkspur Rd. ME5 ... 31 E4
Lascelles Rd. CT17 ... 166 A6
Laser Quay. ME2 ... 9 D6
Latchgate. CT20 ... 177 C3
Lathe Barn (Mus). TN29 ... 186 D5
Latimer Cl. CT6 ... 22 B2
Latimer Pl. **3** ME7 ... 10 C7
Launder Way. ME15 ... 74 E2
Laundry Rd. CT12 ... 50 D7
Laureate Cl. CT9 ... 8 B2
Laurel Ave. TN29 ... 194 F4
Laurel Cl. CT20 ... 177 E6
Laurel Gr. ME17 ... 99 D2
Laurel Ho. ME12 ... 1 C2
Laurel Rd. ME7 ... 10 C7
Laurel Wlk. ME8 ... 33 E6
Laurels The. ME6 ... 74 C2
Laureston Pl. CT16 ... 166 E8
Laurie Gray Ave. ME5 ... 31 D1
Lauriston Cl. CT11 ... 52 A5
Lauriston Mount. CT10 ... 30 A5
Lausanne Rd. CT9 ... 7 J2
Lausanne Terr. **11** CT9 ... 7 J2
Lavenda Cl. ME7 ... 33 A4
Lavender Cl. **1** Chatham ME5 ... 31 E4
Lavender Cl. Margate CT9 ... 28 C8
Lavender Cl. Whitstable CT5 ... 21 C2
Lavender Ct. ME10 ... 37 A3
Laverstoke Rd. ME16 ... 74 C8
Lawley Cl. CT12 ... 29 C1
Lawn Cl. ME4 ... 10 B2
Lawn Cl. Broadstairs CT10 ... 30 A4
Lawn Rd. Deal CT14 ... 117 C1
Lawns The. **13** CT11 ... 52 F7
Lawrence Cl. Folkestone CT19 ... 177 F6
Lawrence Cl. Maidstone ME15 ... 97 A7
Lawrence Ct. CT19 ... 178 E6
Lawrence Gdns. CT6 ... 23 C4
Lawrence St. ME7 ... 10 C5
Laws La. TN25 ... 172 D7
Lawson Cl. CT4 ... 86 D2
Laxey The. ME15 ... 74 E1
Laxton Cl. ME15 ... 75 F3
Laxton Dr. ME17 ... 98 A1
Laxton Way. Canterbury CT1 ... 88 C7
Laxton Way. Faversham ME13 ... 62 C5
Laxton Way. Sittingbourne ME10 ... 36 C6
Laxton Way. Whitstable CT5 ... 21 C1
Lay La. CT3 ... 71 D2
Layfield Rd. ME7 ... 10 F7
Laylam Cl. CT10 ... 29 D5

Lea Cl. CT21 ...... 176 B4
Lea Ct. ME4 ...... 9 E1
Leacon Cotts. TN27 ...... 120 E4
Leacon Cotts The. TN27 ...... 120 E4
Leacon Rd. TN23 ...... 138 F2
Leafield. TN25 ...... 159 D1
Leafy Glade. ME8 ...... 33 B6
Leahurst Ct. CT16 ...... 148 E4
Leander Rd. ME1 ...... 31 C7
Learoyd Rd. TN28 ...... 200 C6
Leas Cl. CT10 ...... 29 D4
Leas Rd. CT14 ...... 117 B4
Leas The. Faversham ME13 ...... 62 B8
Leas The. Folkestone CT20 ...... 178 C4
Leas The. Kingsdown CT14 ...... 134 D3
Leas The. Minster ME12 ...... 4 C8
Leas The. Sheerness ME12 ...... 1 I1
Leas The. Whitstable CT5 ...... 21 C1
Leaside Cotts. CT21 ...... 176 B3
Leatt Cl. CT10 ...... 29 F4
Leaveland Cl. Ashford TN23 ...... 155 E6
Leaveland Cl. Ashford TN23 ...... 155 F6
Leaveland Cotts. ME13 ...... 83 B2
Leda Cotts. TN25 ...... 120 F3
Leeds & Broomfield
  CE Prim Sch. ME17 ...... 99 A7
Leeds Castle. ME17 ...... 99 D7
Leeds Rd. ME17 ...... 98 E3
Leeds Sq. ME8 ...... 11 B3
Leelands Ho. CT14 ...... 117 B1
Lees Cl The. TN25 ...... 158 D5
Lees Court Rd. ME13 ...... 83 C5
Lees Rd. Ashford TN24 ...... 140 A1
Lees Rd. Brabourne Lees TN25 ...... 158 E6
Lees Terr. CT4 ...... 85 C2
Lees The. Herne Bay CT6 ...... 23 C5
Lees The. Herne Bay CT6 ...... 23 D5
Leet Cl. ME7 ...... 10 E6
Leeward Rd. ME1 ...... 9 C1
Leggett's La. [4] CT5 ...... 20 D2
Leicester Ave. CT9 ...... 8 C2
Leicester Gdns. ME12 ...... 6 E3
Leicester Rd. ME15 ...... 97 D7
Leigh Ave. ME15 ...... 97 B6
Leigh Cl. ME12 ...... 3 F5
Leigh Green Ind Est. TN30 ...... 179 E6
Leighton Cl. [3] CT16 ...... 149 C1
Leighton Rd. CT16 ...... 149 C1
Leighville Dr. CT6 ...... 22 D4
Leivers Rd. CT14 ...... 117 A3
Len Valley Wlk. ME15 ...... 75 F1
Lenacre Ave. CT16 ...... 148 F7
Lenacre La. CT16 ...... 148 F8
Lenacre St. TN25 ...... 122 B2
Lenfield Ave. ME14 ...... 75 B4
Length The. CT7 ...... 25 F2
Lenham Cl. ME10 ...... 30 A2
Lenham Cty Prim Sch. ME17 ...... 101 C5
Lenham Forstal Rd. ME17 ...... 119 B8
Lenham Gdns. CT9 ...... 28 B8
Lenham Heath Rd. ME17 ...... 101 C2
Lenham Ho. ME17 ...... 101 E5
Lenham Rd. ME17 ...... 100 C1
Lenham Sta. ME17 ...... 101 C4
Lenham Way. ME8 ...... 11 A3
Lennard Ct. [3] CT20 ...... 178 E5
Lennard Rd. CT20 ...... 178 E5
Lenside Dr. ME15 ...... 76 A2
Leona Ct. [8] CT9 ...... 8 B2
Leonard Cl. ME16 ...... 74 B6
Leonard Rd. Chatham ME4 ...... 10 B3
Leonard Rd.
  Greatstone-on-S TN29 ...... 204 E7
Leonard's Ave. CT11 ...... 29 E1
Leopold Ct. [2] Chatham ME4 ...... 10 A3
Leopold Rd. Ramsgate CT11 ...... 52 E8
Leopold St. CT11 ...... 52 E6
Lerryn Gdns. CT10 ...... 29 F8
Les Spickett Cl. ME13 ...... 62 E6
Lesley Ave. CT1 ...... 88 A6
Leslie Ave. CT9 ...... 28 B8
Leslie Cres. TN30 ...... 167 B2
Leslie Pl. ME16 ...... 74 E5
Leslie Rd. Birchington CT7 ...... 27 A8
Leslie Rd. Gillingham ME7 ...... 10 D7
Leslie Smith Dr. ME13 ...... 62 C7
Lested La. ME17 ...... 98 B2
Lester Rd. ME4 ...... 10 A3
Letchworth Ave. ME4 ...... 9 F1
Lewd La. TN27 ...... 135 A3
Lewis Ave. ME8 ...... 11 B2
Lewis Cl. ME13 ...... 62 A7
Lewis Court Dr. ME17 ...... 97 C3
Lewis Cres. CT9 ...... 8 B3
Lewis Ct. TN23 ...... 155 F7
Lewisham Rd. CT17 ...... 148 E4
Leybourn Rd. CT10 ...... 30 B2
Leybourne Cl. ME5 ...... 32 A2
Leybourne Dr. CT9 ...... 28 B8
Leyburne Rd. CT16 ...... 166 D8
Leycroft Cl. CT2 ...... 66 E3
Leys The. CT12 ...... 28 D1
Leysdown Rd. Eastchurch ME12 ...... 5 E3
Leysdown Rd.
  Leysdown-on-S ME12 ...... 6 C1
Leyton Ave. ME7 ...... 10 E1
Libya Terr. [6] ME14 ...... 75 A7
Lichfield Ave. CT1 ...... 88 B6
Lichfield Cl. ME8 ...... 11 D2
Lidsing Rd. ME14 ...... 54 E6
Liege Cl. ME10 ...... 37 A7
Lighthouse Rd. CT15 ...... 151 A5
Lilac Ho. ME12 ...... 1 C2
Lilk Hill. ME14 ...... 76 C3
Lillian Rd. CT11 ...... 52 F8
Lilyvale Cotts. TN25 ...... 158 F4

Lime Cl. TN23 ...... 138 F3
Lime Ct. ME8 ...... 33 C3
Lime Gr. Halfway Houses ME8 ...... 3 D5
Lime Gr. Sittingbourne ME10 ...... 37 A4
Lime Kiln Rd. CT1 ...... 87 F6
Lime Kiln Wharf. ME11 ...... 3 A5
Lime Villas. CT4 ...... 144 F5
Limes Cl. TN30 ...... 179 C8
Limes Pl. [15] ME13 ...... 62 D7
Limes Rd. Dover CT16 ...... 149 C1
Limes Rd. Folkestone CT19 ...... 177 F6
Limes The. Lenham ME17 ...... 101 D5
Limes The. Old Romney TN29 ...... 199 A7
Limetree Cl. ME5 ...... 32 B8
Limetree Terr. ME17 ...... 101 E6
Linces The. CT16 ...... 149 B4
Lincoln Ave. CT1 ...... 88 B7
Lincoln Cl. CT5 ...... 21 D3
Lincoln Gdns. CT7 ...... 26 F7
Lincoln Rd. ME15 ...... 97 D8
Lincon Rd. ME7 ...... 10 D7
Linden Ave. Broadstairs CT10 ...... 30 B5
Linden Ave. Herne Bay CT6 ...... 22 E4
Linden Ave. Whitstable CT5 ...... 20 F1
Linden Chase. CT2 ...... 66 E1
Linden Cl. Sittingbourne ME10 ...... 36 D3
Linden Cl. Westgate-on-S CT8 ...... 27 E7
Linden Cres. CT19 ...... 178 D6
Linden Dr. ME12 ...... 3 A7
Linden Gr. CT2 ...... 66 E1
Linden Grove
  Cty Prim Sch. TN23 ...... 155 F6
Linden Ho. [5] ME5 ...... 31 F4
Linden Rd. Ashford TN24 ...... 139 D1
Linden Rd. Coxheath ME17 ...... 96 C4
Linden Rd. Gillingham ME7 ...... 11 C1
Linden Rd. Westgate-on-S CT8 ...... 27 F8
Lindens. CT21 ...... 176 D2
Lindenthorpe Rd. CT10 ...... 30 A6
Lindfield Cotts. ME13 ...... 62 A6
Lindridge Cl. CT6 ...... 46 A8
Lineacre Cl. ME5 ...... 33 D6
Lines Terr. ME4 ...... 10 A4
Linington Rd. CT7 ...... 27 A6
Link Hill La. TN27 ...... 118 D3
Link La. CT1 ...... 88 A8
Link Rd. Broadstairs CT10 ...... 29 F7
Link Rd. Tyler Hill CT2 ...... 66 E6
Link The. TN23 ...... 155 E7
Links Cl. CT6 ...... 23 A3
Links Cl. CT6 ...... 23 A3
Links Cres. TN29 ...... 195 A4
Links Ct. CT14 ...... 95 C1
Links The. ME5 ...... 32 B8
Links Way. TN28 ...... 200 D6
Linksfield Rd. CT8 ...... 27 D7
Linksway. CT19 ...... 178 B8
Linksway Cl. CT19 ...... 178 B8
Linkway. ME9 ...... 14 D4
Linley Ho. CT10 ...... 29 E7
Linley Rd. CT10 ...... 29 E7
Linnet Ave. CT5 ...... 43 B6
Linton Gore. ME17 ...... 96 D3
Linton Hill. ME17 ...... 96 E1
Linton Hospl. ME17 ...... 96 C2
Linton Rd. ME15 ...... 96 F4
Lion Field. ME13 ...... 62 B7
Lion Yd. Faversham ME13 ...... 62 A6
Lion Yd. [3] Sittingbourne ME10 ...... 36 F4
Lion's Rd. TN28 ...... 200 A6
Lionard Ho. [3] CT2 ...... 66 E1
Liphook Way. ME16 ...... 74 C8
Lisa Ct. CT5 ...... 21 A2
Lismore Cl. ME15 ...... 97 A7
Lismore Rd. Herne Bay CT6 ...... 23 D5
Lismore Rd. Whitstable CT5 ...... 44 B8
Liss Rd. CT13 ...... 93 A1
List The. CT3 ...... 69 C2
Lister Cl. Deal CT14 ...... 117 C5
Lister Cl. Dover CT17 ...... 149 B1
Lister Ho. CT10 ...... 29 A8
Lister Rd. CT9 ...... 29 A8
Lister Way. CT20 ...... 177 F3
Listmas Rd. ME4 ...... 10 B3
Listways Cotts. CT3 ...... 113 B6
Little Ave. CT14 ...... 116 F3
Little Brook Rd. TN23 ...... 139 A3
Little Buckland Ave. ME16 ...... 74 D6
Little Charles St. CT16 ...... 22 F5
Little Chequers. TN25 ...... 123 E2
Little Cl. ME16 ...... 74 D2
Little Glovers. ME10 ...... 36 F3
Little Hempen. TN23 ...... 155 D8
Little Hill. TN30 ...... 167 B2
Little John Ave. ME5 ...... 31 F2
Little Kit's Coty Ho. ME20 ...... 53 C5
Little Knoll. TN23 ...... 155 F8
Little Meadow. CT2 ...... 65 E1
Little Orch. ME17 ...... 96 D3
Little Paddocks. CT5 ...... 44 D7
Little Stone Stile Cotts. ME13 ...... 84 F4
Little Walton. CT13 ...... 93 C3
Littlebourne Ave. ME8 ...... 11 B4
Littlebourne CE Prim Sch. CT3 ...... 89 F8
Littlebourne Rd.
  Canterbury CT1 & CT3 ...... 88 E8
Littlebourne Rd.
  Maidstone ME14 ...... 75 C6
Littlebrook Cl. TN23 ...... 139 A3
Littlemead. CT19 ...... 178 A7
Littlestone Golf Course.
  TN28 ...... 200 E8
Littlestone Rd. TN28 ...... 200 D6
Liverpool Lawn. [15] CT11 ...... 52 E6

Liverpool Rd. CT14 ...... 117 D2
Livingstone Circ. ME7 ...... 10 D5
Livingstone Cl. TN29 ...... 187 B4
Livingstone Rd.
  Broadstairs CT10 ...... 29 E6
Livingstone Rd. Gillingham ME7 ...... 10 E5
Livingstone Wlk. [4] ME15 ...... 97 F5
Llamas Gate. ME13 ...... 62 D8
Lloyd Rd. CT10 ...... 30 A4
Lloyds Gn. TN30 ...... 188 D4
Loach Ho. ME1 ...... 9 D1
Loading Bay App. CT12 & CT13 ...... 73 A8
Loaland Bsns Ctr. ME2 ...... 9 D8
Lobelia Cl. ME7 ...... 10 E6
Locarno Ave. ME8 ...... 11 A2
Lock La. ME4 & ME16 ...... 53 D1
Lock St. ME7 ...... 10 C5
Lockenden Cotts. CT3 ...... 89 D6
Lockholt Cl. TN23 ...... 138 E3
Lockington Gr. ME1 ...... 9 C5
Locksley Cl. ME5 ...... 31 E2
Lockswood. ME16 ...... 74 D7
Loddington La. ME17 ...... 97 A1
Loder Cl. ME17 ...... 101 B5
Lodge Cl. CT2 ...... 66 A7
Lodge Rd. ME14 ...... 75 D5
Lodge The. TN24 ...... 139 D7
Lomas Rd. ME10 & ME9 ...... 37 D4
Lombard St. CT9 ...... 7 I3
Lombardy Cl. ME7 ...... 33 A6
Lombardy Dr. ME14 ...... 75 C5
London Rd. Canterbury CT2 ...... 66 D1
London Rd. Deal CT14 ...... 117 B5
London Rd.
  Dover CT16 & CT17 ...... 149 B1
London Rd.
  Faversham ME13 & ME9 ...... 61 C7
London Rd. Faversham ME13 ...... 63 A5
London Rd.
  Gillingham ME8 ...... 11 C1
London Rd.
  Hartlip Hill ME8 & ME9 ...... 34 D7
London Rd. Hythe CT21 ...... 175 F3
London Rd. Maidstone ME16 ...... 74 C6
London Rd. Newington ME9 ...... 35 A6
London Rd. Ramsgate CT11 ...... 52 B6
London Rd. Rochester ME2 ...... 9 A7
London Rd. Sittingbourne ME10 ...... 36 C4
London Rd.
  Temple Ewell CT15 & CT16 ...... 148 B6
London Rd. Teynham ME9 ...... 38 C1
London Road (River).
  CT16 & CT17 ...... 148 F4
London Road Temple Ewell.
  CT16 ...... 148 D5
London Road Trad Est. ME10 ...... 36 D4
London St. CT20 ...... 178 E5
Lone Barn Rd. ME17 ...... 102 B8
Lonefield. TN26 ...... 155 B1
Long Acre Cl. CT2 ...... 66 E2
Long Barrow The. TN24 ...... 156 E6
Long Beech. TN23 ...... 138 E1
Long Catlis Rd. ME8 ...... 33 D4
Long Dr. CT13 ...... 93 C2
Long Hill. CT4 ...... 85 C1
Long La. CT13 ...... 130 D7
Long Length. TN23 ...... 155 D4
Long Market. [2] TN23 ...... 88 A8
Long Meadow Way. CT2 ...... 67 A4
Long Reach Cl. CT5 ...... 43 C6
Long Rede La. ME16 ...... 74 A3
Long Rock. CT5 ...... 21 C3
Long Row. TN25 ...... 157 D2
Long Wlk. TN23 ...... 138 E4
Long's Acre. TN25 ...... 123 E1
Longacre. CT5 ...... 21 D1
Longacre Rd. TN23 ...... 155 D7
Longage Hill. CT18 & CT4 ...... 144 A1
Longbridge. TN24 ...... 140 B1
Longbridge Terr. CT21 ...... 175 F1
Longfellow Rd. ME7 ...... 10 C3
Longfield. TN30 ...... 179 A6
Longfield Cl. CT5 ...... 21 D2
Longfield Pl. ME15 ...... 97 C8
Longfield Rd. CT17 ...... 166 B7
Longfields Dr. ME14 ...... 76 A5
Longford Cl. ME8 ...... 34 A8
Longford Ct. ME8 ...... 34 A8
Longford Terr. [9] CT20 ...... 178 D4
Longford Way. [10] CT20 ...... 178 D4
Longham Copse. ME15 ...... 75 F1
Longhill Ave. ME7 ...... 10 B3
Longhurst Dr. ME5 ...... 31 F2
Longley Rd. Gillingham ME8 ...... 11 F1
Longley Rd. Rochester ME1 ...... 9 C4
Longmead Cl. CT6 ...... 22 C3
Longmete Rd. CT3 ...... 70 C5
Longmore Dr. ME8 ...... 5 C1
Longparish Cl. ME15 ...... 97 E5
Longport. CT1 ...... 88 B8
Longridge. ME10 ...... 37 B2
Longsfield. TN25 ...... 173 A6
Longshaw Rd. ME15 ...... 97 F5
Longtye Dr. CT5 ...... 44 C7
Longwood. ME5 ...... 32 B1
Lonsdale Ave. CT9 ...... 8 C3
Lonsdale Dr. Gillingham ME8 ...... 33 E7
Lonsdale Dr. Herne Bay CT6 ...... 22 B5
Lonsdale Dr.
  Sittingbourne ME10 ...... 36 C5
Lookers La. CT21 ...... 176 B3
Loop Court Mews. CT13 ...... 72 F1
Loop St. CT13 ...... 72 F1
Loose Cty Prim Sch. ME15 ...... 97 A6
Loose Down Rd. ME13 ...... 104 F7
Loose Rd. ME15 ...... 97 A7
Lord Romney's Hill. ME14 ...... 75 F3

Lord Warden Ave. CT14 ...... 117 D2
Lord Warden Sq. CT17 ...... 166 D5
Lords Cl. ME9 ...... 37 E2
Lords Cotts. ME13 ...... 83 C4
Lords Wood Cl. ME5 ...... 32 B3
Lords Wood La. ME5 ...... 32 B3
Lordswood Cty Prim Sch. ME5 ...... 32 B3
Lordswood Ind Est. ME5 ...... 54 C8
Lorina Rd. CT12 ...... 52 C8
Lorne Cotts. CT14 ...... 117 C7
Lorne Rd. Dover CT16 ...... 149 B2
Lorne Rd. Ramsgate CT11 ...... 52 C6
Lorraine Cl. [1] CT19 ...... 178 E6
Loudon Ct. TN23 ...... 138 E3
Loudon Path. TN23 ...... 138 E3
Loudon Way. TN23 ...... 138 E3
Loughborough Ct. [2] CT11 ...... 52 E7
Louisville Ave. ME7 ...... 10 D4
Love La. Adisham CT3 ...... 90 D7
Love La. Canterbury CT1 ...... 88 A8
Love La. Faversham ME13 ...... 62 F6
Love La. Margate CT9 ...... 7 I3
Love La. Minster ME12 ...... 4 D7
Love La. Rochester ME1 ...... 9 C5
Love Street Cl. CT6 ...... 22 C2
Lovelace Cl. ME8 ...... 33 D4
Lovelace Ct. TN26 ...... 153 C5
Lovell Rd. Minster ME12 ...... 4 A5
Lovell Rd. Rough Common CT2 ...... 66 B3
Lower Blackhouse Hill. CT21 ...... 176 D3
Lower Boxley Rd. [8] ME14 ...... 75 A3
Lower Bridge St. CT1 ...... 88 A8
Lower Chantry La. CT1 ...... 88 A8
Lower Denmark Rd. TN23 ...... 156 E8
Lower East Rd. ME4 ...... 10 B8
Lower Ensden Rd. CT4 ...... 85 D4
Lower Fant Rd. ME16 ...... 74 D2
Lower Gore La. CT13 ...... 93 B3
Lower Halstow
  Cty Prim Sch. ME9 ...... 13 B2
Lower Hartlip Rd. ME9 ...... 34 E5
Lower Herne Rd. CT6 ...... 45 E8
Lower Lees Rd. CT4 ...... 85 D2
Lower Mill La. CT14 ...... 117 C5
Lower Northdown Ave. CT9 ...... 8 B2
Lower Rainham Rd.
  Gillingham ME8 ...... 12 A3
Lower Rainham Rd.
  Gillingham, Lower Twydall ME7 ...... 11 D5
Lower Rd. East Farleigh ME15 ...... 96 B7
Lower Rd. Faversham ME13 ...... 61 C8
Lower Rd. Maidstone ME15 ...... 75 B3
Lower Rd. Minster ME12 ...... 3 E4
Lower Rd. Minster ME12 ...... 4 E4
Lower Rd. River CT16 & CT17 ...... 148 B8
Lower Rd. Staple CT3 ...... 92 B6
Lower Rd. Temple Ewell CT16 ...... 148 D5
Lower Rd. Teynham ME9 ...... 38 B3
Lower Rd.
  Teynham ME9 & ME13 ...... 38 E2
Lower Rd. Wittersham TN30 ...... 189 D5
Lower Rd. Woodchurch ME26 ...... 169 B1
Lower Rd E. CT16 ...... 166 H8
Lower Rd W. CT16 ...... 166 G8
Lower Sandgate Rd. CT20 ...... 178 C4
Lower Sands. TN29 ...... 186 E2
Lower Santon La. CT3 ...... 70 D7
Lower St. Eastry CT13 ...... 93 B1
Lower St. Leeds ME17 ...... 99 A7
Lower St. Tilmanstone CT14 ...... 115 A2
Lower Stone St. ME15 ...... 75 A3
Lower Tovil. ME15 ...... 74 E2
Lower Twydall La. ME7 & ME8 ...... 11 C4
Lower Vicarage Rd. TN24 ...... 139 D7
Lower Wall Rd.
  CT21 & TN29 & TN25 ...... 186 D8
Lower Warren Rd.
  ME5 & ME14 ...... 53 E6
Lower Woodlands Rd. ME7 ...... 11 A6
Lowfield Rd. ME12 ...... 3 E6
Lowslip Hill. CT15 ...... 165 A5
Lowther Rd. CT17 ...... 166 B8
Loxwood Cl. CT16 ...... 149 B7
Lubbock Cl. ME15 ...... 97 E5
Lubbock Wlk. ME15 ...... 33 D5
Lucerne Cl. CT5 ...... 42 F6
Lucerne Dr. CT5 ...... 42 F6
Lucerne La. CT5 ...... 133 C2
Lucerne St. ME14 ...... 75 A5
Luckhurst Gdns. CT9 ...... 8 E3
Luckhurst Rd. Ashford TN24 ...... 157 A2
Luckhurst Rd. River TN17 ...... 148 E3
Lucknow Cl. CT16 ...... 149 F3
Lucy Ave. CT19 ...... 178 B7
Lucy's Hill. CT21 ...... 176 B2
Luddenham Cl. Ashford TN24 ...... 155 F6
Luddenham Cl.
  Maidstone ME14 ...... 75 C6
Luddenham
  Cty Prim Sch. ME13 ...... 39 E1
Ludgate Rd. ME9 ...... 59 F5
Lukes Cl. CT17 ...... 149 B1
Lullingstone Cl. ME7 ...... 33 B3
Lullingstone Ct. [15] CT1 ...... 87 F8
Lullingstone Rd. ME16 ...... 74 C7
Lumsden Terr. ME4 ...... 9 E4
Lushington Rd. ME14 ...... 74 E7
Luton Ave. CT10 ...... 29 F3
Luton Cl. CT10 ...... 29 F3
Luton Cty Inf Sch. ME5 ...... 10 C2
Luton Cty Jun Sch. ME4 ...... 10 C2
Luton High St. ME5 ...... 10 C2
Luton Rd. Chatham ME5 ...... 10 C2
Luton Rd. Faversham ME13 ...... 62 E7
Lyall Way. ME8 ...... 33 E4
Lychfield Dr. ME2 ...... 9 A8
Lydbrook Cl. ME10 ...... 36 D4
Lydd Airport. TN28 ...... 204 A7

Lydd Cty Prim Sch. TN29 ...... 203 C6
Lydd Golf Course. TN29 ...... 199 F1
Lydd Rd. Camber TN31 ...... 201 C1
Lydd Rd. Chatham ME5 ...... 32 B5
Lydd Rd. New Romney TN28 ...... 199 F6
Lydd Town Crossing. TN29 ...... 203 D8
Lydden Cty Prim Sch. CT15 ...... 147 F8
Lydden Hill. CT15 ...... 130 C1
Lydden International
  Motor Racing Circuit. CT4 ...... 129 F3
Lydia Rd. CT14 ...... 117 A2
Lydos Cl. TN29 ...... 204 E5
Lyeat Ct. CT2 ...... 66 C4
Lyell Cl. CT21 ...... 176 A1
Lyell Cl. [5] CT7 ...... 26 F8
Lyell Rd. CT7 ...... 26 F8
Lyle Cl. ME2 ...... 9 B8
Lyle Ct. ME16 ...... 74 C5
Lyminge CE Prim Sch. CT18 ...... 161 C7
Lyminge Cl. ME8 ...... 11 C2
Lyminge Way. CT9 ...... 8 C1
Lymington Cl. ME15 ...... 97 F4
Lymington Rd. CT8 ...... 27 E7
Lympne Castle. CT21 ...... 174 F2
Lympne CE Prim Sch. CT21 ...... 175 A3
Lympne Hill. CT21 ...... 175 A2
Lympne Ind Est. CT21 ...... 174 E3
Lyndhurst Ave. Gillingham ME8 ...... 33 C7
Lyndhurst Ave. Margate CT9 ...... 8 B2
Lyndhurst Cl. CT2 ...... 66 E3
Lyndhurst Gr. ME10 ...... 36 E2
Lyndhurst Rd. Broadstairs CT10 ...... 30 A6
Lyndhurst Rd.
  Dymchurch TN29 ...... 195 C8
Lyndhurst Rd. Maidstone ME15 ...... 97 C8
Lyndhurst Rd. Ramsgate CT11 ...... 52 F7
Lyndhurst Rd. River CT17 ...... 148 E3
Lyndon Way. CT18 ...... 161 C7
Lyngate Ct. CT9 ...... 8 D2
Lynmouth Dr. ME12 ...... 4 C7
Lynstead Ho. ME16 ...... 74 A1
Lynsted Cl. TN23 ...... 155 F6
Lynsted La. ME9 ...... 60 B7
Lynsted & Norton
  Cty Prim Sch. ME9 ...... 60 B7
Lynsted Rd. Gillingham ME8 ...... 11 B3
Lynsted Rd. Halfway Houses ME8 ...... 3 E7
Lynton Court Mansions. CT9 ...... 8 B3
Lynton Dr. ME5 ...... 32 B3
Lynton Pl. CT4 ...... 89 A1
Lynton Rd. CT21 ...... 176 C1
Lynwood. CT19 ...... 178 C7
Lysander Cl. Broadstairs CT10 ...... 29 C3
Lysander Cl. Littlebourne CT4 ...... 89 E4
Lysander Wlk. CT18 ...... 163 A4
Lytham Ave. CT6 ...... 22 D1

Mabledon Ave. TN24 ...... 139 D1
Mabledon Cl. TN28 ...... 200 B6
Macdonald Par. CT5 ...... 43 A6
Macdonald Rd. Dover CT17 ...... 149 A1
Macdonald Rd. Gillingham ME7 ...... 10 D6
Mace Ind Est. TN24 ...... 139 C3
Mace La. TN23 & TN24 ...... 139 C2
Mace Terr. TN26 ...... 155 A1
Mackenders Cl. ME20 ...... 53 A6
Mackenders Gn. ME20 ...... 53 A6
Mackenders La. ME20 ...... 53 A6
Mackenzie Dr. CT20 ...... 177 E5
Mackeson Ct. [6] CT21 ...... 176 B2
Macklands Way. ME8 ...... 12 A2
Madden Ave. ME5 ...... 31 E5
Madeira Ct. CT20 ...... 178 B3
Madeira Rd.
  Littlebourne-on-S TN28 ...... 200 E6
Madeira Rd. Margate CT9 ...... 8 A2
Madeira Wlk. CT11 ...... 52 E6
Madginford Cl. ME15 ...... 76 A2
Madginford Park
  Cty Inf Sch. ME15 ...... 76 A2
Madginford Park
  Cty Jun Sch. ME15 ...... 76 A2
Madginford Rd. ME15 ...... 75 F2
Madras Ho. [2] ME15 ...... 97 E5
Mafeking Rd. ME5 ...... 31 F3
Magazine Rd. TN24 ...... 139 B3
Magdala Rd. Broadstairs CT10 ...... 29 E6
Magdala Rd. Dover CT17 ...... 149 B1
Magdalen Cl. ME7 ...... 33 A4
Magdalen Ct. Broadstairs CT10 ...... 30 A6
Magdalen Ct. Canterbury CT1 ...... 88 B7
Magness Rd. CT14 ...... 117 A2
Magnolia Ave. Gillingham ME8 ...... 33 B8
Magnolia Ave. Margate CT9 ...... 8 D2
Magnolia Rise. CT6 ...... 23 D2
Magpie Cl. ME12 ...... 4 A6
Magpie Hall Rd. Chatham ME4 ...... 10 A2
Magpie Hall Rd.
  Stubb's Cross TN26 ...... 155 E2
Magpie La. Rhodes Minnis CT4 ...... 144 B3
Magpie La.
  Yelstead ME9 & ME14 ...... 33 F1
Magwitch Cl. ME1 ...... 9 B4
Maida Rd. ME4 ...... 10 B2
Maidstone Barracks Sta. ME16 ...... 74 E5
Maidstone East Sta. ME14 ...... 74 F5
Maidstone Gram Sch. ME15 ...... 75 B2
Maidstone Gram Sch
  for Girls. ME16 ...... 74 E5
Maidstone Hospl The. ME16 ...... 74 A4
Maidstone Ind Ctr. ME14 ...... 74 F5
Maidstone Mus & Art Gallery.
  ME14 ...... 74 F5
Maidstone Rd. Ashford
  TN23 & TN24 & TN25 & TN26 ...... 138 D7

224 Mai – Mil

Maidstone Rd.
Charing TN25 & TN26 & TN27 ... 120 D6
Maidstone Rd. Chatham ME4 .... 9 F2
Maidstone Rd.
Chatham,Walderslade ME5 .... 31 D4
Maidstone Rd.
Chestnut Street ME9 .... 35 D4
Maidstone Rd. Five Wents ME17 98 E2
Maidstone Rd. Gillingham ME8 ... 33 C6
Maidstone Rd.
Gillingham,Bredhurst ME7 .... 33 B2
Maidstone Rd. Lenham ME17 ... 101 D5
Maidstone Rd. Rochester ME1 ... 9 C3
Maidstone St Francis Sch.
ME14 .... 75 A5
Maidstone West Sta. ME16 .... 74 F3
Mailyns The. ME8 .... 33 D7
Main Gate Rd. ME4 .... 9 F7
Main Rd.
Queenborough ME11 & ME12 .... 3 B5
Main Rd. Sheerness ME12 .... 1 B3
Maine Cl. CT16 .... 149 B3
Maison Des Fleurs. ME16 .... 74 C2
Maison Dieu Pl. 4 CT16 .... 166 D8
Maison Dieu Rd. CT16 .... 166 D8
Maitland Ct. ME13 .... 40 B1
Makenade Ave. ME13 .... 62 E6
Malcolm Sargent Rd. TN23 .... 156 B5
Malden Dr. ME14 .... 75 A8
Mall The. ME13 .... 62 C6
Mallard Apartments. 12 ME15 .. 97 E5
Mallard Ct. ME12 .... 4 A6
Mallards. TN24 .... 156 D7
Mallards Way. ME15 .... 76 A1
Malling Terr. ME16 .... 74 C4
Mallings Dr. ME14 .... 76 C4
Mallings La. ME14 .... 76 C4
Mallory Cl. CT12 .... 29 C2
Mallow Way. 1 ME5 .... 31 F4
Mallows The. ME14 .... 74 E7
Malmains Rd. CT17 .... 166 A6
Malt House La. TN30 .... 179 A7
Malta Ave. ME5 .... 32 A7
Malta Ho. 17 CT1 .... 67 B2
Malta Terr. 5 ME14 .... 75 A7
Malthouse Cl. ME17 .... 101 D5
Malthouse Cotts. TN28 .... 200 A6
Malthouse Hill. 10 Hythe CT21 . 176 B2
Malthouse Hill. Loose ME15 .... 96 F4
Malthouse La.
Boughton Aluph TN25 .... 123 A4
Malthouse La.
Hamstreet TN26 .... 170 D1
Malthouse Rd. CT2 .... 66 F2
Maltings The. Faversham ME13 .. 62 D8
Maltings The. Gillingham ME8 ..... 34 A8
Maltings The. Littlebourne CT3 ... 89 F7
Maltings The. Maidstone ME14 ... 75 E5
Maltings The. Ramsgate CT11 .... 52 D7
Maltings The.
The Quarries ME17 .... 97 B4
Malus Cl. ME5 .... 32 B1
Malvern Meadow. CT16 .... 148 E5
Malvern Pk. CT6 .... 23 D4
Malvern Rd. Ashford TN24 .... 139 B4
Malvern Rd. Dover CT17 .... 166 C7
Malvern Rd. Gillingham ME7 .... 10 E3
Malvern Rd. Temple Ewell CT16 148 E5
Mamignot Cl. ME14 .... 76 A5
Manchester Cl. ME5 .... 32 C6
Manciple Cl. CT2 .... 87 C8
Mandeville Ct. 1 ME14 .... 75 A5
Mandeville Rd. CT2 .... 66 E2
Mangers La. CT16 .... 149 A2
Mangers Pl. CT16 .... 149 A3
Mangravet Ave. ME15 .... 97 C7
Manktelow Ct. CT10 .... 29 F2
Manley Cl. CT16 .... 149 A7
Mannering Cl. CT17 .... 148 F3
Mannock Ho. 6 CT1 .... 67 B1
Manns Hill. CT4 .... 127 A6
Manor Ave. CT14 .... 117 B4
Manor Cl. Canterbury CT1 .... 87 C5
Manor Cl. Deal CT14 .... 117 A4
Manor Cl. Herne Bay CT6 .... 23 F6
Manor Cl. Maidstone ME14 .... 76 B3
Manor Cl. Rushenden ME11 .... 3 A3
Manor Cotts. Hernhill ME13 .... 64 B6
Manor Cotts. Langley ME17 .... 98 C5
Manor Ct. Canterbury CT1 .... 87 F7
Manor Ct. Gillingham ME7 .... 11 C4
Manor Ct. Maidstone ME14 .... 76 B3
Manor Dr. CT7 .... 26 F6
Manor Gdns. ME5 .... 31 F4
Manor Gr. ME10 .... 36 E3
Manor Ho. 8 ME7 .... 10 A6
Manor House Dr. ME16 .... 74 D3
Manor La. ME1 .... 9 A2
Manor Lea Rd. CT7 .... 25 F1
Manor Leaze. TN25 .... 158 F5
Manor Mews. CT14 .... 133 F5
Manor Pound La. TN25 .... 158 F7
Manor Rd. Broadstairs CT10 .... 30 A4
Manor Rd. Chatham ME4 .... 9 F4
Manor Rd. Deal CT14 .... 117 A4
Manor Rd. Dover CT17 .... 166 A6
Manor Rd. Folkestone CT20 .... 178 C4
Manor Rd. Herne Bay CT6 .... 23 F6
Manor Rd. Lydd TN29 .... 203 C6
Manor Rd. Milstead ME9 .... 58 F2
Manor Rd. Monkton CT12 & CT7 .. 49 A8
Manor Rd. Rushenden ME11 .... 3 A3
Manor Rd. Whitstable CT5 .... 21 A2
Manor Rise. Dover CT17 .... 166 A6
Manor Rise. Maidstone ME14 ...... 76 B3
Manor St. ME7 .... 10 A6
Manor Way. Ashford TN23 .... 138 F4
Manor Way.
Leysdown-on-S ME12 .... 6 H2
Manor Way. Warden ME12 .... 6 D6
Manorfield. Ashford TN23 .... 155 F8
Manorfield. Elham CT4 .... 144 F4
Manse Field. TN25 .... 158 E5
Mansel Dr. ME1 .... 9 A2
Mansell La. CT15 .... 146 B4
Mansfield Ct. CT4 .... 89 A1
Mansfield Wlk. ME16 .... 74 E2
Mansion Gdns. CT16 .... 149 A4
Mansion Row. ME7 .... 10 A6
Mansion St. CT9 .... 7 I3
Manston Court Cotts. CT12 .... 28 C2
Manston Court Rd. CT12 & CT9 . 28 D3
Manston Park Bglws. CT12 .... 27 F2
Manston Rd. Acol CT12 & CT7 .... 27 D4
Manston Rd. Lydden CT12 & CT9 . 28 C4
Manston Rd.
Ramsgate CT11 & CT12 .... 52 A8
Mantles Hill. CT14 .... 116 D1
Manwood Ave. CT2 .... 66 F3
Manwood Cl. ME10 .... 36 F2
Manwood Rd. CT13 .... 94 A8
Maple Ave. Gillingham ME7 .... 10 E6
Maple Ave. Maidstone ME16 .... 74 C6
Maple Cl. Ashford TN23 .... 138 E3
Maple Cl. Rough Common CT2 ...... 66 B3
Maple Ct. CT3 .... 68 E8
Maple Dr. TN29 .... 194 F4
Maple Gdns. CT3 .... 68 E8
Maple St. ME12 .... 1 D1
Maples The. Broadstairs CT10 .... 29 D4
Maples The. Minster ME12 .... 4 B6
Maplesden Noakes Sch The.
ME16 .... 74 E6
Maplins Cl. ME8 .... 11 F1
Marathon Paddock. ME7 .... 10 D4
Mardale Cl. ME8 .... 12 A1
Marden Ave. CT12 .... 52 B8
Mardol Rd. TN24 .... 139 C5
Maresfield Cl. CT16 .... 149 B2
Margaret Ct. CT6 .... 22 F4
Margaret St. 8 CT20 .... 178 E5
Margarets Rd. CT15 .... 134 A1
Margate Cl. ME7 .... 10 E6
Margate Hill. CT7 .... 27 C4
Margate Rd. Herne Bay CT6 .... 23 C3
Margate Rd.
Herne Bay, Broomfield CT6 .... 23 D2
Margate Rd.
Ramsgate CT10 & CT12 & CT11 .... 29 B3
Margate Sta. CT9 .... 7 H2
Marian Ave. ME12 .... 4 A7
Marilyn Cres. CT7 .... 27 B7
Marina Ct. CT14 .... 117 D8
Marina Dr. ME12 .... 4 A7
Marina Espl. CT11 .... 52 F7
Marina Rd. CT11 .... 52 F7
Marina The. CT14 .... 117 D8
Marine Ave. TN29 .... 186 F3
Marine Cres. 7
Folkestone CT20 .... 178 D4
Marine Cres. Whitstable CT5 .... 21 B3
Marine Ct. 13 CT16 .... 166 E7
Marine Dr. Broadstairs CT10 .... 8 G3
Marine Dr. Margate CT9 .... 7 I2
Marine Gap. CT5 .... 20 C1
Marine Gdns. CT9 .... 7 I2
Marine Par. Dover CT16 .... 166 E7
Marine Par. Dover CT16 .... 166 F8
Marine Par. Folkestone CT20 .... 178 E4
Marine Par. Hythe CT21 .... 176 C1
Marine Par.
Littlestone-on-S TN28 .... 200 E5
Marine Par. Sheerness ME12 .... 1 F2
Marine Par. Whitstable CT5 .... 21 A3
Marine Parade Mews. CT20 .... 178 E4
Marine Point. CT20 .... 178 A3
Marine Rd. CT14 .... 117 D4
Marine Terr. Folkestone CT20 ... 178 E4
Marine Terr. Margate CT9 .... 7 H2
Marine Terr. Whitstable CT5 .... 20 C1
Marine Walk St. CT21 .... 176 C2
Marion Cl. ME5 .... 32 A2
Marion Cres. ME15 .... 97 B8
Maritime Cl. ME2 .... 9 D8
Maritime Way. ME4 .... 10 A8
Marjan Cl. CT17 .... 149 A1
Mark Ave. CT11 .... 52 B5
Market Bldgs. 4 ME14 .... 74 F4
Market Colonnade. 3 ME14 .... 74 F4
Market Hill. CT21 .... 176 C2
Market La. 12 TN23 .... 139 B2
Market Pl. Aylesham CT3 .... 112 F5
Market Pl. Charing TN27 .... 120 C7
Market Pl. 1 Faversham ME13 ..... 62 D7
Market Pl. 16 Folkestone CT20 . 178 D5
Market Pl. Margate CT9 .... 7 I3
Market Sq. 12 CT16 .... 166 D7
Market St. Deal CT14 .... 117 D6
Market St. Faversham ME13 .... 62 D7
Market St. Herne Bay CT6 .... 22 F5
Market St. 2 Maidstone ME14 .... 74 F4
Market St. Margate CT9 .... 7 I3
Market St. Sandwich CT13 .... 73 A1
Market View. CT3 .... 112 F5
Market Way. CT2 .... 67 A2
Markland Rd. CT15 & CT17 .... 165 F7
Marlborough Cl.
Broadstairs CT10 .... 29 E3
Marlborough Cl.
Littlestone-on-S TN28 .... 200 D6
Marlborough Ct.
Folkestone CT20 .... 178 B4
Marlborough Ct. Hythe CT21 ... 176 D1
Marlborough Ho. ME8 .... 33 F8
Marlborough Rd. Deal CT14 ..... 117 A2
Marlborough Rd.
Dover CT15 & CT17 .... 165 F7
Marlborough Rd.
Gillingham ME7 .... 10 B5
Marlborough Rd. Margate CT9 ..... 7 I1
Marlborough Rd. 6
Ramsgate CT11 .... 52 D6
Marlborough Rd.
Whitstable CT5 .... 43 D5
Marlborough Way. TN24 .... 139 F7
Marler Rd. CT19 .... 177 E6
Marley Ct. CT2 .... 66 C4
Marley La. Chislet CT3 .... 47 A5
Marley La. Finglesham CT14 ..... 116 A8
Marley La. Kingston CT4 .... 111 B1
Marley La. Westwood CT4 .... 127 F8
Marley Rd. ME17 .... 100 F6
Marley Way. ME1 .... 9 C2
Marlow Cl. CT5 .... 21 B1
Marlow Copse. ME5 .... 31 F1
Marlowe Arc. 11 CT1 .... 87 F8
Marlowe Ave. CT1 .... 87 F8
Marlowe Ct. 15 CT1 .... 87 F8
Marlowe Rd. Ashford TN23 .... 139 B2
Marlowe Rd. Dover CT16 .... 149 B3
Marlowe Rd. Margate CT9 .... 29 C8
Marlpit Cotts. ME17 .... 97 E2
Marquis Dr. ME7 .... 33 B3
Marr Cl. ME12 .... 3 F7
Marrose Ave. CT12 .... 29 B3
Marrowbone Hill. ME12 .... 5 B5
Marsh Cres. TN28 .... 200 B6
Marsh Farm Rd. CT12 .... 50 B4
Marsh La. CT14 .... 117 A7
Marsh St. ME2 .... 9 B7
Marsh View. CT21 .... 187 C8
Marshall Cres.
Broadstairs CT10 .... 29 E4
Marshall Cres. Rushenden ME11 ... 2 F3
Marshall Rd. ME8 .... 33 C8
Marshall St. CT19 .... 178 E7
Marshalls Land. TN30 .... 167 A3
Marsham Cres. ME17 .... 98 B1
Marsham St. ME14 .... 75 A4
Marshborough Rd. CT13 .... 93 B7
Marshlands. TN29 .... 195 B7
Marshlands Cl. TN29 .... 195 B7
Marshwood Cl. CT1 .... 67 C3
Marstan Cl. ME9 .... 12 E2
Marston Cl. ME5 .... 31 E3
Marston Dr. ME14 .... 75 C5
Marston Wlk. ME5 .... 31 E3
Martello Cotts. CT21 .... 187 E8
Martello Dr. CT21 .... 175 F1
Martello Ind Ctr. CT19 .... 178 F6
Martello Rd. Folkestone CT20 ... 178 E6
Martello Rd.
Folkestone, Sandgate CT20 .... 177 E3
Martello Terr. 1 CT20 .... 177 F3
Marten Rd. CT20 .... 178 B5
Martha Cl. CT19 .... 178 B7
Martin Ct. ME7 .... 33 A3
Martin Dale Cres. CT15 .... 133 C2
Martin Ho. TN25 .... 123 E2
Martin Mill Sta. CT15 .... 133 C2
Martin Rd. ME2 .... 9 B8
Martin's Cl. CT12 .... 29 C2
Martin's Way. CT21 .... 187 D8
Martindale Cl. CT1 .... 88 A7
Martindown Rd. CT5 .... 43 C7
Martins Cl. TN30 .... 179 C8
Martins The. TN26 .... 168 A8
Martyrs' Field Rd. CT1 .... 87 F7
Mary Green Wlk. 5 CT1 .... 67 B2
Mary Haugham Almshouses.
CT14 .... 117 D7
Mary Rd. CT14 .... 117 A3
Maryland Ct. ME8 .... 33 E5
Mason's Rise. CT10 .... 30 A5
Masons Rd. CT17 .... 149 B1
Mate Hall Villas. ME14 .... 76 C4
Matfield Cres. ME14 .... 75 C5
Matilda Cl. ME7 .... 33 B8
Matthew's Pl. 9 CT16 .... 149 C1
Matthews Cl. CT14 .... 117 C6
Matthews Rd. CT6 .... 22 C2
Mattinson Pl. ME9 .... 78 F7
Matts Hill Rd. ME9 .... 33 E2
Maugham Ct. CT5 .... 43 D8
Maundene Cty Prim Sch. ME5 . 32 B5
Maunders Cl. ME5 .... 32 C8
Maunsell Pl. TN24 .... 156 D7
Maxine Gdns. CT10 .... 29 F5
Maxted Ct. CT6 .... 23 C4
Maxton Cl. Dover CT17 .... 166 A6
Maxton Cl. Maidstone ME14 .... 75 F5
Maxton Ct. CT17 .... 166 A6
Maxton Rd. CT17 .... 166 A6
Maxwell Dr. ME16 .... 74 B6
Maxwell Pl. CT14 .... 117 C4
Maxwell Rd. ME7 .... 10 A6
May Lodge. CT14 .... 117 D5
May Rd. Gillingham ME7 .... 10 C4
May Rd. Rochester ME1 .... 9 C3
May St. CT6 .... 23 F4
May Terr. 2 ME4 .... 10 A7
Maybrook Ind Est. CT1 .... 67 C3
Maydowns Rd. CT5 .... 21 D2
Mayers Rd. CT14 .... 117 A1
Mayfair. ME2 .... 9 C8
Mayfair Ave. ME15 .... 97 A8
Mayfield Ave. CT16 .... 149 C2
Mayfield Cl. Chatham ME5 .... 32 A1
Mayfield Cl. Gillingham ME8 .... 11 E2
Mayfield Ct. 3 CT16 .... 149 B2
Mayfield Gdns. CT16 .... 149 C2
Mayfield Rd. Herne Bay CT6 .... 23 A3
Mayfield Rd. Lyminge CT18 .... 161 C6
Mayfield Rd. Whitfield CT16 .... 149 A7
Mayfly Dr. CT18 .... 163 A4
Mayford Rd. ME5 .... 32 D2
Mayforth Gdns. CT11 .... 52 B6
Mayhew Cl. TN23 .... 156 A8
Maymills Cotts. CT13 .... 93 B2
Maynard and Cotton's Spital. 9
CT1 .... 87 F8
Maynard Ave. CT9 .... 28 B8
Maynard Pl. ME5 .... 10 D2
Maynard Rd. CT1 .... 87 E7
Mayor's Pl. 9 TN30 .... 179 A7
Maypits. TN23 .... 155 F8
Maypole La. CT3 .... 46 E6
Maypole Rd. CT3 .... 46 E6
Mays Rd. CT11 .... 52 C6
Maystreet Cross. CT6 .... 23 F3
Mayton La. CT2 .... 45 C1
Maytree Cotts. CT14 .... 133 D8
Mayville Rd. CT10 .... 29 E6
Mayweed Ave. ME5 .... 31 E4
Mc Kenzie Rd. ME5 .... 32 A3
McAlpine Cres. ME15 .... 96 F3
McCarthy Ave. CT2 .... 67 F7
McClean Wlk. ME12 .... 17 C8
McCudden Row. 4 ME4 .... 10 A6
McKinlay Ct. CT7 .... 26 D8
Mead Rd. Ashford TN24 .... 156 E7
Mead Rd. Folkestone CT19 .... 178 D6
Mead Way. CT2 .... 66 E1
Mead Wlk. TN23 .... 155 E8
Meade The. CT18 .... 162 F4
Meadow Bank. ME13 .... 61 F2
Meadow Brook Ct. CT20 .... 177 E4
Meadow Cl. Bagham CT4 .... 107 E8
Meadow Cl. Bridge CT4 .... 89 A1
Meadow Cl. Chatham ME5 .... 31 F5
Meadow Cl. Herne Bay CT6 .... 23 C4
Meadow Cl. Iwade ME9 .... 14 D4
Meadow Cotts.
East Studdal CT15 .... 132 D8
Meadow Cotts.
Goodnestone CT3 .... 92 A2
Meadow Ct. TN25 .... 175 B6
Meadow Dr. CT5 .... 44 D8
Meadow Gr. TN25 .... 174 D8
Meadow Rd. Ashford TN23 .... 139 A4
Meadow Rd. Canterbury CT2 .... 66 C2
Meadow Rd. Margate CT9 .... 7 F1
Meadow Rd. Sturry CT2 .... 67 F6
Meadow Rise. ME9 .... 14 D4
Meadow View. TN26 .... 138 A6
Meadow View Industries.
TN26 .... 183 C7
Meadow View Rd.
Boughton Monchelsea ME17 .... 97 B3
Meadow View Rd.
Shepherdswell CT15 .... 130 E5
Meadow Wlk. Maidstone ME15 ... 75 B3
Meadow Wlk. Whitstable CT5 .... 43 C6
Meadowbank Rd. ME4 .... 10 A4
Meadowbrook. CT20 .... 177 E4
Meadowbrook Cl. TN24 .... 139 D6
Meadowbrook Rd. TN24 .... 139 D6
Meadowdown. ME14 .... 75 E4
Meadowdown Cl. ME7 .... 33 A4
Meadows The. Herne Bay CT6 .... 23 D2
Meadows The. Maidstone ME15 . 74 E2
Meadows The.
Sittingbourne ME10 .... 36 F2
Meads Ave The. ME10 .... 36 D7
Meads Way. TN29 .... 194 E3
Meadside Wlk. ME5 .... 31 F6
Meadway. CT17 .... 148 E3
Medina Ave. CT5 .... 43 B7
Medlar Cl. ME9 .... 58 A6
Medlar Gr. ME7 .... 33 A4
Medlars The. ME14 .... 75 D6
Medway Cl. ME10 .... 36 D4
Medway Com Coll. ME4 .... 10 A1
Medway Ent Ctr. ME2 .... 9 D8
Medway Gdns. ME4 .... 9 F7
Medway Heritage Ctr. ME4 .... 9 F5
Medway Ho. 1 ME15 .... 97 D8
Medway Hospl. ME7 .... 10 B4
Medway Rd. Gillingham ME7 .... 10 C7
Medway Rd.
Gillingham,Rainham ME8 .... 11 F1
Medway Rd. Sheerness ME12 .... 1 C1
Medway Service Area. ME8 .... 33 F3
Medway St. Chatham ME4 .... 9 F5
Medway St. Maidstone ME14 .... 74 F4
Medway Trad Est. ME16 .... 74 F3
Medway Villas. ME15 .... 96 B7
Meehan Rd. TN28 .... 200 E4
Meehan Rd S. TN28 .... 200 E3
Meeres Court La. ME10 .... 37 C5
Meeson's Cl. ME13 .... 81 E6
Meeting House La. ME4 .... 9 F4
Meeting St. CT11 .... 52 E7
Megby Cl. ME8 .... 33 D6
Megone Cl. CT18 .... 163 A4
Meirs Court Rd. ME8 .... 33 E6
Melbourne Ave. Dover CT16 .... 149 C4
Melbourne Ave. Ramsgate CT12 29 B1
Melbourne
Cty Prim Sch. CT16 .... 149 C4
Melbourne Rd. ME4 .... 10 A3
Melbury Mews. TN28 .... 200 C8
Melford Dr. ME16 .... 74 C4
Mellanby Cl. CT7 .... 27 A6
Mellor Row. ME10 .... 14 F1
Melody Cl. Gillingham ME8 .... 33 C4
Melody Cl. Warden ME12 .... 6 E4
Melon La. TN26 & TN29 .... 193 B6
Melrose Cl. ME15 .... 97 A7
Melsetter Cl. CT7 .... 27 B7
Melville Ct. ME4 .... 9 F6
Melville Lea. CT13 .... 93 C7
Melville Rd. ME15 .... 75 A3
Memorial (General) Hospl.
ME10 .... 36 F3
Mendfield St. 5 ME13 .... 62 C7
Mendip Rise. TN24 .... 139 B4
Menin Rd. ME10 .... 14 F1
Mentmore Ho. CT12 .... 29 C3
Mentmore Rd. CT10 & CT12 .... 29 C3
Menzies Ave. CT14 .... 117 B1
Menzies Ct. ME12 .... 4 A5
Mercer Dr. ME17 .... 100 F6
Mercer Way. ME17 .... 98 B1
Mercery La. 5 CT1 .... 87 F8
Merchants Way. CT2 .... 87 C8
Mercury Cl. ME1 .... 9 A3
Mere Gate. CT9 .... 7 I1
Meredale Cty Inf Sch. ME8 .... 12 A1
Meresborough Cotts. ME8 .... 33 F5
Meresborough La. ME8 & ME9 .. 34 B5
Meresborough Rd. ME8 .... 34 A7
Mereworth Cl. ME8 .... 11 A3
Meridian Ct. TN23 .... 155 E7
Meridian Pk. ME2 .... 9 E6
Merivale Gr. ME5 .... 32 B4
Merleburgh Dr. ME10 .... 36 F8
Merlin Cl. ME10 .... 37 A3
Mermaid Cl. ME5 .... 32 A6
Merritt Rd. TN28 .... 200 E2
Mersham Cty Prim Sch. TN25 157 E3
Merton Cl. ME5 .... 32 C5
Merton La. CT1 & CT4 .... 87 F4
Merton Rd. ME15 .... 75 F2
Meryl Gdns. CT14 .... 117 C1
Metcalfe Mews. 1 CT1 .... 67 B2
Meteor Ave. CT5 .... 43 B7
Metropole Rd E. CT20 .... 178 B3
Metropole Rd W. CT20 .... 178 B3
Meverall Ave. CT12 .... 51 E5
Mews The. Maidstone ME16 .... 74 E5
Mews The. Sittingbourne ME10 .... 36 F2
Meyrick Rd. ME12 .... 1 D2
Micawber Cl. ME5 .... 32 A1
Michael Ave. CT11 .... 52 G8
Michelle Gdns. CT9 .... 28 A8
Mickleburgh Ave. CT6 .... 23 B4
Mickleburgh Hill. CT6 .... 23 B4
Mid Kent Coll (City Way Ctr).
ME1 .... 9 E4
Mid Kent Coll of H & F Ed.
Maidstone ME16 .... 74 E3
Mid Kent Coll of H & F Ed.
Maidstone,Cherry Orchard ME16 . 74 C3
Mid Kent Coll of Higher
& F Ed. ME1 & ME4 .... 31 E6
Mid Kent Sch for Girls. ME14 ... 75 A5
Mid Kent Sh Ctr The. ME16 ...... 74 C7
Middelburg Ho. CT19 .... 177 D6
Middelburg Sq. CT20 .... 178 D4
Middle Cl. TN23 .... 138 C1
Middle Deal Rd. CT14 .... 117 B5
Middle Mead. CT19 .... 178 B7
Middle Row. Ashford TN23 .... 139 C2
Middle Row. 2
Faversham ME13 .... 62 D7
Middle Row. 6
Maidstone ME15 .... 74 F4
Middle St. Ashford TN23 .... 139 B2
Middle St. Deal CT14 .... 117 D6
Middle St. 5 Gillingham ME4 ...... 10 A6
Middle Wall. CT5 .... 20 D2
Middle Way. ME10 .... 37 B3
Middlefields. ME8 .... 34 A8
Middlesex Rd. ME15 .... 97 D7
Middleton Cl. ME8 .... 33 E4
Middleton Cotts. TN25 .... 122 E3
Middleton Ct. 8 ME10 .... 36 E4
Middletune Ave. ME10 .... 36 E7
Midhurst Ct. ME15 .... 75 A3
Midley Cl. ME16 .... 74 C7
Midsummer Hill. TN24 .... 139 D6
Miers Court
Cty Prim Sch. ME8 .... 33 F7
Mierscourt Cl. ME8 .... 34 A8
Mierscourt Rd. ME8 .... 33 E6
Mikyle Ct. CT1 .... 88 A6
Milbourne Gr. ME10 .... 36 E7
Milburn Rd. ME7 .... 10 C7
Mildred Cotts. CT19 .... 177 F7
Mile Rd. CT12 & CT3 .... 48 F6
Miles Ct. CT3 .... 91 A8
Miles Pl. ME1 .... 9 D3
Miles Way. CT7 .... 26 F7
Milestone Cl. CT19 .... 178 A7
Milestone Rd. CT14 .... 117 B5
Milford Cl. ME16 .... 74 D5
Military Rd. Canterbury CT1 .... 67 A1
Military Rd. Canterbury CT1 .... 67 B1
Military Rd. Chatham ME4 .... 9 F5
Military Rd. 2 Dover CT17 ...... 166 D7
Military Rd. Folkestone CT20 ..... 177 E4
Military Rd. Hythe CT21 .... 176 B2
Military Rd. Ramsgate CT11 .... 52 E6
Military Rd.
Stone in Oxney TN26 & TN30 ...... 190 B4
Mill Bank. TN29 .... 203 B6
Mill Bank Cotts. CT13 .... 93 A2
Mill Bay. CT20 .... 178 E5
Mill Cl. Lenham ME17 .... 101 C4
Mill Cl. River CT17 .... 148 F2
Mill Cl. Sandwich CT13 .... 72 E2
Mill Cotts. Ramsgate CT11 .... 52 D6
Mill Cotts. Worth CT14 .... 94 A4
Mill Ct. ME10 .... 37 A3
Mill Field. Ash CT3 .... 71 E1
Mill Field. Broadstairs CT10 .... 29 F5

Mill Fields Rd. CT21 .... 175 F2
Mill Gn. CT13 .... 93 A2
Mill Hamlet. CT3 .... 69 C2
Mill Hill. CT14 .... 117 A3
Mill La. Aldington TN25 .... 172 E5
Mill La. Ashford TN24 .... 140 A1
Mill La. Bagham CT4 .... 107 D7
Mill La. Biddenden Green TN27 . 135 A2
Mill La. Birchington CT7 .... 26 F6
Mill La. Bridge CT4 .... 88 F1
Mill La. Canterbury CT1 .... 66 F1
Mill La.
    Canterbury, Harbledown CT2 .. 87 C8
Mill La.
    Chatham,Bluebell Hill ME5 .... 31 D1
Mill La. Chatham,Luton ME5 ..... 10 C1
Mill La. Coxheath ME17 .... 96 D4
Mill La. 8 Dover CT16 .... 166 E7
Mill La. Eastry CT13 .... 93 B2
Mill La. Hartlip Hill ME9 .... 34 E6
Mill La. Hawkinge CT18 .... 163 B5
Mill La. Herne Bay CT6 .... 23 B2
Mill La. Lynsted ME9 .... 60 C5
Mill La. Maidstone ME14 .... 74 F6
Mill La. Margate CT9 .... 7 I2
Mill La. Nonington CT15 .... 113 F4
Mill La. Northbourne CT14 ..... 115 F4
Mill La. Preston CT3 .... 70 D6
Mill La. Shepherdswell CT15 ... 130 F5
Mill La. Stelling Minnis CT4 ... 126 F2
Mill La. Tenterden TN30 .... 167 B1
Mill La. Whitfield CT16 .... 149 A8
Mill La. Worth CT14 .... 94 A4
Mill Lane Cotts. CT14 .... 116 A4
Mill Mews. CT14 .... 117 B4
Mill Pl. ME13 .... 62 D8
Mill Rd. Bethersden TN26 .... 153 E5
Mill Rd. Bramling CT3 .... 90 E6
Mill Rd. Deal CT14 .... 117 C4
Mill Rd. Dymchurch TN29 .... 195 B7
Mill Rd. Gillingham ME7 .... 10 C6
Mill Rd. Hoath CT3 .... 46 F5
Mill Rd. Hythe CT21 .... 176 D2
Mill Rd. Lydd TN29 .... 203 D7
Mill Rd. Rochester ME2 .... 9 B8
Mill Rd. Staple CT3 .... 92 B5
Mill Rd. Sturry CT2 .... 67 F5
Mill Row. CT7 .... 26 F6
Mill St. Loose ME15 .... 96 F5
Mill St. Maidstone ME15 .... 74 F4
Mill St. Sittingbourne ME10 ..... 36 E5
Mill St. Temple Ewell CT16 .... 148 D5
Mill Terr. Bridge CT4 .... 88 F1
Mill Terr. Chartham CT4 .... 86 D3
Mill View. Ashford TN24 .... 156 F8
Mill View. Woodchurch TN26 ... 169 A3
Mill View Rd. CT6 .... 23 A1
Mill Wall Pl. CT13 .... 94 A8
Mill Way. ME10 .... 36 F6
Mill Wlk. ME16 .... 74 A3
Millais Rd. CT16 .... 149 C1
Millbank La. TN29 .... 198 E7
Millbank Rd. TN23 .... 155 F5
Millbrook. CT21 .... 176 D2
Millbrook Cl. ME15 .... 74 F1
Millbrook Meadow. TN23 ...... 138 E1
Milldale Cl. CT14 .... 117 B4
Millen Rd. ME10 .... 36 E5
Millen's Row. ME13 .... 83 B3
Miller Ave. CT2 .... 87 D8
Miller Cl. ME10 .... 37 A8
Miller Ct. ME12 .... 4 A5
Millers Ct. CT5 .... 43 D7
Millers La. CT12 .... 49 C7
Millers Wharf. ME16 .... 74 E2
Millfield. Ashford TN23 .... 155 D8
Millfield. Folkestone CT20 ..... 178 D5
Millfield. Hawkinge CT18 .... 163 C6
Millfield. High Halden TN26 ... 167 D7
Millfield. Sittingbourne ME10 .. 37 A3
Millfield.
    St Margaret's at Cliffe CT15 . 150 F7
Millfield Cl. CT18 .... 163 B5
Millfield Manor. CT5 .... 20 E1
Millfield Rd. Faversham ME13 .. 62 E7
Millfield Rd. Ramsgate CT12 .... 29 B3
Millfields. Chatham ME5 .... 32 D2
Millfields. Shepherdswell CT15 . 130 E4
Millmead Ave. CT9 .... 8 D1
Millmead Gdns. CT9 .... 8 D1
Millmead Rd. CT9 .... 8 C1
Millpond Cl. ME2 .... 9 B8
Mills Cl. ME12 .... 3 F6
Mills Terr. ME4 .... 10 A3
Millstock Terr. ME15 .... 74 E2
Millstream Cl. Faversham ME13 . 62 C7
Millstream Cl. Whitstable CT5 ... 20 E1
Millstrood Rd. CT5 .... 43 E8
Milne Rd. TN24 .... 156 F8
Milner Cl. CT15 .... 114 B1
Milner Cres. CT3 .... 112 E5
Milner La. CT2 .... 67 F5
Milner Rd. Elvington CT15 ..... 114 B1
Milner Rd. Gillingham ME7 ..... 10 D7
Milner Rd. Whitstable CT5 ...... 43 A6
Milstead Cl. Maidstone ME14 ... 75 C5
Milstead Cl. West Minster ME12 . 3 B7
Milstead & Frinstead
    CE Prim Sch. ME9 .... 58 E1
Milsted Rd. ME8 .... 11 C3
Milton Ave. CT9 .... 7 J1
Milton Cl. Canterbury CT1 ...... 88 C6
Milton Cl. Dover CT16 .... 149 B4
Milton Rd. Ashford TN23 .... 139 B2
Milton Rd. Canterbury CT1 ..... 88 A6
Milton Rd. Dover CT16 .... 149 B4
Milton Rd. Gillingham ME7 ..... 10 C3
Milton Rd. Sittingbourne ME10 . 36 E4

Milton Sq. 4 CT9 .... 7 J1
Milton St. ME16 .... 74 C2
Mincers Cl. ME5 .... 32 C2
Minerva Ave. CT16 .... 149 C2
Minerva Ho. CT11 .... 52 D7
Minerva Rd. ME2 .... 9 A8
Minnis Field. CT4 .... 126 E3
Minnis Gn. CT4 .... 126 E2
Minnis La. CT15 & CT17 . 148 C2
Minnis Rd. CT7 .... 26 E7
Minnis Terr. CT17 .... 149 A2
Minnis Way. CT14 .... 94 B5
Minster Abbey. Minster ME12 ... 4 D6
Minster Abbey. Minster,Thanet
    CT12 .... 50 C5
Minster CE Prim Sch. CT12 ..... 50 B5
Minster Cl. CT10 .... 30 A2
Minster Coll. ME12 .... 3 F6
Minster Dr. Herne Bay CT6 ..... 22 D4
Minster Dr. Minster ME12 .... 4 A8
Minster Lodge. CT11 .... 52 C6
Minster Rd. Acol CT12 & CT7 .. 27 C2
Minster Rd. Faversham ME13 ... 62 E7
Minster Rd. Gillingham ME8 .... 11 C3
Minster Rd. Minster ME12 .... 4 B6
Minster Rd. Ramsgate CT11 .... 52 B5
Minster Rd. Westgate-on-S CT8 . 27 F7
Minster (Thanet) Sta. CT12 .... 50 C5
Minster-in-Sheppey
    Cty Prim Sch. ME12 .... 4 C7
Mint The. CT2 .... 66 C1
Mintching Wood La. ME9 .... 58 F2
Minter Ave. CT18 .... 162 F7
Minter Cl. CT18 .... 162 F7
Minterne Ave. ME10 .... 36 D2
Minterne Cty Jun Sch. ME10 ... 36 D2
Miranda Ct. ME12 .... 1 C1
Misling La. CT4 & TN25 .... 143 C7
Missenden Ct. 6 CT20 .... 178 D5
Mitcham Rd. TN29 .... 195 C8
Mitchell Ave. ME4 .... 9 F2
Mitchell Cl. ME17 .... 101 C5
Mitchell St. CT19 .... 177 D6
Mitre Rd. ME1 .... 9 B4
Mittell Ct. TN29 .... 203 B6
Moat Farm Cl. CT19 .... 178 C7
Moat Farm Rd. CT19 .... 178 C7
Moat Ho. Canterbury CT1 .... 87 F7
Moat Ho. Charing TN27 .... 120 C7
Moat La. Ash CT3 .... 71 E1
Moat La. Fordwich CT2 & CT3 .. 68 A3
Moat La. Rough Common CT2 ... 66 B4
Moat Pk. TN27 .... 120 C6
Moat Sole. CT13 .... 72 F1
Moat The. TN27 .... 120 C7
Moat Way. ME11 .... 3 A5
Moatfield Meadow. TN23 ...... 156 B4
Mock La. TN23 .... 155 B6
Mockett Ct. 4 ME10 .... 36 E4
Mockett Dr. CT10 .... 29 F7
Molehill Cnr. CT5 .... 44 D8
Molehill Copse
    Cty Prim Sch. ME15 .... 97 D7
Molehill Rd.
    Herne Bay CT6 & CT5 .... 22 A1
Molehill Rd.
    Whitstable CT5 & CT6 .... 44 E8
Molineux Rd. CT12 .... 50 B6
Molland Cl. CT3 .... 71 C2
Molland La. Ash CT3 .... 71 E1
Molland La. Westmarsh CT3 ..... 71 D6
Molland Lea. CT3 .... 71 C2
Molloy Rd. TN26 .... 155 B1
Monarch Cl. ME5 .... 32 A6
Monastery St. CT1 .... 88 A8
Monckton's Ave. ME14 .... 74 F7
Monckton's Dr. ME14 .... 74 E7
Moncktons La. ME14 .... 74 F7
Moncrif Cl. ME14 .... 76 B4
Mongeham Church Cl. CT14 .. 116 D3
Mongeham
    Cty Prim Sch. CT14 .... 116 F4
Mongeham Rd. CT14 .... 116 E3
Monins Rd. CT17 .... 166 B7
Monkdown. ME15 .... 76 A1
Monkery La. ME13 & TN25 ... 104 C3
Monks Cl. Canterbury CT2 ...... 67 A2
Monks Cl. Faversham ME13 ..... 62 B8
Monks Way. CT16 .... 149 A3
Monks Wlk. TN27 .... 120 C7
Monkshill Rd. ME13 .... 42 B2
Monkton CE Prim Sch. CT12 ... 49 D7
Monkton Court La. CT15 ...... 131 C7
Monkton Gdns. CT9 .... 8 E3
Monkton Manor. CT12 .... 49 D7
Monkton Pl. CT11 .... 52 D7
Monkton Rd. CT12 .... 50 A6
Monkton Rdbt. CT12 .... 49 D8
Monkton St. CT12 .... 49 D7
Monkwood Cl. ME1 .... 31 B8
Monmouth Cl. ME8 .... 11 C2
Mons Ct. ME10 .... 14 F1
Montacue Ct. CT20 .... 178 B4
Montague Cl. ME12 .... 1 C1
Montague Rd. CT11 .... 52 E8
Montague St. CT6 .... 22 D5
Montefiore Ave. CT11 .... 29 F1
Montefiore Cotts. CT11 .... 52 F8
Montfort Cl. Ashford TN23 .... 155 F7
Montfort Cl. Canterbury CT2 ... 67 A4
Montfort Rd. Chatham ME5 ..... 31 F2
Montfort Rd. Rochester ME2 ..... 9 A8
Montgomery Ave. ME5 .... 32 A7
Montgomery GM Sch. CT3 ..... 68 C8
Montgomery Rd. ME7 .... 10 C3
Montgomery Way. CT19 .... 178 E8
Montpelier Ave. CT5 .... 43 D6
Montpelier Bsns Pk. TN23 .... 138 F1

Montpelier Gate. ME16 .... 74 B5
Montreal Cl. 8 CT16 .... 149 B3
Montrose Ave. ME5 .... 10 E2
Monument Way. TN24 .... 156 F5
Moon Hill. CT15 .... 130 E4
Moonstone Dr. ME5 .... 32 B2
Moor La. Ivychurch TN29 ...... 192 D4
Moor La.
    Woodchurch TN26 & TN30 ... 180 E6
Moor Lane Cotts. TN26 .... 181 C2
Moor Park Ct. ME8 .... 34 A8
Moor St. ME8 .... 34 B8
Moore Cl. TN29 .... 192 A3
Moore St. ME2 .... 9 A8
Moorfield. CT2 .... 66 F4
Mooring Rd. ME1 .... 9 D1
Moorings The. ME9 .... 38 E6
Moorland Rd. CT15 .... 130 E4
Moorstock La. TN25 .... 159 C2
Moorwell Dr. CT15 .... 130 D5
Moray Ave. CT7 .... 26 F8
Mordaunt Ave. CT8 .... 27 E8
Morden St. ME1 .... 9 C4
Morehall Ave. CT19 .... 177 F6
Morehall Cty Prim Sch. CT19 . 177 F6
Morella Wlk. ME17 .... 101 C5
Morello Cl. ME9 .... 38 C2
Moreton Terr. TN26 .... 155 A1
Morgan Kirby's Gdn. ME13 ..... 83 D5
Morris Ave. CT6 .... 21 F4
Morris Court Cl. ME9 .... 37 D2
Morrison Rd. CT20 .... 178 E6
Morry La. ME17 .... 99 D1
Mortimer Cl. TN23 .... 156 B7
Mortimer Rd. CT16 .... 166 F8
Mortimer St. CT6 .... 22 F5
Mossbank. ME5 .... 32 A3
Mossend Mews. CT11 .... 29 E2
Mossy Glade. ME8 .... 33 E6
Mostyn Rd. ME14 .... 75 C4
Mote Ave. ME15 .... 75 B3
Mote Pk. ME15 .... 75 D2
Mote Rd. ME15 .... 75 A3
Motney Hill Rd. ME8 .... 12 A4
Mouat Ct. ME5 .... 32 A3
Mount Charles Wlk. CT4 .... 88 F1
Mount Dr. ME14 .... 76 B4
Mount Ephraim. ME13 .... 64 A4
Mount Field. Faversham ME13 .. 62 B6
Mount Field.
    Queenborough ME11 .... 3 A5
Mount Green Ave. CT12 .... 51 D5
Mount La. Hartlip ME9 .... 34 D4
Mount La. Maidstone ME14 ..... 76 B4
Mount Lodge. ME1 .... 9 B2
Mount Pleasant.
    Aldington TN25 .... 173 A6
Mount Pleasant.
    Aylesford ME20 .... 53 A3
Mount Pleasant. Blean CT2 ..... 66 A6
Mount Pleasant.
    Gillingham ME4 .... 10 B3
Mount Pleasant.
    Kingsdown CT14 .... 134 D5
Mount Pleasant. Oare ME13 .... 40 B2
Mount Pleasant.
    Tenterden TN30 .... 179 C8
Mount Pleasant Dr. ME14 .... 76 A5
Mount Pleasant Rd. 4 CT20 .. 178 D5
Mount Pleasant Terr. ME17 ... 100 C2
Mount Rd. Canterbury CT1 ...... 88 C6
Mount Rd. Chatham ME4 .... 9 F3
Mount Rd. Dover CT17 .... 166 A6
Mount Rd. Rochester ME1 .... 9 B2
Mount St. CT21 .... 176 C2
Mount View. ME13 .... 62 A5
Mount View Rd. CT6 .... 23 A2
Mountain St. CT4 .... 107 B6
Mountbatten Ave. ME5 .... 32 A7
Mountbatten Way. TN25 ...... 158 E6
Mountfield Cl. ME16 .... 74 D5
Mountfield Rd. TN28 .... 200 C6
Mountfield Row. TN28 .... 200 C6
Mountfield Way. CT8 .... 27 D6
Mountpleasant Cl. CT18 .... 161 C7
Mounts Cl. CT14 .... 117 A5
Mountsfield Cl. ME16 .... 74 D5
Mountview. ME9 .... 36 B2
Moyle Cl. ME8 .... 33 D4
Mozart Ct. ME4 .... 9 E3
Muddy Bush Cnr. CT5 .... 90 F2
Muir Rd. Maidstone ME15 .... 75 A2
Muir Rd. Rochester ME1 .... 9 E4
Mulberry Cl. Gillingham ME7 ... 33 A4
Mulberry Cl. Ramsgate CT11 ... 52 F8
Mulberry Ct. Canterbury CT1 ... 87 F8
Mulberry Ct.
    Littlestone-on-S TN28 .... 200 E5
Mulberry Field. CT13 .... 72 F1
Mulberry Hill. CT4 .... 85 D1
Munday Bois Cotts. TN27 ..... 135 F8
Munday Bois Rd. TN27 .... 118 E1
Mundella
    Cty Prim Sch. CT19 .... 178 D6
Mungeam Ho. ME1 .... 9 C4
Munn's La. ME9 .... 34 E6
Murrain Dr. ME15 .... 76 A1
Murray Rd. ME2 .... 9 C8
Murston Cty Inf Sch. ME10 ..... 37 B4
Murston Jun Sch. ME10 .... 37 B5
Murston Rd. ME10 .... 37 B4
Murthwaite Ct. ME12 .... 4 A5
Murton Pl. ME13 .... 41 E1
Museum of Kent Rural Life.
    ME14 .... 53 D1
Museum St. ME14 .... 74 F4
Musgrave Cl. CT12 .... 27 F2
Musgrave Rd. ME10 .... 36 F6
Musgrove. TN23 .... 156 A8

Musket La.
    Eyhorne Street ME17 .... 77 B2
Musket La. Silver Hill ME17 .... 77 A2
Mustards Rd. ME12 .... 6 D2
Mutrix Gdns. CT9 .... 7 E1
Mutrix Rd. CT9 .... 28 B8
Mutton La. ME13 .... 62 A6
Mymms Cl. CT5 .... 44 C8
Mynn Cres. ME14 .... 76 A4
Myrtle Cres. ME5 .... 31 F5
Myrtle Rd. 4 CT19 .... 178 E6
Mystole Cl. CT4 .... 108 C8
Mystole Rd. CT4 .... 108 A8

Nacholt Cl. CT5 .... 21 A2
Nackington Ct. CT1 .... 88 B6
Nackington Pk. CT1 .... 88 A4
Nackington Rd. CT1 & CT4 ...... 88 A3
Nag's Head La. ME1 .... 9 D4
Nagpur Ho. 4 ME15 .... 97 E5
Nags Head La. ME1 .... 9 D4
Nailbourne Cl. CT1 .... 111 D3
Nailbourne Ct. CT18 .... 161 C7
Naildown Cl. CT21 .... 177 A3
Naildown Rd. CT21 .... 177 A3
Nairne Cl. TN26 .... 170 A8
Namur Pl. CT16 .... 149 F3
Napchester Rd. CT15 & CT16 .. 149 A8
Napier Cl. ME10 .... 36 C4
Napier Ct. ME14 .... 74 F7
Napier Cty Prim Sch. ME7 .... 10 D4
Napier Gdns. CT21 .... 176 C1
Napier Rd. Broadstairs CT10 ... 29 E6
Napier Rd. Dover CT16 .... 149 B2
Napier Rd. Gillingham ME7 ..... 10 D4
Napleton Cl. CT11 .... 52 C6
Napleton Rd. Faversham ME13 . 62 C7
Napleton Rd. Ramsgate CT11 ... 52 C6
Napoleon Wlk. ME17 .... 101 C5
Napwood Cl. ME8 .... 33 D6
Nares Rd. ME8 .... 33 D4
Nargate Cl. CT3 .... 90 A8
Nargate St. CT3 .... 90 A8
Narrabeen Rd. CT19 .... 177 E6
Narrowbush La. TN29 .... 198 B7
Naseby Ave. CT20 .... 177 D5
Nash Cl. ME5 .... 32 C2
Nash Court Gdns. CT9 .... 28 E8
Nash Court Rd. CT9 .... 28 E8
Nash Gdns. CT10 .... 30 B4
Nash Hill. CT18 .... 161 D6
Nash La. CT9 .... 28 F7
Nash Rd. CT9 & CT10 .... 28 F7
Nashenden Farm La. ME1 .... 31 A8
Nasmyth Rd. CT7 .... 27 A8
Nat's La. TN25 .... 141 A5
Natal Rd. Chatham ME4 .... 10 A3
Natal Rd. Dover CT16 .... 149 C4
Nativity Cl. ME14 .... 36 E4
Nautilus Cl. ME12 .... 4 A6
Nautilus Dr. ME12 .... 4 A6
Naval Terr. ME12 .... 4 A6
Naylands. CT9 .... 7 H1
Naylor's Path. CT2 .... 66 C3
Neal's Place Rd. CT2 .... 66 C3
Neale St. ME4 .... 9 F2
Neame Rd. CT7 .... 27 A7
Neames Forstal. ME13 .... 84 E7
Neason Ct. CT19 .... 178 F6
Neason Way. CT19 .... 178 F6
Neath Ct. 2 ME15 .... 97 E8
Neath Rd. TN29 .... 202 A2
Neatscourt Cotts. ME12 .... 3 C4
Nelson Ave. ME12 .... 4 D5
Nelson Cl. Ashford TN24 .... 157 B8
Nelson Cl. West Minster ME12 ... 3 A8
Nelson Cres. CT11 .... 52 E6
Nelson Ho. 5 ME15 .... 97 F5
Nelson Park Rd. CT15 .... 150 E8
Nelson Pl. CT10 .... 30 B5
Nelson Rd. Gillingham ME7 ..... 10 D4
Nelson Rd. Whitstable CT5 ...... 20 D7
Nelson St. Deal CT14 .... 117 D7
Nelson St. Faversham ME13 ..... 62 E7
Nelson Terr. ME15 .... 10 C1
Nelson Wlk. ME10 .... 36 B5
Neptune Bsns Pk. ME2 .... 9 E7
Neptune Cl. ME2 .... 9 E7
Neptune Terr. ME12 .... 1 E2
Nesbit Rd. TN29 .... 194 F4
Ness Rd. TN29 .... 203 C6
Ness The. CT1 .... 88 B5
Nether Ave. TN28 .... 200 D6
Nethercourt Cir. CT12 .... 52 A6
Nethercourt Farm Rd. CT11 ... 52 B7
Nethercourt Gdns. CT11 .... 52 B6
Nethercourt Hill. CT11 .... 52 B6
Nethergong Hill. CT3 .... 47 D3
Netherhale Farm Rd. CT7 .... 26 B3
Nethersole Cl. CT2 .... 67 A4
Nethersole Rd. CT4 .... 112 F1
Netley Cl. ME14 .... 75 D6
Nettlefield. TN24 .... 139 E5
Nettlepole La. TN27 .... 119 D1
Nevill Gdns. ME14 .... 117 B1
Neville Cl. ME14 .... 75 B8
Neville Rd. ME4 .... 9 F2
New Barns Rd. ME14 .... 75 A8
New Beverley Ho. CT2 .... 66 F2
New Bridge. 10 CT15 .... 166 E7
New Cotts. Guston CT15 .... 149 E6
New Cotts. Harbledown CT2 ..... 87 A5
New Cotts. Teynham ME9 .... 38 A4
New Covenant Pl. ME1 .... 9 D4
New Cross St. CT9 .... 7 I2
New Cut. Chatham ME4 .... 9 F4
New Cut. Dean Street ME15 .... 96 D7

New Cut Rd.
    Chilham CT4 & ME13 .... 85 A3
New Cut Rd. Maidstone ME14 ... 75 D5
New Delhi Ho. 5 ME15 .... 97 E5
New Dover Rd.
    Canterbury CT1 & CT4 .... 88 C6
New Dover Rd.
    Capel-le-F CT18 .... 164 C2
New Forest La. CT4 & ME13 .... 85 B3
New Gardens Rd. ME9 .... 38 C2
New Hall Cl. TN29 .... 195 C8
New Hall Mus. TN29 .... 195 C8
New House Cl. CT1 .... 87 E4
New House La. CT1 & CT4 ...... 87 C2
New Inn Cotts. ME15 .... 96 C7
New La. TN29 .... 203 C6
New Rd. Calcott CT2 & CT6 ..... 45 C4
New Rd. Chatham ME1 .... 9 D4
New Rd. Chatham ME4 .... 9 F4
New Rd. Egerton TN27 .... 119 A2
New Rd. Elham CT4 .... 144 F4
New Rd. Eythorne CT15 .... 131 C7
New Rd.
    Harbledown CT2 & ME13 ...... 65 D3
New Rd. Hythe CT21 .... 176 B1
New Rd. Hythe, Saltwood CT21 . 176 B4
New Rd. Langley ME17 .... 98 C5
New Rd. Minster ME12 .... 4 C6
New Rd. Rough Common CT2 ... 66 B3
New Rd. Sheerness ME12 .... 1 B1
New Rectory La. TN23 .... 156 B4
New Rents. 5 TN23 .... 139 B2
New Road Ave. ME4 .... 9 E4
New Road Cotts. CT6 .... 45 C5
New Road Cty Prim Sch. ME4 .. 10 A3
New Road Hall. TN25 .... 172 F4
New Road Ind Est. ME12 .... 1 B1
New Romney CE Jun Sch.
    TN28 .... 200 B7
New Romney Cty Inf Sch.
    TN28 .... 200 B7
New Romney Pl. CT13 .... 93 F8
New Romney Sta. TN28 .... 200 C6
New Ruttington La. CT1 .... 67 A1
New St. Ash CT3 .... 71 E1
New St. Ashford TN23 & TN24 . 139 B2
New St. Canterbury CT2 .... 66 E1
New St. Canterbury CT1 .... 87 E7
New St. Chatham ME4 .... 9 E3
New St. Deal CT14 .... 117 D7
New St. 12 Dover CT16 .... 166 D8
New St. Folkestone CT20 ...... 178 D5
New St. Herne Bay CT6 .... 22 F5
New St. Lydd TN29 .... 203 C6
New St. Margate CT9 .... 7 I2
New St. Sandwich CT13 .... 94 A8
New St. Sheerness ME12 .... 1 C1
New St. 2 Whitstable CT5 ...... 20 C2
New Strs. ME4 .... 9 F6
New Town Gn. TN24 .... 156 D8
New Town St. Canterbury CT1 .. 67 B2
New Town St. Chartham CT4 .... 86 C5
New Villas. ME5 .... 96 C7
Newark Ct. 1 ME2 .... 9 B7
Newark Yd. ME2 .... 9 B7
Newbridge Ave. ME10 .... 36 E7
Newbury Ave. ME16 .... 74 C6
Newbury Cl. Birchington CT7 ... 27 B6
Newbury Cl. Dover CT17 ...... 165 F7
Newbury Cl. Folkestone CT20 . 177 D5
Newcastle Hill. 5 CT11 .... 52 F7
Newchurch La. TN29 & TN26 . 193 A7
Newchurch Rd. ME15 .... 75 A1
Newcomen Rd. ME12 .... 1 D2
Newenden Cl. Ashford TN23 ... 155 F6
Newenden Cl. Maidstone ME14 . 75 D6
Newgate Gap. CT9 .... 8 A3
Newgate Lower Prom. CT9 ...... 8 A3
Newgate Prom. CT9 .... 8 A3
Newham St. ME4 .... 10 B3
Newhouse Cnr. CT5 .... 48 D1
Newhouse La. ME13 .... 83 D7
Newing Cl. CT3 .... 89 E8
Newington CE Prim Sch. ME9 . 35 B7
Newington Cty Inf Sch. CT12 .. 52 B8
Newington Ent Ctr. ME9 .... 35 C8
Newington Ind Est. ME9 .... 34 F6
Newington Jun Sch. CT12 ...... 52 A8
Newington Rd.
    Newington CT18 .... 177 A8
Newington Rd.
    Ramsgate CT12 & CT11 .... 29 B1
Newington Sta. ME9 .... 35 B6
Newington Wlk. ME14 .... 75 C6
Newland Green La. TN27 ...... 135 D8
Newland Rd. ME12 .... 2 F7
Newlands. Ashford TN23 .... 155 D6
Newlands. St Mary's Bay TN29 . 194 F3
Newlands. Whitfield CT16 ..... 149 B6
Newlands Ave. ME10 .... 36 B5
Newlands Cty Prim Sch. CT11 .. 29 B1
Newlands Dr. CT14 .... 134 B8
Newlands Farm Cotts. ME13 . 104 C4
Newlands Ho. CT11 .... 29 C2
Newlands La. CT12 .... 29 D2
Newlands Rd. Charing TN27 ... 119 F5
Newlands Rd.
    Ramsgate CT11 & CT12 .... 29 D1
Newlyn Ct. 1 ME14 .... 75 A4
Newlyn's Meadow. CT15 ...... 147 D1
Newman Dr. ME10 .... 37 A8
Newman Rd. CT3 .... 112 E5
Newnham Cl. ME8 .... 11 C2
Newnham La. ME13 & ME9 ..... 81 D7
Newport Ct. CT1 .... 88 B6

Newton Cl. Chatham ME5 .... **32** C2
Newton Cl. **1** Maidstone ME16 .. **74** E3
Newton Rd. Faversham ME13 ...... **62** D7
Newton Rd. Whitstable CT5 ...... **21** B2
Newtown Rd.
　Ashford TN23 & TN24 .... **156** D7
Nicholas Cl. Chatham ME5 .... **74** A3
Nicholas Dr. CT12 .... **51** D5
Nicholas Rd. TN24 .... **139** R6
Nicholls Ave. CT10 .... **29** F2
Nicklaus Dr. ME5 .... **31** F3
Nickle Cotts. CT4 .... **86** A3
Nickleby Cl. ME1 .... **9** C2
Nickley Wood Rd. TN26 .... **170** C6
Nightingale Ave. Hythe CT21 ... **187** D8
Nightingale Ave.
　Whitstable CT5 .... **43** B6
Nightingale Cl. Chartham CT4 .. **86** C6
Nightingale Cl. Gillingham ME8 .. **33** E6
Nightingale Cl. Sevington TN24 **157** B2
Nightingale La. CT13 .... **113** C2
Nightingale Rd. Dover CT16 .... **149** C3
Nightingale Rd.
　Faversham ME13 .... **62** C7
Nile Rd. ME7 .... **10** C4
Nine Acres. TN24 .... **139** C5
Nine Ash La. ME13 .... **63** D3
Ninn La. TN23 & TN26 .... **138** B2
Nixon Ave. CT12 .... **29** C1
No Name St. **3** CT13 .... **73** A1
Noah's Ark Rd. CT17 .... **166** A8
Noah's Ark Terr. CT17 .... **166** B8
Noakes Meadow. TN23 .... **156** A8
Nobel Cl. ME9 .... **38** C2
Nobel Cl. ME13 .... **62** C7
Noble Ct. CT9 .... **28** A8
Noble Gdns. CT9 .... **28** A8
Nonington
　CE Prim Sch. CT15 .... **113** C5
Nonsuch Cl. CT1 .... **88** C8
Nore Cl. ME7 .... **10** E1
Noreen Ave. ME12 .... **4** A6
Norfolk Cl. Chatham ME5 .... **32** C3
Norfolk Cl. Gillingham ME8 ...... **11** D2
Norfolk Dr. TN23 .... **139** A2
Norfolk Rd. Canterbury CT1 .... **87** E6
Norfolk Rd. Lydden CT9 .... **28** D5
Norfolk Rd. Maidstone ME15 .... **97** C8
Norfolk Rd. Margate CT9 .... **8** B3
Norfolk Sq. CT12 .... **29** B2
Norfolk St. CT5 .... **43** D8
Norman Cl. Gillingham ME8 ...... **33** B5
Norman Cl. Maidstone ME14 .... **75** B6
Norman Rd. Ashford TN23 ...... **156** B7
Norman Rd. Broadstairs CT10 .. **29** F6
Norman Rd. Canterbury CT1 .... **88** A7
Norman Rd. Faversham ME13 .. **62** C7
Norman Rd. Ramsgate CT11 .... **52** B6
Norman Rd.
　St Margaret's at Cliffe CT15 .. **151** B6
Norman Rd. Warden ME12 .... **6** A6
Norman Rd.
　Westgate-on-S CT8 & CT9 ...... **7** D1
Norman Rd. Whitstable CT5 .... **43** E8
Norman St. **8** CT16 & CT17 .. **166** B8
Norman Tailyour Ho. CT14 .... **117** D5
Norreys Rd. ME8 .... **33** E7
Norrie Rd. CT7 .... **27** A6
Norrington Mead. **3** CT19 .... **178** A7
Norrington Rd. ME15 .... **97** B6
North Ave. CT11 .... **52** D6
North Barrack Rd. CT14 .... **117** D4
North Borough
　Cty Jun Sch. ME14 .... **75** A6
North Camber Way. CT16 ...... **150** B1
North Cl. CT20 .... **177** D4
North Close Bsns Ctr. CT20 .. **177** D4
North Court Ave. CT3 .... **91** A8
North Court La. CT14 .... **115** A4
North Court Rd. CT3 .... **91** A8
North Cres. ME17 .... **96** D4
North Ct. Deal CT14 .... **117** C7
North Ct. Ramsgate CT12 .... **29** B2
North Dane Way. ME5 .... **32** C4
North Downs Cl. CT4 .... **85** C2
North Eastling Rd. ME13 & ME9 **81** F8
North Exit Rd. CT16 .... **166** H8
North Foreland Ave. CT10 ...... **30** B7
North Foreland Golf Course.
　CT10 .... **30** A8
North Foreland Hill. CT10 ...... **30** B8
North Foreland Rd. CT10 .... **30** B7
North Holmes Rd. CT1 .... **88** B8
North La. Boughton Street ME13 .. **84** F8
North La. Canterbury CT2 .... **66** F1
North La. Faversham ME13 ...... **62** C8
North La. **7** Folkestone CT20 .... **177** E3
North Lea. CT14 .... **117** C7
North Lockside Rd. ME4 .... **10** D8
North Lyminge La. CT18 .... **161** C7
North Military Rd. CT17 .... **166** C7
North Pasley Rd. ME4 .... **10** B7
North Pends. TN24 .... **139** E5
North Pondside Rd. ME4 .... **10** A8
North Rd. Dover CT17 .... **166** C8
North Rd. Folkestone CT20 .... **177** D4
North Rd. Gillingham ME4 & ME7 .. **10** A7
North Rd. Hythe CT21 .... **176** B2
North Rd. Kingsdown CT14 .... **134** D6
North Rd. Queenborough ME11 .... **2** F5
North Rd. Richborough CT12 .... **51** A1
North Rd. Sandwich CT13 .... **95** A7
North Rd W. CT21 .... **176** A3
North Return Rd. CT16 .... **166** G8

North Sch The. TN24 .... **139** D1
North Side Three Rd. ME4 ...... **10** C8
North St. Ashford TN23 .... **139** C2
North St. Ashford TN24 .... **139** C3
North St. Deal CT14 .... **117** D7
North St. Dover CT17 .... **166** B7
North St. Folkestone CT19 .... **178** E5
North St. Herne Bay CT6 .... **23** A5
North St. New Romney TN28 .... **200** A6
North St. Rochester ME2 .... **9** B7
North St. Sittingbourne ME10 .. **37** E1
North St. Sutton Valence ME17 .. **98** E1
North View. Hersden CT3 .... **46** F1
North View. Maidstone ME15 .. **75** B1
North View Cotts. ME15 .... **96** C7
North Way. Finglesham CT14 .. **116** A7
North Way. Maidstone ME14 .... **75** B7
Northbourne Ave. CT17 .... **166** B8
Northbourne
　CE Prim Sch. CT14 .... **115** F5
Northbourne Court Gdns.
　CT14 .... **116** B5
Northbourne Park Sch
　(Annexe). CT14 .... **115** D6
Northbourne Park Sch
　(Prep). CT14 .... **115** C6
Northbourne Rd.
　East Studdal CT14 & CT15 .... **115** E1
Northbourne Rd.
　Gillingham ME8 .... **11** B4
Northbourne Rd.
　Great Mongeham CT14 .... **116** C4
Northbourne Way. CT9 .... **8** E2
Northbrooke. TN24 .... **139** C3
Northbrooke La. TN24 .... **139** C3
Northcliffe Gdns. CT10 .... **30** A7
Northcote Rd. Deal CT14 ...... **117** D5
Northcote Rd. Kingsdown CT14 **134** D4
Northcote Rd. Rochester ME2 .... **9** A7
Northdown. Ashford TN24 ...... **139** C4
Northdown. Doddington ME9 .... **80** F7
Northdown. Stockbury ME9 ...... **56** D8
Northdown Ave. CT9 .... **8** B2
Northdown Cl.
　East Studdal CT15 .... **132** B6
Northdown Cl. Maidstone ME14 .. **75** B7
Northdown Cty Prim Sch. CT9 .... **8** C1
Northdown Hill. CT10 & CT9 .... **29** D7
Northdown Park Rd. CT9 .... **8** C1
Northdown Rd. Broadstairs CT10 **29** E6
Northdown Rd. Margate CT9 ...... **8** B2
Northdown View. ME17 .... **100** F6
Northdown Way. CT9 .... **8** C1
Northern By-Pass. TN27 .... **120** C3
Northfleet Cl. ME14 .... **75** C5
Northgate. Canterbury CT1 ...... **67** A1
Northgate. Rochester ME1 .... **9** C6
Northleigh Cl. ME14 .... **97** A6
Northpoint Bsns Est. ME9 .... **9** D8
Northumberland Ave.
　Ashford TN24 .... **139** D5
Northumberland Ave.
　Gillingham ME8 .... **11** E1
Northumberland Ave.
　Margate CT9 .... **8** C2
Northumberland Ct.
　Maidstone ME15 .... **97** D7
Northumberland Ct.
　Margate CT9 .... **8** C3
Northumberland Rd. ME15 ...... **97** D8
Northwall Ct. CT14 .... **117** C7
Northwall Mews. CT14 .... **117** C7
Northwall Rd. CT14 .... **117** B8
Northwood Dr. ME10 .... **36** F1
Northwood Rd. Broadstairs,
　Ramsgate CT10 & CT12 .... **29** C7
Northwood Rd. Whitstable CT5 .. **20** F2
Norton Ave. CT6 .... **46** A8
Norton Dr. CT12 .... **50** B6
Norton Gr. ME5 .... **31** E3
Norton Knatchbull Sch The.
　TN24 .... **139** E2
Norton La. TN24 .... **153** D5
Norton Rd. Five Wents ME17 .... **98** D1
Norton Rd. Lynsted ME13 & ME9 .. **60** E5
Norview Rd. CT5 .... **43** B7
Norway Dro. CT15 .... **151** A8
Norway Terr. **4** ME14 .... **75** A7
Norwood Gdns. TN23 .... **139** B2
Norwood Cl. TN29 .... **193** E7
Norwood Rise. ME12 .... **4** C7
Norwood St. TN23 .... **139** B2
Norwood Wlk E. ME10 .... **36** C5
Norwood Wlk W. ME10 .... **36** B5
Notley St. CT1 .... **67** A1
Notley Terr. **3** CT1 .... **67** A1
Nottingham Ave. ME15 .... **97** D7
Nottingham Rd. CT7 .... **26** F5
Nouds Rd. ME9 .... **60** D7
Nunnery Fields. CT1 .... **88** A7
Nunnery Fields Hospl. CT1 .... **88** A6
Nunnery Rd. CT1 .... **88** A7
Nursery Ave. Maidstone ME16 .. **74** B6
Nursery Ave.
　Maidstone,Bearsted ME14 ...... **76** B3
Nursery Cl. Densole CT18 ...... **163** A4
Nursery Cl. Ramsgate CT11 .... **52** C7
Nursery Cl. Sheerness ME12 .... **1** E1
Nursery Cl. Whitstable CT5 .... **21** A1
Nursery Fields. Acol CT7 .... **27** B3
Nursery Fields. Hythe CT21 .... **176** A2
Nursery La. Densole CT18 ...... **163** A4
Nursery La. Sheldwich ME13 .... **83** D5
Nursery La. Whitfield CT16 .... **148** F7
Nursery Rd. ME8 .... **33** D8
Nursery Wlk. CT7 .... **66** F2
Nurserylands. CT6 .... **22** F3
Nutberry Cl. ME9 .... **38** D2

Nutfield Cl. ME5 .... **32** B8
Nutfields. ME10 .... **37** B3
Nutley Cl. TN24 .... **139** C3
Nutts Ave. ME12 .... **6** G2
Nutwood Cl. ME14 .... **75** E4

Oak Ave. Eythorne CT15 .... **131** D5
Oak Ave. Gillingham ME7 .... **10** E6
Oak Ave. Minster ME12 .... **4** F6
Oak Bglws. ME29 .... **203** C6
Oak Caer. ME25 .... **172** F4
Oak Cotts. East Studdal CT15 .. **132** E8
Oak Cotts. Sellindge IN25 ...... **174** D7
Oak Cotts. Selling ME13 .... **84** D4
Oak Dr. Boughton Street ME13 .. **64** A3
Oak Dr. Hawkinge CT18 .... **163** B5
Oak Dr. St Mary's Bay TN29 .. **194** F3
Oak Gr. CT15 .... **114** B2
Oak Hall Pass. CT21 .... **176** C2
Oak Hill. CT13 .... **93** B6
Oak Ho. **6** ME5 .... **31** F4
Oak La. Lydd TN29 .... **203** B6
Oak La. Minster ME12 .... **4** F7
Oak La. Upchurch ME9 .... **12** D2
Oak Lodge Rd. TN28 .... **200** B7
Oak Rd. ME10 .... **37** C5
Oak Ridge. TN25 .... **183** F8
Oak St. CT14 .... **117** D6
Oak Tree Ave. ME15 .... **97** C7
Oak Tree Cty Prim Sch. TN29 **155** F8
Oak Tree Gr. CT9 .... **28** A8
Oak Tree Rd. TN23 .... **155** F8
Oak Trees Cty Prim Sch. ME7 **97** C7
Oak Wlk. CT21 .... **176** C2
Oakapple La. ME16 .... **74** A3
Oakdale Rd. CT6 .... **23** A4
Oakdene Rd. CT12 .... **29** C1
Oakenpole. TN23 .... **138** E1
Oakfield Ct. CT12 .... **52** B8
Oakfield Rd. TN24 .... **139** D5
Oakfields. ME10 .... **36** C3
Oakhurst Cl. ME5 .... **31** F3
Oakland Cl. ME5 .... **31** F3
Oakland Ct. CT6 .... **22** E5
Oaklands. Ashford TN23 .... **138** F1
Oaklands. Mersham TN25 ...... **157** E4
Oaklands Ave. CT10 .... **29** E5
Oaklands Cty Prim Sch. ME5 .... **31** F4
Oaklands Way. CT2 .... **68** B7
Oakleigh Cl. ME5 .... **31** E2
Oakleigh Ho. TN23 .... **155** E8
Oakleigh La. CT4 .... **89** B5
Oakleys The. CT15 .... **130** D5
Oakridge. CT10 .... **8** G1
Oaks Ave. CT6 .... **22** D2
Oaks Bsns Village The. ME5 .. **32** C1
Oaks Cty Inf Sch The. ME10 .. **36** D2
Oaks Dene. ME5 .... **31** F1
Oaks Pk. CT2 .... **66** B3
Oaks Rd. Folkestone CT20 .... **177** D6
Oaks Rd. Tenterden TN30 ...... **179** B8
Oaks The. Broadstairs CT10 .... **29** F7
Oaks The. Hersden CT3 .... **46** F1
Oaks The.
　St Nicholas at Wade CT7 ...... **25** F2
Oaks View. CT21 .... **187** C8
Oakside Rd. CT17 .... **112** E5
Oaktree Ho. ME10 .... **37** B3
Oakum Ct. ME4 .... **10** B2
Oakvale Cl. CT17 .... **166** B6
Oakwood Ct. ME16 .... **74** D3
Oakwood Dr. CT5 .... **21** A1
Oakwood Hospl. ME16 .... **74** B3
Oakwood Park Gram Sch.
　ME16 .... **74** C3
Oakwood Rd. Maidstone ME16 .. **74** D3
Oakwood Rd. Sturry CT2 .... **68** A4
Oare Rd. ME13 .... **40** C1
Oast Cotts. Dargate ME13 ...... **64** D8
Oast Cotts. Sheldwich ME13 .... **83** C8
Oast Ct. Margate CT9 .... **28** F8
Oast Ct. Sittingbourne ME10 .... **36** E2
Oast Ho. CT4 .... **85** C2
Oast La. ME13 .... **104** E6
Oast Meadow. TN24 .... **139** F1
Oast Paddock The. CT3 .... **92** A6
Oast The. Canterbury CT1 ...... **88** B4
Oast The. Staple CT3 .... **92** A6
Oasthouse Field. TN29 .... **192** F4
Oasts The. ME17 .... **76** C4
Oastview. ME8 .... **34** A8
Oaten Hill. CT1 .... **88** A7
Oaten Hill Pl. CT1 .... **88** A7
Occupation Rd. TN25 .... **123** F2
Ocean Cl. CT7 .... **27** B8
Ocean View. Broadstairs CT10 .. **30** A1
Ocean View. Herne Bay CT6 .... **23** F6
Octavia Cl. ME5 .... **32** B3
Octavian Dr. CT21 .... **175** A3
Odiham Dr. ME14 .... **74** C7
Odo Rd. CT17 .... **166** C8
Officers' Rd. ME4 .... **10** B8
Offley Cl. CT9 .... **8** C1
Ogilvy Ct. CT10 .... **29** E2
Okehampton Cl. TN24 .... **139** F7
Olantigh Ct. CT7 .... **27** A7
Olantigh Rd. TN25 .... **123** F3
Olave Rd. CT9 .... **8** B1
Old Ash St. TN29 .... **139** C5
Old Ashford Rd. Charing TN27 .. **120** C2
Old Ashford Rd. Lenham ME17 .. **101** E5
Old Badgins Rd. ME13 .... **83** B6
Old Bakery Cl. CT15 .... **113** B4
Old Bakery The. ME12 .... **3** F5
Old Barn Cl. ME7 .... **32** F6
Old Billet La. ME12 .... **5** C6
Old Boundary Rd. CT9 .... **7** D1
Old Bridge Rd. CT5 .... **20** E1

Old Carriageway The. ME7 .... **32** F4
Old Castle Wlk. ME8 .... **33** D4
Old Charlton Rd. CT16 .... **149** D2
Old Chatham Rd.
　Kit's Coty ME20 .... **53** D6
Old Chatham Rd.
　Maidstone ME14 .... **53** F1
Old Court Hill. CT15 .... **113** C6
Old Crossing Rd. **1** CT9 ...... **28** B8
Old Dairy Cl. **3** CT11 .... **52** F7
Old Dover Rd. Barham CT4 .... **112** B1
Old Dover Rd. Canterbury CT1 .. **88** B6
Old Dover Rd. Capel-le-F CT18 .. **164** C1
Old Dr. ME15 .... **96** F6
Old Farm Cl. CT5 .... **43** C6
Old Farm Rd. CT7 .... **26** D7
Old Ferry Rd. ME9 .... **14** E7
Old Fold. CT15 .... **44** C8
Old Folkestone Rd. CT17 ...... **166** A4
Old Forge La. ME9 .... **56** F3
Old Gate Rd. ME13 .... **62** B8
Old Green Rd. Broadstairs CT10 **29** F7
Old Green Rd. Margate CT9 ...... **8** C1
Old Hall Dr. CT12 .... **51** C5
Old Ham La. ME17 .... **101** A4
Old High St The. CT20 .... **178** E5
Old Hockley Rd. ME13 .... **82** C2
Old Hook Rd. ME12 .... **4** F2
Old House Rd. ME9 .... **34** E4
Old Kingsdown Cl. CT10 .... **29** E3
Old Lain. ME17 .... **100** F6
Old London Rd. CT20 .... **175** F2
Old Loose Hill. ME15 .... **96** F4
Old Mead. CT19 .... **178** A7
Old Mill La. ME20 .... **53** C3
Old Mill Rd. ME17 .... **76** F1
Old Oast Bsns Ctr The. ME20 .. **53** A1
Old Orch. ME3 .... **155** D8
Old Orch The. ME8 .... **34** A8
Old Park Ave. CT1 .... **67** C2
Old Park Cl. CT16 .... **149** A4
Old Park Ct. CT1 .... **67** C2
Old Park Hill. CT16 .... **149** B4
Old Park Rd. CT16 .... **149** B2
Old Park Way. CT16 .... **149** A3
Old Pattens La. ME1 .... **9** D2
Old Pond Rd. TN23 .... **155** E8
Old Railway Works
　(Ind Est). TN24 .... **156** D8
Old Rd. Chatham ME4 .... **9** F4
Old Rd. Elham CT4 .... **144** F4
Old Rectory Cl. CT18 .... **163** B4
Old Rectory The. TN25 .... **122** E2
Old Roman Rd. CT15 .... **133** C1
Old Ruttington La. CT1 .... **67** A1
Old Saltwood La. CT21 .... **176** A4
Old Saw Mill The. TN26 ...... **153** E6
Old School Cl. ME17 .... **101** D4
Old School Ct. Egerton TN27 .. **118** F3
Old School Ct. Folkestone CT20 **178** B4
Old School Gdns. CT9 .... **8** A1
Old School Mews. CT4 .... **86** C2
Old School The. TN24 .... **156** D8
Old Surrenden Manor Rd.
　TN26 .... **154** C5
Old Tovil Rd. ME15 .... **75** A2
Old Trafford Cl. ME16 .... **74** B6
Old Tree La. ME17 .... **97** D3
Old Tree Rd. CT3 .... **47** B7
Old Valley Rd. CT4 .... **128** F7
Old Vicarage The. CT13 .... **93** C7
Old Way. TN26 .... **190** D7
Oldborough Manor Com Coll.
　ME15 .... **97** B6
Oldchurch Ct. **3** ME16 .... **74** E3
Oldfield Cl. Gillingham ME8 .... **33** D8
Oldfield Cl. Maidstone ME15 .... **76** F1
Oldhawe Hill. CT3 & CT6 ...... **46** D7
Oldhouse La. TN29 .... **191** E1
Oldstairs Rd. CT14 .... **134** D4
Oliver Cl. ME4 .... **10** B2
Oliver Twist Cl. ME1 .... **9** B4
Olivers Cotts. ME14 .... **76** C4
Olivine Cl. ME5 .... **54** A8
Olliffe Cl. ME5 .... **31** F2
Omer Ave. CT9 .... **9** D3
Onslow Rd. ME1 .... **9** D3
Ontario Way. CT16 .... **149** B3
Opal Gn. ME5 .... **32** B2
Orache Dr. ME14 .... **75** E5
Orange St. CT1 .... **87** F8
Orange Terr. ME1 .... **9** D5
Orbit Cl. ME5 .... **54** A8
Orchard Ave. CT14 .... **117** B5
Orchard Bank. ME17 .... **98** B1
Orchard Bsns Ctr. ME16 .... **74** C8
Orchard Cl. Canterbury CT2 .... **66** F4
Orchard Cl. Coxheath ME17 .... **96** C3
Orchard Cl. Langley Heath ME17 .. **98** E4
Orchard Cl. Littlebourne CT3 .. **89** F7
Orchard Cl. Mersham TN25 .... **157** E3
Orchard Cl. Minster,Thanet CT12 **50** B7
Orchard Cl. Ramsgate CT12 .... **29** B3
Orchard Cl. Whitfield CT16 .... **148** F8
Orchard Cl. Whitstable CT5 .... **20** F2
Orchard Cl. Wingham CT3 ...... **91** A7
Orchard Cotts. ME16 .... **74** C8
Orchard Cotts. Chillenden CT3 .. **113** F8
Orchard Cotts. Herne Bay CT6 .. **22** F1
Orchard Dr. Ashford TN23 .... **138** F4
Orchard Dr.
　Littlestone-on-S TN28 .... **200** E6
Orchard Dr. Newington ME9 .... **35** A5
Orchard Dr. River CT17 .... **148** F1
Orchard Dr. Wye TN25 .... **123** F1
Orchard Field. TN26 .... **153** D4

Orchard Fields. CT21 .... **160** E2
Orchard Flats. CT1 .... **88** D7
Orchard Gdns. CT9 .... **28** A8
Orchard Gr. ME12 .... **4** C6
Orchard Hts. TN23 .... **138** F5
Orchard Ind Est. ME15 .... **97** F3
Orchard La. Ashford TN24 .... **139** F6
Orchard La. Challock TN25 .... **105** B2
Orchard Mews. CT14 .... **117** D5
Orchard Pk. CT6 .... **23** D4
Orchard Pl. Faversham ME13 .. **62** B7
Orchard Pl. **2** Maidstone ME16 .. **74** E3
Orchard Pl. Sittingbourne ME10 .. **37** A3
Orchard Rd. Eastry CT13 .... **93** B3
Orchard Rd. Herne Bay CT6 .... **22** F3
Orchard Rd. Maidstone ME15 .. **75** E4
Orchard Rd. Margate CT9 .... **28** A8
Orchard Rd.
　St Mary's Bay TN29 .... **195** A5
Orchard Rd. St Michaels TN30 **167** A3
Orchard Residences The. CT1 .. **88** A5
Orchard Row. CT6 .... **23** A1
Orchard Sch. CT1 .... **87** F6
Orchard St. Canterbury CT2 .... **66** E1
Orchard St. Gillingham ME8 .... **33** E8
Orchard St. Maidstone ME15 .. **75** A3
Orchard The. ME14 .... **76** B4
Orchard Valley. CT21 .... **176** A2
Orchard View. Ash CT3 .... **71** F1
Orchard View.
　Tenterden TN30 .... **179** B8
Orchard View. Teynham ME9 .. **38** C3
Orchard Villas. CT16 .... **148** E4
Orchard Way. ME12 .... **5** D1
Orchards The. CT4 .... **144** F4
Ordnance St. ME4 .... **9** E3
Ordnance Terr. ME4 .... **9** E4
Orgarswick Ave. TN29 .... **195** C2
Orgarswick Way. TN29 .... **195** C7
Oriel Rd. TN23 .... **138** F4
Orient Pl. CT2 .... **66** F1
Orion Rd. ME1 .... **31** C7
Orion Way. TN24 .... **156** B2
Ormonde Ct. CT21 .... **176** C1
Ormonde Rd.
　Folkestone CT20 .... **178** B6
Ormonde Rd. Hythe CT21 .... **176** C1
Ormsby Gn. ME8 .... **33** E3
Orwell Pl. **6** ME15 .... **97** E8
Osborne Gdns. CT6 .... **23** D4
Osborne Rd. Ashford TN24 .... **156** F8
Osborne Rd. Gillingham ME7 .. **10** C5
Osborne Rd. Kingsdown CT14 **134** C6
Osborne Terr. CT9 .... **7** J1
Osbourn Ave. CT8 .... **27** E8
Osbourne Rd. CT10 .... **29** F4
Oscar Rd. CT10 .... **30** B4
Osier Field. TN24 .... **139** E2
Osier Rd. ME9 .... **38** E3
Osprey Ave. ME5 & ME7 .... **10** E2
Osprey Cl. CT5 .... **43** C7
Osprey Ct. **2** Dover CT16 .... **149** B2
Osprey Ct. Sittingbourne ME10 .. **37** A3
Ospringe CE Prim Sch. ME13 .. **62** A6
Ospringe Pl. ME13 .... **62** B6
Ospringe Rd. ME13 .... **62** B7
Ospringe St. ME13 .... **62** A6
Ostend Ct. ME10 .... **14** F1
Ostlers La. CT7 .... **48** D6
Oswald Pl. CT17 .... **149** B2
Oswald Rd. CT17 .... **149** B2
Otham Cl. CT2 .... **67** A4
Otham La. ME15 .... **76** C2
Otham St. Maidstone ME15 .... **76** C2
Otham St. Otham ME15 .... **98** B7
Ottawa Cres. CT16 .... **149** C3
Ottawa Way. CT16 .... **149** B3
Otterbourne Pl. ME15 .... **75** E1
Otterden Cl. TN23 .... **155** F6
Otterden Rd. ME13 .... **81** D3
Otterham Quay La. ME8 .... **12** B2
Otteridge Rd. ME14 .... **76** A3
Otterpool La. CT21 & TN25 .. **174** D4
Otway St. ME4 .... **10** A3
Otway Terr. **1** ME4 .... **10** A3
Out Elmstead La. CT4 .... **111** F2
Oval The. TN29 .... **186** D1
Overland La. CT3 .... **71** A3
Owen Sq. CT14 .... **117** B2
Owen's Cl. CT21 .... **177** B3
Owens Court Cotts. ME13 .... **83** F8
Owens Way. ME7 .... **11** A6
Owl's Hatch Rd. CT6 .... **22** C1
Ox La. TN30 .... **167** B2
Oxen Lease. TN23 .... **155** E8
Oxenden Cnr. CT3 .... **23** F1
Oxenden Cres. CT3 .... **91** A8
Oxenden Park Dr. CT6 .... **22** E4
Oxenden Rd. CT20 .... **177** C4
Oxenden St. CT6 .... **22** E5
Oxenden Way. CT4 .... **128** F8
Oxenturn Rd. TN25 .... **140** E8
Oxford Cl. CT1 .... **87** F7
Oxford Rd. Canterbury CT1 .... **87** F7
Oxford Rd. Gillingham ME7 .... **10** D3
Oxford Rd. Maidstone ME15 .. **97** D8
Oxford St. **6** Margate CT9 ...... **7** J2
Oxford St. Whitstable CT5 .... **20** D1
Oxford Terr. CT20 .... **178** D4
Oxney Cl. CT7 .... **26** F7
Oxney Cotts. TN30 .... **190** A4
Oyster Cl. ME10 .... **36** E6

Packer Pl. ME5 .... **32** A8
Packer's La. CT11 .... **52** E7
Pad's Hill. ME15 .... **75** A4
Padbrook La. CT3 .... **70** D6
Paddock Cl. Deal CT14 .... **116** F5

Paddock Cl. Folkestone CT20 ...... **177** F5
Paddock Cl. Lydd TN29 ...... **203** B6
Paddock Rd. Ashford TN23 ...... **155** C2
Paddock Rd. Birchington CT7 ...... **27** A7
Paddock The. Canterbury CT1 ...... **88** B8
Paddock The. Chatham ME4 ...... **9** F4
Paddock The. Chilham CT4 ...... **85** C2
Paddock The. Dover CT16 ...... **166** D8
Paddock View. CT5 ...... **43** E7
Paddocks The.
Broadstairs CT10 ...... **29** F7
Paddocks The. Gillingham ME7 ...... **33** A5
Paddocks The.
Great Chart TN23 ...... **138** C1
Paddocks The. Herne Bay CT6 ...... **23** F5
Padsole La. ME15 ...... **75** A4
Padstow Manor. ME7 ...... **10** C6
Padwell La. TN23 ...... **155** C8
Paffard Cl. CT2 ...... **67** F6
Paffard Ct. CT2 ...... **67** F6
Page Pl. CT19 ...... **178** D8
Paget Row. ME7 ...... **10** C5
Paget St. ME7 ...... **10** C5
Pagitt St. ME4 ...... **9** E3
Paine Ave. TN29 ...... **203** C6
Painesfield Cl. TN29 ...... **186** C4
Painter's Forstal Rd. ME13 ...... **61** E3
Palace Ave. ME15 ...... **75** A4
Palace Cl. CT5 ...... **21** B2
Palace Cotts. ME9 ...... **80** F8
Palace Ct. Chatham ME5 ...... **10** D2
Palace Ct. Hythe CT21 ...... **176** C2
Palace St. **17** CT1 ...... **67** A1
Palace Wood
Cty Inf Sch. ME16 ...... **74** C6
Palace Wood
Cty Jun Sch. ME16 ...... **74** C6
Palm Bay Ave. CT9 ...... **8** D3
Palm Bay Cty Prim Sch. CT9 ...... **8** D3
Palm Bay Gdns. CT9 ...... **8** C3
Palm Tree Cl. CT15 ...... **131** D7
Palm Tree Way. CT18 ...... **161** B7
Palmar Rd. ME16 ...... **74** D6
Palmarsh Ave. CT21 ...... **187** D7
Palmarsh Cres. CT21 ...... **187** D7
Palmarsh
Cty Prim Sch. CT21 ...... **187** D8
Palmbeach Ave. CT21 ...... **187** D6
Palmer Cl. CT6 ...... **46** B8
Palmer Cres. CT9 ...... **29** C8
Palmer Rd. CT3 ...... **91** A8
Palmers Cross Hill. CT2 ...... **66** A1
Palmerston Ave.
Broadstairs CT10 ...... **30** B3
Palmerston Ave. Deal CT14 ...... **117** C2
Palmerston Ct. CT14 ...... **117** D2
Palmerston Rd. ME4 ...... **9** F1
Palmerston St. **4** CT19 ...... **178** D6
Palmerston Wlk. ME10 ...... **37** C4
Palting Way. CT20 ...... **178** B4
Panteny La. ME9 ...... **37** E2
Panton Cl. ME5 ...... **32** C4
Papion Gr. ME5 ...... **31** E2
Papworth Cl. **1** CT19 ...... **178** A7
Parade. CT1 ...... **87** F8
Parade Rd. CT20 ...... **177** F3
Parade The. Birchington CT7 ...... **26** D8
Parade The. Folkestone CT20 ...... **178** E5
Parade The.
Greatstone-on-S TN28 & TN29 ...... **204** E3
Parade The. Margate CT9 ...... **7** I3
Parade The. Sevington TN24 ...... **156** F5
Paradise. CT11 ...... **52** D7
Paradise Cotts. ME9 ...... **34** E5
Paradise Row CT13 ...... **72** F1
Paragon. CT11 ...... **52** E5
Paragon St. CT11 ...... **52** D5
Paraker Way. CT21 ...... **177** B4
Pardoner Cl. CT2 ...... **87** C7
Pardoners Way. CT16 ...... **149** A5
Parfitt Way. CT16 ...... **149** B2
Parham Cl. CT1 ...... **67** B2
Parham Rd. Canterbury CT1 ...... **67** B2
Parham Rd. Chatham ME4 ...... **9** F2
Paris Cnr. TN26 ...... **153** F6
Parish Ct. Chartham CT4 ...... **86** C3
Parish Rd. Minster ME12 ...... **4** A5
Park Ave. Birchington CT7 ...... **27** A6
Park Ave. Broadstairs CT10 ...... **29** E2
Park Ave. Deal CT14 ...... **117** C5
Park Ave. Dover CT16 ...... **149** D1
Park Ave. Gillingham ME7 ...... **10** D3
Park Ave. Leysdown-on-S ME12 ...... **6** G1
Park Ave. Loose ME17 ...... **96** E2
Park Ave. Maidstone ME14 ...... **75** B6
Park Ave. Queenborough ME11 ...... **3** B4
Park Ave. Sittingbourne ME10 ...... **36** E1
Park Ave. Whitstable CT5 ...... **20** F3
Park Barn Rd. ME17 ...... **99** C5
Park Chase. CT10 ...... **29** E2
Park Cl. CT9 ...... **8** D1
Park Cotts. CT11 ...... **29** E2
Park Cres. ME4 ...... **31** F8
Park Crescent Rd. CT9 ...... **8** A1
Park Ct. ME13 ...... **62** E7
Park Dr. Hothfield TN26 ...... **138** A6
Park Dr. Sittingbourne ME10 ...... **36** D1
Park Farm Cl.
Shadoxhurst TN26 ...... **155** A1
Park Farm Cl. Tyler Hill CT2 ...... **66** E6
Park Farm Prim Sch. CT19 ...... **178** C6
Park Farm Rd. CT19 ...... **178** C2
Park Gate. CT10 ...... **29** F2
Park Ho. ME4 ...... **75** B6
Park La. Bethersden TN26 ...... **154** C8
Park La. Birchington CT7 ...... **27** A6
Park La. Bishopsbourne CT4 ...... **111** C5

Park La. Cock Street ME17 ...... **97** D2
Park La. Elham CT4 ...... **144** F5
Park La. Maidstone ME14 ...... **74** F7
Park La. Margate CT9 ...... **8** A2
Park Lea. CT14 ...... **117** C5
Park Mall. **2** TN23 ...... **139** B2
Park Manor. ME7 ...... **10** B5
Park Mews. **6** CT16 ...... **166** D8
Park Pl. Ashford TN24 ...... **156** F8
Park Pl.
Ashford, Willesborough TN23 ...... **156** B7
Park Pl. Dover CT16 ...... **166** D8
Park Pl. Herne CT6 ...... **46** A8
Park Pl. Margate CT9 ...... **7** I1
Park Rd. Ashford TN24 ...... **139** D6
Park Rd. Broadstairs CT10 ...... **30** B6
Park Rd. Dover CT16 ...... **149** B2
Park Rd. Faversham ME13 ...... **62** D7
Park Rd.
Folkestone CT19 & CT20 ...... **177** E6
Park Rd. Herne Bay CT6 ...... **22** F4
Park Rd. Hythe CT21 ...... **176** B1
Park Rd. Littlestone-on-S TN28 ...... **200** E5
Park Rd. Margate CT9 ...... **8** A2
Park Rd. Preston CT3 ...... **70** D7
Park Rd. Queenborough ME11 ...... **2** F5
Park Rd. Ramsgate CT11 ...... **52** C7
Park Rd. Sheerness ME12 ...... **1** E1
Park Rd. Sittingbourne ME10 ...... **36** E3
Park Rd. Temple Ewell CT16 ...... **148** D5
Park Rd.
Westgate-on-S CT7 & CT8 & CT9 ...... **27** D6
Park St. Ashford TN23 & TN24 ...... **139** C2
Park St. Deal CT14 ...... **117** C6
Park St. Dover CT16 ...... **166** D8
Park St. Lydd TN29 ...... **203** C6
Park Terr. Throwley ME13 ...... **82** D1
Park Terr.
Woodnesborough CT13 ...... **93** D7
Park Vale. TN24 ...... **139** D6
Park View. Folkestone CT19 ...... **178** E7
Park View. Sturry CT2 ...... **67** F6
Park View Ct. CT3 ...... **91** D2
Park View Ct. ME15 ...... **75** E1
Park View Rise. CT15 ...... **113** D4
Park Way. Coxheath ME17 ...... **96** D3
Park Way. Maidstone ME15 ...... **75** B1
Park Way
Cty Prim Sch. ME15 ...... **75** B1
Park Wood Cl. TN23 ...... **156** B5
Park Wood
Cty Prim Schs. ME8 ...... **33** E5
Park Wood Gn. ME8 ...... **33** D5
Park Wood Par. ME8 ...... **33** D6
Park Wood Trad Est. ME15 ...... **97** F4
Parker Cl. Gillingham ME8 ...... **33** E5
Parker Cl. Hamstreet TN26 ...... **183** A7
Parkfield Rd. Folkestone CT19 ...... **178** C6
Parkfield Rd. Gillingham ME8 ...... **11** F1
Parkland Ct. CT10 ...... **29** F6
Parkside Cty Prim Sch. CT1 ...... **67** D2
Parkway The. CT7 ...... **27** B7
Parkwood Cl. CT10 ...... **29** F2
Parr Ave. ME7 ...... **10** D6
Parrs Head Mews. ME1 ...... **9** C6
Parsonage Chase. ME12 ...... **3** F5
Parsonage Cotts. ME9 ...... **58** A5
Parsonage Farm
(Rural Heritage Ctr) CT4 ...... **145** A6
Parsonage Fields. CT12 ...... **49** C7
Parsonage La. Bobbing ME9 ...... **14** A1
Parsonage La. Rochester ME2 ...... **9** B8
Parsonage Rd. CT6 ...... **23** A3
Parsonage Stocks Rd. ME13 ...... **82** F5
Parsonage Villas. CT15 ...... **165** C5
Partridge La. ME13 ...... **62** D7
Pasley Rd. ME7 ...... **10** A7
Pasley Rd E. ME7 ...... **10** B7
Pasley Rd W. ME4 ...... **10** A7
Pasture The. TN24 ...... **139** D6
Patchways. TN29 ...... **184** E3
Path Field Cotts. CT15 ...... **164** E5
Patricia Way. CT10 ...... **29** D3
Patrixbourne Ave. ME8 ...... **11** C2
Patrixbourne Rd. CT4 ...... **89** B2
Pattens Gdns. ME4 ...... **9** E2
Pattens La. ME4 ...... **9** E1
Pattens Pl. ME1 ...... **9** D2
Paul's Pl. **8** CT16 ...... **149** C1
Pavement The. TN30 ...... **167** B3
Pavilion Ct. CT20 ...... **178** E4
Pavilion Dr. ME10 ...... **14** F1
Pavilion Meadow. CT17 ...... **148** E4
Pavilion Rd. CT19 ...... **178** D6
Pay St. CT18 ...... **162** F7
Payden St. ME7 & ME9 ...... **102** D8
Payers Pk. CT20 ...... **178** D5
Payne's La. ME15 ...... **97** B7
Pays La. TN25 ...... **104** D1
Payton Cl. CT9 ...... **29** A7
Payton Mews. **4** CT1 ...... **67** B1
Peacock Mews. **7** ME16 ...... **74** E4
Peacock Pl. ME12 ...... **84** A6
Peafield Wood Rd. CT4 ...... **127** E4
Peak Dr. CT13 ...... **93** B3
Pean Court Rd. CT5 ...... **43** D3
Pean Hill. CT5 ...... **43** D2
Pear Tree Alley. **2** ME10 ...... **36** E5
Pear Tree Cl. CT10 ...... **29** C4
Pear Tree La.
Dymchurch TN29 ...... **186** D1
Pear Tree La. Gillingham ME7 ...... **32** E7
Pear Tree La. Maidstone ME15 ...... **97** B6
Pear Tree Wlk. ME9 ...... **35** A5
Pearmain Wlk. CT1 ...... **88** C7
Pearman Cl. ME8 ...... **12** A1

Pearson's Way. CT10 ...... **29** E7
Peartree Cotts. ME8 ...... **34** B8
Peartree Rd. CT6 ...... **23** C3
Peckham Cl. ME2 ...... **9** C8
Pedding Hill. CT3 ...... **71** A1
Pedding La. CT3 ...... **92** A8
Peel Dr. ME10 ...... **37** C4
Peel St. ME14 ...... **75** A6
Peene Cotts. CT18 ...... **162** B1
Pegwell Ave. CT11 ...... **52** A5
Pegwell Cl. CT11 ...... **52** A5
Pegwell Rd. CT11 ...... **52** B5
Pegwell Rd. CT11 ...... **52** B5
Pelham Gdns. CT20 ...... **178** A4
Pelwood Rd. TN31 ...... **201** A2
Pemberton Ct. CT21 ...... **177** B3
Pemberton Rd. TN24 ...... **139** D2
Pemberton Sq. ME2 ...... **9** C8
Pembroke. ME4 ...... **10** B8
Pembroke Ave. CT5 ...... **7** F1
Pembroke Ct. Chatham ME4 ...... **10** A4
Pembroke Ct. **1**
Ramsgate CT11 ...... **52** E7
Pembroke Gdns. ME8 ...... **33** E4
Pembroke Mews. TN28 ...... **200** C8
Pembroke Rd. ME17 ...... **96** C3
Pembury Ct. **6** ME10 ...... **36** E4
Pembury Gdns. ME16 ...... **74** D3
Pembury St. ME10 ...... **36** E4
Pembury Way. ME8 ...... **11** E2
Pencester Ct. CT16 ...... **166** E8
Pencester Rd. CT16 ...... **166** D8
Penderel Mews. TN30 ...... **179** B8
Penenden Ct. ME14 ...... **75** B7
Penenden Heath Rd. ME14 ...... **75** C7
Penenden St. ME14 ...... **75** A6
Penfield La. ME9 ...... **59** A4
Penfold Cl. Chatham ME5 ...... **32** B7
Penfold Cl. Park Wood ME15 ...... **97** E5
Penfold Gdns. CT15 ...... **130** E5
Penfold Hill. ME17 ...... **99** B8
Penfold Rd. CT19 ...... **178** F6
Penfold Way. ME15 ...... **96** F6
Penhurst Cl. ME14 ...... **75** F5
Penlee Point. TN24 ...... **139** D5
Penn Cl. ME10 ...... **37** B2
Penn Hill. TN23 ...... **155** E6
Pennant Rd. ME1 ...... **31** C7
Pennine Way. Ashford TN24 ...... **139** B4
Pennine Way. Maidstone ME15 ...... **76** A1
Pennington Cl. CT2 ...... **68** C7
Penny Pot La. CT4 ...... **108** B4
Pennypot Ind Est. CT21 ...... **175** F1
Penrose Ct. CT21 ...... **176** C1
Penryn Manor. ME7 ...... **10** C6
Pensand Ho. CT21 ...... **176** D1
Penshurst Cl. Canterbury CT2 ...... **67** A3
Penshurst Cl. Gillingham ME8 ...... **11** C2
Penshurst Gdns. CT9 ...... **8** F2
Penshurst Rd. CT11 ...... **52** F7
Penshurst Rise. ME13 ...... **62** B8
Penstocks The. ME16 ...... **74** D2
Pent Vale Cl. CT19 ...... **178** A6
Pent Valley High Sch. CT19 ...... **177** F7
Pent Valley Sch (annexe).
CT19 ...... **177** F6
Pepys Ave. ME12 ...... **1** C2
Percival Terr. CT17 ...... **166** B7
Percy Ave. CT10 ...... **8** F2
Percy Rd. Broadstairs CT10 ...... **29** F5
Percy Rd. Margate CT9 ...... **8** A3
Percy Rd. Ramsgate CT11 ...... **52** D8
Peregrine Dr. ME10 ...... **37** A2
Peri Ct. CT1 ...... **87** E6
Perimeter Rd. CT16 ...... **166** G8
Periwinkle Cl. ME10 ...... **36** E5
Periwinkle Ct. **5** ME10 ...... **36** E5
Perkins Ave. CT9 ...... **28** F8
Perries Mead. CT19 ...... **178** B7
Perry Court
Rudolf Steiner Sch. CT4 ...... **108** E7
Perry Rd. CT3 ...... **70** C3
Perry St. Chatham ME4 ...... **9** E3
Perry St. Maidstone ME14 ...... **74** F6
Perryfield St. ME14 ...... **74** F6
Perth Gdns. ME10 ...... **36** C4
Perth Way. CT16 ...... **149** C3
Pested Bars Rd. ME17 ...... **97** D5
Pested La. CT4 & TN25 ...... **105** C4
Petchell Mews. **11** CT1 ...... **67** B2
Peter St. Deal CT14 ...... **117** D7
Peter St. Dover CT16 & CT17 ...... **166** C8
Peter St. Folkestone CT20 ...... **178** E5
Petfield Cl. ME12 ...... **4** C6
Petham Cty Prim Sch. CT4 ...... **109** C3
Pett Bottom Rd. CT4 ...... **110** C5
Pett Hill. CT15 ...... **88** F1
Pett La. TN27 ...... **120** D7
Pett's Cres. CT12 ...... **50** B5
Pettfield Hill Rd. ME13 ...... **82** B1
Pettitts Row. ME13 ...... **62** B7
Peverel Dr. ME14 ...... **76** A5
Peverel Gn. ME8 ...... **33** D4
Peverell Rd. CT16 ...... **149** B4
Pheasant La. ME15 ...... **97** B8
Pheasant Rd. ME4 ...... **10** C2
Pheasants' Hall Rd. CT4 ...... **110** F2
Philip Corby Cl. CT9 ...... **8** B2
Philippa Ho. CT19 ...... **178** F6
Phillip Rd. CT19 ...... **177** D7
Phillipine Village Craft Ctr.
TN29 ...... **197** A6
Phillippa Ct. ME10 ...... **36** E8
Phillips Ct. ME8 ...... **11** B2

Phillips Rd. CT7 ...... **27** A6
Phoenix Ind Est. ME2 ...... **9** D7
Phoenix Pk. ME15 ...... **97** F4
Phoenix Rd. ME5 ...... **32** B2
Piccadilly The. **4** ME4 ...... **10** B3
Pickelden La. CT4 ...... **107** F8
Pickering St. ME15 ...... **97** B6
Pickhill Oast. TN30 ...... **179** B4
Pickneybush La. TN29 ...... **194** A7
Pickwick Cres. ME1 ...... **9** C3
Picton Rd. CT11 ...... **52** C7
Pier Approach Rd. ME7 ...... **10** D7
Pier Ave. Herne Bay CT6 ...... **22** E4
Pier Ave. Whitstable CT5 ...... **21** A2
Pier Rd Ind Est. ME7 ...... **10** D7
Pier The. CT16 ...... **148** F8
Pierpoint Rd. CT5 ...... **43** D7
Pierremont Ave. CT10 ...... **30** A4
Pigeon La. CT6 ...... **23** A2
Pigtail Cnr. ME12 ...... **4** E6
Pike Cl. CT19 ...... **178** A7
Pike Rd. CT14 & CT15 ...... **114** E4
Pikefields. ME8 ...... **11** C2
Pilcem Cl. CT1 ...... **67** D1
Pilgrim Spring. CT19 ...... **178** D8
Pilgrims Ct. TN27 ...... **120** C7
Pilgrims La. Chilham CT4 ...... **85** E1
Pilgrims La. Whitstable CT5 ...... **43** B4
Pilgrims Lakes. ME17 ...... **100** E6
Pilgrims Rd. CT1 ...... **88** C7
Pilgrims View. ME14 ...... **53** E3
Pilgrims Way. Boxley ME14 ...... **54** C3
Pilgrims' Way.
Brabourne TN25 ...... **159** E8
Pilgrims Way.
Broad Street ME14 & ME17 ...... **77** C6
Pilgrims Way. Canterbury CT1 ...... **88** C7
Pilgrims Way. Charing TN27 ...... **120** C8
Pilgrims Way. Detling ME14 ...... **55** B1
Pilgrims Way. Dover CT16 ...... **149** A3
Pilgrims Way. Eccles ME20 ...... **53** B6
Pilgrims Way.
Hollingbourne ME17 ...... **77** F3
Pilgrims Way. Lenham ME17 ...... **101** B7
Pilgrims Way. Westwell TN25 ...... **121** D5
Pilgrims Way
Cty Prim Sch The. CT1 ...... **88** C7
Pilot Rd. ME1 ...... **31** C8
Pilot's Farm Rd. CT4 ...... **110** A4
Pilots Ave. CT14 ...... **117** A4
Pimp's Court Cotts. ME15 ...... **96** E6
Pimp's Court Farm Ctr. ME15 ...... **96** E6
Pimpernel Cl. ME14 ...... **76** B4
Pimpernel Way. ME5 ...... **31** E4
Pin Hill. CT1 ...... **87** F7
Pine Cotts. ME14 ...... **74** E8
Pine Gr. Gillingham ME7 ...... **33** A5
Pine Gr. Maidstone ME14 ...... **75** B6
Pine Ho. **3** ME5 ...... **31** F5
Pine Lodge. ME16 ...... **74** C3
Pine Tree Ave. CT2 ...... **66** E2
Pine Way. CT19 ...... **177** D7
Pine Wlk. CT6 ...... **23** E5
Pineham Rd. CT15 ...... **149** D6
Pines Gdns The. CT15 ...... **151** B5
Pines The. CT10 ...... **29** D4
Pineside Rd. CT3 ...... **89** E8
Pinetree Ct. CT5 ...... **20** C3
Pinewood Cl. CT12 ...... **29** C1
Pinewood Dr. ME14 ...... **54** B8
Pink's Cnr. ME9 ...... **14** E3
Pinks Cnr. CT12 ...... **50** D6
Pinners Hill. CT15 ...... **113** C6
Pinners La. CT15 ...... **113** C5
Pinous Ho. ME10 ...... **36** D5
Pintail Way. CT6 ...... **23** C2
Pioneer Rd. CT16 ...... **149** A3
Pippin Ave. CT4 ...... **111** B8
Pippin Cl. Coxheath ME17 ...... **96** B2
Pippin Cl. Sittingbourne ME10 ...... **36** D6
Pippin Croft. ME7 ...... **33** A6
Pirbright Cl. ME5 ...... **32** D2
Pitstock Rd. ME9 ...... **59** B5
Pitt Rd. Langley Heath ME17 ...... **99** A2
Pitt Rd. Maidstone ME16 ...... **74** B1
Pittlesden. TN30 ...... **179** A7
Pittlesden Pl. **1** TN30 ...... **179** A7
Pittock Ho. CT14 ...... **117** B3
Pivington La. CT4 ...... **119** C3
Pivington Mill Ind Est. TN27 ...... **119** C2
Pixwell La. CT14 ...... **116** D3
Place La. Hartlip ME9 ...... **34** D4
Place La. Woodchurch TN26 ...... **169** B3
Place The. CT4 ...... **112** F1
Plain Rd. Brabourne Lees TN25 ...... **158** F5
Plain Rd. Folkestone CT20 ...... **178** B4
Plains Ave. ME15 ...... **75** C1
Plains Of Waterloo. CT11 ...... **52** F7
Plaistow Sq. ME14 ...... **75** C6
Plantation Cl. TN26 ...... **138** A7
Plantation La. ME14 ...... **76** A3
Plantation Rd. Faversham ME13 ...... **62** C7
Plantation Rd. Gillingham ME7 ...... **11** A6
Plantation Rd. Whitstable CT5 ...... **21** D2
Platt's Heath
Cty Prim Sch. ME17 ...... **100** F2
Platters The. ME8 ...... **33** C7
Playstool Cl. ME9 ...... **35** B6
Playstool Rd. ME9 ...... **35** A6
Plaza Ct. ME10 ...... **37** A4
Pleasance Rd N. TN29 ...... **204** E5
Pleasance Rd S. TN29 ...... **204** F2
Pleasance Road Central.
TN29 ...... **204** F3
Pleasant Row. **2** ME4 ...... **10** A6
Pleasant Pl. ME12 ...... **3** E6
Plenty Brook Dr. CT6 ...... **22** F3

Plewis Ho. ME7 ...... **10** E7
Pleydell Cres. CT2 ...... **67** F7
Pleydell Gdns. CT20 ...... **178** D4
Plimsoll Ave. CT19 ...... **178** E8
Plomley Cl. ME8 ...... **33** D4
Plough Cotts. ME17 ...... **98** E2
Plough Ct. CT6 ...... **23** D2
Plough Hill. CT15 ...... **165** C4
Plough La. CT5 ...... **21** D3
Plough Rd. ME12 ...... **5** C5
Plough Wents Rd. ME17 ...... **98** B2
Ploughmans Way.
Chatham ME5 ...... **32** A1
Ploughmans Way.
Gillingham ME8 ...... **33** E6
Plover Cl. ME5 ...... **32** D1
Pluckley CE Prim Sch. TN27 ...... **136** D7
Pluckley Cl. ME8 ...... **11** C3
Pluckley Gdns. CT9 ...... **8** E2
Pluckley Rd.
Bethersden TN26 & TN27 ...... **153** D7
Pluckley Rd. Charing TN27 ...... **120** B5
Pluckley Rd. Hothfield TN26 ...... **137** B4
Pluckley Rd.
Maitman's Hill TN27 ...... **135** D2
Pluckley Sta. TN27 ...... **136** C3
Plum Tree Gdns. TN26 ...... **169** B1
Plum Tree Rd. ME9 ...... **56** B8
Plumford Rd. ME13 ...... **62** A2
Plumpton Wlk. **5**
Canterbury CT1 ...... **67** B1
Plumpton Wlk. **9**
Maidstone ME15 ...... **97** F6
Plumpudding La. ME13 ...... **42** E1
Plumstone Rd. CT7 ...... **26** F1
Plumtree Gr. ME7 ...... **33** A4
Plumtrees. ME16 ...... **74** A2
Plurenden Manor Farm Cotts.
TN26 ...... **168** E7
Plurenden Rd. TN26 ...... **168** E7
Poachers Cl. ME5 ...... **32** C5
Podkin Wood. ME5 ...... **53** F8
Poets Cnr. CT14 ...... **7** J1
Poets Wlk. CT14 ...... **117** C1
Poison Cross. CT13 ...... **93** B4
Poldark Ct. **14** CT11 ...... **52** F7
Poles The. ME9 ...... **12** E4
Polhill Dr. ME5 ...... **31** F2
Pollard Cl. TN23 ...... **155** F8
Pollard Ct. ME7 ...... **10** C5
Polo Way. CT5 ...... **21** D1
Pomfret Ho. CT4 ...... **86** D1
Pomfret Rd. CT4 ...... **86** D1
Pommeus La. CT14 ...... **133** D7
Poncia Rd. TN23 ...... **156** A7
Pond Cotts. Herne Bay CT6 ...... **23** D2
Pond Cotts. Sittingbourne ME10 ...... **58** D8
Pond Dr. ME10 ...... **37** A2
Pond Farm Rd. Hucking ME17 ...... **56** F1
Pond Farm Rd. Oad Street ME9 ...... **35** F1
Pond Hill. CT3 ...... **90** D1
Pond Hill Rd. CT20 ...... **177** C5
Pond La.
St Margaret's at Cliffe CT15 ...... **150** D7
Pond La.
Womenswold CT3 & CT4 ...... **112** D3
Pondfield. TN25 ...... **139** C8
Poorhole La. CT10 ...... **29** B5
Poot La. ME9 ...... **12** E5
Pope House La. TN30 ...... **167** B4
Pope St. Godmersham CT4 ...... **107** E4
Pope St. Maidstone ME16 ...... **74** C2
Popes La. CT2 ...... **67** F7
Poplar Cl. TN23 ...... **138** F3
Poplar Dr. Elvington CT15 ...... **114** B2
Poplar Dr. Herne Bay CT6 ...... **22** D2
Poplar Field. TN30 ...... **188** D4
Poplar Gr. ME14 ...... **74** C5
Poplar Ho. ME12 ...... **1** C2
Poplar La. TN29 ...... **203** D7
Poplar Rd. Broadstairs CT10 ...... **29** E6
Poplar Rd. Ramsgate CT11 ...... **52** D7
Poplar Rd. Wittersham TN30 ...... **188** D4
Poplar View. ME13 ...... **63** E3
Poplars. TN26 ...... **182** A7
Poplars The. Ashford TN23 ...... **156** A7
Poplars The. Bethersden TN26 ...... **153** E5
Poplars The. Hersden CT3 ...... **46** F1
Poppy Cl. ME7 ...... **10** E5
Popsal Cl. CT3 ...... **91** B6
Porchester Cl. ME15 ...... **97** A6
Port Cl. Chatham ME5 ...... **32** B3
Port Cl. Maidstone ME14 ...... **76** A5
Port Lympne Zoo. CT21 ...... **174** C2
Port Rise. ME4 ...... **9** F3
Portal House Sch. CT15 ...... **151** A6
Portebello Ct. CT14 ...... **117** D7
Porter Cl. ME12 ...... **4** A6
Porter's La. ME13 ...... **62** B2
Porters Wlk. ME17 ...... **98** E4
Portland Ave. ME10 ...... **37** C4
Portland Cl. Ashford TN24 ...... **139** C7
Portland Cl. Hythe CT21 ...... **176** B2
Portland Ct. **3** Hythe CT21 ...... **176** B2
Portland Ct. Ramsgate CT11 ...... **52** E7
Portland Rd. Gillingham ME7 ...... **10** E6
Portland Rd. Hythe CT21 ...... **176** B2
Portland St. ME14 ...... **10** B2
Portland Terr. Ripple CT14 ...... **133** D8
Portland Terr. Sheerness ME12 ...... **1** D2
Portsdown Cl. ME14 ...... **74** B2
Portway. CT5 ...... **43** C8
Post Barn Rd. ME4 ...... **9** F2
Postley Commercial Ctr. ME15 ...... **75** A2
Postley Rd. ME15 ...... **75** A1

Postling. TN23 .... 138 E1
Postling Rd. CT19 .... 177 E7
Postling Wents. CT21 .... 175 F8
Postmill Dr. ME15 .... 74 F1
Potten Street Rd. CT7 .... 25 E3
Potter St. CT13 .... 73 A1
Potters Cl. TN24 .... 138 E6
Potters Cnr. TN24 .... 138 E6
Pottery Cotts. TN25 .... 140 E5
Potyn Ho. ME1 .... 9 C4
Pouces Cotts. CT12 .... 27 F1
Poulders Gdns. CT13 .... 93 E8
Poulders Rd. CT13 .... 93 E8
Poulsen Ct. ME10 .... 37 B4
Poulton Cl. CT17 .... 165 F8
Poulton Close Bsns Pk. CT17 . 148 E1
Poulton La. CT3 .... 92 C8
Pound Ct. TN23 .... 156 A3
Pound Farm Cotts. CT18 .... 177 A7
Pound Ho. TN23 .... 156 B8
Pound La. Ashford TN23 .... 155 F4
Pound La.
   Brabourne Lees TN25 .... 158 F5
Pound La.
   Canterbury CT1 & CT2 .... 66 F1
Pound La. Elham CT4 .... 144 F4
Pound La. Molash CT4 .... 105 F4
Poundhurst Rd. TN26 .... 171 C3
Powell Cl. ME20 .... 53 A3
Powell Cotton Dr. CT7 .... 27 B6
Powell Cotton Mus. CT7 .... 27 B5
Powell Sch (Prim) The. CT16 . 149 B4
Power Station Rd. ME12 .... 3 E7
Pratling St. ME20 .... 53 C4
Precincts The. 16
   Canterbury CT1 .... 67 A1
Precincts The. Canterbury CT1 .. 88 A8
Prentis Cl. ME10 .... 36 C5
Prentis Quay. ME10 .... 36 E5
Prescott Cl. CT15 .... 149 E6
Prescott Ho. TN28 .... 200 A4
Prestedge Ave. CT10 & CT11 ..... 29 E2
Preston Ave. Faversham ME13 ... 62 E6
Preston Ave. Gillingham ME7 ... 10 E1
Preston Gr. ME13 .... 62 D6
Preston Hall Gdns. ME12 .... 6 E4
Preston Hill. CT3 .... 70 B1
Preston La. Faversham ME13 ... 62 D6
Preston La. Preston CT3 .... 70 B5
Preston Malt Ho. ME13 .... 62 D6
Preston Par. ME13 .... 42 F7
Preston Pk. ME13 .... 62 D6
Preston Rd. Manston CT12 ...... 28 E2
Preston Rd. Stourmouth CT3 .... 48 D1
Preston Rd. Wingham CT3 .... 70 B2
Preston St. ME13 .... 62 D7
Preston-next-Wingham
   Cty Prim Sch. CT3 .... 70 C6
Pretoria Ho. 8 ME14 .... 97 E5
Pretoria Rd. Canterbury CT1 .... 88 B8
Pretoria Rd. Chatham ME4 .... 9 F2
Pretoria Rd. Gillingham ME7 ... 10 D3
Price's Ave. Margate CT9 .... 8 B2
Price's Ave. Ramsgate CT11 ... 52 E6
Priest Ave. CT2 .... 87 C7
Priest Fields. CT6 .... 23 F5
Priest & Sow Cnr. CT5 .... 21 B3
Priest Wlk. CT5 .... 21 C3
Priestfield Rd. ME7 .... 10 E5
Priestfield Stad
   (Gillingham FC). ME7 .... 10 E1
Priestfields. ME1 .... 9 B3
Primrose Ave. ME8 .... 33 B5
Primrose Cl. ME1 .... 31 E7
Primrose Dr. TN23 .... 156 B4
Primrose Gr. ME9 .... 58 A6
Primrose Hill. CT4 .... 86 B7
Primrose La. ME9 .... 58 A6
Primrose Pl. CT17 .... 149 B1
Primrose Rd. CT17 .... 149 A1
Primrose Way. Cliffs End CT12 .. 51 C5
Primrose Way. Whitstable CT5 ... 21 C1
Prince Andrew Rd. CT10 .... 29 E7
Prince Arthur Rd. ME7 .... 10 B6
Prince Charles Ave.
   Chatham ME5 .... 32 B4
Prince Charles Ave.
   Minster ME12 .... 4 C6
Prince Charles Ave.
   Sittingbourne ME10 .... 37 C3
Prince Charles Rd. CT10 .... 29 E7
Prince of Wales Terr. CT14 .... 117 D5
Prince's Ave. CT12 .... 29 B1
Prince's Gdns. CT9 .... 8 C2
Prince's Golf Links. CT13 .... 73 E5
Prince's Rd. CT11 .... 52 D8
Prince's St. Margate CT9 .... 7 J2
Prince's St. 7 Ramsgate CT11 .. 52 E6
Prince's St. Rochester ME1 .... 9 C4
Prince's Wlk. CT9 .... 8 D3
Princes Ave. Chatham ME5 ...... 32 B5
Princes Ave. Minster ME12 .... 4 D7
Princes Cl. CT7 .... 26 D7
Princes Cres. 10 CT9 .... 7 J2
Princes Dr. Sandwich CT13 ..... 73 F2
Princes Dr. Sandwich CT13 ..... 95 A8
Princes Par. CT21 .... 176 E2
Princes St. Deal CT14 .... 117 D7
Princes St. 11
   Dover CT16 & CT17 .... 166 D7
Princes St. Maidstone ME14 ... 75 A5
Princes Terr. CT21 .... 175 F1
Princes Way. Canterbury CT2 ... 66 E1
Princes Way. Detling ME14 ...... 55 A1

Princess Anne Rd. CT10 .... 29 E7
Princess Cl. CT5 .... 21 C3
Princess Margaret Ave.
   Margate CT9 .... 8 E2
Princess Margaret Ave.
   Ramsgate CT12 .... 29 A1
Princess Mary Ave. ME7 .... 10 B7
Princess Mary's
   Day Hospl. CT9 .... 8 A2
Princess Rd. CT5 .... 21 C3
Princess St. CT19 .... 178 E6
Prinys Dr. ME8 .... 33 C4
Prior Rd. TN29 .... 204 E8
Prior's Lees. 8 CT20 .... 178 D4
Prioress Rd. CT2 .... 87 D8
Priory Cl. Broadstairs CT10 ..... 29 F3
Priory Cl. East Farleigh ME15 .. 96 B8
Priory Cl. New Romney TN28 .. 199 F6
Priory Ct. Gillingham ME8 .... 11 A2
Priory Ct. Leysdown-on-S ME12 .. 6 G1
Priory Cty Inf Sch.
   Ramsgate CT11 .... 52 D6
Priory Cty Inf Sch.
   Ramsgate CT11 .... 52 D7
Priory Gate. 4 ME14 .... 75 A5
Priory Gate Rd. CT17 .... 166 C8
Priory Gdns. CT20 .... 178 D4
Priory Gr. CT17 .... 166 C8
Priory Hill. CT16 & CT17 .... 166 C8
Priory Ho. CT17 .... 166 C7
Priory La. Herne Bay CT6 .... 23 A3
Priory La. Sellindge TN25 ...... 159 D4
Priory of St Jacob. CT1 .... 87 E6
Priory Rd. Bilsington TN25 .... 172 C4
Priory Rd. Dover CT16 & CT17 .. 166 D8
Priory Rd. Faversham ME13 ... 62 C8
Priory Rd. Gillingham ME8 ...... 11 A2
Priory Rd. Maidstone ME15 .... 75 A3
Priory Rd. Ramsgate CT11 ...... 52 D6
Priory Rd. Rochester ME2 .... 9 A6
Priory Row. ME14 .... 62 C8
Priory St. 10 CT16 & CT17 ..... 166 D8
Priory Sta. CT17 .... 166 C8
Priory Station Approach Rd.
   CT17 .... 166 C7
Priory Way. TN30 .... 179 C7
Progress Est The. ME15 .... 98 A4
Promenade. Birchington CT7 .... 26 F8
Promenade. Deal CT14 .... 117 D3
Promenade The. ME12 .... 6 G2
Prospect Ave. ME2 .... 9 B8
Prospect Cl. CT8 .... 27 E7
Prospect Cotts.
   Boughton Lees TN25 .... 122 E3
Prospect Cotts.
   Harbledown CT2 .... 65 E1
Prospect Gdns. CT12 .... 50 B7
Prospect Hill. CT6 .... 23 A5
Prospect Mews. CT21 .... 176 C2
Prospect Pl. 7
   Broadstairs CT10 .... 30 B4
Prospect Pl. Canterbury CT1 ... 88 A7
Prospect Pl. Dover CT17 .... 149 B1
Prospect Pl. Eastling ME13 ..... 81 E6
Prospect Pl. Maidstone ME16 .. 74 E3
Prospect Pl.
   St Nicholas at Wade CT7 .... 25 E1
Prospect Rd. Birchington CT7 .. 26 F7
Prospect Rd. Broadstairs CT10 .. 30 B4
Prospect Rd. Folkestone CT20 .. 177 D3
Prospect Rd. Hythe CT21 ...... 176 C2
Prospect Rd. Minster CT12 ..... 50 B6
Prospect Row. Chatham ME4 .. 10 A3
Prospect Row. Gillingham ME4 .. 10 A6
Prospect Terr. Elham CT4 ..... 144 F4
Prospect Terr. 17
   Ramsgate CT11 .... 52 E6
Prospect Way. TN25 .... 158 C5
Provender Rd. ME13 & ME9 .... 61 A6
Provender Way. ME14 .... 75 E5
Providence La. ME1 .... 9 C5
Providence St. TN23 .... 156 C8
Puckle La. CT1 .... 88 A6
Pudding La. Ash CT3 .... 71 D1
Pudding La. Maidstone ME14 .. 74 F4
Pudding Rd. ME8 .... 33 F8
Pullman Cl. CT12 .... 52 C8
Pump La. Gillingham ME8 .... 11 D2
Pump La. Gillingham ME7 & ME8 . 11 D3
Pump La. 1 Margate CT9 .... 7 J2
Purbeck Rd. ME4 .... 9 E2
Purchas Ct. CT2 .... 66 C4
Purchase La. TN26 .... 154 E8
Purr Wood. CT4 .... 107 B2
Purser Way. ME7 .... 10 C7
Puttney Dr. ME10 .... 37 A8
Pyatt Mews. 3 CT1 .... 67 B1
Pye Alley La. CT5 .... 43 C3
Pym Ho. TN27 .... 120 D7
Pyrus Cl. ME5 .... 54 A8
Pyson's Rd. CT10 & CT12 .... 29 D3
Pyson's Road Ind Est. CT10 ... 29 D3

Quain Ct. CT20 .... 178 C4
Quantock Dr. TN23 & TN24 ... 139 B4
Quantock Gdns. CT12 .... 29 B3
Quarries The. ME17 .... 97 C4
Quarrington La. TN25 .... 158 A7
Quarry Cotts. TN30 .... 189 C3
Quarry Rd. Hythe CT21 .... 176 B3
Quarry Rd. Maidstone ME15 ... 75 A2
Quarry Sq. ME14 .... 75 A5
Quarry View. TN23 .... 155 D7
Quarry Wlk. CT21 .... 177 A3
Quarry Wood. ME5 .... 173 A6
Quay Cotts. ME9 .... 38 E6
Quay La. Faversham ME13 .... 62 D8
Quay La. Sandwich CT13 .... 73 A1

Quay The. ME9 .... 38 E6
Quayside. ME4 .... 10 B8
Queen Bertha Rd. ME14 .... 75 B4
Queen Bertha's Ave.
   CT7 & CT8 .... 27 C8
Queen Elizabeth Ave. CT9 .... 8 D1
Queen Elizabeth Rd. CT6 ...... 166 F8
Queen Elizabeth Sq. ME15 ..... 97 D6
Queen Elizabeth the
   Queen Mother Hospl. CT9 ..... 28 F8
Queen Elizabeth's Sch. ME13 .. 62 D8
Queen Mother Ct The. ME1 .... 9 B4
Queen St. Ashford TN23 .... 139 B2
Queen St. Chatham ME4 .... 10 A4
Queen St. Deal CT14 .... 117 D6
Queen St. Dover CT16 .... 166 D7
Queen St. Folkestone CT20 ... 178 E5
Queen St. Herne Bay CT6 .... 22 F5
Queen St. Margate CT9 .... 7 I2
Queen St. Ramsgate CT11 ...... 52 E6
Queen St. Rochester ME1 .... 9 C4
Queen Victoria Meml Hospl.
   CT6 .... 23 B4
Queen's Ave. Birchington CT7 .. 26 D7
Queen's Ave. Broadstairs CT10 .. 30 B6
Queen's Ave. Maidstone ME16 .. 74 D5
Queen's Ave. Margate CT9 .... 7 I1
Queen's Ave. Ramsgate CT12 .. 29 B1
Queen's Gate Rd. CT11 .... 52 C8
Queen's Gdns. CT16 .... 166 D8
Queen's Lea. CT15 .... 164 E5
Queen's Prom. CT9 .... 8 B3
Queen's Rd. Ash CT3 .... 71 D2
Queen's Rd. Ashford TN24 .... 140 A1
Queen's Rd. Broadstairs CT10 .. 30 B4
Queen's Rd. Chatham ME5 ...... 10 D1
Queen's Rd. Faversham ME13 .. 62 B7
Queen's Rd. Gillingham ME7 ... 10 C4
Queen's Rd.
   Littlestone-on-S TN28 .... 200 D6
Queen's Rd. Lydd TN29 .... 203 D5
Queen's Rd. Maidstone ME16 .. 74 C4
Queen's Rd. Ramsgate CT11 ... 52 F7
Queen's Rd. Westgate-on-S CT8 .. 27 F8
Queen's Rise. CT14 .... 133 F5
Queen's Way. ME12 .... 3 A8
Queenborough
   Cty Prim Sch. ME11 .... 3 B5
Queenborough Dr. ME12 .... 4 B7
Queenborough Rd.
   Halfway Houses ME12 .... 3 C6
Queenborough Rd.
   Queenborough ME11 & ME12 ... 3 C4
Queenborough Sta. ME11 .... 3 A5
Queendown Ave. ME8 .... 33 D5
Queendown Rd. CT7 .... 28 A3
Queens Ave. Canterbury CT2 ... 66 E1
Queens Ave. Dover CT17 ...... 166 A7
Queens Ave. Herne Bay CT6 .... 23 D5
Queens Ave. Hythe CT20 ...... 177 B6
Queens Ct. Ashford TN24 ..... 139 C3
Queens Ct. Hythe CT21 .... 176 B1
Queens Ct. Margate CT9 .... 8 B3
Queens Gdns. Broadstairs CT10 . 30 B3
Queens Gdns. Herne Bay CT6 .. 22 F5
Queens Mews. CT14 .... 117 D6
Queens Par. 12
   Faversham ME13 .... 62 D7
Queens Par. Margate CT9 .... 8 A3
Queens Par. West Minster ME12 .. 3 A8
Queens Rd. Ashford TN24 ..... 139 C3
Queens Rd. Aylesham CT3 ..... 112 F5
Queens Rd. Minster ME12 .... 4 D7
Queens Way. ME14 .... 55 A1
Queensbridge Dr. CT6 .... 22 C4
Queensdown Rd. CT14 .... 134 D4
Queensway. Dymchurch TN29 .. 186 E2
Queensway. Lydd TN29 .... 203 C6
Queenswood Rd. ME20 .... 53 D7
Quern Rd. CT14 .... 117 A2
Quern The. ME15 .... 74 E1
Querns Pl. CT1 .... 88 B8
Querns Rd. CT1 .... 88 C8
Quested Rd. CT19 .... 177 E6
Quested Way. ME17 .... 100 C6
Quetta Rd. CT12 .... 28 F1
Quex Rd. CT8 .... 27 F8
Quex View Rd. CT7 .... 27 A5
Quickthorn Cres. ME5 .... 31 E5
Quince Orch. TN26 .... 183 A7
Quinion Cl. ME5 .... 54 A8
Quinnell St. ME8 .... 11 E1
Quinton Rd. ME10 .... 36 C7

Rabbit Hole. CT4 .... 129 A7
Radfall Cnr. CT5 .... 44 C6
Radfall Gate. CT5 .... 44 C6
Radfall Hill. CT5 .... 44 D5
Radfall Rd. CT2 & CT5 & CT6 ... 44 D4
Radfall Ride. CT5 .... 44 C5
Radleigh Gdns. ME4 .... 9 E1
Radley Cl. CT10 .... 30 A6
Radnor Bridge Rd.
   CT19 & CT20 .... 178 E5
Radnor Cl. CT6 .... 23 B1
Radnor Cliff. CT20 .... 178 A3
Radnor Cliff Cres. CT20 .... 178 A3
Radnor Park Ave. CT19 .... 178 C6
Radnor Park Cres. CT19 .... 178 C5
Radnor Park Gdns. CT19 ...... 178 C6
Radnor Park Rd. CT19 .... 178 C6
Radnor Pk W. CT19 .... 178 B6
Radnor St. 17 CT19 .... 178 E5
Raggatt Pl. ME15 .... 75 B2
Raglan Pl. 10 CT10 .... 30 B4
Ragstone Hollow. TN25 .... 173 A6

Ragstone Rd. ME15 .... 76 A2
Railway Ave. CT5 .... 20 E1
Railway Cotts. ME9 .... 38 D3
Railway Hill. CT4 .... 128 E8
Railway Rd. ME12 .... 1 C2
Railway St. Chatham ME4 .... 9 F4
Railway St. Gillingham ME7 .... 10 D6
Railway Terr. Margate CT9 .... 7 H1
Railway Terr.
   Queenborough ME11 .... 3 A5
Rainham Cl. ME15 .... 75 A1
Rainham Mark
   Gram Sch. ME8 .... 11 D2
Rainham Rd. ME5 & ME7 .... 10 C3
Rainham Sch for Girls. ME8 .... 33 C8
Rainham Sh Ctr. ME8 .... 33 F8
Rainham St. ME13 .... 11 F1
Raleigh Cl. Ashford TN24 ..... 157 A8
Raleigh Cl. Chatham ME5 .... 32 A6
Raleigh Way. ME12 .... 3 E6
Ralph Grimshaw Ct. CT8 .... 27 E8
Ram La. TN26 .... 137 C8
Ramillies Cl. ME5 .... 32 A6
Ramp A. CT16 .... 166 H8
Ramp B. CT16 .... 166 H8
Ramp C. CT16 .... 166 G8
Rampart Rd. CT21 .... 176 B2
Rampion Cl. ME14 .... 75 E5
Ramsey Cl. CT2 .... 66 E1
Ramsey Ho. 8 CT1 .... 87 F7
Ramsgate Hospl (Geriatric).
   CT11 .... 52 D6
Ramsgate Rd.
   Broadstairs CT10 & CT11 .... 29 F2
Ramsgate Rd. Broadstairs CT10 . 30 B4
Ramsgate Rd.
   Margate CT10 & CT9 .... 29 A6
Ramsgate Rd.
   Sandwich CT12 & CT13 .... 73 A7
Ramsgate Sch The. CT12 .... 29 A2
Ramsgate Sta. CT12 .... 52 C8
Ramstone Cl. TN25 .... 158 E5
Rancorn Rd. CT9 .... 7 G1
Randall Rd. ME4 .... 9 E1
Randall St. ME14 .... 74 F6
Randalls Row. ME15 .... 96 F5
Randolph Cl. CT1 .... 88 A7
Randolph Gdns. TN24 .... 139 E5
Randolph Ho. 13 CT20 .... 178 E5
Randolph Rd. Dover CT17 .... 149 B1
Randolph Rd. Gillingham ME7 .. 10 C5
Randolph Sq. CT9 .... 7 J3
Ranelagh Gdns. CT10 .... 29 E5
Ranelagh Gr. CT10 .... 29 E5
Ranelagh Rd. Deal CT14 .... 117 D5
Ranelagh Rd. Sheerness ME12 ... 1 D2
Range Rd. Eastchurch ME12 ...... 5 D1
Range Rd. Hythe CT21 .... 176 B1
Range Road Ind Est. CT21 .... 176 E1
Ransley Gn. TN26 .... 183 F8
Raspberry Hill La. ME9 .... 14 D6
Ratling Rd. CT3 .... 112 F7
Rattington St. CT4 .... 86 E2
Ravenlea Rd. CT20 .... 178 A5
Ravens Dane Cl. ME15 .... 76 A1
Ravensbourne Ave. CT6 .... 23 B3
Ravenscourt Rd. Deal CT14 .. 117 C5
Ravenscourt Rd.
   Rough Common CT2 .... 66 B3
Ravenswood Ave. ME2 .... 9 B8
Rawdon Rd. Maidstone ME15 .. 75 A3
Rawdon Rd. Ramsgate CT11 ... 52 C6
Rawling St. ME9 .... 58 F3
Rayham Rd. CT5 .... 44 A8
Raymer Rd. ME14 .... 75 B8
Raymond Ave. CT1 .... 88 A6
Raymoor Ave. TN29 .... 195 A4
Rayners Hill. ME17 .... 102 C5
Reach Cl. CT15 .... 150 F5
Reach Meadow. CT15 .... 151 A6
Reach Rd. Lympne CT21 .... 174 D2
Reach Rd.
   St Margaret's at Cliffe CT15 ... 150 F5
Reachfields. CT21 .... 176 A1
Reading Cl. CT14 .... 117 B1
Reading Rd. CT17 .... 165 F7
Reading St. Broadstairs CT10 .. 29 F8
Reading St. Tenderden TN30 .. 180 C2
Reading Street Rd. CT10 & CT9 . 29 E8
Readscroft Rd. ME8 .... 33 D5
Rebecca Ct. 6 CT9 .... 8 B2
Recreation Cl. ME14 .... 75 B6
Recreation Ground Rd. TN30 . 179 B7
Rectory Bglws. TN26 .... 169 F8
Rectory Cl. TN26 .... 169 A2
Rectory Gdns. CT5 .... 21 D2
Rectory Grange. ME1 .... 9 C2
Rectory La. Barham CT4 .... 112 A1
Rectory La. Harrietsham ME17 . 100 E5
Rectory La. Hythe CT21 .... 176 B5
Rectory La. Lyminge CT18 .... 161 C6
Rectory La. Maidstone ME16 .. 74 A1
Rectory Rd. Broadstairs CT10 .. 30 B5
Rectory Rd. Deal CT14 .... 116 F4
Rectory Rd. Sittingbourne ME10 . 37 B3
Rectory Rd.
   St Mary in the Marsh TN29 .... 194 B4
Rectory Way. TN24 .... 139 C5
Reculver Ave. CT7 .... 26 E8
Reculver CE Prim Sch. CT6 .... 24 A4
Reculver Cl. CT6 .... 23 F5
Reculver Dr. CT6 .... 23 E5
Reculver Rd. CT6 .... 23 D5
Reculver Wlk. Maidstone ME15 . 97 F6
Reculvers Rd. CT8 .... 27 F7

Red Lion La. 5 CT5 .... 20 D2
Red Lion Sq. 7 CT21 .... 176 B2
Red Rd. CT32 & ME13 .... 64 D5
Red Robin Cotts. ME9 .... 35 B6
Red Tree Orch. TN23 .... 155 F6
Redbridge Cl. ME5 .... 32 C4
Redbrook St. TN26 .... 168 D5
Redbrooks Way. CT21 .... 175 F2
Redcliffe La. ME14 .... 75 B7
Redcot La. CT2 & CT3 .... 68 B7
Redfern Ave. ME7 .... 10 E5
Redgates. CT6 .... 23 A5
Redhill Rd. CT8 .... 27 E8
Redhouse La. CT4 .... 109 D6
Redhouse Wall. CT14 .... 95 B1
Redington. TN24 .... 139 C3
Redland Shaw. ME4 .... 9 E1
Redlands Ct. CT17 .... 148 E4
Redmill Cl. CT20 .... 177 E5
Redoubt Way. TN29 .... 187 B4
Redruth Manor. ME7 .... 10 C6
Redsells Cl. ME15 .... 76 A1
Redsull Ave. CT14 .... 117 A3
Redvers Cotts. CT16 .... 148 E5
Redvers Rd. ME4 .... 10 A2
Redwing Rd. ME5 .... 32 B7
Redwood Cl. Canterbury CT2 .. 66 E2
Redwood Cl. Chatham ME5 .... 32 B2
Redyear Cotts. TN24 .... 140 A1
Redyear Ct. TN24 .... 140 A1
Reed Ave. CT1 .... 67 D3
Reed Cres. TN23 .... 156 C3
Reedland Cres. ME13 .... 62 C8
Reedmace Cl. TN23 .... 155 D8
Reeds Cl. CT6 .... 23 C4
Reeves Alley. 1 CT5 .... 20 D1
Reeves Pas. 7 ME13 .... 62 C7
Reeves Way. CT5 .... 21 C2
Reform Rd. ME4 .... 10 B2
Regency Cl. Gillingham ME8 ... 33 C3
Regency Cl. Sheerness ME12 .... 1 B3
Regency Cl. Whitstable CT5 .... 43 F7
Regency Ct. ME10 .... 36 D4
Regency Pl. CT1 .... 67 B2
Regency Villas. CT4 .... 129 C5
Regent Dr. ME15 .... 97 A8
Regent Rd. ME7 .... 10 C4
Regent St. CT5 .... 20 D2
Regents Pl. TN23 .... 139 B2
Regents Wlk. CT6 .... 23 D5
Reginald Rd. ME16 .... 74 E3
Regis Cres. ME10 .... 36 F7
Regis Manor
   Cty Prim Sch. ME10 .... 36 E7
Reglvlbivm Roman Fort. CT6 ... 24 D7
Reinden Gr. ME15 .... 75 F1
Remston Mews. 12 CT1 .... 67 B2
Renault Cl. CT6 .... 22 A4
Rendezvous St. CT20 .... 178 D5
Rendezvous The. CT9 .... 7 I3
Renown Rd. ME5 .... 32 C2
Rentain Rd. CT4 .... 86 D2
Repton Cl. CT10 .... 29 F6
Repton Manor Rd. TN23 .... 139 A3
Repton Way. ME5 .... 31 F4
Resolution Cl. ME5 .... 32 A6
Resrvoir Rd. CT5 .... 20 E2
Rest Harrow. ME13 .... 83 D6
Restharrow Rd. ME14 .... 75 E4
Retreat The. Birchington CT7 .. 27 B8
Retreat The. Doddington ME9 .. 80 D7
Retreat The. Ramsgate CT12 .. 52 B8
Revenge Rd. ME5 .... 54 C8
Reynolds Cl. CT6 .... 23 B4
Rhee Wall. TN26 .... 190 D7
Rheims Ct. CT2 .... 66 D1
Rheims Way. CT1 & CT2 .... 87 E8
Rhodaus Cl. CT1 .... 87 F7
Rhodaus Ho. CT1 .... 87 F7
Rhodaus Town. CT1 .... 87 F7
Rhode St. ME4 .... 10 A4
Rhodes Gdns. CT10 .... 30 A6
Rhodes Ho. ME5 .... 10 C2
Rhodewood Cl. ME15 .... 76 A1
Richard Cl. 7 CT9 .... 8 B2
Richard St. Chatham ME4 .... 9 F4
Richard St. Rochester ME1 .... 9 C3
Richborough Bsns Pk. CT13 ... 73 A3
Richborough Castle. CT13 ...... 72 E5
Richborough Rd. CT8 .... 27 F7
Richbourg Rd. CT13 .... 72 E3
Richdore Rd. CT4 .... 125 C6
Richmond Ave. CT9 .... 8 B1
Richmond Cl. ME5 .... 32 B4
Richmond Ct. CT16 .... 149 D1
Richmond Cty Inf Sch. ME7 ... 10 C6
Richmond Cty Prim Sch. ME12 . 1 E2
Richmond Dr. Herne Bay CT6 ... 23 E5
Richmond Dr.
   New Romney TN28 .... 200 C3
Richmond Dr.
   Sittingbourne ME10 .... 36 E7
Richmond Gdns. CT2 .... 66 C2
Richmond Rd. Gillingham ME7 .. 10 C7
Richmond Rd. Ramsgate CT11 . 52 D6
Richmond Rd. Whitstable CT5 .. 21 B1
Richmond St. Folkestone CT19 . 177 D6
Richmond St. Herne Bay CT6 ... 22 F5
Richmond St. Sheerness ME12 ... 1 C2
Richmond Way. ME15 .... 97 A8
Riddles Rd. ME10 & ME9 .... 36 C3
Ridge Meadow
   Cty Prim Sch. ME5 .... 31 F6
Ridge The. TN24 .... 139 E6
Ridgeway. Lympne CT21 .... 175 A3
Ridgeway. Whitstable CT5 ...... 21 C1
Ridgeway Cliff. CT6 .... 22 C5
Ridgeway Rd. CT6 .... 46 A7

Ridgeway Terr. TN25 .... 158 C5
Ridgeway The.
　Boughton Street ME13 .... 64 A3
Ridgeway The.
　Broadstairs CT10 .... 29 F3
Ridgeway The. Chatham ME4 ... 31 F1
Ridgeway The. Gillingham ME7 ... 10 C7
Ridgeway The. Margate CT9 ...... 8 B1
Ridgeway The. River CT17 ...... 148 E2
Ridgeway The. Smeeth TN25 ... 158 B5
Ridgeway Wlk. CT6 .... 46 A7
Ridgway. ME16 .... 74 B2
Ridham Ave. ME10 .... 15 A1
Riding Hill. TN24 .... 139 C6
Ridings The. Canterbury CT1 ... 67 B1
Ridings The. Margate CT9 .... 8 F3
Ridings The. Whitstable CT5 ..... 21 C1
Ridlands. CT1 .... 88 A5
Ridley Cl. CT6 .... 46 A8
Ridley Rd. ME1 .... 9 C4
Rigden Rd. TN23 .... 156 B7
Rigshill Rd. ME13 .... 103 B6
Riley Ave. CT6 .... 21 F4
Ring Wall. CT14 .... 94 E2
Ringlestone Cres. ME14 .... 74 F8
Ringlestone Rd. ME17 .... 78 D4
Ringold Ave. CT12 .... 52 A8
Ringsloe Ct. CT7 .... 26 D8
Ringwood Cl. Canterbury CT2 ... 66 E3
Ringwood Cl. Gillingham ME8 ... 33 D8
Ringwood Rd. ME15 .... 97 C8
Ringwould Rd.
　Kingsdown CT14 .... 134 B5
Ringwould Rd.
　Ringwould CT14 & CT15 ...... 133 D4
Ripley Rd. TN24 .... 157 A8
Ripon Cl. ME8 .... 11 D3
Ripper's Cross. TN26 .... 137 D4
Ripple Cross. CT14 .... 133 F6
Ripple Cty Prim Sch. CT14 ... 133 D8
Ripple Rd. CT14 .... 133 F7
Ripplevale Sch. CT14 .... 133 E8
Risborough La. CT19 & CT20 ... 177 D5
Risborough Way. CT20 .... 177 E6
Risdon Cl. CT2 .... 67 F6
Rise The. Ashford TN23 .... 155 E7
Rise The. Borden ME9 .... 36 B2
Rise The. Gillingham ME7 .... 33 A3
Rise The. Halfway Houses ME12 ... 3 C5
Rise The. Kingsdown CT14 ..... 134 D5
Rise The. Rochester ME1 .... 9 D3
Rise The.
　St Margaret's at Cliffe CT15 ... 151 B6
River Cl. ME15 .... 96 A7
River Ct. Chartham CT4 .... 86 D3
River Ct. River CT17 .... 148 E2
River Cty Prim Sch. CT17 ...... 148 E3
River Dale. CT17 .... 148 F3
River Dr. CT17 .... 148 E2
River Meadow. CT17 .... 148 F3
River St. Gillingham ME4 .... 10 A6
River St. River CT17 .... 148 E3
River Valley Golf Course.
　ME8 & ME9 .... 12 D2
River View. Gillingham ME8 ..... 11 D3
River View. Maidstone ME15 ... 74 F2
River View. Rushenden ME11 ..... 2 F3
River View. Sturry CT2 .... 67 F7
Riverdale Rd. CT1 .... 67 B2
Riverhead Cl. Maidstone ME16 ... 74 D6
Riverhead Cl. Margate CT9 .... 8 B1
Riverhead Cl.
　Sittingbourne ME10 .... 36 C3
Rivers Rd. ME9 .... 38 D2
Rivers Wlk. ME17 .... 101 C5
Riversdale Rd. Ashford TN23 ... 156 C8
Riversdale Rd. Ramsgate CT12 ... 29 E1
Riverside. CT4 .... 86 C3
Riverside Bsns Pk. TN24 .... 139 D2
Riverside Cl. Bridge CT4 .... 89 A1
Riverside Cl. Kingsnorth TN23 ... 156 A4
Riverside Ct. CT2 .... 66 F1
Riverside Ctry Pk. ME7 .... 11 D5
Riverside Ind Est. CT21 .... 175 B1
Riverside Mews. CT4 .... 89 A1
Riverside Rd. CT12 .... 51 A1
Riverside Sch. TN23 .... 138 F1
Riverview. TN23 .... 138 E1
Riviera Cl. CT20 .... 177 E3
Riviera Rd. CT20 .... 178 A3
Riviera The. CT20 .... 177 F3
Roach St. ME2 .... 9 A7
Road Five. CT8 .... 7 D1
Road of Remembrance. CT20 ... 178 D4
Robert Napier Sch The. ME7 ... 10 E3
Robert St. CT14 .... 117 D7
Roberts Cl. ME10 .... 36 D7
Roberts Rd. Gillingham ME8 ..... 33 E8
Roberts Rd.
　Greatstone-on-S TN28 .... 200 E1
Roberts Rd. Whitstable CT5 ..... 42 F6
Robeshaw. ME8 .... 58 E2
Robin Ho. ME16 .... 74 E4
Robins Ave. ME17 .... 101 C5
Robins Cl. ME17 .... 101 C4
Robins Ct. ME14 .... 75 B7
Robson's Yd. CT17 .... 166 C8
Robus Cl. CT18 .... 161 C7
Robus Terr. CT18 .... 161 C7

Rochester Airport. ME1 & ME5 ... 31 C6
Rochester Ave. Canterbury CT1 ... 88 B7
Rochester Ave. Rochester ME1 ... 9 C4
Rochester Cath. ME1 .... 9 C6
Rochester Ct. ME2 .... 9 E8
Rochester Gram Sch
　for Girls The. ME1 .... 9 C2
Rochester Ho. ME15 .... 97 D7
Rochester Rd. Chatham ME5 ... 31 C4
Rochester Rd.
　Pratling Street ME20 .... 53 B4
Rochester St. ME4 .... 9 E3
Rochester Sta. ME1 .... 9 D5
Rock Ave. ME7 .... 10 C3
Rock Hill Rd. TN27 .... 118 E2
Rock Rd. Maidstone ME14 .... 75 A6
Rock Rd. Sittingbourne ME10 ... 36 E4
Rockingham Pl. CT6 .... 23 B2
Rockstone Way. CT12 .... 29 A1
Rocky Bourne Rd. TN25 .... 172 D5
Rocky Hill. ME16 .... 74 E4
Rocky Hill Terr. ME16 .... 74 E4
Rodmer Cl. ME14 .... 4 C8
Rodmersham Cty Prim Sch.
　ME9 .... 59 B7
Rodmersham Gn. ME9 .... 59 B7
Rodney St. CT11 .... 52 D6
Roebuck Rd. Faversham ME13 ... 62 A7
Roebuck Rd. Rochester ME1 ...... 9 C5
Roentgen Ho. ME10 .... 36 D5
Roethorne Gdns. TN30 .... 179 B8
Roffen Rd. ME1 .... 9 C2
Rogersmead. TN30 .... 179 A7
Rokesley Rd. CT16 .... 149 B5
Rolfe Cl. TN28 .... 200 B7
Roll's Ave. ME12 .... 5 C1
Rolvenden Ave. ME8 .... 11 C3
Rolvenden Dr. ME10 .... 36 B5
Roly Eckhoff Ho. CT16 .... 149 B3
Roman Cl. Chatham ME5 .... 31 D1
Roman Cl. Deal CT14 .... 117 B6
Roman Hts. ME14 .... 75 C6
Roman Rd. East Studdal CT15 ... 132 C5
Roman Rd. Faversham ME13 ... 62 C7
Roman Rd. Ramsgate CT12 ..... 29 C2
Roman Rd. Whitfield CT15 ..... 149 D8
Roman Sq. ME10 .... 36 F3
Roman Way. Elvington CT15 ... 114 B2
Roman Way. Folkestone CT19 ... 177 C6
Roman Way. Kingsnorth TN23 ... 156 C4
Roman Way.
　St Margaret's at Cliffe CT15 ... 150 F5
Romany Ct. ME5 .... 10 C1
Romany Rd. ME8 .... 11 C2
Romden Rd. TN27 .... 135 D1
Rome House Cnr. TN28 .... 200 A6
Rome Rd. TN28 .... 200 A6
Romilly Gdns. CT12 .... 29 C2
Romney Ave. CT20 .... 177 F5
Romney Cl. Birchington CT7 ..... 27 A7
Romney Cl. Maidstone ME14 ... 76 A3
Romney Ct. ME10 .... 36 E5
Romney Marsh Rd. TN23 .... 156 B6
Romney Pl. ME15 .... 75 A4
Romney Rd. Ashford TN24 ..... 139 E1
Romney Rd. Sheerness ME12 ... 32 B5
Romney Rd. Hamstreet TN26 ... 183 A7
Romney Rd. New Romney TN29 ... 199 E3
Romney Sands
　Holiday Village. TN28 .... 204 D8
Romney Sands Sta. TN28 ...... 204 E8
Romney Warren
　Golf Course. TN28 .... 200 E7
Romney Way. TN21 .... 175 F1
Ronalds Ct. ME10 .... 37 A4
Rook La. ME9 .... 35 F6
Rookery Cl. Ashford TN24 ...... 139 D7
Rookery Cl. Bredgar ME9 .... 58 A6
Rookston Cnr. CT3 .... 48 D1
Roonagh Ct. ME10 .... 36 E2
Roosevelt Ave. ME5 .... 32 A8
Roosevelt Rd. CT16 .... 149 B3
Rope Walk Mews. CT13 .... 93 F8
Rope Wlk. ME4 .... 9 F5
Ropemakers Ct. ME4 .... 10 A1
Roper Cl. Canterbury CT2 .... 66 E1
Roper Cl. Gillingham ME8 .... 33 C3
Roper Rd. Canterbury CT2 ...... 66 E1
Roper Rd. Teynham ME9 .... 38 D3
Rose Acre Rd. CT3 .... 89 F7
Rose Cotts. Hythe CT21 .... 176 B4
Rose Cotts.
　Lenham Heath ME17 .... 119 B8
Rose Ct. ME7 .... 96 D1
Rose Gdns. Birchington CT7 ..... 26 F6
Rose Gdns. Eythorne CT15 ... 131 D7
Rose Gdns. Herne Bay CT6 ..... 23 C4
Rose Gdns. Minster CT12 .... 50 B6
Rose Hill. Ramsgate CT11 .... 52 E6
Rose Hill. Wittersham TN30 ... 189 B5
Rose La. Bishopsbourne CT4 ... 111 C6
Rose La. Canterbury CT1 .... 87 F8
Rose La. Lenham Heath ME17 ... 119 B8
Rose St. Rochester ME1 .... 9 D3
Rose St. Sheerness ME12 .... 1 C2
Rose Street
　Cty Prim Sch. ME12 .... 1 C2
Rose Terr. ME13 .... 62 D5
Rose Yd. ME14 .... 75 A4
Roseacre Cl. CT14 .... 66 E1
Roseacre Ct. CT9 .... 8 E2
Roseacre Gdns. ME14 .... 76 A4
Roseacre Jun Sch. ME14 .... 76 A4
Roseacre La. ME14 .... 76 A4
Rosebery Ave. Herne Bay CT6 ... 23 E5
Rosebery Rd. Ramsgate CT11 ... 29 F1
Rosebery Cl. ME10 .... 37 A4
Rosebery Rd. Chatham ME4 ...... 9 E2

Rosebery Rd. Gillingham ME7 ... 10 D7
Rosedale Rd. CT9 .... 8 A1
Roseholme. ME16 .... 74 D2
Roselands. CT14 .... 117 C1
Roselands Gdns. CT2 .... 66 D2
Roseleigh Ave. ME16 .... 74 C5
Roseleigh Rd. ME10 .... 36 D2
Rosemary Ave.
　Broadstairs CT10 .... 30 A3
Rosemary Ave.
　Halfway Houses ME12 .... 3 D6
Rosemary Cl. ME5 .... 31 F4
Rosemary Cnr. TN29 .... 197 D8
Rosemary Gdns.
　Broadstairs CT10 .... 29 F2
Rosemary Gdns.
　Whitstable CT5 .... 44 A8
Rosemary La. CT1 .... 87 F8
Rosemary Rd. ME15 .... 76 A3
Rosemount Cl. ME10 .... 36 D2
Rosetower Ct. CT10 .... 29 F8
Rosiers Ct. CT2 .... 66 E1
Ross Gdns. CT2 .... 66 B3
Ross St. ME1 .... 9 A4
Ross Way. CT20 .... 177 E5
Rossendale Ct. CT20 .... 178 E6
Rossendale Gdns. CT20 .... 178 E6
Rossendale Rd. CT20 .... 178 E6
Rossetti Rd. CT7 .... 26 F8
Rossland Rd. CT12 .... 52 A8
Rosslyn Gn. ME16 .... 74 B5
Rothbrook Dr. TN24 .... 139 C7
Rother Ho. ME15 .... 97 D8
Rother Vale. ME5 .... 32 C3
Rothley Cl. TN30 .... 179 B8
Rothsay Ct. CT11 .... 29 F1
Rough Common Rd. CT2 .... 66 B3
Roundel Cl. ME9 .... 38 D2
Roundel The. ME9 .... 36 F7
Roundwell. ME14 .... 76 D3
Rover Rd. ME5 .... 32 B2
Row The. Ash CT3 .... 71 E5
Row The. Elham CT4 .... 144 F5
Rowan Cl. Ashford TN23 .... 138 E2
Rowan Cl. Staple CT3 .... 92 A6
Rowan Cl. Sturry CT2 .... 67 F6
Rowan Ct. CT10 .... 30 A5
Rowan Ho. Chatham ME5 .... 31 F5
Rowan Ho. Sheerness ME12 ..... 1 C2
Rowan Lea. ME5 .... 10 B1
Rowan Wlk. ME4 .... 9 E3
Rowans The. ME12 .... 4 B3
Rowbrocke Cl. ME8 .... 33 D3
Rowe Cl. CT9 .... 28 F7
Rowena Rd. CT8 .... 7 C1
Rowetts Way. ME12 .... 5 D3
Rowland Ave. ME7 .... 10 E2
Rowland Cl. ME5 .... 10 E1
Rowland Cres. CT6 .... 23 E5
Rowland Dr. CT6 .... 22 C2
Roxburgh Rd. CT8 .... 7 D1
Royal Ave. CT5 .... 43 C5
Royal Cinque Ports
　Golf Links. CT13 .... 95 B4
Royal Cl. CT13 .... 29 F4
Royal Cres. Margate CT9 .... 7 H2
Royal Cres. Ramsgate CT11 .... 52 D5
Royal Eagle Cl. ME2 .... 9 E7
Royal Engineers' Rd. ME14 ... 74 F7
Royal Espl. Margate CT9 .... 7 F1
Royal Espl. Ramsgate CT11 .... 52 C5
Royal Military Ave. CT20 ...... 177 D5
Royal Military Rd.
　Aldington TN25 .... 173 D1
Royal Military Rd.
　Hythe CT21 .... 175 D1
Royal Par. CT11 .... 52 E6
Royal Rd. Ramsgate CT11 .... 52 D6
Royal Rd. Sheerness ME12 .... 1 D2
Royal Sch for
　Deaf Children. CT9 .... 7 J2
Royal Sea Bathing Hospl. CT9 ... 7 G2
Royal Sovereign Ave. ME7 ..... 10 B7
Royal St George's
　Golf Links. CT13 .... 73 E2
Royal Star Arc. ME14 .... 74 F4
Royal Victoria Hospl. CT19 ... 178 C6
Royal Victoria Pl. CT16 .... 166 B8
Royds Rd. TN24 .... 156 D6
Royston Gdns. CT15 .... 150 F6
Royston Rd. ME15 .... 76 A3
Roystons Cl. ME8 .... 11 F2
Royton Ave. ME17 .... 101 D5
Rubery Dro. CT3 .... 72 C7
Ruckinge Cnr. TN25 .... 183 F8
Ruckinge Rd. TN26 .... 183 A7
Ruckinge Way. ME8 .... 11 C3
Rudge Cl. ME5 .... 32 D2
Rugby Cl. Broadstairs CT10 ..... 29 F5
Rugby Cl. Chatham ME5 .... 31 F4
Rugby Gdns. TN23 .... 156 C8
Rugby Rd. CT17 .... 166 A6
Ruins Barn Rd. ME10 & ME9 ... 58 D6
Rule Ct. ME12 .... 3 B8
Rumfields Rd. CT10 .... 29 D4
Rumstead La. ME17 & ME 9 ... 56 D4
Rumstead Rd. ME9 .... 56 E4
Rumwood Ct. ME17 .... 98 B5
Runcie Ho. CT1 .... 87 F7
Runcie Pl. CT1 .... 66 D1
Runham La. ME17 .... 100 E3
Running Horse Rndbt The.
　ME20 .... 53 E1
Rush Cl. Chatham ME5 .... 32 A3
Rush Cl. Dymchurch TN29 ... 195 B6
Rusham Rd. CT3 .... 70 C1

Rushenden Ct. ME11 .... 2 F3
Rushenden Rd. ME11 .... 3 A4
Rushmead Ct. ME2 .... 66 D2
Rushmead Dr. ME15 .... 97 A7
Russel Dr. CT5 .... 21 D3
Russell Cl. ME10 .... 36 C3
Russell Ct. ME4 .... 10 B3
Russell Pl. ME13 .... 40 B3
Russell Rd. Folkestone CT19 ... 178 D6
Russell Rd. Kit's Coty ME20 .... 53 D7
Russell St. Dover CT16 .... 166 E7
Russell St. Sheerness ME12 ..... 1 C2
Russells Ave. ME8 .... 34 A8
Russet Ave. ME13 .... 62 E5
Russet Ct. ME17 .... 96 C3
Russet Rd. CT1 .... 88 C8
Russets The. Maidstone ME16 ... 74 B5
Russets The. Whitstable CT5 ... 21 D1
Ruth Ho. ME16 .... 74 E5
Rutherford Coll. CT2 .... 66 E4
Rutherford Rd. TN24 .... 139 B5
Rutland Ave. CT9 .... 8 C2
Rutland Cl. CT1 .... 88 D7
Rutland Gdns. Birchington CT7 ... 26 F7
Rutland Gdns. Margate CT9 ..... 8 C2
Rutland Ho. CT9 .... 8 B2
Rutland Pl. ME8 .... 33 C3
Rutland Rd. CT16 .... 149 B3
Rutland Way. ME15 .... 97 E8
Ryan Dr. ME15 .... 76 A3
Rycaut Cl. ME8 .... 33 D3
Rydal Ave. CT11 .... 52 B7
Ryde Cl. ME5 .... 32 B8
Ryde St. CT2 .... 66 E1
Ryder's Ave. CT8 .... 27 D8
Rye Ct. TN30 .... 155 D7
Rye Rd. TN30 .... 189 A2
Rye Wlk. CT5 .... 23 C2
Ryecourt Cl. ME16 .... 74 C3
Ryeglass Cl. ME5 .... 32 C6
Ryegrass Cl. ME5 .... 32 C6
Ryland Cl. ME20 .... 178 E5
Ryland Pl. ME20 .... 178 E5
Rylands Rd. TN24 .... 139 D5
Rype Cl. TN29 .... 203 C5
Ryswick Mews. TN28 .... 200 C8

Sabre Ct. ME7 .... 11 A1
Sackett's Gap. CT9 .... 8 C3
Sacketts Hill. CT10 .... 29 C6
Sackville Ct. TN26 .... 138 C2
Sackville Cres. TN23 .... 139 A2
Saddler's Wall La. TN29 .... 191 B1
Saddlers Cl. ME14 .... 75 E5
Saddlers Hill. CT3 .... 91 D2
Saddlers Mews. CT5 .... 21 D1
Saddlers Way. TN23 .... 156 B5
Saddleton Gr. CT5 .... 43 D8
Saddleton Rd. CT5 .... 43 D8
Sadlers Cl. ME5 .... 31 D2
Saffron Way. Chatham ME5 .... 31 F5
Saffron Way.
　Sittingbourne ME10 .... 36 F7
Saffron's Pl. CT20 .... 178 E5
Sailfield Ct. ME4 .... 9 F7
Sailmakers Ct. ME4 .... 10 B2
St Agnes Gdns. ME12 .... 1 D1
St Alban's Rd. CT3 .... 46 E1
St Albans Rd. ME7 .... 10 E7
St Alphege CE Inf Sch. CT5 .... 20 D1
St Alphege Cl. CT5 .... 43 B7
St Alphege La. CT1 .... 66 F1
St Alphege Rd. CT5 .... 149 C1
St Ambrose Gn. TN25 .... 123 E3
St Andrew Rd. ME7 .... 10 D7
St Andrew Terr. CT17 .... 149 A2
St Andrew's Cl.
　Maidstone ME16 .... 74 A2
St Andrew's Cl. Whitstable CT5 ... 43 E7
St Andrew's Gdns. CT15 .... 130 E5
St Andrew's Lees. CT13 .... 94 A3
St Andrew's Rd. Deal CT14 ... 117 C6
St Andrew's Rd.
　Littlebourne-in-S TN28 .... 200 E6
St Andrew's Rd.
　Maidstone ME16 .... 74 A3
St Andrew's Rd.
　Ramsgate CT11 .... 52 F8
St Andrews. CT19 .... 178 E5
St Andrews Cl. Canterbury CT1 ... 87 E7
St Andrews Cl. Herne Bay CT6 ... 23 A4
St Andrews Cl. Margate CT9 ... 28 F7
St Andrews Gdns. CT17 .... 149 B2
St Andrews Way. CT14 .... 115 A3
St Ann's Rd. Dymchurch TN29 ... 195 B2
St Ann's Rd.
　Faversham ME13 .... 62 B7
St Anne Ct. ME16 .... 74 E4
St Anne's Ct. Dover CT16 ..... 149 B2
St Anne's Ct. Herne Bay CT6 ... 22 E5
St Anne's Dr. CT6 .... 22 D4
St Anne's Gdns. CT9 .... 28 F8
St Anne's Rd. Ashford TN23 ... 155 F7
St Anne's Rd. Whitstable CT5 ... 20 F2
St Anselm's
　Catholic Comp Sch. CT1 ...... 88 C5
St Anthony's Sch. CT9 .... 8 C1
St Anthony's Way. CT9 .... 8 C1
St Augustine of Canterbury
　RC Prim Sch. ME8 .... 33 D3
St Augustine's Abbey. CT1 ..... 52 D5
St Augustine's Ave. CT9 .... 28 F8
St Augustine's Coll. CT1 .... 88 A8
St Augustine's Cres. CT5 .... 21 D1
St Augustine's Ct. CT1 .... 88 B8
St Augustine's Golf Course.
　CT12 .... 51 C4
St Augustine's Pk. CT11 .... 52 C6

St Augustine's RC Prim Sch.
　CT21 .... 176 E2
St Augustine's Rd.
　Canterbury CT1 .... 88 B7
St Augustine's Rd. Deal CT14 ... 116 F4
St Augustine's Rd.
　Ramsgate CT11 .... 52 D5
St Barnabas Cl. Ashford TN23 ... 155 F7
St Barnabas Cl. Gillingham ME7 ... 10 D3
St Barnabas Cl.
　Maidstone ME16 .... 74 C8
St Bart's Rd. CT13 .... 93 F8
St Barnabas Cl.
　Maidstone ME16 .... 74 C8
St Bartholomew's Hospl. ME1 ... 9 E4
St Bartholomew's La. ME1 .... 9 E4
St Bartholomew's Sch. ME10 ... 36 F7
St Bartholomew's Terr. ME1 ..... 9 E4
St Benedict's Lawn. CT11 ...... 52 D5
St Benedicts
　RC Prim Sch. ME5 .... 32 C2
St Benet's Rd. CT8 .... 27 E7
St Benets Ct. TN30 .... 179 B8
St Benets Way. TN30 .... 179 B8
St Catherine's Dr. ME13 .... 62 D6
St Catherine's Gr. CT12 .... 28 D1
St Catherine's Hospl. ME1 .... 9 D4
St Catherines. TN29 .... 199 A2
St Catherines Ct. CT11 .... 29 F1
St Christopher Cl. CT9 .... 29 D8
St Christopher's Sch. CT1 ...... 88 B6
St Christophers Gn. CT10 ...... 29 F5
St Clare Rd. CT14 .... 117 C6
St Clement's Ct. CT6 .... 23 A3
St Clement's Ho. ME1 .... 9 D5
St Clement's Rd. CT8 .... 7 C1
St Clements. CT13 .... 73 A1
St Clements Cl. ME12 .... 29 E6
St Clements Ct. ME12 .... 29 E6
St Clements Rd. ME12 .... 6 E3
St Cosmus St. TN25 .... 105 B1
St Crispin's Cty Inf Sch. CT8 ... 27 E7
St Crispin's Rd. CT8 .... 27 E7
St David's Cl. Birchington CT7 ... 27 B8
St David's Cl. Whitstable CT5 ... 43 E8
St David's Rd. Deal CT14 ...... 117 C6
St David's Rd. Ramsgate CT11 ... 29 F1
St Davids Ave. CT17 .... 166 A5
St Denys Rd. CT18 .... 163 B5
St Dunstan's Cl. CT2 .... 66 E1
St Dunstan's Rd. CT9 .... 8 A2
St Dunstan's St. CT2 .... 66 E1
St Dunstan's Terr. CT2 .... 66 E1
St Eanswythe Way. CT20 ...... 178 D5
St Eanswythe's
　CE Prim Sch. CT20 .... 178 D4
St Edmund's RC Sch. CT16 ... 149 B2
St Edmund's Rd. CT14 .... 116 E4
St Edmund's Sch. CT2 .... 66 C3
St Edmunds Rd. CT11 .... 87 F8
St Edmunds Way. ME8 .... 12 B1
St Edward's
　RC Prim Sch. ME12 .... 1 C2
St Ethelbert's
　RC Prim Sch. CT11 .... 52 F8
St Faith's La. ME14 .... 76 B4
St Faith's St. ME14 .... 74 F4
St Faiths Sch. CT3 .... 71 C1
St Francis Cl. Deal CT14 .... 116 F4
St Francis Cl. Margate CT9 .... 29 D8
St Francis
　RC Prim Sch. ME14 .... 75 D7
St Francis Rd. CT19 .... 177 F6
St Francis Sch. ME14 .... 75 B7
St Gabriel's. CT20 .... 178 E6
St George's Ave.
　Herne Bay CT6 .... 22 D4
St George's Ave.
　Sheerness ME12 .... 1 C1
St George's Bsns Ctr. TN23 ... 138 F2
St George's
　CE High Sch. CT10 .... 29 C5
St George's CE Mid Sch. ME12 ... 1 D1
St George's Cl. CT5 .... 43 E7
St George's Cl. ME12 .... 3 B8
St George's Lees. CT13 .... 94 A8
St George's Pass. CT14 .... 117 D6
St George's Pl. Canterbury CT1 ... 88 A8
St George's Pl. Hythe CT21 ... 187 D8
St George's Rd.
　Broadstairs CT10 .... 30 A4
St George's Rd. Deal CT14 ..... 117 D6
St George's Rd.
　Folkestone CT19 .... 177 F6
St George's Rd.
　Gillingham ME7 .... 10 C6
St George's Rd.
　Ramsgate CT11 .... 52 F8
St George's Rd.
　Sandwich CT13 .... 94 A8
St George's Sq.
　Ashford TN23 .... 139 B2
St George's Sq.
　Maidstone ME16 .... 74 E3
St George's St. CT1 .... 88 A8
St George's Terr. CT6 .... 22 E5
St Georges Ave. ME12 .... 5 D2
St Georges Cres. CT17 .... 166 B5
St Georges Ct. CT7 .... 149 A2
St Georges Ct. CT1 .... 88 A8
St Georges Pl. CT15 .... 150 F6
St Georges St. CT1 .... 88 A8
St Giles Cl. CT17 .... 166 B5
St Giles Rd. CT17 .... 166 B5
St Giles Wlk. CT17 .... 166 B5
St Gregory's. CT1 .... 67 A1
St Gregory's. CT14 .... 116 F4

St Gregory's
RC Prim Sch. CT9 .... 28 E8
St Gregory's Rd. CT1 .... 67 B1
St Helen's Rd. ME12 .... 1 E1
St Helier's Rd. ME16 .... 74 B2
St Hilda Rd. CT19 .... 177 E6
St Hilda's Rd. CT21 .... 176 B1
St Jacob's Pl. CT1 .... 87 D6
St James' Ave.
Broadstairs CT10 .... 29 E5
St James' Ave. Ramsgate CT12 .. 29 B1
St James Cl. ME12 .... 6 E4
St James' Gdns. CT5 .... 43 D8
St James La. **5** CT16 .... 166 E7
St James' Park Rd. CT9 .... 28 A8
St James Rd. CT14 .... 134 D5
St James St. CT16 .... 166 E7
St James's Terr. CT7 .... 27 B8
St Jean's Rd. CT8 .... 27 E7
St John Fisher
Cath Comp Sch. ME4 .... 9 F3
St John Fisher
Cath Sch (Lower Sch). ME4 ..... 9 F2
St John's Ave. Ramsgate CT12 .. 29 A1
St John's Ave.
Sittingbourne ME10 .... 37 B3
St John's CE Inf Sch. ME4 ...... 9 E3
St John's
CE (VA) Prim Sch. ME14 .... 75 E4
St John's Church Rd. CT19 ... 178 C6
St John's Cl. CT18 .... 163 A7
St John's Commandery
(rems of) CT15 .... 146 E4
St John's Ct. TN24 .... 157 A6
St John's Hospl. CT1 .... 67 A1
St John's La. Ashford TN23 ..... 139 C2
St John's La. Canterbury CT1 .... 87 F8
St John's Pl. CT1 .... 67 A1
St John's Rd. Dover CT17 ..... 166 C7
St John's Rd.
Faversham ME13 .... 62 D7
St John's Rd. Gillingham ME7 .. 10 C3
St John's Rd. Margate CT9 ...... 7 J2
St John's Rd.
New Romney TN28 .... 200 A6
St John's Rd. Whitstable CT5 .... 21 D3
St John's St. Folkestone CT20 .. 178 E5
St John's St. **7** Margate CT9 .... 7 J2
St John's Way. CT18 .... 163 A7
St Johns Cres. CT2 .... 66 D6
St Johns Rd. Elvington CT15 ... 114 B2
St Johns Rd. Hythe CT21 ..... 176 A3
St Johns Way. ME1 .... 9 A2
St Joseph's
RC Prim Sch. CT3 .... 113 A5
St Julien Ave. CT1 .... 67 D1
St Katherine Rd. ME12 .... 3 E7
St Laurence Ave. ME16 .... 74 C8
St Laurence CE Jun Sch. CT12 .. 52 B8
St Laurence Cl. ME9 .... 37 D2
St Laurence Cl. CT11 .... 52 C7
St Lawrence Ave. CT11 .... 52 B5
St Lawrence Cl. CT11 .... 88 B6
St Lawrence Coll. CT11 .... 52 D8
St Lawrence Coll
(Jun Sch) CT11 .... 52 E8
St Lawrence Ct. TN28 .... 200 A6
St Lawrence Forstal. CT1 ...... 88 B6
St Lawrence Gdl
(Kent Cty Cricket Club). CT1 .. 88 B6
St Lawrence Ind Est. CT11 ..... 52 E7
St Lawrence Rd. CT1 .... 88 B6
St Leonard's
CE Jun Sch. CT21 .... 176 B2
St Leonard's Rd. CT14 .... 117 B4
St Leonards Ave. ME4 .... 9 F2
St Leonards Ct. CT21 .... 176 B1
St Leonards Rd. Hythe CT21 ... 176 B1
St Leonards Rd.
Maidstone ME16 .... 74 C8
St Louis Gr. CT6 .... 22 C4
St Luke's Ave. Maidstone ME14 .. 75 B5
St Luke's Ave. Ramsgate CT11 .. 52 E8
St Luke's Cl. CT5 .... 27 E8
St Luke's Rd. Maidstone ME14 .. 75 B5
St Luke's Rd. Ramsgate CT11 ... 52 E8
St Luke's Wlk. CT18 .... 162 F4
St Lukes Cl. CT5 .... 43 E7
St Lukes Ct. TN23 .... 155 F7
St Magnus Cl. CT7 .... 27 A8
St Margaret's at Cliffe
Cty Prim Sch. CT15 .... 151 A6
St Margaret's at Troy Town
CE Prim Sch. ME1 .... 9 C4
St Margaret's Banks. ME1 ...... 9 D5
St Margaret's CE Inf Sch. ME8 .. 33 E8
St Margaret's
CE Jun Sch. ME8 .... 33 E8
St Margaret's Cl. CT5 .... 43 A6
St Margaret's Mews. ME1 ...... 9 C5
St Margaret's Rd.
St Margaret's at Cliffe CT15 ... 151 A5
St Margaret's Rd.
Westgate-on-S CT8 .... 27 E7
St Margaret's St.
Canterbury CT1 .... 87 F8
St Margaret's St.
Rochester ME1 .... 9 C5
St Margarets Cl. ME16 .... 74 B2
St Margarets Ct. **1** CT1 ...... 87 F8
St Margarets Dr. Deal CT14 .... 134 B8
St Margarets Dr.
Gillingham ME8 .... 33 C5
St Margarets Rd. CT7 .... 27 F3
St Mark's Cl. CT20 .... 177 D5

St Marks Cl. CT5 .... 43 E8
St Marks Ho. ME7 .... 10 C5
St Martin's
CE Prim Sch. CT18 .... 177 B5
St Martin's Cl. Detling ME14 ... 55 A1
St Martin's Cl. Dover CT17 .... 166 B5
St Martin's
Cty Prim Sch. CT17 .... 166 A7
St Martin's Hill. CT1 .... 88 C8
St Martin's Hospl. CT1 .... 88 D8
St Martin's Pl. CT1 .... 88 B8
St Martin's Rd. Canterbury CT1 .. 67 B1
St Martin's Rd. Deal CT14 ..... 116 F4
St Martin's Rd. Guston CT15 ... 149 E4
St Martin's Terr. CT1 .... 88 B8
St Martin's View. CT6 .... 46 A8
St Martins Ave. CT1 .... 88 B8
St Martins Cl. Canterbury CT1 .. 88 B8
St Martins Cl. Newington ME9 .. 35 C7
St Martins Rd.
Folkestone CT20 .... 177 D6
St Martins Rd.
New Romney TN28 .... 200 B6
St Mary St. **13** ME13 .... 62 D7
St Mary of Charity
CE Inf Sch. ME13 .... 62 D7
St Mary of Charity
CE Jun Sch. ME13 .... 62 D7
St Mary's Ave. CT9 .... 8 D1
St Mary's CE Prim Sch.
Ashford TN23 .... 139 A3
St Mary's CE Prim Sch.
Chilham CT4 .... 107 B8
St Mary's CE Prim Sch.
Dover CT16 .... 166 E8
St Mary's CE Prim Sch.
Folkestone CT19 .... 178 F6
St Mary's Church. CT6 .... 24 D7
St Mary's Cl. Eastry CT13 ..... 93 C2
St Mary's Cl. Hamstreet TN26 .. 183 A8
St Mary's Cl. Nonington CT15 ... 113 C5
St Mary's Cl.
Woodnesborough CT13 .... 93 B6
St Mary's Coll.
Folkestone CT20 .... 178 A5
St Mary's Coll. Herne Bay CT6 .. 22 E4
St Mary's Ct. **17** CT1 .... 87 F8
St Mary's Cty Prim Sch. ME2 .. 9 B7
St Mary's Gdns.
St Mary's Bay TN29 .... 195 A5
St Mary's Gdns. Upstreet CT3 ... 47 E3
St Mary's Gr.
Tilmanstone CT14 .... 115 A4
St Mary's Gr. Whitstable CT5 ... 42 F7
St Mary's Hospl. CT18 .... 161 D3
St Mary's Meadow. CT3 ...... 91 A8
St Mary's Pl. ME9 .... 35 C7
St Mary's RC Prim Sch.
Deal CT14 .... 116 F3
St Mary's RC Prim Sch.
Gillingham ME7 .... 10 D6
St Mary's RC Prim Sch.
Whitstable CT5 .... 20 F2
St Mary's Rd. 5
Broadstairs CT10 .... 30 B4
St Mary's Rd. Deal CT14 ..... 117 C1
St Mary's Rd. Elham CT4 ..... 144 F4
St Mary's Rd. Faversham ME13 .. 62 D7
St Mary's Rd. Gillingham ME7 ... 10 C6
St Mary's Rd. Minster CT12 ..... 50 B6
St Mary's Rd. Patrixbourne CT4 .. 89 B3
St Mary's Rd. Rochester ME2 .... 9 B7
St Mary's Rd. St Mary
in the Marsh TN28 & TN29 .. 194 C5
St Mary's Rd. West Hythe CT21 .. 175 B1
St Mary's Row. ME12 .... 4 A6
St Mary's St. CT1 .... 87 F8
St Mary's View. ME9 .... 35 C7
St Mary's Terr. **2** CT20 .... 178 E5
St Marys View. TN24 .... 139 E7
St Marys Mews. TN24 .... 156 F8
St Matthew's
CE (VC) Inf Sch. ME1 .... 9 A2
St Matthew's Cl. ME1 .... 35 C7
St Matthews Dr. ME1 .... 9 A2
St Michael's Alley. **11** CT11 .... 52 E8
St Michael's CE Inf Sch. ME16 .. 74 E3
St Michael's
CE Jun Sch. ME16 .... 74 E3
St Michael's
CE Prim Sch. TN30 .... 167 A3
St Michael's Cl. Chatham ME4 ... 9 F3
St Michael's Cl. 5
Sittingbourne ME10 .... 36 F4
St Michael's Ct. 6
Folkestone CT20 .... 178 E5
St Michael's Ct. Rochester ME2 .. 9 B8
St Michael's Pl. CT2 .... 66 E2
St Michael's
RC Prim Sch. ME4 .... 9 F3
St Michael's Rd.
Canterbury CT2 .... 66 E2
St Michael's Rd.
Maidstone ME16 .... 74 D3
St Michael's Rd.
Sittingbourne ME10 .... 36 E4
St Michael's Rd.
Sittingbourne ME10 .... 37 A4
St Michael's St. CT20 .... 178 E5
St Michael's Terr. TN30 ..... 167 B3
St Michael's Wlk. CT18 ..... 162 F4
St Michaels Ave. CT9 .... 29 D8
St Michaels Cl. Canterbury CT2 .. 66 A1
St Michaels Rd.
Pratling Street ME14 & ME20 .. 53 C3
St Mildred's Ave.
Birchington CT7 .... 26 E8

St Mildred's Ave.
Broadstairs CT10 .... 30 A4
St Mildred's Ave.
Ramsgate CT11 .... 52 B5
St Mildred's Cl. **2** TN30 ..... 179 A7
St Mildred's Cty Inf Sch. CT10 .. 30 A4
St Mildred's Gdns. CT8 & CT9 .. 7 D1
St Mildred's Rd. Margate CT9 .... 8 A2
St Mildred's Rd. Minster CT12 .. 50 B5
St Mildred's Rd.
Ramsgate CT11 .... 52 C6
St Mildred's Rd.
Westgate-on-S CT8 .... 7 C1
St Mildreds Ct. Canterbury CT1 .. 87 E8
St Mildreds Ct. Deal CT14 ..... 117 C1
St Mildreds Pl. CT1 .... 87 E7
St Monicas. CT17 .... 166 C7
St Monicas Rd. CT14 .... 134 D6
St Nicholas at Wade
CE Prim Sch. CT7 .... 25 E2
St Nicholas CE Inf Sch. ME2 .... 9 A7
St Nicholas Cl. Deal CT14 ..... 116 F4
St Nicholas Cl. Sturry CT2 ..... 67 F7
St Nicholas Cnr. CT7 .... 25 F1
St Nicholas Hospl. CT2 .... 66 C1
St Nicholas Rd. Canterbury CT1 . 87 D6
St Nicholas Rd.
Faversham ME13 .... 62 A7
St Nicholas Rd. Hythe CT21 ... 176 A2
St Nicholas Rd.
Littlestone-on-S TN28 .... 200 E6
St Nicholas Rdbt. CT7 .... 26 B2
St Nicholas Sch. CT1 .... 87 F6
St Nicholas & St John's
CE Prim Sch. CT14 .... 134 C5
St Nicholas Terr. **1** CT21 .... 176 B2
St Patrick's Cl. Deal CT14 ..... 117 C6
St Patrick's Cl. Whitstable CT5 .. 43 E7
St Patrick's Rd. Deal CT14 ..... 117 C6
St Patrick's Rd. Ramsgate CT11 .. 52 F8
St Patricks Rd. CT17 .... 166 A4
St Paul's Ave. ME13 .... 62 A7
St Paul's Ct. CT20 .... 177 E4
St Paul's Rd. CT9 .... 8 A3
St Paul's St. **1** ME10 .... 36 E5
St Paul's Way. CT20 .... 177 F4
St Pauls Cres. ME13 .... 64 A3
St Pauls Cty Inf Sch. ME14 ... 75 A7
St Pauls Rd. ME13 .... 64 A3
St Pauls Terr. CT1 .... 88 A8
St Peter St. ME1 .... 9 D4
St Peter's Bridge. ME16 ...... 74 F4
St Peter's CE Prim Sch.
Aylesford ME20 .... 53 A3
St Peter's CE Prim Sch.
Folkestone CT19 .... 178 E5
St Peter's Cl. ME12 .... 3 D6
St Peter's Cl. Broadstairs CT10 .. 29 F5
St Peter's Ct. Faversham ME13 .. 62 A7
St Peter's Cty Inf Sch. ME1 .... 9 C3
St Peter's Footpath.
Margate CT9 .... 7 J1
St Peter's Footpath.
Margate CT9 .... 29 A8
St Peter's Gr. CT1 .... 87 E8
St Peter's La. CT1 & CT2 ...... 66 F1
St Peter's Meth Prim Sch. CT1 .. 87 E8
St Peter's Park Rd. CT10 ...... 29 F5
St Peter's Path. ME1 .... 9 D5
St Peter's Pl. CT1 & CT2 ...... 87 E8
St Peter's RC Prim Sch.
Sittingbourne ME10 .... 36 D2
St Peter's RC Prim Sch.
Sittingbourne ME10 .... 36 E4
St Peter's Rd.
Boughton Street ME13 .... 64 A3
St Peter's Rd. Broadstairs CT10 .. 29 F5
St Peter's Rd. Margate CT9 ..... 29 A7
St Peter's Rd. Whitstable CT5 ... 20 D2
St Peter's St.
Canterbury CT1 & CT2 .... 87 F8
St Peter's St. Sandwich CT13 ... 73 A1
St Peter's Way. TN26 .... 170 A8
St Peter's-in-Thanet
CE Jun Sch. CT10 .... 29 E5
St Peters Pl. ME9 .... 60 A6
St Peters St. ME16 .... 74 F4
St Philip Howard
RC Prim Sch. CT6 .... 22 F5
St Philip's Ave. ME15 .... 75 B2
St Philip's CE Prim Sch. ME15 .. 75 A3
St Radigund's
Cty Prim Sch. CT17 .... 149 A1
St Radigund's Pl. CT17 .... 67 A1
St Radigund's Rd. CT17 ...... 149 A1
St Radigunds St. **22** CT1 ..... 67 A1
St Richard's
RC Prim Sch. CT16 .... 149 D1
St Richard's Rd. CT14 .... 116 F3
St Richard's Wlk. CT17 ..... 166 A4
St Ronan's Cl. ME15 .... 97 C7
St Saviour's Cl. ME13 .... 62 E7
St Saviour's Hospl. CT21 ..... 176 F2
St Saviours CE Jun Sch. CT8 ... 27 E8
St Saviours Ct. CT19 .... 178 D7
St. Saviours Rd. ME15 ...... 97 D6
St Simon of England
RC Prim Sch. TN29 .... 156 A8
St Simon Stock RC Sch. ME16 .. 74 C4
St Stephen's CE Inf Sch. ME15 .. 74 E2
St Stephen's Cl. Canterbury CT2 .. 66 F2
St Stephen's Cl. Newington ME9 .. 35 C7
St Stephen's Cty Inf Sch. CT2 .. 66 F3
St Stephen's Cty Jun Sch. CT1 .. 66 F3
St Stephen's Fields. CT2 ..... 66 F1
St Stephen's Gn. CT2 .... 66 F3
St Stephen's Hill. CT2 .... 66 E4

St Stephen's Lodge. CT2 ...... 66 F2
St Stephen's Rd. CT2 .... 66 F2
St Stephen's Sq. ME15 .... 74 E2
St Stephen's Way. CT20 ..... 177 F4
St Stephen's Wlk. TN23 ..... 155 F7
St Swithin's St. CT5 .... 21 B3
St Teresa's
RC Prim Sch. TN24 .... 139 B4
St Theresa's Cl. TN24 .... 139 B3
St Thomas' Cross. TN26 ..... 170 E3
St Thomas Hill. CT2 .... 66 D3
St Thomas More
RC Prim Sch. ME5 .... 32 A5
St Thomas of Canterbury
Cath Prim Sch. ME1 .... 11 B2
St Thomas' RC Prim Sch. CT1 .. 67 A1
St Thomas's Hospl. CT13 ..... 72 F1
St Thomas's Sch. ME10 ...... 36 E7
St Vincent Rd. CT15 .... 150 F7
St Vincent's Cl. Littlebourne CT3 .. 68 F1
St Vincent's Cl. Whitstable CT5 .. 43 E7
St Welcume's Way. ME17 ..... 100 E6
St William of Perth
RC Prim Sch. ME1 .... 9 B2
St William's Way. ME1 .... 9 D2
St Williams Hospl. ME1 .... 9 D2
St Winifred Rd. CT19 .... 177 F6
Salem St. ME15 .... 75 A3
Salisbury Ave. Broadstairs CT10 .. 29 F2
Salisbury Ave. Gillingham ME8 ... 33 D8
Salisbury Ave. Ramsgate CT11 ... 52 F8
Salisbury Cl. ME10 .... 37 C4
Salisbury Ho. **5** ME15 ...... 97 D7
Salisbury Rd. Canterbury CT2 ... 66 E2
Salisbury Rd. Chatham ME4 ..... 10 A3
Salisbury Rd. Deal CT14 ..... 117 B2
Salisbury Rd. Dover CT16 ..... 149 D1
Salisbury Rd. Folkestone CT19 .. 177 E7
Salisbury Rd. Herne Bay CT6 ... 23 C5
Salisbury Rd. Kit's Coty ME20 ... 53 D7
Salisbury Rd. Maidstone ME4 ... 75 A6
Salisbury Rd.
St Margaret's at Cliffe CT15 ... 151 B6
Sally Port. ME7 .... 10 A6
Sally Port Gdns. ME7 .... 10 B6
Salmestone
Cty Prim Sch. CT9 .... 28 E8
Salmestone Grange. CT9 ..... 28 E8
Salmestone Rd. CT9 .... 28 E8
Salmestone Rise. CT9 .... 28 E8
Salmon Cres. ME4 .... 3 F6
Salt Marsh La. **15** CT5 ...... 20 D2
Salt's Ave. ME15 .... 96 F3
Salt's Dr. CT10 .... 29 E3
Salter's La. TN29 .... 197 C8
Salters La. ME13 .... 62 D4
Salthouse Cl. TN29 .... 197 D8
Saltings The.
Littlestone-on-S TN28 .... 200 E6
Saltings The. **10** Whitstable CT5 .. 20 D2
Salts Cl. CT5 .... 20 D1
Salts La. ME15 .... 97 A4
Saltwood CE Prim Sch. CT21 .. 176 B4
Saltwood Gdns. CT9 .... 8 E2
Saltwood Rd. ME15 .... 74 F1
Samara Cl. ME5 .... 32 A1
Samian Cres. CT19 .... 177 C6
Samphire Cl. ME14 .... 75 E4
Sancroft Ave. CT2 .... 66 C1
Sanctuary Cl. CT10 .... 29 F2
Sanctuary Rd. ME8 .... 11 A3
Sand Ct. ME12 .... 6 G2
Sandbanks Rd. ME13 .... 41 C2
Sandbourne Dr. ME14 .... 53 F1
Sanders Ct. ME12 .... 4 A5
Sandford Rd. ME10 .... 36 B5
Sandgate Ct. ME8 .... 33 F4
Sandgate
Cty Prim Sch. CT20 .... 177 F4
Sandgate Espl. CT20 & CT21 .. 177 D2
Sandgate High St. CT20 ..... 177 E3
Sandgate Hill. CT20 .... 178 A4
Sandgate Rd. Folkestone CT20 .. 178 C4
Sandgate Rd. Folkestone CT20 .. 178 D4
Sandhurst Cl. Canterbury CT2 ... 67 A4
Sandhurst Cl. Gillingham ME8 ... 11 C3
Sandhurst Rd. CT9 .... 8 F2
Sandilands. TN24 .... 139 E2
Sandle's Rd. CT7 .... 26 F7
Sandlewood Dr. CT7 .... 25 F1
Sandling Cl. TN23 .... 155 F7
Sandling Cty Prim Sch. ME14 .. 75 B8
Sandling La. ME14 .... 75 A8
Sandling Rd. Hythe CT21 ..... 175 F6
Sandling Rd. Maidstone ME14 ... 74 F6
Sandling Rd.
Maidstone,Ringlestone ME14 .... 74 F7
Sandling Sta. CT21 .... 175 F6
Sandown Cl. CT14 .... 95 D1
Sandown Cotts. Margate CT9 ... 8 A3
Sandown Cotts. Teynham ME9 ... 38 E1
Sandown Ct. CT14 .... 117 C7
Sandown
Cty Prim Sch. CT14 .... 117 C7
Sandown Dr. Gillingham ME8 ... 33 D7
Sandown Dr. Herne Bay CT6 ... 22 D4
Sandown Lees. CT13 .... 94 D8
Sandown Rd. Deal CT14 ..... 117 D8
Sandown Rd. Sandwich CT13 ... 94 B8
Sandpiper Ct. 3
Birchington CT7 .... 26 F8
Sandpiper Ct. Margate CT9 .... 7 J3
Sandpiper Rd. Chatham ME5 ... 32 D2
Sandpiper Rd. Whitstable CT5 ... 43 B7
Sandpit Hill. CT3 .... 47 C4
Sandringham Ho. ME1 .... 9 B4
Sandringham Rd. ME8 .... 33 E3

Sandstone Ct. CT20 .... 178 A1
Sandstone Rise. ME14 .... 54 C8
Sandway Rd. ME17 .... 100 F9
Sandway Bay
Bird Obsy. CT13 .... 94 E3
Sandwich Cl. CT20 .... 177 F9
Sandwich Cty Inf Sch. CT13 ... 72 F7
Sandwich Cty Jun Sch. CT13 .. 93 F8
Sandwich Hill. CT3 .... 70 B7
Sandwich Ind Est. CT13 .... 73 B7
Sandwich Rd. Ash CT3 .... 71 F7
Sandwich Rd. Ash CT3 .... 72 A4
Sandwich Rd. Cliffs End CT12 .. 51 D4
Sandwich Rd. Eastry CT13 ..... 93 C3
Sandwich Rd. Eythorne CT15 .. 131 C6
Sandwich Rd.
Nonington CT15 & CT3 .... 113 F6
Sandwich Rd. Sandwich CT13 ... 93 D2
Sandwich Rd.
Tilmanstone CT14 & CT15 ..... 115 B2
Sandwich Rd. Whitfield CT15 ... 132 A2
Sandwich Rd. Whitfield CT16 ... 149 A2
Sandwich Rd.
Woodnesborough CT13 .... 93 D9
Sandwich Sta. CT13 .... 94 A8
Sandwich Tech Sch. CT13 ..... 93 F6
Sandwood Rd. Ramsgate CT10 ... 29 F2
Sandwood Rd. Sandwich CT13 .. 93 F8
Sandy Cnr. ME7 .... 154 F7
Sandy Dell. ME7 .... 33 A2
Sandy La. Ashford TN24 .... 140 B7
Sandy La. Daniel's Water TN26 .. 154 E4
Sandy La. Hythe CT20 & CT21 .. 177 B3
Sandy La.
Maidstone,Harbourland ME14 ... 75 C8
Sandy La.
Maidstone,Penenden Heath ME14 75 C2
Sandy La.
Maidstone,Ware Street ME14 .... 76 B3
Sandy La. Tenterden TN30 ..... 179 B3
Sandy Mount. ME14 .... 76 B9
Sandy Pl. TN25 .... 158 D9
Sangro Pl. CT1 .... 67 D3
Sanspareil Ave. ME12 .... 4 A6
Santon La. CT3 .... 70 E4
Saracen Cl. ME7 .... 11 A1
Saracen Fields. ME5 & ME14 .. 54 C4
Sarah Gdns. CT9 .... 29 D6
Sark Cl. TN29 .... 195 C2
Sarre Ct. CT7 .... 48 D6
Sarre Mill. CT7 .... 48 D2
Sarre Pl. CT13 .... 93 F6
Sarsen Hts. ME5 .... 31 F7
Satis Ave. ME5 .... 36 E1
Satmar La. CT15 & CT18 ...... 164 E4
Saunders La. CT3 .... 71 F7
Saunders St. ME7 .... 10 C6
Saunders Way. TN31 .... 201 A1
Savage Rd. ME5 .... 32 B3
Savernake Dr. CT6 .... 23 B3
Saw Lodge Field. TN23 .... 156 C4
Sawpit Rd. ME9 .... 59 B5
Sawyers Ct. ME4 .... 10 B1
Saxon Ave. ME12 .... 4 B6
Saxon Cl. CT21 .... 176 E5
Saxon Ct. CT14 .... 71 C
Saxon Rd. Bridge CT4 .... 89 A4
Saxon Rd. Faversham ME13 ..... 62 C7
Saxon Rd. Ramsgate CT11 ..... 52 B6
Saxon Rd. Westgate-on-S CT8 .. 7 J2
Saxon St. **9** CT17 .... 166 D8
Saxons Cl. CT14 .... 117 C6
Saxons Dr. ME14 .... 75 B7
Saxton Rd. TN29 .... 204 E8
Saxton St. ME7 .... 10 C5
Sayer Rd. TN27 .... 120 C4
Sayers La. **4** TN30 .... 179 A7
Scanlons Bridge Rd. CT21 ..... 176 A4
Scarborough Dr. ME12 .... 4 C8
Scarlett Cl. ME5 .... 32 C1
Scene Cotts. CT21 .... 176 E4
Sceptre Way. CT5 .... 43 B7
School Ave. ME7 .... 10 E4
School Cl The. CT8 .... 7 C
School Hill. CT4 .... 107 B8
School La. Bapchild ME9 .... 37 D7
School La. Bekesbourne CT4 ... 89 C4
School La. Blean CT2 .... 66 A6
School La. Borden ME9 .... 35 F6
School La.
Boughton Street ME13 .... 63 F8
School La. Fordwich CT2 ..... 68 A4
School La. Goodnestone CT3 ... 91 D2
School La. Herne Bay CT6 ..... 23 B7
School La. Hoath CT3 .... 46 E6
School La. Ickham CT3 .... 90 C6
School La. Iwade ME9 .... 14 C
School La. Lower Halstow ME9 .. 13 B
School La. Lower Hardres CT4 .. 110 B4
School La. Maidstone ME15 ..... 75 E4
School La. Newington ME9 ..... 35 C7
School La. Platt's Heath ME17 .. 100 F8
School La. Ramsgate CT11 ..... 52 E
School La.
Stalisfield Green ME13 .... 103 D
School La. Staple CT3 .... 92 A
School La. Stourmouth CT3 ..... 48 E
School La. Wingham CT3 ..... 91 A
School Rd. Appledore TN26 ... 181 C
School Rd. Ash CT3 .... 71 C
School Rd. Bethersden TN26 ... 153 D
School Rd. Charing TN27 ..... 120 C
School Rd. Densole CT18 ..... 162 E
School Rd. Faversham ME13 ... 62 C
School Rd. Hothfield TN26 ..... 138 A
School Rd. Hythe CT21 ..... 176 B
School Rd. Sandwich CT13 ..... 72 B

School Rd. Sittingbourne ME10 37 B3
School Rd. Tilmanstone CT14 114 F4
School View. ME9 58 C8
Scimitar Cl. ME7 11 A1
Scocles Cotts. ME12 4 C5
Scocles Rd. ME12 4 C5
Scoggers Hill. ME13 85 A7
Scot's La. TN25 159 F8
Scotby Ave. ME5 32 B4
Scott Ave. ME8 12 A1
Scott St. ME14 74 F6
Scott's Terr. ME4 9 F3
Scotteswood Ave. ME4 9 F2
Scotton St. TN25 123 F2
Scragged Oak Rd. Detling ME14 55 C5
Scragged Oak Rd. Hucking ME14 56 C1
Scraps Hill. ME9 37 F4
Scrapsgate Rd. ME12 4 A7
Scrubbs La. ME16 74 D4
Sea App. ME12 6 E4
Sea Rd. Hythe CT21 177 A2
Sea Rd. Kingsdown CT14 134 D6
Sea Rd. Westgate-on-S CT7 & CT8 7 C1
Sea St. Herne Bay CT6 22 C3
Sea St. St Margaret's at Cliffe CT15 151 A6
Sea St. Whitstable CT5 20 D2
Sea View Ave. CT7 26 E8
Sea View Cl. CT18 164 B1
Sea View Gdns. ME12 6 E3
Sea View Hts. CT7 26 D8
Sea View Rd. Birchington CT7 26 E8
Sea View Rd. Broadstairs CT10 30 A6
Sea View Rd. Cliffs End CT12 51 D6
Sea View Rd. Herne Bay CT6 23 C5
Sea View Rd. St Margaret's at Cliffe CT15 150 F4
Sea View Sq. CT6 22 F5
Sea View Terr. Folkestone CT20 177 D3
Sea View Terr. Margate CT9 7 G2
Sea View Terr. Minster ME12 5 A5
Sea Wall. Dymchurch TN29 195 D8
Sea Wall. Whitstable CT5 20 D2
Seabourne Way. TN29 195 B7
Seabrook Ct. CT21 177 B3
Seabrook Gdns. CT21 177 B2
Seabrook Gr. CT21 177 A2
Seabrook Rd. CT21 176 E2
Seabrook Vale. CT21 177 B4
Seacroft Rd. CT10 30 A1
Seadown Cl. CT21 177 A4
Seafield Rd. Broadstairs CT10 30 A8
Seafield Rd. Ramsgate CT11 52 C6
Seafield Rd. Whitstable CT5 21 B3
Seaford Ct. ME1 9 B5
Seagar Rd. ME13 40 B1
Seager Rd. ME12 1 F2
Seagrave Cres. CT19 178 F6
Sealand Ct. ME1 9 B5
Seamark Cl. CT12 49 D7
Seamark Rd. CT12 & CT7 26 E2
Seapoint Rd. CT10 30 B3
Seasalter Beach. CT5 43 A7
Seasalter Cl. ME12 6 E4
Seasalter La. CT5 43 A5
Seasalter Rd. CT5 & ME13 41 E3
Seaside Ave. ME12 4 C8
Seathorpe Ave. ME12 4 C8
Seaths Cr. CT3 91 A7
Seaton Ave. CT21 176 B3
Seaton Cotts. TN25 122 E3
Seaton Rd. Gillingham ME7 10 E3
Seaton Rd. Wickhambreaux CT3 69 D2
Seaview Ave. ME12 6 H1
Seaview Cotts. 6 CT10 30 B4
Seaview Ct. CT10 30 B3
Seaview Rd. Gillingham ME7 10 C4
Seaview Rd. Greatstone-on-S TN28 200 E1
Seaville Dr. CT6 23 E5
Seaway Cres. TN29 194 F4
Seaway Gdns. TN29 194 F4
Seaway Rd. TN29 195 A4
Second Ave. Broadstairs CT10 8 G2
Second Ave. Chatham ME4 & ME5 10 C1
Second Ave. Eastchurch ME12 5 F5
Second Ave. Gillingham ME7 10 E3
Second Ave. Margate CT9 8 B3
Second Ave. Rushenden ME11 2 F3
Second Ave. Sheerness ME12 1 C1
Secretan Rd. ME1 9 B1
Sedge Cres. ME5 31 E4
Sedley Cl. ME8 33 C3
Seesalter Cross. CT5 43 A6
Seeshill Cl. CT5 43 E8
Segrave Rd. CT19 178 F5
Selby Cl. CT6 23 C4
Selborne Rd. CT9 29 B8
Selbourne Rd. ME7 10 D7
Selbourne Wlk. ME15 97 F6
Selby Rd. ME15 97 F4
Selkirk Rd. CT16 149 B3
Sellens Cotts. ME12 1 E2
Sellindge Cty Prim Sch. TN25 159 C1
Selling CE Prim Sch. ME13 84 B5
Selling Ct. ME13 84 C5
Selling Rd. Chilham CT4 85 B3
Selling Rd. Faversham ME13 62 F3
Selling Rd. Selling ME13 84 E6
Sellinge Gn. ME8 11 C3
Selsea Ave. CT6 22 D4
Selstead Cl. ME8 11 C2
Selsted CE Prim Sch. CT15 146 C6
Selway Ct. CT14 117 B3
Selwood Cl. ME12 3 E6
Selwyn Ct. CT10 29 F5
Selwyn Dr. CT10 29 F5
Semaphore Rd. CT7 26 F8
Semple Cl. CT12 50 C7
Semple Gdns. ME4 9 E3
Senacre La. ME15 97 E6
Senacre Sq. ME15 97 F7
Senacre Tech Coll. ME15 97 D6
Senacre Wood Cty Prim Sch. ME15 97 F7
Sene Pk. CT21 176 D3
Sene Valley Golf Course. CT21 176 E4
Senlac Cl. CT11 52 B6
Serene Ct. 12 CT10 30 B4
Serene Pl. 9 CT10 30 B4
Setford Rd. ME5 32 C6
Setterfield Ho. CT21 176 D2
Setterfield Rd. CT9 7 J1
Settington Ave. ME5 10 C1
Sevastopol Pl. CT1 67 D1
Seven Stones Dr. CT10 30 A1
Sevenacre Rd. ME13 62 C8
Sevenscore Farm Cotts. CT12 51 A5
Severn Rd. ME5 32 C5
Sevington La. TN24 157 A7
Sevington Pk. ME15 96 F6
Sewell Cl. CT7 27 A6
Sexburga Dr. ME12 4 B8
Sextant Pk. ME2 9 E6
Seymour Ave. Westgate-on-S CT9 7 D1
Seymour Ave. Whitstable CT5 20 E1
Seymour Cl. CT6 23 B1
Seymour Pl. CT1 87 E7
Seymour Rd. 1 Chatham ME4 10 B3
Seymour Rd. Gillingham ME8 12 C1
Seymour Rd. St Margaret's at Cliffe CT15 150 F8
Shackleton Cl. ME5 32 B6
Shadoxhurst Rd. TN26 169 C7
Shaftesbury Ave. CT19 177 E7
Shaftesbury Ct. CT14 117 D2
Shaftesbury Dr. ME16 74 C4
Shaftesbury Rd. Canterbury CT2 66 F3
Shaftesbury Rd. Hersden CT3 46 E1
Shaftesbury Rd. Whitstable CT5 20 D1
Shaftsbury St. CT11 52 F7
Shah Pl. CT11 52 D7
Shakespeare Ct. CT17 166 B7
Shakespeare Pas. CT9 7 H2
Shakespeare Rd. Birchington CT7 27 A8
Shakespeare Rd. Dover CT17 166 B6
Shakespeare Rd. Gillingham ME7 10 C3
Shakespeare Rd. Margate CT9 7 J1
Shakespeare Rd. Sittingbourne ME10 37 A4
Shakespeare Terr. 8 CT20 178 C4
Shalder Ho. ME7 10 D7
Shalloak Rd. CT2 67 D6
Shallows Rd. CT10 29 D6
Shalmsford Ct. CT4 86 C2
Shalmsford Rd. CT4 85 F2
Shalmsford St. CT4 86 B2
Shamel Bsns Ctr. ME2 9 C7
Shamley Rd. ME5 32 D2
Shamrock Ave. CT5 43 B7
Shanklin Cl. ME5 32 C8
Shapland Cl. CT6 23 C3
Share and Coulter Rd. CT5 21 D1
Sharon Cres. ME5 31 F4
Sharsted Hill. ME9 81 C8
Sharsted Way. Gillingham ME7 33 A7
Sharsted Way. Maidstone ME14 76 B5
Shatterlocks Cty Inf Sch. CT17 149 B2
Shaw Cross. TN24 139 D5
Shawdon Ave. CT13 95 A7
Shaws Way. ME1 9 C3
Shawstead Rd. ME7 & ME7 32 D5
Sheal's Cres. ME15 75 A2
Sheals Ct. ME15 75 A2
Shear Way. TN29 186 C5
Shearers Cl. ME14 75 E4
Shearwater. ME16 74 B5
Shearwater Ave. CT5 43 C7
Shearwater Ct. ME12 3 B8
Shearwater Ho. TN29 195 A3
Shearway Rd. CT19 177 F8
Sheepfold La. TN23 156 C4
Sheerness Golf Course. ME12 3 F8
Sheerness Harbour Est. ME12 1 A3
Sheerness-on-Sea (Terminus). ME12 1 C2
Sheerstone. ME9 14 D4
Sheerwater Rd. CT3 70 F5
Sheerways. ME13 62 A6
Sheet Glass Rd. ME11 3 A3
Shelden Dr. ME8 33 F8
Sheldon Bsns Ctr. ME2 9 D8
Sheldon Cl. CT3 113 A6
Sheldwich Cl. TN23 156 A6
Shellbeach. ME12 19 D6
Shelley Ave. CT1 67 C2
Shelley Rd. ME16 74 C2
Shellness Rd. ME12 19 D7
Shellons St. CT20 178 D5
Shelvin La. CT4 129 C3
Shenley Gr. ME14 53 F2
Shepherd Dr. TN24 157 A8
Shepherd's Close Rd. CT4 89 E1
Shepherd's Cross. CT15 132 B1
Shepherds Gate. ME7 32 F5
Shepherds Gate Dr. ME14 75 E6
Shepherds Way. Langley Heath ME17 98 E4
Shepherds Way. Whitstable CT5 44 C8
Shepherds Well Sta. CT15 130 D5
Shepherds Wlk. Hythe CT21 175 E1
Shepherds Wlk. Whitstable CT5 44 C8
Shepherdsgate. CT2 66 F1
Shepherdsgate Dr. CT6 46 A8
Shepherdswell Rd. CT15 131 A7
Shepperton Cl. ME5 32 C4
Sheppey Cl. CT7 27 A7
Sheppey Cotts. ME12 1 E2
Sheppey Hospl. ME12 4 C7
Sheppey Rd. ME15 97 A7
Sheppey St. ME12 1 B2
Sheppey Terr. ME12 4 F5
Sheppey View. CT5 43 C6
Sheppey Way. Bobbing ME10 & ME9 36 B7
Sheppey Way. Iwade ME9 14 F6
Sheppey Way. Queenborough ME12 & ME9 3 D2
Shepway. TN24 139 E5
Shepway Cl. CT19 178 D6
Shepway Cross. CT21 175 B3
Shepway Ct. ME15 97 C8
Shepway Cty Inf Sch. ME15 97 E8
Shepway Cty Jun Sch. ME15 97 E8
Sheraton Ct. ME5 31 F1
Sherbourne Dr. ME16 74 B2
Sheridan Cl. Chatham ME5 32 C7
Sheridan Cl. Maidstone ME14 74 E8
Sheridan Rd. CT16 149 B3
Sheriff Dr. ME5 32 A2
Sherman Cl. ME7 11 B1
Shernold Sch. ME16 74 D5
Shernolds. ME15 97 B7
Sheron Cl. CT14 117 A5
Sherriffs Court La. CT12 49 E6
Sherwood Ave. ME5 32 A2
Sherwood Cl. Ashford TN24 139 D7
Sherwood Cl. Faversham ME13 40 B1
Sherwood Cl. Herne Bay CT6 23 C2
Sherwood Cl. Whitstable CT5 43 C6
Sherwood Ct. CT8 7 C1
Sherwood Dr. CT5 43 C6
Sherwood Gdns. CT11 29 E1
Sherwood Ho. ME5 32 A3
Sherwood Rd. CT7 26 F5
Shillingheld Cl. ME14 75 F5
Ship Cl. TN29 195 C8
Ship La. ME1 9 E4
Ship St. CT19 178 D6
Shipland Hos. TN27 136 D8
Shipley Ct. ME14 75 A4
Shipman Ave. CT2 87 C8
Shipmans Way. CT16 149 A3
Shipwrights Ave. ME4 10 B2
Shipwrights Lee. CT5 20 C2
Shire La. ME13 103 C6
Shireway Cl. CT19 178 A7
Shirley Ave. Chatham ME5 31 D5
Shirley Ave. Ramsgate CT11 29 E1
Shirley Way. ME15 76 A3
Shoebury Terr. ME12 5 A5
Sholden Bank. CT14 116 E4
Sholden CE Prim Sch. CT14 116 F5
Sholden New Rd. CT14 116 F6
Shooter's Hill. 5 CT16 & CT17 149 C1
Shooters Hill. CT15 131 C8
Shorefields. ME8 12 B2
Shoregate La. ME9 12 F6
Shoreham La. TN30 167 A3
Shoreham Wlk. ME15 97 F7
Shoreland Ct. ME1 9 B5
Shorncliffe Cres. CT20 177 E5
Shorncliffe Ind Est. CT20 177 D4
Shorncliffe Rd. Folkestone CT20 177 F5
Shorncliffe Rd. Folkestone CT20 178 B5
Short La. Alkham CT15 147 D1
Short La. Gillingham ME7 11 A6
Short La. Snargate TN29 191 D6
Short St. 3 Chatham ME4 10 B3
Short St. Chillenden CT3 114 A8
Short St. 5 Sandwich CT13 73 A1
Short St. Sheerness ME12 1 C2
Short's Prospect. ME12 17 C8
Shortlands Gn. ME15 97 F5
Shortlands Rd. ME10 37 B4
Shorts Way. ME1 9 A3
Shottendane Rd. CT9 & CT7 & CT8 28 C7
Shottenden Rd. Gillingham ME7 10 D7
Shottenden Rd. Leaveland CT4 & ME13 105 D8
Shottenden Rd. Shottenden CT4 84 B1
Shrimpton Cl. CT4 85 B3
Shropshire Terr. 3 ME15 97 E7
Shrub Hill Rd. CT5 44 D7
Shrubbery The. Barham CT4 111 F1
Shrubbery The. Deal CT14 117 C1
Shrubcote. TN30 179 C7
Shrubsole Ave. ME12 1 D1
Shrubsole Dr. ME14 53 F3
Shuart La. CT7 25 F4
Shurland Ave. Leysdown-on-S ME12 6 H1
Shurland Ave. Minster ME12 4 B6
Shurland Ave. Sittingbourne ME10 36 F1
Shuttle Rd. CT10 30 B5
Sibert's Cl. CT15 130 F5
Sibertswold CE Prim Sch. CT15 130 E4
Sibton Park Prep Sch. CT18 161 B8
Sidings The. CT18 161 C7
Sidney Rd. Gillingham ME7 10 C7
Sidney Rd. Rochester ME1 9 A2
Sidney St. Folkestone CT19 178 E7
Sidney St. Maidstone ME16 74 C2
Silchester Ct. ME14 75 C7
Silecroft Ct. TN23 138 E1
Silvanus Ho. CT11 52 D7
Silver Ave. CT7 27 B6
Silver Bank. ME5 32 A6
Silver Birch Gr. TN23 156 B4
Silver Birches. Chatham ME5 32 A3
Silver Birches. Ruckinge TN26 171 A5
Silver Birches. Sheerness ME12 1 H1
Silver Hill. Chatham ME4 9 F3
Silver Hill. Tenterden TN30 167 B1
Silver Hill Gdns. Ashford TN24 140 A1
Silver Hill Gdns. Chatham ME4 9 F3
Silver Hill Rd. TN24 140 A1
Silver St. Deal CT14 117 D7
Silver St. Silver Street ME9 57 F5
Silver Tree. ME5 32 B1
Silverdale. ME16 74 A2
Silverdale Ave. ME12 4 A6
Silverdale Dr. Gillingham ME8 33 F7
Silverdale Dr. Herne Bay CT6 23 D2
Silverdale Gr. ME10 36 D3
Silverdale Rd. CT11 52 A5
Silverlands Rd. CT18 161 C7
Silvers The. CT10 29 C4
Silverspot Cl. ME8 33 F7
Silverweed Rd. ME5 31 F4
Simmonds La. ME15 98 B6
Simmonds Rd. CT1 87 E7
Simon Ave. CT9 8 D2
Simon Langton Sch for Boys. CT1 88 A4
Simon Langton Sch for Girls. CT1 88 C5
Simon's Ave. TN23 155 F7
Simone Weil Ave. TN24 139 B4
Simpson Rd. ME10 36 C5
Sinclair Cl. ME8 33 E5
Singapore Dr. ME7 10 B5
Singer Ave. CT6 22 B4
Singledge Ave. CT16 148 F6
Singledge La. CT15 131 C2
Singleton Cl. CT12 50 B6
Singleton Ctr The. TN23 155 D8
Singleton Hill. TN23 155 D8
Singleton Rd. TN23 138 C1
Sion Hill. CT11 52 E6
Sir Evelyn Rd. ME1 9 B1
Sir John Hawkins Way. ME4 9 F4
Sir John Moore Ave. CT21 176 B2
Sir John Moore Ct. 5 CT20 177 E3
Sir Joseph Williamson's Mathematical Sch. ME1 9 C1
Sir Roger Manwood's Sch. CT13 94 B8
Sir Thomas Longley Rd. ME2 9 E6
Sir William Nottidge Tech Sch. CT5 43 F8
Siskin Cl. CT18 162 F4
Sissinghurst Dr. ME16 74 B4
Sittingbourne Comm Coll. ME10 37 C2
Sittingbourne & Kemsley Light Rly. ME10 37 A7
Sittingbourne Rd. Maidstone,Detling ME14 75 E8
Sittingbourne Rd. Maidstone, Penenden Heath ME14 75 B6
Six Fields Path. TN30 179 A7
Sixth Ave. ME12 6 A5
Skeete Rd. CT18 & TN25 160 E7
Skene Cl. ME8 12 A1
Skinner Rd. TN29 203 C6
Skinner St. Chatham ME4 9 F3
Skinner St. Gillingham ME7 10 C5
Skinner St. Gillingham ME7 10 C6
Skinner Street Cty Prim Sch. ME7 10 C6
Skinner's Alley. 3 CT5 20 D1
Skinner's Way. ME17 98 E4
Skinners Cl. ME20 53 A6
Skye Cl. ME15 97 A7
Slade Cl. ME5 32 B2
Slade Rd. ME17 & ME9 & ME13 102 D8
Slades Cl. CT5 44 C8
Slatin Rd. ME2 9 B8
Sleigh Rd. CT2 67 F6
Slicketts Hill. ME4 10 A4
Slip La. CT15 147 C2
Slip Rd. ME4 10 A8
Slipway Rd. ME12 1 A3
Sloe La. CT10 & CT9 29 B6
Slough Rd. ME9 59 A3
Smack Alley. ME13 62 D8
Small Hythe Rd. TN30 179 C3
Smallhythe Rd. TN30 179 A6
Smarden Cty Prim Sch. TN27 135 A1
Smarden Rd. TN27 136 B6
Smarden Wlk. ME8 12 B1
Smarts Cotts. ME14 76 C4
Smeed Cl. ME10 37 B4
Smeed-Dean Ctr The. ME10 37 A4
Smeeth Cty Prim Sch. TN25 158 D5
Smith Rd. ME5 32 B3
Smith St. ME2 9 A6
Smuggler's Way. CT7 27 A8
Snakes Hill. CT3 91 A5
Snargate La. TN29 191 C5
Snargate St. CT17 166 D7
Snell Gdns. CT6 22 B2
Snodhurst Ave. ME5 31 E5
Snow Ho. ME7 10 E7
Snowbell Rd. TN23 156 B4
Snowdon Ave. ME14 75 B5
Snowdon Cl. ME5 32 B7
Snowdown Caravan Site. CT15 113 A4
Snowdown Ct. CT3 112 F5
Snowdown Sta. CT15 113 B3
Snowdrop Cl. CT19 178 C8
Sobraon Way. CT1 67 D1
Sole Street Cotts. CT4 125 B7
Solent Gdns. ME5 32 B8
Soleshill Rd. CT4 84 E1
Solihull Cotts. CT12 49 E6
Solomon Ho. CT14 117 B3
Solomon Rd. ME8 12 A1
Solomons La. ME13 62 D7
Solomons Rd. ME4 9 F4
Somerfield Barn Ct. TN25 174 C8
Somerfield Cl. ME16 74 D5
Somerfield Hospl The. ME16 74 E5
Somerfield La. ME16 74 D4
Somerfield Rd. ME16 74 D4
Somerset Cl. Chatham ME5 32 C8
Somerset Cl. Sittingbourne ME10 36 C4
Somerset Cl. Whitstable CT5 43 B7
Somerset Ct. Deal CT14 117 B3
Somerset Ct. Ramsgate CT12 29 B2
Somerset Rd. Ashford TN23 & TN24 139 B3
Somerset Rd. Canterbury CT1 88 D8
Somerset Rd. Deal CT14 117 C3
Somerset Rd. Folkestone CT19 177 E6
Somerset Rd. Maidstone ME15 97 C8
Somme Ct. CT1 67 D1
Sommerville Cl. ME13 62 E7
Somner Cl. CT2 66 D1
Somner Wlk. ME15 97 F4
Sondes Cl. CT6 23 A2
Sondes Rd. CT14 117 D5
Sorrell Rd. ME5 31 F4
Sotherton. TN24 156 E7
Souberg Cl. CT14 117 C8
South Ave. Aylesham CT15 113 A3
South Ave. Gillingham ME8 11 B2
South Ave. Sittingbourne ME10 37 A3
South Avenue Cty Jun & Inf Schs. ME10 37 A3
South Barham Rd. CT4 128 E6
South Borough Cty Prim Sch. ME15 75 A2
South Brooks Rd. TN29 202 F2
South Bush La. ME8 34 B6
South Camber Way. CT16 150 B1
South Canterbury Rd. CT1 88 A6
South Cl. CT1 88 A8
South Cliff Par. CT10 30 B1
South Court Dr. CT3 91 A7
South Cres. ME17 96 C4
South Ct. Deal CT14 117 D6
South Ct. Ramsgate CT12 29 B2
South Cty Prim Sch. TN23 156 A8
South Deal Cty Prim Sch. CT14 117 B4
South Eastern Rd. Ramsgate CT11 52 D7
South Eastern Rd. Rochester ME2 9 C7
South Exit Rd. CT16 166 G8
South Goodwin Ct. CT14 117 D8
South Green La. ME9 56 F6
South Kent Coll of Tech. Ashford TN23 139 C1
South Kent Coll of Tech. Ashford TN23 156 A8
South Kent Coll of Tech. Dover CT16 166 D8
South Kent Coll of Tech. Folkestone CT20 178 B5
South Lea. TN23 156 A3
South Lodge Cl. CT5 20 E3
South Military Rd. CT17 166 C5
South Motto. TN23 156 B5
South of England Rare Breeds Ctr The. TN26 169 D1
South Park Bsns Village. ME15 75 A1
South Park Rd. ME15 75 C1
South Pondside Rd. ME4 10 A8
South Rd. Dover CT17 166 B8
South Rd. Faversham ME13 62 C7
South Rd. Gillingham ME7 10 A7
South Rd. Gillingham ME4 10 B7
South Rd. Herne Bay CT6 23 A5
South Rd. Hythe CT21 176 D1
South Rd. Kingsdown CT14 134 D5
South Rd. Sandwich CT12 & CT13 73 A8
South Side Three Rd. ME4 10 C8
South St. Boughton Street ME13 84 F8
South St. Canterbury CT1 67 C2
South St. Deal CT14 117 D6
South St. Lydd TN29 203 C6
South St. Queenborough ME11 2 F5
South St. Whitstable CT5 44 A7
South Stour Ave. TN23 156 C8
South Street Crossing. CT5 44 A7
South Street Rd. ME9 56 C7
South View. CT3 46 F1
South View Gdns. ME12 1 D1
South View Rd. CT5 43 D6
South Wall. CT14 117 B7
Southall Cl. CT12 50 C7
Southbourne. TN23 155 E5
Southbourne Gr. ME5 32 A4
Southbourne Rd. CT19 178 E5

Southdown Rd. ME12 .... 3 E6
Southenay La. TN25 .... 159 C4
Southernwood Rise. CT20 ... 177 F4
Southfields. ME1 .... 9 C3
Southgate Rd. TN30 .... 179 C7
Southill Rd. ME4 .... 9 F3
Southlands Comm
   Comp Sch. TN28 .... 200 B7
Southlees La. ME9 .... 56 F3
Southmead Cl. CT19 .... 178 A6
Southover Ct. 2 CT20 .... 177 E3
Southsea Ave. ME12 .... 4 C8
Southsea Dr. CT6 .... 22 D4
Southwall Rd. CT14 .... 117 B6
Southwood Gdns. CT11 .... 52 B7
Southwood Gdns. CT11 .... 52 B6
Southwood Rd. Ramsgate CT11 . 52 C6
Southwood Rd. Whitstable CT5 .. 21 B2
Sovereign Bvd. Gillingham ME7 .. 10 F2
Sovereign Bvd.
   Gillingham,Twydall ME8 ..... 11 A2
Sovereigns The. ME16 .... 74 D4
Sowell St. CT10 .... 29 F5
Spade La. ME8 & ME9 .... 34 C6
Spanton Cres. CT21 .... 176 A3
Sparrow Castle 3 CT9 .... 7 J1
Spearhead Rd. ME14 .... 74 F7
Spearpoint Cnr. TN24 .... 139 F5
Spectrum Bsns Ctr. ME2 ...... 9 E8
Spectrum Bsns Est. ME15 ..... 97 F4
Speedwell Ave. ME5 .... 31 F4
Speedwell Cl. Gillingham ME7 .. 10 E5
Speedwell Cl. Maidstone ME14 .. 75 E5
Speke Rd. CT10 .... 29 E6
Spekes Rd. ME7 .... 33 B6
Speldhurst Cl. TN23 .... 155 E5
Speldhurst St. ME16 .... 74 D4
Speldhurst Gdns. CT9 .... 8 F3
Spencer Cl. ME5 .... 32 A5
Spencer Flats. ME5 .... 32 B8
Spencer Ho. 3 CT20 .... 177 F5
Spencer Rd. CT7 .... 27 A8
Spencer Sq. CT11 .... 52 D6
Spencer St. 9 CT11 .... 52 D6
Spencer Way. ME15 .... 97 E7
Spenlow Dr. ME5 .... 54 A8
Spenser Rd. CT6 .... 22 F4
Spicer Homes. ME10 .... 36 F2
Spicer's Pl. CT3 .... 69 C2
Spiers The. ME7 .... 11 C5
Spillett Cl. ME13 .... 62 B6
Spillway The. ME15 .... 74 D2
Spindle Glade. ME14 .... 75 C5
Spindlewood Cl. ME5 .... 32 B3
Spinnaker Ct. 3 ME1 .... 9 C1
Spinnens Acre
   Cty Jun Sch. ME5 .... 32 C1
Spinney La. Aylesham CT3 .. 112 E4
Spinney La. Aylesham CT3 .. 112 F5
Spinney The. Ashford TN23 . 138 E3
Spinney The. Chatham ME5 .. 32 B1
Spinney The. Maidstone ME15 .. 75 B2
Spinney The. Margate CT9 ..... 8 E1
Spinney The. River CT17 .... 148 E2
Spire Ave. CT5 .... 44 A8
Spires The. ME16 .... 74 D4
Spitalfield La. TN28 .... 199 F6
Spitfire Cl. ME5 .... 32 B6
Spitfire & Hurricane
   Memls Mus. CT12 .... 28 A2
Split La. CT4 .... 127 A5
Sportsfield. ME14 .... 75 B5
Spot La. ME15 .... 76 A2
Spratling La. CT12 .... 28 F1
Spratling St. CT12 .... 28 E1
Sprig The. ME4 .... 76 A4
Spring Farm Rd. TN29 .... 192 C5
Spring Grove Sch. TN25 .... 123 C2
Spring Ho. CT21 .... 176 C2
Spring Hollow. TN29 .... 195 A4
Spring La. Canterbury CT1 ... 88 C7
Spring La. Fordwich CT2 ...... 68 A4
Spring La. Hythe CT21 .... 177 A4
Spring Vale. ME16 .... 74 E4
Spring Wlk. CT5 .... 43 C7
Springett Way. ME17 .... 96 D3
Springfield Ave.
   Maidstone ME14 .... 74 F7
Springfield Ave.
   St Michaels TN30 .... 167 C2
Springfield Cl. CT11 .... 29 E2
Springfield Pass. CT21 ...... 176 B2
Springfield Rd. Dover CT16 .. 149 B2
Springfield Rd. Gillingham ME7 .. 10 E6
Springfield Rd. Margate CT9 ... 8 E3
Springfield Rd.
   Sittingbourne ME10 .... 36 D5
Springfield Way. CT21 ...... 177 B3
Springhead Rd. ME13 .... 40 D1
Springside Terr. CT18 .... 161 C6
Springvale. Gillingham ME8 .. 33 C6
Springvale. Iwade ME9 .... 14 D4
Springwood Cl. Ashford TN23 .. 138 E3
Springwood Cl.
   Maidstone ME16 .... 74 A3
Springwood Ct. TN28 .... 200 B6
Springwood Dr. TN23 .... 138 E3
Springwood Rd. ME16 .... 74 A3
Sprotlands Ave. TN24 .... 139 F1
Sprotshill Cl. ME10 .... 36 E6
Spurgeons Cotts. ME17 .... 96 E2
Spurway. ME14 .... 76 A4
Square Hill. ME15 .... 75 B4
Square Hill Rd. ME14 & ME15 .. 75 B4

Square The. Birchington CT7 .. 27 A7
Square The. Chilham CT4 .... 107 B8
Square The. Elham CT4 ...... 144 F4
Square The. Lenham ME17 ... 101 D5
Square The. Selling ME13 .... 84 A6
Square The. Sittingbourne ME10 .. 14 F1
Squeeze Gut Alley. 8 CT5 ... 20 D2
Squire Ave. CT2 .... 87 C8
Squires Ct. ME12 .... 5 E3
Squires Way. ST16 .... 149 A3
Stable Cl. ME5 .... 32 C5
Stable Ct. ME13 .... 62 D6
Stable Mews. ST18 .... 161 D4
Stablemead. CT19 .... 178 A7
Stace Cl. TN30 .... 179 C8
Staceys St. ME14 .... 74 F5
Stade St. CT21 .... 176 C1
Stade The. CT21 .... 178 E5
Staffa Rd. ME15 .... 97 A7
Stafford Cl. TN23 .... 138 F2
Stafford St. ME7 .... 10 C5
Staffordshire St. 8 CT11 .... 52 E7
Stag Rd. ME5 .... 32 B5
Staines Hill. CT2 .... 68 B7
Staines Pl. CT10 .... 30 B5
Stalham Ct. ME7 .... 33 B4
Stalin Ave. ME5 .... 32 B8
Stalisfield Ave & TN27 .... 103 E3
Stalisfield Rd. Stalisfield Green
   ME13 & ME17 & TN27 ...... 103 C5
Stalisfield Rd.
   Throwley, Eastling ME13 ..... 82 C6
Stampers The. ME15 .... 74 D2
Stanbury Cres. CT19 .... 178 F7
Stancomb Ave. CT11 .... 52 C5
Standard Ave. 1 CT6 .... 22 A4
Standen Cl. ME8 .... 33 E4
Standen La. CT18 .... 163 E5
Staner Ct. CT12 .... 52 A8
Staner Hill. CT12 .... 51 F8
Stanford Dr. ME16 .... 74 C3
Stanhope Ave. ME10 .... 37 A3
Stanhope Cl. ME14 .... 74 E7
Stanhope Rd. Ashford TN23 .. 155 F7
Stanhope Rd.
   Ashford, Stanhope TN23 .... 155 E6
Stanhope Rd. Deal CT14 .... 117 D6
Stanhope Rd. Dover CT16 .. 149 C2
Stanhope Rd. Rochester ME2 .. 9 A7
Stanhope Sq. TN23 .... 155 F6
Stanley Ave. Minster ME12 ... 4 D7
Stanley Ave.
   Queenborough ME11 .... 3 A4
Stanley Cl. TN29 .... 187 B4
Stanley Gdns. CT6 .... 22 F3
Stanley Pl. Broadstairs CT10 .. 30 A4
Stanley Pl. Ramsgate CT11 ... 52 E7
Stanley Rd. Broadstairs CT10 .. 30 A6
Stanley Rd. Chatham ME5 .... 32 C6
Stanley Rd. Deal CT14 ...... 117 D5
Stanley Rd. Folkestone CT19 .. 177 E6
Stanley Rd. Gillingham ME7 .. 10 C6
Stanley Rd. Herne Bay CT6 .. 22 F4
Stanley Rd. Margate CT9 .... 8 A3
Stanley Rd. Ramsgate CT11 ... 52 D8
Stanley Rd. Whitstable CT5 ... 43 D7
Stanley Sykes Cl. CT9 .... 29 B8
Stanmore Ct. CT11 .... 88 B7
Stansted Cl. ME16 .... 74 D7
Staple Cl. ME10 .... 36 E5
Staple Rd. CT3 .... 91 C6
Staple St. ME13 .... 63 F5
Staple Vineyard. CT3 .... 91 F5
Staplehurst Ave. CT10 .... 30 A2
Staplehurst Gdns. CT9 .... 8 E2
Staplehurst Rd. Gillingham ME8 .. 11 B3
Staplehurst Rd.
   Sittingbourne ME10 .... 36 D5
Staplers Ct. ME14 .... 75 B8
Staplestreet Rd. ME13 .... 64 A4
Star Hill. ME1 .... 9 D5
Star La. Folkestone CT19 .... 177 D7
Star La. Gillingham ME7 ...... 33 A7
Star La. Margate CT10 & CT9 .. 29 A5
Star Mill La. ME5 .... 10 D2
Star Mill La. ME5 .... 10 D2
Star Rd. TN24 .... 139 D2
Starle Cl. CT1 .... 67 B1
Starnes Ct. 5 ME14 .... 75 A5
Starvation Cnr. 1 CT5 .... 20 D2
Station App. Adisham CT3 .. 112 E8
Station App. Birchington CT7 .. 26 F7
Station App. Maidstone ME16 .. 74 F3
Station App. Martin Mill CT15 .. 133 C2
Station App. Minster,Thanet
   CT12 .... 50 C5
Station App.
   New Romney TN28 .... 200 C6
Station Approach Rd. CT11 .. 52 D8
Station Cotts. ME13 .... 84 E7
Station Dr. CT14 .... 117 A1
Station Rd. Adisham CT3 .... 90 E1
Station Rd. Ashford TN23 .. 139 C2
Station Rd. Birchington CT7 .. 27 A7
Station Rd. Bridge CT4 .... 88 F2
Station Rd. Charing TN27 ... 120 C7
Station Rd. Deal CT14 ...... 117 B1
Station Rd. Dymchurch TN29 .. 195 B4
Station Rd. East Farleigh ME15 .. 96 A7
Station Rd. Faversham ME13 .. 62 D6
Station Rd. Folkestone CT19 .. 177 F5
Station Rd. Gillingham ME8 .. 12 A2
Station Rd. Harrietsham ME17 .. 100 D6
Station Rd. Herne Bay CT6 .. 22 E4
Station Rd. Hythe CT21 ..... 176 D3
Station Rd. Lydd TN29 .... 203 D7
Station Rd. Lyminge CT18 .. 161 C6

Station Rd. Maidstone ME14 .. 74 F5
Station Rd. Margate CT9 .... 7 H2
Station Rd. Martin Mill CT15 .. 133 D1
Station Rd. Minster CT12 ..... 50 C5
Station Rd. New Romney TN28 .. 200 C6
Station Rd. Newington ME9 .. 35 B6
Station Rd. Petersbourne CT4 .. 89 C4
Station Rd. Pluckley TN27 .. 136 C5
Station Rd. Rochester ME2 ..... 9 C7
Station Rd.
   Shepherdswell CT15 .... 130 D5
Station Rd. Smeeth TN25 .... 158 B3
Station Rd.
   St Margaret's at Cliffe CT15 .. 150 E8
Station Rd. Tenterden TN30 .. 179 A7
Station Rd. Teynham ME9 ..... 38 D2
Station Rd. Westgate-on-S CT8 .. 7 D1
Station Rd. Whitstable CT5 ... 20 E2
Station Rd E. CT1 .... 87 F7
Station Rd W. CT2 .... 66 F1
Station Row. ME9 .... 38 D3
Station St. ME10 .... 36 F4
Stede Hill. ME17 .... 78 F3
Steed Cl. CT6 .... 46 B8
Steeds Cl. TN23 .... 156 A1
Steeds La. TN23 & TN26 .... 156 B1
Steele St. ME7 .... 9 A8
Steerforth Cl. ME1 .... 9 C2
Stella Maris
   RC Prim Sch. CT19 .... 178 C6
Stelling Minnis
   CE Prim Sch. CT4 .... 126 F6
Stembrook. CT16 .... 166 D8
Stembrook Ct. 4 CT16 ...... 166 D7
Step Style. ME10 .... 37 B2
Stephen Cl. CT10 .... 30 A4
Stephen Ct. 2 CT20 .... 178 D5
Stephen's Cl. CT7 .... 28 B7
Stephens Cl. Faversham ME13 .. 62 B8
Stephens Cl. Ramsgate CT11 .. 52 C8
Stephenson Rd. CT2 .... 66 F3
Steps Hill Rd. ME9 .... 56 D6
Sterling Ave. ME16 .... 74 C5
Sterling Cl. CT10 .... 29 E5
Sterling Rd. Queenborough ME11 .. 3 A5
Sterling Rd. Sittingbourne ME10 .. 36 D1
Stevens Cl. ME15 .... 74 F3
Stickfast La. ME9 .... 14 A1
Stiles Cl. CT19 .... 178 A2
Stirling Cl. Gillingham ME8 ... 33 E4
Stirling Cl. Rochester ME1 ..... 9 A3
Stirling Way. CT12 .... 29 A2
Stirlng Rd. TN24 .... 156 D7
Stisted Way. TN27 .... 118 F3
Stock La. TN25 .... 158 A4
Stockbury Dr. ME16 .... 74 D7
Stockbury Gdns. CT9 .... 8 E2
Stockdale Gdns. CT14 .... 117 C4
Stocker's Hill. ME13 .... 63 E4
Stockers Brow. ME9 .... 59 A7
Stockers Hill. ME10 & ME9 .. 59 A7
Stockett La. ME15 .... 96 B6
Stockham La. ME9 .... 14 E4
Stockham Ct. CT19 .... 177 E7
Stocks Rd. TN30 .... 188 F3
Stocks The. ME13 .... 83 C6
Stockton Cl. ME14 .... 75 B8
Stockwood Chase. CT2 .... 66 A2
Stoddart Rd. CT19 .... 177 E6
Stodmarsh National
   Nature Reserve. CT3 .... 69 D8
Stodmarsh Rd. CT3 .... 68 C3
Stombers La. CT18 .... 163 C6
Stonar Cl. Ramsgate CT11 ... 29 E1
Stonar Cl. Sandwich CT13 ... 73 A1
Stonar Gdns. CT13 .... 73 A2
Stone Abbage. TN27 .... 136 D4
Stone Barn Ave. CT27 .... 27 A6
Stone Bay Sch. CT10 .... 30 B6
Stone Cnr. TN30 .... 189 A6
Stone Cross Lees. CT13 ...... 93 F7
Stone Gdns. CT10 .... 30 B5
Stone Gn. TN30 .... 189 F4
Stone Hill. TN25 .... 159 A2
Stone Hill Rd. TN27 .... 118 F2
Stone Ho. CT10 .... 30 B5
Stone Rd. CT10 .... 30 B5
Stone St. Faversham ME13 ... 62 C7
Stone St. Lympne CT21 & TN25 .. 175 A4
Stone St. Stanford TN25 .... 160 C3
Stone St. Stelling Minnis
   CT4 & CT18 & TN25 .... 126 D4
Stoneacre Cl. ME8 .... 33 D5
Stoneacre La. ME15 .... 98 B7
Stoneacre (NT). ME15 .... 98 B7
Stonebridge Cotts. TN23 ... 156 B8
Stonebridge Green Rd. TN27 .119 A4
Stonebridge Way. ME13 ...... 62 B7
Stonecross Lea. ME5 .... 10 C1
Stonedane Ct. ME13 .... 62 C8
Stonehall Rd. CT15 .... 131 A5
Stoneheap Rd. CT14 & CT15 .. 115 E1
Stonestile Farm Rd. TN27 .. 103 A3
Stoney Bank. ME7 .... 10 F1
Stoney Rd. ME13 .... 64 B3
Stony La. ME5 .... 31 C5
Stonyway La. CT15 .... 165 C5
Stopford Rd. ME7 .... 10 D4
Storehouse Wharf. ME12 ...... 1 A3
Stour Cl. Ashford TN23 ..... 138 E1
Stour Cl. Chartham CT4 .... 86 D2
Stour Cres. CT1 .... 67 D3
Stour Ct. 7 Canterbury CT1 .. 87 F8
Stour St. Sandwich CT13 ..... 72 F1
Stour Valley Cl. CT3 .... 47 D3

Stourmouth Rd. CT3 .... 70 C8
Stourside Studios. 2 CT2 ... 66 F1
Stowting CE Prim Sch. TN25 .. 160 B8
Stowting Hill. TN25 .... 143 A1
Straight La. TN29 .... 191 F1
Strakers Hill. CT15 .... 132 D0
Strand Approach Rd. ME7 ... 10 E7
Strand St. CT13 .... 72 F1
Strand The. CT14 .... 117 D4
Stranger's Cl. CT1 .... 87 C6
Stranger's La. CT1 .... 87 C6
Strangford Pl. CT6 .... 23 B2
Strangford Rd. CT5 .... 20 F2
Strasbourg St. CT9 .... 29 A6
Stratford Ave. ME8 .... 33 D8
Stratford La. ME8 .... 33 F8
Straw Mill Hill. ME15 .... 74 E1
Stream Wlk. CT5 .... 20 D2
Street End. CT3 .... 71 E1
Street End Rd. ME5 .... 10 B1
Street The. Acol CT7 .... 27 B3
Street The. Adisham CT3 .... 112 C8
Street The. Appledore TN26 .. 190 B8
Street The. Ash CT3 .... 71 D1
Street The. Ashford TN24 .. 139 E6
Street The.
   Ashford, Kennington TN24 .. 139 E6
Street The. Bapchild ME9 .... 37 E3
Street The. Barfrestone CT15 .. 113 D1
Street The. Barham CT4 ..... 111 F1
Street The. Bethersden TN26 .. 153 D5
Street The. Bishopsbourne CT4 .. 111 C6
Street The. Borden ME9 ...... 36 B2
Street The. Bossingham CT4 .. 127 A7
Street The.
   Boughton Street ME13 .... 64 A3
Street The. Boxley ME14 .... 54 C3
Street The. Brabourne TN25 .. 159 C8
Street The. Bredgar ME9 ..... 58 A5
Street The. Bredhurst ME7 .. 33 B1
Street The. Brook TN25 ..... 141 B6
Street The. Chilham CT4 .... 107 B8
Street The. Deal CT14 .... 116 F6
Street The. Denton CT4 .... 129 B3
Street The. Detling ME14 .... 55 A1
Street The. Doddington ME9 .. 80 E7
Street The. East Langdon CT15 .. 133 A1
Street The. Eastling ME13 ... 81 E6
Street The. Egerton TN27 .. 118 F3
Street The. Eythorne CT15 .. 131 D7
Street The. Finglesham CT14 .. 116 B8
Street The. Godmersham CT4 .. 107 B2
Street The. Goodnestone CT3 .. 91 D2
Street The. Great Chart TN23 .. 138 C1
Street The. Guston CT15 .... 149 E6
Street The. Hamstreet TN26 .. 183 A4
Street The. Hartlip ME9 ...... 34 D5
Street The. Hastingleigh TN25 .. 142 B6
Street The. Hawkinge CT18 .. 163 B5
Street The. Hothfield TN26 .. 138 A6
Street The. Ickham CT3 .... 69 C2
Street The. Iwade ME9 .... 14 E4
Street The. Kingston CT4 ... 111 D3
Street The. Lower Halstow ME9 .. 13 B3
Street The. Lympne CT21 .... 174 F2
Street The. Lynsted ME9 ..... 60 A6
Street The. Maidstone ME14 .. 76 C4
Street The. Martin CT15 .... 133 B3
Street The. Mersham TN25 .. 157 E4
Street The. Newington CT18 .. 177 A7
Street The. Newnham ME9 .. 81 C8
Street The. Northbourne CT14 .. 116 A5
Street The. Oare ME13 .... 40 B2
Street The. Patrixbourne CT4 .. 89 B3
Street The. Petham CT4 ..... 109 B3
Street The. Postling CT21 .. 160 F2
Street The. Preston CT3 ...... 70 C6
Street The. Shadoxhurst TN26 .. 170 A8
Street The. Silver Street ME9 .. 57 F5
Street The.
   St Nicholas at Wade CT7 .... 25 F2
Street The. Staple CT3 .... 91 F6
Street The.
   Stone in Oxney TN30 .... 190 A5
Street The. Stourmouth CT3 .. 48 E1
Street The. Upchurch ME9 .. 12 F4
Street The.
   West Hougham CT15 .... 164 F5
Street The. Wickhambreaux CT3 . 69 C1
Street The. Wittersham TN30 .. 188 D3
Street The. Womenswold CT4 .. 112 D2
Street The.
   Woodnesborough CT13 .... 93 C2
Street The. Wormshill ME9 .. 79 A7
Street The. Worth CT14 ...... 94 B5
Streete Court Rd. CT8 .... 27 F8
Streete Ct. CT8 .... 27 F8
Streetfield. CT6 .... 46 B8
Streetfield Rd. ME8 .... 11 F1
Stringer Dr. CT7 .... 27 A6
Strode Cres. ME12 .... 1 D2
Strode Park Rd. CT6 .... 23 A2
Strond St. CT17 .... 166 D6
Strood Sta. ME2 .... 9 C7
Strouts Rd. TN23 .... 155 D7
Strover St. ME7 .... 10 C7
Stuart Cl. ME14 .... 75 C6
Stuart Ct. CT1 .... 166 C8
Stuart Ho. CT14 .... 117 A5
Stuart Rd. Folkestone CT19 .. 178 E6
Stuart Rd. Gillingham ME7 .. 10 D3
Studds Cotts. CT6 .... 22 A3
Studfall Cl. CT21 .... 187 D8
Studio. CT14 .... 139 E6
Stumble La. TN23 & TN26 .. 156 D6
Stuppington Court Farm. CT1 . 87 E4
Stuppington La. CT1 .... 87 F5
Sturdee Ave. ME7 .... 10 E4

Sturdy Cl. CT21 .... 176 D2
Sturges Rd. TN24 .... 139 B3
Sturla Rd. ME4 .... 10 A3
Sturmer Cl. CT1 .... 88 C2
Sturry CE Prim Sch. CT2 ..... 68 A7
Sturry Court Mews. CT2 ...... 67 F5
Sturry Hill. CT2 .... 67 E5
Sturry Rd. CT1 & CT2 .... 67 C5
Sturry Sta. CT2 .... 67 F5
Sturry Way. ME8 .... 11 C2
Stutfall Castle
   (rems of). CT21 .... 174 F1
Style Cl. ME8 .... 33 E4
Sudbury Pl. CT8 .... 27 E1
Suffolk Ave. Gillingham ME8 .. 11 F1
Suffolk Ave. Westgate-on-S CT8 .. 27 D1
Suffolk Dr. TN23 .... 139 A3
Suffolk Gdns. CT17 .... 165 F2
Suffolk Rd. Canterbury CT1 .. 88 D4
Suffolk Rd. Maidstone ME15 .. 97 D8
Suffolk St. CT5 .... 43 D6
Sugarloaf Wlk. CT19 .... 178 D6
Sultan Rd. ME5 .... 32 C6
Summer Cl. Hythe CT21 ..... 175 F2
Summer Cl. Tenterden TN30 .. 166 C7
Summer Ct. CT2 .... 66 C3
Summer Hill. CT2 .... 66 C3
Summer Hill Pk. TN24 .... 157 C4
Summer La. CT2 .... 66 E4
Summer Leeze. TN24 .... 156 E8
Summer Leeze Gdns. TN24 .. 156 E8
Summer Rd. CT7 .... 25 B7
Summerfield Ave. CT5 .... 20 F2
Summerfield Rd. CT9 .... 8 E5
Summerhill. TN23 .... 155 E6
Summerville Ave. ME12 .... 4 A4
Sumpter Way. ME13 .... 61 F2
Sun La. Hythe CT21 .... 176 C3
Sun La. St Nicholas at Wade CT7 .. 25 F
Sun St. CT1 .... 87 F7
Sun Terr. ME5 .... 32 B
Sunbeam Ave. CT6 .... 21 F
Sunderland Cl. ME1 .... 9 A
Sunderland Dr. ME1 .... 34 A
Sunderland Ho. 2 ME7 ...... 10 C
Sundew Gr. CT11 .... 52 E
Sundridge Cl. CT2 .... 67 A
Sundridge Dr. ME5 .... 32 A
Sunningdale Ave. 4 CT19 .. 178 A
Sunningdale Cl. ME8 .... 33 D
Sunningdale Cl. ME15 .... 75 B
Sunningdale Dr. ME8 .... 33 D
Sunningdale Wlk. CT6 .... 22 C
Sunny Bank. Hythe CT21 ... 175 F
Sunny Bank.
   Sittingbourne ME10 .... 37 B
Sunny Cnr. CT17 .... 166 B
Sunnyfields Cl. ME8 .... 33 E
Sunnyfields Dr. ME12 .... 3 C
Sunnyhill Rd. CT6 .... 22 C
Sunnymead. CT2 .... 66 D
Sunnymead Ave. ME7 .... 10 E
Sunnyside. Doddington ME9 .. 80 E
Sunnyside.
   Littlestone-on-S TN28 .... 200 D
Sunnyside. Lydd TN29 .... 203 B
Sunnyside Ave. ME12 .... 4 A
Sunnyside Cl. CT14 .... 116 C
Sunnyside Gdns. CT13 .... 93 E
Sunnyside Rd. CT20 .... 177 D
Sunray Ave. CT5 .... 43 B
Sunrise
   Ind Pre-Prep Sch. ME17 ..... 98 C
Sunset Cl. Eastchurch ME12 ... 5 F
Sunset Cl. Whitstable CT5 .... 43 C
Superabbey Est. ME20 .... 53 B
Surf Cres. ME12 .... 5 F
Surrenden. TN27 .... 136 F
Surrenden Cl. CT19 .... 177 F
Surrey Gdns. CT7 .... 26 F
Surrey Rd. Canterbury CT1 .. 88 D
Surrey Rd. Maidstone ME15 .. 97 D8
Surrey Rd. Margate CT9 .... 8 B
Susan's Hill. TN26 .... 168 E
Sussex Ave. Ashford TN24 .. 139 B
Sussex Ave. Canterbury CT1 .. 88 D
Sussex Ave. Margate CT9 ...... 7 J
Sussex Cl. CT6 .... 22 A
Sussex Dr. ME5 .... 32 A
Sussex Gdns. Birchington CT7 .. 26 F
Sussex Gdns. Herne Bay CT6 .. 22 B
Sussex Gdns.
   Westgate-on-S CT8 .... 7 D
Sussex Mansions. CT8 .... 7 D
Sussex Rd. 5
   Folkestone CT19 .... 178 D
Sussex Rd. Maidstone ME15 .. 97 D
Sussex Rd. New Romney TN28 .. 200 A
Sussex St. CT11 .... 52 E
Sussex Wlk. CT1 .... 88 D
Sutherland Cl. CT21 .... 176 A
Sutherland Dr. CT7 .... 27 B
Sutherland Gdns. ME8 .... 33 E
Sutherland Rd. CT14 .... 117 C
Sutton Cl. Folkestone CT19 .. 178 A
Sutton Cl. Gillingham ME8 ... 34 A
Sutton Cotts. ME13 .... 84 C
Sutton La. Ringwould CT14 .. 133 F
Sutton La. Ripple CT14 ...... 133 C
Sutton Rd. Hersden CT3 ...... 46 E
Sutton Rd. Langley ME17 .... 98 C
Sutton Rd. Maidstone ME15 .. 97 D8
Sutton Rd. ME14 .... 76 C
Suttons The. TN31 .... 201 A
Swadelands Cl. ME17 .... 101 C
Swadelands Sch. ME17 ...... 101 C
Swain Rd. Gillingham ME8 ... 33 B
Swain Rd. St Michaels TN30 .. 167 A

Swakeley Wlk. CT5 .... 21 D3
Swale Ave. Rushenden ME11 ...... 2 F3
Swale Ave. Sheerness ME12 .... 1 C1
Swale Cl. CT4 .... 23 A3
Swale Halt. ME9 .... 15 A7
Swale Ho. **1** ME15 .... 97 E7
Swale View. ME13 .... 64 B6
Swalecliffe Ave. CT6 .... 22 B4
Swalecliffe Court Dr. CT5 .... 21 D3
Swalecliffe Cty Prim Sch. CT5 ... 21 B2
Swalecliffe Rd. CT5 .... 21 B2
Swallow Ave. CT5 .... 43 B6
Swallow Cl. CT9 .... 28 C8
Swallow Ho. **4** ME16 .... 74 E4
Swallow Rise. ME5 .... 32 A5
Swallowfield. TN24 .... 156 E7
Swamp Rd. TN29 .... 199 B4
Swan Apartments. **10** ME15 ... 97 E5
Swan Cl. ME10 .... 37 B4
Swan Cotts. TN30 .... 188 D4
Swan Gn. TN25 .... 159 D1
Swan La. TN25 .... 159 E2
Swan St. TN30 .... 188 C3
Swanfield Rd. CT5 .... 43 D8
Swanstree Ave. ME10 .... 37 B2
Swanton La. Canterbury CT3 ..... 68 D2
Swanton La. Lydden CT15 .... 147 C6
Swanton Mill. TN25 .... 157 B2
Swarling Hill Rd. CT4 .... 109 C7
Swaynes Way. CT13 .... 93 B2
Sweechbridge Rd. CT6 .... 23 F3
Sweechgate. CT2 & CT3 .... 67 E7
Sweetbriar La. CT15 .... 114 B2
Sweetlove Pl. CT3 .... 91 A8
Sweyn Rd. CT9 .... 8 A3
Swift Cres. ME5 .... 32 C6
Swift Ho. **6** ME16 .... 74 E4
Swinburne Ave. CT10 .... 30 A3
Swinford Gdns. CT9 .... 29 C8
Swingate Cl. ME5 .... 32 B2
Swingate Cty Inf Sch. ME5 .... 32 C1
Sycamore Ave. CT3 .... 112 E5
Sycamore Cl. Broadstairs CT10 .. 29 C4
Sycamore Cl.
  Dymchurch TN29 .... 195 C8
Sycamore Cl. Herne Bay CT6 .... 23 C5
Sycamore Cl. Hythe CT21 .... 175 E1
Sycamore Cl. Lydd TN29 .... 203 D7
Sycamore Cl. Margate CT9 .... 28 E7
Sycamore Cres. CT15 .... 74 C5
Sycamore Gdns. TN29 .... 195 C8
Sycamore Ho. ME12 .... 1 C2
Sycamores The. CT3 .... 68 E8
Sydcot Dr. CT14 .... 117 D8
Sydenham Rd. CT14 .... 117 D7
Sydenham St. CT5 .... 20 D2
Sydney Ave. ME10 .... 36 C4
Sydney Cooper Cl. CT2 .... 66 B2
Sydney Rd. Chatham ME4 .... 10 A3
Sydney Rd. Deal CT14 .... 117 A1
Sydney Rd. Ramsgate CT11 ...... 52 F8
Sydney Rd. Whitstable CT5 ...... 43 E8
Sydney St. TN23 .... 156 C8
Sylewood Cl. ME1 .... 31 B8
Sylvan Glade. ME5 .... 54 A8
Sylvan Rd. ME8 .... 33 C8
Symmonds Dr. ME10 .... 37 A6
Symons Ave. ME4 .... 10 A2
Syndale Pl. **1** CT11 .... 52 F7

Tabret Cl. TN24 .... 139 D6
Tadburn Gn. ME5 .... 32 B4
Taddington Wood La. ME5 .... 31 E2
Taddy Gdns. CT9 .... 29 C8
Tadley Ct. ME7 .... 10 F6
Tadworth Rd. TN24 .... 139 D5
Tail Race The. ME15 .... 74 E2
Taillour Cl. ME10 .... 36 F7
Talavera Rd. CT1 .... 88 D8
Talbot Ave. CT6 .... 22 B3
Talbot Rd. Maidstone ME16 ..... 74 C6
Talbot Rd. Margate CT9 .... 8 B2
Tall Trees Cl. ME17 .... 99 D2
Tally Ho Rd. TN26 .... 155 C2
Tamar Ho. **4** ME15 .... 97 E8
Tamarind Cl. ME7 .... 33 A4
Tamarisk. ME12 .... 19 E5
Tame La. TN29 .... 185 F6
Tamley La. TN25 .... 142 B6
Tams Gdns. ME12 .... 4 D6
Tangier Cl. CT16 .... 149 E3
Tanglewood Cl. ME8 .... 33 C6
Tangmere Cl. ME7 .... 10 F5
Tanker Hill. ME8 .... 33 D6
Tankerton Cir. CT5 .... 20 F3
Tankerton Ct. CT5 .... 21 B3
Tankerton Mews. CT5 .... 20 E3
Tankerton Rd. CT5 .... 20 F3
Tanner's Hill. CT21 .... 176 C3
Tanner's Hill Gdns. CT21 .... 176 C3
Tanners St. ME13 .... 62 C7
Tannery Cl. **3** ME10 .... 36 E5
Tannery La. TN23 & TN24 .... 139 C2
Tapleys Hill. CT4 .... 110 B5
Target Bsns Ctr. ME15 .... 97 F4
Target Firs. CT16 .... 148 D5
Tariff Reform Cotts. ME13 .... 62 D5
Tartane La. TN29 .... 195 C8
Tasker Cl. ME15 .... 76 B3
Tassell's Wlk. CT5 .... 21 D3
Taswell Cl. CT16 .... 166 E8
Taswell Rd. ME8 .... 12 A1
Taswell St. CT16 .... 166 E8
Tatler Cl. ME5 .... 32 D2
Tatsfield Cl. ME14 .... 11 A2
Taunton Cl. ME15 .... 97 F6
Taverners Rd. ME8 .... 33 E7
Tavistock Cl. Chatham ME5 ..... 31 F1

Tavistock Cl. Gillingham ME8 .....: 33 E7
Tavistock Cl.
  Sittingbourne ME10 .... 36 D4
Tavistock Rd. CT11 .... 29 E1
Tay Cl. ME5 .... 32 B5
Taylor Rd. Folkestone CT19 ..... 177 E6
Taylor Rd. Lydd-on-S TN29 ...... 204 E6
Taylor Rd. Minster CT12 .... 50 B6
Taylor's La. ME2 .... 9 B7
Taylors Cl. TN29 .... 194 F3
Taylors Hill. CT4 .... 107 B8
Taylors La. TN29 .... 194 F3
Taylors Yd. TN25 .... 123 E2
Taywood Rd. TN24 .... 139 F1
Teasaucer Hill. ME15 .... 96 F8
Teasel Cl. ME14 .... 75 F4
Teasel Rd. ME5 .... 31 F4
Teddars Leas Rd. CT18 .... 161 E4
Tedder Ave. ME5 .... 32 A7
Teddington Cl. CT1 .... 67 B2
Teelin Cl. TN29 .... 195 A4
Tees Ho. **9** ME15 .... 97 E7
Telegraph Rd. CT14 .... 117 B3
Telford Cl. Folkestone CT19 ..... 178 E6
Telford Ct. Herne Bay CT6 .... 22 C2
Telford Ho. **1** ME14 .... 75 A6
Telford St. CT5 .... 22 E5
Telham Ave. CT12 .... 52 B8
Templar Rd. CT16 .... 148 D5
Templar St. CT17 .... 166 C8
Temple Cl. CT16 .... 148 D6
Temple Ct. CT2 .... 66 D1
Temple Ewell
  CE Prim Sch. CT16 .... 148 D5
Temple Gdns. Rochester ME2 .... 9 A6
Temple Gdns.
  Sittingbourne ME10 .... 37 B3
Temple Mews. **10** CT1 .... 87 F8
Temple Rd. CT2 .... 66 D1
Temple Side. CT16 .... 148 D6
Temple Way. CT14 .... 94 A4
Templeman Liby. CT2 .... 66 E4
Ten Acre Way. ME8 .... 12 B1
Ten Perch Rd. CT1 .... 87 D6
Tennyson Ave. CT1 .... 67 D3
Tennyson Gdns. CT3 .... 112 F6
Tennyson Pl. CT19 .... 178 E7
Tennyson Rd. Ashford TN23 .... 156 A6
Tennyson Rd. Gillingham ME7 ... 10 C3
Tenterden CE Jun Sch. TN30 ... 179 B7
Tenterden Cty Inf Sch. TN30 ... 179 B7
Tenterden Dr. CT2 .... 67 A4
Tenterden Rd.
  Appledore TN26 & TN30 ...... 181 B1
Tenterden Rd. Chatham ME5 .... 32 B5
Tenterden Town Sta. TN30 ...... 179 A8
Tenterden Way. CT9 .... 8 C1
Terence Cl. ME4 .... 10 A2
Terminus Dr. CT6 .... 23 D5
Terminus Rd. ME16 .... 74 A2
Terrace Cotts. CT4 .... 127 A6
Terrace Rd. Elvington CT15 ..... 114 B1
Terrace Rd. Maidstone ME16 ... 74 E3
Terrace Rd. Sittingbourne ME10 . 37 B3
Terrace The. Canterbury CT2 ... 66 F3
Terrace The. Chatham ME4 ...... 9 F7
Terrace The. Faversham ME13 .. 62 A7
Terrace The. Little Chart TN26 .. 120 A1
Terrace The. Rochester ME1 .... 9 C5
Terrace The.
  Shepherdswell CT15 .... 130 D5
Terry's La. CT5 .... 20 D2
Teynham Cl. TN24 .... 8 F2
Teynham Dr. CT9 .... 20 F7
Teynham Parochial
  CE Prim Sch. ME9 .... 38 C2
Teynham Rd. CT5 .... 20 F2
Teynham Sta. ME9 .... 38 D3
Thames Ave. Gillingham ME8 ... 33 E8
Thames Ave. Sheerness ME12 ... 1 C1
Thames Ct. ME2 .... 6 G2
Thames Ho. **3** ME15 .... 97 D8
Thames View
  Cty Inf Sch. ME8 .... 11 D2
Thanet Cl. CT10 .... 30 B5
Thanet Coll. Broadstairs CT10 .. 30 A3
Thanet Coll. Margate CT9 .... 7 I2
Thanet Gdns. CT19 .... 178 F6
Thanet Place Gdns. CT10 .... 30 B6
Thanet Rd. Broadstairs CT10 ... 30 B4
Thanet Rd. Margate CT9 .... 7 J2
Thanet Rd. Ramsgate CT11 ..... 52 F7
Thanet Rd. Westgate-on-S CT8 . 27 D8
Thanet Terr. TN26 .... 138 A6
Thanet View. Eythorne CT15 ... 131 B8
Thanet View.
  St Nicholas at Wade CT7 ...... 25 F2
Thanet Way.
  Boughton Street ME13 .... 63 D6
Thanet Way.
  Hawthorn Cnr CT3 & CT6 & CT7 .. 24 C4
Thanet Way.
  Herne Bay CT6 & CT5 .... 22 D3
Thanet Way. Whitstable CT5 .... 21 C2
Thanet Way. Whitstable CT5 .... 43 D6
Thanet Way.
  Yorklets CT5 & ME13 .... 42 E2
Thanington Rd. CT1 .... 87 C6
Thatchers The. ME4 .... 74 B5
Theatre Sq. **5** TN30 .... 179 A7
Theatre St. CT21 .... 176 C2
Theresa Cl. CT21 .... 176 B1
Theodore Pl. ME7 .... 10 C5
Theresa Cl. CT21 .... 176 B1
Third Ave. Chatham ME4 & ME5 .. 10 C1
Third Ave. Eastchurch ME12 .... 5 F6

Third Ave. Gillingham ME7 .... 10 F4
Third Ave. Margate CT9 .... 8 B3
Thirlmere. TN24 .... 139 D6
Thirlmere Cl. CT11 .... 52 A7
Thirlmere Cl. ME7 .... 11 A5
Thirlmere Gdns. CT3 .... 112 F6
Thistle Wlk. ME10 .... 37 B5
Thistlebank. ME5 .... 32 A3
Thistledown. ME14 .... 75 F4
Thistledown Cl. ME7 .... 33 A4
Thomas Aveling
  Sch The. ME1 .... 31 C8
Thomas Ct. ME10 .... 37 B4
Thomas Rd. Faversham ME13 ... 62 D7
Thomas Rd.
  Sittingbourne ME10 .... 37 B4
Thomas St. ME1 .... 9 C3
Thompson Cl. Deal CT14 .... 134 B8
Thompson Cl. Folkestone CT19 . 178 B7
Thompson Cl. Gillingham ME8 ... 34 A8
Thorn Cl. ME5 .... 31 D1
Thorn Est The. TN27 .... 136 B6
Thorn Gdns. CT11 .... 29 E1
Thorn Hill Rd. ME12 .... 6 D4
Thorn Wlk. ME10 .... 37 C5
Thorn La. CT4 .... 126 C2
Thornbridge Rd. CT14 .... 117 B2
Thorndale Cl. ME5 .... 31 D4
Thornden Ct. CT6 .... 22 B2
Thornden Ct. CT2 .... 66 C4
Thornden Wood Rd.
  Herne Bay CT6 .... 22 B1
Thornden Wood Rd.
  Whitstable CT2 & CT6 .... 44 E4
Thorndike Cl. ME4 .... 31 F8
Thorndike Rd. TN29 .... 186 C4
Thorne Hill. CT12 .... 51 A6
Thorne Rd. CT12 .... 50 B6
Thorney Croft Cl. ME17 .... 99 D2
Thorneycroft Rd. ME13 .... 103 D5
Thornham Rd. ME8 .... 11 C3
Thornhill Pl. ME14 .... 75 A6
Thornhurst. CT6 .... 23 D4
Thornlea. TN23 .... 138 E2
Thornton La. CT13 & CT14 ..... 114 E7
Thornton's La. **7** TN16 ...... 166 E7
Thorold Rd. ME4 .... 10 B3
Thorpe Wlk. ME8 .... 33 D3
Thrale Way. ME8 .... 33 E4
Thread La. ME13 .... 64 B4
Three Acres Site. CT19 .... 178 B8
Three King's Yd. CT13 .... 73 A1
Threshers Dr. ME14 .... 75 E5
Throwley Dr. CT6 .... 22 C4
Throwley Rd. ME13 .... 82 D5
Thrupp Paddock. CT10 .... 8 G1
Thrush Cl. ME5 .... 32 B7
Thruxted La. CT4 .... 86 B1
Thunderland Rd. CT6 .... 23 B4
Thurlow Ave. CT6 .... 23 C5
Thurnham CE Inf Sch. ME14 ... 76 A4
Thurnham La. ME14 .... 76 C6
Thurston Pk. CT5 .... 20 E1
Thurstone Ct. ME14 .... 74 F6
Tiber Cl. CT19 .... 177 C6
Tichborne Cl. ME16 .... 74 C6
Tickham La. ME9 .... 60 C5
Tickner's La. TN29 .... 192 B1
Tideway The. ME1 .... 31 C8
Tilbury Rd. ME8 .... 12 A2
Tilden Cl. TN26 .... 167 D7
Tilden Gill Rd. TN30 .... 179 C7
Tile Fields. ME7 .... 77 D2
Tile Ho The. CT21 .... 176 C2
Tile Kiln Hill. CT2 .... 66 B5
Tile Kiln La. CT19 .... 177 F7
Tile Kiln Rd. TN24 .... 139 C7
Tile Lodge Cotts. TN27 .... 119 E8
Tile Lodge Rd. TN27 .... 119 E8
Tillard Cl. CT4 .... 109 B3
Tillery La. TN29 .... 198 A8
Timber Tops. ME14 .... 54 D8
Timberbank. ME5 .... 32 A6
Timperley Cl. CT14 .... 117 B6
Tina Gdns. CT10 .... 30 A6
Tinbridge Pk. ME13 .... 63 A5
Tintagel Manor. ME7 .... 10 C6
Tintern Rd. ME16 .... 74 D7
Titchfield Cl. **5** ME15 .... 97 F6
Titchfield Rd. ME15 .... 97 F6
Tithe Barn La. TN23 .... 155 D8
Tithe Yd. ME17 .... 101 D5
Tivoli Brooks. CT9 .... 7 I1
Tivoli Park Ave. CT9 .... 7 H1
Tivoli Rd. CT9 .... 28 E8
Tobruk Way. ME5 .... 31 F6
Toby Rd. TN29 .... 204 E6
Todd Cres. ME10 .... 37 A8
Toddington Cres. ME5 .... 31 D1
Toke Cl. TN23 .... 138 C1
Tolgate Cl. ME2 .... 9 B7
Tolgate Way. ME14 .... 53 E4
Toll Gate. CT14 .... 117 A4
Toll La. TN27 .... 120 E7
Tollemache Cl. CT12 .... 27 F2
Tollgate Cl. CT5 .... 43 C8
Tolsford Cl. Etchinghill CT18 .. 161 D3
Tolsford Cl. Folkestone CT19 .. 177 D6
Tomay Cotts. CT6 .... 24 A3
Tomlin Dr. CT9 .... 29 C8
Tonbridge Cl. ME16 .... 74 D3
Tonford La. Canterbury CT1 ... 87 B6
Tonford La. Harbledown CT2 ... 87 A7
Tong Rd. ME10 .... 37 B4
Tonge Rd. ME10 .... 37 C4
Tontine St. CT20 .... 178 E5
Tookey Rd. TN28 .... 200 B6
Top Rd. TN30 .... 189 D3

Tormore Mews. CT14 .... 117 A4
Tormore Pk. CT14 .... 117 A4
Toronto Cl. **6** CT16 .... 149 B3
Toronto Rd. ME7 .... 10 E4
Torrington Cotts. CT12 .... 50 D7
Torrington Rd. TN23 .... 156 C8
Tothill St. CT12 .... 50 C7
Tournay Cl. TN23 .... 155 F8
Tourney Cl. CT21 .... 174 F3
Tourney Rd. TN29 .... 203 C5
Tourtel Rd. CT1 .... 67 A1
Tovil Gn. ME15 .... 74 E2
Tovil Green Bsns Pk. ME15 .... 74 E1
Tovil Hill. ME15 .... 74 E2
Tovil Rd. ME15 .... 74 F2
Tower Bglws. CT7 .... 27 A8
Tower Ct. **4** CT20 .... 177 E3
Tower Est. TN29 .... 186 E2
Tower Gdns. Hythe CT21 .... 176 C1
Tower Gdns. Maidstone ME14 .. 76 B4
Tower Hamlets Rd. CT17 .... 166 C8
Tower Hamlets St. **1** CT17 .. 166 C8
Tower Hill. Dover CT17 .... 166 C8
Tower Hill. Whitstable CT5 ..... 20 E3
Tower La. ME14 .... 76 B4
Tower Par. CT5 .... 20 E3
Tower Rd. CT5 .... 20 E2
Tower St. CT17 .... 166 C8
Tower Way. **1** CT1 .... 87 F8
Towers Sch The. TN24 .... 139 D8
Towers The. TN21 .... 103 E1
Towers View. TN24 .... 139 C7
Town La. CT4 .... 86 C6
Town Wlk. CT20 .... 178 D4
Townley St. CT11 .... 52 D6
Townsend Farm Rd. CT15 ...... 150 F6
Townsend Terr. CT17 .... 166 B5
Townwall St. CT16 .... 166 E7
Tracies The. ME9 .... 35 C6
Trafalgar Pl. ME12 .... 4 B6
Trafalgar Rd. CT7 .... 27 F3
Trafalgar St. ME7 .... 10 C5
Tram Rd The. CT20 .... 178 E5
Transom Ho. **2** ME1 .... 9 C1
Trapfield Cl. ME14 .... 76 C4
Trapfield La. ME14 .... 76 C4
Trapham Rd. ME16 .... 74 D5
Travers Gdns. ME9 .... 57 F5
Travers Rd. CT14 .... 117 A5
Travertine Rd. ME5 .... 32 B1
Treasury View. CT3 .... 90 C8
Trefoil Cl. ME9 & ME13 .... 60 E6
Trefor Jones Ct. CT16 .... 149 B2
Trelawn Cres. ME5 .... 32 B2
Trent Ho. **2** ME15 .... 97 E7
Trent Rd. ME5 .... 32 B5
Trenton Cl. ME16 .... 74 B7
Trevale Rd. ME1 .... 9 C2
Trevino Dr. ME5 .... 31 F2
Trevor Dr. ME16 .... 74 C5
Tribune Cl. ME12 .... 3 B8
Tribune Dr. ME10 .... 36 F6
Trident Cl. ME2 .... 9 D7
Trigg's Row. ME5 .... 38 D2
Trimworth Rd. CT19 .... 177 F6
Trinity Cres. CT20 .... 178 B4
Trinity Cl. Aylesford ME20 .... 53 A3
Trinity Ct. Margate CT9 .... 7 J3
Trinity Gdns. CT20 .... 178 C4
Trinity Homes. CT14 .... 117 C1
Trinity Pl. Deal CT14 .... 117 A4
Trinity Pl. Ramsgate CT11 ..... 52 F7
Trinity Rd. Ashford TN24 ...... 139 B6
Trinity Rd. Folkestone CT20 ... 178 B4
Trinity Rd. Gillingham ME7 ... 10 C6
Trinity Rd. Sheerness ME12 ... 1 D2
Trinity Rd. Sittingbourne ME10 . 36 F7
Trinity Sq. CT10 .... 29 F7
Trinity Trad Est. ME10 .... 36 F6
Trinty Hill. CT9 .... 7 J3
Trinty Sq. CT9 .... 7 J3
Tritton Cl. TN24 .... 139 F7
Tritton Fields. TN24 .... 139 F7
Tritton Gdns. TN29 .... 186 D1
Tritton La. TN28 .... 200 B6
Troodos Hill. ME14 .... 74 F8
Trotts Hall Gdns. ME10 .... 36 F3
Trotwood Cl. ME5 .... 54 A8
Troubridge Cl. TN24 .... 157 B7
Troughton Mews. CT9 .... 7 H1
Trove Ct. **5** CT11 .... 52 F7
Troy Town La. TN25 .... 141 B5
Troys Mead. ME17 .... 77 D2
Trueman Cl. CT2 .... 66 A7
Trumpet Ho. TN23 .... 156 B8
Truro Cl. ME10 .... 11 D3
Truro Rd. CT11 .... 52 F7
Tudor Ave. Dymchurch TN29 .. 186 D1
Tudor Ave. Maidstone ME14 ... 75 B6
Tudor Byway. TN24 .... 139 B6
Tudor Cl. CT7 .... 27 B8
Tudor End. CT15 .... 149 D5
Tudor Gr. ME8 .... 33 F8
Tudor Ho. CT14 .... 117 A5
Tudor Rd. Ashford TN24 .... 139 D5
Tudor Rd. Canterbury CT1 ..... 87 E7
Tudor Rd. Folkestone CT19 .... 177 D6
Tufa Cl. ME5 .... 32 B1
Tufton Rd. Ashford TN24 ...... 139 D2
Tufton Rd. Gillingham ME8 .... 11 F1
Tufton Rd. Hothfield TN26 ..... 138 A7
Tufton St. Ashford TN23 .... 139 B2
Tufton St. Maidstone ME14 ... 75 A4
Tufton Wlk. **9** TN23 .... 139 B2
Tunbury Ave. Chatham ME5 ... 31 F1
Tunbury Ave. Chatham ME5 ... 31 F2
Tunbury Ave S. ME5 .... 31 F1

Tunbury Cty Prim Sch. ME5 ... 31 F1
Tunis Ct. CT1 .... 67 D1
Tunis Row. CT10 .... 30 B5
Tunstall CE Prim Sch. ME9 .... 58 C8
Tunstall Rd. Canterbury CT2 ... 67 A4
Tunstall Rd.
  Sittingbourne ME10 & ME9 .. 58 D8
Tupman Cl. ME1 .... 9 B4
Turgis Cl. ME17 .... 98 E4
Turketel Rd. CT20 .... 178 A4
Turmine Cl. ME12 .... 4 A5
Turnagain La. **3** CT1 .... 87 F8
Turnden Gdns. CT9 .... 8 E2
Turner Cl. ME10 .... 37 A7
Turner Ct. **5** Folkestone CT20 . 177 F5
Turner Ct. Margate CT9 .... 8 A2
Turner St. CT11 .... 52 E7
Turners Ave. TN30 .... 179 B8
Turners Cl. ME12 .... 1 D1
Turnpike Cl. CT21 .... 176 A2
Turnpike Hill. CT21 .... 176 A3
Turnstone Cl. TN29 .... 195 A3
Turnstone Rd. ME5 .... 32 C1
Tuscan Dr. ME5 .... 32 C1
Twelve Acres. TN24 .... 156 F8
Twiss Ave. CT21 .... 176 D2
Twiss Gr. CT21 .... 176 D2
Twiss Rd. CT21 .... 176 D2
Two Chimneys
  Holiday Pk. CT7 .... 27 E5
Twydall Cty Inf Sch. ME8 ...... 11 B2
Twydall
  Cty Prim Jun Sch. ME8 ...... 11 B2
Twydall Gn. ME8 .... 11 B3
Twydall La. ME8 .... 11 B2
Twyford Cl. ME8 .... 12 A2
Twyford Ct. ME14 .... 75 D6
Twyne Cl. CT2 .... 68 A6
Tydeman Rd. ME15 .... 75 F2
Tydeman's Ave. CT5 .... 21 C1
Tyland La. ME14 .... 53 F3
Tyler Cl. CT2 .... 66 F3
Tyler Dr. ME8 .... 33 E4
Tyler Hill Rd. CT2 .... 66 C6
Tyler Way. CT5 .... 21 E3
Tyndale Pk. CT6 .... 23 B5
Tyne Cl. ME5 .... 32 C5
Tyne Ho. **10** ME15 .... 97 E7
Tysoe Cl. ME12 .... 4 A5
Tyson Ave. CT9 .... 7 E1
Tyson Rd. CT19 .... 178 E7

Uden Rd. TN29 .... 187 B4
Uffington Ct. CT3 .... 91 A7
Ufton Cl. ME15 .... 75 E1
Ufton La. ME10 .... 36 E3
Ulcombe Gdns. CT2 .... 67 A3
Ulcombe Hill. ME17 .... 99 F1
Ulcombe Rd. ME17 .... 98 C3
Ulley Rd. TN24 .... 139 D7
Ullswater Gdns. CT3 .... 112 F6
Ulster Rd. CT9 .... 28 F8
Undercliff. CT20 .... 177 E3
Undercliffe Rd. CT14 .... 134 D5
Underdown Ave. ME4 .... 9 F1
Underdown La. CT6 .... 22 F2
Underdown Rd. Dover CT17 ... 166 B7
Underdown Rd. Herne Bay CT6 . 22 F5
Underhill Cotts. CT18 .... 177 B8
Underhill Rd. CT20 .... 177 B5
Underwood. CT18 .... 163 C6
Underwood Cl. Ashford TN24 . 139 D6
Underwood Cl. Canterbury CT1 . 88 B5
Underwood Cl.
  Maidstone ME15 .... 74 F2
Underwood Ct. CT1 .... 88 B6
Unicorn Cotts. CT4 .... 89 B5
Unicumes La. ME16 .... 74 C2
Union Cres. CT9 .... 7 J2
Union Pk. ME15 .... 97 F4
Union Pl. **4** CT1 .... 67 A1
Union Rd. Bridge CT4 .... 88 F1
Union Rd. Deal CT14 .... 117 D6
Union Rd. Minster ME12 .... 4 C7
Union Rd. Ramsgate CT11 ..... 52 F8
Union Row. CT9 .... 7 J2
Union Sq. **3** CT10 .... 30 B4
Union St. Canterbury CT1 ..... 67 A1
Union St. Chatham ME4 .... 10 A3
Union St. Dover CT17 .... 166 D6
Union St. Faversham ME13 ... 62 C7
Union St. Maidstone ME14 ... 75 A5
Union St. **9** Ramsgate CT11 . 52 E7
Union St. Rochester ME1 ...... 9 C5
Union St. Sheerness ME12 .... 1 B2
Unity Pl. **2** CT11 .... 52 F7
Unity St. Sheerness ME12 ..... 1 E3
Unity St. Sittingbourne ME10 . 36 E3
Univ of Kent at Canterbury.
  CT2 .... 66 D4
University Rd. CT2 .... 66 D3
Unwin Cl. CT2 .... 66 F4
Upbury Manor High Sch. ME7 . 10 B4
Upbury Way. ME4 .... 10 A4
Upchurch Wlk. CT9 .... 8 E2
Uphill. CT18 .... 163 B4
Uplands. CT2 .... 66 F4
Uplands Way. ME12 .... 3 C5
Uplees Cotts. ME13 .... 39 F5
Uplees Rd. ME13 .... 40 A3
Upnor Rd. ME2 .... 9 D8
Upper Approach Rd. CT10 .... 30 A3
Upper Brents. ME13 .... 62 D8
Upper Bridge St.
  Canterbury CT1 .... 88 A8

Upper Bridge St. Wye TN25 ..... 123 F2
Upper Britton Pl. ME7 .... 10 B5
Upper Chantry La. CT1 .... 88 A7
Upper Corniche. CT20 .... 177 C3
Upper Dane Rd. CT9 .... 8 B1
Upper Denmark Rd. TN23 ..... 156 B8
Upper Dumpton Park Rd.
 CT11 .... 52 E8
Upper East Rd. ME4 .... 10 B8
Upper Fant Rd. ME16 .... 74 D2
Upper Field Rd. ME10 .... 37 B5
Upper Free Down CT6 .... 23 B2
Upper Gore La. CT13 .... 93 A2
Upper Gr. CT9 .... 7 J2
Upper Hunton Hill. ME15 ..... 96 A3
Upper Luton Rd. ME4 & ME5 .. 10 C2
Upper Malthouse Hill. CT21 .. 176 B2
Upper Rd. Dover CT15 & CT16 .. 150 C2
Upper Rd. Dover CT16 .... 166 H8
Upper Rd. Maidstone ME15 ... 75 B2
Upper St. Hollingbourne ME17 .. 77 E3
Upper St. Kingsdown CT14 .... 134 D5
Upper St. Leeds ME17 .... 98 F5
Upper St. Tilmanstone CT14 .. 115 A3
Upper St Ann's Rd. ME13 ..... 62 B6
Upper Stone St. ME15 .... 75 A3
Upper Strand St. CT13 .... 73 A1
Upper Tickham Cotts. ME9 .... 60 D6
Upper Vicarage Rd. TN24 ..... 139 D7
Upstreet. CT18 .... 161 D3
Upton Cl. CT19 .... 178 A7
Upton Cty Jun Sch. CT10 ..... 29 F4
Upton Rd. CT10 .... 29 F5
Urquhart Cl. ME5 .... 32 A5
Ursuline Dr. CT8 .... 27 D7

Vale Cotts. ME9 .... 57 A8
Vale Dr. ME5 .... 31 E6
Vale Pl. CT11 .... 52 D6
Vale Rd. Broadstairs CT10 .... 29 F4
Vale Rd. Loose ME15 .... 96 E4
Vale Rd. Ramsgate CT11 ...... 52 D6
Vale Rd. Ripple CT14 & CT15 .. 133 B8
Vale Rd. Whitstable CT5 ...... 43 D8
Vale Sq. CT11 .... 52 D6
Vale The. CT10 .... 30 A4
Vale View
 Cty Prim Sch. CT17 .... 166 B7
Vale View Rd. Aylesham CT3 .. 112 E5
Vale View Rd. Dover CT17 .... 166 B7
Valebrook Cl. CT20 .... 177 C5
Valenciennes Rd. ME10 ...... 36 E3
Valentine Cl. ME7 .... 11 A1
Valentine Rd. ME15 .... 97 E7
Valerian Cl. ME5 .... 31 E4
Valestone Cl. CT20 & CT21 ... 177 B4
Valiant Rd. ME4 .... 32 C2
Valkyrie Ave. CT5 .... 43 C7
Vallance The. ME9 .... 60 A6
Valley Cotts. Alkham CT15 .... 147 C1
Valley Cotts.
 Stalisfield Green ME13 ..... 103 D8
Valley Dr. ME15 .... 96 F6
Valley Rd. Barham CT4 .... 111 E2
Valley Rd. Canterbury CT1 .... 87 E6
Valley Rd. Folkestone CT20 ... 177 E4
Valley Rd. Gillingham ME7 .... 10 E4
Valley Rd. Lydden CT9 .... 28 E4
Valley Rd. River CT17 .... 148 E3
Valley Rise. ME5 .... 31 F1
Valley The. ME7 .... 96 D3
Valley View. CT15 .... 131 C8
Valley View Rd. ME1 .... 9 F8
Valley Wlk. CT21 .... 177 B3
Vancouver Dr. ME8 .... 11 C1
Vancouver Rd. CT16 .... 149 C3
Vange Cottage Mews. ME1 .... 9 B4
Vanity La. ME17 .... 96 D1
Vanity Rd. ME12 .... 6 F2
Varne Ct. CT20 .... 177 F3
Varne Lodge. CT20 .... 177 F3
Varne Pl. CT19 .... 178 F5
Varne Rd. CT19 .... 178 F5
Vaughan Dr. ME10 .... 36 F8
Vauxhall Ave. Canterbury CT1 .. 67 C3
Vauxhall Ave. Herne Bay CT6 .. 22 A3
Vauxhall Cres. CT1 .... 67 C3
Vauxhall Industrial Rd. CT1 ... 67 D4
Vauxhall Lakes
 (Nature Reserve). CT1 ...... 67 B3
Vauxhall Rd. CT1 & CT2 ...... 67 C4
Vectis Dr. ME10 .... 36 F8
Ventnor Cl. ME5 .... 32 C8
Ventnor La. CT9 .... 7 J2
Venture Cl. TN29 .... 186 D1
Vere Rd. CT10 .... 30 A4
Vereth Rd. CT11 .... 52 D6
Vernon Holme (Kent Coll
 Inf & Jun Sch). CT2 .... 66 A1
Vernon Pl. Canterbury CT1 .... 88 A7
Vernon Pl. Deal CT14 .... 117 D8
Verwood Cl. CT2 .... 66 E2
Vesper Ct. TN27 .... 135 A1
Vestey Ct. CT5 .... 7 C1
Viaduct Cl. CT12 .... 52 C8
Viaduct Terr. TN26 .... 182 F7
Viaduct The. CT17 .... 166 D5
Viburnum Cl. TN23 .... 138 E2
Vicarage Cl. ME20 .... 53 A3
Vicarage Cres. CT9 .... 7 J1
Vicarage Gdn. CT12 .... 49 C7
Vicarage Gdns. CT3 .... 91 A7
Vicarage Hill. CT4 .... 109 B4

Vicarage La. Ashford TN23 .... 139 C2
Vicarage La. Blean CT2 ...... 66 A6
Vicarage La. Deal CT14 ...... 116 F5
Vicarage La.
 East Farleigh ME15 .... 96 B6
Vicarage La. Elham CT4 ...... 144 F4
Vicarage La. Faversham ME13 .. 62 A4
Vicarage La.
 Lower Halstow ME9 .... 13 C3
Vicarage La. Nonington CT15 .. 113 C5
Vicarage La. Sandwich CT13 .. 72 F1
Vicarage La. Selling ME13 .... 84 F2
Vicarage La. Tilmanstone CT14 . 115 A3
Vicarage Pl. CT9 .... 7 J1
Vicarage Rd. Folkestone CT20 .. 177 F3
Vicarage Rd. Gillingham ME7 .. 10 C5
Vicarage Rd. Minster ME12 ... 4 D7
Vicarage Rd. Rochester ME2 .. 9 B8
Vicarage Rd.
 Sittingbourne ME10 .... 36 E6
Vicarage St. Broadstairs CT10 .. 29 E5
Vicarage St. Faversham ME13 . 62 D8
Vicary Way. ME16 .... 74 D5
Vickers Cl. CT18 .... 163 A4
Victor Ave. CT9 .... 8 D2
Victoria Ave. Broadstairs CT10 .. 29 E8
Victoria Ave. Hythe CT21 .... 176 B2
Victoria Ave. Margate CT9 ... 8 B1
Victoria Ave.
 St Margaret's at Cliffe CT15 . 151 B6
Victoria Ave.
 Westgate-on-S CT8 .... 27 F8
Victoria Cl. ME5 .... 31 D2
Victoria Cres. Ashford TN23 .. 139 B1
Victoria Cres. Dover CT16 ... 166 D8
Victoria Ct. Hythe CT21 ..... 176 C1
Victoria Ct. Maidstone ME16 . 74 E3
Victoria Dr. CT6 .... 22 C5
Victoria Gr.
 Folkestone CT20 .... 178 D5
Victoria Gr. Hythe CT21 ..... 177 B2
Victoria Ho. CT5 .... 20 D2
Victoria Hospl. CT14 .... 117 B5
Victoria Par. Broadstairs CT10 . 30 B4
Victoria Par. Ramsgate CT11 .. 52 F7
Victoria Pk. Dover CT16 ..... 166 E8
Victoria Pk. Herne Bay CT6 .. 23 A5
Victoria Pl. Faversham ME13 . 62 C7
Victoria Pl. Hythe CT21 ..... 176 B4
Victoria Rd. Ashford TN23 ... 139 B1
Victoria Rd. Broadstairs CT10 . 29 E6
Victoria Rd. Canterbury CT1 .. 87 E7
Victoria Rd. Capel-le-F CT18 . 164 B1
Victoria Rd. Chatham,Luton ME4 . 10 B2
Victoria Rd.
 Chatham,Walderslade ME5 .. 31 E3
Victoria Rd. Deal CT14 ...... 117 D5
Victoria Rd. Folkestone CT19 . 178 C5
Victoria Rd. Hythe CT21 ..... 176 C1
Victoria Rd. Kingsdown CT14 . 134 C4
Victoria Rd.
 Littlestone-on-S TN28 ...... 200 E5
Victoria Rd. Lydden CT9 ..... 28 D4
Victoria Rd. Margate CT9 .... 7 J2
Victoria Rd. Ramsgate CT11 .. 52 F7
Victoria Rd. Sittingbourne ME10 . 36 D4
Victoria Rd W. TN28 .... 200 E5
Victoria Road Cty Prim Sch.
 TN23 .... 139 B1
Victoria Row. CT1 .... 67 A1
Victoria St. Dover CT17 ..... 149 B1
Victoria St. Gillingham ME7 .. 10 D6
Victoria St. Maidstone ME16 . 74 E3
Victoria St.
 New Romney TN28 .... 200 A6
Victoria St. Rochester ME2 .. 9 B7
Victoria St.
 Rochester,Troy Town ME1 ... 9 D5
Victoria St. Sheerness ME12 . 1 D1
Victoria St. Whitstable CT5 .. 20 D2
Victoria Terr. Minster ME12 .. 5 A5
Victoria Terr. Rochester ME1 . 9 A2
Victoria Terr.
 Sittingbourne ME10 .... 36 D4
Victory Pk. ME2 .... 9 E7
Victory Rd. CT15 .... 133 F1
Victory St. ME12 .... 1 C2
Vidal Manor. ME7 .... 10 C5
Vigo Terr. ME9 .... 38 B1
Viking Cl. CT7 .... 26 D8
Viking Ct. Broadstairs CT10 .. 30 B3
Viking Ct. Canterbury CT2 ... 66 F2
Viking Ct. Margate CT9 ...... 8 A2
Village Way. TN26 .... 183 A7
Villas The. CT3 .... 47 A1
Villiers Ct. CT17 .... 166 C7
Villiers Ho. CT10 .... 30 B7
Villiers Rd. CT1 .... 67 D1
Vincent Cl. Broadstairs CT10 . 29 C3
Vincent Cl. Folkestone CT20 .. 177 E5
Vincent Ct. ME12 .... 1 D1
Vincent Gdns. ME12 .... 1 D1
Vincent Rd. Kit's Coty ME20 .. 53 C7
Vincent Rd. Lydden CT9 ..... 28 C4
Vincent Rd. Sittingbourne ME10 . 37 C3
Vine Cl. CT11 .... 29 C2
Vine End. CT11 .... 29 E2
Vine Lands. TN29 .... 203 B6
Vineries The. ME7 .... 10 E5
Viners Cl. ME10 .... 36 F1
Vines La. ME1 .... 9 C5
Viney's Gdns. TN30 .... 167 C1
Vineyard Cres. ME8 .... 12 B1
Vinson Cl. ME13 .... 41 D1
Vinten Cl. CT6 .... 46 B8
Vinters Rd. ME14 .... 75 B4
Vinters Sch for Boys. ME14 .. 75 E4
Vintners Way. ME14 .... 75 E4

Violet Ave. CT12 .... 29 C2
Violet Cl. ME5 .... 54 A8
Virginia Rd. Gillingham ME7 .. 10 C7
Virginia Rd. Whitstable CT5 .. 44 A8
Vixen Cl. ME5 .... 32 C6
Vlissingen Dr. CT14 .... 117 C8
Volante Dr. ME10 .... 36 F7
Vulcan Cl. Chatham ME5 ..... 32 B7
Vulcan Cl. Whitstable CT5 ... 43 C7

Wacher Cl. CT2 .... 66 F2
Waddenhall Farm. CT4 ...... 126 B6
Waddle Cnr. TN30 .... 189 D3
Wades Cl. TN29 .... 194 B4
Wadham Pl. ME10 .... 37 B2
Waghorn St. ME4 .... 10 B3
Wagoners Cl. ME14 .... 75 E4
Wain Ct. ME12 .... 4 A5
Wainwright Pl. TN24 .... 156 D8
Wake Rd. ME1 .... 31 C8
Wakefield Way. CT21 .... 176 B1
Wakefield Wlk. CT21 .... 176 D1
Wakehurst Cl. ME17 .... 96 B3
Wakeley Cty Jun Sch. ME8 ... 12 A1
Wakeley Rd. ME8 .... 12 A1
Wakelys Cotts. ME8 .... 34 B8
Walcheren Cl. CT14 .... 117 C8
Waldens The. ME17 .... 99 E2
Waldershare Ave. CT13 ..... 95 A7
Waldershare Rd. CT15 ...... 132 A5
Walderslade
 Cty Prim Sch. ME5 .... 32 A3
Walderslade Girls Sch. ME5 .. 31 F5
Walderslade Rd. ME5 .... 31 F6
Walderslade Woods.
 Chatham ME5 .... 31 E2
Walderslade Woods.
 Chatham ME5 & ME14 ..... 54 B8
Waldron Dr. ME15 .... 96 F6
Waldron Rd. CT10 .... 30 B2
Walk The. ME17 .... 99 E2
Walker La. ME7 .... 26 D8
Walkers Outland
 (RSPB Reserve). TN28 ..... 204 B1
Wall Rd. TN24 .... 139 B3
Wall The. ME10 .... 36 E5
Wallace Mews. CT19 .... 178 D7
Wallace Rd. ME1 .... 31 E8
Wallace Way. CT10 .... 29 E4
Wallbridge La. ME8 & ME9 ... 12 D3
Waller Rd. TN29 .... 204 E7
Wallers Rd. ME13 .... 62 A7
Wallis Ave. ME15 .... 97 E5
Wallis Rd. TN24 .... 139 D2
Wallwood Rd. CT11 .... 52 F8
Walmer Castle. CT14 .... 117 D1
Walmer Castle Rd. CT14 .... 117 C1
Walmer Ct. ME14 .... 75 A5
Walmer Gdns. Cliffs End CT12 . 51 D5
Walmer Gdns. Deal CT14 ... 117 A2
Walmer Gdns.
 Sittingbourne ME10 .... 36 D5
Walmer & Kingsdown
 Golf Links. CT14 .... 134 D2
Walmer Rd. CT5 .... 43 E8
Walmer Sch. CT14 .... 117 B2
Walmer Sta. CT14 .... 117 A1
Walmsley Ho. CT19 .... 178 E6
Walmsley Rd. CT10 .... 29 F5
Walner Gdns. TN28 .... 200 B7
Walner La. TN28 .... 200 B7
Walnut Cl. Ashford TN24 ... 139 D6
Walnut Cl. Chatham ME5 ... 32 B8
Walnut Ridge. TN25 .... 173 A6
Walnut Tree Ave. ME15 .... 97 A5
Walnut Tree Cotts. ME13 ... 84 E8
Walnut Tree Dr. ME10 ..... 36 D4
Walnut Tree La. Loose ME15 . 97 A5
Walnut Tree La. Westbere CT2 . 68 D7
Walpole Rd. CT9 .... 7 J3
Walsby Dr. ME10 .... 37 A8
Walseley Terr. TN29 .... 203 C5
Walsham Rd. ME5 .... 31 F1
Walsingham Ave. ME8 ..... 33 D3
Walsingham Ho. ME14 ..... 75 A6
Waltham Cl. CT9 .... 8 E2
Waltham Rd. Gillingham ME8 . 11 C3
Waltham Rd. Waltham CT4 .. 108 F1
Walton Gdns. CT19 .... 178 D7
Walton Manor Cl. CT19 .... 178 D7
Walton Rd. CT19 .... 178 D6
Waltons The. CT19 .... 178 D6
Wanden La. TN27 .... 135 C8
Wanstall Ct. CT7 .... 27 A7
Wansted House Sch. CT9 ... 8 A3
Wantsum Mews. CT13 ...... 72 F1
Wantsum Way. CT7 .... 25 E3
Wantsume Lees. CT13 ...... 72 E2
Warblers Cl. ME2 .... 9 A7
Warden Bay Rd. ME12 ..... 6 E3
Warden Cl. ME16 .... 74 C4
Warden Pl. CT17 .... 149 C1
Warden House
 Cty Prim Sch. CT14 .... 117 A5
Warden Rd. Rochester ME1 . 9 C2
Warden Rd. Warden ME12 .. 6 D5
Warden Terr. ME12 .... 5 A6
Warden View Gdns. ME12 .. 6 D1
Warden Way. ME12 .... 6 B5
Wardour Cl. CT10 .... 30 B4
Wards Hill Rd. ME12 .... 4 C8
Wardwell La. ME9 .... 13 C1
Ware St. ME14 .... 76 A5
Warehorne Rd. TN26 ...... 183 A7
Warlingham Cl. ME8 .... 12 A1
Warmlake. ME17 .... 98 F1

Warmlake Est. ME17 .... 98 E1
Warmlake Rd. ME17 .... 98 C1
Warner St. ME4 .... 9 F3
Warnford Gdns. ME15 ..... 97 A8
Warre Ave. CT11 .... 52 C5
Warren Cl. Folkestone CT19 . 178 F6
Warren Cl. Sittingbourne ME10 . 37 B2
Warren Dr. CT10 .... 29 E5
Warren Dr The. CT8 .... 27 D7
Warren Hos. TN27 .... 119 E8
Warren Hts. TN25 .... 158 E5
Warren La.
 Ashford TN23 & TN24 ..... 139 A4
Warren La. Hartlip ME9 .... 34 C3
Warren La. Lydden CT15 ... 147 D6
Warren Rd. Folkestone CT19 . 178 F6
Warren Rd.
 Kit's Coty ME5 & ME20 .... 53 D7
Warren Rd.
 Littlestone-on-S TN28 ..... 200 D6
Warren Ret Pk. TN24 ...... 139 B4
Warren St.
 Stalisfield Green TN27 .... 103 A3
Warren St.
 Warren Street ME17 ...... 102 D7
Warren The.
 Brabourne Lees TN25 ..... 158 E5
Warren The. Whitstable CT5 . 43 C6
Warren View. TN23 .... 138 F4
Warren Way. CT19 .... 178 F6
Warren Wood
 Cty Prim Sch. ME1 .... 31 C8
Warren Wood Rd. ME1 .... 31 C7
Warten Rd. CT10 & CT11 .. 29 F1
Warwick Cres. ME10 ...... 36 C5
Warwick Dr. CT11 .... 52 B5
Warwick Pl. ME16 .... 74 E3
Warwick Rd. Ashford TN24 . 139 E5
Warwick Rd. Canterbury CT1 . 88 C8
Warwick Rd. Deal CT14 .... 117 D2
Warwick Rd. Margate CT9 .. 8 B2
Warwick Rd. Whitstable CT5 . 20 D2
Washford Farm Rd. TN23 ... 155 E5
Washington Cl. CT16 ...... 149 B3
Washington La. TN29 ...... 198 C6
Wass Dro. CT3 .... 71 B7
Wat Tyler Way. ME15 ..... 75 A4
Watchester Ave. CT11 ..... 52 C5
Watchester La. CT12 ...... 50 B5
Water Farm. CT4 .... 144 F4
Water La. Bayfield ME13 ... 61 B3
Water La. Canterbury CT1 .. 87 F8
Water La. Faversham ME13 . 62 C7
Water La. Harrietsham ME17 . 100 B5
Water La. Kingswood ME17 . 99 F3
Water La. Maidstone ME15 .. 75 A4
Water La.
 Maidstone,Bearsted ME14 .. 76 E6
Water La. Smarden TN2 .... 135 A2
Water St. CT14 .... 117 D7
Watercress La. TN23 ...... 155 F8
Waterditch La. ME17 & TN27 . 102 E5
Waterfall Rd. TN26 .... 138 B6
Waterham Rd. ME13 ...... 42 C1
Waterlock Cotts. CT3 ..... 91 A7
Waterloo Cres. CT16 & CT17 . 166 E7
Waterloo Hill. ME12 ...... 4 D6
Waterloo Mansions.
 CT16 & CT17 .... 166 E7
Waterloo Pl. CT11 .... 52 F7
Waterloo Rd. Folkestone CT20 . 177 D5
Waterloo Rd. Gillingham ME7 . 10 C4
Waterloo Rd.
 Sittingbourne ME10 ...... 36 D5
Waterloo Rd. Whitstable CT5 . 20 D2
Waterloo St. ME15 .... 75 A3
Waterloo Terr. ME15 ..... 5 A5
Waterlow Rd. ME14 ...... 75 A6
Waterman Ho. TN23 ..... 156 B8
Watermead Cl. ME7 ...... 32 F6
Watermill Cl. Maidstone ME16 . 74 B5
Watermill Cl. Rochester ME2 . 9 C8
Waters Edge. ME15 ...... 74 F2
Waters Pl. ME7 .... 33 A6
Watersend. CT16 .... 148 D5
Waterside. TN24 .... 139 F1
Waterside Ct. CT21 ...... 176 B2
Waterside Dr. CT8 .... 7 D1
Waterside La. ME7 ...... 10 F7
Waterside View. ME12 ... 6 E4
Waterstone Pl. ME13 .... 62 A6
Waterworks Hill. CT15 ... 133 B3
Waterworks La. CT15 .... 133 B3
Watery La. CT4 .... 109 C5
Watkin Rd. CT19 .... 178 C6
Watling Ave. ME5 ...... 10 D2
Watling Pl. ME10 ...... 37 A3
Watling St. Canterbury CT1 . 87 F8
Watling St.
 Chatham ME5 & ME7 .... 10 D2
Watling St.
 Gillingham ME5 & ME7 ... 10 D2
Watson Ave. ME5 ...... 31 D5
Watsons Cl. TN29 ...... 139 C8
Watsons Hill. ME10 .... 36 E5
Wattle Cnr. TN30 ...... 189 D3
Watts' Ave. ME1 ...... 9 C4
Watts Cotts. TN24 .... 139 D7
Watts' St. ME4 .... 9 E3
Watts Yd. CT13 ...... 72 F1
Wauchope Rd. CT5 ... 42 F6
Wave Crest. CT5 .... 20 C1
Waveney Ho. ME15 .. 97 E8
Waverley Ave. ME12 . 5 A6
Waverley Cl. Chatham ME5 . 32 A5
Waverley Cl. Coxheath ME17 . 96 C3
Waverley Rd. CT9 ... 28 C8

Way Farm Cotts. CT12 .... 50 E7
Way Hill. CT12 .... 50 E7
Wayborough Hill. CT12 ... 50 D7
Wayfield City Prim Sch. ME5 . 32 A7
Wayfield Rd. ME5 .... 32 A7
Wayne Cl. CT10 .... 29 E5
Wayside. TN30 .... 167 B3
Wayside Ave. TN30 ..... 167 B3
Wayside Flats. TN30 .... 167 B2
Weald Cl. ME15 .... 97 C6
Weald Cl. ME10 .... 36 D2
Weald The. TN24 ...... 139 C3
Wealden Ave. TN30 .... 167 B1
Wealden Ct. ME4 ...... 10 B3
Wealden Forest Pk. CT2 &CT6 . 45 D4
Wealdhurst Pk. CT10 ... 29 D5
Wear Bay Cres. CT19 .. 178 F6
Wear Bay Rd. CT19 .... 178 F5
Weatherly Cl. ME1 ..... 9 C4
Weatherly Dr. CT10 .... 29 F2
Weavering Cotts. ME14 . 75 E3
Weavering St. ME14 ... 75 F4
Weavers The. ME16 .... 74 B5
Weavers Way. Ashford TN23 . 155 E2
Weavers Way. Dover CT16 . 149 A3
Webb Cl. CT19 .... 178 A7
Webster Rd. ME8 ..... 11 F1
Weddington La. CT3 ... 71 E2
Wedgewood Cl. ME16 .. 74 B5
Wedgewood Dr. ME5 .. 32 A7
Weeds Wood Rd. ME5 . 31 F4
Week St. ME14 .... 75 A4
Weeks Ct. ME11 ..... 3 A5
Weigall Pl. CT11 ..... 52 C7
Weighbridge Way. CT16 . 166 H8
Welcombe Ct. ME8 ... 33 D8
Well Cl. CT2 .... 68 A6
Well La. Bayfield ME13 . 61 B3
Well La. Fordwich CT2 & CT3 . 68 A3
Well La.
 St Margaret's at Cliffe CT15 . 150 F5
Well Rd. Lyminge CT18 . 161 C6
Well Rd. Maidstone ME14 . 75 A5
Well Rd. Queenborough ME11 . 3 A5
Well Rd. Rushenden ME11 . 2 F3
Well St. ME15 & ME17 .. 96 E4
Well Winch Rd. ME10 .. 36 D5
Welland Rd. ME15 .... 97 E8
Weller Ave. ME1 ..... 9 D2
Wellesley Cl. Broadstairs CT10 . 29 E3
Wellesley Cl.
 Westgate-on-S CT8 ... 27 E7
Wellesley Rd. Ashford TN23 . 139 C2
Wellesley Rd. Dover CT16 . 166 E7
Wellesley Rd. Margate CT9 . 8 B1
Wellesley Rd. Sheerness ME12 . 1 C2
Wellesley Rd.
 Westgate-on-S CT8 ... 27 E7
Wellesley Villas. TN24 . 139 C3
Wellfield Rd. CT20 .... 178 A5
Wellington Cl. CT8 .... 7 C1
Wellington Cres. CT11 . 52 F6
Wellington Ct. CT14 ... 117 D3
Wellington Gdns.
 Dover CT16 .... 149 B3
Wellington Gdns. Margate CT9 . 7 J3
Wellington Ho. ME15 .. 97 E5
Wellington Par.
 Kingsdown CT14 ...... 134 D7
Wellington Par.
 Kingsdown CT14 ...... 134 E6
Wellington Pl.
 Folkestone CT20 ...... 177 D3
Wellington Pl. Maidstone ME14 . 74 F5
Wellington Rd. Deal CT14 . 117 D5
Wellington Rd.
 Folkestone CT20 ...... 177 D5
Wellington Rd. Gillingham ME7 . 10 C4
Wellington Rd. Lydden CT9 . 28 D4
Wellington Rd.
 Sittingbourne ME10 .... 36 B5
Wellington Rd.
 Temple Ewell CT16 .... 148 D5
Wellington St.
 Westgate-on-S CT8 .... 27 E7
Wellington St. CT5 .... 43 C5
Wellington St. CT5 .... 43 C5
Wellington Terr. CT20 . 177 D3
Wellis Gdns. CT9 ..... 7 G1
Wells Ave. CT1 ...... 88 B7
Wells Cl. New Romney TN28 . 200 C6
Wells Cl. Tenterden TN30 . 179 B8
Wells Ho. ME10 ..... 37 B4
Wells Rd. CT19 ..... 177 F6
Wells Way. ME13 ... 40 B1
Welsdene Rd. CT9 .. 28 B8
Welson Rd. CT20 ... 178 A5
Wemmick Cl. ME1 .. 31 D7
Wemyss Ct. CT1 ... 67 B2
Wemyss Ho. CT1 .. 67 B2
Wemyss Way. CT1 . 67 C1
Wenham's La. TN29 . 192 E2
Wents Wood. ME14 . 75 F5
Wentworth Ave. CT9 . 7 E1
Wentworth Cl. CT18 . 161 C6
Wentworth Dr. Gillingham ME8 . 33 E7
Wentworth Dr. Ramsgate CT12 . 29 A1
Wentworth Dr.
 Sittingbourne ME10 ... 36 C5
Wentworth Gdns. CT6 . 22 C8
Wentworth Ho. ME10 . 36 C5
Wesley Terr. CT18 .. 161 C7
West Beach. CT5 .. 20 C1
West Borough
 Cty Prim Sch. ME16 . 74 B3
West Cliff. CT5 .... 20 D1
West Cliff Arc. CT11 . 52 E6

West Cliff Ave. CT10 30 B3
West Cliff Dr. CT6 22 B4
West Cliff Gdns.
Folkestone CT20 178 D4
West Cliff Gdns.
Herne Bay CT6 22 B4
West Cliff Prom. CT11 52 D5
West Cliff Rd. Broadstairs CT10 30 B3
West Cliff Rd. Ramsgate CT11 52 D6
West Cliff Terr. CT11 52 B5
West Dr. ME5 31 D5
West Dumpton La.
CT10 & CT11 29 E1
West End. TN26 168 F3
West End Cotts. ME9 80 D7
West Gn. ME10 14 F1
West Hill Rd. CT6 22 C5
West Hythe Rd. CT21 187 A8
West La. Sheerness ME12 1 B2
West La. Sittingbourne ME10 37 A4
West Lane Trad Est. ME10 37 A4
West Minster
Cty Prim Sch. ME12 3 B8
West Norman Rd. CT16 166 E8
West Par. CT21 176 B1
West Park Ave. CT9 8 D1
West Park Farm North
Ret Pk. CT19 178 B8
West Park Rd. ME15 75 B2
West Pas. ME12 1 B2
West Pl. TN29 197 D8
West Ramp. CT16 166 G8
West Rd. Folkestone CT20 177 C4
West Rd. Gillingham ME4 10 A7
West Rd. Sandwich CT12 51 A1
West Ridge. ME10 36 D3
West Rise. CT12 29 B1
West Side. CT15 133 A1
West St. Ashford TN23 139 B2
West St. Deal CT14 117 D6
West St. Dover CT17 166 C8
West St. Faversham ME13 62 C7
West St. Gillingham ME7 10 D6
West St. Harrietsham ME17 100 C6
West St. Hothfield TN26 137 F7
West St. Lenham ME17 79 E1
West St. New Romney TN28 200 A6
West St. Queenborough ME11 2 F5
West St. Sheerness ME12 1 B2
West St. Sittingbourne ME10 36 E4
West Street Cotts. CT13 94 A1
West Terr. CT20 178 D4
West View. CT19 178 D8
West View Cl. CT6 22 C2
West Wlk. ME16 74 B3
West Wood Rd. ME9 56 B8
Westbere La. CT2 68 B7
Westbourne. TN23 155 D6
Westbourne Gdns. CT20 178 B4
Westbourne St. ME10 36 E4
Westbrook Ave. CT9 7 F1
Westbrook Cotts. CT9 7 G1
Westbrook Gdns. CT9 7 G1
Westbrook House Sch. CT20 178 B5
Westbrook La. CT6 22 B3
Westbrook Prom. CT9 7 G2
Westbrook Rd. CT9 7 G2
Westbrook Wlk. 8 ME13 62 C7
Westbrooke Cl. ME4 10 A2
Westbury Cres. CT17 166 B6
Westbury Hts. CT17 166 B6
Westbury Rd. Dover CT17 166 B6
Westbury Rd.
Westgate-on-S CT8 27 E8
Westcliff Dr. ME12 4 D8
Westcliff Gdns. CT9 7 F1
Westcliff Ho. 4 CT20 178 D4
Westcliff Rd. CT9 7 G1
Westcourt La. CT15 130 C5
Westcourt Rd. ME4 10 A6
Westdean Cl. CT17 148 E2
Westenhanger Sta. TN25 175 B7
Westerham Cl. Broadstairs CT9 8 F1
Westerham Cl. Canterbury CT2 67 A4
Westerham Cl. Gillingham ME8 11 B3
Westerham Rd. ME10 36 C3
Westerhill Rd. ME17 96 C1
Westerhout Cl. CT14 117 C8
Western Ave. Ashford TN23 139 A3
Western Ave. Bridge CT4 89 A1
Western Ave.
Halfway Houses ME12 3 D6
Western Ave. Herne Bay CT6 22 E4
Western Cl. CT17 166 C6
Western Espl.
Broadstairs CT10 30 B2
Western Espl. Herne Bay CT6 22 C5
Western Gdns. TN24 156 E8
Western Heights Rdbt. CT17 166 C5
Western Ho. CT14 117 C7
Western Link. ME13 62 A8
Western Rd. Deal CT14 117 C7
Western Rd. Maidstone ME16 74 C2
Western Rd. Margate CT9 29 C8
Western Service Rd. CT16 166 G8
Western Undercliff. CT11 52 C5
Westfield. CT2 66 A6
Westfield Bsns Ctr. ME2 9 C7
Westfield Cotts. ME9 13 A2
Westfield La. CT18 161 C3
Westfield Rd. Birchington CT7 27 A7
Westfield Rd. Margate CT9 28 C8
Westfield Sole Rd. ME14 54 D8
Westfields. TN27 136 D8
Westgate Ave. CT7 28 A4
Westgate Bay Ave. CT8 & CT9 7 C1
Westgate & Birchington
Golf Course. CT7 27 C8
Westgate Cl. CT2 66 C1
Westgate Court Ave. CT2 66 D1
Westgate Garden Flats. CT2 87 E8
Westgate Gr. CT2 66 F1
Westgate Hall Rd. 3
CT1 & CT2 66 F1
Westgate Rd. ME13 62 E7
Westgate Terr. CT5 20 E2
Westgate-on-Sea Sta. CT8 27 E8
Westlands Ave. ME10 36 B4
Westlands
High Sch The. ME10 36 B4
Westlands Rd. CT6 22 C3
Westleigh Rd. CT8 27 D8
Westmarsh Cl. ME15 97 F7
Westmarsh Dr. CT9 8 E2
Westmeads Cty Inf Sch. CT5 20 E2
Westmeads Rd. CT5 20 E2
Westminster Rd. CT1 67 C4
Westminster Wlk. CT12 29 C1
Westmoors. TN23 155 E6
Westmoreland Dr. ME9 13 C3
Westmorland Cl. ME15 97 E7
Westmorland Gn. ME15 97 E7
Westmorland Rd. ME15 97 E7
Westmount Ave. ME4 9 F3
Westmount Ho. 4 CT9 8 B2
Weston Rd. ME2 9 A8
Westonville Ave. CT9 7 F1
Westover Gdns. CT10 29 E7
Westover Rd. CT10 29 E6
Westree Rd. ME16 74 E3
Westway. ME17 96 C3
Westwell La.
Charing TN25 & TN27 120 F5
Westwell La.
Potters Corner TN24 & TN25 138 E7
Westwell La. Westwell TN25 121 B4
Westwood Ind Est. CT9 29 A6
Westwood Pl. ME13 62 D5
Westwood Rd.
Broadstairs CT10 29 C4
Westwood Rd.
Maidstone ME15 97 A7
Wetheral Dr. ME5 32 B4
Wey Cl. ME5 32 C5
Wey St. TN26 183 D3
Weybridge Cl. ME5 32 C4
Weyburn Dr. CT12 29 A1
Weyhill Cl. ME14 75 C6
Weymouth Cl. CT19 177 D7
Weymouth Rd. CT19 177 D6
Weymouth Terr. CT19 177 D7
Wharf Rd. Gillingham ME7 10 C7
Wharf Rd. Maidstone ME15 74 E2
Wharfedale Rd. CT9 8 A1
Wharton Gdns. TN24 156 E8
Whatman Cl. ME14 75 C6
Whatmer Cl. CT2 68 A6
Wheatcroft Cl. ME10 37 B4
Wheatcroft Gr. ME8 33 F7
Wheatear Way. ME5 32 B7
Wheatfields. Chatham ME5 32 D2
Wheatfields. Maidstone ME14 75 D4
Wheatley Rd. Ramsgate CT12 29 C1
Wheatley Rd. Whitstable CT5 20 E2
Wheatsheaf Cl.
Boughton Street ME13 64 A3
Wheatsheaf Cl.
Maidstone ME15 97 B8
Wheatsheaf Gdns. ME12 1 C1
Wheeler St. ME14 75 A5
Wheelers The. ME8 33 B6
Wheelwrights Way. CT13 93 B2
Wheler Rd. TN27 120 C8
Whewell Terr. 1 CT20 178 E5
Whiffen's Ave. ME4 9 F5
Whiffen's Ave W. ME4 9 F5
Whigham Cl. TN23 155 D7
Whimbrel Cl. ME10 36 F8
Whimbrel Wlk. ME5 32 C1
Whinfell Ave. CT11 51 F7
Whinless Rd. CT17 166 A8
Whiston Ave. TN26 153 C4
Whitby Rd. CT20 177 D6
Whitchurch Cl. ME16 74 E4
Whitcombe Cl. ME5 32 C3
White Acre Dr. CT14 134 B8
White Cliffs. 11 CT20 178 D4
White Cliffs Bsns Pk. CT16 149 A6
White Ct. 8 CT20 177 E3
White Hart Mansions. CT9 7 I3
White Hill.
Boughton Aluph TN25 & CT4 123 B6
White Hill. Challock TN25 105 E1
White Hill Cl. CT4 110 A8
White Hill Rd. ME14 33 D1
White Horse La. 6
Canterbury CT1 87 F8
White Horse La.
Otham Hole ME15 98 A6
White Horse La.
Rhodes Minnis CT4 144 A3
White House Farm Ct. CT15 113 E5
White Marsh Ct. CT5 20 E2
White Mill Folk Mus. CT13 72 E2
White Post. ME17 78 B5
White Post Gdns. CT3 71 E1
White Rd. ME4 10 A2
White Rock Ct. ME16 74 E3
White Rock Pl. 5 ME16 74 E3
White Wood Rd. CT13 93 B1
Whiteacre La. CT4 125 E4
Whitebeam Dr. ME17 96 B3
Whitecliff Way. CT19 178 F6
Whitefriars Meadow. CT13 94 A8
Whitefriars Way. CT13 72 F1
Whitehall. TN29 197 E8
Whitehall Bridge Rd. CT2 87 E8
Whitehall Cl. CT2 87 E8
Whitehall Dr. ME17 99 D3
Whitehall Gdns. CT2 66 E1
Whitehall Rd.
Broad Street ME14 77 A6
Whitehall Rd. Canterbury CT2 87 D7
Whitehall Rd. Canterbury CT2 87 E8
Whitehall Rd. Ramsgate CT12 29 C1
Whitehall Rd.
Sittingbourne ME10 36 E2
Whitehall Way. TN25 159 D1
Whiteheads La. ME14 76 B4
Whitehorse Hill. ME4 10 B3
Whitehouse Cres. ME1 53 A8
Whitehouse Dro. CT13 & CT3 72 D7
Whitelocks Cl. CT4 111 D3
Whitenbrook. CT21 177 A3
Whiteness Gn. CT10 8 F1
Whiteness Rd. CT10 8 G1
Whites Hill. CT14 115 B2
Whitewall Ctr. ME2 9 D8
Whitewall Rd. ME2 9 D7
Whitewall Way. ME2 9 D7
Whiteway Rd. ME11 2 F6
Whitfeld Rd. TN23 156 B8
Whitfield Ave.
Broadstairs CT10 29 E7
Whitfield Ave. Dover CT16 149 B2
Whitfield Cotts. TN23 156 B8
Whitfield Cty Prim Sch. CT16 149 A7
Whitfield Hill.
Temple Ewell CT16 148 F4
Whitfield Hill. Whitfield CT16 148 F5
Whitfield Rdbt. CT16 149 A6
Whitgift Ct. CT2 66 D1
Whiting Cres. ME13 62 A8
Whiting Ho. TN29 203 C5
Whitmore St. ME16 74 D2
Whitstable Cty Jun Sch. CT5 20 D1
Whitstable Rd. Canterbury CT2 66 D2
Whitstable Rd.
Faversham ME13 62 E7
Whitstable Rd.
Faversham, Goodnestone ME13 63 B6
Whitstable Rd.
Herne Bay CT5 & CT6 21 F3
Whitstable Rd.
Herne Bay, Studd Hill CT6 22 B3
Whitstable Rd.
Rough Common CT2 66 B4
Whitstable & Seasalter
Endowed CE Jun Sch. CT5 20 D1
Whitstable & Tankerton
Hospl. CT5 21 A2
Whitstable & Tankerton Sta.
CT5 20 E1
Whittaker St. ME4 10 A4
Whittington Terr. CT15 130 D4
Whybornes Chase. ME12 4 C7
Whyman Ave. ME4 10 A1
Whytecliffs. CT10 30 A2
Wichling Cl. CT2 67 A3
Wick La. CT4 129 E7
Wicken Ho. ME16 74 E4
Wicken La. TN25 & TN27 120 E6
Wickenden Cres. TN24 157 A8
Wickets The. TN24 156 F7
Wickham Ave. CT11 52 G8
Wickham Cl. ME9 35 B6
Wickham Court La. CT3 69 B3
Wickham La. CT3 69 B1
Wickham Mill. CT3 69 C2
Wickham Pl. ME17 101 D5
Wickham Rd. CT3 69 B2
Wickham St. ME1 9 D3
Wickhambreaux
CE Prim Sch. CT3 69 C2
Widred Rd. CT17 166 C8
Wierton La. ME17 97 E1
Wife Of Bath Hill. CT2 87 C8
Wigmore La. CT15 131 C8
Wigmore Rd. Gillingham ME8 33 B4
Wigmore Rd. Gillingham ME8 33 B5
Wigwam Paddocks. CT7 27 A8
Wihtred Rd. ME9 37 D2
Wilberforce Rd.
Coxheath ME17 96 D3
Wilberforce Rd.
Folkestone CT20 177 E3
Wilbrough Rd. CT7 27 A7
Wilcox Cl. CT3 112 D5
Wilderness Hill. CT9 8 A2
Wildfell Cl. ME14 54 C8
Wildish Rd. ME13 62 A8
Wildman Cl. ME8 33 D3
Wildwood Cl. ME17 99 E2
Wildwood Glade. ME7 33 B4
Wildwood Rd. CT2 67 F6
Wiles Ave. TN28 200 B6
Wiles Ho. TN28 200 B6
Wilfred Rd. CT11 52 C8
Wilgate Green Rd. ME13 82 F6
Wilkes Rd. CT10 29 E4
Wilkie Rd. CT7 27 A8
Will Adams Ct. ME7 10 C6
Will Adams Way. ME7 10 F1
Willement Rd. ME13 62 B7
Willesborough Ct. TN24 140 A2
Willesborough
Cty Inf Sch. TN24 157 A8
Willesborough Ind Pk.
TN24 140 A1
Willesborough Rd. TN24 139 F4
Willetts Hill. CT12 49 D7
William Ave. Folkestone CT19 178 B7
William Ave. Margate CT9 29 C8
William Gibbs Ct. 14 ME13 62 D7
William Harvey Hospl The.
TN24 140 C1
William Judge Cl. TN30 179 D7
William Pitt Ave. CT14 117 B6
William Pitt Cl. CT21 176 D2
William Rd. TN23 156 B8
William St. Faversham ME13 62 D7
William St. Gillingham ME8 12 A1
William St. Herne Bay CT6 22 F5
William St. Sittingbourne ME10 36 E4
William St. Whitstable CT5 20 D2
Williamson Rd. TN29 204 E5
Willingdon. TN23 155 E5
Willingdon Pl. CT14 117 C1
Willington Gn. ME15 97 E7
Willington St. ME15 75 F2
Willis Ct. ME12 3 F5
Willis Ho. ME1 9 C4
Willop Cl. TN29 186 F3
Willop Way. TN29 186 F3
Willoughby Ct. 14 CT1 87 F8
Willow Ave. Broadstairs CT10 29 D4
Willow Ave. Faversham ME13 62 A7
Willow Cl. Canterbury CT2 67 A2
Willow Cl. Hythe CT21 175 E1
Willow Cl. Margate CT9 8 C2
Willow Ct. Broadstairs CT10 30 A5
Willow Ct. Folkestone CT20 177 E4
Willow Dr. Hamstreet TN26 183 A7
Willow Dr. St Mary's Bay TN29 194 F3
Willow Ho. 2 Chatham ME5 31 F5
Willow Ho. Sheerness ME12 1 C2
Willow Ho. Sittingbourne ME10 37 B3
Willow Rd.
Great Mongeham CT14 116 C3
Willow Rd. Whitstable CT5 43 C5
Willow Rise. ME15 75 F1
Willow Tree Cl. Ashford TN24 139 F1
Willow Tree Cl.
Herne Bay CT6 23 D5
Willow Way. Maidstone ME15 75 B3
Willow Way. Margate CT9 28 C8
Willow Way. Whitstable CT5 44 C8
Willow Waye. CT15 131 D7
Willowbank Cl. TN29 195 A4
Willowby Gdns. ME8 33 E4
Willows Ct. CT2 66 C4
Willows The. Gillingham ME8 11 E2
Willows The. Newington ME9 35 B6
Willows The. Sheerness ME12 1 I1
Willows The.
Sittingbourne ME10 14 F1
Willson's Rd. CT11 52 D6
Wilmecote Ct. ME8 33 D8
Wilmington Way. ME8 11 B2
Wilmott Pl. CT13 93 B2
Wilson Ave. Chatham ME1 31 E7
Wilson Ave. Deal CT14 116 F4
Wilson Cl. Ashford TN24 140 A1
Wilson Cl. Maidstone ME15 97 E7
Wilsons La. ME15 96 A5
Wiltie Gdns. CT19 178 C5
Wilton Cl. CT14 117 C5
Wilton Rd. Folkestone CT19 178 B6
Wilton Rd. Margate CT12 28 F1
Wilton Terr. ME10 36 B5
Wiltshire Cl. ME5 32 C8
Wiltshire Way. ME15 97 E8
Wimborne Pl. CT12 52 B8
Wimbourne Dr. ME8 33 D6
Win Pine Ho. CT21 176 A1
Winant Way. CT16 149 B3
Wincheap. CT1 87 E7
Wincheap Gn. 4 CT1 87 F7
Wincheap Ind Est. CT1 87 D7
Wincheap Prim Sch. CT1 87 E6
Winchelsea Ct. CT17 166 C7
Winchelsea Rd. Chatham ME5 32 B5
Winchelsea Rd. Dover CT17 166 B7
Winchelsea St. CT17 166 B7
Winchelsea Terr. CT17 166 B7
Winchester Ave. ME5 31 F4
Winchester Gdns. CT1 88 A6
Winchester Ho. 4 ME15 97 D7
Winchester Pl. 7 ME14 75 A5
Winchester Way. ME8 34 A8
Wind Hill. TN27 119 E7
Wind Hill La. TN27 119 E7
Windermere. ME13 62 E6
Windermere Ave. CT11 52 A7
Windermere Ct. TN24 139 C4
Windermere Dr. ME8 33 D7
Windermere Gdns. CT3 112 F6
Windermere Gr. ME10 36 D3
Winding Hill. ME13 83 F6
Windmill Ave. CT12 29 B3
Windmill Cl. Ashford TN24 140 A1
Windmill Cl. Bridge CT4 89 A1
Windmill Cl. Canterbury CT1 88 C8
Windmill Cl. Herne Bay CT6 23 A2
Windmill Ct.
Boughton Monchelsea ME17 97 B3
Windmill Ct. Whitstable CT5 43 C7
Windmill Hill. ME17 100 B1
Windmill Hts. ME14 76 B4
Windmill Quay Rd. ME12 4 E2
Windmill Rd. Canterbury CT1 88 C8
Windmill Rd. Gillingham ME7 10 C4
Windmill Rd. Herne Bay CT6 23 A2
Windmill Rd.
Sittingbourne ME10 36 D6
Windmill Rd. Whitstable CT5 43 D7
Windmill Rise. ME12 4 E6
Windmill Row. ME17 98 D2
Windmill St. CT21 176 B1
Windmill View. CT9 29 A8
Windmill Wlk. CT12 29 B1
Windsor Ave. Chatham ME4 9 F2
Windsor Ave. Margate CT9 8 B1
Windsor Cl. Broadstairs CT10 29 E5
Windsor Cl. Maidstone ME14 75 B6
Windsor Ct. Deal CT14 117 C2
Windsor Ct. Margate CT9 8 B1
Windsor Dr. ME10 36 D2
Windsor Gdns. Herne Bay CT6 22 B3
Windsor Gdns. Warden ME12 6 D4
Windsor Ho. Deal CT14 117 A5
Windsor Ho. 6 Dover CT17 166 D7
Windsor Ho. Whitstable CT5 20 D1
Windsor Mews. 9
Margate CT9 7 J2
Windsor Mews.
New Romney TN28 200 C8
Windsor Rd. Canterbury CT1 87 C6
Windsor Rd. Cliffs End CT12 51 D7
Windsor Rd. Gillingham ME7 10 D5
Windward Rd. ME1 9 C1
Windyridge. ME7 10 E1
Winehouse La. CT18 164 D3
Wineycock. ME9 81 C8
Wing Ho. ME12 6 H1
Wing Rd. ME12 6 H1
Wingate Rd. CT19 178 D7
Wingham Bird Pk. CT3 70 C1
Wingham Cl. Gillingham ME8 11 C3
Wingham Cl. Maidstone ME15 97 F7
Wingham Cty Prim Sch. CT3 91 A7
Wingham Rd. CT3 90 D8
Wingrove Dr. Maidstone ME14 75 E5
Wingrove Dr. Rochester ME2 9 C8
Wingrove Hill. CT17 148 E2
Wings Ct. CT10 30 B5
Winifred Ave. CT12 29 C2
Winifred Rd. ME15 75 F3
Winnipeg Cl. CT16 149 C3
Winstanley Cres. CT11 52 D8
Winstanley Rd. ME12 1 D2
Winston Cl. CT1 88 C7
Winston Ct. CT7 27 A8
Winston Gdns. CT6 23 D4
Winston Ho. 4 CT20 177 F5
Winterage La. CT18 162 C7
Winterstoke Cres. CT11 52 G8
Winterstoke Way. CT11 52 F8
Winton Way. TN29 195 A5
Wirrals The. ME5 32 A4
Wises La. ME10 & ME9 36 A4
Wish The. TN26 181 F6
Wissenden La. TN26 153 B6
Withersdane Cotts. TN25 124 A2
Witley Wlk. CT16 149 B7
Wittersham
CE (VA) Prim Sch. TN30 188 D2
Wittersham Cl. ME5 32 B5
Wittersham Rd.
Stone in Oxney TN30 189 C3
Wittersham Rd.
Wittersham TN30 188 C5
Wivenhoe. TN23 155 E5
Wivenhoe Cl. ME8 12 A2
Wolfe Rd. ME16 74 B2
Wollaston Cl. ME8 33 D3
Wollaston Rd. CT14 117 D4
Wolmer Way. 1 CT20 177 F5
Wolseley Ave. CT6 22 A4
Wolseley Pl. 4 TN24 139 B3
Wood Ave. CT19 178 E7
Wood Cottage La. CT19 177 D7
Wood Hill. CT2 66 E6
Wood Rd. CT21 176 B1
Wood St. Dover CT16 166 D8
Wood St. Gillingham ME7 10 A6
Wood St. Lynsted ME9 59 F8
Wood St. Sheerness ME12 1 D2
Wood View. CT3 46 E5
Wood Yd. CT14 117 D6
Wood's Pl. CT17 149 B2
Woodberry Dr. ME10 37 C3
Woodbridge Dr. ME15 74 F1
Woodbrook. TN27 120 D7
Woodbury La. TN30 179 A7
Woodbury Rd. ME5 31 F1
Woodchurch
CE Prim Sch. TN26 169 A2
Woodchurch Cl. ME5 32 B5
Woodchurch Cres. ME8 11 C2
Woodchurch Ho. ME8 11 C2
Woodchurch Rd.
Appledore TN26 & TN30 181 C4
Woodchurch Rd.
Margate CT7 & CT9 28 A5
Woodchurch Rd.
Shadoxhurst TN26 155 A1
Woodchurch Rd.
Tenterden TN30 179 D8
Woodchurch Rd.
Westgate-on-S CT12 & CT7 27 F3
Woodcock Gdns. CT18 163 A4
Woodcote. CT5 21 D1
Woodcourt Cl. ME10 36 E2
Woodcut. ME14 75 A8
Woodfield Ave. CT19 177 E7
Woodfield Cl. CT19 177 E7
Woodford Ave. CT11 & CT12 29 D1
Woodford Ct. CT7 27 A7
Woodford Rd. ME16 74 B2
Woodgate. CT4 110 E3
Woodgate Cl. ME13 62 C8
Woodgate Ct. ME13 84 E7
Woodgate La. ME9 35 C2
Woodhall Terr. ME11 3 A5

Woodhurst. ME5 .... 31 D4
Woodland Ave. Aylesham CT3 .. 112 E5
Woodland Ave.
  Birchington CT7 .... 27 B6
Woodland Cl. CT17 .... 148 E2
Woodland Cotts. CT18 .... 161 B7
Woodland Dr. ME12 .... 4 B7
Woodland Rd. Herne Bay CT6 ..... 22 B2
Woodland Rd.
  Lyminge CT18 & TN25 .... 160 E8
Woodland View. TN30 .... 188 E4
Woodland Way.
  Broadstairs CT10 .... 8 G1
Woodland Way.
  Canterbury CT2 .... 66 D4
Woodland Way.
  Dymchurch TN29 .... 187 A5
Woodland Way.
  Maidstone ME14 .... 75 B7
Woodland Way.
  Woodnesborough CT13 .... 93 C6
Woodlands. Blean CT2 .... 65 F7
Woodlands. Chatham ME5 ...... 32 A2
Woodlands. Coxheath ME17 ...... 96 B3
Woodlands. Hernhill ME13 ...... 64 C7
Woodlands Cl. ME14 .... 75 B7
Woodlands Cty Prim Sch. ME7 .. 10 F4
Woodlands Dr. CT21 .... 177 A4
Woodlands High Sch. ME7 ...... 10 F4
Woodlands Rd. Adisham CT3 ... 112 C8
Woodlands Rd. Ashford TN24 ... 139 F2
Woodlands Rd. Gillingham ME7 .. 10 F4
Woodlands Rd.
  Sittingbourne ME10 .... 37 B3
Woodlawn St. CT5 .... 20 D2
Woodlea. TN24 .... 139 C3
Woodman Ave. CT5 .... 21 E3
Woodnesborough La. CT13 ...... 93 B3
Woodnesborough Rd. CT13 ...... 93 E7

Woodpecker Glade. ME8 .... 33 D6
Woodrow Chase. CT6 .... 23 A1
Woodruff Cl. ME8 .... 12 D4
Woods Hill. CT4 .... 125 C5
Woods Ley. CT3 .... 71 D2
Woodshale Cotts. ME9 .... 14 D1
Woodside. Ashford TN23 .... 155 E6
Woodside.
  Boughton Street ME13 .... 64 B2
Woodside. Gillingham ME8 .... 33 C6
Woodside Ave. CT4 .... 86 D2
Woodside Cl. CT16 .... 148 E4
Woodside Gdns. ME10 .... 36 D2
Woodside Rd. Maidstone ME15 .. 97 C7
Woodside Rd. Sturry CT2 .... 67 F7
Woodstock Rd. Deal CT14 ...... 117 C4
Woodstock Rd. Rochester ME2 ..... 9 A7
Woodstock Rd.
  Sittingbourne ME10 .... 36 E1
Woodstock Way. TN24 .... 139 C6
Woodvale Ave. CT5 .... 44 C8
Woodville Cl. CT1 .... 87 D6
Woodville Rd. Maidstone ME15 .. 75 A2
Woodville Rd. Ramsgate CT12 .... 29 C1
Woolaston Cl. ME15 .... 74 F1
Woolcomber St. CT16 .... 166 E7
Wooldeys Rd. ME8 .... 11 F2
Woolett Rd. ME10 .... 36 C5
Woollets Cl. CT6 .... 22 C3
Woollett St. ME14 .... 75 A5
Woolley Rd. ME15 .... 97 F7
Woolmer Dr. TN24 .... 157 A7
Woolpack Hill. TN25 .... 158 D5
Woolreeds Rd. TN23 .... 156 A4
Woolwich Cl. ME5 .... 32 A7
Wootton Gn. ME8 .... 11 D3
Wootton La. CT15 & CT4 ...... 146 C7
Wopsle Cl. ME1 .... 31 D7
Worcester Cl. Faversham ME13 .. 62 E6
Worcester Cl. Minster ME12 ...... 4 C6
Worcester Dr. ME10 .... 36 D6
Worcester La. CT3 & CT4 .... 88 E7

Worcester Rd. ME15 .... 97 D7
Wordsworth Cl. ME5 .... 32 C7
Wordsworth Gdns. CT3 .... 112 F6
Wordsworth Rd. ME14 .... 75 B7
Workhouse La. ME15 .... 96 C4
Workhouse Rd.
  Sutton Valence ME17 .... 99 A1
Workhouse Rd. Throwley ME13 .. 82 F1
World's End. ME9 .... 60 E7
Wormdale Hill. ME9 .... 35 B3
Wormdale Rd. ME9 .... 35 B4
Worth Cty Prim Sch. CT14 ...... 94 B5
Worth La. CT20 .... 177 E3
Worthgate Pl. ❷ CT1 .... 87 F7
Worthington St. ⓫ CT16 .... 166 D8
Wotton Cl. ME15 .... 97 E5
Wotton Rd. TN23 .... 156 B6
Wraightsfield Ave. TN29 ...... 195 D8
Wraik Hill. CT5 .... 43 C5
Wrangleden Cl. ME15 .... 97 E5
Wrangleden Rd. ME15 .... 97 E5
Wreight Ct. ME13 .... 40 B1
Wren Ind Est. ME15 .... 97 F4
Wren Way. ME5 .... 32 B6
Wrens Ct. ME9 .... 58 A8
Wrens Rd. ME9 .... 58 A7
Wrentham Ave. CT6 .... 22 B2
Wright Cl. ME8 .... 11 C2
Wright's Way. ME12 .... 17 C8
Wrights Cl. TN30 .... 179 A8
Wrotham Ave. ⓰ CT10 .... 30 B4
Wrotham Rd. CT10 .... 30 B4
Wyatt Ho. ❷ ME2 .... 9 A7
Wyatt Pl. ME2 .... 9 A7
Wyatt St. ME14 .... 75 A4
Wych Elm Way. CT21 .... 187 E8
Wycherley Cres. CT16 .... 149 B4
Wye Coll (Univ of London).
  TN25 .... 123 F2
Wye Gdns. CT9 .... 8 F2
Wye High Sch (Prep). TN25 ... 123 E2
Wye Rd. TN25 .... 122 F3

Wye Sta. TN25 .... 123 D2
Wyke Manor Rd. ME14 .... 75 A4
Wykeham Cl. ME11 .... 2 F3
Wykeham Cotts. ME17 .... 96 F2
Wykeham Gr. ME17 .... 99 A7
Wykeham Rd. MF10 .... 37 B4
Wykeham St. ME2 .... 9 B8
Wyles Rd. ME4 .... 9 E2
Wyles St. ME7 .... 10 C7
Wyllie Ct. ME10 .... 36 E7
Wynd The. TN27 .... 103 D1
Wyndam Rd. ME4 .... 9 E2
Wyndham Ave. CT9 .... 8 B2
Wyndham Rd. CT17 .... 166 B8
Wynn Ellis Ho. CT5 .... 20 E3
Wynn Rd. CT5 .... 21 A2
Wytherling Cl. ME14 .... 75 F5
Wyvern Way. TN24 .... 139 E3
Wyvill Cl. ME8 .... 33 E5

Yard The. CT4 .... 111 F1
Yardhurst Gdns. CT9 .... 8 F3
Yardley Ho. CT10 .... 30 B7
Yarrow Cl. CT10 .... 30 A3
Yarrow Ct. ME14 .... 75 F5
Yarrow Rd. ME5 .... 31 F4
Yates Cl. TN31 .... 201 A2
Yaugher La. ME9 .... 34 C3
Yeates Dr. ME10 .... 37 A8
Yellow Sands. ME12 .... 19 E5
Yelsted La. Chatham ME14 ...... 54 D7
Yelsted La. Yelsted ME9 .... 34 A1
Yelsted Rd. ME9 .... 56 A7
Yeoman Ct. ME14 .... 76 B3
Yeoman Dr. ME7 .... 10 F1
Yeoman Gdns. TN24 .... 157 B8
Yeoman La. ME14 .... 76 B4
Yeoman Way. ME15 .... 76 A2
Yeomans Sq. TN23 .... 155 D8
Yevele Cl. ME11 .... 3 A5
Yew Cl. TN23 .... 138 E2

Yew Tree Cl. Broadstairs CT10 .. 29 D4
Yew Tree Cl. Chatham ME5 ...... 32 D3
Yew Tree Cl. Deal CT14 .... 117 A4
Yew Tree Cl. Stanford TN25 .... 160 B3
Yew Tree Cotts. ME14 .... 53 F7
Yew Tree Farm. CT3 .... 114 A8
Yew Tree Gdns. Birchington CT7 . 27 A2
Yew Tree Gdns. Fordwich CT2 ... 68 A4
Yew Tree Pl. ME7 .... 33 B3
Yew Tree Rd. TN29 .... 194 F2
Yewhedges. ME13 .... 81 E4
Yewtree Cross. CT18 .... 161 C8
Yoakes La. TN29 .... 192 F3
Yoakley Sq. CT9 .... 28 F8
York and Albany Cl. CT14 ..... 117 B3
York Ave. ⓱ Broadstairs CT10 .. 30 B4
York Ave. Chatham ME5 .... 31 F3
York Ave. Gillingham ME7 ...... 10 C4
York Cl. CT6 .... 22 D4
York Hill. ME4 .... 10 C2
York Ho. ⓾ CT17 .... 166 D2
York Mews. CT19 .... 177 E2
York Rd. Ashford TN24 .... 139 D5
York Rd. Canterbury CT1 .... 87 E2
York Rd. Deal CT14 .... 117 D4
York Rd. Herne Bay CT6 .... 22 D9
York Rd. Maidstone ME15 ...... 75 C2
York Rd. Rochester ME1 .... 9 C3
York St. Broadstairs CT10 ...... 30 B4
York St. Dover CT16 & CT17 .. 166 D2
York St. Ramsgate CT11 .... 52 E6
York Street Rdbt. CT16 .... 166 D2
York Terr. CT7 .... 27 B2
Young Cl. CT14 .... 117 B6
Young's Pl. CT15 .... 164 F5
Ypres Ct. CT1 .... 67 D3
Ypres Dr. ME10 .... 14 F3

Zarena Ct. ❽ CT20 .... 177 F3
Zealand Rd. CT1 .... 87 F6
Zetland Ave. ME7 .... 10 E3
Zion Pl. CT9 .... 7 J3

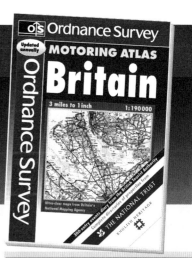

The best-selling *OS Motoring Atlas Britain* uses unrivalled and up-to-date mapping from the Ordnance Survey digital database. The exceptionally clear mapping is at a large scale of 3 miles to 1 inch (Orkney/Shetland Islands at 5 miles to 1 inch).

A special feature of the atlas is its wealth of tourist and leisure information. It contains comprehensive directories, including descriptions and location details, of the properties of the National Trust in England and Wales, the National Trust for Scotland, English Heritage and Historic Scotland. There is also a useful diary of British Tourist Authority Events listing more than 300 days out around Britain during the year.

Available from all good bookshops or direct from the publisher:
Tel: 01933 443863

The atlas includes:

- 112 pages of fully updated mapping
- 45 city and town plans
- 8 extra-detailed city approach maps
- route-planning maps
- restricted motorway junctions
- local radio information
- distances chart
- county boundaries map
- multi-language legend

STREET ATLASES
ORDER FORM

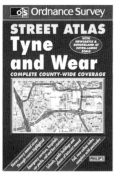

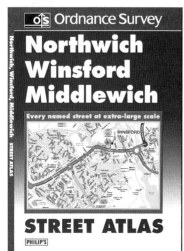

PHILIP'S

The Street Atlases are available from all good bookshops or by mail order direct from the publisher. Orders can be made in the following ways. **By phone** Ring our special Credit Card Hotline on **01933 443863** during office hours (9am to 5pm) or leave a message the answering machine, quoting your full credit card number plus expiry date and your fu name and address. **By post or fax** Fill out the order form below (you may photocopy it) and post it to: **Philip's Direct, 27 Sanders Road, Wellingborough, Northants NN 4NL** or fax it to: **01933 443849.** Before placing an order by post, by fax or on the answering machine, please telephone to check availability and prices.

COLOUR LOCAL ATLASES

	PAPERBACK	
	Quantity @ £3.50 each	£ Total
CANNOCK, LICHFIELD, RUGELEY	☐ 0 540 07625 2	➤ ☐
DERBY AND BELPER	☐ 0 540 07608 2	➤ ☐
NORTHWICH, WINSFORD, MIDDLEWICH	☐ 0 540 07589 2	➤ ☐
PEAK DISTRICT TOWNS	☐ 0 540 07609 0	➤ ☐
STAFFORD, STONE, UTTOXETER	☐ 0 540 07626 0	➤ ☐
WARRINGTON, WIDNES, RUNCORN	☐ 0 540 07588 4	➤ ☐

COLOUR REGIONAL ATLASES

	HARDBACK	SPIRAL	POCKET	
	Quantity @ £10.99 each	Quantity @ £8.99 each	Quantity @ £5.99 each	£ Total
BERKSHIRE	☐ 0 540 06170 0	☐ 0 540 06172 7	☐ 0 540 06173 5	➤ ☐
	Quantity @ £10.99 each	Quantity @ £8.99 each	Quantity @ £4.99 each	£ Total
MERSEYSIDE	☐ 0 540 06480 7	☐ 0 540 06481 5	☐ 0 540 06482 3	➤ ☐
	Quantity @ £12.99 each	Quantity @ £9.99 each	Quantity @ £4.99 each	£ Total
DURHAM	☐ 0 540 06365 7	☐ 0 540 06366 5	☐ 0 540 06367 3	➤ ☐
HERTFORDSHIRE	☐ 0 540 06174 3	☐ 0 540 06175 1	☐ 0 540 06176 X	➤ ☐
EAST KENT	☐ 0 540 07483 7	☐ 0 540 07276 1	☐ 0 540 07287 7	➤ ☐
WEST KENT	☐ 0 540 07366 0	☐ 0 540 07367 9	☐ 0 540 07369 5	➤ ☐
EAST SUSSEX	☐ 0 540 07306 7	☐ 0 540 07307 5	☐ 0 540 07312 1	➤ ☐
WEST SUSSEX	☐ 0 540 07319 9	☐ 0 540 07323 7	☐ 0 540 07327 X	➤ ☐
SOUTH YORKSHIRE	☐ 0 540 06330 4	☐ 0 540 06331 2	☐ 0 540 06332 0	➤ ☐
SURREY	☐ 0 540 06435 1	☐ 0 540 06436 X	☐ 0 540 06438 6	➤ ☐
	Quantity @ £12.99 each	Quantity @ £9.99 each	Quantity @ £5.50 each	£ Total
GREATER MANCHESTER	☐ 0 540 06485 8	☐ 0 540 06486 6	☐ 0 540 06487 4	➤ ☐
TYNE AND WEAR	☐ 0 540 06370 3	☐ 0 540 06371 1	☐ 0 540 06372 X	➤ ☐
	Quantity @ £12.99 each	Quantity @ £9.99 each	Quantity @ £5.99 each	£ Total
BIRMINGHAM & WEST MIDLANDS	☐ 0 540 07603 1	☐ 0 540 07604 X	☐ 0 540 07605 8	➤ ☐
BUCKINGHAMSHIRE	☐ 0 540 07466 7	☐ 0 540 07467 5	☐ 0 540 07468 3	➤ ☐

STREET ATLASES
ORDER FORM

COLOUR REGIONAL ATLASES

	HARDBACK	SPIRAL	POCKET	£ Total
	Quantity @ £12.99 each	Quantity @ £9.99 each	Quantity @ £5.99 each	
CHESHIRE	☐ 0 540 07507 8	☐ 0 540 07508 6	☐ 0 540 07509 4	➤ ☐
DERBYSHIRE	☐ 0 540 07531 0	☐ 0 540 07532 9	☐ 0 540 07533 7	➤ ☐
SOUTH HAMPSHIRE	☐ 0 540 07476 4	☐ 0 540 07477 2	☐ 0 540 07478 0	➤ ☐
NORTH HAMPSHIRE	☐ 0 540 07471 3	☐ 0 540 07472 1	☐ 0 540 07473 X	➤ ☐
OXFORDSHIRE	☐ 0 540 07512 4	☐ 0 540 07513 2	☐ 0 540 07514 0	➤ ☐
WARWICKSHIRE	☐ 0 540 07560 4	☐ 0 540 07561 2	☐ 0 540 07562 0	➤ ☐
WEST YORKSHIRE	☐ 0 540 06329 0	☐ 0 540 06327 4	☐ 0 540 06328 2	➤ ☐
	Quantity @ £14.99 each	Quantity @ £9.99 each	Quantity @ £5.99 each	£ Total
LANCASHIRE	☐ 0 540 06440 8	☐ 0 540 06441 6	☐ 0 540 06443 2	➤ ☐
NOTTINGHAMSHIRE	☐ 0 540 07541 8	☐ 0 540 075426 6	☐ 0 540 07543 4	➤ ☐
STAFFORDSHIRE	☐ 0 540 07549 3	☐ 0 540 07550 7	☐ 0 540 07551 5	➤ ☐

BLACK AND WHITE REGIONAL ATLASES

	HARDBACK	SOFTBACK	POCKET	£ Total
	Quantity @ £11.99 each	Quantity @ £8.99 each	Quantity @ £3.99 each	
BRISTOL AND AVON	☐ 0 540 06140 9	☐ 0 540 06141 7	☐ 0 540 06142 5	➤ ☐
	Quantity @ £12.99 each	Quantity @ £9.99 each	Quantity @ £4.99 each	£ Total
CARDIFF, SWANSEA & GLAMORGAN	☐ 0 540 06186 7	☐ 0 540 06187 5	☐ 0 540 06207 3	➤ ☐
EDINBURGH & East Central Scotland	—	☐ 0 540 06181 6	☐ 0 540 06182 4	➤ ☐
EAST ESSEX	☐ 0 540 05848 3	☐ 0 540 05866 1	☐ 0 540 05850 5	➤ ☐
WEST ESSEX	☐ 0 540 05849 1	☐ 0 540 05867 X	☐ 0 540 05851 3	➤ ☐
	Quantity @ £12.99 each	Quantity @ £9.99 each	Quantity @ £5.99 each	£ Total
GLASGOW & West Central Scotland	☐ 0 540 06183 2	☐ 0 540 06184 0	☐ 0 540 06185 9	➤ ☐

Post to: Philip's Direct,
27 Sanders Road, Wellingborough,
Northants NN8 4NL

◆ Free postage and packing

◆ All available titles will normally be dispatched within 5 working days of receipt of order but please allow up to 28 days for delivery

☐ Please tick this box if you do not wish your name to be used by other carefully selected organisations that may wish to send you information about other products and services

Registered Office: Michelin House, 81 Fulham Road, London SW3 6RB

Registered in England number: 3597451

I enclose a cheque / postal order, for a **total** of ➤ ☐
made payable to *Octopus Publishing Group Ltd*, or please debit my

☐ Access ☐ American Express ☐ Visa ☐ Diners

account by ☐

Account no
☐☐☐☐☐ ☐☐☐☐ ☐☐☐☐ ☐☐☐☐

Expiry date ☐☐ ☐☐

Signature...

Name..

Address..

....

....

....POSTCODE

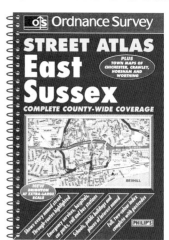

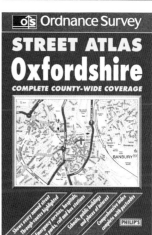